AMERICAN JOURNAL OF NUMISMATICS

32

Second Series, continuing
The American Numismatic Society Museum Notes

THE AMERICAN NUMISMATIC SOCIETY
NEW YORK
2020

ISSN: 1053-8356
ISBN 978-0-89722-369-0

Printed in Canada

Contents

AJN Second Series 32 (2020) pp. 1–30

Compositional Analysis of Sixth–Fifth Century BC Silver Coins from the Larnaca Hoard (*IGCH* 1272) (Cyprus) using pXRF Spectrometry

A. Charalambous*, E. Markou** and V. Kassianidou***

The elemental composition of 436 silver coins from a hoard of the fifth century BC, minted by the Iron Age Cypriot city-kingdoms of Kition, Idalion, Lapethos, Paphos and Salamis, as well as a small number of coins from unidentified mints, was determined by pXRF spectrometry in order primarily to study the silver alloys used for their manufacture. The specific technique was applied because it allows for a non-destructive analysis, taking into consideration its inherent limitations as a surface analysis technique and the possibility of the existence of surface enrichment elements that do not reflect the materials' actual bulk composition. This is the first time such a large number of ancient Cypriot silver coins has been analyzed providing numismatists and archaeologists with new insights into this important component of ancient material culture. The results of the compositional analysis show that the various groups of coins were made of a similar Ag-Cu alloy with

*Archaeological Research Unit, Department of History and Archaeology, University of Cyprus, P.O. Box 20537, CY1678, Nicosia, Cyprus (anchar@ucy.ac.cy).

**Institute of Historical Research (KERA), National Hellenic Research Foundation (NHRF). 48, Vassileos Constantinou Ave., 11635, Athens, Greece (emarkou@eie.gr).

***Archaeological Research Unit, Department of History and Archaeology, University of Cyprus, P.O. Box 20537, CY1678, Nicosia, Cyprus (v.kassianidou@ucy.ac.cy).

silver concentration in the range of 96.5–98.5%. The proportion of copper, larger than the approximately 0.5% that would be expected from ordinary ancient methods of refining silver, is likely justified as an attempt to increase the hardness of the alloy and to improve its casting and minting processing, rather than as an attempt of debasement or a form of adulteration. Furthermore, the analysis has shown that most of the analyzed coins have a lead concentration below 0.5%, indicating a very efficient silver refining process. Gold is in most instances present in a concentration range between 0.1 and 0.5%. The presence of detectable bismuth in most of the coins, at lower concentrations than gold, provides information about the type of ores that were used for the production of silver metal. The interpretation of the chemical elements content reveals similarities and differences between the mints of the Cypriot city-kingdoms and the several coin issues.

1. INTRODUCTION

Coinage in Cyprus was an early phenomenon. The fact that in the Persepolis foundation deposits, which were buried in the late sixth century BC, three out of the five Greek coins were from Cypriot mints (Kraay 1976; Kagan 1994) comes as an interesting observation of how early the Cypriot monetary phenomenon was.

During the Archaic and Classical periods (eighth–fourth centuries BC) the island was divided into a number of kingdoms (Gjerstad 1948; Stylianou 1989; Iacovou 2002; Iacovou 2008; Iacovou 2014; Satraki 2012) and to most of them have been attributed coinages with coin legends in the local script (Fig. 1). The study of the coinages of the city-kingdoms that were included in hoards is of great significance, as it provides researchers with important information regarding coin circulation and the dating of the various coin issues (Pilides and Destrooper-Georgiades 2008; Markou 2011c). Following the successful analytical study and publication of gold coins issued by the local kings of the Iron Age Cypriot city kingdoms via a handheld pXRF (Markou et al. 2014), a new research project was launched. The new project focuses on the silver coin issues of the local Cypriot kings of the Archaic and early Classical period that were included in well-dated hoards. In this paper we present and discuss the results of the analysis of the silver coins from the Larnaca Hoard (*IGCH* 1272), one of the most important hoards of the early fifth century BC on Cyprus.

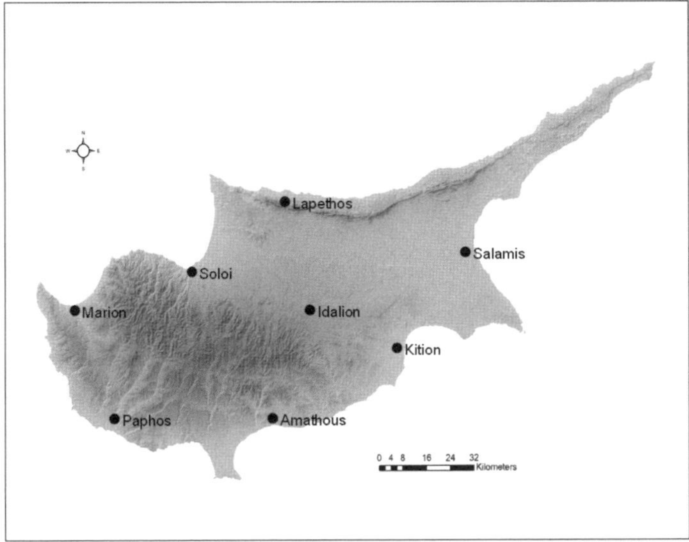

Figure 1. Map of located mints on Cyprus.

The Larnaca Hoard (*IGCH* 1272)

The Larnaca Hoard was discovered accidentally in July 1933 during digging for the foundations of a new wing of the municipal hospital of Larnaca (Dikaios 1935; Robinson 1935; Destrooper-Georgiades 1984). It originally contained at least 700 coins (Kraay 1976), but just before the local antiquities authorities reached the discovery site, a significant number of the silver coins was kept or sold by the workers who discovered them. Most of the scattered coins were recovered in the following months, but 99 coins found their way to the London antiquities market and two coins came into the possession of a Cypriot resident in South Africa (Dikaios 1935).

The coins of the specific hoard were all Cypriot *sigloi* (weight ca. 11 g), for the most part well preserved, and have been dated to the latter part of the sixth century and the first part of the fifth century BC. The combined coin die study of silver issues of the royal coinages of Cyprus is currently in progress, but based on some preliminary observations, it appears that the silver coins of the Archaic and early Classical period were following a common "local" weight standard based on a *siglos* of *circa* 11 grams that was divided into thirds, sixths, twelfths, and so on (Markou 2011b). The *terminus ante quem* of the Larnaca Hoard is around 480 BC or perhaps a little later. The coins (a total of 564) were initially attributed by Porphyrios Dikaios to several city-kingdoms of Cyprus as follows: Kition, 3; Idalion, 36; Lapethos, 143; Paphos, 292; Salamis, 51; uncertain series, 29; and unidentified due to their poor state of preservation, 10 (Dikaios 1935). Interestingly, despite the fact that the hoard was discovered in the modern city of Larnaca, which was built on the location of the ancient city of Kition, the majority of these coins has been attributed to cities other than Kition. The re-examination of 468 coins from the hoard (Destrooper-Georgiades 1984) has shown that more than three coins can be attributed to the city of Kition. In fact, in the Cyprus Museum collections there are eight coins from the hoard, which can be attributed to Kition, and they are all included in the present study (LH1–8).

The coins of the Larnaca Hoard cover a very important historical period and reveal the complexity of Cypriot coinage of the late Archaic–Early Classical period. A number of historical events took place in the Eastern Mediterranean at this time and it is reasonable to expect that they would have also affected the monetary practice of the Cypriot city-kingdoms. Cyprus was encompassed in the Persian Empire in 525 BC and formed part of the fifth satrapy of the Persian Empire, along with Phoenicia, Syria and Palestine. Some years later, in 498 BC, most of the Cypriot cities joined in the Ionian Revolt against the Persian Empire, and together attacked the city of Amathous (Hdt. 5.104.3). Following the collapse of the revolt, Persian authority continued to rule the island of Cyprus, down to the middle of the fourth century BC (Stylianou 1989; Kagan 1999; Iacovou 2008).

The procurement of silver for the production of coins

As has already been mentioned, the Larnaca Hoard consists exclusively of silver coins. But what was the origin of the silver used to produce these coins? Was silver available to the island and easily accessible to the Cypriot kings or did silver have to be imported? Cyprus is well known for its mineral wealth and its massive copper sulfide deposits, which were extensively exploited from antiquity up to the present (Constantinou 1992). Silver, on the other hand, does not appear to have been exploited on the island in ancient times. The reason behind this is that silver is found in Cypriot ores in a colloidal form and in very low concentrations that are not visible to the naked eye and, thus, cannot be collected by panning (Bear 1963). Instead, silver must be extracted through a series of fairly complex metallurgical procedures, none of which are recorded on the island (Kassianidou 2012).

Therefore, we must seek the sources of the silver used to produce the Larnaca Hoard coins overseas. In the Eastern Mediterranean region, important silver ore deposits are located in Laurion (Attica) and in the Aegean area, specifically on the islands of Siphnos (Gale and Stos-Gale 1981; Pernicka et al. 1985) and Thasos (Grabolle 1988; Papadopoulos 2008). Silver production at Laurion, at the site of Thoricos, had already begun in the second half of the fourth millennium (Kakavogianni et al. 2008), reaching its peak in the fifth and fourth centuries BC, before it was finally abandoned in the first century BC (Conophagos 1980). Anatolia also possesses numerous important argentiferous ore deposits that were extensively exploited in antiquity (Bayburtoğlu and Yildirim 2008; Moorey 1994).

No argentiferous deposits are known from the Levant or Mesopotamia, although from the end of the eighth century BC Phoenicia was supplying both of these regions with raw material, including silver (Aubet 2001). The need for silver, made even more imperative due to the pressing demands of the Assyrian Empire, is believed to have led the Phoenicians to the Iberian Peninsula and the extremely rich silver deposits (Aubet 1993; Eshel et al. 2019) of the so-called "Iberian Pyrite Belt," which extends from Seville to the south of Lisbon (Salkield 1987). It is possible that Iberian silver could have reached Cyprus through the extended trade networks of the Phoenicians, in exchange for Cypriot copper or locally produced luxury goods, such as metal vessels (Kassianidou 1992). The Phoenicians established a foothold on Cyprus in the ninth century BC (Gjerstad 1948; Teixidor 1975; Aubet 1993; Stylianou 1989; Iacovou 2006) and the presence of a Phoenician royal authority in Kition is well attested from the fifth to the fourth century BC (Gjerstad 1948; Iacovou 2014).

Moreover, a possible source of silver could have been the island of Sardinia, where significant argentiferous lead-zinc ore deposits can be found (Valera et al. 2005). Indeed, in antiquity Sardinia was well known as a source of lead and silver, and was given the name of αργυρόφλεψ νήσος or "the island of silver veins" (Schol. Plat. *In Tim.* 25b) by the ancient Greeks. Sardinian silver could have reached Cyprus through trade and in exchange for Cypriot copper (Kassianidou 2006).

Aim of the research study

The aim of the present study is the non-destructive pXRF chemical analysis of the silver coins of Larnaca Hoard and the determination of their composition, in order to identify the silver alloys chosen for their manufacture. Determining the silver alloys utilized will allow us to answer important archaeological questions and provide essential new information regarding the specific coin issues of the Cypriot mints included in the hoard. The non-destructive pXRF technique was chosen due to the fact that it was not permitted to (a) take the coins out of the museum for conventional (and usually destructive) laboratory analysis, and

(b) sample them, which would have made possible the application of additional analytical techniques. We are aware of the limitations of pXRF technique regarding surface versus bulk composition, but the high concentration of silver in the assemblage under study seems to minimize the enrichment effect. It has been argued that silver-enriched surface layers are not found in alloys with 96–98 wt% Ag (Ager et al. 2013).

It is important to note that no analytical study of silver coins from the Iron Age Cypriot city-kingdoms has been undertaken on this scale before. Only two studies of the gold coins of the Iron Age Cypriot city-kingdoms have been conducted in the last 20 years. The first one was conducted on 53 coins from the collection of the Cabinet des Médailles de la Bibliothèque Nationale de France in Paris, with the application of two different analytical techniques, Proton Activation Analysis (PAA) (Gondonneau and Amandry 2002) and Laser Ablation Inductively Coupled Plasma Mass Spectrometry (LA-ICP-MS) (Gratuze et al. 2004). The results from both analytical techniques were included together with supplementary examples analyzed by the same methods in 2011 (Markou 2011a). The second study was performed on 48 coins from the coin collections of the Department of Antiquities of Cyprus (27 coins) and the Bank of Cyprus Cultural Foundation (21 coins) using pXRF spectrometry (Markou et al. 2014).

A number of studies on silver coins either from hoards or large coin collections, dated from the fourth century BC up to the seventeenth century AD, from several areas and with the application of various techniques, among them XRF spectrometry, have been published the last years (Constantinescu et al. 2003; Civici et al. 2007; Pitarch and Queralt 2010; Rodrigues et al. 2011). Some of the most important issues that the specific studies address are: (a) the concentration of copper and other elements in the silver coins, (b) the provenance and methods of production of the silver metal, and (c) the advantages and limitations of the analytical techniques applied on the surface and bulk analysis of the coins.

The current analytical approach focuses on the study and interpretation of the compositional results of the main types of coins, which are present in numbers higher than 5 (the smallest group is the Kition group with eight coins) rather than individual pieces or groups of two to three coins. We opted for this approach as it allows for more statistically meaningful results, not affected by small sample size. The current study does not address the question of provenance, as it is well known that a simple chemical composition analysis is not adequate to determine the origin of the raw material (Pollard and Bray 2014), namely the silver metal used to produce the coins. Lead Isotope Analysis (LIA) is currently the best technique for studying metal provenance, although it is not without limitations (Pollard and Bray 2014). Lead Isotope Analysis was, however, not possible in the case of the assemblage under study, as we were not allowed to take any samples.

2. MATERIAL AND METHODS

2.1. Silver coins

The assemblage analyzed for this study includes 436 Cypriot silver *sigloi* attributed to several city-kingdoms. The coins are distributed as follows: Kition, 8; Idalion, 29; Lapethos, 107; Paphos, 224; Salamis, 46; unidentified series, 22. The eight coins of Kition, issued by early kings, are dated to the end of the 6th – beginning of the fifth century BC and they illustrate a recumbent lion turning his head on the obverse and a smooth reverse (no type imprinted on it). The iconography of the lion is quite common in Cyprus and is attested at several unknown mints of the fifth century BC, as well as in Amathous, where it becomes the exclusive numismatic type (Amandry 1984; Amandry 1997; Markou 2015). In the case of Idalion there are two groups of coins: the first group (Idalion 1 henceforth) contains 21 coins, issued by an unknown king at the beginning of the fifth century BC and depicting a sphinx with curved wings seated right on the obverse and an incuse square on the reverse. The second group (Idalion 2 henceforth), composed of 8 coins issued by an unknown king Ki(-) after 480 BC, depicts a sphinx with curved wings seated right on the obverse and a lotus flower on two spiral tendrils on the reverse side.

The coins from the kingdom of Lapethos form the second largest group in the Larnaca Hoard. There are four different types: the first and probably earliest issue is represented only by two specimens, issued by an unknown king beginning of fifth century B), and has a kneeling-wounded (?) giant (the type is poorly preserved) on the obverse and a running-kneeling Herakles with bow and club on the reverse (Robinson 1935; Kagan 1994). One early example of this type was included in the Persepolis foundation deposit (ca. 511 BC) (Kraay 1976). Similarly, the second issue is represented only by two specimens, issued by an unknown king (ca. 525 BC) with an unrecognizable pattern on the obverse side and the bearded head of Herakles on the reverse (Robinson 1935; Zapiti and Michaelidou 2010; Markou 2015). The remaining 102 coins belong to two large groups, both issued by an unknown king(s), dating to the beginning of the fifth century BC (after 490 BC). They depict the head of Aphrodite facing to the right on the obverse side and the head of Athena in screstted Corinthian helmet, facing either to the right (this group of 56 *sigloi* will be named Lapethos 1 henceforth) or to the left (this group of 46 *sigloi* will be named Lapethos 2 henceforth) on the reverse side.

The 224 coins of Paphos comprise the largest assemblage of the hoard. Of these, 223 were issued by King Pu(-) or Pny(-) (early fifth century BC) and depict a bull standing to the left on the obverse and a head of an eagle facing to the left on the reverse. One early example of this type was included in the Persepolis foundation deposit (ca. 511 BC) (Kraay 1976). The only example issued by King A(-) (early fifth century BC) depicts a bull walking to the left on the obverse and the same iconography as the other coins of Paphos on the reverse. There are three different types of coins from Salamis: the first group of 31 coins (Salamis 1 henceforth) was issued by King Evelthon (end of sixth century BC) and depicts a ram lying to the left on the obverse side and a smooth reverse side (no type imprinted on it), while the second group of 14 coins (Salamis 2 henceforth) was issued by Evelthon's Successors (early fifth century BC) and depicts a ram lying to the left on the obverse and an ankh in an incuse square on the reverse side. There is only one coin issued by King Nicodamos or King Evanthes (second quarter of the fifth century BC or earlier) that depicts a ram lying to the left on the obverse side (same iconography as the other coins of Salamis) and the head of a ram facing left on the reverse.

The Larnaca Hoard also includes some coins, which cannot be attributed with certainty to a kingdom, but form three different groups, while there are two coins, which are unique. The first group consists of two coins, minted by an unknown king, probably dated to the first quarter of the fifth century (Kagan 1994). These depict a lion forepart on the obverse and a Gorgon head on the reverse. The second and larger group (Unidentified 1 henceforth) consists of 12 coins, issued by an unknown king or kings (there are five different versions of the same iconography on both the obverse and the reverse side of the coins), dated to the first quarter of the fifth century (Kagan 1994; Zapiti and Michaeli-dou,2010), and they depict a lion head with open jaws on the obverse and a bull head on the reverse side. The third group (Unidentified 2 henceforth) consists of 6 coins, minted by an unknown king, probably dated to the first quarter of the fifth century (Kagan 1994). These depict a lion head (similar to that of the second group) on the obverse and an octopus on the reverse side. The octopus depiction, most probably copied from Eretria coins, is suggestive of a connection with the Ionian Revolt and precisely to 499/8 BC, when Cyprus participated for a short time in the movement (Robinson 1935; Kraay 1976). It has been suggested that the city-kingdom of Kourion could have minted the last two groups of coins (Kagan 1999).

The main groups of the analyzed coins (obverse and reverse sides) are shown in Figure 2.

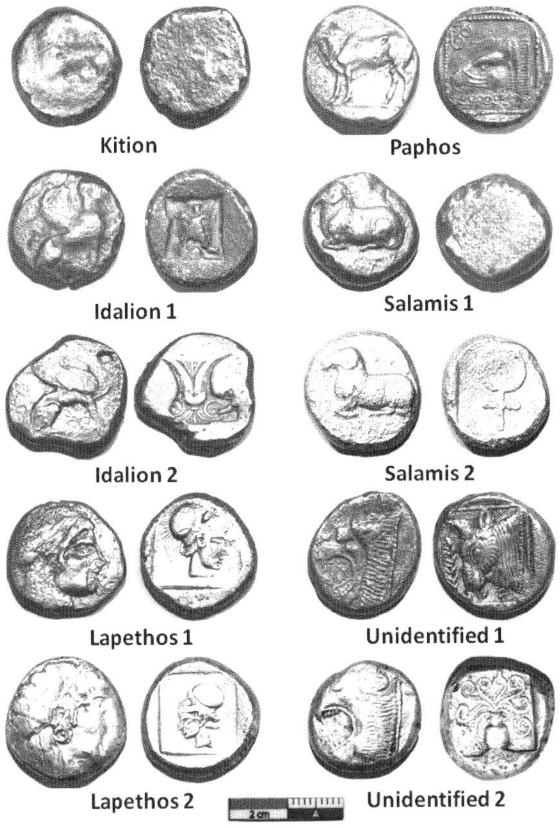

Figure 2. The main groups of the analyzed coins.

2.2. Chemical analysis and methodology

The numismatic study of the silver coins included the determination of the weight, diameter and axis. Some general characteristics are presented in Table 1 (below). Moreover, photos of both sides of the coins, obverse and reverse were taken, in order to mark the selected areas of analysis and to avoid areas with surface corrosion. Generally, all the studied coins were in a very good condition and free from surface depositions and corrosion, as the hoard had previously been treated by a museum conservator. Areas on the surface of the coins where some corrosion was still visible were avoided for analysis, although measurements were conducted on a small number of corroded areas as a means of recording differences between the corroded and uncorroded areas on the same coins. Due to the very good preservation condition of the coins and the very thin layer of the corrosion (usually defined by black coloring of the surface of the coins), the differences in the composition between the various analyzed areas of the same coin in most of the cases were very small and did not affect the general composition of the coins (only the concentration of iron and lead was slightly higher on the darker areas).

Table 1. Overview of the characteristics of the Larnaca Hoard coin groups

Coin Group	Number of Coins	Weight (g)	Diameter (mm)	Period
Kition	8	9.99–10.79	18–20	End of 6th–beginning of 5th century BC
Idalion 1	21	9.43–10.91	20–24	Beginning of 5th century BC
Idalion 2	8	9.83–11.30	21–24	After 480 BC
Lapethos 1	56	9.14–11.26	20–25	Beginning of 5th century BC, after 490 BC
Lapethos 2	46	7.23–11.21	20–25	Beginning of 5th century BC, after 490 BC
Paphos	224	9.30–11.19	18–25	Early 5th century BC
Salamis 1	31	8.75–11.17	18–22	End of 6th century BC
Salamis 2	14	9.39–11.09	20–23	Early 5th century BC
Unidentified 1	12	9.79–10.86	19–23	First quarter of 5th century BC
Unidentified 2	6	9.43–10.74	21–22	First quarter of 5th century BC

The analytical measurements were made using a portable, handheld Innov-X Delta Energy-Dispersive XRF analyzer (pXRF). Energy-Dispersive X-ray Fluorescence (EDXRF) spectrometry is a well-known, non-destructive, fast and multi-element analytical method. The portable XRF was selected for the *in situ* analysis and the determination of the chemical composition of the coins as the only non-destructive and non-invasive analytical technique available. Thus, the application of other more reliable laboratory analytical techniques, such as Laser Ablation Inductively Coupled Plasma Mass Spectrometry (LA-ICP-MS) or Proton Activation Analysis (PAA), which have lower detection limits than the EDXRF technique, especially for trace elements (Guerra 2008), were not an option in our case. The portability and non-destructive nature of portable handheld XRF has resulted in the widespread use of the specific technique for the chemical analysis of ancient precious artefacts, despite the fact that it only provides a chemical profile for the surface, which may not be representative of the whole (Ager et al. 2013). However, one should bear in mind that particularly with regards to silver coins, there are certain conditions that may result in increased values of the items' silver content as far as surface composition is concerned (Schmitt-Korte and Cowell 1989; Butcher and Ponting 1995; Butcher and Ponting, 2012; Ager et al. 2013). These conditions pertain particularly to the alloy composition, means of manufacture, burial conditions and the extent of cleaning and polishing of the artefact (Tate 1986; Araújo et al. 1993; Craddock et al. 1998; Guerra 1998; Cowell and Hyne 2000; Karydas et al. 2004; Ager et al. 2013).

The instrument used in our analyses is equipped with a 4W, 50kV tantalum anode X-Ray tube and a high performance Silicon Drift Detector (SDD) with a resolution of 155 eV (Mo-Kα), covered by a 20-mm detector window. The X-rays are emitted by a miniaturized X-ray tube, located in the internal structure of the instrument, behind a polypropylene film window. The diameter of the X-Ray beam, adjusted by the use of a collimator, is 3 mm.

Six measurements, three on each side, covering a large part of the surface, were performed on each of the coins and the elements concentrations represent the average values of all measurements. This way of measurement takes into account surface irregularities and heterogeneity effects of the coins (Al-Kofahi and Al-Tarawneh 2000; Constantinescu et al. 2003). Measurement time for each spot analysis was 70 seconds.

The analytical mode chosen is Alloy Plus. For this mode Beam 1 (40 kV) analyses the elements Ti, V, Cr, Mn, Fe, Co, Ni, Cu, Zn, As, Hf, Ta, W, Re, Au, Pb, Bi, Zr, Nb, Mo, Pd, Ag, Sn and Sb, whereas Beam 2 (10 kV) is used for the determination of Mg, Al, Si, P and S. The calibration of the instrument was done by the Fundamental Parameters (FP) method designed by the manufacturer (Innov-X). This method calculates chemistry from the spectral data, without the requirement of stored fingerprints. More specifically, Fundamental Parameters involves iterative corrections to raw X-ray counts based on the measured chemical composition, accounting for expected differences in various X-ray phenomena like X-ray emission, diffraction and secondary fluorescence (Frahm 2013).

A silver certified reference material (CRM) 133X AGQ1 (MBH ANALYTICAL LTD, England) was used to test the analytical procedure and the accuracy of the applied analytical mode. The results of the analysis of the silver certified reference material along with the uncertainty and the detection limits of the instrument are provided in Table 2 (below). There was a good agreement between the recommended and measured concentrations for Ag, but higher concentrations for Cu, Au and Pb. The differences were taken into consideration and small corrections were made on the final values of Cu, Au and Pb concentrations of the analyzed coins.

Table 2. The results of the analysis of the silver certified reference material

Element	Silver certified reference material 133X AGQ1		Uncertainty (%)		Detection Limits (ppm)
	Certified value (%) ± std	Measured value (%) ± std	Absolute	Relative	
Ag	96.972 (bal)	96.44 ± 0.3	0.532	0.05	200
Cu	2.532 ± 0.016	2.64 ± 0.05	0.108	4.2	200
Au	0.251 ± 0.003	0.26 ± 0.01	0.09	3.6	200
Pb	0.245 ± 0.002	0.26 ± 0.02	0.015	6.1	250
Fe		0.05 ± 0.005			250

3. RESULTS AND DISCUSSION

Before presenting the results of the chemical analysis of the silver coins, it will be very helpful to provide some information about the cupellation process, the main method of silver extraction and purification during antiquity, and how this process could have affected the composition of the coins and the presence or absence of certain elements.

This process was used in antiquity, as indeed until today, in order to extract the silver from argentiferous lead ores such as galena, the lead sulphide, or cerussite, the lead carbonate (Nriagu 1985). Lead was also used to collect silver from polymetallic ores (Craddock, 1995; Anguilano et al. 2010). Cupellation was and is still used as an assay method for the determination of silver content in ores and metals (Tylecote 1987; Craddock 1995; L'Héritier et al. 2015). The result is metallic silver of high purity. More specifically, the lead cupellation process involves the oxidation of the silver-containing lead bullion in air at a temperature of about 900–950° C, producing silver metal and litharge (lead oxide, PbO). The litharge is absorbed by the reaction vessel, usually made of clay and/or bone ash, called a cupel, while the silver is left within the vessel (Tylecote 1987; Martinón-Torres et al. 2009). Trace elements that were initially contained in the lead bullion are separated from the silver because of their affinity to oxygen. Litharge dissolves and absorbs the oxides of most of elements including silicon (Si), calcium (Ca) and iron (Fe). On the other hand, noble metals like platinum (Pt), palladium (Pd) and gold (Au), and nonreactive metals like bismuth (Bi) tend to remain in the silver bullion (Craddock 1995; Karydas et al. 2004).

Besides silver (Ag), copper (Cu), lead (Pb), gold (Au) and bismuth (Bi), which are related to the silver ores and metallurgy (Butcher and Ponting 2012), iron (Fe) and in some coins small amounts of zinc (Zn) were also detected. Iron will not be included in the discussion as it is most often the result of surface contamination or found as inclusions in the coins (Constantinescu et al. 2003; Civici et al. 2007; Pitarch and Queralt 2010). The concentration ranges of the elements Ag, Cu, Pb, Au and Bi, which are found in most of the coins, are presented in Table 3, with the number of coins analyzed from each group in parentheses.

The results of the chemical analysis show that all coin groups from the various mints under examination are made of a similar silver-copper (Ag-Cu) alloy and in each group most of the coins have a silver concentration in the range 96.5–98.5%. The two groups of coins from Salamis differ, as most examples from both groups have a silver concentration, which is higher than 98% (Table 3, below).

Copper is the main alloying element of the silver metal used for the manufacture of the analyzed coins. Some scholars have argued that copper concentrations in silver (extracted from most types of ores) can reach 1.5%. A copper concentration higher than 1.5% is, therefore, believed to indicate a deliberate addition (Ogden 1992). Others, however, state that the usual natural concentration levels of copper in extracted silver do not exceed 0.5% (Tylecote 1987; Craddock 1995; Karydas et al. 2004). On the other hand, the results of the analysis here show a relatively low copper concentration, which does not support the possibility of an attempt at debasement or some form of adulteration. Therefore, the fact that the concentration of copper is at a higher level than expected after an efficient purification method (around 0.5% Cu) can be justified as a deliberate addition in an attempt to increase the hardness of the alloy and to improve its mechanical properties for the manufacture of coins (Karydas et al. 2004). Moreover, the strong negative correlation between Ag and Cu shown in the plots of silver and copper content of the coins (Fig. 3, below) provides further support to the notion of a deliberate addition of copper in the alloy.

The average copper concentration of the analyzed coins is in the range 1.15–1.9%, with the exception of the two groups from Salamis where the copper concentration is 0.65 and 0.7% respectively (Table 3, below). Interestingly, the issues of the same city-kingdoms have similar or very close average concentrations of copper (e.g., Idalion 1 and Idalion 2 groups have average concentrations 1.7 and 1.55%, respectively). Let us assume that the highest concentration of copper in the silver that can be considered not to have been a deliberate addition is 1.5% (Ogden 1992). In this case, we can divide the coins for each series into those that do and those that do not exceed this limit. We see that Cu concentrations above 1.5% are found in 2 out of 8 coins of Kition (25% of the total), 8 out of 21 coins of Idalion 1 (38% of the total), 4 out of 8 coins of Idalion 2 (50% of the total), 15

Table 3. Elemental concentration range and average value of the analyzed coins from different groups measured by pXRF

Coin Group	Ag (%)			Cu (%)			Pb (%)			Au (%)			Bi (%)		
	Min	Max	Average	Min	Max	Average	Min	Max	Average	Min	Max	Average	Min	Max	Average
Kition (8)	96.8	99	97.65	0.45	2	1.4	0.2	0.8	0.4	0.1	0.8	0.3	0.05	0.09	0.07
Idalion 1 (21)	95.5	98.7	97.25	0.8	3.5	1.7	0.2	1.1	0.5	0.1	0.8	0.35	0.05	0.2	0.1
Idalion 2 (8)	95.3	98.1	96.75	0.95	2.2	1.55	0.4	0.9	0.55	0.1	1.9	0.9	0.05	0.2	0.1
Lapethos 1 (56)	96.5	98.8	97.6	0.4	3.6	1.3	0.15	0.8	0.4	0.2	0.7	0.4	0.05	0.4	0.1
Lapethos 2 (46)	96	99	97.65	0.3	2.3	1.15	0.15	0.9	0.45	0.1	0.8	0.45	0.05	0.2	0.07
Paphos (223)	94	99.1	97.1	0.4	3.8	1.9	0.15	1.4	0.5	0.1	1.2	0.25	0.05	0.5	0.1
Salamis 1 (31)	93.5	99.6	98.3	0.05	1.5	0.65	0.07	1.6	0.4	0.1	1.5	0.4	0.05	0.3	0.1
Salamis 2 (14)	97.5	99.3	98.7	0.1	1	0.7	0.1	1	0.3	0.05	0.6	0.3	0.05	0.2	0.1
Unidentified 1 (12)	95.8	99.1	97.1	0.3	2.5	1.4	0.2	1.4	0.75	0.1	0.9	0.35	0.05	0.3	0.15
Unidentified 2 (6)	96.6	99	98	0.06	2.8	1.2	0.1	0.5	0.3	0.05	0.4	0.25	0.07	0.2	0.15

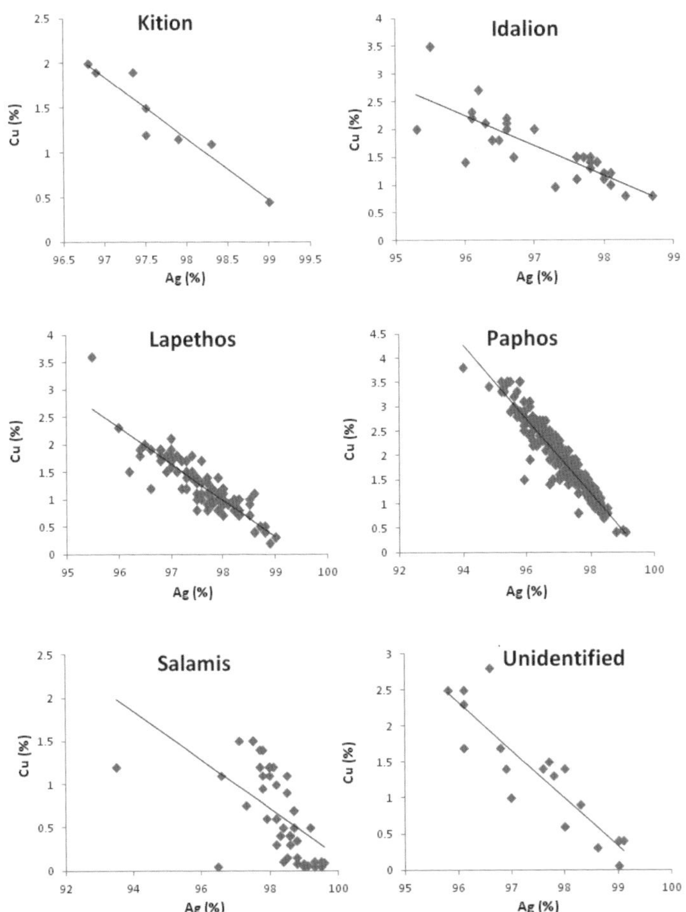

Figure 3. Silver and copper content of the coins from different groups.

out of 56 coins of Lapethos 1 (27% of the total), 9 out of 46 coins of Lapethos 2 (20% of the total), 139 out of 224 coins of Paphos (62% of the total), none of the coins of Salamis, 5 out of 12 of Unidentified Mint 1 (42% of the total) and 1 out of 6 of Unidentified Mint 2 (17% of the total) (Table 4, below). Based on this, the assemblage assigned to Salamis is particularly interesting: all coins, from both issues, have a copper content lower than 1.5%. Equally interesting is the assemblage from Paphos as more than half of the coins (62% of the total) have a copper content above 1.5%, possibly indicating a rather different manufacturing technique for the alloy, compared to the rest of the studied mints.

Lead (Pb) may have been introduced to the silver alloy either as a result of the smelting procedure of the silver ores and the associated cupellation method or from the deliberate addition of copper. In the first instance, the lead concentration in the silver alloy depends on the type of mineral that was used for the production of silver. If argentiferous lead ores, and particularly galena (PbS), cerussite ($PbCO_3$) and anglesite ($PbSO_4$), were smelted (the case of Laurion, Greece), the lead contents in the silver alloy could range between 0.05% and 2.5% (Gale and Stos-Gale 1981) or between 0.001% and 3% (Moorey 1985; Karydas et al. 2004). Tylecote (1987) has mentioned a range of Pb concentration between 0.1 and 1%; the concentration of copper in the case of silver coming from argentiferous galena is usually no more than 0.5% (Gale and Stos-Gale 1981; Tylecote 1987). Moreover, in the case of argentiferous jarosite ores (hydrated sulphates) (the case of Rio Tinto, Spain), the use of lead was obligatory in order to collect the silver (Craddock 1995). Generally, it is well accepted that a low lead concentration (below 0.5%) indicates a good refining process (Civici et al. 2007). It is worth mentioning that the addition of lead for the accumulation of silver from some types of minerals (a process called liquation) could be very misleading in provenance studies on silver artifacts using lead isotope analysis, in cases where they take for granted that lead originates with the silver (Craddock 1995).

In this study, most of the analyzed coins have a Pb concentration below 0.5%, indicating a very efficient silver refining process. More specifically (Table 4), a Pb concentration ≤ 0.5% was detected in 6 out of 8 coins from Kition, 20 out of 29 coins from Idalion (15 out of 21 coins for Idalion 1 and 5 out of 8 coins for Idalion 2), 78 out of 104 coins from Lapethos (42 out of 56 coins for Lapethos 1 and 35 out of 46 coins for Lapethos 2), 145 out of 224 coins from Paphos, 36 out of 46 coins from Salamis (24 out of 31 coins for Salamis 1 and 12 out of 14 coins for Salamis 2), 4 out of 12 coins from Unidentified Mint 1 and 6 out of 6 coins from Unidentified Mint 2. So, the more efficient refining process was observed in the coins of the two groups from Salamis and the second group of unidentified coins (Unidentified Mint 2), while the least efficient process was noted in the coins of Idalion 2, Paphos and Unidentified Mint 1.

Gold (Au) was detected in all coins, ranging from 0.05 up to 1.9% (Table 3, above), although in most coins, its concentration varies between 0.1 and 0.5%. The case of the Idalion coins is very interesting in this regard. In the Idalion 2 group, 6 out of the 8 coins have a gold concentration above 0.6% (Au: 0.65–1.9%, the remaining two coins have 0.1% Au). On the contrary, 18 out of the 21 coins of Idalion 1 group have a gold concentration in the range of 0.1–0.4% (the remaining three coins have 0.7–0.8% Au). These differences in the gold concentra-

Table 4. The comparison of Cu, Pb, Au concentration thresholds and Bi, Zn presence for each group

Coin Group	Cu (%)		Pb (%)		Au (%)		Bi		Zn	
	< 1.5%	> 1.5%	≤ 0.5%	> 0.5%	≤ 0.5%	> 0.5%	Detected	Undetected	Detected	Undetected
Kition (8)	6	2	6	2	7	1	6	2	0	8
Idalion 1 (21)	13	8	15	6	18	3	21	0	3	18
Idalion 2 (8)	4	4	5	3	2	6	6	2	1	7
Lapethos 1 (56)	41	15	42	14	46	10	50	6	7	49
Lapethos 2 (46)	37	9	35	11	35	11	39	7	3	43
Paphos (224)	85	139	145	79	216	8	215	9	45	179
Salamis 1 (31)	31	0	24	7	22	9	30	1	1	30
Salamis 2 (14)	14	0	12	2	9	5	9	5	1	13
Unidentified 1 (12)	7	5	4	8	10	2	12	0	1	11
Unidentified 2 (6)	5	1	6	0	6	0	6	0	0	6

tion between the two groups most likely indicate two different silver sources for the coin issues of Idalion. In the other groups, the gold concentration shows the same trend where the majority of the coins have a gold content below 0.5% and only a small number of coins exceed that concentration. Specifically, as shown in Table 4, in Kition, 7 out of the 8 coins have a gold content in the range 0.1–0.4% (the only exception has 0.8% Au), in Lapethos 1, 46 out of the 56 coins have a gold content in the range 0.2–0.5% (the rest 10 coins have 0.55–0.7% Au), in Lapethos 2, 35 out of the 46 coins have a gold content in the range of 0.1–0.5% (the remaining 11 coins have 0.6–0.8% Au), in the large group of Paphos, only eight coins have a gold content above 0.5%, in Salamis 1, 22 out of the 31 coins have a gold content in the range of 0.1–0.5%, in Salamis 2, 12 out of the 14 coins have a gold content in the range of 0.05–0.45% (the two exceptions have 0.6% Au), in Unidentified Mint 1, 10 out of the 12 coins have a gold content in the range of 0.1–0.45% (the two exceptions have 0.6% and 0.9% Au) and in Unidentified Mint 2 the six coins have a gold content in the range 0.05–0.4%. So it is obvious, in the cases where we have two mints from the same city, that only in the case of Idalion we can suggest the differentiation of the two mints. In the cases of Lapethos, Salamis and the unidentified mints, the two mints have a similar gold concentration range.

But how can the presence of gold in silver coins be explained? Even though ancient silver commonly contains substantial concentrations of gold (Au) and its presence was almost certainly known in antiquity, along with the technology of separating the two precious metals, there seems to have been little effort to recover the gold (Craddock 1995). Specifically, the gold contained in the original argentiferous ores survives the melting process and the manufacture of the coins and is present in the silver metal in its original amount. The gold content of silver depends on the type of ore that was smelted for the production of silver. If argentiferous galena was employed, silver would contain zero up to about 1% Au (Gale and Stos-Gale 1981; Karydas et al. 2004), while the use of oxidized lead ores, like cerussite and anglesite, would have resulted on a gold content of 0.1 up to about 0.5% (Meyers 1983; Craddock 1995; Karydas et al. 2004). Another possible silver source could have been electrum, the natural gold-silver alloy (Craddock 1995; Ramage and Craddock 2000; Butcher and Ponting 2012). In electrum, the concentration of silver varies enormously but typically lies between 5% and 40% by weight (Tylecote 1987; Wallace 1987; Ramage and Craddock 2000). The specific alloy was applied in its natural form for the manufacture of the first coins (electrum issues) in the area of Asia Minor (Lydia) in the seventh century BC or it was processed in order to provide pure gold and pure silver for coins in the sixth century BC (Wallace 1987; Ramage and Craddock 2000).

Similarly to lead, bismuth (Bi) can be found in the silver metal either from the primary source of silver or as an accidentally added impurity. In the first case, if dry ores (ores which contain very small or no amount of elements like copper, lead or zinc) (Hayes and Waldemar Lindgren 1908) or native silver was used for the production of silver metal the bismuth concentration would be less than 0.05% (Craddock 1995; Karydas et al. 2004). If argentiferous galena was used, then the concentration of bismuth in the silver would be between 0.1 and 1% (Gale and Stos-Gale 1981; Karydas et al. 2004). In the second case, bismuth would have entered the silver metal through the deliberate addition of copper, if it was present in the original copper ores. Based on the results of the chemical analysis and the relatively low copper content in the silver coins in most of the analyzed cases, along with the suggested use of pure copper, it is highly possible that bismuth was entering the silver metal through the cupellation process. Bismuth can, thus, be considered as an ore source tracer for silver material (L'Héritier et al. 2015). The analysis of the assemblage under study, showed that bismuth is not present in all the coins. It was found in 6 coins from Kition (0.05–0.09%), in all coins from Idalion 1 (only 6 out of 21 coins have a Bi content higher than 0.1%), in 6 coins from Idalion 2 (only 1 coin exceeds 0.1%), in 50 coins from Lapethos 1 (only in 7 coins Bi content exceeds 0.1%), in 39 coins from Lapethos 2 (only in 4 coins Bi content exceeds 0.1%), in 215 coins from Paphos (49 coins have Bi content 0.15–0.3%, only one coin has 0.5% Bi), in 30 coins from Salamis 1 (only in 9 coins Bi content exceeds 0.1%), in 9 coins from Salamis 2 (only in 2 coins Bi content exceeds 0.1%), and in all coins from Unidentified 1 (in 5 coins Bi content exceeds 0.1%) and Unidentified 2 (in 4 out of the 6 coins Bi content exceeds 0.1%) (Table 4, above). If we convert the presence of bismuth into percentages of the analyzed coins (Kition, 75%; Idalion 1, 100%; Idalion 2, 75%; Lapethos 1, 89%; Lapethos 2, 85%; Paphos, 96%; Salamis 1, 97%; Salamis 2, 64%; Unidentified 1, 100%; Unidentified 2, 100%), we see a clear differentiation between the two Idalion issues (similar to the case of gold) and the two issues of Salamis, a relatively small differentiation in the case of Lapethos and no differentiation in the case of the two unidentified issues. Moreover, if we observe the number of coins that have a bismuth concentration above 0.1% we can see that the two unidentified issues have the higher percentage, 41% and 66%, respectively, followed by Salamis 1 (30%) and Idalion 1 (28.6%).

And what about zinc (Zn)? The intensely oxidizing cupellation process would totally eliminate any zinc (Craddock 1995), thus the presence of even small traces of this metal in silver, would indicate that the zinc entered the silver metal most probably through the addition of copper. In fact, the small amount of zinc found in some of the coins (62 coins, 0.05–0.2%), and the absence of tin possibly indicate that copper was added as pure metal and not as copper alloy, a practice known from Roman times onwards (McKerrell and Stevenson 1972; Civici et al. 2007). In our case, the addition of copper as pure metal, and not as a copper alloy, seems to have started much earlier (fifth century BC). Also, the possibility that part of zinc could be attributed to external pollution, like in the case of iron, cannot be rejected on current evidence. In the present study, zinc was detected in 4 coins from Idalion (3 of Idalion 1 and 1 of Idalion 2 group, 0.05–0.07% Zn), 10 coins from Lapethos (7 of Lapethos 1 and 3 of Lapethos 2 group, 0.05–0.2% Zn), 45 coins from Paphos (0.05–0.2% Zn), 2 coins from Salamis (one from each group, 0.05% Zn) and in one coin from Unidentified Mint 1 (0.05% Zn), while the specific metal was not detected in the cases of Kition and Unidentified Mint 2 groups (Table 4, above).

In closing, it is worth mentioning the results of the analysis of the two small groups of coins that are probably attributed to Lapethos (kneeling-wounded (?) giant/running-kneeling Herakles and unrecognizable pattern/bearded head of Herakles) and the small unidentified group (lion forepart/gorgon head) that were not included in the general discussion and presentation of the results. Starting with the first small Lapethos group, the results of our analyses showed similar composition for all coins and element values very close to the average values of the two bigger groups from Lapethos (Ag: 97.7% and 97.4%; Cu: 1.2% and 1.4%; Pb: 0.15% and 0.5%; Fe: 0.25% and 0.15%; Au: 0.55% and 0.4%; Bi: 0.15% and 0.08%; no Zn). Almost identical is the composition of the two coins of the second small group that was attributed to Lapethos, even though it shows slightly higher silver and lower gold and bismuth concentrations (Ag: 98.5% and 98.2%; Cu: 1% and 1.1%; Pb: 0.2% and 0.15%; Fe: 0.08 and 0.15%; Au: 0.15% and 0.3%; Bi: 0.05%; no Zn). As for the unidentified group, the analysis showed a similar composition for the two coins, with relatively high silver content and low concentrations for the remaining elements (Ag: 98.3% and 98.5%; Cu: 1% and 0.9%; Pb: 0.3% and 0.2%; Fe: 0.15%; Au: 0.15% and 0.1%; Bi: 0.1%; no Zn).

4. CONCLUSIONS

The analytical study of the silver coins in the Larnaca Hoard, by means of a non-destructive portable XRF methodology, has generated useful new information with regards to the composition and manufacture of Cypriot silver coins dating to the sixth–fifth century BC. This is the first time ever that such a high number of Cypriot coins of this period, from a secure archaeological context, has been analyzed in any way.

The pXRF analysis of the 434 silver coins has shown that all the groups of coins are made of a similar silver-copper (Ag-Cu) alloy despite originating from different mints. Furthermore, the majority of coins from every analyzed group is characterized by silver concentration in the range 96.5–98.5%. Only in the two Salamis groups the concentration of silver is higher than 98% (in the majority of coins). With regards to copper—the main alloying component—of much interest are the cases of Salamis, where all coins, from both issues, have a copper content lower than 1.5%, and the case of Paphos where more than half of the coins (62% of the total) have a copper content above 1.5%, indicating a much different manufacture technology for the alloy, compared to the rest of the studied mints. The copper content indicates that this element was deliberately added to silver, most probably for the improvement of silver processing and the increase of its hardness rather than for debasement or adulteration reasons.

The concentration of lead provides useful information with regards to the efficiency of the silver production method. Most of the coins analyzed in this study have a lead concentration below 0.5%, suggesting a very efficient silver refining process. The most efficient silver refining process was observed in the coins of the two groups from Salamis and the Unidentified 2 group, while the coins of Idalion 2, Paphos and Unidentified 1 groups are the result of the least efficient refining process.

Gold (Au) and bismuth (Bi) are two elements that originated in the primary source of the silver minerals and can provide some information about the possible origin of the silver. The two elements can also reveal similarities and differences between the several coin issues coming from the same city. Starting with gold, the majority of the analyzed coins have a gold concentration in the range of 0.1 to 0.5%. The most interesting conclusion we can reach based on the gold content of the silver coins is that the two coin issues of Idalion (different gold concentration range, possibly due to different silver sources) are differentiated from one another, while in the cases of Lapethos, Salamis and the Unidentified mints, the two different issues have a similar gold concentration range. As for bismuth, the results of the analysis show that there is a differentiation between the two issues of Idalion (as in the case of the interpretation of the gold content) and between the two issues of Salamis, a relatively small differentiation in the case of Lapethos coin issues and no differentiation between the two Unidentified issues.

The sources of silver that were used for the manufacture of the coins is a critical issue and one of the main still unanswered archaeological questions regarding Cypriot archaeology. In our study, the results of the analysis and mainly the presence and concentration levels of lead, bismuth, and, principally, gold, suggest that the silver metal of the majority of the coins was most probably processed by argentiferous galena. The closest source of argentiferous galena to Cyprus is the Lavrion mine in Attica area (Athens, Greece), a mine that was highly active during the period that the mints of Larnaca Hoard are covering (sixth–fifth centuries BC) (Conophagos 1980; Kary et al. 2004) and, thus, a possible source for at least part of the raw metal used for the specific coins. At this point we should underline that Athenian coins—as well as Aeginetan coins—have been found in Cyprus mainly as overstrikes, which means that those foreign coins circulated on the island and were used as flans for the minting of local coins (Milne 1945; Destrooper-Georgiades 1996; Markou 2011c). The Athenian coins were made of silver from Laurion and could have been melted and used—as metal—for the issuing of the local Cypriot coinages at different times. However, it must be kept in mind that during this period we also note the documented presence of extensive trade networks organized by the Phoenicians between Cyprus and the rest of the Mediterranean. The establishment and maintenance of such networks in the area indicates that other silver production sources must not be excluded without prior investigation.

Finally, it is worth repeating that the studied coins albeit from different mints were buried together at the same time and they were cleaned, restored and stored in the same way and under the same conditions. Because of that and despite the fact that the applied surface analytical technique is not considered to be the most appropriate one for the study of coins, the pXRF study of the specific Cypriot silver coins has been a very fruitful exercise. By undertaking this study, we have been able to provide numismatists and archaeologists with new and significant information with regards to the minting technology of a series of silver coins produced during a very interesting period in the history of the Cypriot city-kingdoms.

ACKNOWLEDGMENTS

The elemental analysis of the coins was conducted by Dr. Andreas Charalambous within the framework of a project entitled "Interdisciplinary Study of Silver Coins of the Cypriot Iron Age City Kingdoms (6th–4th Centuries BC)". The project was funded with a "Post doctoral Researchers for Cyprus—Grant Supporting Post-doctoral Researchers in Memory of Naso Papaellina" scheme of the University of Cyprus. The project was coordinated by Professor Vasiliki Kassianidou and was carried out in collaboration with Dr. Evangeline Markou. We would like to sincerely thank the University of Cyprus and the family of Naso Papaellina for providing us with the opportunity to study this important material.

The authors wish to thank Dr. Marina Solomidou-Ieronymidou, Director of the Department of Antiquities of Cyprus for the permission to analyze the silver coins from the Larnaca Hoard, as well as Eutychia Zachariou, Archaeological Officer of the Department, and the staff of the storerooms of the museums, for making the coins accessible. The authors would also like to thank the anonymous reviewer for the constructive criticism, which resulted in a much improved paper.

REFERENCES

Ager, F. J., A. I. Moreno-Suárez, S. Scrivano, I. Ortega-Feliu, B. Gómez-Tubío and M. A.Respaldiza. 2013. "Silver surface enrichment in ancient coins studied by micro-PIXE." *Nuclear Instruments and Methods in Physics Research B* 306: 241–244.

Al-Kofahi, M. M., and K. F. Al-Tarawheh. 2000. "Analysis of Ayyubid and Mamluk dirhams using X-Ray Fluorescence Spectrometry." *X-Ray Spectrometry* 29: 39–47.

Amandry, M. 1984. "Le monnayage d'Amathonte." In *Amathonte I, Testimonia I, Auteurs anciens, Monnayage, Voyageurs, Fouilles, Origines, Géographie*, edited by P. Aupert and M.-C. Hellmann, 57–76. Recherche sur les Civilisations, 4. Paris: Études Chypriotes.

———. 1997. "Le monnayage d'Amathonte revisité." *Cahier du Centre d'Études Chypriotes* 27: 35–44.

Anguilano, L., T. Rehren, W. Müller and B. Rothenberg. 2010. "The importance of lead in the silver production at Riotinto (Spain)." *ArchaeoSciences, Revue d' archéométrie* 34: 269–276.

Araújo, M. F., L. C. Alves and J. M. P. Cabral. 1993. "Comparison of EDXRF and PIXE in the analysis of ancient gold coins." *Nuclear Instruments and Methods in Physics Research B* 75: 450–453.

Aubet, M. E. 1993. *The Phoenicians and the West*. Cambridge: Cambridge University Press.

———. 2001. *The Phoenicians and the West. Politics, Colonies and Trade*. Second Edition. Cambridge: Cambridge University Press.

Bayburtoğlu, B., and S. Yildirim. 2008. "Gold and silver in Anatolia." In *Anatolian Metal* IV, edited by Ü. Yalçin, 43–45. Der Anschnitt Beiheft 21. Bochum: Bergbau-Museum.

Bear, L. M. 1963. *The Mineral Resources and Mining Industry of Cyprus*, Bulletin 1. Nicosia: Geological Survey Department.

Butcher, K., and M. Ponting.1995. "Rome and the East: Production of Roman provincial silver coinage for Caesarea in Cappadocia under Vespasian, AD 69–79." *Oxford Journal of Archaeology* 14.1: 63–77.

———. 2012. "The Beginning of the End? The Denarius in the Second Century." *Numismatic Chronicle* 172: 63–83.

Civici, N., S. Gjonngecaj, F. Stamati, T. Dilo, E. Pavlidou, E. K. Polychroniadis and Z. Smit. 2007. "Compositional study of IIIrd century BC silver coins from Kreshpan hoard (Albania) using EDXRF spectrometry." *Nuclear Instruments and Methods in Physics Research B* 258: 414–420.

Conophagos, C. 1980. *Το Αρχαίο Λαύριο (Ancient Laurion)*. Athens: Ekdotike Hellados.

Constantinescu, B., A. Săşianu and R. Bugoi. 2003. "Adulterations in first century BC: the case of Greek silver drachmae analyzed by X-ray methods." *Spectrochimica Acta Part B* 58: 759–765.

Constantinou, G. 1992. "The mining industry of Cyprus in modern times." In *Cyprus, Copper and the Sea,* edited by A. Marangou and K. Pitsillides, 328–367. Nicosia: Government of Cyprus.

Cowell, M. R., and K. Hyne. 2000. "Scientific examination of the Lydian precious metal coinages." In *King Croesus' Gold. Excavations at Sardis and the History of Gold Refining*, edited by A. Ramage and P. Craddock, 169–174. London: British Museum Press.

Craddock, P. T. 1995. *Early Metal Mining and Production*. Edinburgh: Edinburgh University Pres.

Craddock, P., N. Meeks, M. Cowell, A. Middleton, D. Hook, A. Ramage and E. Geçkinli. 1998. "The Refining of Gold in the Classical World." In *The Art of the Greek Goldsmith*, edited by D. Williams, 111–138. London: British Museum Press.

Destrooper-Georgiades, A. 1984. "Le trésor de Larnaca (*IGCH*) 1272 réexaminé." *Report of the Department of Antiquities, Cyprus*:140–61.

———. 1993. "Continuités et ruptures dans le monnayage chypriote a l'époque achéménide." *Transeuphratène* 6: 87–101.

———. 1996. "Les tortues d'Égine à Chypre." In *Χαρακτήρ. Αφιέρωμα στη Μάντω Οικονομίδου*, edited by E. Kypraiou, 103–109. Δημοσιεύματα του Αρχαιολογικού Δελτίου 57. Athens: TAP.

Dikaios, P. 1935. "A hoard of silver Cypriot staters from Larnaca." *Numismatic Chronicle* 15: 165–179.

Eshel, T., Y. Erel, N. Yahalom-Mack, O. Tirosh and A. Gilboa. 2019. "Lead isotopes in silver reveal earliest Phoenician quest for metals in the west Mediterranean." *Proceedings of the National Academy of Sciences of the United States of America*, https://doi.org/10.1073/pnas.1817951116.

Frahm, E. 2013. "Validity of 'off-the-shelf' handheld portable XRF for sourcing New Eastern obsidian chip debris." *Journal of Archaeological Science* 40: 1080–1092.

Gale, N. H., and Z. A. Stos-Gale. 1981. "Cycladic Lead and Silver Metallurgy." *Annual of the British School at Athens* 76: 169–224.

Gjerstad, E. 1948. *The Swedish Cyprus Expedition: The Cypro-Geometric, Cypro-Archaic and Cypro-Classical Periods*, Vol. IV, Part 2. Stockholm: The Swedish Cyprus Expedition.

Gondonneau, A., and M. Amandry. 2002. "Le monnayage en or de Melkiathon et Pumiathon de Kition. Apports de l'analyse élémentaire." *Cahier du Centre d'Études Chypriotes* 32: 339–349.

Grabolle, I., 1988. "The production of precious metals and nonferrous metals on Thasos in Antiquity. Summary." In *Antike Edel-und Buntmetall-gewinnung auf Thasos*, edited by G. A. Wagner and G. Weisgerber, 262–265. Der Anschnitt Beiheft 6. Bochum: Deutschen Bergbau-Museums.

Gratuze, B., M. Blet-Lemarquand and J.-N. Barrandon. 2004. "Caractérisation des alliages monétaires à base d'or par LA-ICP-MS." *Bulletin de la Société Française de Numismatique*: 163–169.

Guerra, M. F. 1998. "Analysis of Archaeological Metals. The Place of XRF and PIXE in the Determination of Technology and Provenance." *X-Ray Spectrometry* 27: 73–80.

———. 2008. "An overview on the ancient goldsmith's skill and the circulation of gold in the past: the role of x-ray based techniques." *X-Ray Spectrometry* 37: 317–327.

Hadjicosti, M. 1997. "The kingdom of Idalion in the light of new evidence." *Bulletin of the American Schools of Oriental Research* 308: 49–63.

Hayes, C. W., and W. Lindgren. 1908. *Contributions to Economic Geology 1907, Part I—Metals and Nonmetals, Except Fuels*. United States Geological Survey Bulletin 340. Washington, DC: Washington Government Printing Office.

Hornblower, S. (ed.). 2013. *Herodotus Histories, Book V, 104.3*. Cambridge: Cambridge University Press.

Iacovou, M. 2002. "From Ten to Naught: Formation, Consolidation and Abolition of Cyprus' Iron Age Polities." *Cahier du Centre d' Etudes Chypriotes* 32: 73–87.

———. 2006. "'Greeks', 'Phoenicians' and 'Eteocypriots'. Ethnic Identities in the Cypriote Kingdoms." In *Sweet Land...: Lectures on the History and Culture of Cyprus*, edited by J. Chrysostomides and C. Dendrinos, 27–59. Camberly: Porphyrogenitus.

———. 2008. "Cultural and Political Configurations in Iron Age Cyprus: The Sequel to a Protohistoric Episode." *American Journal of Archaeology* 112: 625–657.

———. 2014. "Cyprus during the Iron Age through the Persian periods." In *The Oxford Handbook of the Archaeology of the Levant (ca. 8000–332 BCE)*, edited by M. L. Steiner, A. E. Killebrew, 795–824. Oxford: Oxford University Press.

Kakavogianni, O., K. Douni and F. Nezeri. 2008. "Silver metallurgical finds dating from the end of the Final Neolithic period until the Middle Bronze Age in the area of Mesogeia." In *Aegean Metallurgy in the Bronze Age. Proceedings of an International Symposium Held at the University of Crete, Rethymnon, Greece, on November 19–21, 2004,* edited by I. Tzachilli, 45–57. Athens: Ta Pragmata.

Kagan, J. H. 1994. "An Archaic Greek Coin Hoard from the Eastern Mediterranean and Early Cypriot Coinage." *Numismatic Chronicle* 154: 17–52.

———. 1999. "The Archaic and Early Classical coinage of Kourion." *Cahiers du Centre d'Etudes Chypriotes* 29: 33–44.

Karydas, A. G., D. Kotzamani, R. Bernard, J. N. Barrandon, and C. Zarkadas. 2004. "A compositional study of a museum jewellery collection (7th–1st BC) by means of a portable XRF analyser." *Nuclear Instruments and Methods in Physics Research B* 226: 15–28.

Kassianidou V. 1992. "Cyprus and SW Spain. Connections." In *Cyprus, Copper and the Sea,* edited by A. Marangou and K. Psillides, 129–148. Nicosia: Government of Cyprus.

———. 2006. The production, use and trade of metals in Cyprus and Sardinia: so similar and yet so different, in Archaeometallurgy in Sardinia: from the origins to the early Iron Age – 10th and 11th September 2004 (Italy), Instrumentum: Bulletin du Groupe de Travail Européen sur l' Artisanat et les Productions Manufacturées dans l' Antiquité, 23, Chauvigny, pp. 34–37.

———. 2012. The origin and use of metals in Iron Age Cyprus, in Iacovou, M. (ed.), Cyprus and the Aegean in the Early Iron Age. The legacy of Nicolas Coldstream, Cultural Foundation of the Bank of Cyprus, Nicosia, pp. 229–259.

Kraay, C. M., 1976. *Archaic and Classical Greek Coins.* London: Methuen.

L'Héritier, M., S. Baron, L. Cassayre and F. Téreygeol. 2015. "Bismuth behavior during ancient processes of silver-lead production." *Journal of Archaeological Science* 57: 46–68.

Lipiński , E. 2004. *Itineraria Phoenicia.* Leuven: Peeters.

Markou, E., 2011a. *L' or des rois de Chypre. Numismatique et histoire à l'époque classique.* Μελετήματα 64. Athens: Centre de Recherches de l'Antiquité Grecque et Romaine .

———. 2011b. "Gold and silver weight standards in fourth-century Cyprus : a resume." In *Proceedings of the XIVth international Numismatic Congress held in Glasgow 2009,* ed. N. Holmes, 280–284. Glasgow: INC.

———. 2011c. "Le voyage de la monnaie chypriote archaïque et classique dans le temps et dans l'espace." In *Nomisma: La circulation monétaire dans le monde grec antique. Actes du colloque international (Athènes, 14–17 avril 2010)*, edited by T. Faucher, M.-C. Marcellesi et al. 397–416. Bulletin de Correspondance Hellénique, Supplément, 53. Athens: École française d'Athènes.

———. 2015. *Coinage and History. The Case of Cyprus during the Archaic and Classical periods. Lectures on the History of Numismatics* 6. Nicosia: Bank of Cyprus Cultural Foundation.

Markou, E., Charalambous, A., and V. Kassianidou. 2014. "pXRF analysis of Cypriot gold coins of the Classical Period." *American Journal of Numismatics* 26: 33–60.

Martinón-Torres, M., T. Rehren, N. Thomas and A. Mongiatti. 2009. "Identifying materials, recipes and choices: some suggestions for the study of archaeological cupels." In *Archaeometallurgy in Europe 2007: Selected papers from 2nd International Conference, Aquileia, Italy, 17–21 June 2007*, 435–445. Milano: Associazione Italiana di Metallurgia.

Masson, O., and M. Sznycer. 1972. *Recherches sur les Phéniciens à Chypre.* Paris: Droz.

McKerrell, H., and R. B. K. Stevenson. 1972. "Some analyses of Anglo-Saxon and associated oriental silver coinage." In *Methods of Chemical and Metallurgical Investigation of Ancient Coinage*, edited by E. T. Hall and D. M. Metcalf, 195. Royal Numismatic Society Special Publication 8. London: Royal Numismatic Society.

Meyers, P. 1983. *Production, distribution and characterization of silver in the ancient Near East, preprints for the Second International Symposium, Historische Technologie der Edelmetalle, Meersburg 25–28 April 1983.* Meersburg.

Milne, J. G. 1945. "Overstruck Cypriote Staters." *Numismatic Chronicle* 5: 78–79.

Moorey, P. R. S. 1985. *Materials and manufacture in Ancient Mesopotamia: the evidence of archaeology and art. Metals and metalwork, glazed materials and glass.* BAR International Series, Vol. 237. Oxford: BAR.

———. 1994. *Ancient Mesopotamian Materials and Industries: The Archaeological Evidence.* Oxford: Oxford University Press.

Nriagu, J. O. 1985. "Cupellation: The oldest quantitative chemical process." *Journal of Chemical Education* 62.8: 668–674.

Ogden, J. 1992. *Ancient Jewellery.* London: British Museum Press.

Papadopoulos, S. 2008. "Silver and copper production practices in the prehistoric settlement at Limenaria, Thasos." In *Aegean Metallurgy in the Bronze Age*, edited by I. Tzachilli, 59–67. Athens: Ta Pragmata.

Pernicka, E., C. Lutz, H. G. Bachmann, G. A. Wagner, C. Elitzsch and E. Klein. 1985. "Alte Blei-Silber-Verhüttung auf Sifnos." In *Silber, Blei und Gold auf*

Sifnos, edited by G. A. Wagner and G. Weisgerber, 185–199. Der Anschnitt Beiheft 3. Bochum: Deutsches Bergbau-Museum.

Pilides, D., and A. Destrooper-Georgiades. 2008. "A hoard of silver coins from the plot on the corner of Nikokreontos and Hatjopoullou Streets, (east extension of the settlement of the Hill of Agio Georgios, Lefkosia)." *Report of the Department of Antiquities, Cyprus:* 307–335.

Pitarch, A., and I. Queralt. 2010. "Energy dispersive X-ray fluorescence analysis of ancient coins: The case of Greek silver drachmae from the Emporion site in Spain." *Nuclear Instruments and Methods in Physics Research B* 268: 1682–1685.

Pollard A. M., and P. J. Bray. 2014. "Chemical and isotopic studies of ancient metals." In *Archaeometallurgy in Global Perspective. Methods and Syntheses*, edited by B. W. Roberts and C. P. Thornton, 217–238. New York: Springer.

Ramage, A., and P. T. Craddock. 2000. *King Croesus' Gold. Excavations at Sardis and the History of Gold Refining*, London: British museum Press.

Robinson, E.S.G., 1935. "Notes on the Larnaca Hoard." *Numismatic Chronicle* 15: 180–190.

Rodrigues, M., M. Schreiner, M. Melcher, M. Guerra, J. Salomon, M. Radtke, M. Alram and N. Schindel. 2011. "Characterization of the silver coins of the Hoard of Beçin by X-ray based methods." *Nuclear Instruments and Methods in Physics Research B* 269: 3041–3045.

Salkield, L. U. 1987. *A Technical History of the Rio Tinto Mines: Some Notes on Exploitation from Pre-Phoenician Times to the 1950s*. London: Institute of Mining and Metallurgy.

Satraki, A. 2012. *Κύπριοι Βασιλείς από τον Κόσμασο μέχρι το Νικοκρέοντα.* Αρχαιογνωσία 9. Athens.

Schmitt-Korte, K., and M. Cowell. 1989. "Nabatean coinage-Part I: the silver content measured by x-ray fluorescence analysis." *Numismatic Chronicle* 149: 33–58.

Stylianou, P. J. 1989. "The Age of the Kingdoms: A Political History of Cyprus in the Archaic and Classical Periods." *Μελέται και Υπομνήματα* II: 375–530.

Tate, J. 1986. "Some problems in analysing museum material by nondestructive surface sensitive techniques." *Nuclear Instruments and Methods in Physics Research B* 14: 20–23.

Teixidor, J. 1975. "Early Phoenician Presence in Cyprus." In *The Archaeology of Cyprus*, edited by N. Robertson, 121–122. New York: Noyes Press.

Tylecote, R. F. 1987. *The Early History of Metallurgy in Europe*. London/New York: Longman Publishing.

Valera, R. G., P. G. Valera and A. Rivoldini. 2005. "Sardinian ore deposits and metals in the bronze age." In *Archaeometallurgy in Sardinia from the Origins to the Beginning of the Early Iron Age*, edited by F. Lo Schiavo, A. Giumlia-Mair, U. Sanna, and R. Valera, 49–105. Monograpies Instrumentum 30. Montagnac: Monique Mergoil.

Wallace, R. W. 1987. "The origin of electrum coinage." *American Journal of Archaeology* 91.3: 385–397.

Zapiti, E., and L. Michaelidou. 2010. *Coins of Cyprus from the collection of the Bank of Cyprus Cultural Foundation.* Nicosia: Bank of Cyprus Cultural Foundation.

AJN Second Series 32 (2020) pp. 31–92

On the Reattribution of some Byblos Alexanders to Arados II

Plates 1–15 Lloyd W. H. Taylor*

This study makes the case for the reattribution from Byblos to a second mint at Arados (Arados II) of the coinage of Alexander the Great bearing the AR mintmark. The majority of the early output from this mint was gold staters. Most probably the mint was established to accommodate the expansion of gold coinage production from ca. 328/7 BC, while silver Alexandrine coinage remained the priority of the first mint (Arados I), which had its origins in the old Achaemenid mint at Arados. After the initial striking of a substantial gold stater coinage, accompanied by a minor silver tetradrachm mintage, Arados II then issued a sizeable silver tetradrachm coinage. Both mints at Arados produced Macedonian imperial coinage until ca. 321/0 BC at which time Arados I ceased operation. Based on the hoard record, it is likely that Arados II continued to strike Alexander tetradrachms until around 301/0 BC when the city passed from Antigonid to Seleukid control following the Battle of Ipsos.

INTRODUCTION

In his discussion of the coinage attributed to Byblos, Price wrote "The coinage at this mint had certainly ended by 320 BC but attribution of 3422–3428 to Byblos is very doubtful."[1] This applied to those coins bearing the AR monogram

* Independent scholar (lloyd_taylor@bigpond.com).

1. M. J. Price, *The Coinage in the Name of Alexander the Great and Philip Arrhidaeus* (London: British Museum/Swiss Numismatic Society, 1991), 430, with the quote corrected for the typographic error in Price's text where types 2422–2428 are referenced rather than 3422–3428.

(a ligature of the Greek letters A and P), which he attributed to Byblos following the reasoning of Newell.[2] The latter associated these coins with a unique tetradrachm (Price 3421; ANS 1947.98.296; *Demanhur* 3586) of nominally similar style, bearing the Phoenician letters ∿○ (*ayin-yod*) that he read as an abbreviation of the name of Aynel (Enylos in Greek), the king of Byblos at the time of its surrender to Alexander the Great in 333/2 BC. Newell then deciphered the Greek Ᵽ monogram of Price types 3422–3428 as the abbreviation of the name Addirmilk (Adramelek in Greek) whom he inferred must have succeeded Aynel as the vassal king of Byblos under the rule of Alexander the Great.[3]

Recently, Newell's notion of the succession of these two kings under the suzerainty of Alexander has been discredited. Addirmilk preceded Aynel, prior to the Macedonian conquest.[4] With the nexus of regnal succession proposed by Newell severed, the association of the coinage represented by Price 3422–3428 with that of Price 3421 is unsustainable. With this historical understanding, some in the numismatic trade have come to attribute Price 3422–3428 to Arados rather than Byblos.[5] This reattribution is supported by the fact that the Ᵽ mintmark served to identify the autonomous coinage of Arados from the mid third century BC. It reverts to Newell's original interpretation of this coinage in his preliminary assessment of the Demanhur Hoard (*IGCH* 1664); an attribution that followed the reasoning of Müller almost sixty years earlier.[6] Newell pondered the relationship between this coinage and that bearing the ⚹ monogram, which like Müller before him, he also attributed to Arados. He suggested that the former may have been "local or city issues" while the latter "were regal or military issues struck by Alexander's generals or successors at Arados, but under separate management and in a separate mint. This might account, in degree, for the great divergence of

2. E. T. Newell, Alexander Hoards II Demanhur, 1905, ANS NNM 19 (New York: The American Numismatic Society, 1923), 52 and 122–125.

3. Newell, Alexander, 125 "Is it not at once apparent that, Ᵽ, the monogram on the subsequent tetradrachms is but the ligature of the letters AΔPA, the first portion of Adramelek's name in Greek?"

4. J. Elayi, "An Updated Chronology of the Reigns of Phoenician Kings During the Persian Period (539–333 BC)," *Transeuphratene* 32 (2006), 11–44, 25–28, 37, table 3, and 41–42, table 5.

5. For example, Classical Numismatic Group Inc., www.cngcoins.com.

6. E. T. Newell, "Reattribution of Certain Tetradrachms of Alexander the Great," *AJN* 45/46 (1912), 5–62: "Coin types 126 [Price 3424] and 127 [Price 3426] have long been given to Arados—an attribution supported by the monogram (which is found on later undoubted Aradian Alexanders), and by the fact that the style on some is very similar to the above-mentioned coin published by Babelon as certainly struck at Arados." See also L. Müller, *Numismatique d'Alexandre le Grand, Suive d'un Appendice Contenant les Monnaies de Philippe II et III.* (Copenhagen: Imprimerie de Bianco Luno, 1855).

the two series in style, execution, monograms, and other details."[7] Eleven years later, in his final publication of the Demanhur Hoard, he abandoned this construct in favor of the Byblos attribution, based on the erroneous inference of the succession of Aynel by Addirmilk.[8] In doing so, he overlooked the significance of the fact that both mintmarks ℟ and ⚶ are but two variant ligatures of the same Greek letters, A and P, potentially signifying two different mints in the same city.

The relationship between the issues reattributed from Byblos (Price 3422–3428) to Arados and those previously attributed Arados (Price 3303–3335)[9] remains uncertain, with the added confusion of dating now entering the picture as some in the numismatic trade seek to assign Price 3426 to Arados under Ptolemy I.[10] The latter is improbable, for Ptolemaic forces only controlled the city for a matter of months in each of 319/18, 312 and perhaps 301 BC.[11] This paper seeks to address these uncertainties via a die study of the large denomination gold and silver coinage attributed to Byblos by Newell and Price. The study draws on the American Numismatic Society's PELLA online database,[12] supplemented by coins in commerce. No attempt was made to assemble a corpus, a task well beyond the scope of this study. Rather, the catalogue provides a statistically meaningful database with which to analyze and estimate the volume and significance of the coinage. To further clarify the basis of the reattribution of this coinage, a review of the iconographic detail of the tetradrachm issue attributed to Byblos under Aynel and the basis of the reattribution precedes the catalogue of coins.

AYNEL (ENYLOS) TETRADRACHM

The only known example of the tetradrachm issue bearing the Phoenician letters ⋏○ (Price 3421) came from the Demanhur Hoard (*IGCH* 1664). It is now housed in the American Numismatic Society collection, a component of the Newell bequest (Pl. 4, C). The letters ⋏○ beneath the *diphros* upon which Zeus

7. Newell, *Reattribution*, 47.

8. Newell, *Alexander*, 52, 122–125.

9. See also F. Duyrat, *Arados hellénistiqué étude historique et monétaire* (Beirut: Institut Français du Proche-Orient, 2005).

10. For examples refer to Classical Numismatic Group Inc., www.cngcoins.com.

11. G. Le Rider, *Alexander the Great: Coinage, Finances and Policy*, trans. W. E. Higgins (Philadelphia: American Philosophical Society, 2007), 152, citing Diodorus 18.43.1–2 with respect to 319/8 BC; O. D. Hoover, "A Second Look at the Aradian Bronze Coinage Attributed to Seleucus I (*SC* 72–73)," *AJN* 18 (2006), 43–50, 48–49, citing Diodorus 19.58.1–5 and footnote 6, citing Diodorus 19.79.6–7 and 19.80.3 with respect of 312 BC, and E. T. Newell, *The Coinages of Demetrius Poliorcetes* (Chicago: Obol International, 1978), 54, with respect to 301 BC.

12. http://numismatics.org/pella/, accessed for this study prior to 8 October 2018.

is seated are clearly legible and beyond doubt. Whether these identify Aynel as the issuing authority is open to question, but it remains the best interpretation offered to date. The overall style of the coin is that of an early Alexander III issue, a derivative of Kilikian style as noted by Newell.[13] Notwithstanding Newell's assertion,[14] the obverse style of the coin diverges significantly in detail from that of Price 3424, represented in the catalogue of tetradrachms (Series 3; Pls. 4–7). In particular, the portrayal of the brow of Herakles with a heavy bulbous form on the Aynel coin is totally absent in the catalogue of dies of Price 3424. The orientation of the ear on the lion skin headdress is also atypical of the latter, being rotated 45 degrees clockwise from the disposition of the ear on the tetradrachms of Price 3424. The closest coins in overall style and detail are some of the early issues of Sidon, located 77 km south of Byblos. It may have been from this mint that a die engraver was deployed to Byblos for the "Aynel" issue. The absence of a close stylistic counterpart to Price 3421 in the catalogue of Series 3 (Price 3424) tetradrachms substantiates the conclusion from the historical record that these are unlikely to be associated issues from a single mint. Price 3421 remains the only Alexander issue of those under consideration that might be attributed to Byblos.[15]

REATTRIBUTION

The style and fabric of the coinage under study, plus the distribution of find locations detailed below, firmly place its origin in northern Phoenicia, or Syria commencing in the time of Alexander the Great. While the Ʀ mintmark is relatively common on later Hellenistic coinage, its appearance unaccompanied by other mintmarks, or controls, is exceptional. The attribution of Alexander's coinage to specific Phoenician and Syrian mints relies on the interpretation of the significance of mintmarks. Except for Tyre, these mints used a primary mintmark that identified the mint with Greek letters, or monograms, an abbreviation of the name of the city in which the mint was located.[16] Usually this was accompanied

13. Newell, *Alexander*, 123 "modified 'Cilician' style very similar to the earliest issues of Sidon and Ake."

14. Newell, *Alexander*, 122–123 "Its style and fabric is so close to the earliest issues of Nos. 3587–3623 [Price 3424 and 3426] that it must be considered as the immediate precursor of those pieces and struck in the same mint."

15. In addition to this single issue we must consider the possible reattribution to Byblos of the coinage formerly attributed to Berytos by Newell and Price.

16. At Tyre (Ake of Price), the abbreviated name of the vassal king Ozmilk (Azemilkos) in Phoenician letters accompanied the regnal date. This served to distinguish the dating era of Tyre from that of Sidon, and to identify the mint.

by either a secondary letter mint control, or alternatively a regnal year date at each of Sidon and Tyre. In the coinage under study, the R monogram is not accompanied by any other mint control. Therefore, the R monogram can only be the identifying mark of the issuing mint. This mintmark is established to be abbreviation of the name of the city of Arados[17] on the later autonomous coinage of the city from the mid-third century BC. Prior to 300 BC, there was no other major center of population in northern Phoenicia that could have hosted a major mint, let alone one that can be associated with the Greek letter abbreviation AP. Based on the mintmark, the attribution of Price 3422–3428 to a second mint located at Arados (Arados II) is most probable.

The attribution of the coinage bearing the $⩍$ monogram (Price 3303–3335)[18] to Arados is not impacted by this reattribution, for as initially postulated by Newell[19] this coinage must have been struck in a separate facility (Arados I) in the same city. The presence of two separate mints is based on the clear demarcation between the two coinages, each defined by their own unique elements of iconographic style, mintmarks, fabric and other details. The first of these Alexander mints (Arados I) appears to have had its origins in the pre-existing Achaemenid mint in the city, evidenced by the continuity of the Phoenician letter mintmarks ⴲⵍ (*mem-aleph*)[20] from the Achaemenid coinage of the city onto some of the Alexandrine coinage, one example of which (Price 3306) also carries the $⩍$ monogram in addition to the ⴲⵍ mint control.[21] This suggests that the mint responsible for the coinage of Arados during the Achaemenid period also produced Alexander the Great's coinage following submission to the Macedonians. On this basis, the second mint, Arados II, must have been newly established following the Macedonian conquest in order to supplement the mintage from the continuing former Achaemenid facility. The practice of establishing two mints in the one city was not unusual. Newell described such at the opening of the mint at Tarsos.[22] Later, the commissioning stage of the Alexander mint at Damaskos involved two apparently separate facilities that were consolidated into a single operation as production ramped up using six anvils within a process

17. The ancient Greek name for the island bearing the modern day Arabic name Arwad, or Ruad, derived from the old Phoenician name Arvad.

18. See also Duyrat, *Arados*, 9–30.

19. Newell, "Reattribution," 47.

20. Variously interpreted to be the abbreviation of the phrase "of the king of Arwad," or "of the kingdom of Arwad" thus identifying in general terms the issuing authority and city of origin. Price, *Coinage*, 414 and Elayi, "Updated," 29–30.

21. Price, *Coinage*, 414 and Newell, *Alexander*, 119–120.

22. E. T. Newell, "Tarsos under Alexander," *AJN* 52 (1918), 69–115.

control environment that obviated the necessity to maintain separate facilities in order to achieve high output.[23] The earliest coinage of Babylon appears to have originated from two separate lines of production, if not separate facilities, that like those of Damaskos were consolidated into a single operation after about six months.[24] Later, two mints operated intermittently at Babylon between c. 320–316 BC and again in the period c. 308–304 BC.[25] The motivation for the establishment of two mints in one city appears to have been the need for a large volume of coinage in a short period of time and/or the necessity for different administrative structures. The latter applied in the case of Babylon following the death of Alexander the Great which saw the emergence of a clear division between the imperial and satrapal administration of two mints in Babylonia.[26]

The dating and/or marking of issues with short lived secondary mint controls in addition to a primary mintmark was a long-standing practice at the Phoenician mints, one that carried over into the Macedonian era. Fourteen different mintmarks, or symbols, in multiple combinations are recognized on the Macedonian imperial coinage of Arados I (Price 3303–3335).[27] In contrast, the coinage of Arados II carries the solitary Ꝑ mintmark throughout. This may reflect the fact that the mint was newly established under Macedonian administration, with no prior Phoenician, or Achaemenid precedent to influence its operating conventions. Alternatively, it may reflect the fact that two different types of mint administration necessitated different process controls, checks and balances to ensure the integrity of each of their operations. Certainly, the absence of either a regnal year date, or a succession of mint controls at Arados II sets this mint apart from all of the other Phoenician mints of Alexander. It points to a different administrative construct for this mint, a point reinforced by the analysis and interpretation of the following catalogue of coins.

23. L. W. H. Taylor, "The Damaskos Mint of Alexander the Great," *AJN* 29 (2017), 47–100.

24. L. W. H. Taylor, "The Earliest Alexander III Tetradrachm Coinage of Babylon: Iconographic Development and Chronology," *AJN* 30 (2018), 1–43.

25. Houghton and Lorber, *Seleucid Coins*, 39–48, 481–483. For the downdating of the start of the second phase of operation of the Babylon II mint, see L. W. H. Taylor, "From Triparadeisos to Ipsos: Seleukos I Nikator's Uncertain Mint 6A in Babylonia," *AJN* 27 (2015), 41–97

26. Houghton and Lorber, *Seleucid Coins*, 39–50.

27. Previously attributed to Arados I, the later issues of Price P138–P158 and Price 3336–3364 have been reattributed to the Babylon II mint: Houghton and Lorber, *Seleucid Coins*, 39–48 and 479–483.

CATALOGUE

Because the coinage carries a single primary mintmark, unaccompanied by secondary mint controls, it is not amenable to categorization into a sequence of issues based on a progression of mint controls. Rather, the catalogue sequence relies on the progression of evolving iconographic elements, plus a handful of die links. The catalogue is divided into four series. Series 1 and 2 are gold staters, each distinguished by the placement of the Ꝑ mintmark, either to the left of, or below Nike's right wing, respectively. Series 3 and 4 consist of tetradrachms. Both bear the Ꝑ mintmark in the reverse left field and are distinguished from each other by the depiction of Zeus with either parallel legs (Series 3) or crossed legs (Series 4). Within each of the series, minor types defined by variant iconographic or epigraphic elements are identified by a second digit in the sequence type number. For example, Series 2.2 is defined by the Ꝑ monogram below Nike's wing accompanied by an obverse on which Athena's helmet is decorated by a griffin, rather than the more usual serpent motif that characterizes Series 2.1. Dies are numbered sequentially in each denomination. Gold stater obverse dies are denoted by the prefix Av to distinguish them from the tetradrachm obverse dies prefixed with an A. Coin weights (column four) are in grams. The coins were struck with dies adjusted towards 12 o'clock. An asterisk adjacent to the catalogue number denotes a coin illustrated in the accompanying plates.

Gold Staters

Series 1

Proposed date: ca. 328/7–326/5 BC

Plates 2–3

Obv.: Head of Athena right, wearing crested helmet decorated with serpent (Series 1.1), or griffin (Series 1.2), or sphinx (Series 1.3).

Rev.: ΑΛΕΞΑΝΔΡΟΥ on r., Nike standing left, holding wreath and stylis; Ꝑ in left field, to left of Nike's right wing.

1.1 Ꝑ monogram in left field. Serpent on Athena's helmet. (Price 3423)

1.	Av1	P1	8.49	Oeconomides, 1999, no. 43, pl. 22, 43; Epidauros 1977 Hoard.
2.	Av1	P2	8.55	Numismatik Naumann 40 (7 Feb. 2016), lot 66.
3.*	Av1	P3	8.53	London, 1927,0504.12; Price 3423a.

1.2 Ᵽ monogram in left field. Griffin on Athena's helmet. (Price -)

| 4.* | Av2 | P4 | 8.58 | Peus 396 (5 Nov. 2008), lot 296. Av2 is a near identical die to Series 2 Av18 (Cat. No. 35). |

1.3 Ᵽ monogram in left field. Serpent on Athena's helmet. (Price 3423)

5.*	Av3	P5	8.54	CNG 94 (18 Sep. 2013), lot 242. Av3 is an obverse die link to Series 2 (Cat. No. 36). Av3 here in later, worn state.
6.*	Av4	P6	8.56	Heritage 3041 (13 Aug. 2015), lot 32019. Vertical die break across left field transects hand and laurel wreath giving the impression of laurel branch.
7.	Av4	P7	8.55	Paris, BNF41746217; Luynes 1613.
8.	Av4	P8	8.54	London, 1994,0915.37.
9.*	Av4	P9	8.68	London, 1928,0103.5; Price 2423b.
10.*	AV5	P10	8.60	Triton XIII (4 Jan. 2010), lot 105. Av5 is an obverse die link to Series 2 (Cat. No. 37). Av5 here in unworn state.
11.	AV5	P11	8.53	Triton IV (5 Dec. 2000), lot 168.
12.	AV5	P12	8.60	Triton XIII (4 Jan. 2010), lot 1116.
13.*	Av6	P13	8.61	CNG 860175. Av6 is a near identical die to Series 2 Av19 (Cat. No. 38).
14.	Av6	P13	8.70	CNG eAuction 394 (19 Mar. 2017), lot 128.
15.*	Av7	P14	8.61	ANS 1965.77.86.
16.*	Av8	P15	8.61	ANS 1944.100.34975.
17.	Av8	P15	8.61	Berlin, Münzkabinett 18253343; Larnaka Hoard, *IGCH* 1472.
18.*	Av9	P16	8.56	Vienna, Münzkabinett Wien GR 28559.
19.	Av9	P17	8.55	Spink 7023 (27 Sep. 2007), lot 34.
20.*	Av10	P18	8.56	Künker 62 (13 Mar. 2001), lot 60.
21.	Av11	P19	8.61	Gorny & Mosch 224 (13 Oct. 2014), lot 141.
22.*	Av11	P19	8.64	CNG 731923.
23.*	Av12	P19	8.44	Triton VI (14 Jan. 2003), lot 178. Av12 subsequently transferred to Miletos to strike examples of Price 2078.
24.	Av13	P20	8.62	Hess Divo 326 (28 May 2014), lot 32; Hess Divo 325 (23 Oct. 2013), lot 187; Maison Palombo 11 (30 Nov. 2012), lot 13.
25.*	Av13	P20	8.55	Stack's Bowers and Ponterio 2018 NYINC Auction (16 Jan. 2018), lot 2101; Roma Numismatics IX (22 Mar. 2015), lot 226; TimeLine Auctions (Aug, 2012).

26.	Av13	P21	8.47	Forum Ancient Coins SH15299; Coin Galleries (20 Nov. 1975), lot 1098; Colosseum Coin Exchange. P21 first appearance of Nike's extended r. hand in profile. Av13 extensive die breaks.
27.*	Av14	P22	8.58	CNG 99 (13 May 2015), lot 72.
28.	Av15	P23	8.58	Berlin, Münzkabinett 18253344.
29.*	Av15	P23	8.60	Heritage 3037 (4 Jan. 2015), lot 30901; Roma Numismatics VIII (28 Sep. 2014), lot 447.
30.	Av15	P23	8.59	CNG eAuction 300 (10 Apr. 2013), lot 80.

1.3   Ꝛ monogram in left field. Sphinx on Athena's helmet. (Price -)

31.*	Av16	P24	8.54	CNG 64 (24 Sep. 2003), lot 107.

Series 2

Proposed date: ca. 328/7–326/5 BC
Plates 3–4

Obv.: Head of Athena right, wearing crested helmet decorated with serpent (Series 2.1), or griffin (Series 2.2).

Rev.: ΑΛΕΞΑΝΔΡΟΥ on r., Nike standing left, holding wreath and stylis; Ꝛ below Nike's right wing.

2.1   Ꝛ monogram below Nike's wing. Serpent on Athena's helmet. (Price 3422)

32.	Av17	P25	8.37	ANS 1944.100.34977. The progression of die breaks on linking reverse die P25 sequences Series 2 obverse dies Av17 and Av18.
33.*	Av17	P25	8.58	CNG 99 (13 May 2015), lot 71; CNG 96 (14 May 2014), lot 48.
34.	Av17	P25	8.55	Berlin, Münzkabinett 18253345.

2.2   Ꝛ monogram below Nike's wing. Griffin on Athena's helmet. (Price -)

35.*	Av18	P25	8.56	ANS 1944.100.34978. Av18 is a near identical die to Series 1 Av2 (Cat. No. 4).

2.1   Ꝛ monogram below Nike's wing. Serpent on Athena's helmet. (Price 3422)

36.*	Av3	P26	8.54	ACR Auctions 6 (10 Dec. 2012), lot 375; CNG eAuction 54 (4 Dec. 2002), lot 22. Av3 is an obverse die link to Series 1 (Cat. No. 5). Av3 here in early, unworn state.
37.*	Av5	P27	8.56	CNG eAuction 403 (9 Aug. 2017), lot 37. Av5 is an obverse die link to Series 1 (Cat. Nos. 10–12). Av5 here in a well-worn state.

38.*	Av19	P28	8.46	Peus 369 (31 Oct. 2001), lot 145. Av19 is a near identical die to Series 1 Av6 (Cat. Nos. 13–14).
39.*	Av20	P29	8.60	London, 1872,0713.26; Price 3422a.
40.*	Av21	P30	8.58	ANS 1944.100.34976; Naville I (4 Apr. 1921), lot 873.
41.*	Av22	P31	8.62	CNG 860686; Stack's Bowers 3483 (1 Jun. 2014), lot 22964; Stack's Bowers 3479 (5 May 2014), lot 21120; Stack's Bowers 3470 (2 Mar. 2014), lot 20639.
42.*	Av23	P32	8.52	London, 1866,1201.1053; Price 3422b.
43.	Av23	P32	8.58	CGB.fr Monnaies 25 (26 Jan. 2006), lot 56.

Silver Tetradrachms

Series 3

Proposed date: ca. 327/6–326/5 BC

Plates 4–7

Obv.: Head of Herakles r. in lion skin headdress, dotted border.

Rev.: ΑΛΕΞΑΝΔΡΟΥ on r., Zeus seated l. on *diphros*, holding eagle and scepter, Ρ to l., dotted border. Zeus's legs disposed side by side, in parallel.

3.1   Ρ (Price 3424)

44.	A1	P1	16.90	Museum Surplus 11594.
45.*	A1	P2	17.08	LWHT Coll.; Pars Coins PCW-G5970. Reverse die shift imprints the ligate AP as if the Phoenician letter Sade.
46.	A1	P2	16.78	Gorny & Mosch 170 (13 Oct. 2008), lot 1260.
47.	A1	P2	16.92	Goldberg 96 (14–15 Feb. 2017), lot 1587.
48.	A1	P3	17.13	CNG XXX (11 Jun. 1994), lot 66.
49.	A1	P3	16.84	Berlin, Münzkabinett 18253348.
50.	A1	P4	16.80	ANS 1944.100.34997.
51.	A1	P5	17.21	Berlin, Münzkabinett 18253347.
52.	A1	P6	17.19	Rauch 105 (16 Nov. 2017), lot 56; Rauch eAuction 18 (6 Nov. 2015), lot 34.
53.	A1	P7	17.15	ANS 1944.100.34998.
54.	A1	P7	17.17	Le Rider and Olçay, 1958, 74, pl. VII, 74; Akçakale Hoard, *CH* 8.201, *CH* 10.251.
55.	A1	P8	16.25	Numismatics 28 (22 Jan. 2017), lot 136.
56.*	A1	P9	17.12	ANS 1944.100.34999.
57.	A1	P10	17.19	CNG eAuction 265 (5 Oct. 2011), lot 217.

58.	A1	P10	17.18	Berlin, Münzkabinett 18253350; Abusir Hoard, *IGCH* 1672.
59.*	A2	P11	17.16	CNG 87 (18 May 2011), lot 344.
60.	A2	P12	17.06	ANS 1944.100.35000.
61.	A2	P12	16.73	Cambridge, *SNGuk_0601_0505*.
62.	A2	P13	17.12	Christoph Gärtner 32 (24 Oct. 2015), lot 34137.
63.	A3	P14	17.12	NAC Auction O (13 May 2004), lot 1545.
64.*	A3	P14	17.21	ANS 1944.100.34992; Demanhur Hoard *IGCH* 1664.
65.	A3	P14	17.10	ANS 1944.100.34993.
66.*	A4	P15	17.17	CNG 72 (14 Jun. 2006), lot 408; "Seleucus I" Hoard, *CH* 10.265.
67.	A4	P16	17.17	ANS 1944.100.34994.
68.	A4	P17	17.12	CNG 88 (14 Sep. 2011), lot 118.
69.*	A5	P17	17.16	CNG eAuction 350 (6 May 2015), lot 96.
70.	A5	P17	17.18	Le Rider and Olçay, 1958, 76, pl. VII, 76; Akçakale Hoard, *CH* 8.201, *CH* 10.251.
71.	A6	P18	17.15	Gorny & Mosch 196 (7 Mar 2011), lot 1403.
72.*	A6	P18	17.14	Heritage (3 Jan. 2012), lot 23050.
73.	A6	P19	17.24	Elsen 93 (15 Sep. 2007), lot 146.
74.	A6	P19	17.10	CNG eAuction 102 (24 Nov. 2004), lot 4.
75.	A6	P20	17.24	ANS 1944.100.34996.
76.	A6	P21	17.15	Heritage (12 Sep. 2011), lot 25864.
77.	A6	P21	17.13	CNG 78 (14 May 2008), lot 411.
78.*	A6	P21	17.15	ANS 1944.100.34995.
79.*	A7	P22	16.67	ANS 1944.100.35002.
80.*	A8	P22	17.02	Noble Numismatics 71 (22 Nov. 2002), lot 4564.
81.	A8	P23	16.05	Amandry and Callot, 1988, 9, pl. XIII, 9; Failaka Hoard, *CH* 8.256.
82.*	A9	P24	17.25	ANS 1944.100.84669.
83.*	A10	P25	17.21	Rauch 84 (13 May 2009), lot 97.
84.	A10	P26	17.19	Germania Inferior Numismatics HBR-1330; Heritage Europe 50 (24 May 2016), lot 204.
85.	A10	P26	17.04	ANS 1944.100.35009.
86.	A10	P27	16.99	Aureo & Calicó 258 (20 Mar. 2014), lot 3029.
87.	A10	P27	17.13	Naville Numismatics 19 (13 Dec. 2015), lot 37.
88.*	A11	P28	17.14	Künker 193 (26 Sep. 2011), lot 141.

89.	A11	P29	17.13	Gorny & Mosch 196 (7 Mar. 2011), lot 1402. P29 depicts the last facing open palm for the right hand of Zeus.
90.*	A11	P30	17.20	CNG 61 (25 Sep. 2002), lot 462. P30 depicts the first upward oriented hand in profile for the right hand of Zeus. A constant from here in the sequence.
91.	A11	P30	16.93	Peus 401 (3 Nov. 2010), lot 233; Gorny & Mosch 186 (8 Mar. 2010), lot 1257.
92.	A11	P30	17.17	Ars Time Company eAuction 2 (17 Dec. 2013), lot 119.
93.	A11	P30	17.15	ANS 1944.100.35006.
94.*	A12	P31	17.17	CNG eAuction 105 (10 May 2017), lot 73.
95.	A12	P31	17.20	Gorny & Mosch 160 (9 Oct. 2007), lot 1321.
96.	A12	P31	17.15	CNG eAuction 255 (4 May 2011), lot 48.
97.	A12	P32	16.90	ANS 1944.100.35010; Abu Hommos Hoard, *IGCH* 1667.
98.	A12	P32	17.08	ANS 1944.100.35011.
99.	A13?	P33?	17.17	Wildwinds.com database entry Price 3424 A; www.wildwinds.com/coins/greece/macedonia/kings/alexander_III/t.html accessed on 1 May 2017. Die determination based on poor quality image of a worn coin.
100.*	A14	P34	17.27	CNG eAuction 105 (10 May 2017), lot 72; Numismatica Ars Classica 92 (23 May 2016), lot 1440; Gorny & Mosch 156 (5 Mar. 2007), lot 1279.
101.	A14	P34	17.25	Gorny & Mosch 233 (6 Oct. 2015), lot 1303.
102.	A14	P34	17.17	ANS 1944.100.34981; Demanhur Hoard, *IGCH* 1664.
103.	A14	P34	17.12	London, 2002,0101.782; Hersh Coll.
104.	A14	P34	17.14	London, 1911,0409.47; Price 3424c.
105.	A14	P35	17.18	ANS 1944.100.34991.
106.	A14	P35	16.97	CNG eAuction 168 (11 Jul. 2007), lot 34.
107.	A14	P36	17.18	ANS 1944.100.34990.
108.	A14	P36	17.22	Oxford, Ashmolean HCR23653; *SNGuk_0503_3006*.
109.	A15	P37	17.24	Heritage 3032 (10 Apr. 2014), lot 23118.
110.	A15	P37	17.19	Heritage 3046 (14 Apr.2016), lot 31060.
111.	A15	P38	17.20	ANS 1944.100.34982.
112.*	A15	P38	17.18	ANS 1947.98.297.
113.	A15	P38	17.11	ANS 1944.100.34983.
114.	A15	P39	17.20	ANS 1944.100.34979.

115.	A15	P40	16.91	London, 1913,0518.82; Price 3424a; Demanhur Hoard, *IGCH* 1664.
116.*	A16	P41	17.04	ANS 1944.100.34984.
117.	A16	P42	17.11	ANS 1944.100.34985.
118.	A16	P43	16.86	ANS 1944.100.34986.
119.	A16	P43	17.21	Gorny & Mosch 181 (13 Oct. 2009), lot 1307.
120.	A17	P44	17.23	The New York Sale XXX (9 Jan. 2013), lot 95; Künker 193 (26 Sep. 2011), lot 142.
121.	A17	P45	17.27	ANS 1944.100.34987.
122.*	A17	P45	17.19	ANS 1944.100.34988.
123.	A17	P46	17.10	ANS 1944.100.34989.
124.	A18	P47	17.16	CNG eAuction 350 (6 May 2015), lot 97.
125.	A18	P47	17.11	Maison Palombo 7 (13 Jun. 2009), lot 94.
126.*	A18	P47	17.16	Roma Numismatics VIII (28 Sep. 2014), lot 687.
127.	A19	P48	17.20	ANS 1944.100.35113.
128.	A19	P49	17.14	ANS 1944.100.35007.
129.	A19	P49	17.15	Teutoburger 110 (8–9 Sep. 2017), lot 653.
130.	A19	P50	17.14	Noble Numismatics 71 (20–22 Nov. 2002), lot 4563.
131.*	A19	P51	17.17	LWHT Coll; Naumann 55 (30 Jun. 2017), lot 111. Softly engraved letter X before head of Zeus?
132.*	A20	P52	17.17	Berlin, Münzkabinett 18253349.
133.*	A21	P53	17.18	ANS 1944.100.35008.
134.	A21	P53	16.92	Numismatik Naumann 54 (4 Jun. 2017), lot 106.
135.	A21	P53	17.09	Forum Ancient Coins SH68477; Künker eAuction 23 (30 Oct. 2013), lot 9.
136.*	A22	P54	17.21	ANS 1944.100.35013.
137.	A22	P55	17.00	ANS 1944.100.35012.
138.	A22	P55	14.17	London, 1847,0619.37; Price 3424b.
139.	A22	P56	17.15	Hess Divo 299 (27 Oct. 2004), lot 34.

Excluded from Series 3 is ANS 1944.100.35001 that is listed in the PELLA database as an issue of Byblos. It bears no control mark. Although of a closely similar style to Cat. Nos. 124–131 its association with the series remains uncertain in the absence either a control mark, or a direct die link.

Series 4

Proposed dates:
ca. 325/4–321/0 BC Dies A23–A47
ca. 320/19–311/0 BC Dies A48–A79
ca. 310/09–301/0 BC A80–A97
Plates 7–15

Obv.: Head of Herakles r. in lion skin headdress, dotted border.

Rev.: ΑΛΕΞΑΝΔΡΟΥ on r., Zeus seated l. on *diphros* (or throne on last examples in sequence), holding eagle and scepter; Ꝑ to l., dotted border. Zeus's legs disposed with right leg drawn back behind the left, in a crossed legs style.

4.1   Ꝑ (Price 3426)

140.*	A23	P57	17.18	ANS 1944.100.35019.
141.	A23	P58	17.30	Davesne and Lemaire, 1996, no. 97, pl. VII, 97; Syria or Lebanon Hoard, *CH* 8.185.
142.	A23	P58	17.10	Hirsch 264 (25 Nov. 2009), lot 189.
143.*	A24	P59	17.18	Münzen & Medaillen 9 (4 Oct. 2001), lot 135.
144.	A24	P59	16.93	ANS 1944.100.35020.
145.*	A25	P60	16.96	ANS 1947.98.298.
146.	A25	P61	17.13	ANS 1944.100.35021.
147.	A25	P62	17.21	ANS 1944.100.35023.
148.	A25	P63	17.28	ANS 1944.100.35022.
149.	A25	P64	17.13	London, 1913,0518.83; Price 3426e.
150.*	A26	P65	16.91	CNG eAuction 374 (11 May 2016), lot 305.
151.*	A27	P66	17.15	ANS 1944.100.35024.
152.	A27	P67	17.12	Harald Möller 69 (8–9 Jun. 2017), lot 14; Münzen & Medaillen 44 (25 Nov. 2016), lot 147; Gärtner 32 (24 Oct. 2015), lot 34135.
153.	A27	P67	17.05	Oxford, Ashmolean HCR23658; *SNGuk_0503_3011*.
154.	A27	P67	17.14	Le Rider and Olçay, 1958, 78, pl. VII, 78; Akçakale Hoard, *CH* 8.201, *CH* 10.251.
155.	A27	P68	17.25	Hirsch 266 (11 Feb. 2010), lot 1636.
156.	A27	P69	17.94	ANS 1944.100.35025; Abu Hommos Hoard, *IGCH* 1667.
157.*	A28	P70	17.26	ANS 1944.100.35026.
158.	A29	P71	17.31	Le Rider and Olçay, 1958, 86, pl. VII, 86; Akçakale Hoard, *CH* 8.201, *CH* 10.251.

159.	A29	P71	17.08	Le Rider and Olçay, 1958, 87, pl. VII, 87; Akçakale Hoard, *CH* 8.201, *CH* 10.251.
160.	A29	P72	17.19	Oxford, Ashmolean HCR23655; *SNGuk_0503_3008*; Kuft Hoard, *IGCH* 1670.
161.*	A29	P72	17.20	Noble Numismatics 113 (22–25 Nov. 2016), lot 4293.
162.	A29	P73	17.13	CNG 37 (20 Mar 1996), lot 214.
163.	A29	P74	17.03	CNG XXIII (13 Oct. 1992), lot 124.
164.	A29	P75	17.16	ANS 1944.100.35027; Abu Hommos Hoard, *IGCH* 1667.
165.	A29	P76	16.97	ANS 1944.100.35028.
166.	A29	P77	17.10	Baldwin's 34 (13 Oct. 2003), lot 534.
167.	A29	P78	17.15	Hirsch 293 (25 Sep. 2013), lot 2212; Hirsch 287 (7 Feb. 2013), lot 1834; Hirsch 271 (17 Feb. 2011), lot 1899.
168.	A29	P78	17.21	Hirsch 293 (25 Sep 2013), lot 2211.
169.*	A30	P78	17.10	Roma Numismatics E-Sale 38 (29 Jul. 2017), lot 287.
170.	A30	P79	17.15	Hirsch 293 (25 Sep. 2013), lot 2213; Hirsch 287 (7 Feb. 2013), lot 1835; Hirsch 281 (2 May 2012), lot 281, Hirsch 271 (17 Feb. 2011), lot 1898; Hirsch 267 (5 May 2010), lot 181.
171.*	A31	P80	17.22	ANS 1944.100.35031.
172.	A31	P80	17.06	Munthandel G. Henzen 410902010.
173.	A31	P81	17.20	ANS 1944.100.35029; Andritsaena, Elis, c. 1923 Hoard, *IGCH* 0083
174.	A31	P81	17.05	CNG eAuction 370 (9 Mar. 2016), lot 215.
175.	A31	P81	17.10	ANS 1944.100.35034.
176.	A31	P82	17.12	ACR eAuction 32 (11 Jan. 2016), lot 341.
177.	A31	P82	17.80	ANS 1944.100.35050.
178.	A31	P83	17.11	Ars Classica XVII (3 Oct. 1934), lot 375.
179.	A31	P83	17.22	ANS 1944.100.35032.
180.	A31	P83	17.22	Le Rider and Olçay, 1958, 81, pl. VII, 81; Akçakale Hoard, *CH* 8.201, *CH* 10.251.
181.	A31	P84	17.30	ANS 1944.100.35030.
182.*	A32	P85	17.06	Bertolami Fine Arts eAuction 44 (10 Sep. 2017), lot 314; ACR eAuction 4 (19 Mar. 2012), lot 52.
183.*	A33	P86	16.88	London Coin Galleries 4 (1 Jun. 2017), lot 615.
184.*	A34	P87	17.17	ANS 1944.100.35033.

185.	A34	P88	17.22	ANS 1944.100.35035.
186.	A34	P89	17.15	ANS 1944.100.35036.
187.*	A35	P90	17.14	Stack's Coin Galleries (18 Dec. 2007), lot 95.
188.	A35	P90	17.22	CNG eAuction 398 (31 May 2017), lot 343.
189.	A35	P91	16.88	ANS 1944.100.35041.
190.	A35	P91	17.15	CNG 810147; Stack's Bowers 150 (8 Aug. 2009), lot 8365.
191.	A35	P92	17.20	Hirsch 275 (22 Sep. 2011), lot 3489.
192.	A35	P93	16.93	ANS 1944.100.35043; Abu Hommos Hoard, *IGCH* 1667.
193.	A35	P93	17.17	Stack's Bowers Baltimore Auction (15 Nov. 2012), lot 11585.
194.	A35	P94	17.30	ANS 1944.100.35042.
195.	A35	P94	17.14	London, 1958,0304.26; Price 3426a.
196.	A35	P95	17.20	ANS 1944.100.35044.
197.	A35	P96	17.17	Le Rider and Olçay, 1958, 79, pl. VII, 79; Akçakale Hoard, *CH* 8.201, *CH* 10.251.
198.	A35	P97	17.10	Le Rider and Olçay, 1958, 80, pl. VII, 80; Akçakale Hoard, *CH* 8.201, *CH* 10.251.
199.*	A36	P98	17.30	ANS 1944.100.35045.
200.	A36	P99	17.16	Eukratides Ancient Numismatics T042; CNG eAuction 341 (7 Dec. 2014), lot 249.
201.	A36	P100	17.21	Hirsch 266 (11 Feb. 2010), lot 1635
202.	A36	P101	17.20	ANS 1944.100.35046.
203.*	A37	P102	17.17	ANS 1944.100.35047.
204.	A37	P102	16.98	Roma Numismatics May 2013 Auction (21 May 2013), lot 351.
205.*	A38	P103	16.90	London Coin Galleries 4 (1 Jun. 2017), lot 614.
206.*	A39	P104	17.13	Roma Numismatics E-Sale 31 (26 Nov. 2016), lot 64.
207.	A39	P105	17.13	CNG 63 (21 May 2003), lot 186.
208.	A39	P105	17.07	CNG eAuction 283 (25 Jul. 2012), lot 134.
209.	A39	P105	17.16	Oxford, Ashmolean HCR23660; *SNGuk_0503_3013*; Kuft Hoard, *IGCH* 1670
210.	A39	P105	14.89	Cox, 1953, 31, pl. III, 31; Gordion Hoard, *IGCH* 1406
211.	A40	P106	17.13	ANS 1944.100.35048.
212.*	A40	P106	17.02	ANS 1944.100.35049.

213.	A40	P107	17.08	Berlin, Münzkabinett 182533532.
214.	A40	P108	17.09	Paris, FRBNF41838003.
215.*	A41	P109	17.09	ANS 1944.100.35051; Andritsaena, Elis, c. 1923 Hoard, *IGCH* 0083
216.	A41	P109	17.00	Praefectus Coins GRA2328.
217.	A41	P109	17.13	ANS 1944.100.35052; Abu Hommos Hoard, *IGCH* 1667.
218.	A41	P110	17.11	ANS 1944.100.35053.
219.	A41	P110	17.15	Le Rider and Olçay, 1958, 89, pl. VII, 89; Akçakale Hoard, *CH* 8.201, *CH* 10.251.
220.	A41	P110	17.14	Le Rider and Olçay, 1958, 90, pl. VII, 90; Akçakale Hoard, *CH* 8.201, *CH* 10.251.
221.	A42	P110	17.25	CNG 63 (21 May 2003), lot 183.
222.*	A42	P110	16.63	ANS 1944.100.35054; Abu Hommos Hoard, *IGCH* 1667.
223.	A42	P110	16.98	Heritage 419, (15 Sep. 2016), lot 51013.
224.	A42	P111	17.05	Pegasi Numismatics 12120081; Pegasi XXXIV (24 May 2016), lot 94.
225.	A42	P112	16.90	ANS 1944.100.35055.
226.*	A43	P113	17.10	CNG eAuction 256 (25 May 2011), lot 149.
227.	A43	P114	17.28	Peus 418 (2 Nov. 2016), lot 949.
228.	A44	P115	17.27	Le Rider and Olçay, 1958, 85, pl. VII, 85; Akçakale Hoard, *CH* 8.201, *CH* 10.251.
229.	A45	P116	17.21	UBS Gold & Numismatics 52 (11 Sep. 2001), lot 40.
230.*	A45	P117	17.13	ANS 1944.100.35057.
231.	A45	P117	17.09	CNG 38 (6 Jun. 1996), lot 212.
232.	A45	P118	17.22	CNG eAuction 347 (25 Mar. 2015), lot 289.
233.	A45	P118	17.20	ANS 1944.100.35056; Abu Hommos Hoard, *IGCH* 1667
234.*	A46	P119	17.12	London, 2002,0101.783; Hersh Coll.
235.	A46	P120	16.91	ANS 1944.100.35061.
236.*	A47	P121	16.89	Chaponnière & Firmenich 6 (26 Nov. 2014), lot 13.
237.	A47	P122	17.18	Blackburn Museum; *SNGuk* 0800_0482.
238.	A47	P123	17.05	Hirsch 256 (5 May 2008), lot 55.
239.	A47	P123	17.12	Paris, FRBNF41838004.
240.	A47	P123	17.12	Oxford, Ashmolean HCR23654; *SNGuk* 0503_3007; Kuft Hoard, *IGCH* 1670.

241.	A47	P123	16.76	CNG eAuction 354 (1 Jul. 2015), lot 257.
242.	A47	P123	17.07	Zurqieh mk662.
243.	A47	P124	16.98	Solidus Numismatik 6 (19 Jul. 2015), lot 63.
244.	A47	P125	17.17	CGB.fr 47 (19 Mar. 2011), lot 59; Vinchon (14–15 Mar. 1989), lot 89.
245.	A47	P126	17.09	The New York Sale XXXIV (6 Jan. 2015), lot 75.
246.	A47	P126	17.18	Hirsch 296 (13 Feb 2014), lot 1696; Hirsch 303 (25 Sep. 2014), lot 2674.
247.	A47	P126	17.10	Gorny & Mosch 200 (10 Oct. 2011), lot 1425.
248.	A47	P127	16.81	Gorny & Mosch 118 (15 Oct. 2002), lot 1250.
249.	A47	P127	17.09	Elsen 91 (24 Mar. 2007), lot 36.
250.	A47	P128	17.00	ANS 1947.98.299.
251.	A47	P129	16.91	CNG eAuction 391 (15 Feb. 2017), lot 315.
252.	A47	P129	17.14	Peus 396 (5 Nov. 2008), lot 297.
253.	A47	P129	17.09	VAuctions 249 (15 Jul. 2010), lot 2.
254.	A47	P129	16.90	CNG eAuction 243 (27 Oct. 2010), lot 68; CNG eAuction 218 (9 Sep. 2009), lot 143.
255.	A47	P129	17.10	CNG 54 (14 Jun. 2000), lot 480.
256.	A47	P130	17.10	ANS 1944.100.35074.
257.	A47	P131	16.87	Savoca Numismatik 15 (28 May 2017), lot 341.
258.	A47	P132	16.38	VAuctions 257 (30 Dec. 2010), lot 8.
259.	A47	P133	n.r.	Troxell, 1997, 132 no. 70, pl. 28, 70; Unknown Findspot (in Asia Minor) 1993 Hoard, *CH* 10.246.
260.	A47	P133	16.81	Elsen 94 (15 Dec. 2007), lot 518.
261.	A47	P133	17.04	CNG eAuction 325 (23 Apr. 2014), lot 277.
262.	A47	P133?	16.15	Cox, 1953, 32, pl. III, 32; Gordion Hoard, *IGCH* 1406.
263.	A47	P134	16.50	Herbert Grün 54 (16 Nov. 2010), lot 34.
264.*	A47	P135	16.43	ANS 1944.100.35076.
265.	A47	P136	16.67	ANS 1944.100.35077.
266.	A47	P137	15.59	CNG eAuction 272 (25 Jan. 2012), lot 164.
267.	A47	P138	16.44	Münz Zentrum Rheinland 181 (17 May 2017), lot 59; Kölner Münzkabinett Tyll Kroha Nachfolger 104 (12 Feb. 2016), lot 38.
268.	A48	P139	17.13	Elsen 93 (15 Sep. 2007), lot 147.
269.	A48	P140	17.01	Forum Ancient Coins SH15299.
270.	A48	P140	16.92	Stack's Bowers NYINC Auction (10 Jan. 2014), lot 33.

271.	A48	P140	16.82	Gorny & Mosch 156 (5 Mar. 2007), lot 1280.
272.	A48	P141	16.97	Hess Divo 314 (4 May 2009), lot 1083.
273.	A48	P142	17.15	CNG eAuction 389 (18 Jan. 2017), lot 377; Peus 393 (31 Oct. 2007), lot 208.
274.	A48	P142	16.71	CNG 53 (15 Mar. 2000), lot 214.
275.	A48	P143	17.08	Künker 133 (11 Oct. 2007), lot 8024.
276.	A48	P144	16.95	Vienna, Münzkabinett Wien GR 10286.
277.*	A48	P145	16.98	Triton XVI (7 Jan. 2013), lot 584.
278.	A48	P145	16.94	CNG 64 (24 Sep. 2003), lot 106.
279.	A48	P145	17.03	Eukratides Ancient Numismatics vb32.
280.	A48	P145	16.85	V. Gadoury Auction 2016 (14 Dec. 2016), lot 6.
281.	A48	P146	16.90	Goldberg 80 (3 Jun. 2014), lot 3277.
282.	A48	P147	17.07	Hirsch 313 (23 Sep. 2015), lot 2026; Hess-Leu 45 (1970), lot 149.
283.	A48	P148	16.58	Stack's Bowers 2014 NYINC Auction (10 Jan. 2014), lot 34.
284.	A48	P149	16.97	Forum Ancient Coins SH71154.
285.	A48	P150	16.82	CNG 63 (21 May 2003), lot 185.
286.	A48	P151	16.68	Stack's Bowers 2015 ANA Auction (12 Aug. 2015), lot 33021.
287.	A48	P151	17.06	ANS 1944.100.35114.
288.	A49	P152	17.06	CNG eAuction 337 (22 Oct. 2014), lot 157.
289.	A49	P152	16.94	Numismatica Ars Classica 92 (23 May 2016), lot 1441.
290.	A49	P152	17.39	CNG eAuction 364 (2 Dec. 2015), lot 501.
291.*	A49	P153	17.13	LWHT Coll.; Roma Numismatics E-Sale 35 (3 May 2017), lot 178.
292.	A49	P154	16.64	Oxford, Ashmolean HCR23659 *SNGuk_0503_3012*.
293.	A49	P155	16.69	Rauch Summer Auction 2012 (20 Sep. 2012), lot 237.
294.	A50	P156	17.01	CNG eAuction 199 (19 Nov. 2008), lot 106.
295.*	A50	P156	17.16	Numismatik Lanz München 163 (7 Dec 2016), lot 50.
296.	A50	P156	16.92	CNG eAuction 216 (12 Aug. 2009), lot 78.
297.	A50	P156	17.07	Hirsch 313 (23 Sep. 2015), lot 2026.
298.	A50	P156	17.08	CNG eAuction 399 (14 Jun. 2017), lot 292.
299.	A50	P156	17.04	Naville Numismatics 21 (20 Mar. 2016), lot 55.
300.	A50	P157	16.84	CNG eAuction 307 (24 Jul. 2013), lot 113.

301.	A50	P158	17.11	CNG 72 (14 Jun. 2006), lot 411; "Seleucus I" Hoard *CH* 10.265.
302.	A50	P158	16.96	Stack's Coin Galleries September 2008 (10 Sep. 2008), lot 54.
303.	A50	P159	16.96	Heritage 3046 (14 Apr. 2016), lot 31062.
304.	A50	P160	17.12	VAuctions 266 (12 Mar. 2015), lot 2004.
305.	A50	P160	16.86	CNG 78 (14 May 2008), lot 412.
306.	A50	P160	16.97	CGB.fr 57 (20 Feb. 2013), lot 87; CGB.fr 53 (19 Apr 2012), lot 47.
307.	A50	P161	17.14	ANS 1944.100.35078.
308.	A51	P162	17.21	CNG 263539.
309.	A51	P163	17.01	Triton XIV (3 Jan 2011), lot 384.
310.	A51	P163	16.92	London, G.2494; Price 3426c.
311.	A51	P164	n.r.	Heritage 311 (11 Jan. 2003), lot 14128.
312.	A51	P164	17.11	Hess Divo 320 (26 Oct. 2011), lot 110.
313.	A51	P165	17.07	Aureo & Calicó 296 (21 Sep. 2017), lot 25.
314.*	A51	P166	17.18	Roma Numismatics XIII (23 March 2017), lot 186.
315.	A51	P167	16.96	CNG eAuction 225 (13 Jan. 2010), lot 54.
316.	A51	P168	16.96	CNG 41 (19 Mar. 1997), lot 302.
317.	A51	P169	17.03	Heritage 3045 (12 Jan. 2016), lot 32064.
318.	A51	P169	16.97	Berlin, Münzkabinett 18253356.
319.	A51	P170	17.15	CNG eAuction 400 (28 Jun .2017), lot 349.
320.	A51	P170	17.08	Agora 68 (15 Aug. 2017), lot 20; CNG eAuction 388 (14 Dec. 2016), lot 183.
321.	A52	P171	17.20	Stacks Coin Galleries December 2007 (18 Dec. 2007), lot 96.
322.	A52	P172	17.15	Hirsch 238 (10 May 2017), lot 97.
323.	A52	P172	16.64	CNG eAuction 244 (10 Nov. 2010), lot 45.
324.	A52	P173	16.97	CNG 192006; CNG eAuction 218 (9 Sep. 2009), lot 141.
325.	A52	P174	17.10	C.J. Martin Coins EC280.
326.*	A52	P175	17.20	Roma Numismatics E-Sale 9 (28 Jun. 2014), lot 235.
327.	A52	P176	17.13	Berlin, Münzkabinett 18253355.
328.	A52	P177	17.17	CNG eAuction 398 (31 May 2017), lot 342.
329.	A52	P177	17.08	CNG eAuction 347 (25 Mar. 2015), lot 287.
330.	A52	P178	16.50	CNG eAuction 218 (9 Sep. 2009), lot 142.

331.	A52	P178	17.08	ANS 1944.100.35080.
332.	A52	P178	17.10	VAuctions 259 (10 Feb. 2011), lot 7.
333.	A53	P179	16.85	CNG eAuction 124 (12 Oct. 2005), lot 18.
334.	A53	P179	17.00	CNG eAuction 347 (25 Mar. 2015), lot 288.
335.	A53	P180	17.11	Roma Numismatics eSale 4 (28 Dec. 2013), lot 185.
336.*	A53	P181	16.10	ANS 1977.158.152.
337.*	A54	P182	16.66	Goldberg 96 (14 Feb. 2017), lot 1590.
338.	A54	P183	16.50	CNG eAuction 271 (11 Jan. 2012), lot 23; Triton II (1 December 1998), lot 327.
339.	A54	P183	17.11	CNG eAuction 390 (1 Feb. 2017), lot 226.
340.	A54	P183	16.41	CNG eAuction 341 (7 Dec. 2014), lot 248.
341.	A54	P184	17.02	CNG 57 (4 Apr. 2001), lot 227.
342.	A54	P184	17.34	CNG 810148.
343.	A54	P184	17.21	New Haven, Yale University Art Gallery 2001.87.10094.
344.	A54	P185	17.32	Triton IX (9 Jan. 2006), lot 798.
345.	A54	P185	16.86	CNA XX (25 Mar. 1992), lot 51.
346.	A54	P186	17.09	CNG eAuction 383 (28 Sep. 2016), lot 240.
347.	A54	P187	17.13	CNG 49 (17 Mar. 1999), lot 223.
348.	A54	P188	17.12	Roma Numismatics (21 May 2013), lot 352.
349.	A54	P189	17.13	Berlin, Münzkabinett 18253354.
350.	A54	P190	15.70	Oxford, Ashmolean HCR23661, *SNGuk_0503_3013A*; Pasagarde Hoard, *IGCH* 1794.
351.	A54	P191	16.93	Peus 395 (7 May 2008), lot 124.
352.	A54	P191	16.76	CNG eAuction 403 (9 Aug. 2017), lot 288.
353.	A54	P192	17.02	Sternberg 23 (29 Oct. 2000), lot 233.
354.	A54	P193	17.15	Paul-Francis Jacquier 40 (16 Oct. 2015), lot 100.
355.	A54	P194	17.13	ANS 1944.100.35082; Abu Hommos Hoard, *IGCH* 1667.
356.	A54	P194	17.13	ANS 1944.100.35096.
357.	A54	P195	17.24	CGB.fr (13 Jun. 2017), lot 13.
358.	A54	P195	17.13	London, 1878,0301.155; Price 3426f.
359.	A54	P195	16.87	Elsen 93 (15 Sep.2007), lot 675.
360.	A54	P196	16.60	CNG eAuction 198 (5 Nov. 2008), lot 55; CNG 41 (19 Mar. 1997), lot 303.

361.	A55	P197	14.50	ANS 1944.100.35083.
362.*	A55	P198	17.10	ANS 1944.100.45132; Armenak Hoard, *IGCH* 1423.
363.*	A56	P199	17.03	CNG eAuction 398 (31 May 2017), lot 341.
364.	A56	P200	16.96	ACR eAuction 32 (11 Jan. 2016), lot 340.
365.*	A57	P201	17.15	ANS 1944.100.35071.
366.	A57	P201	17.26	CNG eAuction 336 (8 Oct. 2014), lot 130.
367.	A57	P201	17.14	UBS Gold & Numismatics 59 (27 Jan. 2004), lot 5399.
368.	A57	P201	16.61	Heritage 3035 (3 Sep. 2014), lot 32039.
369.	A57	P202	16.59	Künker 295 (25 Sep. 2017), lot 249.
370.	A57	P203	17.13	Stack's Bowers NYINC (6 Jan. 2012), lot 162; CNG 72 (14 Jun. 2006), lot 409.; "Seleucus I" Hoard, *CH* 10.265
371.	A57	P203	17.31	CNG 61 (25 Sep. 2002), lot 465.
372.	A57	P204	17.24	CNG 49 (17 Mar. 1999), lot 222.
373.	A57	P204	16.94	Christoph Gärtner 32 (24 Oct. 2015), lot 34136.
374.	A57	P205	17.33	Aureo & Calicó, 293 (24 May 2017), lot 2025; Stack's Bowers Galleries (16 Nov. 2012), lot 11579.
375.	A57	P205	17.01	Münzen & Medaillen 27 (28 May 2008), lot 2046.
376.	A57	P206	16.79	Künker eAuction 42 (18 Oct. 2016), lot 40.
377.*	A58	P207	16.93	Künker 226 (11 Mar. 2013), lot 325; Hess Divo 317 (27 Oct 2010), lot 147.
378.	A58	P208	17.06	Heritage 3042 (17 Sep. 2015), lot 29040.
379.	A58	P209	17.12	ANS 1944.100.35079; Ankara Hoard, *IGCH* 1399.
380.	A58	P210	17.17	CNG 42 (29–30 May 1997), lot 260.
381.*	A59	P211	17.00	C.J. Martin Coins EC153.
382.*	A60	P212	17.12	CNG 79 (17 Sep. 2008), lot 173; Baldwin's 47 (25 Sep. 2006), lot 41.
383.	A60	P213	16.43	ANS 1944.100.35089; Abu Hommos Hoard, *IGCH* 1667.
384.	A60	P213	15.15	ANS 1953.150.22; Büyükçekmece Hoard, *IGCH* 0867.
385.	A60	P214	17.04	Peus eAuction 4 (14 Jan. 2017), lot 73.
386.	A60	P214	17.04	CNG 66 (19 May 2004), lot 246.
387.	A60	P214	17.10	ANS 1944.100.35085; Abu Hommos Hoard, *IGCH* 1667.
388.	A60	P214	16.82	ANS 1944.100.35086; Abu Hommos Hoard, *IGCH* 1667.

389.	A60	P215	15.87	Amandry and Callot, 1988, 11, pl. XIII, 11; Failaka Hoard, *CH* 8.256.
390.	A60	P215	17.20	Baldwin's 39 (11 Oct. 2004), lot 1217.
391.	A61	P216	16.94	London, 2002,0101.784; Hersh Coll.
392.*	A61	P216	17.10	ANS 1944.100.35084.
393.	A61	P217	17.00	Herbert Grün 65 (12 May 2015), lot 69.
394.	A61	P218	17.35	The New York Sale XXV (5 Jan. 2011), lot 36.
395.	A61	P218	17.15	CNG 61 (25 Sep. 2002), lot 464.
396.*	A62	P219	17.18	ACR 15 (27 Apr. 2016), lot 208; Triton XVIII (5 Jan. 2015), lot 776.
397.	A62	P220	17.04	Noble Numismatics 109 (28–30 Jul. 2015), lot 3597.
398.	A62	P220	17.16	Sedwick 21 (3–4 May 2017), lot 1274.
399.	A62	P221	16.67	ANS 1944.100.35097.
400.	A62	P221	16.18	ANS 1944.100.35098.
401.	A62	P222	17.00	ANS 1944.100.35099.
402.	A63	P223	17.18	Triton XVI (7 Jan 2013), lot 583.
403.*	A63	P223	17.07	CNG eAuction 224 (16 Dec. 2009), lot 95.
404.	A63	P223	17.00	Naumann 37 (1 Nov. 2015), lot 102.
405.	A63	P223	16.77	Adolph E. Cahn 84 (29 Nov. 1933), lot 251.
406.	A64	P224	16.63	CGB.fr 45 (14 Oct. 2010), lot 63.
407.	A64	P224	14.18	ANS 1944.100.35069; Abu Hommos Hoard, *IGCH* 1667.
408.	A64	P225	17.22	Heritage Europe 34 (23 May 2012), lot 90.
409.*	A64	P226	17.06	ANS 1944.100.35070.
410.	A64	P226	16.69	Berlin, Münzkabinett 182533531.
411.	A64	P227	17.14	CGB.fr 36 (23 Oct. 2006), lot 94.
412.	A64	P228	17.00	CNG 397 (17 May 2017), lot 223.
413.	A64	P228	16.78	Hirsch 281 (2 May 2012), lot 224; Hirsch 275 (22 Sep. 2011), lot 3490.
414.	A64	P229	17.27	CNG eAuction 336 (8 Oct. 2014), lot 131.
415.	A64	P229	17.07	Obolos eAuction 6 (28Nov. 2016), lot 318.
416.	A64	P229	16.68	CNG eAuction 375 (1 Jun. 2016), lot 450.
417.	A64	P230	17.18	Calgary Coin vcoin5350; VAuctions 218 (18 Dec. 2008), lot 10.
418.	A64	P230	17.16	Pegasi Numismatics XXII (20 Apr. 2010), lot 107.

419.*	A65	P231	17.37	VAuctions 242 (25 Feb. 2010), lot 2.
420.	A65	P231	17.17	UBS Gold & Numismatics 61 (14 Sep. 2004), lot 4267.
421.	A65	P231	17.17	Münzen & Medaillen 30 (28 May 2009), lot 219.
422.	A66	P232	17.07	Gorny & Mosch 118 (15 Oct. 2002), lot 1251.
423.*	A66	P232	16.68	ANS 1944.100.35104.
424.*	A67	P233	16.81	Kölner 105 (16 Sep. 2016), lot 91; Naumann 21 (7 Sep. 2014), lot 123.
425.	A67	P233	17.24	CGB.fr (15 Dec. 2015), lot 372084.
426.	A67	P233	16.94	CNG 61 (25 Sep. 2002), lot 463.
427.	A67	P234	17.18	Roma Numismatics XII (29 Sep. 2016), lot 207.
428.	A67	P235	17.07	Paris, BNF41848327.
429.	A67	P236	16.89	ANS 1944.100.45131; Armenak Hoard, *IGCH* 1423.
430.	A67	P236	17.15	Meister & Sonntag 10 (18 Nov. 2010), lot 10.
431.	A67	P236	17.01	CNG eAuction 322 (12 Mar. 2014), lot 396.
432.	A67	P237	16.77	Naumann 52 (2–3 April 2017), lot 226.
433.	A67	P237	16.96	Heritage 3046 (14 Apr. 2016), lot 31061.
434.	A68	P238	16.61	CNG eAuction 301 (24 Apr. 2013), lot 100.
435.*	A68	P238	16.97	Naumann 40 (7 Feb. 2016), lot 72.
436.	A68	P238	17.03	Vilmar Numismatics 10868.
437.	A68	P238	16.92	CNG eAuction 194 (20 Aug. 2008), lot 28.
438.	A68	P238	17.19	ANS 1974.26.573.
439.	A68	P239	17.14	Noble Numismatics 80 (22–24 Nov. 2008), lot 3173; Noble Numismatics 70 (9–11 Jul. 2002), lot 3139.
440.	A68	P240	17.26	ANS 1944.100.35095.
441.	A69	P241	16.83	CNG 88 (14 Sep. 2011), lot 535.
442.	A69	P241	16.91	ANS 1952.57.5.
443.	A69	P242	17.15	CGB. fr (May 2017), MA-ID 12020000898.
444.	A69	P243	16.91	Künker eAuction 23 (20 Oct. 2013), lot 10; Hirsch 256 (5 May 2008), lot 56
445.	A69	P243	17.26	iNumis 8 (20 Mar. 2009), lot 16.
446.*	A69	P243	16.96	ANS 1944.100.35090; Abu Hommos Hoard, *IGCH* 1667.
447.	A70	P244	17.05	CNG eAuction 69 (23 Jul. 2003), lot 17.
448.*	A70	P245	17.00	ANS 1944.100.35088.

449.	A70	P246	16.97	Münz Zentrum Rheinland 168 (27 Dec. 2013), lot 102.
450.*	A71	P247	17.05	Numismatik Lanz München 132 (27 Nov. 2006), lot 131.
451.	A71	P248	16.92	Bolaffi 26 (10 Jun. 2015), lot 1053.
452.	A71	P249	17.05	ANS 1944.100.35059; Egypt Hoard, 1912, *IGCH* 1668.
453.*	A72	P250	16.94	CNG eAuction 310 (4 Sep. 2013), lot 143.
454.	A72	P250	17.09	ANS 1944.100.35060; Andritsaena Hoard, *IGCH* 0083.

4.2   A rather than Ꞧ (Price B24)

455.	A72	P251	16.21	CNG eAuction 310 (4 Sep. 2013), lot 144. Tooled coin.
456.*	A72	P252	17.06	London, 1888,0614.26; Price B24.

4.3   △ rather than Ꞧ (Price -)

457.*	A73	P253	17.10	CGB.fr inventory no. bgr_374425; CGB.fr (29 Sep. 2015), lot 364766; Abdo Ayoub Coll. Coin image ©CGB Numismatique Paris.

4.1   Ꞧ (Price 3426)

458.*	A74	P254	16.24	VAuctions 323 (17 Mar. 2017), lot 93.
459.*	A75	P255	15.80	ANS 1944.100.35062.
460.*	A76	P256	16.70	ANS 1944.100.35081.
461.*	A77	P257	17.10	Bertolami Fine Arts 3 (31 May 2011), lot 85.
462.	A77	P257	17.20	ANS 1944.100.35063; Abu Hommos Hoard, *IGCH* 1667.
463.	A77	P258	16.88	Oxford, Ashmolean HCR23657; *SNGuk_0503_3010*.
464.	A77	P258	17.02	Comptoir des Monnaies 31735; Rauch Summer Auction 2013 (18 Sep. 2013), lot 31.
465.*	A78	P259	16.94	CNG eAuction 343 (28 Jan. 2015), lot 266.
466.	A78	P259	16.43	ANS 1944.100.35058.
467.*	A79	P260	17.15	Nomos 12 (22 May 2016), lot 39; Münzen & Medaillen 41 (11 Dec. 2014), lot 52; Münzen & Medaillen 35 (17 Nov. 2011), lot 36.
468.	A79	P261	17.13	Münzen & Medaillen 8 (10 May 2001), lot 109.
469.	A79	P262	17.17	Oxford, Ashmolean HCR23656; *SNGuk_0503_3009*; Kuft Hoard, *IGCH* 1670.
470.	A79	P263	16.75	Noble Numismatics 66 (22–30 Mar. 2001), lot 3285.

471.	A79	P264	17.22	Hess Divo 314 (4 May 2009), lot 1082.
472.	A79	P264	16.94	Peus 286 (26 Apr. 2006), lot 187.
473.	A79	P265	17.20	Heritage 3032 (10 Apr. 2014), lot 23119; Forum Ancient Coins SH46941.
474.*	A80	P266	17.61	Freeman & Sear Mail Bid 15 (27 Jun. 2008), lot 53.
475.*	A81	P267	17.04	Roma Numismatics E-Sale 7 (26 Apr. 2014), lot 388.
476.*	A82	P268	16.56	ANS 1944.100.35102.
477.*	A83	P269	17.10	ANS 1944.100.35091.
478.*	A84	P270	16.96	Leu Numismatik Web Auction 1 (18 Jun. 2017), lot 321.
479.	A85	P271	17.14	iNumis 16 (16 Oct. 2011), lot 23.
480.*	A85	P272	16.27	ANS 1944.100.35103.
481.	A85	P272	16.56	ANS 1944.100.35101; Olympia Hoard, *IGCH* 176.
482.*	A86	P273	17.07	CNG eAuction 224 (16 Dec. 2009), lot 94.
483.	A86	P274	17.14	VAuctions 247 (3 Jun. 2010), lot 4; CNG 205 (25 Feb. 2009) lot 69.
484.*	A87	P275	16.89	CNG eAuction 255 (4 May 2011), lot 141.
485.	A88	P276	17.04	Pars Coins PCW-G4462.
486.*	A88	P276	17.01	CNG eAuction 285 (22 Aug. 2012), lot 149.
487.*	A89	P277	17.10	CNG eAuction 216 (12 Aug. 2009), lot 77.
488.	A89	P277	17.13	ANS 1944.100.35092; Ankara Hoard, *IGCH* 1399.
489.	A89	P277	16.57	Spink 14006 (22 Sep. 2014), Lot 653.
490.	A89	P278	17.10	ANS 1944.100.35093.; Zemun Hoard, *IGCH* 0458.
491.	A89	P279	16.57	CNG eAuction 193 (6 Aug. 2008), lot 42.
492.	A89	P279	16.59	Amandry and Callot, 1988, 10, pl. XIII, 10; Failaka Hoard, *CH* 8.256.
493.	A89	P279	17.0	ANS 1944.100.35094.
494.*	A90	P280	17.19	Nomos 15 (22 Oct. 2017), lot 67.
495.	A90	P280	17.10	Berlin, Münzkabinett 18253353.
496.*	A91	P281	n.r.	Peus 410 (31 Oct. 2013), lot 798 (one of 3 coins).
497.	A91	P282	17.06	Gorny & Mosch 118 (15 Oct. 2002), lot 1249.
498.	A92	P227	16.94	London, 1882,0803.3; Price 3426b.
499.	A92	P283	17.25	CNG 63 (21 May 2003), lot 184.
500.*	A92	P283	17.04	CNG eAuction 403 (9 Aug. 2017), lot 287.

501.	A92	P284	16.52	Miller 2010, 7, pl. 6, 7; East Arachosia (Quetta) Hoard, *CH* 10. 275.
502.*	A93	P285	17.12	Naumann 63 (4 Mar. 2018), Lot 593.
503.	A94	P286	16.80	Palmyra Heritage VCoins store 122133842599.
504.*	A94	P286	16.99	CNG 79 (17 Sep. 2008), lot 172.
505.	A94	P286	17.02	CNG eAuction 318 (15 Jan. 2014), lot 316.
506.*	A95	P287	16.73	Künker 295 (25 Sep. 2017), lot 248.
507.*	A96	P288	16.98	Triton IX (9 Jan. 2006), lot 799.
508.*	A97	P289	16.96	CNG eAuction 402 (26 Jul. 2017, lot 348.
509.	A97	P290	16.99	CNG 72 (14 Jun. 2006), lot 410; "Seleucus I" Hoard, *CH* 10.265.

Excluded from the catalogue of Series 4:

ANS 1989.114.1 too worn and corroded for definitive die identification.
ANS 1956.28.138 appears to be a silver plated fourrée.
ANS 1944.100.35100 bearing a ΛA mintmark; a Celtic (?) imitative of Series 4. Another example from the same obverse die, Hirsch 338 (9 May 2018), lot 4.

COMMENTARY

Series 1 and 2 (Gold Staters)

Series 1 and 2 consist of gold staters distinguished by the placement of the Ɑ mintmark. It is located to the left of Nike's right wing on Series 1 (Cat. Nos. 1–31), while positioned beneath the wing on Series 2 (Cat. Nos. 32–43). The two series were struck contemporaneously, as evidenced by two obverse die links and a parallel progression of iconographic development summarized in Table 1 (below). Sixteen obverse and 24 reverse dies are represented in Series 1, which includes two previously unrecorded varieties with distinguishing decorative elements on Athena's helmet; 1.2 bearing a griffin and 1.3 with a sphinx. Nine obverse and eight reverse dies are represented in Series 2, which includes a previously unrecorded variety (2.2) struck from an obverse die with a griffin rather than a serpent on Athena's helmet. In Series 2, the progression of small die breaks on the Ɑ monogram and behind Nike's trailing leg on a linking reverse die (P25) serve to sequence varieties 2.1 and 2.2. The latter from obverse die Av18 mirrors the same iconographic development on Series 1 die Av2, to the extent that both dies are nearly identical, evidently from the same engraver's hand. This is the first of four occurrences in the catalogue linking the two types by the presence of a shared die engraver, or shared die. Series 1 and 2 are linked by two obverse dies, Av3 and Av5. Die Av3 was in its earliest unworn state when used to strike Series 2, while the reverse applied with die Av5, which was initially put into use for Series 1. This indicates that shared dies were commissioned during the striking of both series, excluding the possibility that one series was struck after the other using old dies from the former. Two almost identical pairs of obverse dies, each pair from the hand of a single engraver, serve to reinforce the association of the two types; the previously noted example of Av2 and Av18, plus Av6 and Av19. Within Series 1, one reverse die link serves to sequence dies Av11 and Av12.

Table 1. Series 1 and 2: dies, links and relative chronology

Series 1 Dies	Links and Iconography	Series 2 Dies
Av1	Paired to reverse dies depicting Nike's right hand with an open facing palm. Series 2: Av17 and Av18 reverse die linked.	Av17
Av2	Griffin on helmet—near identical dies.	Av18
Av3	Obverse die link between Series 1 & 2.	Av3
Av4		-
Av5	Obverse die link between Series 1 & 2.	AV5
Av6	Near identical obverse dies.	Av19
Av7–Av15	Nike's right hand depicted in profile on the last of the reverse dies in each series. Series 1: Av11 and Av12 reverse die linked. Av12 die link to Miletos (Price 2078)	Av20–23
Av16	Sphinx on helmet.	

The sequence is defined in the broadest sense by a progression of the detail in the depiction of the extended right hand of Nike. It evolves from the initial depiction of a crudely defined facing open palm with splayed fingers (Pl. 4, A), eventually to that of a well-defined hand in profile oriented upward (Pl. 4, B) on the last reverse dies of Series 1 and 2. Clumsily engraved intermediate forms of representation are present, indicating that the die engravers struggled to develop the depiction of the hand in profile. This change finds a parallel in the altered depiction of the extended right hand of Zeus that occurs midway through the tetradrachm sequence of Series 3. This parallel suggests that the gold emission finished around the time this change took effect early in the tetradrachm sequence.

The die analysis demonstrates that Series 1 and 2 were struck in parallel (Table 1) so that the differing placement of the Ꞃ mintmark does not define separate issues. Rather, the placement of the Ꞃ monogram, either below the wing of Nike, or in the left field, is likely to have been of some significance in the mint's internal control process. Most plausibly, it may have served to identify the output from each of two anvils during parallel striking. If so, the reverse dies were purpose cut for use on each anvil, the latter uniquely identified by the placement of the Ꞃ monogram. On a daily basis, the struck product from each anvil, identifiable to the specific coin level, could be reconciled precisely by weight to the amount of gold, or gold blanks, apportioned to each anvil at the start of the day. This would have reduced the risk of fraud, malfeasance, or debasement via the ability to match a coin with those responsible for its production, notwithstanding the fact that two production teams operated side by side in the same facility.

Transfers between mints

The diversity of engraving styles of the head of Athena (Pls. 1–4) across the gold emission is notable. The work of up to thirteen engravers is identified in the catalogue of staters. Most notably, as demonstrated on Pl. 1, the work of at least five of these engravers is also recognized in the output of other mints. Common to both Series 1 and 2, obverse die Av5 is of a uniquely distinctive style and detail, also found on an example of the first dated stater issue of Sidon (Price 3482). Dated regnal year 7 (RY 7), equivalent to 327/6 BC, it is the first stater from the mint to depict a serpent, rather than a griffin,[28] on Athena's helmet (Pl. 1, 1). The Sidon die used to strike this example of RY 7 was not recorded by Newell,[29] but was identified from coins in commerce.[30] The use of this die was limited to the RY 7 emission; an important chronological marker. Whether the engraving of Av5 preceded, or post-dated, the engraving of the Sidon RY 7 die is not immediately apparent. However, the first presence at Sidon of the serpent rather than the griffin motif on Athena's helmet argues for the introduction of a new die engraver to Sidon at this time. Based on this, plus the consideration of the movement of other die engravers and an obverse die from Arados II to other mints, it is likely that the engraver of Av5 was transferred from Arados II to Sidon.

28. Le Rider, *Coinage*, 134–139. The earliest staters formerly attributed to Sidon (Price 3456–3466) are reattributed to Tarsos so that Price 3482 is the first issue in the Sidon series to bear the serpent motif.

29. E. T. Newell, *The Dated Alexander Coinage of Sidon and Ake* (Oxford: Oxford University Press, 1916), 12, no. 21 and pl. II, 5.

30. CNG 87 (18 May 2011), lot 347 (illustrated in Pl. 1, 1) and CNG 100 (7 Oct. 2015), lot 45.

Series 1 die Av6 and its Series 2 counterpart Av19 find a very close match with four of the Sidon dies used for stater issues dated regnal years 13 (321/0 BC; Price 3500; Newell *Sidon* 38, dies Y and Z), 14 (320/19 BC; Price P170–P171; Newell *Sidon* 42, die CC), 16 (318/7 BC; Price P176; Newell *Sidon* 46, die CC) and 18 (316/5 BC; Price 3503; Newell *Sidon* 49, dies CC and DD). Pl. 1, 2 compares Av 6 (Cat. No. 13) with a Sidon year 13 example[31] from Newell's obverse die Z. The detailing of the helmet plumes and structure, Athena's hair, and the three locks of hair protruding from beneath the helmet rim obscuring Athena's ear are so distinctive that it is most likely that these dies all originated from one engraver's hand. The congruity of these elements, plus the outline and form of Athena's head, with those of dies Av6 (Series 1) and Av19 (Series 2) is inescapable, pointing to the transfer of the engraver responsible for these dies to Sidon in advance of the issues commencing in 321/0 BC.

Obverse die Av11 finds an extremely close match with the obverse die of Thompson's, Miletos Series III, 129[32] that was used to strike examples of Price 2096, dated to 323–322 BC (Pl. 1, 3). The match is so close that it is concluded that the die engraver responsible for Arados die Av11 was transferred to Miletos. It may have been by this means that obverse die Av12, reverse die linked to Av11, was transported to Miletos, where it was used to strike one of the Miletos Series I staters dated to the period 325–323 BC. Obverse die Av12 is an unequivocal die-link to an example of Price 2078 from Miletos (Pl. 1, 4).[33] The style and detail of this die, and others from the hand of the same engraver, is so distinctive that it stands well apart from others. This occurs in the treatment and fine detailing of the crossed form of the proximal and medial plumes of Athena's helmet, plus the relatively unstructured, falling locks of Athena's hair. Die Av12 was in its unworn state when the Arados II coin (Cat. No. 23) was struck, whereas die wear is present on the Miletos coin, unequivocally identifying the direction of die transfer. Miletos Series I, including Price 2078, was dated by Thompson to the period 325–323 BC. The Arados stater sequence must either precede, or partially overlap this date range. No other comparably styled dies have been identified in the Miletos sequence, from which it might be concluded that the engraver of Av12 did not accompany the die transfer to Miletos.

---

31. Triton XVI (8 Jan. 2013), lot 295.

32. M. Thompson, *Alexander's Drachm Mints I: Sardes and Miletus* (New York: American Numismatic Society, 1983), pl. 24, 129. British Museum coin 1878,0301.57.

33. This coin is from a die unrecorded by Thompson, *Drachm Mints*. Illustrated coin is Dimitry Markov 11 (3 Sep. 2003), lot 26; the same coin as Gorny & Mosch 122 (10 Mar. 2003), lot 1230. It is reverse die linked to another example of Price 2078.

However, the work of the same engraver is later recognized at Tyre (Ake of Newell and Price), where an almost identical obverse die was used to strike some of the staters dated year 33 (317/6 BC;[34] Price 3284 and 3285; Newell *Dated Ake* 36, die O), illustrated on Pl. 1, 4.[35] This die marks the sole introduction into the Tyre series of the serpent motif in place of the griffin on Athena's helmet, suggesting that it may have been the result of the engagement of a new die engraver at the mint. A progression in the iconography involving a slight refinement of the falling locks of Athena's hair, in particular the leading edge of the hair style, plus the addition of a necklace suggest that the Tyre die post-dates the Arados II/Miletos example from the same engraver's hand. It appears that sometime after the transfer of die Av12 to Miletos, the engraver of this die must have transferred to Tyre where he engraved a near identical obverse die for the gold emission of 317/6 BC.

Series 2 obverse die Av17 is of the same portrait model, style and detail, from the same hand as an engraver engaged in cutting of some of the dies for the earliest Alexander III gold issues (Price 164 and 179) of Macedonia (Pl. 1, 5).[36] This distinctive portrait model is limited to Arados II and Macedonia, with the execution at the former apparently in its earliest incarnation, as evidenced by embellishments of minor details on the Macedonian series. It is possible that what we are seeing is the transfer of a portrait model, but when weighed with the evidence of other transfers from Arados, it is likely that the transfer was accommodated by means of an engraver transfer. The start date of the Macedonian gold issuance is uncertain, although a *terminus ante quem* of 323/2 BC is established by the presence of the staters in the Saida Hoard (*IGCH* 1508). Price concluded that it is likely that the Macedonian production of Alexander III gold staters commenced in the later part of the period 330–323 BC,[37] while Le Rider deduced a start date in early 323 BC,[38] post-dating the first gold issue of Arados II. It appears that the engraver responsible for Av17 was transferred from Arados to Macedonia at the start of the Macedonian mintage of gold staters in the name of Alexander III.

---

34. Based on the dating era of Ozmilk, the vassal king of Tyre: J. Elayi and A. G. Elayi, *The Coinage of the Phoenician City of Tyre in the Persian Period (5th–4th cent. BCE)* (Leuven: Peeters, 2009), 371–395. Also, Elayi, "Updated," Table 5.

35. Illustrated example is BM 1908,0110.1214; Price, *Coinage*, pl. XI, 3284.

36. Illustrated on Pl. 1, 5 is CNG 87 (18 May 2011), lot 354.

37. Price, *Coinage*, 106.

38. Le Rider, *Coinage*, 54–56.

The identification of various die engraver and die transfers to other mints serves to constrain the chronology of the Arados II gold emission. Based on the probable transfer of the engraver of die Av5 to Sidon for the RY 7 (327/6 BC) issue, the gold mintage at Arados II is likely to have commenced around 328 BC, while the transfer of die Av12 to Miletos to strike Price 2078 dates at least the first 75 percent of the gold emission to earlier than ca. 325–323 BC. The transfers also shed some light on the *modus operandi* of Alexander's mints. They are the first documented cases involving the mintage of gold staters.[39] Newell noted the transfer of two tetradrachm dies, plus the die engraver responsible for one of these, from Sidon to Tyre (Ake of Newell).[40] This occurred during the commissioning of the Alexander mint at Tyre, immediately following the protracted siege of the city in 332 BC. Subsequently, this engraver was transferred to Tarsos in 329 BC where his distinctive style is recognizable on a number of tetradrachm obverse dies.[41] The additional examples identified in this study expand on this underappreciated movement of skilled workers and confirm the suspicion of Le Rider when discussing Newell's example of the Sidon to Tyre transfers, "This is probably not an isolated example. Not only iconographic models, in all likelihood, passed from mint to mint: the artisans did too."[42]

39. The transfer of a die from Arados II to Miletos may not have been a unique circumstance at the latter mint. Thompson Drachm Mints: 46 and 50 (Series I.28–I.32) identified a possible obverse die link between an Alexander III "eagle on fulmen" drachm (Price 153) and an "enthroned Zeus" drachm of Miletos (Price 2088). Price (*Coinage*, 88, 103–105, 276) disagreed with Thompson's attribution of a small mintage of Alexander "eagle" drachms to Miletos, and assigned these coins to Macedonia, noting that "The general similarity of style of the early silver of this mint [Miletos] to that of lifetime Macedonia issues makes it very likely that there was some contact between the mints of the two areas, and the possibility that an engraver, perhaps with a die, transferred between the two cannot be discounted." He stated that "It is preferable to view this isolated link between Macedonia and Miletus as the result of a member of the mint personnel travelling to Asia Minor to prepare the imperial coinage of the newly opened Alexander mint" and concluded that "It seems much more probable that skilled mint personnel were moved from Macedonia to Miletus at a time when an exceptionally large coinage was required in a city which did not previously contain an Alexander mint."

40. Newell, *Dated*, 53, and Price, *Coinage*, 436.

41. Newell, "Tarsos," 81.

42. Le Rider, *Coinage*, 138.

Series 3 and 4 (Tetradrachms)

The catalogue of tetradrachms separates into two series distinguished by the portrayal of Zeus on the reverse. Series 3 depicts Zeus seated on a *diphros* with legs disposed side by side, in a parallel fashion (Cat. Nos. 44–139). This portrayal of Zeus is consistent with that found on the earliest output of the other Phoenician mints. Series 4 (Cat. Nos 140–509) portrays the right leg of Zeus drawn back behind the left leg in a crossed legs style that spread widely throughout the eastern mints, commencing around 324 BC. The sequence of Series 3 and 4 is poorly constrained by four reverse die links between obverse dies A4–A5, A7–A8, A29–A30 and A41–A42. As a result, groupings of obverse of style were used to define the sequence in its broadest sense.[43]

No obverse die link was identified between Series 3 and 4. However, as sequenced the change between the two occurs with reverse dies paired to the second of two distinctively engraved obverse dies (A22: Pl. 7, 136 and A23: Pl. 7, 140), both the work of the same engraver. Although a significant time break between Series 3 and 4 cannot be completely excluded there is no evidence in the die study to suggest such might have occurred. The large number of engravers represented in the mint's output implies frequent turnover, so that the continuity of an engraver across the end of Series 3 and the start of Series 4 suggests that there was not a major time break (i.e., multiple years or more) between the two series, despite the change in style of depiction of Zeus. This is consistent with that observed at the mints of Sidon, Tyre, Babylon and Susa where the transition from the older, parallel legs depiction, to the later crossed legs portrayal is not associated with a chronological break.[44]

Two previously unrecorded varieties are identified in Series 4. The letter A rather than the Ꝛ monogram defines series 4.2 (Cat. No. 455–456) struck from two different reverse dies. Price considered one of these coins (Cat. No. 456) to be a "barbarous" imitation, Price B24.[45] However, 4.2 is from the same obverse die (A72) as two other coins in the catalogue (Cat. Nos. 453–454) bearing the

43. Each style group is defined by the form, configuration and composition of the component elements of the iconography, particularly the definition of the brow of Herakles, the form of the locks of his hair on the forehead, and the detail of the ear, snout, and mane of the lion skin headdress. Within style groups the work of more than one die engraver can often be recognised.

44. Of the eastern mints, Susa is a notable exception to the pattern of displacement of the archaizing style of parallel legs by the later crossed legs style. Here the two styles alternated on coinage from c. 320, well into the Seleukid era.

45. Price, *Coinage*, 507.

complete Ↄ monogram, while the obverse style is consistent with that of other dies in this part of the sequence. On series 4.3 (Cat. No. 457) the Ↄ monogram is rendered as ⊿. This variant is associated with the mint by virtue of the affinity of style of the obverse die (A73) to that of the immediately preceding coins in the sequence and the consistency of the reverse style with that of series 4.1. The ⊿ monogram may simply be the result of careless engraving of the A component of the monogram.

Iconographic Progression

Series 3 resembles the earliest issues of Myriandros (Price 3217–3230), Arados (Price 3303; Duyrat Groups I and II)[46] and Karne (Price 3429). All are based on the same portrait model for Herakles, derivative of that initiated at Tarsos in 333/2 BC. Although within the framework of a common portrait model, the brow of Herakles, lightly delineated by a single curved line defining an eyebrow, is a distinctive characteristic of Series 3 that sets this type apart from the coinage of contemporary mints, although some specimens of Myriandros come close. This contrasts with the heavier, sometimes bulging, brow depiction on a number of the succeeding Series 4 dies. The obverse dies of Series 3 are of a consistent style, although the influence of three engravers can be detected in the detail of the interpretation of that style. The associated reverse dies variably depict the feet of Zeus either free-floating or resting on a footstool. Beyond this variable, they are of a notably consistent style, but for the change in the depiction of the extended right hand of Zeus from that of a facing open palm to that of an up-ward oriented hand in profile. This occurred mid-way through the emission of Series 3. Only one obverse die (A11) was paired to reverse dies with a mix of the two differing depictions of the right hand of Zeus. All other Series 3 obverse dies were paired to reverse dies that exclusively depicted one, or the other style of hand, without any commingling of the styles. This suggests that the change in the depiction of the right hand of Zeus occurred at a point of time within the working life of a single obverse die. This observation is consistent with that seen at the other Phoenician, Syrian and Babylon mints. It suggests that the change in the portrayal of the right hand of Zeus was a conscious decision taken at each mint, albeit at varying times down to 325 BC, from which time the depiction of the profile hand was the norm throughout the region. This defines a *terminus ante quem* of 326/5 BC for the first half of the Series 3 emission.[47]

---

46. Duyrat, *Arados*, 9–14, pl. 1, 4–28.

47. See Taylor, "Earliest," for a detailed discussion of the chronological significance in the eastern mints of the changed portrayal of the right hand of Zeus.

This change was followed by the evolution of the *diphros* beneath Zeus from a single cross-bracing strut to that of a distinctly double-strut depiction. In this process, the topmost beaded horizontal element, initially part of the seat platform structure, migrated down the legs of the *diphros* to form a clear and distinct second bracing strut. This development is evident in the latter part of Series 3. With few exceptions it is the norm on Series 4. In its earliest development, the depiction of the double-strut *diphros* occurred with the commissioning of the Alexander mints at Babylon and Damaskos in 326/5 BC.[48] This is a chronological reference point for the transition from Series 3 to Series 4. However, the defining characteristic of Series 4 is the changed depiction of Zeus, seated with his right leg (that furthest from the viewer) drawn back behind the left in the fashion of crossing legs. This change was abrupt, with no commingling of the old (parallel legs) and new styles (crossed legs). At Arados I, an apparently contemporaneous change in the style of the depiction of Zeus's legs was made in a different manner. Here the depiction of Zeus changed to that of his left leg (that closest the viewer) rather than his right drawn back, so that the overall disposition of the legs defines an L-shape below the knees (Price 3316; Duyrat Group IV, Series 4). The differing approach to the new treatment of Zeus's legs at the two Arados mints is a notable point of differentiation. It suggests that the change in the style of Zeus's legs may have originated at Arados with two competing styles. The earliest firmly dated examples of the crossed-legs style are found at Sidon on tetradrachms (Price 3487) dated regnal year 9 (325/4 BC). At Tyre (Ake of Price) the same occurs on coinage (Price 3265 and 3267) dated regnal year 26 (ca. 324/3 BC). However, within the uncertainties attached to the definition of the start of the Tyrian year and the approach taken at Sidon, versus Tyre, to counting, or otherwise the accession year,[49] this timing may be synchronous. At these two mints, reverse dies in both the old and new style are identified during the year in which the new style emerged, indicating that the change was implemented in the course of a year rather than at its outset, and that no time break accompanied the change. The latter supports the inference from the die study that at Arados II the transition from Series 3 (parallel legs) to Series 4 (crossed legs) did not

48. Taylor, "Damaskos."

49. Elayi and Elayi, *Coinage*, 373: "The Phoenician lunar calendar is not well-known and it is uncertain whether the year began in the Spring (March/April) or in the Autumn (September/October)." The Macedonian year, by which the coinage of Sidon is dated most certainly commenced in the Autumn (September/October). Sidon followed the accession-year system in which the remaining part of the year in which the royal accession occurred counted as year 1, rather than the first full calendar year following the accession. The system followed at Tyre is less certain and may have varied from ruler to ruler.

involve a substantial time break. It is notable that the L-legs style of Arados I is not found on the coinage of either Sidon or Tyre. The regional uptake of this style was limited to the last of the Babylon Group II coinage (Price 3642–3670), preceding the adoption of the crossed legs style on Babylon Group III coinage around 324/3 BC. These observations combined with the die count at Arados II (discussed below), suggest that the start of Series 4 was no later than 324/3 BC and may have been up to two years earlier.

Series 4 shows little evolution in the reverse style and detail of the iconography until close to the end of the sequence, where the last 16 obverse dies are paired to reverse dies of variable detail and style. On the last 23 reverse dies of the sequence a high-backed throne makes an appearance, commingled with the depiction of the *diphros*. At the same time, a ground line is placed beneath the throne. In a further progression, the footstool beneath the feet of Zeus, is dropped so that his feet rest directly on the ground line. The introduction of new and variable elements into the reverse iconography sets the last fifth of the Series 4 emission apart from the preceding component, possibly the result of the mintage of the last of the coinage at a time when the iconographic conventions of the mint were either relaxed, or not enforced. It suggests the possibility that these coins may date to a much later period than the main body of the emission.

STATISTICS

The utility of statistical methodology to estimate the size of a coin emission is a contentious subject.[50] However, for the following reasons, there is both validity and utility in the statistical estimation of the original population of dies from which a sample of surviving coinage was derived, albeit couched within a widely varying degree of uncertainty dependent on both the size and randomness of a sample of the coinage under study. Uncertainty,[51] properly quantified, does not negate the utility of an estimate of the original population of dies from which a coinage was struck, provided it is considered together with the estimate in making comparisons from one coinage sample to the next. Moving a step beyond the estimation of the original number of dies to make an estimate of the struck vol-

---

50. T. V. Buttrey, "Calculating ancient coin production: Facts and fantasies," *Numismatic Chronicle* 153 (1993), 335–351; T. V. Buttrey, "Calculating ancient coin production II: Why it cannot be done," *Numismatic Chronicle* 154 (1994), 341–352. In response, F. de Callataÿ, "Calculating ancient coin production: seeking a balance," *Numismatic Chronicle* 155 (1995), 289–311.

51. The most appropriate measure of uncertainty is the 95% Confidence Interval that is attached to an estimate: W. W. Esty, "How to estimate the original number of dies and coverage of a sample," *Numismatic Chronicle* 166 (2006), 360, formula 4.

ume of coinage represented by a sample is more problematic, relying as it does on an assumption of average die productivity. Nevertheless, with a full understanding of the assumptions and inherent uncertainties attached to a statistically determined estimate, the result provides an "order of magnitude" estimate of the total volume coined. This can constrain interpretations and facilitate comparison across different coinages and mints. In the absence of such statistical estimation within a framework of a quantified uncertainty, comparison across different coinage emissions, or mints, is limited to observed die counts. The latter are prone to a potentially greater unquantified error and uncertainty, one that arises from variable sample sizes and survival rates.

Table 2. Estimated coinage: gold staters

	Series 1 and 2	
	Av dies	**P dies**
Sample size (n)	43	43
Observed Dies (d)	23	32
Singletons (d_1)	11	26
Characteristic Index (n/d)	1.87	1.34
Coverage (C_{est})	0.74	0.40
Estimated Dies (D_{est})	49.5	125.1
95% Confidence Interval	31.9–77.6	66.9–251.0
Observed P/A	1.39	
Estimated P/A	2.53	
Estimated coinage	500,000	
Attic talents of gold	165.38	
Attic talents silver equivalent	1,653.8	

Table 3. Statistics: tetradrachm emission

	Series 3		Series 4		Total	
	A dies	P dies	A dies	P dies	A dies	P dies
Sample size (n)	96	96	370	370	466	466
Observed Dies (d)	22	56	75	234	97	290
Singletons (d_1)	4	29	20	151	24	180
Characteristic Index (n/d)	4.36	1.71	4.93	1.58	4.80	1.61
Coverage (C_{est})	0.96	0.70	0.95	0.59	0.95	0.61
Estimated Dies (D_{est})	28.5	134.4	94.1	636.6	122.5	767.8
95% Confidence Interval	24.4–33.4	96.3–188.2	87.4–101.3	525.7–771.3	114.6–131.0	649.6–907.8
Observed P/A	2.5		3.1		3.0	
Estimated P/A	4.7		6.8		6.3	
Estimated coinage*	c. 580,000		c. 1,880,000		c. 2,460,000	
Attic talents*	c. 383.7		c. 1,236.5		c. 1,620.2	

*Estimated original dies have been rounded to the nearest whole die for the calculation of the volume coinage struck.

Tables 2 and 3 summarize the statistics of the gold and silver emissions using the approach of Esty to estimate the original population of dies used at the mint,[52] combined with Callataÿ's estimates of die productivity[53] to approximate the volume of coinage produced. An estimated 50 ± 18 original stater obverse dies, plus 123 ± 8 tetradrachm obverse dies were employed at Arados II. Based on this, the coinage is estimated to have totaled $3,274 \pm 700$ Attic talents of silver equivalent, of which approximately 50% was gold staters; the latter determined assuming a 1:10 gold to silver weight equivalent value.[54] Over its life, Arados II produced a significant volume of coinage, which unusually for the time was equally proportioned between gold and silver on a value equivalent basis. Moreover, as will be shown, the gold coinage was struck in the first two to three years of the mint's 28 year life, after which no further gold coinage was issued.

The estimated number of original dies employed in each series also provides a basis for the determination of a potential minimum duration of the coinage. An estimated original population of 50 obverse stater dies, split two-thirds Series 1 and one-third Series 2, were put to use in a parallel striking process. The latter argues strongly for near continuous operation to achieve a requisite volume of coinage in a comparatively short time, otherwise serial striking over a more protracted period would have been a more efficient and less demanding process. With an assumed average daily striking rate of 1,000 staters per anvil, and an average stater die productivity of 10,000 coins, then the gold coinage might have been struck in as little as one year. An estimated original population of 123 obverse tetradrachm dies were commissioned, split one-quarter Series 3 and three-quarters Series 4. All indications are that the tetradrachm coinage was struck serially. Based on an assumed average tetradrachm die productivity of 20,000 coins, combined with a conservatively estimated striking rate of 1,000 coins per day, the entire tetradrachm coinage could have been struck in less 7 years of continuous striking, with Series 3 accounting for as little as 20 months of striking.[55] Despite the large estimated volume of the coinage, the totality of

52. W. W. Esty, "The Geometric Model for Estimating the Number of Dies," in *Quantifying Monetary Supplies in Greco-Roman Times*, ed. F. de Callataÿ (Bari: Edipuglia, 2011), 43–58.

53. An average stater obverse die productivity of 10,000 coins and an average tetradrachm obverse die productivity of 20,000 coins per F. de Callataÿ, "Quantifying monetary production in Greco-Roman times: a general frame," in *Quantifying Monetary Supplies in Greco-Roman Times*, ed. F. de Callataÿ (Bari: Edipuglia, 2011), 23.

54. Le Rider, *Coinage*, 149 "We do not know if the relative value of the two metals, which was theoretically 1:13.33 under the Persians remained the same under Alexander or if it went to 1 to 10, as in Greece."

55. By way of comparison to the conservative assumption of a daily striking rate of 1,000 coins, Callataÿ has determined from a die study of the dated tetradrachm issues of Mithradates

Series 1–4 might have been struck in less than seven years based on a continuous striking operation with a daily mintage of no more than 1,000 coins per anvil. This indicates that Price's dating of the coinage to the period 330–320 BC is a plausible possibility, although, as will be shown, the hoard evidence suggests a more extended, downdated period of mintage.

Another noteworthy aspect to emerge from the statistical analysis of the Arados II coinage is the divergence in the estimated average die pairing ratio (P/A) for gold and silver dies; the former is estimated to have been 2.5 (Table 2), while the latter is calculated to have been 6.3 (Table 3). A peripheral observation from the stater die analysis is that almost all the gold coins show evidence of die rust, indicative of striking from ferrous dies. This contrasts with the complete absence of the effects die rust on the tetradrachms, indicating that the latter were struck from dies of bronze composition. The significantly lower die-pairing ratio in the sample of stater dies may well result from the use of harder and stronger ferrous dies for the gold coinage, versus that of bronze dies for the silver coinage. This is the earliest recorded use of ferrous dies in the Alexander series. The transfer of die engravers and ferrous dies to other mints, as noted to have occurred with obverse die Av12, may have been instrumental in the transfer of this technology throughout the Macedonian Empire, for the effects of die rust becomes more widespread on the staters produced elsewhere after the transfers from Arados II to other mints.

METROLOGY

Table 4 summarizes the weight distribution of the coins in the catalogue. The gold staters were struck to the Attic weight standard of 8.6 g per stater, with no difference between the two series. The weight distribution (Fig. 1) of the staters is tightly constrained indicating precise al pezzo weight adjustment. The tetradrachms of Series 3 appear to have been struck on the Attic standard of 17.2 g per tetradrachm, within a tightly constrained weight distribution (Fig. 2). Series 4 shows a discernible weight reduction over its duration with mean median and modal weights all around 0.8 g less than Series 3. The weight

---

VI Eupator that up to 5 obverse tetradrachm dies were used per month, suggesting an average striking rate of up to ca. 3,000 coins per day: F. de Callataÿ, *L'histoire des guerres mithridatiques vue par les monnaies* (Louvain-la-Neuve: Association de numismatique professeur M. Hoc, 1997), 407; F. de Callataÿ, "The Late Hellenistic Didrachms of Leukas: Another Greek Coinage for the Roman Army," in *Fides: Contributions to Numismatics in Honor of Richard B. Witschonke*, ed. P. G. van Alfen, G. Bransbourg and M. Amandry (New York: American Numismatic Society, 2015), 256.

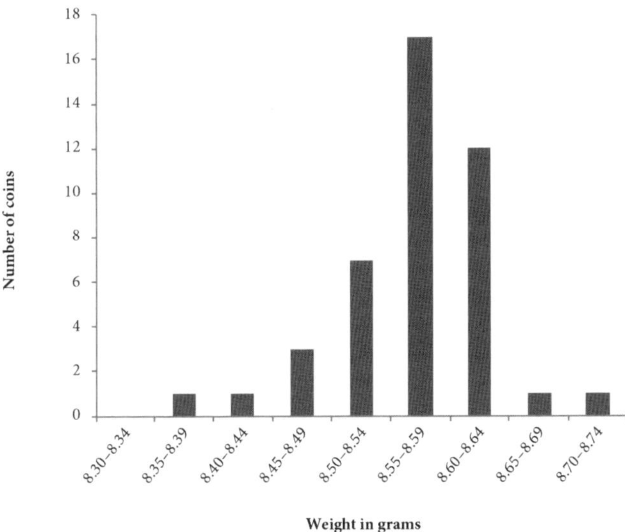

Figure 1. Metrology of AV staters (Price 3422–3423).

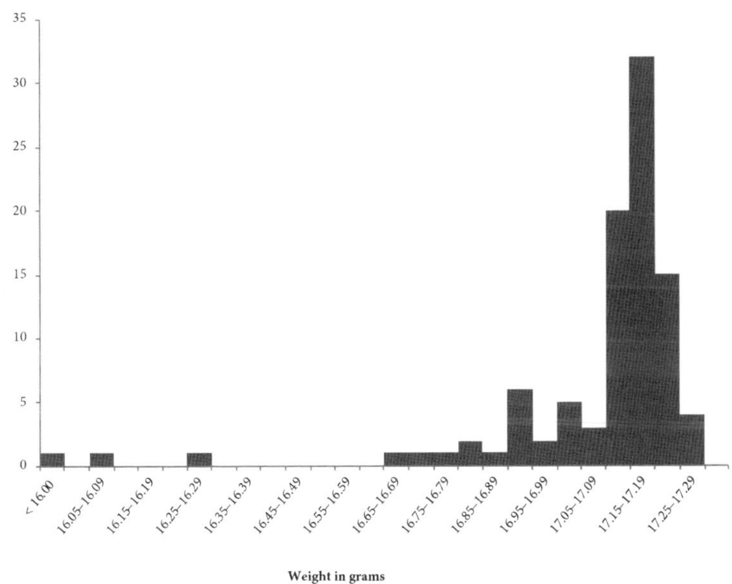

Figure 2. Metrology of Series 3 AR tetradrachms (Price 3424).

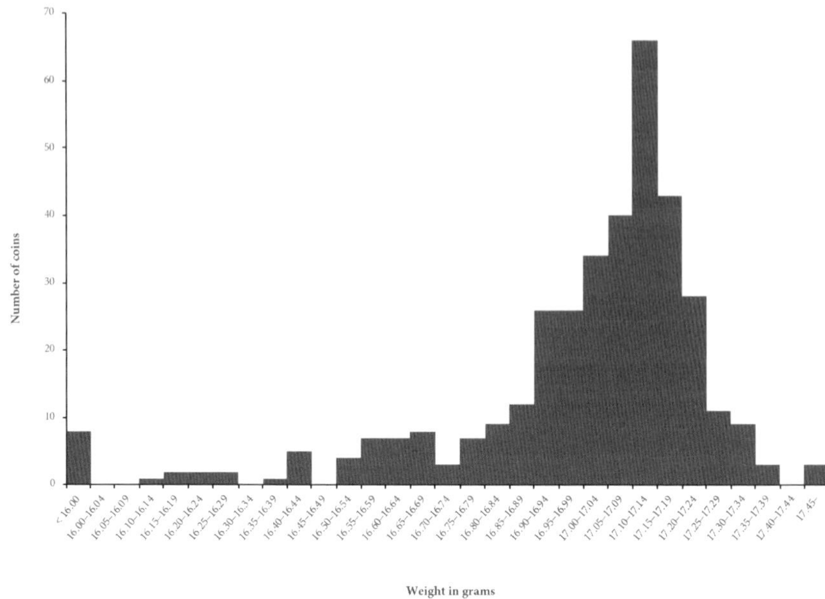

Figure 3. Metrology of Series 4 AR tetradrachms (Price 3426).

distribution suggests a reduced Attic weight standard of about 17.1 g per tetradrachm (Fig. 3). However, most of the weight reduction in Series 4 occurred in the second half of the emission, in which the mean and median weight of the sample are each reduced by 0.1 g relative to that of the first half. The weight reduction suggests that much of Series 4 was struck after the death of Alexander III.

Table 4. Metrological Summary

Series	Number of Coins (n)	Mean (g)	Median (g)	Mode (g)	Standard Deviation (σ)
1	31	8.57	8.58	8.61	0.05
2	12	8.54	8.56	8.58	0.07
3	96	17.06	17.15	17.17	0.35
4	367	16.98	17.07	17.10	0.36

HOARDS

Documented hoards containing examples of the Arados II coinage are listed in Table 5. Recorded finds of gold staters are few, limited to Greece and regions north, plus Cyprus, the earliest of which fall in the period 315–300 BC. The finds of tetradrachms are more geographically and chronologically spread, extending from the eastern region of Arachosia, through the Middle East and Egypt into Asia Minor and Europe, as far west as Greece. These finds date from the last quarter of the fourth century to the closing years of the 3rd century BC. With the exception of three very large Egyptian hoards, the number of Series 3 and 4 coins in hoards decreases rapidly with distance from the region of northern Phoenicia and Syria. In terms of the percentage of content, the Arados II component in the large Egyptian hoards falls at, or below that (less than one percent) of the much smaller hoards found throughout the Middle East and Asia Minor. The highest percentage of Arados II content, up to nineteen percent, occurs in Syrian and Phoenician hoards; the largest percentage occurring in the Sfire 1932 hoard (*IGCH* 1511) found 25 km southeast of Aleppo, around 200 km northeast of Arados. The recorded find locations of Arados II coinage, overlap closely with those of the Arados I series (Table 5). The geographic distribution and content of documented hoards supports the attribution of the coinage to a mint in Northern Phoenicia, or adjacent Syria.

Table 6 identifies the catalogue coins and associated dies with recorded hoard occurrences. Critical to the dating of the Arados II sequence are three hoards, *IGCH* 1672 (Abusir, 1901) with a burial date ca. 325–300 BC,[56] *CH* 8.185 (Syria or Lebanon, 1990) with a closure date of ca. 320 BC[57] and *CH* 10.246 (Unknown Findspot in Asia Minor, 1993) with a reported closure date of c. 323/2 BC.[58] *IGCH* 1672 contained a specimen of Series 3 (Cat. No. 58) from obverse die A1. *CH* 8.185 contained an example of Series 4 (Cat. No. 141) struck from obverse die A23. Another example of Series 4 (Cat. No 259) from die A47 was found in *CH* 10.246. These examples indicate that the mintage of Series 4 coinage started well in advance of 320 BC and that at least half of the Series 4 sequence was struck before this date. Both Series 3 and 4 are well represented in the Deman-

---

56. Online Inventory of Greek Coin Hoards (*IGCH*) http://coinhoards.org/id/*IGCH*1672 accessed 18 October 2018. The burial dates of all other *IGCH* designated hoards noted in the text and tables are from the same source.

57. A. Davesne and A. Lemaire, "Trésors hellénistiques du Proche-Orient I–IV," *RN* 151 (1996), 51–76.

58. Hoover, O., A. Meadows and U. Wartenberg (eds.) *Coin Hoards* X: *Greek Hoards.* (Royal Numismatic Society/American Numismatic Society, 2010), 31.

hur Hoard (*IGCH* 1664) that closed in 318 BC and the Akçakale Hoard (CH 8.201) buried in 318/7 BC. The latter contained coins struck from a range of dies from A1 (Cat. No. 54) to A44 (Cat. No. 228). Dies after A47, down to A79 are represented by catalogue coins in documented hoards that closed from c. 315 BC to around 310 BC, while coins from dies later than this in the sequence are represented only in hoards that were buried early decades of the 3rd century BC or later (Table 6).

The pattern in the hoard record of coins in the catalogue is consistent with the dating of all of Series 3 and the first half of Series 4 to the period down to 320 BC. Based on the catalogue coins, the second half of Series 4 is associated with progressively younger hoard occurrences of coins from later dies after this date. Finds of coins from dies A48 to A79 suggest that these were minted in the decade c. 319–310 BC, while the earliest identified hoard occurrences of coins in the catalogue from dies A80 to A97 are consistent with mintage in the last decade of the third century BC.

Table 5. Hoards

Hoard	Reference	Closure (BCE)	Content	Arados II Series 1-5	Arados I Price 3303–3332
AV Staters					
Europe					
Malko Topolovo, Bulgaria, 1940	*IGCH* 0853	ca. 285–275	96+ AV	1+	1+
Anadol, Ukraine, 1895	*IGCH* 0866	ca. 228–220	1,200 AV	1	3
Lergutsa, Leovo raion, Moldavia, 1956	*IGCH* 0800	ca. 315–300	21+ AV	1	-
Northern(?) Greece, before 1966	*IGCH* 0801	ca. 310–300	c. 350 AV	1	1
Epidauros, 1977	Oeconomides 1999	ca. 295–290	92 AV	1	-
Cyprus					
Larnaka, 1870	*IGCH* 1472	ca. 300–295	1,000+ AV	3	3
AR Tetradrachms					
Europe					
Camarina	*CH* 7.58	ca. 300		1	1
Zemun, Yugoslavia, 1924	*IGCH* 0458	ca. 220	195+ AR	1	-
Prilepec, Yugoslavia, 1950	*IGCH* 0448	ca. 280	208+ AR	1	-
Pontoleibade-Kilkis, Macedonia, 1961	*IGCH* 0445	ca. 280	114+ AR	1	3
Myriophyton, Macedonia,1932-3	*IGCH* 0432	ca. 320	53+ AR	1	1

Turnu Severin (Hinova), Rumania, 1923	IGCH 0452	ca. 275–250	62+ AR	1	-
Büyükçekmece, Thrace, 1952	IGCH 0867	ca. 220	184 AR	1	-
Boeotia, 1935	IGCH 0163	ca. 250	49 AR	1	-
Messene, 1922	IGCH 0095	ca. 305–300	31 AR	1	1
Andritsaena, Elis, 1923	IGCH 0083	ca. 315	150+ AR	4	5
Olympia, Elis, 1922	IGCH 0176	ca. 235–225	82 AR	1	-

Asia Minor

Kizakli, Pontos 1939	IGCH 1369	ca. 235	13 AV,	-	-
			803 AR	3	9
Ankara, c. 1913	IGCH 1399	ca. 290–285	179+ AR	9	5
Aksaray, Cappadokia, 1968	IGCH 1400	ca. 281	19 AR	1	-
Gordion, 1951	IGCH 1406	ca. 205–200	114 AR	2	-
Asia Minor, c 1966	IGCH 1436	ca. 323	52 AR	2	3
Asia Minor, 1964	IGCH 1438	ca. 320	70+ AR	1	6
Asia Minor, 1968	IGCH 1439	ca. 320	80+ AR	2	17
Asia Minor, 1968	IGCH 1440	ca. 320	90+ AR	2	16
Asia Minor, 1965	IGCH 1443	ca. 310	29+ AR	1	2
Manissa, Lydia, 1971	IGCH 1293	ca. 280	24 AR	2	-
Karaman, Lycaonia, 1969	IGCH 1398	ca. 300	49 AR	1	1
Armenak, Kilikia, 1927	IGCH 1423	ca. 280	1957+ AR	2	5
Mersin, Kilikia, 1963	IGCH 1424	ca. 280	150+ AR	7	4

Akçakale, Osrhoene, Turkey, 1958	CH 8.201, CH 10.251	318/7	190 AR	19	10
Unknown Asia Minor, 1993	CH 10.246	ca. 323–322	73 AR	1	1
'Seleucus I' Hoard, 2005	CH 10.265	ca. 280–279	5,000+ AR	28	5

Cyprus

| Kannaviou, 1936 | IGCH 1468 | ca. 310 | 90 AR | 1 | 1 |

Phoenicia, Syria and Judaea

Sfire, 25 km SE of Aleppo, 1932	IGCH 1511	ca. 318	84 AR	16	11
Aleppo, 1893	IGCH 1516	ca. 305	3000+ AR	43	24
Byblos, 1931	IGCH 1515	ca. 309–308	141 AR	7	4
Baalbek, 1885	IGCH 1512	ca. 305	22 + AR	2	2
Tel Tsippor, Judaea, 1960	IGCH 1514	ca. 311	63 AR	3	2
Syria or Lebanon, 1990	CH 8.185	ca. 323	175+ AR	1	20
Ashkelon, 1990	CH 8.220	ca. 305–290	18 AR	3	1

Mesopotamia and East

Chorsabad 1934?	IGCH 1754	ca. 31–305	9 AR	1	–
Tell Halaf, Northern Mepopotamia, 1913	IGCH 1763, CH 8.302	ca. 246–240	353 AR	1	2
Mosul, 1862-3?	IGCH 1756	ca. 305	88+ AR	1	2
Babylonia, c. 1900	IGCH 1761	ca. 280	108+ AR	3	13

Mesopotamia or Babylonia, 1954	*IGCH* 1751	ca. 315	20 AR	1	3
Failaka, Kuwait, 1964	CH 8.256	ca. 290–270	27+ AR	3	-
Pasargadae, 1963	*IGCH* 1794	ca. 280	34 AR	3	5
East Arachosia, Quetta, Pakistan, 2001	CH 10.275	206–200	230+ AR	1	-
Egypt					
Phacous, 1956	*IGCH* 1678	ca. 283	2,400 AR	14	13
Demanhur, 1905	*IGCH* 1664	ca. 318	8,000+ AR	66	317
Abu Hommos, 1919	*IGCH* 1667	ca. 311–310	1,000 AR	14	20
Egypt, 1912	*IGCH* 1668	ca. 310	20 AR	1	2
Kuft, 1875–80	*IGCH* 1670	ca. 310–305	330+ AR	3	12
Abusir, 1901	*IGCH* 1672	ca. 325–300	44 AR	1	-

Table 6. Catalogue coins: recorded hoard occurrences

Hoard	Reference	Burial	Cat. no.	Obverse dies*
Abusir, 1901	*IGCH* 1672	ca. 325–320	58	**A1**
Unknown Findspot, 1993	*CH* 10.246	ca. 323–322	259	**A47**
Syria or Lebanon, 1990	*CH* 8.185	ca. 320	141	A23
Demanhur, 1905	*IGCH* 1664	ca. 318	64, 102, 115	A3, A14, A15
Akçakale, 1958	*CH* 8.201	318/7	54, 70, 154, 158, 159, 180, 197, 198, 219, 220, 228	A1, A5, A27, A29, A29, A31, A35, A35, A41, A41, A44
Andritsaena, 1923	*IGCH* 0083	ca. 315	173, 215, 454	A31, A41, **A72**
Abu Hommos, 1919	*IGCH* 1667	ca. 311–310	97, 156, 164, 192, 217, 222, 233, 355, 383, 387, 388, 407, 446, 462	A12, A27, A29, A35, A41, A42, A45, A54, A60, A60, A60, A64, A69, **A77**
Egypt, 1912	*IGCH* 1668	ca. 310	452	A71
Kuft, 1875-80	*IGCH* 1670	ca. 310–305	160, 209, 240, 469	A29, A39, A47, A79
Ankara, c. 1913	*IGCH* 1399	ca. 290–285	379, 488	A58, **A89**
Failaka, 1964	*CH* 8.256	ca. 290–270	81, 389, 492	A8, A60, **A89**
Armenak, 1927	*IGCH* 1423	ca. 280	362, 429	A55, A67
Pasagarde, 1963	*IGCH* 1794	ca. 280	350	A54
"Seleucus I," 2005	*CH* 10.265	ca. 280–279	66, 301, 379, 509	A4, A50, A57, **A97**
Olympia, 1992	*IGCH* 0176	ca. 235–225	481	A85
Büyükçekmece, 1952	*IGCH* 0867	ca. 220	384	A60
Zemun, 1924	*IGCH* 0458	ca. 220	490	**A89**
East Arachosia (Quetta)	*CH* 10.275	ca. 206–200	501	A92
Gordion, 1951	*IGCH* 1406	ca. 205–200	210, 262	A39, A47

* Dies in bold text: earliest occurrences of progressively later sequence dies.

CHRONOLOGY

The hoard record is imprecise as to the start date of the coinage, other than to suggest that it commenced prior to 325 BC. Refinement relies on the interpretation of the die analysis. The gold staters of Series 1 and 2 were struck in parallel, an argument for near continuous striking, otherwise serial striking would have been more efficient and administratively less demanding. Seven stater dies, five commissioned for Series 1 and two for Series 2, are observed to have preceded the transfer of the engraver of Av5 to Sidon for the year 7 (327/6 BC) issue from that city, making it is unlikely that the gold emission commenced before 328/7 BC. Certainly, the transfer of a stater die and five die engravers to other mints suggest that the gold coinage of Series 1 and 2 commenced no later than 327/6 BC and ended around 326/5 BC. The latter date is consistent with the observation that the final component of the gold emission was coincident with the changed depiction of the extended right hand of Nike from an open facing palm to that of a hand in profile, analogous to the change observed in the portrayal of right hand of Zeus midway through the Series 3 tetradrachms. Based on the evidence from the other Phoenician, Syrian and Babylonian mints this iconographic change occurred no later than 326/5 BC.[59]

The last half of Series 3 and all of Series 4 post-date this iconographic development. The transition from Series 3 to Series 4 is defined by the changed disposition of the legs of Zeus from parallel to crossed. At Sidon and Tyre this is dated to issues in the years 325/4 and ca. 324/3 BC respectively. By analogy with its other Phoenician counterparts, it is probable that the Series 4 emission commenced around 324 BC. This date would allow ample time for the utilization of the last 11 dies of Series 3. The hoard record is consistent with mintage of Series 3 and the first half of Series 4 in the period down to 321/0 BC. Based on the earliest hoard occurrences of coins from dies of the second half of Series 4, it appears most likely that this component of the emission was struck in two phases; the first struck from dies A48–A79 in the period ca. 320/19–311/0 BC, with the second from dies A80–A97 dating to the interval ca. 310/09–301/0 BC.[60]

---

59. Taylor, "Babylon," 31–35.

60. This division into age ranges by obverse dies is approximate due to the partial and incomplete sampling of the hoard process and the limitations of the catalogue sample with respect to the hoard record. For most hoards, the identification of the Arados II content to the specific die level is not possible due to the limitations of documentation.

In summary, the evidence from the die analysis combined with that from early Alexander hoards, points to the mintage of Alexander the Great's gold coinage at Arados II commencing around 328/7 BC. The emission of Series 1 and 2 gold coinage finished in 326/5 BC, overlapping with the first half of the Series 3 tetradrachm emission. Series 3 continued for up to a year after this date, and was then followed by the Series 4 coinage from ca. 325/4 BC. Based on the hoard evidence, the first half of Series 4 was certainly struck by 321/0 BC. However, the hoard data suggests that the mint continued to operate after this date, perhaps intermittently down to ca. 301/0 BC. Within the uncertainty that is attached to the documentation of hoard data to the die specific level, an approximate division of the second half of the Series 4 tetradrachms into two phases is possible; ca. 320/19–311/0 BC for that component from dies A48–A79, and ca. 310/09–301/0 BC for that portion struck from dies A80–A97.

INTERPRETATION

Based on this chronology, the estimated breakdown of the tetradrachm coinage of Series 3 and 4 into the components pre- and post-321/0 BC is summarized in Table 7 (below). Within the uncertainty attached to the statistics, the tetradrachm die count and thus issuance in the period ca. 328–320 BC is the same as that which occurred in the subsequent twenty years. Taking this a step further, Table 8 (below) summarizes the observed and estimated original number of stater and tetradrachm dies at each of the eastern mints of Alexander the Great down to ca. 320 BC based on a sample of 3,328 coins originating from 598 obverse dies, comprising 80 stater dies and 518 tetradrachm dies.[61] Figures 4 and 5 (below) present this data in graphic form, including the 95% confidence interval (high and low) that is attached to each estimate of the original number of dies commissioned at each mint.[62] Figure 6 presents the approximate volume of gold and silver coinage, expressed in Attic talents of silver equivalent, calcu-

61. The observed die counts underpinning this analysis are sourced from Newell, *Dated Sidon and Ake*; Newell, *Myriandros*; Duyrat, *Arados*; Taylor, "Damaskos"; Taylor, "Earliest"; Waggoner, *Alexander Mint*; L. W. H. Taylor ,"The Karne Alexanders," *Journal of the Numismatic Association of Australia* 29 (2018–2019), 1–23; L. W. H. Taylor "The Macedonian Mint at Susa (319/8–312/1 BC)," Koinon II (2019), 28–62; and L. W. H. Taylor, "Reattribution of the Berytos Alexanders to Byblos," forthcoming. The data takes account of the reattribution to Tarsos of the staters formerly attributed to Sidon (Price 3456–3466), as proposed by Le Rider (*Coinage*, 134–139), plus the downdating of the start of the Macedonian mint at Susa to 319/8 BC, detailed in Taylor, "Macedonian Mint at Susa."

62. Statistically, any estimate derived from another random sample of the original coinage will yield a result that will fall within the identified high-low range in 95% of cases.

lated from the statistically estimated original population of dies at each mint.[63] A number of insights as to the origin, nature and function of Arados II arise from the consideration of this analysis.

Table 7. Tetradrachm statistics: pre- and post-320 BC

	ca. 327–320 BC	ca. 319–300 BC
Sample size (n)	224	242
Observed Dies (d)	47	50
Singletons (d_1)	10	14
Characteristic Index (n/d)	4.77	4.84
Coverage (C_{est})	0.96	0.94
Estimated Dies (D_{est})	59.5	63.0
95% Confidence Interval	54.0–65.6	57.4–69.1

Table 8. Obverse die counts: eastern mints to c. 320 BC.

Mint	Stater Dies			Tetradrachm Dies		
	Sample (n)	Observed	Estimated	Sample (n)	Observed	Estimated
Myriandros	1	1	1	97	25	34
Karne	-	-	-	21	5	7
Arados I	51	12	16	750	196	265
Arados II	43	23	50	224	47	60
Byblos	-	-	-	93	8	9
Sidon	62	16	21	109	19	22
Tyre	30	12	20	194	25	29
Damaskos	-	-	-	456	54	61
Babylon	62	16	22	1,135	139	158
Totals	249	80	130	3,079	518	645

Firstly, the disparity in the quantum and composition of the output of Arados II compared to that of Arados I is starkly expressed in Figures 4–6. This is evident whether the basis of comparison is the observed die count, the estimated original number of dies, or the value of the coinage struck in each precious metal. Arados II was first and foremost an issuer of gold staters in the period down to 320 BC while Arados I was minting tetradrachms in large quantity. Sixty-

63. Assuming an average obverse stater die productivity of 10,000 coins and an average tetradrachm obverse die productivity of 20,000 coins per Callataÿ, "Quantifying," plus a 1:10 gold to silver value weight equivalency per Le Rider, Coinage, 149.

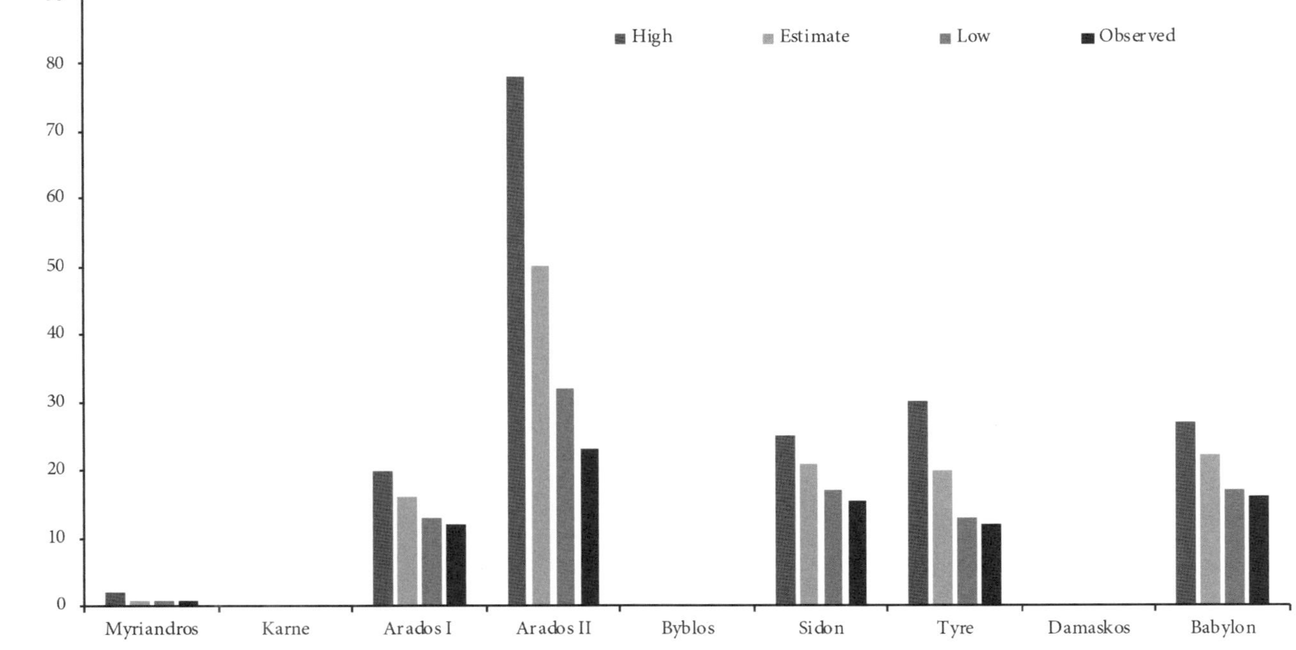

Figure 4. Gold stater obverse die count by mint to ca. 320 BC.

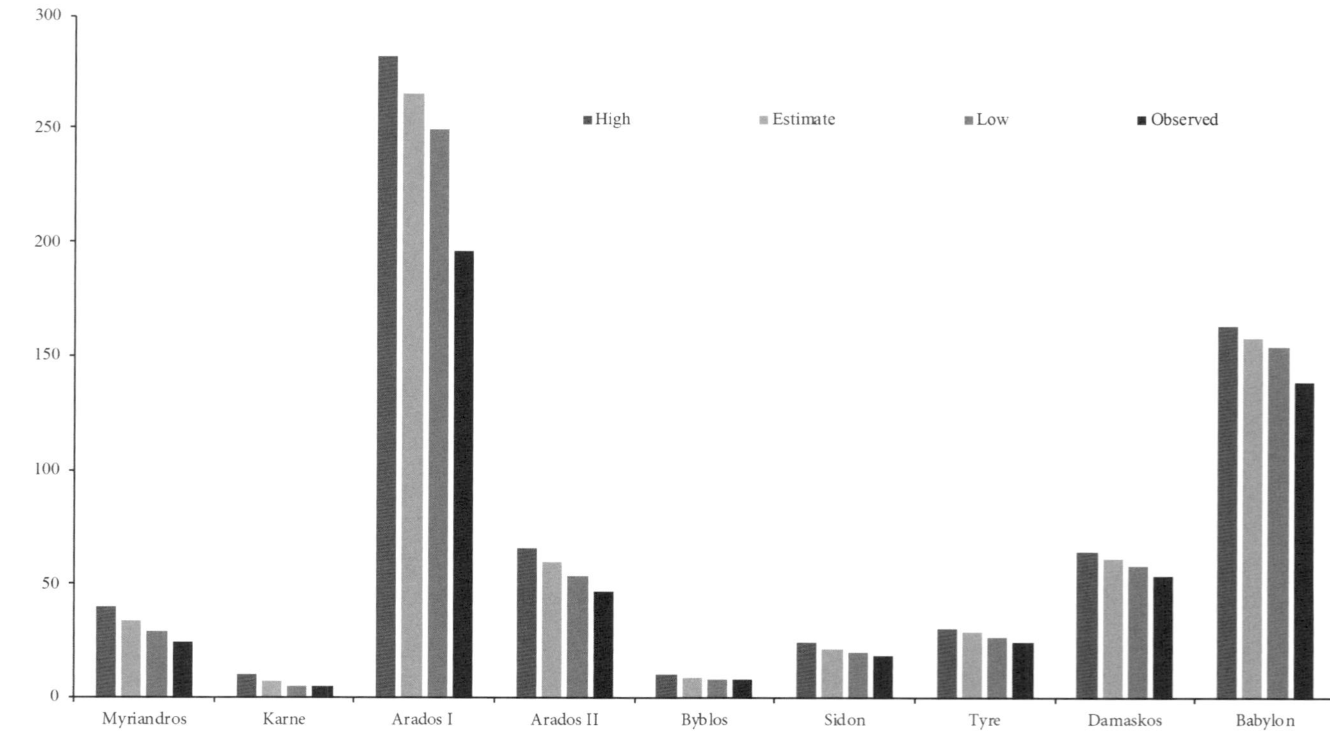

Figure 5. Tetradrachm obverse die count by mint to ca. 320 BC.

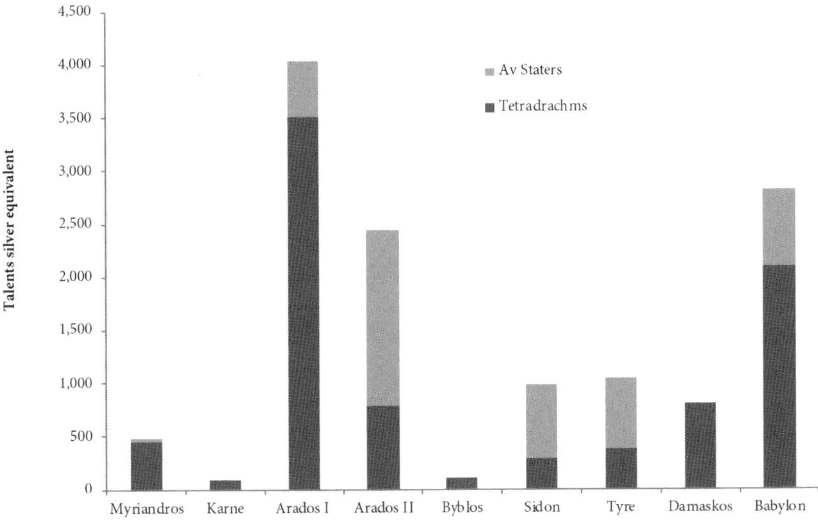

Figure 6. Estimated output by mint to c. 320 BC.

eight percent of the value of the coinage produced at Arados II is estimated to have been gold staters, while only thirteen percent of the value of the Arados I mintage consisted of gold. Notably, with the exception of one issue (Price 3306) from a single obverse die, all of the gold issuance from Arados I is dated to ca. 323–320 BC,[64] after the death of Alexander the Great, and thus postdates the Series 1 and 2 emissions from Arados II. This provides a plausible rationale for the establishment of a second Alexander mint at Arados in 328/7 BC to supplement the continuing operation of the former Achaemenid mint (Arados I) that was striking Alexandrine tetradrachms; the need for a large amount of gold staters in a relatively short time.

Examined in a regional context, the two mints at Arados account for an estimated 51 percent of the gold stater dies and 50 percent of the tetradrachm dies employed across the mints of Phoenicia, Syria and Babylon in the period 333/2–321/0 BC. Arados II alone accounted for an estimated 40 percent of the gold stater dies used in the east. The regional predominance of Arados II gold stater dies (and implicitly the volume of gold coinage struck) remains even at the lower bound of the 95 percent confidence interval attached to the estimate of the original number of dies. Even ignoring the statistically estimated original number of dies and using the observed die counts as an alternative, Arados II

64. Duyrat, *Arados*, 9–30. Most tellingly, all the Arados I stater issues dated to the period ca. 323–320 BC bear the royal title.

used almost 50 percent more stater dies than any other eastern mint. The conclusion is inescapable; Arados II was a significant, if not the most significant center of gold mintage in the easternmost Mediterranean during Alexander the Great's lifetime (Fig. 6).

Another notable aspect that comes from the regional comparison of the number of dies used in each mint is the comparatively minor issuance from each of the mints located in the other Phoenician vassal kingdoms, Byblos, Sidon and Tyre (Figs. 4–6). If the purpose of one of the mints at Arados was to produce coinage for "local or city" purposes as suggested by Newell,[65] then it is difficult to explain why the city of Arados would require so much more coinage for civic purposes than Tyre, which suffered appreciable destruction in the culmination of Alexander the Great's seven-month siege of the city in 332 BC. Logically, the reconstruction of Tyre in the years following the siege would have required the opposite to that which we see in the comparative die counts, if one of the Arados mints was a "local or city" mint. Based on the regional analysis of mint productivity in the period 333/2–321/0 BC, the output of either mint at Arados exceeds what could be construed as a reasonable volume for any local, or city requirement. Therefore, the classification of one of either Arados I or II as a "local or city" mint receives no support from the regional die analysis. The large volume of coinage (manifest in large die counts) from each, struck in a complimentary manner (gold versus silver), accompanied by wide and overlapping circulation patterns (manifest in the hoard record) speak to a common purpose. The establishment and maintenance of two mints at Arados during Alexander's lifetime has one possible explanation, the requirement of a large volume of coinage, beyond the capacity of a single facility. The initial impetus for the establishment of Arados II appears to have been the need for a large volume of gold coinage in a short period.[66] A separate mint, with its own dedicated administration and resources, focused primarily on gold coinage, would have been better positioned to address many of the integrity and security issues associated with a large gold mintage. Two to three years later, with the requisite gold mintage fulfilled, the priority turned to silver tetradrachm mintage, at a scale that was sufficient to justify the maintenance of two mints.

65. Newell, *Reattribution*, 47.

66. This explanation is simply an extension of the previously recognized fact that Alexander's mints often had different production priorities. For example, the drachm mints of Asia Minor documented by M. Thompson and A. R. Bellinger, "Greek Coins in the Yale Collection, IV: A Hoard of Alexander Drachms," *Yale Classical Studies* 14 (1955), 3–45, which identified mints established for the primary purpose of minting drachms, while others struck tetradrachms.

Different administrative structures

Based on the Achaemenid precedents, and analogy with the other Phoenician vassal kingdoms under Macedonian suzerainty, the Arados I mint at its inception was most probably under the supervision and management, but not the absolute control, of the vassal king Gerastart (Gerostratos in Greek), whose son voluntarily surrendered the island city and its mainland territory to Alexander the Great as he advanced down the Phoenician coast in late 333 BC.[67] Indeed the earliest issue from the mint (Price 3303) bears a Γ mintmark has been interpreted to be the first letter abbreviation of the name of Gerostratos the king of Arados, the latter being identified by the letter A beneath the *diphros*.[68] This would be a tacit acknowledgement that Gerostratos was subservient to Alexander whose name figured most prominently on the coins. In contrast, Arados II, established some years later, with its different conventions, notably a single invariable mintmark, must have fallen within a different administrative construct, one more directly responsible to Alexander the Great who retained the absolute authority for the coining of imperial money.[69] The Phoenician and Cypriot mints managed by vassal kings operated on a different basis to those of other cities, astutely and succinctly summarized by Otto Mørkholm,

> It is therefore hardly proper to make a distinction between "imperial" mints and "allied" mints, as Newell was inclined to do. The explanation is rather that, while the other mints were government agencies, the Phoenician and Cypriot city-states under their local kings retained the management of their mints, although they naturally had to operate within the general regulations laid down by the central administration.[70]

---

67. Arrian, *Alexander*, 2.13.7–8, from J. Romm, ed. *The Landmark Arrian* (New York: Pantheon Books, 2010), 79.

68. Elayi, "Updated," 30–31.

69. A. R. Bellinger, *Essays on the Coinage of Alexander the Great* (New York: The American Numismatic Society, 1963), 39–42. In the four years following Alexander the Great's death the exclusive power over the issuance of imperial coinage in the east fell successively to Perdikkas under the Partition Agreement of Babylon (323 BC), then to Antipater via the Treaty of Triparadeisos (320 BC) who delegated this responsibility to Antigonos, as *strategos* of Asia. In following the two decades the empire fragmented in almost continuous conflict. All pretence of a unified empire quickly dissipated and Macedonian imperial type coinage came to be issued by each of the successors, the first step toward establishment of their own royal domains.

70. O. Mørkholm, *Early Hellenistic Coinage from the Accession of Alexander to the Peace of Apamea (336–186 B.C.)*, eds. P. Grierson and U. Westermark (Cambridge: Cambridge University Press, 1991), 47.

In this context, the Arados II mint, established some years after Arados I, was a "government agency" mint directly controlled under instruction from Alexander the Great, without the intercession of an intermediary vassal king. This was the most efficient arrangement for the striking of a substantial gold coinage on the instruction of and for the purposes of Alexander the Great. It afforded the direct control of and accountability for a large gold coinage struck on the direct instruction of the king. It also explains the divergence in the control processes between the two mints, manifest by the multiplicity of mint controls with regular variations at Arados I, versus that of the single $Ꝑ$ mintmark at Arados II. Multiple, regularly changing mint controls would have facilitated the process of checking, or auditing in modern parlance, that a mint under intermediary supervision was operated "within the general regulations laid down by the central administration," including an agreed annual framework of issuance, or a budget. This requirement was simplified, if not reduced, in the case of a "government agency" mint, directly accountable to Alexander the Great; one that drew bullion for striking from a royal treasury only in pre-approved quantities, as and when required by Alexander. Under the latter circumstance, the invariable $Ꝑ$ mintmark, unaccompanied by any form of secondary mint controls throughout the life of Arados II would suffice.

This differentiated administrative construct explains the continued operation of Arados II in the two decades following the Treaty of Triparadeisos. The latter saw Arados fall under the authority of Antigonos, the *strategos* of Asia in 321/0 BC. He was a Macedonian traditionalist, rigidly adhering to Macedonian policy, practice, and controls.[71] By 320 BC, when the justification for the maintenance of two mints at Arados was no longer present, the closure of Arados I,[72] still under non-Macedonian intermediary supervision, would have been the logical option for Antigonos.[73] Two decades later, the Battle of Ipsos in 301 BC saw the death and defeat of Antigonos. Syria and northern Phoenicia fell under the control of Seleukos who moved rapidly to eliminate vestiges of Antigonid control and infrastructure in Syria and northern Phoenicia. Within less than a year he

71. R. A. Billows, *Antigonos the One-Eyed and the Creation of the Hellenistic State* (Berkeley: University of California Press, 1990).

72. Previously attributed to Arados I, the issues of Price P138–P158 and Price 3336–3364, dated to c. 320–300 BC have been reattributed to the Babylon II mint: Houghton and Lorber, Seleucid Coins, 39–48, 479–483.

73. Contemporaneously, at the direction of Antigonos, a similar rationalization of mint operations occurred on Cyprus where most of the mints formerly under the management of vassal kings ceased operation, Salamis being the sole exception. Price, *Coinage*, 482–496. Elsewhere in Phoenicia, the mints at Byblos/Berytos and Karne struck no more imperial coinage after 320 BC.

had established four new foundations in the region.[74] Accompanying this were new mints at Antioch on the Orontes, Seleukeia in Pieria, Laodikeia by the Sea, and Apamea on the Orontes. These fringed, or were within the territory formerly administered by the Aradian vassal kings. The establishment of this Seleukid infrastructure eliminated any justification for the maintenance of a legacy mint at Arados. Thus, the closure of Arados II. Fifty-five years later when Arados was granted autonomy, the city commenced striking a civic coinage (Price 3365–3403) that resurrected Ƥ mintmark of Arados II.

ACKNOWLEDGMENTS

This study was facilitated by the PELLA online database, numismatics.org/pella/. Images of coins in the collections of the American Numismatic Society, the British Museum, the Bibliothèque Nationale de France Cabinet des Médailles and the Münzkabinett Berlin, are reproduced from the PELLA online database under the terms and conditions of the Open Data Commons (ODC) Open Database License (ODbL) v1.0, opendatacommons.org/licenses/odbl/1.0. Other coin images are reproduced with permission of the applicable numismatic dealers noted in the catalogue, including the general consent to reproduction in scholarly works from Classical Numismatic Group Inc., www.cngcoins.com and Roma Numismatics Limited, www.RomaNumismatics.com. Images reproduced from the auctions of Fritz Rudolf Künker GmbH & Co. KG, Osnabrück are owned by Lübke & Wiedemann KG, Leonberg. The image reproduced from CGB.fr is ©CGB Numismatique Paris.

---

74. Houghton and Lorber, *Seleucid Coins*, 18–26.

BIBLIOGRAPHY

Amandry, M. and O. Callot. "Le trésor de Failaka 1984 (Koweit)." *Revue Numismatique* 30 (1998): 64–74.

Bellinger, A. R. *Essays on the Coinage of Alexander the Great.* Numismatic Studies 11. New York: The American Numismatic Society, 1963.

Billows, R. A. *Antigonos the One-Eyed and the Creation of the Hellenistic State.* Berkeley: University of California Press, 1990.

Buttrey, T. V. Calculating ancient coin production: facts and fantasies." *Numismatic Chronicle* 153 (1993): 335–351.

———. "Calculating ancient coin production II: why it cannot be done." *Numismatic Chronicle* 154 (1994): 341–352.

Callataÿ, F. de. "Calculating ancient coin production: seeking a balance." *Numismatic Chronicle* 155 (1995): 289–311.

———. *L'histoire des guerres mithridatiques vue par les monnaies.* Numismatica Lovaniensia 18, Louvain-la-Neuve, 1997.

———. "Quantifying Monetary Production in Greco-Roman Times: A General Frame." In *Quantifying Monetary Supplies in Greco-Roman Times,* edited by F. de Callataÿ, 7–29. Pragmateiai 19. Bari: Edipuglia, 2011.

———. "The late Hellenistic didrachms of Leukas: Another Greek Coinage for the Roman army." In *Fides: Contributions to Numismatics in Honor of Richard B. Witschonke,* edited by P. G. van Alfen, G. Bransbourg and M. Amandry, 239–270. New York: The American Numismatic Society, 2015.

Cox, D. H. *A Third Century Hoard of Tetradrachms from Gordion.* Museum Monographs. Philadelphia: The University Museum, University of Pennsylvania, 1953.

Davesne, A. and A. Lemaire. "Trésors hellénistiques du Proche-Orient I–IV." *Revue Numismatique* 151 (1996): 51–76.

Duyrat, F. *Arados hellénistiqué étude historique et monétaire.* Bibliothèque archéologique et historique 173. Beirut: Institut Français du Proche-Orient, 2005.

Elayi, J. "An Updated Chronology of the Reigns of Phoenician Kings During the Persian Period (539–333 BC)." *Transeuphratene* 32 (2006): 11–44.

Elayi, J., and A. G. Elayi. *The Coinage of the Phoenician city of Tyre in the Persian Period (5th–4th cent. BCE).* Orientalia Lovaniensia Analecta 188; Studia Phoenicia XX. Leuven: Peeters, 2009

Esty, W. W. "How to estimate the original number of dies and the coverage of a sample." *Numismatic Chronicle* 166 (2006): 359–364.

———. "The Geometric Model for Estimating the Number of Dies." In *Quanti-*

fying monetary supplies in Greco-Roman times, edited by F. de Callataÿ, 43-58. Pragmateiai 19. Bari: Edipuglia, 2011.

Hoover, O. D. "A Second Look at the Aradian Bronze Coinage Attributed to Seleucus I (*SC* 72–73)." *American Journal of Numismatics* 18 (2006): 43-50.

Hoover, O., A. Meadows and U. Wartenberg (eds.) *Coin Hoards* X: *Greek Hoards.* New York: Royal Numismatic Society and American Numismatic Society, 2010.

Houghton, A., and C. Lorber. *Seleucid Coins: A Comprehensive Catalogue*, Part I: *Seleucus I through Antiochus III.* 2 vols. New York/Lancaster, PA: American Numismatic Society and Classical Numismatic Group, 2002.

Lemaire, A. "Le monnayage de Tyr et celui dit d'Akko dans la deuxième moitié du IVe siècle avant J.-C." *Revue Numismatique* 18 (1976): 11-24.

Le Rider, G. *Alexander the Great: Coinage, Finances and Policy.* Translated by W. E. Higgins. Philadelphia: American Philosophical Society, 2007.

Le Rider, G., and N. Olçay. "Un trésor de tétradrachmes d'Alexandre trouvé a Akçakale en 1958." *Revue Numismatique* 30 (1988), 42–54.

Mørkholm, O. *Early Hellenistic Coinage from the Accession of Alexander to the Peace of Apamea (336–186 B.C.).* Edited by P. Grierson and U. Westermark. Cambridge: Cambridge University Press, 1991.

Müller, L. *Numismatique d'Alexandre le Grand, suive d'un appendice contenant les monnaies de Philippe II et III.* Copenhagen, 1855.

Newell, E. T. "Reattribution of Certain Tetradrachms of Alexander the Great." *American Journal of Numismatics* 45/46 (1912): 5–62.

―――――. *The Dated Alexander Coinage of Sidon and Ake.* Oxford: Oxford University Press, 1916.

―――――. "Tarsos under Alexander." *American Journal of Numismatics* 52 (1918): 69–115.

―――――. "Myriandros–Alexandria Kat'Isson." *American Journal of Numismatics* 53 (1919): 1–42.

―――――. *Alexander Hoards* II. *Demanhur, 1905.* ANS NNM No. 19. New York: The American Numismatic Society, 1923.

―――――. *The Coinages of Demetrius Poliorcetes.* Chicago: Obol International, 1978 reprint of the London: Oxford University Press, 1927 edition.

Oeconomides, M. "Le trésor d'Épidaure 1977 (Palaia 'Epidauros)." In *Travaux de numismatique Grecque offerts a Georges le Rider.* Edited by M. Amandry and S. Hurter, 307–311. London: Spink and Sons, 1999.

Price, M. J. *The Coinage in the Name of Alexander the Great and Philip Arrhidaeus.* London: British Museum/Swiss Numismatic Society, 1991.

Romm, J. (ed.). *The Landmark Arrian*. New York: Pantheon Books, 2010.

Taylor, L. W. H. "From Triparadeisos to Ipsos: Seleukos I Nikator's Uncertain Mint 6A in Babylonia." *American Journal of Numismatics* 27 (2015): 41–97.

———. "The Damaskos Mint of Alexander the Great." *American Journal of Numismatics* 29 (2017): 47–100.

———. "The Earliest Alexander III Tetradrachm Coinage of Babylon: Iconographic Development and Chronology." *American Journal of Numismatics* (2018): 1–43.

———. "The Karne Alexanders." *Journal of the Numismatic Association of Australia* 29 (2018–2019): 1–23.

———. "The Macedonian Mint at Susa (319/8–312/1 BC)." *Koinon* II (2019): 28–62.

———. "Reattribution of the Berytos Alexanders to Byblos." Forthcoming.

Thompson, M. *Alexander's Drachm Mints* I: *Sardes and Miletus*. Numismatic Studies 16. New York: The American Numismatic Society, 1983.

Thompson, M., and A. R. Bellinger. "Greek Coins in the Yale Collection, IV: A Hoard of Alexander Drachms." *Yale Classical Studies* 14 (1955): 3–45.

Troxell, H. *Studies in the Macedonian Coinage of Alexander the Great*. Numismatic Studies 21. New York: American Numismatic Society, 1997.

Waggoner, N. M. *The Alexander Mint at Babylon*. Ph.D. Diss., Columbia University, 1968.

Wartenberg, U., M. J. Price and K. A. McGregor (eds.). *Coin Hoards*. Volume VIII: *Greek Hoards*. London: The Royal Numismatic Society, 1994.

AJN Second Series 32 (2020) pp. 93–125

The Late Hellenistic Tetradrachms
of Parion and Lampsakos

PLATES 16–20   ANEURIN ELLIS-EVANS*

This article presents die studies of the tetradrachms minted by Parion and Lampsakos in the Hellenistic period. The Parion Group 1 tetradrachms date to the late 160s or 150s, whereas the Parion Group 2 and Lampsakos tetradrachms date not to the second quarter of the second century as previously thought, but rather to the early first century. The overlooked evidence of *IGCH* 1322 (western Asia Minor, 1964/5) provides proof for this later date in the case of Lampsakos. New evidence about the composition of *IGCH* 1322 is presented which allows some progress to be made in identifying the contents of this hoard. The downdating of these two coinages has two broader consequences. Firstly, Lampsakos's decision to depict Priapos on its coins for the first time with this series should be connected to an epiphany of Priapos which occurred during the war with Aristonikos and significantly altered the god's status at Lampsakos for the rest of antiquity. Secondly, the downdating of the Parian and Lampsakene series to a period of direct Roman rule raises the question of the degree to which Rome was involved in the production of these coinages.

1. INTRODUCTION

Our picture of Greek coinage under Rome in the second and first centuries has changed dramatically in recent decades.[1] Many silver coinages have been moved

*Oriel College, University of Oxford (aneurin.ellis-evans@classics.ox.ac.uk).

1. All dates are BC unless otherwise stated. This article follows on from my study of the coinage of the *koinon* of Athena Ilias where die studies of Parion and Lampsakos were promised at A. Ellis-Evans, "The koinon of Athena Ilias and its coinage," *AJN* 28 (2016), 149 n. 129.

down from the first half of the second century to the first half of the first century, thus populating a hitherto sparse period of Greek numismatics with coinages using civic types.[2] Even in the case of coinages already thought to have been minted between the mid-second and mid-first centuries, such as those of Athens, Macedonia, Thasos, and Maroneia, there have been substantial readjustments to the chronologies which have consequently placed these series in new historical contexts.[3] Die studies for these coinages have revealed many to be much larger and more intensively minted than was hitherto suspected and thus strengthened the case for linking them to Roman military expenditure, while systematic work on the weight standards of these coinages is beginning to reveal how they came to be aligned with the *denarius* standard over the course of the first century.[4]

The primary focus of much of this scholarship has been on establishing that there was indeed Roman involvement in Greek coinage, even when the coin types do not make this explicit. This has been important for dispelling the impression, which Greek mints presumably meant to give when they chose coin types, of Roman involvement in their affairs being limited and late.[5] By revealing the true extent of Roman influence over Greek coinage, we have come much closer to resolving the question of how the Romans paid for their presence in the

2. To choose just two examples from the Troad which are thus relevant to Parion and Lampsakos, see F. de Callataÿ, "Abydos sur Aesillas," in Χαρακτηρ. Αφιέρωμα στην Μαντώ Οικονομίδου (Athens: TAP, 1996), 81–91, and F. de Callataÿ, "Les monnaies hellénistiques en argent de Ténédos," in *Studies in Greek Numismatics in Memory of Martin Jessop Price*, ed. R. H. J. Ashton et al. (London: Spink, 1998), 99–114, for Abydos and Tenedos respectively.

3. See O. Picard,"Les tétradrachmes à types thasiens et les guerres thraces au début du Ier siècle avant notre ère," *CRAI* (2008), 465–493; O. Picard, "Rome et la Grèce à la basse période hellénistique: monnaies et impérialisme," *Journal des Savants* (2010), 161–192; and F. de Callataÿ, "The coinages struck for the Romans in Hellenistic Greece: a quantified overview (mid-2nd c.–mid-1st c. BCE)," in *Neue Forschungen zur Münzprägung der Römischen Republik: Beiträge zum internationalen Kolloquium im Residenzschloss Dresden 19.–21. Juni 2014*, ed. F. Haymann et al. (Bonn: Habelt Verlag, 2016), 315–320, 323–325.

4. Overview of die studies: F. de Callataÿ, "More than it would seem: the use of coinage by the Romans in late Hellenistic Asia Minor (133–63 BC)," *AJN* 23 (2011), 55–86; F. de Callataÿ, "The coinages struck for the Romans in Hellenistic Greece: a quantified overview (mid-2nd c.–mid-1st c. BCE)," in *Neue Forschungen zur Münzprägung der Römischen Republik: Beiträge zum internationalen Kolloquium im Residenzschloss Dresden 19.–21. Juni 2014*, ed. F. Haymann et al. (Bonn: Habelt Verlag, 2016), 315–318. Weight standards: A. Meadows, "The Penetration of the *denarius* and *quinarius* standards into Asia Minor in the 1st century BC," in *Graecia Capta? Roman Influence on Coinage and its Circulation in the Aegean Basin in the Second and First Centuries BC*, ed. R. Ashton and N. Badoud (forthcoming).

5. For the story of how Roman rule gradually became visible on Greek coins in the second and first centuries, see P. Thonemann, *The Hellenistic World: Using Coins as Sources* (Cambridge: Cambridge University Press, 2015), 169–190.

Greek world given the relatively late point at which they began to bring *denarii* east with them.[6] A further consequence has been to demonstrate that the Roman authorities by and large did not seek to interfere in how civic mints went about producing the coins which the Romans had requested from them.[7] Thus, while the reason that a city was minting a high value coinage in the first place may have been because the Roman authorities had asked them to do so, the form which this coinage took (its types, denominations, weight standard, and so on) was a choice which remained in the hands of the civic authorities. As such, these coinages can provide a wealth of incidental detail about Greek cities in the late Hellenistic period—how they conceived of their communal identity, how they related to their civic traditions, and how their institutions continued to operate.

The tetradrachms of Parion and Lampsakos provide an interesting case study for exploring all these issues for two reasons. Firstly, in attempting to establish the degree of Roman influence on Greek coinage scholars have understandably focused on very large coinages which are thus the most likely to represent Roman rather than civic expenditure. By contrast, the Parion Group 2 tetradrachms (one obverse die) and the Lampsakos tetradrachms (five obverse dies) appear to be small coinages. As such, they raise questions about how we identify Roman influence at a mint when volume of production does not settle the matter and, if we acknowledge that there was indeed Roman involvement, how to make sense of these small coinages in the context of Roman finances. Secondly, the redating of the Parion Group 2 and Lampsakos tetradrachms to the early first century provides an opportunity, particularly in the latter case, to explore the contribution which these coinages can make to our understanding of these cities in the late Hellenistic period.

2. THE APOLLO AKTAIOS TETRADRACHMS OF PARION

2.1 Introduction

Our knowledge of this series has developed rapidly in the last 20 years. Whereas four of the five examples of Group 2 have been known since the nineteenth century, the coins of Group 1 were almost entirely unknown until the 1990s. Meadows (1998) devoted a short note to the series, which established the existence

6. For the problem, see e.g., M. Crawford, *Coinage and Money under the Roman Republic. Italy and the Mediterranean Economy* (London: Methuen, 1985), 116, 119, and for an estimate of the extent to which Greek coinages may have met this need see Callataÿ, "The coinages struck for the Romans," 329–332.

7. Particularly emphasized by Picard, "Les tétradrachmes à types thasiens," 476–478 and Picard, "Rome et la Grèce," 189–192.

of the two groups and dated the coins to *ca.* 165–143. At the time he knew of two Group 1 coins, one of which was from *CH* X 308 (Gaziantep, Turkey, 1994; hoard closed pre-Aug./Oct. 143). Since then, five more Group 1 coins have appeared, three of which are from *CH* X 301 ("Demetrius I," Commerce, 2003; hoard closed pre-151). In addition, in 2017 the first undamaged example of a Group 2 coin appeared in trade, thus giving a first indication of the weight standard of this issue.

2.2 Catalogue[8]

Group 1

Obv.: Laureate head of Apollo r.

Rev.: Apollo semi-draped standing l. on ground line; palm branch in r. hand in front; l. hand on bow resting on ground behind; <RF and LF> ΑΠΟΛΛΩΝΟΣ | ΑΚΤΑΙΟΥ written vertically downwards; <EX> ΠΑΡΙΑΝΩΝ; <LF and/or RF> two monograms.

Ref.: Meadows 1 (Pl. 15, 10). *Rev.:* <ILF> △ (above), altar (below), <IRF> ⷷ (above).

O1/R1 (1)	39	16.88	*CH* X 308, C216. BM 1996,0107.1 = Spink 106 (11/10/1994), lot 59.
O1/R1 (2)	40	16.61	Künker 236 (7/10/2013), lot 72 = NAC 29 (11/5/2005), lot 197.

Ref.: None. *Rev.:* <OLF> ⷷ, <ILF> △ (above), altar (below).

O1/R2	40	16.95	Nomos 5 (25/10/2011), lot 179 ("From the PGB collection, acquired in the 1970s").

Ref.: None. *Rev.:* <ILF> ⷨ (above), ⷷ (below).

O2/R3	35	16.88	*CH* X 301.127. Gemini 1 (11/1/2005), lot 152 = Freeman & Sear List 9 (Spring 2004), lot 35.

Ref.: Meadows 2 (Pl. 15,11). *Rev.:* <OLF> ⷠ, <ILF> ⷨ (above), altar (below).

O2/R4	36	17.10	ANS 1991.99.1 = Sotheby's NY (19/6/1991), lot 317 (Nelson Bunker Hunt IV, acq. *ca.* 1978–1983).[9]

Ref.: None. *Rev.:* <ILF> ⷫ (above), ⷔ (below).

---

8. Abbreviations: Meadows = A. R. Meadows, "Parion," *NC* 158 (1998), 42–43.

9. For the acquisition dates for this collection see P. Watson and C. Todeschini, *The Medici Conspiracy: The Illicit Journey of Looted Antiquities, from Italy's Tomb Raiders to the World's Greatest Museums* (New York: Public Affairs, 2006), 129–130.

| O3/R5 | 38 | 16.64 | *CH* X **301.129.** Ira & Larry Goldberg (The Pre-Long Beach Sale) 53 (26/5/2009), lot 1680 = Freeman & Sear List 11 (Spring/Summer 2006), lot 45. |

Ref.: None. *Rev.*: <ILF>)€ (above), ℈ (below).

| O3/R6 | 37 | 16.77 | *CH* X **301.128.** Numismatica Genevensis 8 (24/11/2014), lot 47 = 4 (12/12/2006), lot 92—Die fault has begun to develop on forehead. |

Group 2

Obv.: Veiled head of Demeter r. with grain ear in hair, all within dotted border.

Rev.: Apollo semi-draped standing l.; in right hand in front, patera over flaming altar; in left behind, lyre resting on omphalos; <RF and LF> written vertically downwards ΑΠΟΛΛΩΝΟΣ | ΑΚΤΑΙΟΥ; <EX> ΠΑΡΙΑΝΩΝ | (signer's name).

Polykles

Ref.: Meadows 3–4 (Pl. 15,12–13: Fitzwilliam, Paris). *Rev.*: <EX> ΠΟΛΥΚΛΗΣ.[10]

O4/R7 (1)	31 × 28	14.82	*SNG Lewis* 829 (cf. *BMC Mysia*, 99) = Hoffmann (15/1/1882), lot 1399 (F. Bompois) [14.78 g]—Broken.
O4/R7 (2)	30	14.36	*BNF Fonds Général* 893 (*SNG Paris* 1401) = T. M. Dumersan, *Description des médailles antiques du cabinet de feu m. Allier de Hauteroche* (Paris, 1829) 74, Pl. XII,13—Broken.
O4/R7 (3)	29	13.03	Berlin, C. R. Fox 1873 (acq. from C. C. Rollin, 1848)—Broken.

Ref.: None. *Rev.*: <EX> ΠΑΡΙΑΝΩΝ.

| O4/R8 | 29.5 | 15.77 | Triton 20 (9/1/2017), lot 247. |

---

10. *Pace* L. Robert, *Monnaies antiques en Troade* (Paris: Minard, 1966), 44, this individual is not identical with the Polykles in *I. Ilion* 5.5–6: Meadows, "Parion," 45. *LGPN VA*, *s.v.* nos. 6–7 are in fact the same individual from the coins; the reference to M. J. Price and B. L. Trell, *Coins and Their Cities: Architecture on the Ancient Coins of Greece, Rome, and Palestine* (London, 1977), 121, Fig. 216, is to the example in Paris; the reference to *BMC Mysia*, 99 is to the example in the Fitzwilliam.

Mandrodikos

Ref.: Meadows 5 (Pl. 16,14). This individual not in *LGPN*. *Rev.:* <EX> [M] ΑΝΔΡΟΔΙΚ[ΟΣ],[11] <RF> ⚲ (above).

O4/R9	28	13.95	BM 1896,0601.63 = Sotheby, Wilkinson & Hodge (23/3/1896), lot 522 (H. Montagu)—Heavily corroded to point where obverse die identity not certain.

2.3 Dating

Meadows argued that the Group 2 coins were a separate and later issue than Group 1 on the grounds that: 1) the Group 1 coins had broader and thinner flans than the Group 2 coins; 2) the Group 1 coins lacked a signer's name, whereas the Group 2 coins feature one in the exergue.[12] With the expanded sample now available to us we can also note two further diagnostic features: 1) all the Group 1 coins have hammered edges, whereas all the Group 2 coins instead have a dotted border on the obverse; 2) the weights of the Group 1 coins are uniformly higher (16.6 g–17.1 g) and clearly conform closely to the "reduced" Attic standard of 16.9 g common in the mid-second century, whereas the weight of the one intact Group 2 coin is surprisingly low (15.77 g).

The appearance of three Group 1 coins in *CH* X 301 ("Demetrius I," pre-151) allows us to tighten the chronology of this issue still further to the period of the late 160s/150s. Although the sample remains small, we have a ratio of specimens ($n = 7$) to obverse dies ($d = 3$) of 2.33:1 with all three obverse dies represented by more than one specimen, suggesting that our sample is not entirely unrepresentative. These coins may have been produced over a relatively short time span, and the appearance of the monogram ⲉ on reverse dies paired with two separate obverse dies (O1/R1, O1/R2, O2/R4) reinforces this impression.

For want of evidence to the contrary, Meadows also dated the Group 2 coins *ca.* 165–143. The implication of his separate grouping of these coins was that they belonged towards the end of this period. He was appropriately cautious about their non-appearance in *CH* X 308 (Gaziantep, pre-Aug./Oct. 143) along with the Group 1 coin which appeared in that hoard, noting that "not even their absence from the 1994 hoard can be pressed since they are so rare."[13] The Group 2 coins have now also failed to turn up in *CH* X 301 (pre-151) which, by con-

---

11. For the restoration of this name and other (less likely) possibilities see Meadows, "Parion," 45–46.

12. Meadows, "Parion," 43–44.

13. Meadows, "Parion," 45.

trast, produced three Group 1 coins. At the very least, this strengthens the argument that the Group 2 coins postdate the 150s and are indeed a separate and later issue.

However, we may now also want to question whether the Group 2 coins even belong to the first half of the 140s. One consequence of the full publication of *CH* X 301 and 308 has been a general lowering of the dates for the tetradrachms with autonomous types, with series which began as late as *ca.* 143/2 (Herakleia, Lebedos, the "Syros" tetradrachms) still choosing to adopt the spread-flan design with hammered edges.[14] The implication is that even series starting (or, in the case of Parion, restarting) as late as the 140s would still be likely to adopt the spread-flan design with hammered edges, which had been prevalent in the Greek world since the 170s. The adoption of flans with a reduced diameter of *c.* 30 mm, a correspondingly thicker fabric, and a dotted border on the obverse is instead more typical of series which started in the late second/early first century such as Abydos, Lampsakos (see below), and the Apollo Smintheus *cistophoroi* of Alexandreia Troas.[15] The Group 2 coins may therefore date to the last third of the second century or, more probably, to the first half of the first century, and thus to the period of direct Roman rule over Asia Minor.

3. THE PRIAPOS TETRADRACHMS OF LAMPSAKOS

3.1 Introduction

The studies of Gaebler (1923, reflecting work pre-1919) and Baldwin (1924) were necessarily cursory in their treatment of this series, since only nine examples had appeared prior to 1921, not all of which were known to either scholar. However, in 1964/5 a hoard reached the market which had reportedly been found in western Asia Minor (*IGCH* 1322). In the subsequent decade nine new examples appeared in trade, with a further two new examples popping up in 1984 and 1990. No new examples have appeared on the market since 1990, and it seems likely that all eleven coins derive from *IGCH* 1322 (these coins are identified as "*IGCH* 1322?" in the catalogue). Although small, this hoard makes a substantial contribution to our knowledge of the series: in addition to adding two new signers, a new obverse die, a new die link between two signers, and four overstrikes,

14. F. de Callataÿ "The coinages of the Attalids and their neighbours: a quantified overview," in *Attalid Asia Minor: Money, International Relations, and the State*, ed. P. Thonemann (Oxford: Oxford University Press, 2013), 233, Table 6.10.

15. Apollo Smintheus *cistophoroi*: Lanz 163 (7/12/2016), lot 95 (Year 216 = 85 BC); GM 249 (11/10/2017), lot 274 (Year 233 = 68 BC).

it also allows us to downdate this series by almost a century from the first half of the second century to the first half of the first century. This in turn suggests a rather different context for the production of the series than has hitherto been assumed.

3.2 Catalogue[16]

Obv.: Bearded head of Priapos r., wearing an ivy wreath, his hair tightly rolled and down to his shoulders, all within dotted border.

Rev.: Apollo Kitharoidos standing r. on ground line, wearing chiton and mantle, plectrum in r. hand, lyre under l. arm;[17] <RF and LF> ΛΑΜΨΑ|ΚΗΝΩΝ written vertically downwards; <ILF> monogram; <IRF> control mark; <EX> signer's name in the genitive.

Ephesios, son of Theodoros

Ref.: Gaebler Group 5, 71 (Taf. 2,43); Baldwin Pl. 8,4. *Rev.:* <EX> ΕΦΕΣΙΟΥ ΤΟΥ | ΘΕΟΔΩΡΟΥ, <LF> ⩎, <RF> tripod.[18]

O1/R1   32   16.79   *BNF Fonds Général 769* (*SNG Paris* 1230) = Waddington 884.

Promethion, son of Lampon (1)[19]

Ref.: Gaebler Group 5, 74 (Taf. 2.45); Baldwin Pl. 8, 5–6. *Rev.:* <EX> ΠΡΟΜΗΘΙΩΝΟΣ | ΤΟΥ ΛΑΜΠΩΝΟΣ, <LF> ⨎, <RF> Hekate facing, wearing kalathos, holding a torch in each hand.[20]

16. Abbreviations: Gaebler = H. Gaebler, "Die Silberprägung von Lampsakos. Eine chronologische Studie," *Nomisma* 12 (1923), 72–73; Baldwin = A. Baldwin, *Lampsakos: The Gold Staters, Silver and Bronze Coinages* (New York: The American Numismatic Society, 1924), 30–32.

17. This depiction of Apollo Kitharoidos is common throughout Mysia: see L. Robert, "Apollons de Mysie. Apollon Kratéanos." In *Hellenica* X (Paris: Adrien-Maisonneuve, 1955), 134–153, with the reliefs illustrated in Planches XXIII–XXVII.

18. The ethnic appears to read ΛΑΜΨΑ|ΚΕΙΝΩΝ instead of ΛΑΜΨΑ|ΚΗΝΩΝ. However, this is more likely to be a case of die fill, whereby fine details in the die become temporarily filled up by metal fragments that have become detached from the flan of a previous coin, than a genuine change in spelling (in general, the city ethnic is the most conservative aspect of reverse designs). I thank Philip Kinns for discussion on this point.

19. The order of O2/R2–R6 is based on a worsening die break above the head of Priapos on the obverse die.

20. This is the same figure that appears on lifetime Alexanders minted at Lampsakos (Price 1351–1356) where it has been incorrectly identified as Demeter.

O2/R2   29   16.10   BM 1900,1204.3 (W. Wroth, *NC* 20³ [1900] 288–289, no. 21, Pl. XIV) = Sotheby, Wilkinson & Hodge (28/5/1900), lot 327 ("Greek Coins of a Late Collector" [Rothschild]).[21]

O2/R3   30   15.93   ANS 1948.29.3 = Jameson 3 (1924) 2221 = Naville 1 (4/4/1921), lot 2238 (S. Pozzi).

O2/R4   31   16.12   *SNG Lewis* 825 = Hoffmann (15/1/1882), lot 1395 (F. Bompois) [16.05 g].

O2/R5   16.49   *IGCH* **1322**? Elsen 102 (12/9/2009), lot 97 = BM Cast ("Mallers Hd. 1965").[22]

O2/R6 (1)   29   16.63   *IGCH* **1322**? Triton 8 (11/1/2005), lot 379 = Triton 2 (1/12/1998), lot 413 = Kovacs 13 (3/6/1998), lot 48 = Lanz 74 (20/11/1995), lot 197 = Sotheby's London (28/1/1976), lot 31—Die breaks on obverse. **Overstruck** (dotted border of undertype visible on obverse).

O2/R6 (2)   34   15.45   *BNF Fonds Général 770* (*SNG Paris* 1231) = Waddington 885 (Waddington [1853] 74–5, no. 1)—Die breaks on obverse.

Andromachos son of Menophilos

Ref.: None. This individual not in *LGPN*. *Rev.:* <EX> [A]NΔPOMAXOY | [TO]Y MHNOΦIΛOY, <LF> K, <RF> headdress of Isis.[23]

O3/R7   26   15.81   *IGCH* **1322**? ANS 1972.15.1 (acq. from Marcel Salton, 12/10/1971) = R. J. Myers, Ancient Coins Summer Sale (1971), lot 24.

21. For the identity of the owner see J. Spring, *Ancient Coin Auction Catalogues, 1880–1980* (London: Spink and Son, 2009), 299–300.

22. François de Callataÿ drew my attention to this cast in the BM, for which he noted down the information "Mallers Hd. 1965" on his index card (dated summer 1992). No such hoard of Greek coins is known. However, Peter Thonemann has suggested to me that this may be a reused label for the Mallers(tang) hoard of Roman *denarii* found in 1926, part of which was deposited at the BM. If that is correct (and I have no better solution), then presumably this is a coin which was seen in trade in 1965 and thus at precisely the time when *IGCH* 1322 was coming on the market. The Elsen catalogue refers to this coin as, "Provient de Sotheby, vente d'octobre 1992, 51." However, there is no such coin in Sotheby's (8 Oct. 1992).

23. This control mark also appears on issues of Abydos and Tenedos in the first third of these two series: Callataÿ, "Abydos," D10/R1a (Apollonios) and Callataÿ, "Ténédos," D11/R1.

Herodes son of Dorotheus

Ref.: None. This individual not in *LGPN*. *Rev.:* <EX> ΗΡΩΔΟΥ ΤΟΥ | ΔΩΡΟΘΕΟΥ, <LF> ⟨monogram⟩, <RF> snake wrapped round staff.[24]

O4/R8	27	16.35	*IGCH* **1322?** NAC 2 (21/2/1990), lot 182.

Demetrios, son of Demetrios, son of Meikalos

Ref.: Gaebler Group 5, 70 (Taf. 2, 42); Baldwin Pl. 8, 1–2. Meikalos not in *LGPN*. *Rev.:* <EX> ΔΗΜΗΤΡΙΟΥ ΤΟΥ | ΔΗΜΗΤΡΙΟΥ ΤΟΥ | ΜΕΙΚΑΛΟΥ, <LF> ⟨monogram⟩, <RF> bow and arrow r.

O4/R9 (1)	27	16.61	*IGCH* **1322?** Sotheby's Zurich (27/5/1974), lot 311 = Stanley Gibbons Coin List 2 (not dated, pre-1973) 41 = Hess-Leu 31 (7/12/1966), lot 406.
O4/R9 (2)	28.5	16.35	*IGCH* **1322?** *Boston MFA* 1973.294 ("by 1969: with Robert E. Hecht Jr.," acq. from Hecht 13/6/1973)—Overstruck.
O4/R9 (3)	26	15.23	*BNF* K 1832 (*SNG Paris* 1229) (E. de Cadalvène, 1832)—Worn.
O4/R10 (1)	26	16.88	*IGCH* **1322?** *SNG Cop. Suppl.* 306 (acq. 1970).
O4/R10 (2)		16.45	*IGCH* **1322?** Morton & Eden 86 (24/5/2017), lot 27 = The New York Sale 27 (4/1/2012), lot 475 = GM 46 (30/10/1989), lot 220 = Bank Leu 48 (10/5/1989), lot 220 = MM Basel 41 (18/6/1970), lot 149—**Overstruck (?)**.
O4/R10 (3)	26	15.95	BM 1899,0103.1 (W. Wroth, *NC* 20³ [1900] 17, no. 21, Pl. II, 7—"Struck on a somewhat thick *flan*, too small for the die") (W. T. Ready).
O4/R11	30 x 28	16.73	*IGCH* **1322?** Nomos 3 (10/5/2011), lot 111 = Lanz 102 (28/5/2001), lot 257 = Bank Leu 33 (3/5/1983), lot 363 = MM Basel 47 (30/11/1972), lot 493.
O4/R12 (1)	26	16.65	*IGCH* **1322?** Lanz 28 (7/5/1984), lot 250 ("Stempelbruch auf Vs. (wie bei den meisten bekannten Exemplaren)").
O4/R12 (2)	28	16.31	*IGCH* **1322?** Bank Leu 7 (9/5/1973), lot 205—**Overstruck** (wreathed border of undertype visible on reverse).

---

24. This control mark also appears on an issue of Abydos in the middle of the series: Callataÿ, "Abydos," D16/R1, D17/R2 (Menis). This symbol could perhaps be a reference to Asklepios, whose festival at Lampsakos was lavishly endowed in the second century BC (*I. Lampsakos* 9).

Promethion, son of Lampon (2)[25]

Ref.: Gaebler Group 5, 73. *Rev.:* <EX> ΠΡΟΜΗΘΙѠΝΟΣ | ΤΟΥ ΛΑΜΠѠΝΟΣ, <LF> ⋈, <RF> Hekate facing, wearing kalathos, holding a torch in each hand, a pair of recumbent outward-facing lions to either side, all on separate ground line.[26]

O5/R13   30   16.13   Berlin 18245862 (A. Löbbecke, 1906).

Sokrates son of Xenophanes

Ref.: Gaebler Group 5, 72 (Taf. 2,44); Baldwin Pl. 8,3. *Rev.:* <EX> ΣѠΚΡΑΤΟΥ ΤΟΥ | ΞΕΝΟΦΑΝΟΥ, <LF> ⋈, <RF> palm branch.

O5/R14   30   16.41   BM RPK,p131D.1.Lam (*BMC Mysia*, p. 86, no. 68).

3.3.1 *The Arrangement of the Issues*

The arrangement of the issues is highly uncertain. As we shall see below (section 3.3.2), we probably have an unrepresentative sample of the series and, consequently, new discoveries are likely to expose problems with the arrangement I have adopted here.

Obverse die links connect two pairs of signers: Herodes, son of Dorotheus, and Demetrius, son of Demetrius, son of Meikalos (O4), and Promethion, son of Lampon (2) and Sokrates, son of Xenophanes (O5). However, the decision to place these four signers at the end of the sequence is largely based on the assumption that issues where the signer's name shows more "late" forms (i.e., lunate letters, alphas with broken crossbars, thetas with a line across the middle) belong later in the series. The evidence for these "late" forms is set out in Table 1. It should be noted, however, that where we have thorough surveys of well-dated material, the conclusion is that letter forms provide only a very rough indication of dating and do not follow a straightforward trajectory of stylistic development.[27]

25. Several factors suggest that this issue needs to be dissociated from the other coins minted under a Promethion, son of Lampon—1) the obverse die link with Sokrates, son of Xenophanes; 2) the letter forms; 3) the redrawn monogram in left field; 4) the addition of two lions to the Hekate control mark. Either this is a different individual with the same names (perhaps the grandson of the first Promethion), or, more probably, the same individual was signing these coins on more than one occasion as we appear to see on the Apollo Smintheus coinage with Herodikos (92 and 80 BC), Nikandros (85, 84, and 78 BC), and Peisistratos (71 and 68 BC).

26. For discussion of Hekate on this and the issue of Promethion, son of Lampon (1), see F. Imhoof-Blumer, "Beiträge zur Erklärung griechischer Münztypen," *Nomisma* 8 (1913), 14.

27. The most comprehensive recent survey of this kind is P. Kinns, "Lunate letter forms in the 4th century and Hellenistic coinage of Ionia," *NC* 174 (2014), 1–15.

Table 1. Diagnostic letter forms of the ethnic (top letter)
and signer (bottom letter)

Signer	Die					
Ephesios, son of Theodoros	O1	Σ	E	Ω	-	A
		Σ	E	Ω	Θ	-
Promethion, son of Lampon (1)	O2	Σ	-	Ω	-	A
		Σ	-	Ω	Θ	A
Andromachos, son of Menophilos	O3	Σ	-	Ω	-	A
		-	-	-	-	A
Herodes, son of Dorotheus	O4	Σ	-	Ω	-	A
		-	Є	Ω	Θ	-
Demetrios, son of Demetrios, son of Meikalos	O4	Σ	-	Ω	-	A
		-	Є	-	-	A
Promethion, son of Lampon (2)	O5	Σ	-	Ω	-	A
		Σ	-	ω	Θ	A
Sokrates, son of Xenophon	O5	Σ	-	Ω	-	A
		Σ	Є	ω	-	A

Although several factors can be adduced to argue for Ephesios, son of Theodorus, coming first in the series, all have their problems. The most significant factor in favor of placing him first is style, since the die cutting of O1 is appreciably finer than that of O2–O5. However, if we compare the contemporary and much better attested Athena Ilias and Apollo Smintheus series, we see that, while there is an overall decline in the quality of die cutting over the course of the whole series (and above all in the first half of the first century), within this general trend there can be considerable variation from one issue to the next.[28] Secondly, there is the higher weight of the coin (16.79 g). This suggests that it was struck to the reduced Attic standard (16.9 g) which was widespread in the first half of the second century. However, it is obviously problematic to extrapolate the average weight of an issue based on a single example. Moreover, as Table 2 indicates, other signers whose issues display "late" features such as Demetrios and Promethion (1) likewise have weights consistent with a theoretical standard of 16.9 g.[29]

28. See the plates in Ellis-Evans, "The *koinon* of Athena Ilias" for Athena Ilias and A. R. Bellinger, *Troy: The Coins* (Princeton: Princeton University Press, 1961), plates 16–18, for Apollo Smintheus.

29. Two further points could be made. Firstly, Ephesios displays the fewest "late" letter forms despite his name providing opportunities for lunate epsilons, sigmas, and omegas. Secondly, the monogram is reminiscent of one we find on coins minted in the name of Apollo

Table 2. Weight table of the Lampsakos tetradrachms with relevant signers

Weight Ranges	Signers and Weights
16.80–9	Demetrios (16.88)
16.70–9	Ephesios (16.79), Demetrios (16.73)
16.60–9	Promethion 1 (16.63), Demetrios (16.61, 16.65)
16.50–9	-
16.40–9	Promethion 1 (16.48), Demetrios (16.45), Sokrates (16.41)
16.30–9	Herodes (16.35), Demetrios (16.35, 16.31)
16.20–9	-
16.10–9	Promethion 1 (16.10, 16.12), Promethion 2 (16.13)
16.00–9	-
15.90–9	Promethion 1 (15.93), Demetrios (15.95)
X<15.90	Andromachos (15.81), Promethion 1 (15.45), Demetrios (15.23–worn)

3.3.2 The Size of the Series

The sample we have looks to be fairly representative (i.e., it has an $n/d > 3$):

n	d	n/d	Singletons	D (Carter)[30]	D (Esty)[31]
20	5	4	2 (O1, O3)	5.7 ±0.73	6.7 ±2.43

However, this masks issues of both over and underrepresentation within our sample. For example, the obverse die used for the issue of Demetrios, son of Demetrios, son of Meikalos, is significantly overrepresented (9 out of 20) because coins of this signer make up the majority of the Lampsakene portion of *IGCH* 1322 (7 out of 11). Conversely, two of the five obverse dies are only known from a single example (the "singletons" O1 and O3). In addition, our two examples of O5 show considerable wear, raising the possibility that this obverse die had already been in use for some time, perhaps with one or several previous signers who are as yet unattested.

In light of all this, the slightly higher estimate of the original number of obverse dies arrived at using Esty's formula seems more realistic. That said, al-

Smintheus by Alexandreia Troas in 148 BC (Bellinger A 136 = ANS 1967.152.420; cf. Bellinger A 137 = ANS 1947.49.2 [135 BC], CNG 99 (13/5/2015), lot 194 [128 BC], and Roma Numismatics 9 (22/3/2015), lot 270 [127 BC]).

30. G. F. Carter, "A simplified method for calculating the original number of dies from die link statistics," *ANSMN* 28 (1983), 195–206.

31. W. W. Esty, "The geometric model for estimating the number of dies," in *Quantifying Monetary Supplies in Greco-Roman Times*, ed. F. de Callataÿ, (Bari: Edipuglia, 2011), 43–58.

though the current evidence suggests that we have somewhat underestimated the size of the series, both the extremely rare appearance of these coins in trade (see below) and the evidence of the die study (imperfect as it is) do not encourage us to think that we have dramatically underestimated the overall size of this coinage. The number of obverse dies might realistically rise to as many as 10, but more than double that to equal the wreathed tetradrachms of Tenedos, or five times that to surpass the wreathed tetradrachms of Abydos, seems highly unlikely.[32]

3.3.3 The Date of the Series

It was traditionally assumed that the series began either after 196 (Flamininus declaring the freedom of the Greeks) or 190–188 (the end of the war with Antiochos III) and was then minted continuously over the next century until the war with Mithridates in 88–85.[33] Otto Morkhølm instead assumed a date *ca.* 160 in both *IGCH* (1973) and his *Early Hellenistic Coinage* (1991, reflecting work pre-1982).[34] While Morkhølm did not explicitly set out his reasons for this later date, he was presumably influenced by the widescale downdating of autonomous tetradrachm series to the mid-second century in the 1970s.[35] Morkhølm's authority has subsequently encouraged some auction cataloguers to adopt his later date.[36] It is worth noting, finally, that in the mid-nineteenth century William Waddington had instead preferred a late Attalid date, while the catalogue of Robert Jameson's collection had already suggested a date "vers 100" in 1924.[37] As we shall see, the overlooked evidence of *IGCH* 1322 shows that the Jameson catalogue is

---

32. Tenedos (*ca.* 100–70): $n = 86$, $d = 21$, $n/d = 4.1$, D (Esty) = 28. Abydos (*c.* 100–70): $n = 126$, $d = 35$, $n/d = 3.6$, D (Esty) = 48.

33. E.g., *BMC Mysia*, 86, no. 68.

34. O. Mørkholm, *Early Hellenistic Coinage: From the Accession of Alexander to the Peace of Apamea (336–188 BC)* (Cambridge: Cambridge University Press, 1991), 25, 266; cf. G. Le Rider, "Numismatique grecque." *AEPHE 1971–1972* (1972), 235, assuming a date *ca.* 175.

35. Influential here is the work of C. Boehringer, *Zur Chronologie mittelhellenistischer Münzserien, 220–160 v. Chr.* (Berlin: De Gruyter, 1972), and the die studies made possible by the discovery of the Kırıkhan hoard in 1972 (*CH* X 310).

36. See, e.g., Nomos 3 (10/5/2011), lot 111: "The general dates given for this series are c. 190–85 BC: this seems far too long a time span. A date of around 160 seems more likely, though it is certainly possible that it could be later, given the prominent broken-bar alphas in the reverse legend. The elaborate patronymic, Demetrios, son of Demetrios, son of Meikalos, also argues for a late date."

37. W. H. Waddington, *Voyage en Asie-Mineure au point de vue numismatique* (Paris: M. Rollin, 1853), 75 (discussing BNF Fonds Général 770 = *SNG Paris* 1231): "Le style de cette médaille décèle une antiquité peu reculée; elle doit avoir été frappée vers la fin de la dynastie des rois de Pergame".

closest to the mark and that this series belongs not to the second quarter of the second century but rather to the early first century.

Before discussing this hoard in detail, it is worth noting that this later date makes much better sense of a number of the coinage's characteristics which strongly suggest a late Hellenistic date even without the evidence of this hoard. 1) Letter Forms—Although problematic as evidence for a coinage's internal arrangement (as discussed in Section 3.3.1), the presence of "late" letter forms favors a date in the first half of the first century over a date a century earlier; 2) Diameters—In the mid-second century the trend was towards broader, thinner flans with hammered edges (typical diameter: 35–40 mm). In the later second century there is then a return to thicker flans with a reduced diameter (typically around 30 mm) which often replace hammered edges with a dotted border. The coins of Parion Group 2 are a good example of this change, and the Lampsakos tetradrachms also appear to fit here (range of recorded diameters: all but one 26–32 mm); 3) Patronymics—A variety of factors determined whether the signer's patronymic was included (e.g., the rest of the design, available space on the flan, the traditions of the city in question), but broadly speaking when it does appear it is usually a phenomenon of the late second/early first century. For example, it does not appear on the Athena Ilias series until the issue of Diopeithes son of Zenis at the very end of the second century, but after this the inclusion of the patronymic then becomes the fashion for this coinage.[38] The fact, therefore, that all the Lampsakos tetradrachms include the signer's patronymic, and that one issue even goes back to the grandfather's generation, strongly points to these coins having been minted in the late second/early first century; 4) Control Marks—The series shares two distinctive control marks (a headdress of Isis and a staff with a snake wrapped round it) with issues belonging to the wreathed tetradrachms minted by Abydos and Tenedos *ca.* 100–70.[39]

3.3.4 *The Hoard Evidence: IGCH 1322*

Morkholm reported in *IGCH* that the hoard was found in western Asia Minor in 1964/5, that it contained silver tetradrachms of Abydos (20+) and Lampsakos (10+), and that it had been dispersed in trade. Since Morkholm's purview for *IGCH* was the European market, we may presume that this is where the hoard was dispersed, and indeed the earliest provenances we have for the coins likely to derive from the hoard largely support this. In addition, we have two further pieces of information. Firstly, because Priapos tetradrachms turn up so infrequently

38. Ellis-Evans, "The *koinon* of Athena Ilias," 124–125.
39. See nn. 23 and 24 above.

on the market, the appearance of this hoard is fairly easy to trace in auctions. As mentioned above (Section 3.1), prior to 1965 a new example had not appeared since 1921, whereas in the decade after 1965 nine new examples appeared. It is thus fairly clear that these coins are the Lampsakene portion of the hoard (the coins which appeared in 1984 and 1990 probably also belonged to the hoard, but the attribution is of course rather less certain).

Secondly, there are two wreathed tetradrachms of Abydos in the Heberden Coin Room (*SNG Ashmolean* 1002 and 1004) which were purchased in June 1966 from Spink with money from the E. S. G. Robinson Trust "from a small hoard of 4 drs [i.e. tetradrachms], mostly Abydus, but also Tenedus & Lampsacus."[40] It seems highly likely that the hoard in question is *IGCH* 1322, but with the added information (unknown to Morkholm in *IGCH*) that it also contained wreathed tetradrachms of Tenedos. François de Callataÿ has demonstrated beyond doubt that the wreathed tetradrachms of Abydos and those of Tenedos in "phase two" of the mint's production date *ca.* 100–70.[41] The appearance of the Lampsakos tetradrachms in a hoard alongside these two series thus confirms that it belongs in the first half of the first century.

Unfortunately, it is not currently possible to identify the Tenedian portion of the hoard with any confidence, or indeed to establish whether the hoard contained issues from other mints.[42] However, it may be possible to make some progress in reconstructing the Abydene portion of the hoard. This can be attempted by identifying issues which have become overrepresented in our sample since the appearance of *IGCH* 1322 in 1964/5.

The wreathed tetradrachms of Abydos were a fairly sizeable coinage ($d = 35$, D [Esty] = 48). To judge from the substantial die-linking immediately apparent from de Callataÿ's study, the series was intensively minted over a fairly short period of time. Thus, although over forty individuals are named on the coins, it is clear that these were not annual signers covering this many years of production. Rather, the moneyers signing these coins probably formed a board of an as

40. I am grateful to Volker Heuchert for looking up this information for me.

41. Callataÿ, "Abydos," and Callataÿ, "Ténédos." For "phase one" of Tenedian production of this series in the 150s see A. Meadows and A. Houghton, "The Gaziantep Hoard, 1994 (*CH* 9.527; 10.308)," in *Coin Hoards* X: *Greek Hoards*, ed. O. Hoover, A. R. Meadows and U. Wartenberg (New York: American Numismatic Society, 2010), 185, discussing *CH* X 301.140–141 (151/0 BC), and now A. Meadows, "The Penetration of the *denarius*," section 2.e.i.

42. I wonder whether it is merely coincidental that the sale in which one of the Lampsakene hoard coins (an example of O2/R6) first appeared also included the first appearance of an Apollo Smintheus tetradrachm minted under Diophanes in 68 BC: Sotheby's (28/1/1976), lots 31–32.

yet undetermined size which minted the issues in parallel.[43] Within the series, the issue of Iphiades, which de Callataÿ placed penultimate in his arrangement, appears to be a strong candidate for an issue which we have come to know much better since the appearance of *IGCH* 1322. Of the 25 examples of this issue now known, 12 have appeared since the discovery of the hoard. Of these, seven first appeared in the 1970s, and five specifically in the period 1970–1973. There is therefore a good chance that *IGCH* 1322 was responsible for this spike in the appearance of Iphiades coins.

It should be noted, however, that the Abydene portion of the hoard was clearly not just made up of examples of this one issue, since the two coins in the Ashmolean deriving from this hoard belong instead to Philiskos (this coin: O23) and Antigonos (this coin: O27). Given that de Callataÿ places these two issues in the latter half of the series and Iphiades (O32–34) penultimate in his arrangement, it would seem that *IGCH* 1322 primarily included examples from late in the series. This may be significant if Andrew Meadows is correct to argue that the Iphiades issue is a separate and later issue which revived the Abydos coinage of *ca.* 100–70 in the early 40s, since this latter date would thus become the *terminus post quem* for the deposit of the hoard.[44] Comparison with the late Hellenistic hoards which Paunov has collected for Thrace suggests that the possible profile of *IGCH* 1322, with coins from both the early and the mid-first century found circulating together, is typical of tetradrachm hoards from this period.[45]

3.3.5 *Priapos Epiphanes*

The downdating of the Priapos tetradrachms to *ca.* 100–70 raises new questions about the one piece of epigraphic evidence we have for the worship of Priapos at Lampsakos. *I. Lampsakos* 7 republishes two decrees of Lampsakos which were passed in successive years and led to the city granting proxeny to a certain Dionysodoros of Thasos. The copy of these decrees which we have is part of a monument in the Thasian agora which included two more proxeny decrees for Dionysodoros from Assos and Rhodes and one from Samothrace for his brother

---

43. The inclusion of dates on the Apollo Smintheus coins allows us to see that pairs of moneyers started to be responsible for a single year's output from 93 BC onwards. We are presumably looking at a similar arrangement for Abydos, but without the ability to easily discern the pattern because of the lack of dates on the coins.

44. Meadows, "The Penetration of the *denarius*," section 2.e.ii.

45. Compare E. Paunov, "Georgi Dobrevo/2000 reconsidered: note on a 1st-century BC coin hoard from Thrace," *AWE* 12 (2013), 286–291 on late Hellenistic hoards from Thrace, particularly those containing tetradrachms from Troad mints.

Hestiaios.[46] All four decrees used to be dated to the 80s/70s primarily on palaeographic grounds. However, it has now been shown that the eponymous magistrate mentioned in the Rhodian decree dates to 131 and therefore that the Lucius Aurelius referred to there as governor of Macedonia must be L. Aurelius Orestes (*cos.* 126) who was praetor *ca.* 131–129.[47] The likelihood, therefore, is that Dionysodoros and Hestiaios had performed their benefactions for all four cities in the context of the war against Aristonikos (*ca.* 133–129) and that these are the "difficult times" (ἐγ καιροῖς ἀναγκαίοις) referred to in the Assian decree.[48]

The decrees of Lampsakos are of particular interest because in both cases the eponymous magistracy is filled not by a citizen of Lampsakos, but by one of the city's gods: Priapos in the first decree, his mother Aphrodite in the second. Moreover, in both cases the god is described as ἐπιφανής ("manifest").[49] We have numerous examples from throughout the Hellenistic and Imperial periods of a god being declared the eponymous magistrate of a city.[50] In at least some of these cases, this resulted from the fact that the polis was experiencing financial or political difficulties and as a result could not find a citizen willing or able to fulfil the role.[51] For example, a decree of Akraiphia in Boiotia dating to the reign of Claudius explicitly states that Zeus Soter had fulfilled the magistracy for three consecutive years during a period of famine because no one could be found to take up the post.[52]

---

46. *Recherches Thasos* II 169 (Samothrace), 170 (= *I. Assos* 11a), 171 (= *I. Lampsakos* 7), 172 (Rhodes). Patrice Hamon will re-edit these texts in his forthcoming *Corpus des inscriptions de Thasos, III: documents publics du IVe siècle et de l'époque hellénistique*, Études thasiennes XXVI (École française d'Athènes).

47. N. Badoud, *Le temps de Rhodes: une chronologie des inscriptions de la cité fondée sur l'étude de ses institutions* (Munich: C. H. Beck, 2015), 173–174.

48. *I. Assos* 11a.5–6: γενόμενος εὔχρηστος τῆι π[όλει] | ἐγ καιροῖς ἀναγκαίοις. Regarding the end date of the war with Aristonikos, note that the first examples of his year 5 = 130/29 BC coinage minted at Stratonikeia have recently appeared: Naumann 53 (7/5/2017), lot 297, Naumann 79 (7/7/2019), lot 177. M. Perperna captured Aristonikos prior to the arrival of M'. Aquilius in early 129. It has therefore traditionally been assumed Aristonikos was captured in 130, and the fact we only had his coinage up to year 4 = 131/0 BC seemed to confirm this. Since the years of Aristonikos's reign began in September, the new year 5 coins presumably indicate that he hung on at Stratonikeia into the winter of 130/29.

49. *I. Lampsakos* 7.9: Πρυτανεύοντος Πριάπου Ἐπιφανοῦς; 27–28: Πρυτανεύοντος Ἀφροδίτης Ἐπιφανοῦς.

50. List of examples: L. Robert, "Divinités éponymes," in *Hellenica* II (Paris: Adrien-Maisonneuve, 1946), 154–155; J. Robert and L. Robert, "Une inscription grecque de Téos en Ionie. L'union de Téos et de Kyrbissos," *Journal des Savants* (1976), 234.

51. Robert, "Divinités," 54–55 n. 9; J. Tréheux, "Décret de Lampsaque trouvé à Thasos," *BCH* 77 (1953), 434–435; P. Frisch, *Die Inschriften von Lampsakos* (Bonn: Habelt, 1978), 47–48.

52. *SEG* XV 330.45–8: τοῦ γὰρ ἐνστάντος ἐνιαυτοῦ Δι|ὸς Σωτῆρος τοῦ μετὰ Ἀφροδίσιον

On balance, the case of Lampsakos is likely to be a context of crisis for two reasons. Firstly, the city's inability to fill the office for (at least) two consecutive years suggests a persistent problem such as that which prevented Akraiphia from filling their eponymous magistracy for three years running.[53] Secondly, we know that the war with Aristonikos really did precipitate political and financial crises in cities throughout western Asia Minor, especially in the period prior to spring 131, when Roman troops finally arrived in force under P. Licinius Crassus. Before this, the majority of the fighting on both land and sea had been borne by the Greek cities and the allied kingdoms. So far as we can tell, Roman support was limited to the legation led by P. Scipio Nasica which provided overall command of the Greek forces from either late 133 or early 132, and possibly a detachment of troops from Macedonia under the command of the governor M. Cosconius.[54]

The Hellespontine region appears to have been particularly hard hit, especially at the beginning of the war. The decrees for Dionysodoros and Hestiaios indicate that Assos, Lampsakos, and Samothrace were all in some kind of trouble during the war, and, as we have seen, the Assian decree explicitly refers to difficult times. An honorific decree of Kyzikos refers to the city being encircled in *ca.* 133/2 and sending first to M. Cosconius and later to the Senate for help.[55] The honorific decree for Menas of Sestos likewise refers to the city in the context of *ca.* 133/2 facing "a dangerous crisis because of fear of the neighboring Thracians and other difficulties arising from the sudden contingency [i.e., the death of Attalos III]" which prompted Menas to seek an audience with Nasica's legation.[56] Finally, of particular interest is a decree of Methymna which dates to *ca.* 129 but refers to events from throughout the war.[57] The city had found itself hard pressed by a continual grain shortage, the consequent cost of exactions to support the grain fund, and the expense of supporting the Roman war effort. This seems to have precipitated a political crisis at Methymna over whether it was more important to solve the food crisis or show loyalty to Rome by supporting the war effort.

τὸ γ′, | ἐν τῇ τῆς χώρας ἀπωλείᾳ, δεομένης τῆς πό|λεως ἀρχείων. See L. Robert, "Études sur les inscriptions et la topographie de la Grèce centrale. VI. Décrets d'Akraiphia," *BCH* 59 (1935), 441, 446–8.

53. The months mentioned at *I. Lampsakos* 7.10 and 29 appear to suggest that the two decrees were passed over a winter: Tréheux, "Décret de Lampsaque," 435–438; Frisch, *Inschriften von Lampsakos*, 53.

54. See C. P. Jones, "Events surrounding the bequest of Pergamon to Rome and the revolt of Aristonicos: New inscriptions from Metropolis," *JRA* 17 (2004), esp. 483–485, for a persuasive reconstruction of the early years of the war.

55. *IGR* IV 134.

56. *I. Sestos* 1.16–23.

57. *IG* XII Suppl. 116.

At this juncture, the *neoi* of the city made the highly unusual decision to intervene and propose a way out of the political impasse.[58] The case of Methymna illustrates precisely how the disruption caused by war could precipitate the kind of political crisis which might leave civic offices unfilled at Lampsakos.

This context of crisis at Lampsakos in turn helps us understand why Priapos and Aphrodite are both referred to as ἐπιφανής. Given that this term had not yet come to have the more banal meaning it would later have in the Imperial period and does not prosaically refer to the god being "present" in the person of their priest, we should interpret ἐπιφανής here as an epithet which Priapos and Aphrodite had gained as a result of performing an epiphany at Lampsakos.[59] This can be paralleled in a decree of Knidos where it is explicitly stated that Artemis Hyakinthotrophos gained the epithet ἐπιφανής after performing an ἐπιφάνεια.[60] Epiphanies often occurred in the context of warfare when a city was faced with a much more powerful opponent and yet somehow escaped destruction.[61] For example, an inscription from Bargylia in Caria refers to an epiphany of Artemis Kindyas as having saved the city and its whole way of life at a time when Bargylia was threatened by many and great dangers on all sides during the war with Aristonikos.[62] As we have seen, cities in the Hellespontine region such as Lampsakos, Sestos, and Kyzikos faced no shortage of extreme dangers in 133–131. It is therefore entirely plausible that an epiphany of Priapos and Aphrodite (and perhaps also of Priapos' father Dionysos) should have occurred at Lampsakos in the

---

58. P. Gauthier, "Compte rendu: G. Labarre, *Les cités de Lesbos aux époques hellénistique et impériale* (Lyon, 1996)," *Topoi* 7.1 (1997), 359–360.

59. See already F. Prêteux, "Priapos Bébrykès dans la Propontide et les Détroits: succès d'un mythe local," *REG* 118.1 (2005), 251–252; T. Boulay, "Une épiphanie de Zeus Sôter à Clazomènes," *RN*⁶ 165 (2009), 125. For the other two possibilities canvassed here see Frisch, *Inschriften von Lampsakos*, 52.

60. *IG* XII (4,1) 166.7–9 (*ca.* 200–150 BC): διὰ τὰς γεγενημένας ὑπ᾽ αὐτᾶ[ς ἐπιφανεί|ας], καὶ διὰ ταῦτα ποταγορεύσαντος αὐτὰν [θεὸν Ἐπιφα|νῆ] (the restorations here are based on the repeated phrase at lines 29–30). For an inscription using the new epithet see *I. Knidos* 171 (*ca.* 200–150 BC).

61. Boulay, "Une épiphanie," 119–121; V. Platt, *Facing the Gods: Epiphany and Representation in Graeco-Roman Art, Literature and Religion* (Cambridge: Cambridge University Press, 2011), 147–159; C. Müller and F. Prost, "Un décret inédit du koinon des Ioniens trouvé à Claros," *Chiron* 43 (2013), 109–114; G. Petridou, *Divine Epiphany in Greek Literature and Culture* (Oxford: Oxford University Press, 2015), 107–170.

62. *I. Iasos* 613.2–5: ἐ[πειδὴ ἐν τῶι πολέμωι πολλῶν καὶ μεγάλων]| περιστάντων κινδύνων τήν τε πόλιν ἡμῶν καὶ [τὴν χώραν, ὁ δῆμος, διὰ τὴν τῆς Ἀρτέμιδος]| ἐπιφάνειαν τήν τε πάτριον αὐτονομ[ίαν διέσωσε καὶ εἰς τὴν ἐξ ἀρχῆς]| παρεγενήθη κατάστασιν. For discussion of the restorations and the context see L. Robert, *Études anatoliennes: recherches sur les inscriptions grecques de l'Asie mineure* (Paris: Bonard, 1937), 459–465, esp. 465, for the suggestion that this epiphany occurred in the difficult early years of the war.

particularly perilous opening stages of the war, when Roman support seemed very far away. While epiphanies of multiple deities are somewhat unusual, we in fact have a parallel case at nearby Kyzikos. When Mithridates VI was besieging Kyzikos in 73, the city's principal deity, Kore Soteira, appeared in a dream to the city's *grammateus* Aristagoras promising to defend Kyzikos, and the very next day a strong wind blew down the siege engines of Mithridates. At the same time, Athena Ilias, the principal deity of Ilion, likewise appeared in a dream to the Ilians covered in sweat and with her *peplos* torn, saying that she had been helping defend the Kyzikenes.[63]

Priapos has the reputation of being the principal deity of Lampsakos, with Pausanias for example remarking that: "This god is worshipped where goats and sheep pasture or there are swarms of bees; but the Lampsakenes consider him greater than the rest of the gods, saying that he is the son of Dionysos and Aphrodite."[64] The special connection between Priapos and Lampsakos was likewise well known to Latin poets who habitually refer to his origins on the Hellespont.[65] Consequently, his appearance on the tetradrachms studied above and as an eponymous magistrate in *I. Lampsakos* 7 has been taken for granted as a choice which was no less obvious and inevitable at Lampsakos than Athena was at Athens.[66] On the contrary, the numismatic evidence suggests that this epiphany may have been crucial in elevating Priapos to the status of the city's principal deity.

Before the Imperial period, Priapos appears on only four issues of Lampsakene coinage. There are two bronze issues which share the same obverse portrait of Priapos as the tetradrachms and must therefore all date *ca.* 100–70, one with the *parasemon* of Lampsakos, a protome of Pegasos, on the reverse (Fig. 1), the other with the city's ethnic within an ivy wreath (Fig. 2).[67] In addition, there is a bronze issue with a quite different portrait of a crowned Priapos on the obverse and a kantharos on the reverse (Fig. 3).[68] These last coins are difficult to date, but they are conventionally ascribed to the second century, and the fact that the die axes are adjusted to 12 o'clock supports this.[69]

63. Plut. *Luc.* 10 with discussion in Petridou, *Divine Epiphany*, 128–129.

64. Paus. 9.31.2: τούτῳ τιμαὶ τῷ θεῷ δέδονται μὲν καὶ ἄλλως, ἔνθα εἰσὶν αἰγῶν νομαὶ καὶ προβάτων ἢ καὶ ἑσμοὶ μελισσῶν· Λαμψακηνοὶ δὲ ἐς πλέον ἢ θεοὺς τοὺς ἄλλους νομίζουσι, Διονύσου τε αὐτὸν παῖδα εἶναι καὶ Ἀφροδίτης λέγοντες.

65. See Frisch, *Inscriften von Lampsakos*, 150–152, for the testimonia.

66. See, e.g., Gaebler, "Die Silberprägung," 31, on the coins and Frisch, *Die Inscriften von Lamposakos*, 52, on the inscription.

67. Pegasos protome: *SNG Ashmolean* 695. Ivy wreath: *SNG Ashmolean* 700–701.

68. *SNG Ashmolean* 696–699.

69. Many of the coins from this issue appear to be overstruck and a large number were

Figure 1. Lampsakos, *ca.* 100–70 BC. BNF Fonds Général 786 = *SNG Paris* 1248
(20 mm, 12h, 7.20 g). Scale 2:1. © Bibliothèque nationale de France.

Figure 2. Lampsakos, *ca.* 100–70 BC. BNF Fonds Général 787 = *SNG* Paris 1253
(15 mm, 12h, 2.40 g). Scale 2:1. © Bibliothèque nationale de France.

Figure 3. Lampsakos, ca. second century BC? BNF Fonds Général 788 = *SNG Paris*
1249 (20 mm, 12h, 4.21 g). Scale 2:1. © Bibliothèque nationale de France.

This late and rather meager showing for Priapos is all the more surprising given the unusually wide and comprehensive variety of deities which Lampsakos had displayed on its coinage in the Classical and Hellenistic periods.[70] Most telling is the gold coinage that Lampsakos produced in the first half of the fourth century. In the course of its production, this coinage cycled through almost fifty types depicting gods and heroes from myth, including Priapos' parents Aphrodite and Dionysos, yet not once does Priapos himself appear.[71] By contrast, from the reign of Augustus onwards the situation is entirely reversed. Of the 66 types catalogued in the volumes of *Roman Provincial Coinage* published so far, 34 have Priapos as the reverse type.[72]

One is left with the impression that, prior to his epiphany during the war with Aristonikos, the Lampsakenes considered Priapos either too unimportant or, more likely, too inappropriate to appear on coins. Indeed, in the remark of Pausanias quoted above, the point of the contrast he draws between the environmental margins where Priapos is usually worshipped and how the Lampsakenes honor him above all other gods is that it is deeply unusual, and thus noteworthy, to consider Priapos so important a civic deity. Although Lampsakos was identified as the home of Priapos from at least the third century, it was only in the late Hellenistic period that the Lampsakenes elevated him to the status of their principal civic deity.[73] However, once this change in status had taken place, Priapos became a natural choice for civic iconography, with the first opportunity to do so on coins apparently occurring *ca.* 100–70 when Lampsakos minted the

subsequently countermarked with a bunch of grapes in a circular punch (e.g., SNG *Ashmolean* 696–697). This perhaps points to their production in an emergency context.

70. See already Prêteux, "Priapos Bébrykès," 252–254.

71. For discussion of the types see Gaebler, "Die Silberprägung," for the silver and Baldwin, *Lampsacus,* for the gold and bronze.

72. The following does not take account of *RPC* 5/2, 8, and 10 which are as yet unpublished. All *RPC* 4/2 and 6 references are to the temporary numbers. Statue of Priapos: *RPC* 1, 2274–2276 (Augustus); *RPC* 2, 890–891 (Domitian); *RPC* 3,1547–1548, 1550 (Trajan), 1550B, 1552A (Hadrian); *RPC* 4/2, 2562, 2564 (Antoninus Pius), 595, 2366, 11265–11266 (Marcus Aurelius); *RPC* 6, 3895, 3898 (Severus Alexander), 3902–3903 (Maximinus); *RPC* 7/1, 47 (Gordian III); *RPC* 9, 386–387, 389 (Trajan Decius), 394–395 (Trebonianus Gallus). Head of Priapos: *RPC* 1, 2280 (Caligula); *RPC* 3, 1551, 1551A (Hadrian); *RPC* 4/2, 2563 (Marcus Aurelius), 2367, 8206, 9175 (Commodus). Statue of Priapos in temple: *RPC* 6, 3897 (Severus Alexander).

73. The sanctuary of Artemidorus of Perge on Thera (second half of the third century) includes an epigram in which Priapos declares himself to be from Lampsakos: ἥκω Πρίαπος τῆιδε Θηραίωμ πόλει | ὁ Λαμψακηνός πλοῦτον ἄφθιτομ φέρων (*IG* XII.3 421c.1–2). For evidence of Priapos's earlier presence along the Hellespont see Prêteux, "Priapos Bébrykès."

Priapos tetradrachms and the accompanying two issues of bronze coinage with the same image. We can usefully compare the case of Artemis Hyakinthotrophos at Knidos. The epiphany of Artemis probably occurred during Philip V's failed attack on the city in 201.[74] The immediate result was an increased status for the goddess: the Knidians gave her the epithet ἐπιφανής, established a penteteric festival in her honor, and sent to Delphi to request recognition of the festival as isopythian. Consequently, when an opportunity later arose in the 160s/150s to mint tetradrachms with civic types, the Knidians abandoned their traditional Aphrodite and lion types for a depiction of Artemis Hyakinthotrophos with her cult statue.[75]

Perhaps the earliest literary witness to this shift in status is an epigram by Erykios of Kyzikos whose *floreat* was in the mid-first century.[76] In appropriately ribald terms, Erykios talks of Priapos's "heavy ... and well-hardened weapon" and his insatiable desires. However, he ends the poem by advising Priapos to put away his phallus, "for you do not dwell on a lonely mountain, but guard holy Lampsakos by the shore of the Hellespont."[77] In a few short lines, Erykios brilliantly captures the fundamental oddness of having Priapos as one's tutelary deity by systematically subverting the genre conventions of Priapos poetry. Typi-

74. Polyb. 16.11.1.

75. For the date of the Knidian tetradrachms, see R. J. H. Ashton, "The late Alexander tetradrachms of Knidos and ?Nisyros," *NC* 174 (2014), 21 n. 95 and for their relation to the epiphany, see A. Meadows, "The great transformation. Civic coin design in the second century BC," in ΤΥΠΟΙ. *Greek and Roman Coins Seen through Their Images: Noble Issuers, Humble Users?*, ed. P. P. Iossif et al. (Liège: Presses Universitaires de Liège, 2018), 301–303. Another case are the tetradrachms of Klazomenai from the 160s/150s which refer to Zeus Soter Epiphanes: Boulay, "Une épiphanie"; A. Meadows, "The Hellenistic silver coinage of Clazomenae". In *Ancient History, Numismatics and Epigraphy in the Mediterranean World: Studies in Memory of Clemens E. Bosch and Sabahat Atlan and in Honour of Nezahat Baydur*, ed. O. Tekin (Istanbul: Ege Yayınları, 2009), 246–262. Both authors assume that the coins were minted close to the time of the epiphany, but the lag we see between when the epiphany happens and when this is reflected on the coins in the case of Knidos and Lampsakos suggest that this assumption is not valid.

76. R. Reitzenstein, *RE, s.v.* "Erykios."

77. *AP* 16.242: Ὡς βαρὺ τοῦτο, Πρίηπε, καὶ εὖ τετυλωμένον ὅπλον / πᾶν ἀπὸ βουβώνων ἀθρόον ἐκκέχυκας / εἰς γάμον οὐκ ἀνέτοιμον· ἔχει δέ σε δίψα γυναικῶν, / ὦ 'γαθέ, καὶ σπαργᾶς θυμὸν ἅπαντα πόθοις. / ἀλλὰ καταπρήϋνε τὸν ἐξῳδηκότα φαλλὸν / τόνδε, καὶ ἀνθηρῇ κρύψον ὑπὸ χλαμύδι· / οὐ γὰρ ἐρημαῖον ναίεις ὅρος, ἀλλὰ παρ' Ἕλλης / ἠόνα τὴν ἱερὴν Λάμψακον ἀμφιπολεῖς. For the injunction to cover up his phallus in lines 5–6, contrast J. Robert and L. Robert, "Inscriptions de l'Hellespont et de la Propontide," in *Hellenica* IX: *Inscriptions et reliefs d'Asie Mineure* (Paris: Adrien-Maisonneuve, 1950), 82, with Planche V, 5, for a relief of Priapos from Parion where he is in his characteristic pose of lifting his cloak up so as to expose himself.

cally, Priapos inhabits isolated and marginal spaces, guards fruit trees and crops, and does so by impotently threatening sexual violence. By contrast, the Priapos of Lampsakos dwells in a city, is responsible for the city's defence, and must be told by the poet to put away his phallus and show characteristically civic restraint in his desires so as to fulfil his duties. The very notion that the ὅπλον (line 1) with which Priapos defends Lampsakos is in fact his φαλλός (line 5) captures his essential inappropriateness for the role. Deeply unusual as this conception of Priapos is, it makes perfect sense if we assume that the Lampsakenes really did believe that the city had been saved from certain disaster by an epiphany of Priapos, his mother Aphrodite, and perhaps also (though evidence is lacking) his father Dionysos during the war with Aristonikos.[78]

4. CONCLUSIONS

The evidence we now have for the tetradrachm coinages of Parion and Lampsakos allows us to place them in their proper historical context. The Parion Group 1 series was a relatively small coinage (3 obverse dies) which was briefly issued in the late 160s/150s. Given the close similarity in the design of these coins to those of Athena Ilias and Apollo Smintheus, it seems likely that the correct context for these coins is the intra-regional rivalry which existed between the members of the *koinon* of Athena Ilias. On this interpretation, Parion's Apollo Aktaios coins were a short-lived attempt to place the city's Aktaia festival on a par with the region's more eminent Panathenaia and Smintheia festivals.[79] If this is correct, then the coinage was wholly civic in character.

The Parion Group 2 and Lampsakos coinages both belong *ca.* 100–70 as is indicated by the general characteristics of both coinages, the absence of Parion Group 2 from the many mid-second century hoards, and the presence of the Lampsakos coins in *IGCH* 1322. The small size of both coinages means that we cannot argue for Roman involvement in their production on the basis of volume

78. Another possibility is that Priapos was on this occasion being identified with Dionysos, as Ath. 1.30b claims happened at Lampsakos. The ability of Priapos to take on this tutelary role at Lampsakos might be connected to his cult's particular association with protecting seafarers along the Asian shore of the Hellespont: Prêteux, "Priapos Bébrykès," 256–265.

79. For this argument with regard to the Panathenaia and Smintheia see Ellis-Evans, "The *koinon* of Athena Ilias," 146–149 and A. Ellis-Evans, *The Kingdom of Priam. Lesbos and the Troad between Anatolia and the Aegean* (Oxford: Oxford University Press, 2019), 46–55. Boulay ("Une épiphanie," 117) also raises the attractive (but as yet unprovable) hypothesis that the decision to depict Apollo Aktaios, whose sanctuary in fact belonged to Adrasteia, may mark the fact that Parion had recently swallowed up this settlement (perhaps as a prize in the Peace of Apameia?).

of minting. While these coinages may, therefore, reflect civic expenditure, there are nevertheless several reasons to suspect Roman involvement. Firstly, Parion had not minted silver coinage with civic types since the 150s and Lampsakos had not done so since the fourth century. It is therefore striking that both cities chose to return to this practice *ca.* 100–70 at precisely the point when nearby Abydos and Tenedos likewise did so in order to produce their much larger coinages. Since de Callataÿ has made a strong case for Roman involvement in the Abydos and Tenedos coinages, there is a good *prima facie* case for the Parion and Lampsakos coinages likewise having been produced at the behest of the Romans. Secondly, in the case of Parion it is suggestive that all three of the Polykles coins have snapped edges. The breaking of coins by folding their edges over is a phenomenon commonly seen in tetradrachms coming out of hoards from Thrace, and may thus suggest that the Group 2 coins were circulating there. If correct, then Parion's coins were perhaps a small contribution to the great flood of silver coinage from Athens, Macedonia, Maroneia, and above all Thasos, which was used to pay Roman auxiliaries in the Thracian wars between the 120s and 70s.

Thirdly, in the case of Lampsakos it is potentially significant that there is an unusually high proportion of overstrikes (4/20). De Callataÿ has argued that when we encounter coins overstruck on coinages which are firmly attested "Roman" coinages (e.g., First Macedonian Meris, Thasos, Aesillas, and so on) and which do not ordinarily appear in hoards in the region of the overstriking mint, then we should assume Rome has had a hand in moving these coinages from where they were minted to where they were overstruck—examples of this phenomenon are known for Abydos, Tenedos, and Apollo Smintheus.[80] Although we cannot identify any of the undertypes in the case of Lampsakos, one had a dotted border (O2/R6 [1]) while the other had a wreathed border (O4/R12 [2]), thus indicating that Lampsakos was overstriking at least two different coinages. It may also be significant that all four overstrikes come from *IGCH* 1322 and three from the same signer (Demetrios), a pattern we do not see paralleled even in much larger series such as Abydos, Tenedos, and Apollo Smintheus. If we also take into account that the Lampsakene coins were circulating alongside Abydos and Tenedos, then there is a good circumstantial case for arguing that the Priapos tetradrachms were minted at the behest of the Roman authorities.

Despite all these indications of possible Roman involvement, the Parion Group 2 and Lampsakos tetradrachms may nevertheless represent a late and unexpected return to civic minting for civic purposes at these mints. Conversely,

---

80. Callataÿ, "More than it would seem," 68–70.

though, if we accept that the Parion and Lampsakos tetradrachms really were minted at the behest of the Roman authorities, should we therefore call them "Roman coinages"?[81] Such terminology might be deemed unhelpful in several respects. Picard and de Callataÿ have both recently argued that the silver for "Roman" coinages primarily came not from Rome but from the cities, and therefore that "Roman" coinages in large part represent Roman monetary exactions.[82] The sums involved in small coinages such as those of Parion and Lampsakos, and even of larger coinages such as Abydos and Tenedos, were by no means beyond the means of a *polis* and, as de Callataÿ speculates, could have been met by minting stored bullion.[83] Cities clearly did not *prefer* to spend their money in this way, hence, for example, the political tensions which Roman demands caused at Methymna during the war with Aristonikos and the many honorific decrees for benefactors who gained exemptions for their city from such demands. Nevertheless, cities could certainly see the *benefit* of spending their money in this way. If a Roman commander demanded money to pay his troops during wartime so as to deal with a threat such as Aristonikos, the Thracians, or Mithridates, a city could hardly argue that this was not to their ultimate advantage. Equally, the importance of showing loyalty to Rome by acceding to such requests (and the implied risk to the community's standing of failing to do so in wartime) clearly weighed on cities, as we see in the case of Methymna.[84] In sum, while the impetus to mint in the first place may have come from the Roman authorities, the silver was the city's and the decision to spend it in this way may not have been straightforwardly against the city's wishes.

A further difficulty with terming these coinages "Roman" is that all decisions about how to produce them were left in the hands of the civic authorities. Paradoxically, therefore, by imposing extraordinary financial demands on the cities (and thus compromising their fiscal autonomy) the Roman authorities created an opportunity for the cities to articulate their civic identity through coin types which they would not otherwise have had. As the decree for Menas of Sestos famously demonstrates, cities highly prized the opportunity to produce coins with their own types.[85] However, whereas Menas was referring to bronze coin-

81. For example, the term is used throughout Callataÿ, "More than it would seem," and Callataÿ, "The coinages struck for the Romans," although the actual analysis in both articles is a good deal more nuanced than this.

82. Picard, "Rome et la Grèce," 190; Callataÿ, "The coinages struck for the Romans 332–333.

83. Callataÿ, "The coinages struck for the Romans," 333.

84. *IG* XII Suppl. 116.9–20.

85. *I. Sestos* 1.43–9.

age whose coin types would therefore only reach an audience of local users, Attic weight silver tetradrachms such as those Parion and Lampsakos produced would circulate internationally and thus present the city's identity to a much broader cross-section of the Greek world. In the case of Parion, the decision to revive the reverse type of Apollo Aktaios sacrificing at an altar from the Group 1 tetradrachms advertised an important civic cult, asserted continuity with the past, and once again placed Parion in competition with the Athena Ilias and Apollo Smintheus coinages which the koinon of Athena Ilias and Alexandreia Troas continued to produce. In the case of Lampsakos, the portrait of Priapos commemorated a key episode in the city's recent history when the city's piety towards its gods had been rewarded by an epiphany in its hour of need and when the city's loyalty to Rome had been demonstrated in the most testing circumstances. In addition to this, the combination of a detailed portrait of Priapos on the obverse with a full-figure depiction of Apollo Kitharoidos flanked by the city's ethnic on the reverse clearly resembles the types of the Athena Ilias, Apollo Smintheus, and Apollo Aktaios coinages produced in the second century.[86] Lampsakos was therefore not just displaying its close relationship with Priapos, but also participating in peer-polity competition with other members of the *koinon* of Athena Ilias. While coin types and other questions of production were apparently still a matter of indifference to the Roman authorities in the early first century BC, from the perspective of the cities retaining control over these areas of production was a significant advantage. It is thus far from clear that the minting authorities of Lampsakos and Parion would have understood what we mean when we term such coinages "Roman," never mind "pseudo-civic."[87]

ACKNOWLEDGMENTS

It is a pleasure to thank the following curators for help with specimens in their collections: Julien Oliver (Paris), Amelia Dowler (London), Ute Wartenberg (New York), Helle Horsnaes (Copenhagen), Bernhard Weisser and Karsten Dahmen (Berlin). I am grateful to Andrew Meadows, François de Callataÿ, Philip Kinns, and Peter Thonemann for discussion of this paper at various stages and to the anonymous referee for a number of corrections.

86. Le Rider, "Numismatique grecque," 235.
87. For use of the term "pseudo-civic" in relation to such coinages see, e.g., Callataÿ, "The coinages struck for the Romans," 315.

PLATES

Plate 16

Parion Group 1

1. O1/R1 – BM 1996,0107.1.
2. O1/R2 – Nomos 5 (25/10/2011), lot 179.
3. O2/R3 – Gemini 1 (11/1/2005), lot 152.
4. O2/R4 – ANS 1991.99.1.

Plate 17

Parion Group 1

5. O3/R5 – Ira & Larry Goldberg 53 (26/5/2009), lot 1680.
6. O3/R6 – Numismatica Genevensis 8 (24/11/2014), lot 47.

Parion Group 2

7. O4/R7 (Polykles)—*BNF Fonds Général* 893 = *SNG Paris* 1401.
8. O4/R8 (Polykles)—Triton 20 (9/1/2017), lot 247.
9. O4/R9 (Mandrodikos)—BM 1896,0601.63.

Plate 18

Lampsakos: Ephesios, son of Theodoros

10. O1/R1—*BNF Fonds Général* 769 = *SNG Paris* 1230.

Lampsakos: Promethion son of Lampon (1)

11. O2/R2—BM 1900,1204.3.
12. O2/R3—ANS 1948.29.3.
13. O2/R4—*SNG Lewis* 825.
14. O2/R5 [Hoard?]—Elsen 102 (12/9/2009), lot 97.
15. O2/R6 [Hoard?]—Triton 8 (11/1/2005), lot 379.

Plate 19

Lampsakos: Andromachos son of Menophilos

16. O3/R7 [Hoard?]—ANS 1972.15.1.

Lampsakos: Herodes son of Dorotheus

17. O4/R8 [Hoard?]—NAC 2 (21/2/1990), lot 182.

Lampsakos: Demetrios son of Demetrios son of Meikalos

18. O4/R9 (1) [Hoard?]—Sotheby's Zurich (27/5/1974), lot 311.
19. O4/R9 (2) [Hoard?]—Boston MFA 1973.294.
20. O4/R10 (1) [Hoard?]—*SNG Cop.* Suppl. 306.

Plate 20

Lampsakos: Demetrios son of Demetrios son of Meikalos

21. O4/R10 (2) [Hoard?]—Morton & Eden 86 (24/5/2017), lot 27.
22. O4/R11 [Hoard?]—Nomos 3 (10/5/2011), lot 111.
23. O4/R12 (1) [Hoard?]—Lanz 28 (7/5/1984), lot 250.
24. O4/R12 (2) [Hoard?]—Bank Leu 7 (9/5/1973), lot 205.

Lampsakos: Promethion son of Lampon (2)

25. O5/R13—Berlin 18245862.

Lampsakos: Sokrates son of Xenophanes

26. O5/R14—BM RPK,p131D.1.Lam = *BMC Mysia* 86,68.

BIBLIOGRAPHY

Ashton, R. H. J. "The late Alexander tetradrachms of Knidos and ?Nisyros." *Numismatic Chronicle* 174 (2014): 19–22.

Badoud, N. *Le temps de Rhodes: une chronologie des inscriptions de la cité fondée sur l'étude de ses institutions.* Munich: C. H. Beck, 2015.

Baldwin, A. *Lampsakos: The Gold Staters, Silver and Bronze Coinages.* New York: American Numismatic Society, 1924.

Bellinger, A. *Troy: The Coins.* Princeton: Princeton University Press, 1961.

Boehringer, C. *Zur Chronologie mittelhellenistischer Münzserien, 220–160 v. Chr.* Berlin: De Gruyter, 1972.

Boulay, T. "Une épiphanie de Zeus Sôter à Clazomènes." *Revue Numismatique*[6] 165 (2009): 113–127.

Callataÿ, F. de. "Abydos sur Aesillas." In Χαρακτηρ. Αφιέρωμα στην Μαντώ Οικονομίδου, 81–91. Athens: TAP, 1996

―――. "Les monnaies hellénistiques en argent de Ténédos." In *Studies in Greek Numismatics in Memory of Martin Jessop Price*, edited by R. H. J. Ashton et al., 99–114. London: Spink, 1998.

―――. "More than it would seem: the use of coinage by the Romans in late Hellenistic Asia Minor (133–63 BC)." *American Journal of Numismatics* 23 (2011): 55–86.

―――. "The coinages of the Attalids and their neighbours: a quantified overview." In *Attalid Asia Minor: Money, International Relations, and the State*, edited by P. Thonemann, 207–244. Oxford: Oxford University Press.

―――. "The coinages struck for the Romans in Hellenistic Greece: a quantified overview (mid-2nd c.–mid-1st c. BCE)." In *Neue Forschungen zur Münzprägung der Römischen Republik: Beiträge zum internationalen Kolloquium im Residenzschloss Dresden 19.–21. Juni 2014*, edited by F. Haymann et al., 315–338. Bonn: Habelt Verlag, 2016.

Carter, G. F. "A simplified method for calculating the original number of dies from die link statistics." *ANS Museum Notes* 28 (1983): 195–206.

Crawford, M. *Coinage and Money under the Roman Republic. Italy and the Mediterranean Economy.* London: Methuen, 1985.

Ellis-Evans, A. "The koinon of Athena Ilias and its coinage." *American Journal of Numismatics* 28 (2016): 105–158.

―――. *The Kingdom of Priam. Lesbos and the Troad between Anatolia and the Aegean.* Oxford: Oxford University Press, 2019.

Esty, W. W. "The geometric model for estimating the number of dies." In *Quantifying Monetary Supplies in Greco-Roman Times*, edited by F. de Callataÿ, 43–58. Bari: Edipuglia, 2011.

Frisch, P. *Die Inschriften von Lampsakos*. Bonn.: Habelt, 1978.

Gaebler, H. "Die Silberprägung von Lampsakos. Eine chronologische Studie." *Nomisma* 12 (1923): 1–46.

Gauthier, P. "Compte rendu: G. Labarre, *Les cités de Lesbos aux époques hellénistique et impériale* (Lyon, 1996)." *Topoi* 7.1 (1997): 349–361.

Imhoof-Blumer, F. "Beiträge zur Erklärung griechischer Münztypen." *Nomisma* 8 (1913): 1–22.

Jones, C. P. "Events surrounding the bequest of Pergamon to Rome and the revolt of Aristonicos: new inscriptions from Metropolis." *Journal of Roman Archaeology* 17 (2014): 469–485.

Kinns, P. "Lunate letter forms in the 4th century and Hellenistic coinage of Ionia." *Numismatic Chronicle* 174 (2014): 1–15.

Le Rider, G. "Numismatique grecque." *AEPHE 1971–1972* (1972): 227–42.

Meadows, A. R. "Parion." *Numismatic Chronicle* 158 (1998): 41–46.

———. "The Hellenistic silver coinage of Clazomenae". In *Ancient History, Numismatics and Epigraphy in the Mediterranean World: Studies in Memory of Clemens E. Bosch and Sabahat Atlan and in Honour of Nezahat Baydur*, edited by O. Tekin, 247–262. Istanbul: Ege Yayınları, 2009.

———. "The great transformation. Civic coin design in the second century BC." In *ΤΥΠΟΙ. Greek and Roman Coins Seen through Their Images: Noble Issuers, Humble Users?*, edited by P. P. Iossif et al., 297–318. Liège: Presses Universitaires de Liège, 2018.

———. "The Penetration of the *denarius* and *quinarius* standards into Asia Minor in the 1st century BC." In *Graecia Capta? Roman Influence on Coinage and its Circulation in the Aegean Basin in the Second and First Centuries BC*, edited by R. Ashton and N. Badoud. Forthcoming.

Meadows, A. R., and A. Houghton. "The Gaziantep Hoard, 1994 (*CH* 9.527; 10.308)." In *Coin Hoards. X, Greek Hoards*, edited by O. Hoover, A. R. Meadows and U. Wartenberg, 172–223. New York: The American Numismatic Society, 2010.

Mørkholm, O. *Early Hellenistic Coinage: From the Accession of Alexander to the Peace of Apamea (336–188 BC)*. Cambridge: Cambridge University Press, 1991.

Müller, C., and F. Prost. "Un décret inédit du koinon des Ioniens trouvé à Claros." *Chiron* 43 (2013): 93–126.

Paunov, E. "Georgi Dobrevo/2000 reconsidered: note on a 1st-century BC coin hoard from Thrace." *Ancient West and East* 12 (2013): 281–294.

Petridou, G. *Divine Epiphany in Greek Literature and Culture*. Oxford: Oxford University Press, 2015.

Picard, O. "Les tétradrachmes à types thasiens et les guerres thraces au début du Ier siècle avant notre ère." *Comptes rendus de l'Académie des Inscriptions et Belles-Lettres* (2008): 465–493.

———. "Rome et la Grèce à la basse période hellénistique: monnaies et impérialisme." *Journal des Savants* (2010): 161–192.

Platt, V. *Facing the Gods: Epiphany and Representation in Graeco-Roman Art, Literature and Religion.* Cambridge: Cambridge University Press, 2011.

Prêteux, F. "Priapos Bébrykès dans la Propontide et les Détroits: succès d'un mythe local." *Revue d'égyptologie* 118.1 (2005): 246–265.

Robert, L. 1935. "Études sur les inscriptions et la topographie de la Grèce centrale. VI. Décrets d'Akraiphia." *Bulletin de correspondance hellénique* 59 (1935): 438–452 = *Opera Minora Selecta* 1: 279–293.

———. *Études anatoliennes: recherches sur les inscriptions grecques de l'Asie mineure.* Paris: Bonard, 1937.

———. "Divinités éponymes." In *Hellenica. Volume II,* 51–64, 154–155. Paris: Adrien-Maisonneuve, 1946.

———. "Apollons de Mysie. Apollon Kratéanos." In *Hellenica. Volume X,* 134–53. Paris: Adrien-Maisonneuve, 1955.

———. *Monnaies antiques en Troade.* Paris: Minard, 1966.

Robert, J., and L. Robert, "Inscriptions de l'Hellespont et de la Propontide." In *Hellenica. Volume IX: Inscriptions et reliefs d'Asie Mineure,* 78–97. Paris: Adrien-Maisonneuve, 1950.

———. "Une inscription grecque de Téos en Ionie. L'union de Téos et de Kyrbissos." *Journal des Savants* (1976): 153–235 = *Opera Minora Selecta* 7: 297–379.

Spring, J. *Ancient Coin Auction Catalogues, 1880–1980.* London: Spink and Son, 2009.

Thonemann, P. *The Hellenistic World: Using Coins as Sources.* Cambridge: Cambridge University Press, 2015.

Tréheux, J. "Décret de Lampsaque trouvé à Thasos." *Bulletin de correspondance hellénique* 77 (1953): 426–443.

Waddington, W. H. *Voyage en Asie-Mineure au point de vue numismatique.* Paris: M. Rollin, 1853.

Watson, P., and C. Todeschini. *The Medici Conspiracy: The Illicit Journey of Looted Antiquities, from Italy's Tomb Raiders to the World's Greatest Museums.* New York: Public Affairs, 2006.

AJN Second Series 32 (2020) pp. 127–156

New Evidence for the Introduction of the Roman *Denarius* System:
An Unpublished Hoard of Republican Bronzes from Morgantina (Sicily)

 D. Alex Walthall[*] and Anne E. Truetzel[**]

This article publishes a hoard of 23 bronze coins recovered in 1957 during controlled excavations at the site of Morgantina (Sicily). This small hoard primarily contained anonymous Roman Republican types, including coins of semilibral (*RRC* 38 and 40), post-semilibral (*RRC* 42), and sextantal (*RRC* 56, 69, 72) standard.[1] Although the hoard's contents and archaeological context are here fully published for the first time, T. V. Buttrey alluded to the importance of these coins in his two seminal articles on the Morgantina excavations and the date of the Roman *denarius*. Based on our recent analysis of the hoard's contents and archaeological context, we argue that—contrary to Buttrey's initial observations—the coins were buried shortly after the siege of 211 BCE, when the city fell to Roman forces under the command of M. Cornelius Cethegus, and not, as previously believed, in the period immediately preceding the siege.

* Department of Classics, University of Texas at Austin (dwalthall@austin.utexas.edu).

** Classics Department, Davidson College (antruetzel@davidson.edu).

1. For ease of reference, we use "sextantal" in this article as an *omnibus* term, referring to bronze coins struck variously during the Second Punic War on standards based on an *as* weighing between one-sixth and one-twelfth of a Roman pound (56–28 grams). As will be discussed in further detail below, A. McCabe, "The Anonymous Struck Bronze Coinage of the Roman Republic: A Provisional Arrangement," in *Essays in Honour of Roberto Russo*, eds. P. G. van Alfen and R. B. Witschonke (Zurich: Numismatica Ars Classica NAC AG, 2013), 219–22, has challenged the generally accepted idea of a single, official reduction of the Roman weight standard for bronze coinage to "sextantal," instead noting the variety of weight standards for Roman coins issued roughly contemporaneously in different locales during the Second Punic War.

When viewed within the wider context of numismatic deposits found across the archaeological site, the hoard in question joins a mounting body of evidence indicating that Roman bronze coinage of sextantal standard was not in circulation at Morgantina prior to the siege of 211 BCE. We conclude that the archaeological evidence from Morgantina does not support the long-held scholarly position that the Romans introduced the *denarius* and its fractions coincident with the sextantal standard for bronze coinage. Rather, the material record from Morgantina is more compatible with a scenario in which the first issues of the *denarius* or its fractions were in circulation in Sicily some months, or possibly years, prior to bronze coinage struck on the sextantal standard.[2]

INTRODUCTION

At the International Numismatic Congress held in Rome in 1961, T. V. Buttrey first advanced the now well-known argument that the fieldwork of the American Excavations at Morgantina had produced demonstrable evidence that the *denarius* system was introduced during the time of the Second Punic War.[3] In the subsequent publication of this talk in the *Atti del Congresso Internazionale di Numismatica*, Buttrey cited nearly a dozen hoards and stratigraphically-sealed coin deposits from the archaeological site at Morgantina, which collectively supported his conclusion that the *denarius* was introduced only a short time before the city was captured by the Romans in 211 BCE.[4] Among the most

2. We use the phrase "the *denarius* or its fractions" because, as discussed in the conclusion below, there is some evidence from Morgantina indicating that *victoriati* and fractions of the *denarius* (i.e., *quinarii, sestertii*) entered circulation in Sicily before *denarius* coins themselves.

3. T. V. Buttrey, "The Morgantina Excavations and the Date of the Roman Denarius," in *Atti del Congressso Internazionale di Numismatica 1961* (Rome, 1965). Buttrey found himself arguing against the proponents of a conservative chronology, which placed the introduction of the *denarius* around 268 BCE, as well as against the fashionable theory of the time, championed by Mattingly and Robinson, which dated the earliest *denarii* to 187 BCE. On the history of the debate between these two schools of thought, see F. Ronchi, "Il dibattito sulla data d'introduzione del denario nella moderna letteratura numismatica," *RIN* 99 (1998); B. E. Woytek, "The Denarius Coinage of the Roman Republic," in *The Oxford Handbook of Greek and Roman Coinage*, ed. W. E. Metcalf (Oxford: Oxford University Press, 2012), 316. Around the same time as Buttrey, R. Thomsen (*Early Roman Coinage*, 3 vols. [Copenhagen: Nationalmuseet, 1957–1961]) independently arrived at a similar conclusion on the date of the earliest *denarii*, based on his critical reassessment of the available numismatic evidence. M. H. Crawford, in *Roman Republican Coinage* (*RRC*, 28–35), presented the most comprehensive case for dating the introduction of the *denarius* to 211 BCE or immediately before; reassertion of this position can be found in A. M. Burnett and M. H. Crawford, "Coinage, Money, and Mid-Republican Rome: Reflections on a Recent Book by Filippo Coarelli," *AIIN* 60 (2014), 257.

4. Buttrey, "Morgantina Excavations," adopted a position popular at the time that Morgantina was twice recaptured, once in 214 BCE and once in 211 BCE. However, by the time of his

important of these deposits for Buttrey's argument was a hoard comprising 36 anonymous *quinarii* and *sestertii* and one 20-*as* gold piece, which had been thrown into a domestic cistern prior to the Roman siege of the city but was never recovered in antiquity.[5] The house in which this hoard was discovered, aptly named by archaeologists the "House of the Silver Hoard," was abandoned after the siege and never reoccupied. In the same article, Buttrey also noted the existence of a second hoard, composed exclusively of bronze coins, which he believed also had been found within the House of the Silver Hoard.[6] This bronze hoard, hereafter referred to as "the East Hill Hoard," consisted primarily of Roman Republican issues, including bronzes of reduced sextantal standard with grain ear and **KA** mint mark. Although Buttrey's article principally focused on deposits containing silver denominations from the earliest phases of the *denarius* system, this bronze hoard merited inclusion since at that time (as now) it was widely believed that the Romans had initiated production of the *denarius*

next publication on the subject, "Morgantina and the Denarius," *NAC* 8 (1979), 150, Buttrey appears to have changed his mind, accepting what remains the current *communis opinio* among archaeologists of the American Excavations at Morgantina, namely that the city suffered only one violent episode, which took place in 211 BCE following the siege led by the Roman praetor M. Cornelius Cethegus; see also D. A. Walthall, "Numismatic Material from Late Third-Century Contexts at Morgantina (Sicily)," *AJN* 29 (2017), 102, n. 2, with Livy 24.36.8–10, 26.21.14–17. A. M. Burnett's study of Punic coins minted in Akragas in 213–210 BCE ("The Coinage of Punic Sicily during the Hannibalic War," in *La Sicilia tra l'Egitto e Roma. La monetazione siracusana dell'età di Ierone II. Atti del Seminario di Studi, Messina 2–4 Dicembre, 1993*, ed. M. Caccamo Caltabiano [Messina: Accademia Peloritana dei Pericolanti, 1995], 386), confirms that the single episode of destruction at Morgantina must have taken place in 211 BCE rather than 214 BCE, as half-*shekels* and quarter-*shekels* struck at the Punic mint are found below destruction layers at the site; see also R. R. Holloway, "Monete provenienti dagli scavi di Morgantina e già attribuite a Hiempsal II," *AIIN* 7–8 (1960–1961). On the timeline and historical narrative of the siege, also see M. Bell, "A Stamp with the Monogram of Morgantina and the Sign of Tanit," in *Damarato: Studi di antichità offerti a Paola Pelagatti*, ed. I. Berlingò *et al.* (Milan: Electa, 2000).

5. Buttrey, "Morgantina Excavations," 263–264. Additional information on this hoard was later published in *MS* II, Deposit no. 25. In both Buttrey's article and MS II, the coins are called a deposit, but it is clear from the trench supervisor's notebook that these coins belonged together as a discrete hoard.

6. Buttrey ("Morgantina Excavations," 264–265), referring to this bronze hoard, writes, "There is some evidence from Morgantina for the chronology of the earliest sextantal bronze, and it is not surprising to find that this evidence is very like that presented with regard to the denarius. In the house from whose cistern the gold and silver coins were taken a second coin deposit was found, this consisting solely of bronze coins. The four Greek coins are of the third century B.C. The Roman range from a piece of aes grave to a number of sextantal (or better, reduced sextantal) sextantes with grain ear symbol, or grain ear plus **KA** monogram." As with the aforementioned silver hoard, Buttrey uses the term deposit, but the trench supervisor's notebook clarifies that these bronze coins formed a discrete hoard.

and its fractions concurrently with the adoption of the sextantal standard for their bronze coinage.[7] The discovery of both sextantal bronzes and anonymous silver *quinarii* and *sestertii* within this same house thus provided Buttrey with compelling evidence that these issues were in circulation by 211 BCE and that the introduction of the integrated *denarius* system must have predated the siege of Morgantina.

Recognizing the opportunity to advance Buttrey's observations, we undertook a program to study the coins of the East Hill Hoard alongside the archaeologist's notebook in which their initial discovery was recorded. In the course of our research, we found that—contrary to Buttrey's initial belief—archaeologists did not discover this hoard within the House of the Silver Hoard, but instead recovered it from the public street that ran immediately to the south of the house. Additionally, in revisiting the contents of the hoard, we found cause to revise the original identifications for several of the individual coins, based on recent scholarship on anonymous republican bronzes.[8] In what follows, we fully publish for the first time a detailed description of the archaeological context of the hoard and a complete catalog of its contents.[9]

In recent years, numismatists have challenged the now traditional chronology of the *denarius* system, as established in part by Buttrey's analysis of the evidence from Morgantina.[10] Our reassessment of the East Hill Hoard joins this growing

7. *RRC*, 6–7, with citation of earlier scholarship.

8. Most notably, R. Russo, "Unpublished Roman Republican Bronze Coins," in *Coins of Macedonia and Rome: Essays in Honour of Charles Hersh*, eds. A. M. Burnett, U. Wartenberg, and R.B. Witschonke (London: Spink, 1998), and McCabe, "Anonymous Struck Bronze Coinage."

9. Unlike the hoard of silver coins from the House of the Silver Hoard, the East Hill Hoard does not appear among the stratigraphically-related coins published in *MS* II. And, while several of the bronze coins that comprise the hoard were included in the catalog of *MS* II as representative entries of individual types (e.g., Cat. No. 9; inv. 57-2764), no reference is made to their original context.

10. A number of scholars have sought to push back the date for the introduction of the *denarius* and its silver fractions by upwards of several years. See, for instance, P. Marchetti, "La datation du denier romain et les fouilles de Morgantina," *RBN* 117 (1971), and "Numismatique romaine et histoire," *CCG* 4 (1993): 30–35; M. Caccamo Caltabiano, "Il tesoretto di oro 'marziale' da Agrigento e il problema delle origini del sistema denariale," in *Actes du XIe Congrès international de numismatique: organisé a l'occasion du 150e anniversaire de la Société Royale de Numismatique de Belgique, Bruxelles, 8–13 septembre 1991*, eds. T. Hackens and G. Moucharte (Louvain-la-Neuve: Séminaire de Numismatique Marcel Hoc, 1993), and "I ritrovamenti siciliani e l'introduzione del sistema denariale," in *Studi sulla moneta e sulla circolazione monetale in Italia. Tavola Rotonda in margine alla mostra 'Roma e il suo fiume'* (Conference Proceedings Roma 1994), 2004, 1–19; W. T. Loomis, "The Introduction of the Denarius," in *Transitions to Empire: Essays in Greco-Roman History, 360–146 BC, in Honor of E. Badian*, eds. R.W. Wallace

body of scholarship aimed at refining our understanding of the early stages of the *denarius* system. While our research does not impinge upon Buttrey's observations about the date of the introduction of the *denarius*, it has led us to conclude that bronze coinage of sextantal standard was not present at Morgantina before the Roman siege of 211 BCE. To date, no sextantal bronze coins have been identified from 211 BCE destruction and abandonment layers at the site, despite the discovery therein of a large number of early silver *denarii, quinarii, sestertii,* and *victoriati*.[11] Although this circumstance may be an accident of deposition or recovery, the total absence of sextantal bronzes from pre-211 BCE contexts across the site of Morgantina is more likely a reflection of circulation patterns at the time, especially in consideration of the many Roman republican bronzes of heavier standards (semilibral, post-semilibral) that have been found in commercial, domestic, and sacred contexts predating the capture of the city. Thus, the data that have emerged from a renewed investigation of numismatic deposits at Morgantina support the conclusion that in Sicily the *denarius* and its fractions were circulating at an earlier date than bronze coinage of sextantal standard, perhaps by a year or more.[12]

ARCHAEOLOGICAL CONTEXT

During the 1957 campaign of the American Excavations at Morgantina, archaeologists discovered a hoard of bronze coins while excavating on the East Hill, a residential quarter that once rose above the city's agora (Fig. 1). In his field note-

and E. M. Harris (Norman: University of Oklahoma Press, 1996); A. R. Meadows, "The Mars/ eagle and thunderbolt gold and Ptolemaic involvement in the Second Punic War," in Burnett et al,. *Coins of Macedonia and Rome: Essays in Honour of Charles Hersh*, 133; P. Debernardi, "CR 44 e le origini del denario," *Panorama Numismatico* 264 (2011); P. Debernardi and O. Legrand, "The Dates of the Quadragati," *AIIN* 60 (2014): 225; Walthall, "Numismatic Material," 114–15. McCabe ("Anonymous Struck Bronze Coinage") has reexamined the classification and chronology of anonymous struck bronze coins, including those associated with the earliest issues of the *denarius* and its fractions; see note 12 below for further discussion.

11. We are not alone in calling attention to the absence of sextantal bronzes from 211 BCE destruction and abandonment contexts; S. Frey-Kupper (*StIet* X, 197–98, and "Coins and Contacts," in *Tas-Silg, Marsaxlokk (Malta) I: Archaeological Excavations Conducted by the University of Malta, 1996-2005*, eds. A. Bonanno and N. C. Vella [Leuven: Peeters, 2015], 379) has previously noted that specimens of *RRC* 69/6 are conspicuously absent from the 211 BCE contexts published in *MS* II.

12. This conclusion is consistent with recent arguments made by McCabe, "Anonymous Struck Bronze Coinage"; he contends that the "data does not necessarily support the generally accepted story of a 120:1 silver bronze ratio, nor of a decisive sextantal reduction step, nor of a relationship between that reduction step and the very first *denarius* issue" (221), and he discusses links between the early *denarius* and post-semilibral bronzes (222–223).

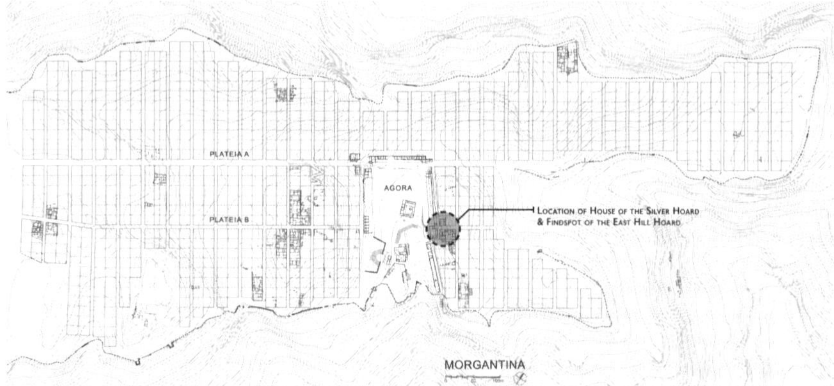

Figure 1. Plan of Morgantina, indicating location of the House of the Silver Hoard and findspot of the East Hill Hoard. Image after E. Thorkildsen 2017.

book entry for 29 April, trench supervisor Kyle M. Phillips, Jr. recorded a hoard containing twenty-three bronze coins recovered during work in the immediate vicinity of a modest residence of Hellenistic date, referred to by its excavators as the "House of the Silver Hoard" (Fig. 2). The coins were found together, though not in a container, in a stratum identified by Phillips as the packing for a beaten-earth pavement that lay over the irregular surface of the East Hill's bedrock.

At the time, Phillips believed that he and his team were working within the limits of the House of the Silver Hoard, where, during the previous season of excavations, the aforementioned hoard of anonymous *sestertii* and *quinarii* had been recovered from a cistern.[13] Phillips's assumption is understandable, given the proximity of the hoard to the previous year's trench, as well as the fact that 1957 was only the third season of American excavations at the site and the archaeologists were not yet aware that they were excavating an urban center organized according to an orthogonal grid plan. The subsequent identification of the urban street grid, composed of two broad east-west avenues (*plateiai*) intersected at right angles by cross-streets (*stenopoi*), has made it clear that, in fact, Phillips and his team were excavating a portion of an ancient avenue (*Plateia* B), which ran east-west between the House of the Silver Hoard to its north and the so-called "House of the Doric Capital" to its south. Based on Phillips's sketches and the measured plan of his excavation, it is evident that the coins of the East Hill Hoard were found close to the middle of the avenue, just below a line of stones forming a step that facilitated foot traffic up and down the slope of the hillside.

---

13. For the contents and context of the cistern hoard, see Buttrey, "Morgantina Excavations," 263–64; *PR* I, 158; *MS* II, Deposit no. 25.

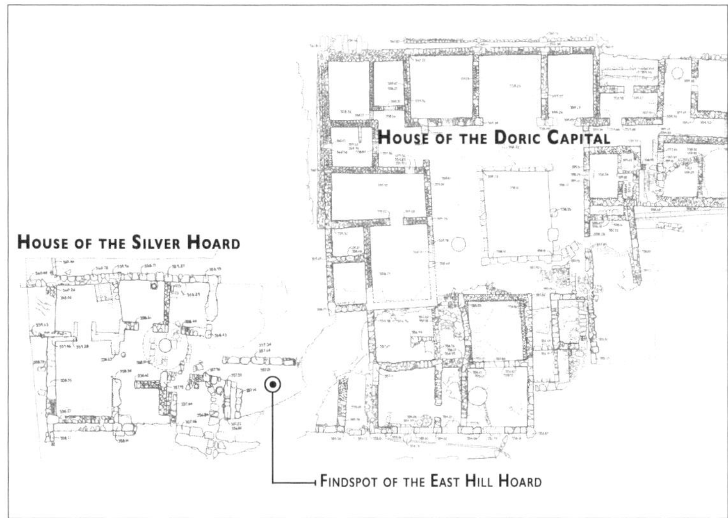

Figure 2. Plan of the House of the Silver Hoard and the House of the Doric Capital, indicating findspot of the East Hill Hoard. Image after D. Bylund 1986.

Contrary to Phillips' initial supposition, which was echoed in Buttrey's published remarks on the hoard, these coins were buried some four meters to the south of the House of the Silver Hoard, not inside it. Recognition of the hoard's location in the street allows its deposition to be decoupled from the fate of the House of the Silver Hoard, for which there is ample evidence of abandonment due to the siege of 211 BCE.[14] And, in fact, while some houses on the East Hill show clear signs of acute violence and abandonment during the time of the siege, others appear to have emerged relatively unscathed. The latter include the neighboring House of the Doric Capital, which saw continued occupation into the 30s BCE.[15]

14. At several points within the House of the Silver Hoard, archaeologists encountered the remains of a tile fall resting above a layer of soil with concentrations of ash and signs of burning. In addition to these clear signs of violence inside the building, the latest numismatic material discovered within and below the destruction layer—including the eponymous silver hoard from the courtyard cistern—dates to the decade of the 210s BCE (*MS* II, Deposit no. 25). Aside from the cistern hoard, excavators found five coins below the layer of fallen tiles inside the house (*MS* II, Deposit no. 26); all five coins date to 211 BCE or earlier. B. Tsakirgis, "The Domestic Architecture of Morgantina in the Hellenistic and Roman Periods" (PhD diss., Princeton University, 1984), 43–46, provides a succinct discussion of the house and its archaeological remains. S.C. Stone (*MS* VI, 37) notes that the ceramics recovered from the cistern support a date of 211 BCE for its closure.

15. The House of the Doric Capital was very likely a victim of a violent episode that befell the city in the 30s BCE, when it is believed that pro-Octavian forces carried out punitive campaigns against Sicilian cities that had supported Sextus Pompey; see S. C. Stone, "Sextus Pompeius,

CATALOGUE

Mamertine

Obverse: Head of Ares r.
Reverse: Athena charging r.

Date: Before 211 BCE.[16]
Ref.: *MS* II, no. 224; Särström X. A; *SNG Cop.*, nos. 844–845.

   1. Inv. 57-2770. (Pl. 21, 1). AE. 23.98 mm, 5.37 g, 9h.

Syracuse

Obverse: Head of Persephone l.
Reverse: Bull butting l.; above, club with T; below, IE.

Denomination: Hemilitron.
Date: c. 276–269/263 BCE.[17]

Ref.: *MS* II, no. 324ii; Gàbrici, nos. 173–77; *SNG München*, nos. 1234–1235; *StIet* X, nos. 594–595.

   2. Inv. 57-2756. (Pl. 21, 2). AE. 19.67 mm, 5.99 g, 7h.

Obverse: Head of Poseidon l., diademed.
Reverse: Ornamental trident head; at either side, a dolphin; below, ΙΕΡΩ-ΝΟΣ, and ΣΩ at lower right.

Denomination: Litra.

Octavianus and Sicily," in *Sextus Pompeius*, eds. A. Powell and K. Welch (Swansea: Classical Press of Wales, 2002), 142–144. Below the tile fall and destruction layers within the house, archaeologists found ceramics datable to the first century BCE (e.g., pre-sigillata, late Campana C) as well as Roman *denarii* of the second half of the first century BCE, including specimens of *RRC* 462/1 (47–46 BCE) and *RRC* 485/1 (43 BCE). For discussion of the archaeological remains of the House of the Doric Capital, see Tsakirgis, "Domestic Architecture," 146–170; see also *PR* I, 156–57 and *PR* II, 161, where it is referred to as "the Villa."

   16. For a recent review of the chronology of Mamertine coinage, see M. H. Crawford, "The Coinage of the Mamertini," in *Studies in Ancient Coinage in Honour of Andrew Burnett*, eds. R. Bland and D. Calomino (London: Spink, 2015).

   17. Regarding the early Hieronian date for the Persephone/Bull series, see M. Bell, "Monete ieroniche in nuovi contesti di scavo a Morgantina," in Caccamo Caltabiano, *La Sicilia*, 291–92; M. Caccamo Caltabiano *et al*, "Il sistema monetale ieroniano: cronologia e problemi," in Caccamo Caltabiano, *La Sicilia*, 214–16. The date is further supported by Frey-Kupper (*StIet* X, 156–159) on the basis of the evidence from Southern Italy.

Date: c. 241–215 BCE.[18] *Small-flan series.*
Ref. *MS* II, no. 368s; Gàbrici, nos. 483–88; *SNG Cop.*, no. 856; *StIet* X, nos. 619–20.

3. Inv. 57-2757. (Pl. 21, 3). AE. 19.98 mm, 6.51 g, 5h.

Punic (Western Sicily)

Obverse: Palm.

Reverse: Pegasos flying l.

Date: c. 290/280–260 BCE.[19]
Ref.: *MS* II, no. 434; *SNG Cop.*, nos. 1018–19; *StIet* X, nos. 1099–1107.

4. Inv. 57-2758. (Pl. 21, 4). AE. 16.71 mm, 2.61 g, 3h.

Rome

Obverse: Head of Roma l.
Reverse: Prow r.; above, ROMA.

Denomination: Semilibral *uncia.*
Date: c. 217–215 BCE.[20]
Ref.: *MS* II, no. 496; *RRC* 38/6; McCabe 2013, Group AA.

5. Inv. 57-2759. (Pl. 21, 5). AE. 24.21 mm, 14.02g, 11h.

Obverse: Head of Hercules l.
Reverse: Prow l.; above, corn-ear.

Denomination: Semilibral *quadrans.*
Date: c. 216 BCE.
Ref.: *MS* II, no. 494; *RRC* 40/1.[21]

---

18. For this date range, see Bell, "Monete ieroniche," 292. Caccamo Caltabiano *et al*, "Il sistema monetale ieroniano," 224–25, and *Siracusa ellenistica: le monete "regali" di Ierone II, della sua famiglia e dei siracusani* (Messina: Accademia Peloritana dei Pericolanti, 1997), 33, have posited 220 / 218 BCE as the start date for the small-flan Poseidon/Trident series, on the basis of similarities between the control-marks on these coins and those minted by Hieronymos (r. 215–214 BCE); for evaluation of Caltabiano's argument and restatement of support for the higher date range, see Frey-Kupper's analysis in *StIet* X, 162–163.

19. For date and discussion, see *StIet* X, 136–138.

20. All dates provided for Roman coins are those established in *RRC*.

21. Traces of a grain ear visible above the prow on the reverse of this coin indicate that it is an example of *RRC* 40/1, rather than *RRC* 38/4, as it is listed in *MS* II. We thank Andrew McCabe for his assistance with the identification of this coin.

6. Inv. 57-2750. (Pl. 21, 6). AE. 36.96 mm, 47.51 g, 12h. Cast.

Obverse: Head of Mercury r.
Reverse: Prow r.; above, grain ear and ROMA.

Denomination: Post-semilibral *sextans*.
Date: c. 214–212 BCE.

Ref.: *MS* II, no. 502; *RRC* 42/3.[22]

7. Inv. 57-2751. (Pl. 21, 7). AE. 25.76 mm, 12.65 g, 4h.

Obverse: Head of Roma r.
Reverse: Prow r.; above, ROMA.

Denomination: Post-semilibral *uncia*.
Date: c. 214–212 BCE.
Ref.: *MS* II –; *RRC* –; McCabe 2013, Group B1.[23]

8. Inv. 57-2762. (Pl. 21, 8). AE. 22.18 mm, 6.38 g, 11h.

Obverse: Head of Saturn r.
Reverse: Prow r.; below, ROMA.

Denomination: *Semis*.
Date: After 211 BCE.
Ref.: *MS* II, no. 511; *RRC* 56/3; McCabe 2013, Group G2.

9. Inv. 57-2764. (Pl. 21, 9). AE. 28.17 mm, 19.59 g, 8h.

Obverse: Head of Mercury r.
Reverse: Prow r.; above, corn-ear and ROMA.

Denomination: *Sextans*.
Date: c. 211–210 BCE.

22. Our attribution as *RRC* 42/3, rather than *RRC* 72/8, is based on this coin's relatively heavy weight. It should be noted, however, that there is increasing scholarly doubt as to whether these two series can be distinguished from one another on the basis of weight or any other criterion; see R. Russo, *The RBW Collection of Roman Republican Coins: Part I* (Zurich: Numismatica Ars Classica NAC AG, 2011), 46; McCabe, "Anonymous Struck Bronze Coinage," 108, n. 23.

23. This group of coins is related to *RRC* 42 and *RRC* 72 but lacks their characteristic corn-ear above the prow on the reverse. Coins of this type do not appear as a separate series in *RRC*, but were first published by Russo, "Unpublished Roman Republican Bronze Coins," nos. 29–36, and are further discussed by McCabe, "Anonymous Struck Bronze Coinage," 130–131. We believe that this specific coin is misidentified in *MS* II, where it is listed as an example of *RRC* 41/10.

Ref.: *MS* II, no. 524; *RRC* 72/8.[24]

   10. Inv. 57-2763. (Pl. 22, 10). AE. 22.05 mm, 6.80 g, 3h.

Obverse: Head of Hercules r.
Reverse: Bull charging r.; above, corn-ear; below, snake.

Denomination: *Quadrans.*
Date: c. 211–208 BCE.
Ref.: *MS* II –; *RRC* 69/5.[25]

   11. Inv. 57-2771. (Pl. 22, 11). AE. 21.26 mm, 5.52 g, 7h. Overstruck on a
bronze *litra* of Hieron II (Undertype: Poseidon/Trident; *MS* II, no. 368;
Gàbrici, nos. 442–89).[26]

Obverse: Head of Mercury r.
Reverse: Prow r.; above, corn-ear; below, ROMA; at right, KA or IC or C.

Denomination: *Sextans.*
Date: c. 211–208 BCE.
Ref.: *MS* II, no. 520; *RRC* 69/6.

   12. Inv. 57-2752. (Pl. 22, 12). AE. 21.00 mm, 5.97 g, 1h.
   13. Inv. 57-2753. (Pl. 22, 13). AE. 20.03 mm, 5.32 g, 3h. Overstruck on a
bronze *litra* of Hieron II (Undertype: Poseidon/Trident; *MS* II, no. 368;
Gàbrici, nos. 442–89).[27]
   14. Inv. 57-2754. (Pl. 22, 14). AE. 19.86 mm, 6.36 g, 11h.

24. Our attribution as *RRC* 72/8, rather than *RRC* 42/3, is based on this coin's relatively light
weight, but see note 22 above for recent debate over the feasibility of distinguishing between
these two series.

25. Due to its style and light weight, we believe that this specific coin is an example of *RRC*
69/5, rather than *RRC* 72/7, as it is incorrectly designated in *MS* II. *RRC* 69 and *RRC* 72 *quadran-
tes* are easily confused, as the former lack the KA / IC / C mintmark that appears on the other
denominations of this series and most clearly distinguishes it from *RRC* 72.

26. For overstrikes of Roman types on small denominations of Hieron II (r. 269–215 BC),
see C. A. Hersh, "Overstrikes as Evidence for the History of Roman Republican Coinage," *NC*
13 (1953), 41–43, 49–50. Examples of *RRC* 69/5 overstruck on Poseidon/Trident undertypes are
well-attested (e.g., *RRC* Table XVIII, nos. 64a–f).

27. This particular overstrike, *RRC* 69/6 struck on a Poseidon/Trident undertype, is very common (e.g., *RRC* Table XVIII, nos. 65a–s). See also the recently published examples from Monte
Iato in northwestern Sicily (*StIet* X, nos. 1200–1204, 1206–1208, 1210, 1213, 1216), as well as
those from Lilybaeum on the island's western coast in S. Frey-Kupper, "I ritrovamenti monetali,"
in *La necropoli di Lilybaeum*, ed. B. Bechtold (Palermo: Regione Siciliana. Assessorato dei Beni
Culturali ed Ambientali e della Pubblica Istruzione, 1999), nos. 131, 137–139, 147, 161–162, 183.

15. Inv. 57-2755. (Pl. 22, 15). AE. 19.73 mm, 5.75 g, 7h. IC visible to r. Overstruck on a bronze *litra* of Hieron II (Undertype: Poseidon/Trident; *MS* II, no. 368; Gàbrici, nos. 442–89)

16. Inv. 57-2760. (Pl. 22, 16). AE. 20.14 mm, 6.89 g, 1h. KA visible to r.

17. Inv. 57-2761. (Pl. 22, 17). AE. 20.13 mm, 5.84 g, 11h. Overstruck on a bronze *litra* of Hieron II (Undertype: Poseidon/Trident; *MS* II, no. 368; Gàbrici, nos. 442–89)

18. Inv. 57-2765. (Pl. 22, 18). AE. 19.76 mm, 5.02 g, 11h. KA visible to r.

19. Inv. 57-2766. (Pl. 22, 19). AE. 21.04 mm, 6.49 g, 6h. KA visible to r.

20. Inv. 57-2767. (Pl. 22, 20). AE. 19.59 mm, 5.70 g, 12h. C visible to r.

21. Inv. 57-2768. (Pl. 22, 21). AE. 21.00 mm, 5.50 g, 1h. Overstruck on a bronze *litra* of Hieron II (Undertype: Poseidon/Trident; *MS* II, no. 368; Gàbrici, nos. 442–89)

22. Inv. 57-2769. (Pl. 22, 22). AE. 20.77 mm, 6.12 g, 3h. IC visible to r.

23. Inv. 57-1089. (Pl. 22, 23). AE. 19.00 mm, 5.70 g, 5h.

DATE OF DEPOSITION

The archaeological context of the East Hill Hoard does not provide conclusive evidence for its date of deposition. The associated archaeological materials produced by Phillips' excavation in the vicinity of the hoard point to a general date around the last two decades of the third century BCE but do not contribute substantially to refining this date range, as the hoard itself is the latest datable deposit from the trench.[28] Moreover, because our reevaluation of Phillips' archaeological findings revealed that the hoard was deposited in the avenue running to the south of the House of the Silver Hoard rather than within the house itself, this building's well-supported abandonment date of 211 BCE can no longer provide a definitive *terminus ante quem* for the hoard's deposition. This, of course, does not preclude burial prior to 211 BCE, but a post-211 BCE closing

28. Apart from the hoard, Phillips' excavations produced ceramics described as being of mid-third-century BCE date, as well as a few fragmentary terracotta figurines, also of third-century manufacture. Additionally, Phillips recorded several other individual coin finds from the area of the street, the latest of which, a *sextans* of sextantal standard (*RRC* 69/6), is of the same type as twelve of the coins in the East Hill Hoard. From the uppermost stratum (stratum 1), Phillips records three Syracusan coins (1: inv. 57-1020, Agathokles, *MS* II, no. 329; 2: inv. 57-1026, Hieron II, *MS* II, no. 368; 3: inv. 57-1060, Hieron II, *MS* II, no. 368); one Siculo-Punic coin (inv. 57-1059, *MS* II, no. 433), one coin from the mint of Tauromenium (inv. 57-1064, *MS* II, no. 409); and two Roman republican *unciae* of post-semilibral standard (inv. 57-1061 and 57-1063, *RRC* 42/4). In the lower stratum (stratum 2), from which the East Hill Hoard was recovered, Phillips records one Roman republican *sextans* of sextantal standard (inv. 57-1062, *RRC* 69/6); it is evident from his notebook entry that this *sextans* was found several meters away from the hoard and thus was not part of the hoard.

date for the hoard emerges as the more compelling option in light of the hoard's composition.

The latest coins of the East Hill Hoard are Roman Republican bronzes of sextantal standard, all struck during the Second Punic War, including an anonymous *semis* (*RRC* 56/3), a *sextans* with grain ear (*RRC* 72/8), a *quadrans* with grain ear (*RRC* 69/5), and twelve *sextantes* with grain ear and mintmark KA, IC, or C (*RRC* 69/6). Although it is generally accepted that the adoption of the sextantal standard coincided with the introduction of the *denarius*, and Buttrey marshaled convincing evidence from Morgantina for a pre-211 BCE date for the latter, the site has not produced comparable evidence for sextantal bronzes.[29] In fact, despite their prevalence in later contexts at Morgantina, bronze coins of sextantal standard have yet to be recovered in or below 211 BCE destruction and abandonment layers.[30] Post-semilibral *unciae* (*RRC* 42/4) are the latest and most common Roman bronze coins that appear in these contexts (Table 1).[31] This stratigraphic pattern is quite pronounced and obtains across the ancient site, suggesting that bronzes of sextantal standard first arrived at Morgantina only in the wake of the siege and not before (Fig. 3).

The notable absence of sextantal bronzes from deposits formed prior to 211 BCE at Morgantina is echoed in the hoard evidence found elsewhere in Sicily. Bronze coins of sextantal standard are rarely attested in Sicilian hoards of the Second Punic War, and specimens of the *RRC* 56 and *RRC* 69 series are not found in any hoards thought to predate 211 BCE (Fig. 4).[32] Post-semilibral

29. For Buttrey's line of argumentation, see pp. 1–2 above, with citations.

30. Fifty-nine bronze coins of the *RRC* 69 series, eleven of the *RRC* 72 series, and ten of the *RRC* 56 series are published in *MS* II, but no specimens of these series appear among the stratigraphically-sealed coin deposits associated with the siege of 211 BCE. Similarly, not one of the twenty sextantal bronzes found in controlled excavations since 1982 was recovered from a pre-211 BCE context. Although Buttrey, "Morgantina and the Denarius," 151, asserted that "denominations of the new system in all three metals" had been recovered from destruction layers at Morgantina, in the case of sextantal bronzes this conclusion was based exclusively on the East Hill Hoard and, in light of our findings, can no longer hold.

31. See, for instance, *MS* II, Deposit nos. 27–28, 30, 56, 62, 65; and, more recently, Walthall, "Numismatic Material," 118. Frey-Kupper (*StIet* X, 197–98) makes a similar observation.

32. Omitted from this chart is a hoard briefly seen by G. Manganaro, "Un ripostiglio siciliano del 214–211 a.C. e la datazione del denarius," *JNG* 31–32 (1981–1982): 52, n. 70, before its contents were dispersed on the market. Manganaro states that specimens of *RRC* 56/6 and 72/9 were among the contents of this hoard. However, we find that it is difficult to draw definitive conclusions in the absence of any contextual information or a complete list of the hoard's contents. Also omitted is the Adrano hoard (*RRCH* 69), which was originally thought to include a post-semilibral *quadrans* (*RRC* 42/2). However, subsequent examination of the hoard by P. Marchetti, *Histoire économique et monétaire de la deuxième guerre punique* (Brussels: Palais des Académies, 1978), 492, n. 194, revealed that this coin was mistakenly placed on the tray with the hoard; see also Crawford, "Coinage of the Mamertini," 45.

Table 1. Roman Republican coins found below 211-BCE destruction contexts at Morgantina.

Location	Map Reference	Semilibral Bronze	Post-Semilibral Bronze		Gold and Silver Coins of the *Denarius* System						Sextantal Bronze			Reference
		RRC 38/7	*RRC* 42/3	*RRC* 42/4	*RRC* 44/1 victoriatus	*RRC* 44/5 denarius	*RRC* 44/6 quinarius	*RRC* 44/7 sestertius	*RRC* 72/1 victoriatus	*RRC* 72/2 20-as piece	*RRC* 56 series	*RRC* 69 series	*RRC* 72 series	
House of the Silver Hoard (East Hill)	1						8	27		1				*MSII* Deposit 25
Central Shops (Agora)	2	1		10				2						*MSII* Deposits 27-28 Walthall (2017)
South Shops (Agora)	3			3										*MSII* Deposit 56
South Sanctuary (West Hill)	4			3	4	1	3	3						*MSII* Deposit 29-30
House of the Antefixes (West Hill)	5			1										*MSII* Deposit 58
North Sanctuary Annex (Area IV)	6			1										*MSII* Deposit 35
House (Area V)	7		1											*MSII* Deposit 36
House (Papa Hill)	8								1					Walthall (2017)
House of Two Skeletons (Contrada Agnese)	9		1	2										*MSII* Deposit 65

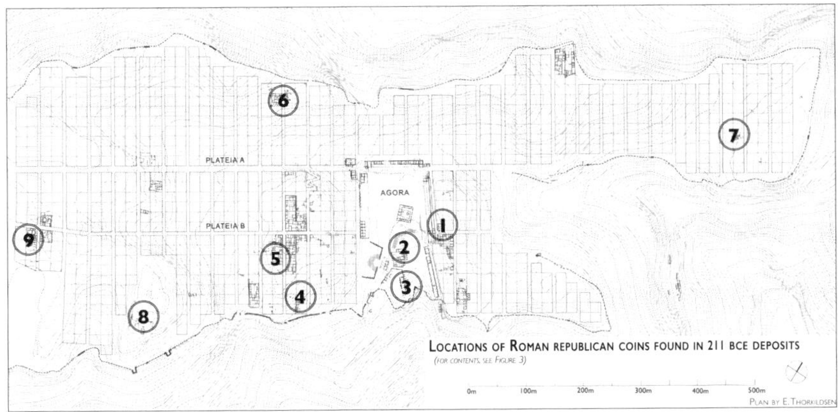

Figure 3. Plan showing locations of Roman Republican coins found in 211-BCE deposits at Morgantina. Image after E. Thorkildsen 2017.

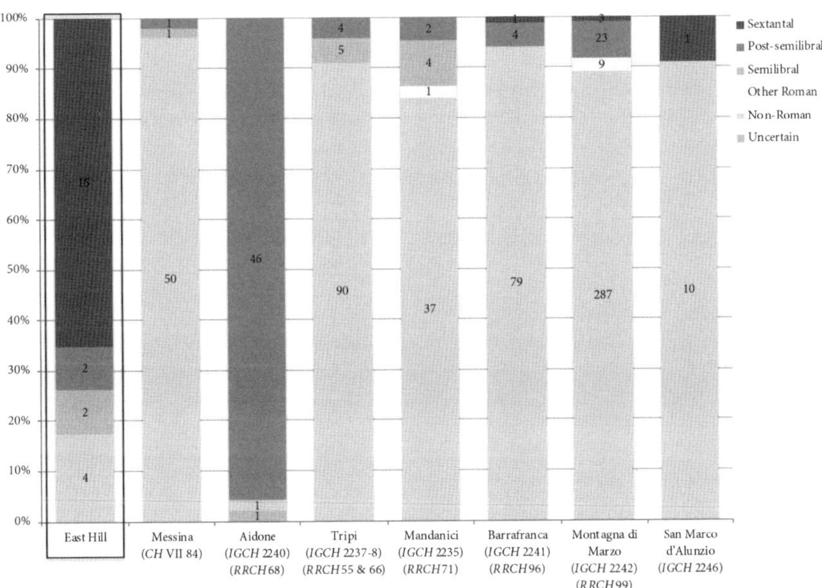

Figure 4. Contents of Sicilian hoards of bronze coins from the era of the Second Punic War.

bronzes are the latest Roman coins in the Messina,[33] Aidone,[34] Tripi,[35] and Mandanici[36] hoards. Among the few contemporary Sicilian hoards which contain coins of sextantal standard, at least two have closing dates later than 211 BCE. These are: (1) the San Marco d'Alunzio hoard,[37] with one reduced sextantal *quadrans* with grain ear (*RRC* 69/5); and (2) the Grammichele hoard,[38] which contains a small number of Roman republican bronzes "to sextantal" standard. Scholars have consistently dated the San Marco d'Alunzio hoard to the end of

33. Messina hoard: *CH* VII, no. 84; Crawford, "Coinage of the Mamertini," 43.

34. Aidone hoard: *IGCH* 2240; *RRCH* 68; *CMRR*, 111, 306; *MS* II, 183; G. Manganaro, *Pace e guerra nella Sicilia tardo-ellenistica e romana (215 a.C.–14 d.C.): Ricerche storiche e numismatiche* (Bonn: Habelt, 2012), 32nXIV. This hoard was found in Aidone, near ancient Morgantina, in 1908. The contents of another hoard of bronze coins reportedly found in Aidone in 1909 (*IGCH* 2239) have been aggregated with the coins of the Aidone 1908 hoard in some scholarship (e.g., *CMRR*, 111). However, both Marchetti, *Histoire économique*, 489–90n98, and Crawford, "Coinage of the Mamertini," 43n17, have noted that extraneous coins were incorrectly registered among the contents of the Aidone 1909 hoard; according to Marchetti, even Paolo Orsi, who originally catalogued the hoard, expressed doubts as to its composition. Due to this uncertainty over the contents of the Aidone 1909 hoard, we have omitted it from Figure 4. It may be noted, however, that the latest Roman coins attributed to this hoard are post-semilibral bronzes.

35. Tripi hoard: *IGCH* 2237–38; *RRCH* 55 and 66; Marchetti, *Histoire économique*, 491; *CMRR*, 111, 306; Manganaro, *Pace e guerra nella Sicilia*, 32nXII; Crawford, "Coinage of the Mamertini," 43. This hoard is also known as the Abacaenum/Abakainon hoard. It was originally treated in *RRCH* as two separate hoards from different neighborhoods of the town (the Pertusi and Chiapazzi hoards), but Marchetti argued that the groups had been confused when they entered the museum, so it is now considered safer to treat these coins as a single hoard; see Crawford, 43n18. Therefore, the data used for this hoard in Figure 4 combines the counts provided by Marchetti for his *1er* dépôt and *2e* dépôt, and excludes those coins whose attribution to these two groups he deems "*incertaine.*"

36. Mandanici hoard: *IGCH* 2235; *RRCH* 71; Marchetti, *Histoire économique*, 490–91; *CMRR*, 111, 306; Manganaro, *Pace e guerra nella Sicilia*, 32nXVII; Crawford, "Coinage of the Mamertini," 44. The counts for this hoard in Fig. 5 are based on those of Marchetti, who revises *RRCH* slightly; the one coin labelled "other Roman" is an *RRC* 70/1 *victoriatus*, per Crawford, 44.

37. San Marco d'Alunzio hoard: *IGCH* 2246; E. Fabbricotti, "Considerazioni su di un tesoretto di monete proveniente da S. Marco d'Alunzio," *AIIN* 15 (1968); *CMRR*, 111, 306; Crawford, "Coinage of the Mamertini," 44. Fabbricotti's original publication of the San Marco d'Alunzio hoard is the basis of the data on the hoard's contents in Figure 4.

38. Grammichele hoard: *IGCH* 2236; *CMRR*, 111, 306; G. Manganaro, "Spigolature nel medagliere del Museo Archeologico di Siracusa," *RIN* 100 (1999), 83, and *Pace e guerra nella Sicilia*, 32nXIII; G. Sarcinelli, "Rinvenimenti monetali da Grammichele," in *Da Terravecchia di Grammichele a Occhiolà. Archeologia di un insediamento della Sicilia centro-orientale: campagne di scavo 2000–2001*, ed. M. Barra Bagnasco (Alessandria: Edizioni dell'Orso, 2006). In his published comments on the Grammichele hoard, Crawford (*CMRR*, 111) notes the presence of Roman bronzes "to sextantal" standard, but the precise identifications of the Roman coins in this hoard have not been published. As a result, we have refrained from including the Grammichele hoard in Figure 4.

the third or early second century BCE, based on the hoard's Mamertine coin and several types produced at the local mint of Haluntium.[39] Although often discussed in the context of the political and military turmoil of the Second Punic War, the Grammichele hoard likewise was almost certainly buried after the close of the war, probably in the first quarter of the second century.[40]

This leaves only two Sicilian hoards from the Second Punic War, the Barrafranca hoard and the Montagna di Marzo hoard, which are thought to contain sextantal coins and to have a closing date prior to 211 BCE.[41] The Barrafranca hoard is reported to have one sextantal *sextans* with corn-ear (*RRC* 72/8)

39. Crawford ("Coinage of the Mamertini," 44) assigns a closing date for the hoard "well after 211 BC" and proposes a *terminus post quem* of 211 BCE for the Mamertine coin (Särström XVI.A) found therein; Särström, 125, had posited a date range of c. 212–200 BCE for this series. It should be noted that Mamertine coins of this type do not appear in 211 BCE destruction and abandonment contexts at Morgantina, despite their general prevalence at the site (264 specimens published in *MS* II, no. 325), including a number of coins found in stratigraphically-sealed deposits postdating the siege of 211 BCE (e.g., *MS* II, Deposit nos. 40, 42–43, 46–48, 66–67, 72). These findings from Morgantina are consistent with Crawford's post-211 BCE date for this series. In his original publication of the San Marco d'Alunzio hoard, Fabbricotti, "Considerazioni," 90, proposed a closing date at the end of the third or beginning of the second century BCE, hypothesizing intervals of time between issuance of each of the three series of Haluntium coins found in the hoard. The only specimens of these Haluntium types (*MS* II, nos. 107–9) found at Morgantina in stratigraphically-sealed contexts postdate 211 BCE (*MS* II, Deposit nos. 43, 67).

40. The Grammichele hoard cannot date earlier than the last decade of the third century or, more likely, the early decades of the second century, since among its contents are small denominations from the mints of Katane (Apollo/Isis = *BMC Sicily*, no. 65; *MS* II, no 142; *StIet* X, no. 161) and Menaeum (Apollo/Lyre = *BMC Sicily*, no. 10; *MS* II, no. 211; regarding date, see H. Mattingly, "Methodology and History in Third Century Sicilian Numismatics," *SNR* 79 [2000], 37–38). These types were struck only after the Sicilian phase of the Second Punic War (*StIet* X, 189, n. 54).

41. Barrafranca hoard: *IGCH* 2241; *RRCH* 96; R.R. Holloway, "Numismatic Notes from Morgantina II. Half Coins of Hieron II in the Monetary System of Roman Sicily," *ANSMN* 9 (1960), 69; G. Manganaro, *Sikelika: Studi di antichità e di epigrafia della Sicilia greca* (Pisa: Istituti Editoriali e Poligrafici Internazionali, 1999), 17–19, and *Pace e guerra nella Sicilia*, 31, n. VIII. Montagna di Marzo hoard: *IGCH* 2242; *RRCH* 99; P. Orsi, "Tesoretto di bronzi greci, sicelioti e romani da Piazza Armerina," *Atti e Memorie dell'Istituto Italiano di Numismatica* 6 (1930); Holloway, 69–70; Marchetti, *Histoire économique*, 489; *CMRR*, 111, 306; Manganaro, *Sikelika*, 18–19, and *Pace e guerra nella Sicilia*, 39–40. Manganaro, *Sikelika*, 18, dates the deposition of both the Barrafranca and the Montagna di Marzo hoards to c. 215–211 BCE, associating their burial with military activity around cities in central Sicily—including Morgantina and Akragas—which continued to resist Roman occupation following the fall of Syracuse to the Roman general M. Claudius Marcellus in 212 BCE. We note that among the contents of the Montagna di Marzo hoard is a bronze coin of the type Veiled head of Demeter (?) r. / Horse galloping r., now commonly attributed to a Carthaginian mint operating at Morgantina between 212 and 211 BCE; see *MS* II, no. 446; Holloway, "Monete." If this identification is correct, the presence of this coin in the Montagna di Marzo hoard would provide a *terminus post quem* for burial of 212 BCE.

among its 84 coins, while the 322 coins comprising the Montagna di Marzo hoard include two specimens of this issue and one sextantal *semis* with grain ear (*RRC* 72/5).[42] However, in light of recent research calling attention to the difficulty in distinguishing coins of the *RRC* 72 series from *RRC* 42 types on the basis of weight alone, it is possible that the "sextantal" coins in these hoards are in fact specimens of the post-semilibral *RRC* 42 series.[43] Since the *sextans* with grain ear (*RRC* 72/8) types are generally struck on flans with modules identical to heavier coins of post-semilibral weights, they may be easily confused with thin and light examples of *RRC* 42/3. Similarly, the *semis* with grain ear typically assigned to the *RRC* 72 series (*RRC* 72/5) is always struck on a large, heavy flan consistent with post-semilibral *semisses* (*RRC* 41/6e) and almost certainly should be associated with the *RRC* 42 coinage instead.[44] Thus, it is not at all certain that the Barrafranca and Montagna di Marzo hoards contain sextantal bronzes, and, even if they do, these coins make up a small fraction of the hoards' contents and do not include specimens of the *RRC* 56 or *RRC* 69 series.

In sum, the general pattern attested among these wartime Sicilian hoards is a preponderance of semilibral and post-semilibral bronzes, to the near or complete exclusion of bronzes of sextantal standard, particularly in those hoards considered to predate 211 BCE. This is consistent with the aforementioned depositional patterns observed across the site of Morgantina, where sextantal bronzes are absent from contexts deposited before the Roman siege. In contrast, the East Hill Hoard is composed predominantly of bronzes of sextantal standard (14 of 23 coins), including coins of the *RRC* 56 series and all three subtypes of the *RRC* 69 series. While we cannot, strictly speaking, rule out a date of deposition prior to 211 BCE, the discrepancy in composition between the East Hill

42. For the Montagna di Marzo hoard, these counts—and the data in Figure 5—are based on Crawford's (*RRCH* 96) description of the hoard's contents; the nine coins labelled "other Roman" are *unciae* for which more precise classifications cannot be made because these coins are no longer extant, having been lost during the Second World War. Dispersal of some of the hoard's contents during the war likewise has resulted in persistent discrepancies among scholars' overall counts and attributions of individual coins in this hoard; see, for example, the slightly different data provided by Manganaro, *Sikelika*, 17, and *Pace e guerra nella Sicilia,* 31, n. VIII. On the other hand, there is general consensus among scholars as to the contents of the Barrafranca hoard, shown in Figure 5.

43. For the problems inherent in using weight as a criterion for distinguishing between issues of *RRC* 42 and *RRC* 72, see Russo, *RBW Collection,* 46; McCabe, "Anonymous Struck Bronze Coinage," 108, n. 23. Only renewed attention to the design elements of the coins in the Barrafranca and Montagna di Marzo hoards would provide definitive evidence for their identification.

44. Personal correspondence from Andrew McCabe; we thank him for these insights based on his current work.

Hoard and pre-211 BCE deposits offers compelling circumstantial evidence that the East Hill Hoard was buried in the wake of the Roman siege of Morgantina.

There are several factors that weigh in favor of placing the hoard's date of deposition, more specifically, in the decade following the siege. First and foremost, while bronze coinage of the *RRC* 56, 69, and 72 series are markedly absent from 211 BCE destruction and abandonment layers at Morgantina, they nonetheless appear in archaeological contexts that accumulated in the period immediately following the siege. In the city's agora, for instance, specimens of the *RRC* 69 series have been recovered from the debris lying directly above destruction contexts associated with the capture of the city.[45] Similarly, recent excavations of a Hellenistic house located near the western edge of the city have yielded some seven *sextantes* with KA mintmark (*RRC* 69/6), along with a *quadrans* and *sextans* of the *RRC* 72 series, all from contexts associated with the building's final phases of occupation. The archaeologists responsible for excavating this house currently date these phases to the last years of the third century BCE, based on evidence of post-211 BCE modifications to the building.[46] Thus, the evidence emerging from recent excavations indicates that bronze coins of the *RRC* 69 and *RRC* 72 series were circulating in the city during the final decade of the century. Given that specimens of these two series predominate in the East Hill Hoard, it very well may have been deposited at about the same time.

Further indication of the hoard's date may be deduced from what is missing from its contents. Notably, the hoard does not include any of the late third-century Roman bronzes with moneyers' marks that are attested in later contexts at Morgantina.[47] Nor, importantly, does it contain any specimens of the most common Sicilian issues dating to the late third and early second centuries BCE, such as the Apollo/Isis *hexantes* of Katane, which arrived at Morgantina in extraordinary numbers during the first quarter of the second century.[48]

45. For example, a sextantal *sextans* with KA mintmark (*RRC* 69/6) was found in the accumulation just above the tile fall in Room 5 of the Central Market in Morgantina's agora; see Walthall, "Numismatic Material," 115–116, inv. 92-222.

46. D. A. Walthall *et al.*, "Preliminary Report on the 2014 Field Season of the American Excavations at Morgantina: Contrada Agnese Project (CAP)," *Fasti Online Documents & Research* 364 (2016): 1–23, http://www.fastionline.org/docs/FOLDER-it-2016-364.pdf; D.A. Walthall *et al.*, "Preliminary Report on the 2015 Field Season of the American Excavations at Morgantina: Contrada Agnese Project (CAP)," *Fasti Online Documents & Research* 408 (2018): 1–23, http://www.fastionline.org/docs/FOLDER-it-2018-408.pdf.

47. Buttrey, "Morgantina Excavations," 266–267. Issues found at Morgantina include *RRC* 80/2, 89/3, 113/2, and 121/3.

48. *MS* II, no. 141 (second issue), and *MS* II, no. 142 (third issue). On the Apollo/Isis series, see M. Casabona, "Le monete di Catana ellenistica fra Roma e le influenze orientali," *RIN* 100

Numbering over one thousand specimens recovered in controlled excavations across the site, these *hexantes* are second in frequency only to the Syracusan coins of Hieron II found at Morgantina.[49] While arguments from absence are rarely conclusive, the fact that the Apollo/Isis *hexantes* do not appear either among the contents of the hoard or among the finds recovered by Phillips in the surrounding archaeological *strata* does suggest to us that the East Hill Hoard was buried prior to these issues' arrival at Morgantina.

Finally, we note that several of the latest coins in the East Hill Hoard show minimal signs of wear, possibly indicating that they were buried not long after being minted. In particular, the Mamertine coin (Cat. no. 1, inv. 57-2770), issued shortly before 211 BCE, is in remarkably good condition compared to the vast majority of Mamertine coinage found at Morgantina, which tends to show extreme wear to the point of illegibility. Other coins from the hoard with little wear include the anonymous *semis* (Cat. no. 9, inv. 57-2764, *RRC* 56/3), the *sextans* with grain ear (Cat. no. 10, inv. 57-2763, *RRC* 72/8), and one of the *sextantes* with grain ear and KA mintmark (Cat. no. 16, inv. 57-2760, *RRC* 69/6).

Taken together, these factors suggest that the East Hill Hoard was removed from circulation—whether by intentional burial or accidental loss—in the first few years following the Roman siege of Morgantina in 211 BCE. In the aftermath of the siege, the Romans handed over the city to a group of Iberian mercenaries, who had betrayed Syracuse to the Roman general M. Claudius Marcellus.[50] Morgantina may have continued to experience some degree of social and political instability in the period following the introduction of the mercenary population, resulting in the burial or loss of assemblages like the East Hill Hoard. Such continued instability is conspicuous in the archaeological record, where there is ample evidence that portions of the city were either slow to recover or were largely abandoned following the siege, perhaps due to a drastic reduction in population.[51] While some restoration was taking place around the urban core, many

(1999), but cf. Mattingly, "Methodology and History," 27, who rightly suggests that Casabona's dates for the introduction of these coins should be shifted down by several decades into the second century; likewise, see Frey-Kupper, *StIet* X, 188–189, and "Coins and Contacts," 379–380, in favor of a date post-211/210 to the early second century BC. Stone (*MS VI*, 247) argues along similar lines for a late-third or early-second-century date for the introduction of the Apollo/Isis series, based on his thorough study of post-211 BCE "clean-up" deposits at Morgantina.

49. 190 specimens of the second issue (*MS* II, no. 141) and 837 of the third issue (*MS* II, no. 142) are published in *MS* II. For total counts of coins, according to mint, that have been identified at Morgantina from 1955 to 1981, see *MS* II, 133–134.

50. Livy 26.21.12, 17.

51. For summary, including comments about decline in population, see Stone's discussion in *MS VI*, 10–17.

buildings remained unoccupied, including several other houses located along the East Hill near the House of the Silver Hoard.[52] Thus, although the stretch of Plateia B where the East Hill Hoard was buried was surely a well-defined public space during the mid-third century BCE, this beaten-earth street may have been less frequented in the aftermath of the Roman siege and, therefore, an ideal location either to conceal or lose—and fail to recover—a small purse of coins. In fact, accidental loss may be just as likely as intentional burial given the low value of the East Hill Hoard, as the total value of these twenty-three coins (total weight = 203.61 g) probably amounted to little more than that of five *asses*, or roughly one *quinarius*.

While concentrations of coin hoards from antiquity are frequently associated with military activity, the East Hill Hoard provides a salutary reminder that this pattern is not without exception.[53] The evidence of the coins and their archaeological context does not support a date of deposition during the most conspicuously turbulent period of Morgantina's history, i.e., the Roman siege of 211 BCE. Instead, the assemblage's deposition and non-recovery likely occurred in the period immediately following the siege, either because of continued socio-political upheaval, due to the personal considerations of the owner, or as a result of accidental loss.

DISCUSSION AND CONCLUSION

Our reevaluation of the East Hill Hoard—and the reassessment of depositional patterns of Roman bronzes at Morgantina occasioned by it—has implications beyond simply establishing this hoard's archaeological context and closing date. Our findings also contribute to refining the chronology of individual issues of Roman bronze coinage traditionally associated with the earliest stages of the *denarius* system. Following our redating of the deposition of the East Hill Hoard,

---

52. See, for example, *MS* VI, 37–38 (Deposit IH); Tsakirgis, "Domestic Architecture," 85–86.

53. On the link between military or political violence and the deposition and non-recovery of hoards, see especially Crawford, "Coin Hoards and the Pattern of Violence in the Late Republic," *PBSR* 37 (1969). With specific reference to Sicilian hoards, see Manganaro, *Pace e guerra nella Sicilia,* 23–42, who attributes the non-recovery of some forty-eight hoards to (often very specific) historical events which took place during the course of the Sicilian phase of the Second Punic War. In their respective reviews of Manganaro's book, both A.M. Burnett, "Review of *Pace e Guerra nella Sicilia tardo-ellenistica e romana (215a.C–14 d.C). Ricerche storiche e numismatiche:* Nomismata. Historisch-numismatische Forschungen 7 by G. Manganaro," *NC* 173 (2013), and P. Morton, "Review of *Pace e Guerra nella Sicilia tardo-ellenistica e romana (215a.C–14 d.C). Ricerche storiche e numismatiche* (Nomismata 7) by G. Manganaro," *JRS* 104 (2014), urge greater caution whenever linking the burial and non-recovery of hoards to specific political, military, or social events.

the absence of bronze coins of the *RRC* 69 and *RRC* 72 series from archaeological contexts predating the siege at Morgantina is in evidence across the site without exception, leading us to conclude that Roman mint(s) in Sicily had yet to issue these series by late 211 BCE, when Roman forces captured the town. Morgantina's central location on the island, as well as its participation in the prevailing trade networks of eastern Sicily, should have ensured representation of these types in contexts predating the siege if, indeed, their production had already begun by late 211 BCE.[54] Coupled with the notable absence of specimens of *RRC* 69 from pre-211 BCE hoards recovered throughout central and eastern Sicily, the available evidence strongly suggests this series began to be struck only after 211 BCE.[55] The evidence from Morgantina points in the same direction for the *RRC* 72 bronzes, although further investigation of the Barrafranca and Montagna di Marzo hoards would be necessary in order to definitively redate production of these issues to the period after 211 BCE.[56]

In addition to clarifying the chronology of these issues, our research has broader significance for the reconstruction of patterns of coin circulation within Sicily during the Second Punic War, as well as for our understanding of the nature of the early *denarius* system itself. Post-semilibral bronzes—especially those of the *RRC* 42 series produced by the Roman mint in Sicily—are well-attested in

54. While low-value coins do tend to circulate more slowly than high-value coins, Morgantina is located less than seventy kilometers from Katane, the mint usually credited with production of the *RRC* 69 series, prompting an expectation for these coins to have entered circulation at Morgantina very quickly after production first began. For the varying speeds at which high-value and low-value coinage travelled in antiquity, see M. H. Crawford, "Money and Exchange in the Roman World," *JRS* 60 (1970), 43. For the proposed mint location for the *RRC* 69 series in Katane, based on the series' KA mintmark, see Hersh, "Overstrikes as Evidence," 49–50; *CMRR*, 110.

55. Crawford dated the *RRC* 69 series to 211–208 BCE and suggested that it "should belong to the very beginning of [the *denarius*] coinage despite its light weight" (*RRC*, 15, 168–169). We also note that specimens of the *RRC* 68 silver *denarius* series likewise do not appear in or below destruction contexts associated with the siege of Morgantina or in other Sicilian hoards dated before 211 BCE. This is significant, as the *RRC* 68 series is generally considered to be a product of the same mint in Katane that struck the *RRC* 69 series (*RRC*, 13–14).

56. Crawford dated the *RRC* 72 series to 211–210 BCE and argued that it continued on directly from the *RRC* 42 coinage and came at the beginning of the *denarius* coinage (*RRC*, 15, 170–71). We note that our tentative suggestion of a post-211 BCE date for the *RRC* 72 bronzes is complicated by the presence in 211 BCE contexts at Morgantina of a small number of gold and silver fractions usually thought to be produced by the same mint in parallel with these bronzes (*RRC*, 13–14). See note 58 below for additional details on specimens of *RRC* 72/1 and *RRC* 72/2 recovered from Morgantina and environs. It is possible that coins of this series in all three metals had begun to be minted by late 211 BCE, but higher velocities of exchange for the precious metal issues resulted in their arrival to Morgantina before the siege while the bronzes only reached the city thereafter.

211 BCE destruction and abandonment layers at Morgantina, as are anonymous *quinarii* (*RRC* 44/6), *sestertii* (*RRC* 44/7), and *victoriati* (*RRC* 44/1) minted in Rome, which occasionally appear in the same contexts as the post-semilibral bronzes.[57] Fractional coinage of the early *denarius* system and post-semilibral bronzes had not only arrived at Morgantina by the time of the siege, they had been integrated into the monetary system, as indicated by their representation in commercial contexts sealed by the violence of 211 BCE. The same cannot be said for anonymous *denarii* struck in Rome (*RRC* 44/5), nor for the earliest silver and gold denominations (e.g., *victoriatus* [*RRC* 72/1] and the 20-*as* gold piece [*RRC* 72/2]) produced by the Roman mint in Sicily; to date, only one specimen of each of these issues has been recovered at Morgantina from secure pre-211 BCE contexts.[58] The picture emerging from this evidence is one in which anonymous fractional coins of the *denarius* system circulated widely alongside locally minted post-semilibral bronzes during the period immediately preceding the siege of Morgantina, while anonymous *denarii* from Rome and fractions and multiples of the *denarius* minted in Sicily had only recently entered circulation. Completely absent from this picture are sextantal bronzes, which turn up neither at Morgantina in contexts predating the siege, nor in other pre-211 BCE hoards found in eastern and central Sicily.[59] Thus, it appears that the weight standard of Roman bronze coins minted in Sicily did not drop to one-sixth of a pound until

57. *MS* II, Deposit nos. 27–30; Walthall, "Numismatic Material," 107–109, 118. See also Fig. 3, with references.

58. For the anonymous *denarius* (*RRC* 44/5): *MS* II, Deposit no. 29; for the 20-*as* gold piece (*RRC* 72/2): *MS* II, Deposit no. 25; for the *victoriatus*: Walthall, "Numismatic Material," 103–105. In 1914, Paolo Orsi purchased eighty-nine *victoriati* contained within a lead pouch, or *marsupium*, that was said to have been discovered on the Serra Orlando, the modern name for the site of Morgantina (*RRCH* 82); for the initial report, see Orsi, "Aidone—scavi nella anonima città a Serra Orlando," *NSc* 12 (1915): 234; also, see Manganaro, *Pace e guerra nella Sicilia*, 38–39, for further description of the contents and discussion of the package as related to Roman military payments. These coins and their pouch are now on display in Syracuse at the Museo Archeologico Regionale "Paolo Orsi" (inv. 35277-78). Two among the eighty-nine *victoriati* within the *marsupium* are of the *RRC* 72/1 type. Manganaro, "Un ripostiglio siciliano," 41, nos. 93–94, also published an example of *RRC* 72/1 from another hoard—now dispersed on the market—that he believed had been buried at Morgantina in the lead-up to the siege. Given that these coins were clandestinely excavated, little can be said about the hoard's contents or find spot. For the *victoriatus* coinage generally, see the recent work by C. Parisot-Sillon, "Soldats, vétérans et monnaies romaines: le cas du victoriat au IIe siècle av. n. è.," *RN* 175 (2018), who offers a sweeping reevaluation of the coinage and its function in Roman military affairs of the second century BCE.

59. The Barrafranca and Montagna di Marzo hoards are possible exceptions to this pattern, but their precise dating is not secure, and uncertainty remains as to the identification of the sextantal bronzes reported among their contents. See pp. 10–11 above for further discussion of these hoards.

after 211 BCE, and, moreover, that any bronze coinages struck elsewhere (e.g., Rome, Sardinia) at or below the sextantal standard likely were not circulating on the island by the time of the capture of Morgantina.

These conclusions support recent observations about the early *denarius* system made by Andrew McCabe, who calls into question the long-held association between the introduction of the *denarius* and that of the sextantal standard for bronze coins, established in part by Buttrey's original analysis of the evidence from Morgantina.[60] Anonymous *quinarii, sestertii,* and *victoriati* appear to have entered circulation well before bronzes struck at or below sextantal standard— at least in Sicily, where instead these silver fractions circulated alongside post-semilibral bronzes. Moreover, differences in recovery rates at Morgantina between these anonymous fractions and anonymous *denarii* themselves may very well point to an earlier date of introduction for the former than the latter.[61] From the evidence at Morgantina, one has the clear impression of a gradual implementation of the new "system" over the course of months or, perhaps, even several years, beginning with anonymous *victoriati* and silver fractions, followed by the *denarius,* and finally—only after 211 BCE—bronzes struck at or below sextantal standard. In sum, depositional patterns from Morgantina are largely inconsistent with the traditional model positing a single moment in or just before 211 BCE for the introduction—imposed by law from Rome—of a new, integrated tri-metallic system, including the *denarius,* its fractions and multiples, and the sextantal standard. Instead, the evidence on the ground speaks to staggered production and highlights the regional diversity of minting practices and circulation patterns during the Second Punic War. For example, while the weight standard appears to have dropped below one-sixth of a pound by 211 BCE for bronze coins minted in Sardinia, a similar reduction did not occur until after this date in Sicily.[62] As individual Roman commanders stationed in different theaters of the Second Punic War grappled with the financial strains imposed by the conflict, they seem to have made decisions about coin production based

60. McCabe, "Anonymous Struck Bronze Coinage," esp. 219–223.

61. We are not the first to suggest that the anonymous fractions (*sestertii* and *quinarii*) of the *denarius* were struck prior to the introduction of the *denarius* coin itself; see A.S. Walker, "Some Hoards from Sicily and a Carthaginian Issue from the Second Punic War," in *Studies in Honor of Leo Mildenberg: Numismatics, Art History, Archaeology,* eds. A. Houghton *et al.* (Wetteren: Editions NR, 1984), 279–281.

62. For example, bronzes of the *RRC* 63 series minted in Sardinia in 211 BCE were struck based on an *as* of about 36 grams, well below the sextantal standard of 56 grams (*RRC,* 165). The Sardinian issues from 211–209 BCE (*RRC* 63–65) can be closely dated, as their reverses include monograms of the Roman praetors presiding over the island in these years; the C ligature on *RRC* 63 issues likely refers to L. Cornelius Lentulus, praetor in 211 BCE (*RRC,* 32, 165).

on their local situations and resources, rather than in adherence to a "standard" established from above by senatorial authorities in Rome.

ACKNOWLEDGMENTS

We thank Malcolm Bell III and Carla Antonaccio, co-Directors of the American Excavations at Morgantina, for allowing us to publish this material and for providing critical feedback on an early draft of the text. Dott.ssa Maria Musumeci, Director of the Museo Archeologico "Paolo Orsi" in Syracuse, kindly granted us access to the coins now held in the museum's Medagliere. We are grateful for the support and assistance offered to us by Dott.ssa Angela Maria Manenti, who assisted our research in the Medagliere of the Paolo Orsi. The final version of this text benefited greatly from the constructive feedback offered to us by Andrew Burnett, Michael Crawford, Andrew McCabe, Rabun Taylor, Suzanne Frey-Kupper, and the *AJN*'s anonymous reviewers.

ABBREVIATIONS

BMC Sicily = Poole, R. S., ed. *A Catalog of the Greek Coins in the British Museum, Sicily*. London, 1876. Reprint, Bologna: Forni, 1963.

CH VII = Price, M., ed. *Coin Hoards*, Volume VII. London: The Royal Numismatic Society, 1985.

CMRR = Crawford, M. H. *Coinage and Money Under the Roman Republic: Italy and the Mediterranean Economy*. Berkeley: University of California Press, 1985.

Gàbrici = Gàbrici, E. *La monetazione del bronzo nella Sicilia antica*. Palermo, 1927. Reprint, Bologna: Forni, 1969.

IGCH = Thompson, M., O. Mørkholm, and C.M. Kraay. *An Inventory of Greek Coin Hoards*. New York: American Numismatic Society for the International Numismatic Commission, 1973.

MS II = Buttrey, T. V., K. T. Erim, R. R. Holloway, and T. D. Groves. *Morgantina Studies*, Volume II: *The Coins*. Princeton: Princeton University Press, 1989.

MS VI = Stone, S. C. *Morgantina Studies*, Volume VI: *The Hellenistic and Roman Fine Pottery*. Princeton: Princeton University Press, 2014.

PR I = Stillwell, R., and E. Sjöqvist. "Excavations at Serra Orlando: Preliminary Report." *American Journal of Archaeology* 61 (1957): 151–159.

PR II = Sjöqvist, E. "Excavations at Serra Orlando (Morgantina), Preliminary Report II." *American Journal of Archaeology* 62 (1958): 155–164.

RRC = Crawford, M. H. *Roman Republican Coinage*. 2 vols. London: Cambridge University Press, 1974.

RRCH = Crawford, M. H. *Roman Republican Coin Hoards*. London: Royal Numismatic Society, 1969.

Särström = Särström, A. *A Study in the Coinage of the Mamertines*. Lund: Gleerup, 1940.

SNG München = *Sylloge Nummorum Graecorum. Deutschland. Staatliche Münzsammlung München. Vol. 6. Sikelia: Nr. 873-1670. Punier in Sizilien: Nr. 1589-1662. Lipara: Nr. 1671-1694. Sardinia: Nr. 1695-1755. Punier in Sardinien: Nr. 1695-1749. Nachträge: Nr. 1756-1774*. Berlin, 1980.

SNG Cop. = *Sylloge Nummorum Graecorum. Copenhagen. The Royal Collection of Coins and Medals. Danish National Museum*. Vols. 4–5. Copenhagen, 1942.

StIet X = Frey-Kupper, S. *Die antiken Fundmünzen vom Monte Iato (1971–1991). Ein Beitrag zur Geldgeschichte Westsiziliens*. Studia Ietina X. Lausanne: Éditions du Zèbre, 2013.

BIBLIOGRAPHY

Bell III, M. "Monete ieroniche in nuovi contesti di scavo a Morgantina." In Caccamo Caltabiano, *La Sicilia*, 289–294.

———. "A Stamp with the Monogram of Morgantina and the Sign of Tanit." In *Damarato: Studi di antichità offerti a Paola Pelagatti*, edited by I. Berlingò, H. Blanck, F. Cordano, P. G. Guzzo and M.C. Lentini, 246–254. Milan: Electa, 2000.

Burnett, A. M. "The Coinage of Punic Sicily during the Hannibalic War." In Caccamo Caltabiano, *La Sicilia*, 383–399.

———. "Review of *La Sicilia da Dionisio I a Sesto Pompeio. Circolazione e funzione della moneta*. Pelorias: Collana del Dipartimento di Scienze dell'Antichità dell'Università di Messina 16, 2009 by M. Puglisi; and *Pace e Guerra nella Sicilia tardo-ellenistica e romana (215a.C–14 d.C). Ricerche storiche e numismatiche*: Nomismata. Historisch-numismatische Forschungen 7 by G. Manganaro." *NC* 173 (2013): 540–546.

Burnett, A. M., and M. H. Crawford. "Coinage, Money, and Mid-Republican Rome: Reflections on a Recent Book by Filippo Coarelli." *Annali dell'Istituto Italiano di Numismatica* 60 (2014): 231–265.

Burnett, A. M., U. Wartenberg and R. B. Witschonke, eds. *Coins of Macedonia and Rome: Essays in Honour of Charles Hersh*. London: Spink, 1998.

Buttrey, T. V. "The Morgantina Excavations and the Date of the Roman Denarius." In *Atti del Congresso Internazionale di Numismatica 1961*, 261–267. Rome, 1965. Reprinted with emendations in *MS* II.

————. "Morgantina and the Denarius." *Numismatica e Antichità Classiche* 8 (1979): 149–157. Reprinted with emendations in *MS* II.

Caccamo Caltabiano, M., ed. *La Sicilia tra l'Egitto e Roma. La monetazione siracusana dell'età di Ierone II. Atti del seminario di studi, Messina 2–4 dicembre 1993*. Messina: Accademia Peloritana dei Pericolanti, 1995.

————. "Il tesoretto di oro 'marziale' da Agrigento e il problema delle origini del sistema denariale." In *Actes du XIe Congrès international de numismatique: organisé a l'occasion du 150e anniversaire de la Société Royale de Numismatique de Belgique, Bruxelles, 8–13 septembre 1991*, edited by T. Hackens and G. Moucharte, 109–116. Louvain-la-Neuve: Séminaire de Numismatique Marcel Hoc, 1993.

————. "I ritrovamenti siciliani e l'introduzione del sistema denariale." In *Studi sulla moneta e sulla circolazione monetale in Italia. Tavola Rotonda in margine alla mostra 'Roma e il suo fiume' (Conference Proceedings Roma 1994)*, 2004, 1–19. http://www.monetaecivilta.it/convegno/caltabiano.pdf.

Caccamo Caltabiano, M., B. Carroccio and E. Oteri. "Il sistema monetale ieroniano: cronologia e problemi." In Caccamo Caltabiano, *La Sicilia*, 195–280.

————. *Siracusa ellenistica: le monete "regali" di Ierone II, della sua famiglia e dei siracusani*. Messina: Accademia Peloritana dei Pericolanti, 1997.

Casabona, M. "Le monete di Catana ellenistica fra Roma e le influenze orientali." *Rivista Italiana di Numismatica e Scienze Affini* 100 (1999): 13–46.

Crawford, M. H. "Coin Hoards and the Pattern of Violence in the Late Republic." *PBSR* 37 (1969): 76–81.

————. "Money and Exchange in the Roman World." *Journal of Roman Studies* 60 (1970): 40–48.

————. "The Coinage of the Mamertini." In *Studies in Ancient Coinage in Honour of Andrew Burnett*, edited by R. Bland and D. Calomino, 41–49. London: Spink, 2015.

Debernardi, P. "CR 44 e le origini del denario." *Panorama Numismatico* 264 (2011): 5–35.

Debernardi, P., and O. Legrand. "The Dates of the Quadragati." *Annali dell'Istituto Italiano di Numismatica* 60 (2014): 209–230.

Fabbricotti, E. "Considerazioni su di un tesoretto di monete proveniente da S. Marco d'Alunzio." *Annali dell'Istituto Italiano di Numismatica* 15 (1968): 83–90.

Frey-Kupper, S. "I ritrovamenti monetali." In *La necropoli di Lilybaeum*, edited by B. Bechtold, 394–457. Palermo: Regione Siciliana. Assessorato dei Beni Culturali ed Ambientali e della Pubblica Istruzione, 1999.

————. "Coins and Contacts." In *Tas-Silg, Marsaxlokk (Malta) I. Archaeological Excavations Conducted by the University of Malta, 1996-2005*, edited by A. Bonanno and N. Vella, 351–400. Leuven: Peeters, 2015.

Hersh, C. A. "Overstrikes as Evidence for the History of Roman Republican Coinage." *Numismatic Chronicle* 13 (1953): 33–68.

Holloway, R. R. "Numismatic Notes from Morgantina II. Half Coins of Hieron II in the Monetary System of Roman Sicily." *ANS Museum Notes* 9 (1960): 65–73.

————. "Monete provenienti dagli scavi di Morgantina e già attribuite a Hiempsal II." *Annali dell'Istituto Italiano di Numismatica* 7–8 (1960–1961): 35–37.

Loomis, W. T. "The Introduction of the Denarius." In *Transitions to Empire: Essays in Greco-Roman History, 360–146 BC, in Honor of E. Badian*, edited by R. W. Wallace and E. M. Harris, 338–55. Norman: University of Oklahoma Press, 1996.

Manganaro, G. "Un ripostiglio siciliano del 214–211 a.C. e la datazione del denarius." *Jahrbuch für Numismatik und Geldgeschichte* 31–32 (1981–1982): 37–54.

————. *Sikelika: Studi di antichità e di epigrafia della Sicilia greca.* Pisa: Istituti Editoriali e Poligrafici Internazionali, 1999.

————. "Spigolature nel medagliere del Museo Archeologico di Siracusa." *Rivista Italiana di Numismatica e Scienze Affini* 100 (1999): 79–92.

————. *Pace e guerra nella Sicilia tardo-ellenistica e romana (215 a.C.–14 d.C.): Ricerche storiche e numismatiche.* Nomismata 7. Bonn: Habelt, 2012.

Marchetti, P. "La datation du denier romain et les fouilles de Morgantina." *Revue Belge de Numismatique et de Sigillographie* 117 (1971): 81–114.

————. *Histoire économique et monétaire de la deuxième guerre punique.* Brussels: Palais des Académies, 1978.

————. "Numismatique romaine et histoire." *Cahiers du Centre Gustave Glotz* 4 (1993): 25–65.

Meadows, A. R. "The Mars/eagle and thunderbolt gold and Ptolemaic involvement in the Second Punic War." In *Coins of Macedonia and Rome*, edited by A. Burnett, U. Wartenberg and R. Witschonke, 125–134. London: Spink, 1998.

Mattingly, H. "Methodology and History in Third Century Sicilian Numismatics." *Schweizerische numismatische Rundschau* 79 (2000): 35–48.

McCabe, A. "The Anonymous Struck Bronze Coinage of the Roman Republic: A Provisional Arrangement." In *Essays in Honour of Roberto Russo*, edited by

P. G. van Alfen and R. B. Witschonke, 101–274. Zurich: Numismatica Ars Classica NAC AG, 2013.

Morton, P. "Review of *Pace e Guerra nella Sicilia tardo-ellenistica e romana (215a.C–14 d.C). Ricerche storiche e numismatiche* (Nomismata 7) by G. Manganaro." *Journal of Roman Studies* 104 (2014): 272–273.

Orsi, P. "Aidone—scavi nella anonima città a Serra Orlando." *Notizie degli Scavi di Antichità* 12 (1915): 233–234.

———. "Tesoretto di bronzi greci, sicelioti e romani da Piazza Armerina." *Atti e Memorie dell'Istituto Italiano di Numismatica* 6 (1930): 105–116.

Parisot-Sillon, C. "Soldats, vétérans et monnaies romaines: le cas du victoriat au IIe siècle av. n. è." *Revue Numismatique* 175 (2018): 241–283.

Ronchi, F. "Il dibattito sulla data d'introduzione del denario nella moderna letteratura numismatica." *Rivista Italiana di Numismatica e Scienze Affini* 99 (1998): 39–88.

Russo, R. "Unpublished Roman Republican Bronze Coins." In A. Burnett *et al*, *Coins of Macedonia and Rome*, 139–150.

———. *The RBW Collection of Roman Republican Coins: Part I*. Zurich: Numismatica Ars Classica NAC AG, 2011.

Sarcinelli, G. "Rinvenimenti monetali da Grammichele." In *Da Terravecchia di Grammichele a Occhiolà. Archeologia di un insediamento della Sicilia centro-orientale: campagne di scavo 2000–2001*, edited by M. Barra Bagnasco, 429–453. Alessandria: Edizioni dell'Orso, 2006.

Stone, S. C. "Sextus Pompeius, Octavianus and Sicily." In *Sextus Pompeius*, edited by A. Powell and K. Welch, 135–165. Swansea: Classical Press of Wales, 2002.

Tsakirgis, B. "The Domestic Architecture of Morgantina in the Hellenistic and Roman Periods." PhD diss., Princeton University, 1984.

Thomsen, R. *Early Roman Coinage*. 3 vols. Copenhagen: Nationalmuseet, 1957–1961.

Walker, A. S. "Some Hoards from Sicily and a Carthaginian Issue from the Second Punic War." In *Studies in Honor of Leo Mildenberg: Numismatics, Art History, Archaeology*, edited by A. Houghton, S. Hurter, P. E. Mottahedeh and J. A. Scott, 269–283. Wetteren: Editions NR, 1984.

Walthall, D. A. "Numismatic Material from Late Third-Century Contexts at Morgantina (Sicily)." *American Journal of Numismatics* 29 (2017): 101–124.

Walthall, D. A., R. Souza and J. Benton. "Preliminary Report on the 2014 Field Season of the American Excavations at Morgantina: Contrada Agnese Project (CAP)." *Fasti Online Documents & Research* 364 (2016): 1–23. http://www.fastionline.org/docs/FOLDER-it-2016-364.pdf

Walthall, D. A., R. Souza, J. Benton, E. Wueste and A. Tharler. "Preliminary Report on the 2015 Field Season of the American Excavations at Morgantina: Contrada Agnese Project (CAP)." *Fasti Online Documents & Research* 408 (2018): 1–23. http://www.fastionline.org/docs/FOLDER-it-2018-408.pdf

Woytek, B. E. "The Denarius Coinage of the Roman Republic." In *The Oxford Handbook of Greek and Roman Coinage*, edited by W. E. Metcalf, 315–334. Oxford: Oxford University Press, 2012.

AJN Second Series 32 (2020) pp. 157–168
© 2020 The American Numismatic Society

The Imperial *Victoriatus* in New Inscriptions from Pompeii and London

Seth Bernard*

This paper points out the consistent use of the term *victoriatus* to describe fractions of the *denarius* in two newly published inscriptions from Pompeii and London. These texts, as well as other epigraphic and literary evidence collected here, suggest that Romans of the Imperial period used the term to describe silver coins worth half a *denarius*. The modern convention of calling this Imperial denomination a *quinarius* finds little basis in the ancient evidence.

Two recently published inscriptions bear significantly on the ancient name of the Imperial silver coin valued at half a *denarius*. Originally a Republican denomination, the coin was minted by Augustus early in his reign, but not by subsequent Julio-Claudian emperors until it was revived under Galba and issued with some regularity through the end of the third century.[1] Scholarship universally calls the Imperial denomination a *quinarius*, but I believe this is wrong, or at least a wholly modern convention.[2] There was perhaps some ambiguity surrounding

---

*University of Toronto (seth.bernard@utoronto.ca).

1. The standard reference is C. E. King, *Roman Quinarii: From the Republic to Diocletian and the Tetrarchy* (Oxford: Ashmolean Museum Press, 2007); see also W. H. Gross in *RE* VIII A.2, *s.v.* "victoriatus," coll. 2542–2557.

2. Recent scholarship sometimes acknowledges confusion, as see A. Burnett, "Le monnayage romain jusqu'à l'époque des guerres civiles, ca. 300–49 av. J.-C.," in *La monnaie antique: Grèce et Rome, VIIe siècle av. J.-C.–Ve siècle apr. J.-C.*, ed. M. Amandry (Paris: Ellipses), 140, but *quinarius* remains standard nomenclature. I have been unable to discover when this first became the case, although H. Cohen, *Description historique des Monnaies frappées sous l'Empire romain, communément appelées Médailles imperials* (Paris: Rollin and Feuerdent, 1880), vol. I,

the name in the Republic; however, in the Empire, Romans called this coin a *victoriatus*.

The first text is a monumental inscription published by Osanna in 2018 from a tomb outside the Porta Stabia at Pompeii. The text, recording a series of benefactions performed by an unnamed patron, is of considerable length, and I cite only the relevant passage in ll. 3–4, which describes a distribution of food at reduced cost during a grain shortage.[3]

> …*cum esset denaris quinis modius tritici, coemit / et ternis victoriatis populo praestitit et, ut ad omnes haec liberalitas eius perveniret viritim populo ad ternos victoriatos per amicos suos panis cocti pondus divisit.*

When a modius of wheat cost five *denarii*, he bought it and offered to the people for three *victoriati* and, so that his liberality reach all, he distributed an amount of baked bread worth up to three *victoriati* individually to the people through his friends.

The next sentence describes gladiatorial games put on by the same individual *ante senatus consult*(*um*), which must refer to Nero's edict outlawing such games in response to a violent amphitheater riot at Pompeii in AD 59, as famously recorded by Tacitus.[4] If the text describes events in chronological order, then the grain sale at a price of three *victoriati* took place before that date. Meanwhile, the monument's exceptional preservation suggests it was erected just before the eruption of AD 79. The document offers our first attestation of *victoriati* in Pompeian epigraphy, although we cannot be certain whether these references belong to the Neronian period in which the grain sale took place, or to the Flavian period when the monument was made.

---

xiii, uses *quinaire*, and from there the term might have passed to the first edition of *RIC* I in 1923, from which it became customary. Before that, Georgius Agricola, *De mensuris et ponderibus Romanorum atque Graecorum* (1533) and Joseph Scaliger, *De re nummaria antiquorum dissertatio* (1616) cite Volusius Maecianus, discussed below, in labelling half-*denarii* as both *quinarius* and *victoriatus*, while J. H. Eckhel (*Doctrina numorum veterum*, Part II, vol. V [Fridericus Volke: Vienna, 1795], 20–22), calls Republican half-*denarii quinarii* but comments on the puzzling relationship to *victoriati* and notes that Pliny's comments in particular *molesta mihi semper*.

3. M. Osanna, "Games, banquets, handouts, and the population of Pompeii as deduced from a new tomb inscription. *JRA* 31 (2018), 310–322; there is much more to say about this inscription, and I have contributed to more expansive discussion in J. Bodel, A. Bendlin, S. Bernard, C. Bruun and J. Edmondson, "Notes on the new elogium of a benefactor at Pompeii." *JRA* 32.1 (2019), 148–182. Justification for my translation here, which differs from that of Osanna, as well as extensive discussion of these and other points appears there.

4. Tac. *Ann.* 14.17; other details in the text further strengthen the connection with this event.

Of course, the inscription uses *victoriati* to relate a price and so cannot confirm on its own that coins called *victoriati* were ever transacted. The noteworthy shift from *denarii* to *victoriati* in the space of a single sentence might relate to preferences otherwise observable in Pompeian epigraphy for expressions of coin in round figures and single metals rather than mixed sums of silver and bronze.[5]

We may compare a second recent epigraphic acquisition of similar date. *Victoriati* are mentioned in a Bloomberg London writing tablet published by Tomlin and dateable to the decade or so after AD 63.[6] The tablet preserves the following letter in Latin.[7]

[traces of another line]
rogo [te] per panem et sal-
em ut quam primum mit-
tas ✗ *(denarios) viginti sex in victoriat(is)*
et ✗ *(denarios) decem Paterionis*

I ask you by bread and salt to send as soon as possible 26 *denarii* in *victoriati*, and the 10 *denarii* of Paterio.

Here, there can be no question that the reference is to actual coins called *victoriati*. Tomlin notes the Neronian debasement of silver *denarii* around the time the letter was written and raises the ingenious idea that the writer was interested in hoarding Augustan coins of higher fineness; however, the fineness of silver half-*denarii* was typically lower than contemporary *denarii*, perhaps as a consequence of the higher production costs of minting smaller denominations.[8]

Both texts relate *victoriati* to *denarii*, confirming the expected but important fact that the former term refers to a fraction of the latter. The two documents also come from very different parts of the Empire, so that neither describes local nomenclature. Above all, I emphasize that the texts converge chronologically not only with each other, but with a consequential moment for silver half-*denarii*

---

5. Cf. M. Bailey, "Roman Money and Numerical Practice." *Revue belge de philologie et d'histoire* 91.1 (2013), 154–162.

6. A timber plank from the same context provides a felling date and thus a *terminus post quem* of AD 63; R. S. O. Tomlin, *Roman London's first voices: Writing tablets from the Bloomberg excavations, 2010–4* (London: Museum of London Archaeology, 2016), 42.

7. WT 31; Tomlin, *Roman London's*, 126 takes more or less the conventional view that *victoriati* were no longer minted but had become a sort of nickname for *quinarii*; in fact, little supports the idea that Romans at that date called any circulating coins *quinarii* to begin with, as I discuss below.

8. K. Butcher and M. Ponting, *The Metallurgy of Roman Silver Coinage: From the Reform of Nero to the Reform of Trajan* (Cambridge: Cambridge University Press, 2015), 23; see already King, *Roman Quinarii*, 103.

just after the death of Nero, when the Imperial mints of Lugdunum and Rome revived production after a lapse of almost a century. These inscriptions now confirm that Romans around that time referred to fractional issues of the *denarius* as *victoriati*.

It is admittedly difficult to determine whether these inscriptions intend to refer to Augustan or even Republican silver fractions still circulating under Nero, or to new issues struck after his reign. Republican and Augustan half-*denarii* continued to circulate in Pompeii up to the eruption, as demonstrated, for example, by a small hoard from the House of Stlaborius Auctus containing an Augustan half-*denarius* along with six Republican *denarii* and a *denarius* of Vespasian.[9] Meanwhile, Republican and early Imperial half-*denarii* circulated in limited numbers in southern Roman Britain, although pre-Claudian Roman coins of any denomination are rare from London itself.[10]

Both texts' reference to *victoriati* corresponds remarkably well with other epigraphic evidence of a later date, as *victoriatus* appears in several other private and public Latin inscriptions. One and possibly two early-second century letters from Vindolanda refer to sums in *victoriati*.[11] And in similar context to the Pompeii inscription, *victoriati* appear in records of municipal benefactions in a second-century document from Cales in Campania and in a late-second or early-third century inscription from Saldae in Mauretania, which describes the distribution of *sportulae* of three *victoriati*. *Sportulae* were typically cash handouts, and we might think this last reference is to actual coins.[12]

In addition, several Imperial Greek inscriptions list values in τροπαϊκά. The Greek term seems derived from *victoriatus*, even if the trophy on the earliest

9. R. Cantilena, *Pompei: Rinvenimenti monetali nella Regio VI* (Rome: Istituto Italiano di Numismatica, 2008), 280–281; see also Hobbs, R. *Currency and Exchange in Ancient Pompeii: Coins from the AAPP Excavations at Regio VI, Insula 1.* (London: Institute of Classical Studies, 2013), 56, 60.

10. The Portable Antiquities Scheme database includes half-*denarii* of Republican date from Essex and of triumviral date from Hampshire, and a plated example of Vespasian from Hertfordshire; note also a rare Gaulish imitation of the denomination from Wiltshire. For London generally, see M. J. Hammerson, "Problems of Roman Coin Interpretation in Greater London," in *Interpreting Roman London: Papers in memory of Hugh Chapman*, ed. J. Bird, M. Hassall and H. Sheldon (Oxford: Oxbow, 1996), 153–164; we lack any systematic study of the Roman settlement's coin finds, but I am not aware of early half-*denarii*, and this makes it a minor puzzle where anyone in Neronian London hoped to get 52 *victoriati*.

11. *Tab Vindol* 323; less securely, *Tab Vindol* 694.

12. *CIL* X 4643 (Cales); *CIL* VIII 8938 = *ILS* 5078 (Saldae); on *sportulae* and cash, see S. Mrozek, *Les distributions d'argent et de nourriture dans les villes italiennes du Haut-Empire romain* (Brussels: Latomus, 1987), 33–37.

Republican *victoriati* appears less commonly on later issues, and there is debate over how such references relate to local Greek coinages.[13] We might point in particular to prices listed in both διvάρια and τροπαϊκά, *denarii* and *victoriati*, found in two Augustan manumission records from Thessaly and a second-century edict from Beroia concerning the funding of a gymnasium.[14]

Now including the inscriptions from Pompeii and London, then, the catalogue of epigraphic references to *victoriati* in Latin and Greek can claim to cover more or less the entire Imperial production of silver half-*denarius* coins. By contrast, I am unaware of a single epigraphic attestation of *quinarius* in reference to coins.

A similar pattern characterizes the literary sources.[15] A handful of authors refer to *victoriati* in passing references to prices, offering plausible testimony for the names of coins in daily use. In chronological order, Cicero describes custom taxes on wine in Roman Gaul reckoned at least partly in *victoriati* (*Font.* 9.19). Quintilian records a story of the emperor Galba purchasing a large eel for *uno victoriato* (*Orat.* 6.3.80). Set in Sicily, the episode will have taken place prior to Galba's reign but remains noteworthy considering his revival of silver half-*denarii*. As late as the third century, Tertullian refers to a trifling donation of a single *victoriatus* (*De virgin. velandis* 13.4). There are no literary references to prices in *quinarii*.

Where we find both *victoriati* and *quinarii* named is in antiquarian writing about Roman money. Varro affirms the value of the *victoriatus* at half a *denarius*, and Pliny gives a history of the coin, which I discuss further below. Neither discussion shows concern with contemporary use or circulation, but rather both treatments are historical and etymological. The same aspects characterize both authors' mentions of *quinarii*. For Varro, "the *denarii* are called such because they are valued at ten *asses*, the *quinarii*, because they are five, the *sestertius*,

---

13. B. Helly, "Deux attestations du 'Victoriat' dans les listes d'affranchissement de Thessalie," in *Proceedings of the 9th International Congress of Numismatics, Berne, September 1979*, ed. T. Hackens and R. Weiller (Louvain-la-Neuve: Association internationale des numismates professionnels, 1982), 165–176; B. Helly, "Le diorthôma d'Auguste fixant la conversion des statères thessaliens en deniers. Une situation de passage à la monnaie unique." *Topoi* 7.1 (1997), 63–91.

14. *SEG* XXXII 599, 603; *EKM* 1 Beroia 7. See also *IDidyma* 291; *SEG* 30.1390. Mentions of τροπαιοφόρα in inventories from Athenian Delos (*IDelos* 1443, 1449, 1450) may refer to early Republican *victoriati*.

15. Liv. 41.31.7; Cato, *Agr.* 15.1, 145.3; and the *Sententia Minuciae* (*ILLRP* 517) all likely refer to *victoriati* of the early second century BC. Otherwise, Festus 492 L, *Reginum victoriati*, reveals nothing about Roman coins.

because it is the half of a third."[16] For Pliny, "it was enacted that the *denarius* is valued at ten libral *asses*, the *quinarius* five, the *sestertius* two and a half."[17] Both passages refer to the brief initial period when the *denarius* was valued at ten *asses* before its retariffing at sixteen *asses* around 141 BC.[18] Elsewhere, Pliny does refer to *quinarii* in relation to the post-tariff Republican *denarius*: "Afterwards when Hannibal was making his presence known, in the dictatorship of Q. Fabius Maximus *asses* were made of uncial weight, and it was enacted that the *denarius* be changed to sixteen *asses*, the *quinarius* eight, the *sestertius* four."[19] As before, however, his perspective in this passage is firmly historical, and it therefore forms less sound evidence for what Romans called coins circulating in Pliny's own day.

Otherwise, *victoriati*, but not *quinarii*, appear as units of weight or price in medical treatises by Scribonius Largus in the Julio-Claudian period and Marcellus Empiricus in fifth-century Gaul. The only remaining source of note to refer to *quinarii* is the numismatic pamphlet written by Volusius Maecianus and dedicated to Marcus Aurelius, the *Distributio item vocabula ac notae partium in rebus quae constant pondere numero mensura*. The relevant passage can be quoted in full (§44–47):[20]

> *Sicut autem assis appellatio ad rerum solidarum hereditatisque totius, divisio autem eius ad partium demonstrationem pertinet, ita etiam ad pecuniam numeratam refertur, quae olim in aere erat, postea et in argento feriri coepti ita, ut omnis nummus argenteus ex numero aeris potestatem haberet. Eo in numero sunt hi argenti nummi: denarius cuius est nota* ✗, *quinarius, cuius est nota* V, *sestertius, cuius nota* HS. *Victoriatus enim, nunc tantundem valet quantum quinarius, olim ut peregrinus nummus loco mercis, ut nunc tetradrachmum et drachma, habebatur. Denarius primo asses decem valebat, unde et nomen traxit; quinarius dimidium eius, id est quinque asses, unde et ipse vocatus; sestertius duos asses et semissem, quasi semis tertius…Nunc denarius XVI, victoriatus et quinarius VIII, sestertius quattuor asses valet.*

16. *De ling.* 5.173: *denarii quod denos aeris valebant; quinarii, quod quinos; sestertius, quod semis tertius.*

17. *HN* 33.44: *et placuit denarium pro x libris aeris valere, quinarium pro v, sestertium pro dunpondio ac semisse.*

18. Similarly, Apul. *apud* Prisc. Inst. Gramm. 6.66: *sed tum sestertius dipondium semissem, quinarius quinquessis, denarius decussis valebat.*

19. *HN* 33.45: *postea Hannibale urguente Q. Fabio Maximo dictatore asses unciales facti, placuitque denarium XVI assibus permutari, quinarium octonis, sestertium quaternis.*

20. Text following F. O. Hultsch, *Scriptores metrologici graeci et romani*, 2 vols (Leipzig: Teubner, 1866).

Just as the name of the *as* has to do with whole sums and bequests in their entirety, while its distribution has to do with a description of its parts, the same can be applied to currency, which once was bronze, and afterwards began to be struck in silver, so that every silver coin holds the value of the number of bronze coins (to which it relates). Among this group are these silver coins: the *denarius* whose symbol is X, the *quinarius* whose symbol is V, the *sestertius* whose symbol is HS. For the *victoriatus*, now worth the same amount as the *quinarius*, once was reckoned as a foreign coin used for commerce, as now are tetradrachms and drachms. At first, the *denarius* was worth ten *asses*, which is how it derived its name; the *quinarius* half of that, that is, five *asses*, after which it was named; the *sestertius* two and a half *asses*, as if half the third…Now the *denarius* is worth sixteen *asses*, the *victoriatus* and *quinarius* eight, and the *sestertius* four."

Recent scholarship on this work points out its deviation from actual minting practice and stresses that it cannot be read as a factual account of the Antonine monetary system. Subdivisions of the *uncia* described elsewhere in the work, for example, find no basis in contemporary coinage, while Maecianus sometimes explicitly claims to discuss obscure denominations.[21] There is thus an antiquarian impulse behind Maecianus's account of Roman money, not dissimilar to that of Pliny and Varro, who have both exerted influence on his writing; in the passage above, observe Maecianus's gloss of Varro's *semis tertius*. Also like these authors, Maecianus offers an historical perspective, starting with the evolution of silver money from bronze at Rome before describing the old *denarius* of ten *asses*. When Maecianus turns to the sixteen-*as denarius*, he inserts *victoriatus* along with *quinarius* to describe its half unit, but I do not think we can rule out that this simply intends to relate for readers the current *denarius* and its fractions to the account he just gave of the earlier system. Aside from Maecianus's work, the only other text in the corpus of ancient metrological writings to refer to half-*denarii*, a Greek work derived from Julius Africanus's *Cesti*, calls such coins τροπαϊκά, i.e., *victoriati*.[22]

21. S. Cuomo, "Measures for an emperor: Volusius Maecianus' monetary pamphlet for Marcus Aurelius," in *Ordering Knowledge in the Roman Empire,* ed. J. König and T. Whitmarsh (Cambridge: Cambridge University Press, 2007), 206–228; A. Riggsby, *Mosaics of Knowledge: Representing Information in the Roman World.* (Oxford/New York: Oxford University Press, 2019), 86.

22. Hultsch, *Scriptores,* I.302 = Julius Africanus Cesti F62.42 (M. Wallraff, C. Scardino, L. Mecella and C. Guignard, eds. *Iulius Africanus Cesti: The Extant Fragments* [Berlin: De Gruyter, 2012]); Hultsch also publishes Celsus of Ravenna's 1525 Latin recension of this text, which refers to *tropaica…quinariosve,* but the history of that text, as well as the mixed reference to Greek and Latin terminology point to likely interpolation. Metrological sections of the Cesti

This passage of Maecianus's work also provides important information on the Republican *lex Clodia*, the law which effected a significant change in the *victoriatus*' production. While he does not name the law, Maecianus's account of old *victoriati* as peregrine coins "for commerce" (*loco mercis*) clearly follows Pliny *HN* 33.46:

> *Is, qui nunc victoriatus appellatur, lege Clodia percussus est; antea enim hic nummus ex Illyrico advectus mercis loco habebatur. est autem signatus Victoria, et inde nomen.*

> The coin now called the *victoriatus* was struck according to the Clodian law; before this coin, brought from Illyria, was used for commerce. It is stamped with an image of Victory and from this derives its name.

Crawford influentially suggested this law, whether intentionally or not, brought about the end of the earlier *victoriatus* and revived the *quinarius*, which would go on to have a "more eventful and longer history."[23] But Pliny and Maecianus might be read the other way around: what the law effected was a change in the long history of the *victoriatus*. In describing the law, Pliny refers nowhere to *quinarii*, but instead to the coin "now" (*nunc*) called *victoriatus*. Maecianus uses the same temporal adverb: once foreign coins, *victoriati* are "now" (*nunc*) worth as much as *quinarii*. As for what the law achieved, Pliny's compact statement requires us to understand how a law of ca. 102 BC authorized the striking of coins, which had already been minted some hundred years prior. I think the key is the often noted strangeness of the first *victoriati*, fossils of the earlier didrachm coinage and seemingly distinct from the *denarius* system emerging around the same time.[24] It is certainly possible as these sources claim that *victoriati* originally had commercial, i.e., unofficial, purposes relating to Roman trade with Illyria.[25]

were excerpted many times as a Greek work περί ταλάντων, but other versions only include reference to τροπαϊκά, never any equivalent of *quinariosve*; cf. Wallraff *et al.*, *Iulius Africanus*, lxv–lxx and *comm. ad loc.* Plausibly, a scribe faced with an obscure Greek word for a coin, which was itself by that point obscure, offered *quinarii* as a gloss for τροπαϊκά, probably based on Maecianus, and this found its way into Celsus's text.

23. *RRC*, pp. 628–630.

24. See already E. A. Sydenham, E. A. "The Victoriate." *NC* 12.46 (1932), 74; H. Zehnacker, "Le quinaire-victoriat et la surévaluation du denier," in *Proceedings of the 8th International Congress of Numismatics, New York-Washington, September 1973*, ed. H. A. Cahn and G. Le Rider (Paris/Bale: Association international des numismates professionals, 1976), 388. Proof of its distinctness to my mind are the double- and half-*victoriati* without relationship to the *denarius*, which had its own fractions.

25. Polyb. 2.8 describes Illyria as a destination for Italian traders, but the issue remains how well Pliny's *ex Illyrico adventus* reflects numismatic evidence. The much-debated topic is more

However, the *denarius* quickly came to dominate not only state expenditures, but the broader Roman monetary economy, while Cato's references to *nummi victoriati* show that by the mid-second century Romans were trying to use old *victoriati* as fractions of *denarii*. After the retariffing of the *denarius*, any *victoriati* still in circulation contained almost a gram more silver than appropriate for a half-*denarius* piece, and the discrepancy became problematic. In this situation, the Clodian law will have merged the old *victoriatus* coinage with the revamped *denarius* system by retariffing its weight to correspond to half the value of new *denarii*, thereby making the coin official tender. Gresham's law will have taken care of any old *victoriati* still in circulation.[26]

The resulting equivalence of *victoriatus* and *quinarius* may have caused confusion as to what to call these coins, and this perhaps led some of the first issues after the Clodian law to display a Q, usually in the exergue of their reverse, as a sort of clarifying reference to *quinarius* below the image of Victoria.[27] It is possibly this same ambiguity in the Republican period, which has left a mark in the antiquarian sources discussed above. But I think that by Pliny's time, the issue was settled, as his description seems unequivocal: Romans referred to the coin as a *victoriatus* because it was struck with the image of Victory. Importantly, the new inscriptions confirm that Romans around that same time but in different parts of the Empire applied the same name to fractions of *denarii*.

It may not be coincidence that around the time Pliny was writing the Imperial mint resumed production of silver half-*denarii* featuring an image of Victory, possibly without exception.[28] In light of the new inscriptions and other evidence assembled here, it is hard not draw the logical conclusion: the fractional silver coins struck after Nero's death did not represent a new chapter in the long history of the *quinarius*; instead, these coins were new issues of the Imperial *victoriatus*.

complex than can be treated here. On the topic, see now the treatment of D. Machado, "The distribution and circulation of the *Victoriatus* in Northern Italy," *AJN* 31 (2019), 117–141. I thank the author for sharing his study with me.

26. E. Lo Cascio, "Il primo denarius." *AIIN* 27–28 (1980–1981), 350 n. 58.

27. *RRC* 326/2, 331/1, 332/1a–c, 333; Zehnacker, "Le quinaire-victoriat," 386; representing a Republican coin's denomination with reference to its name, not value, is unusual; however, the mark of value V might have been confused for *victoriatus*.

28. Cf. King, *Roman Quinarii*, 90, on *RIC* I² 91, the earliest possible exception, a Vitellian issue showing Concordia but of disputed authenticity.

BIBLIOGRAPHY

Bailey, M. "Roman Money and Numerical Practice." *Revue belge de philologie et d'histoire* 91.1 (2013): 153–186.

Bodel, J., Bendlin, A., Bernard, S., Bruun, C., and J. Edmondson. "Notes on the new elogium of a benefactor at Pompeii." *Journal of Roman Archaeology* 32.1 (2019): 148–182.

Burnett, A. "Le monnayage romain jusqu'à l'époque des guerres civiles, ca. 300–49 av. J.-C." In *La monnaie antique: Grèce et Rome, VIIe siècle av. J.-C.–Ve siècle apr. J.-C.*, edited by M. Amandry, 127–153. Paris: Ellipses edition, .

Butcher, K. and M. Ponting. 2015. *The Metallurgy of Roman Silver Coinage: From the Reform of Nero to the Reform of Trajan.* Cambridge: Cambridge University Press, 2017.

Cantilena, R. *Pompei: Rinvenimenti monetali nella Regio VI.* Rome: Istituto Italiano di Numismatica, 2008.

Cohen, H. *Description historique des Monnaies frappées sous l'Empire romain, communément appelées Médailles imperials.* Paris: Rollen and Feuerdent, 1880.

Cuomo, S. "Measures for an emperor: Volusius Maecianus' monetary pamphlet for Marcus Aurelius." In *Ordering Knowledge in the Roman Empire,* edited by J. König and T. Whitmarsh, 206–228. Cambridge: Cambridge University Press, 2007.

Eckhel, J. H. *Doctrina numorum veterum.* Part II, vol. V. Fridericus Volke: Vienna, 1795.

Hammerson, M. J. "Problems of Roman Coin Interpretation in Greater London," in *Interpreting Roman London: Papers in memory of Hugh Chapman,* edited by J. Bird, M. Hassall, and H. Sheldon, 153–164. Oxford: Oxbow, 1997.

Helly, B. "Deux attestations du 'Victoriat' dans les listes d'affranchissement de Thessalie." In *Proceedings of the 9th International Congress of Numismatics, Berne, September 1979,* edited by T. Hackens and R. Weiller, 165–176. Louvain-la-Neuve: Association internationale des numismates professionnels, 1982.

Helly, B. "Le diorthôma d'Auguste fixant la conversion des statères thessaliens en deniers. Une situation de passage à la monnaie unique." *Topoi* 7.1 (1997): 63–91.

Hobbs, R. *Currency and Exchange in Ancient Pompeii: Coins from the AAPP Excavations at Regio VI, Insula 1. BICS* Suppl. 116 London: Institute of Classical Studies, 2013.

Hultsch, F. O. *Scriptores metrologici graeci et romani.* 2 vols. Leipzig: Teubner, 1866.

King, C. E. *Roman Quinarii: From the Republic to Diocletian and the Tetrarchy.* Oxford: Ashmolean Museum Press, 2007.

Lo Cascio, E. "Il primo denarius." *Annali dell'Istituto Italiano di Numismatica* 27–28 (1980–1981): 335–358.

Machado, D. "The distribution and circulation of the Victoriatus in Northern Italy." *American Journal of Numismatics* 31 (2019): 117–141.

Mrozek, S. *Les distributions d'argent et de nourriture dans les villes italiennes du Haut-Empire romain.* Brussels: Latomus, 1987.

Osanna, M. "Games, banquets, handouts, and the population of Pompeii as deduced from a new tomb inscription. *Journal of Roman Archaeology* 31 (2018): 310–322.

Riggsby, A. *Mosaics of Knowledge: Representing Information in the Roman World.* Oxford/New York: Oxford University Press, 2019.

Sydenham, E. A. "The Victoriate." *The Numismatic Chronicle and Journal of the Royal Numismatic Society* 12.46 (1932): 73–95.

Tomlin, R. S. O. 2016. *Roman London's first voices: Writing tablets from the Bloomberg excavations, 2010-4.* London: Museum of London Archaeology, 2016.

Wallraff, M., C. Scardino, L. Mecella, and C. Guignard, eds. *Iulius Africanus Cesti: The Extant Fragments* Berlin: De Gruyter, 2012.

Zehnacker, H. "Le quinaire-victoriat et la surévaluation du denier." In *Proceedings of the 8th International Congress of Numismatics, New York-Washington, September 1973,* edited by H. A. Cahn and G. Le Rider, 389–393. Paris/Bale: Association international des numismates professionals, 1976.

AJN Second Series 32 (2020) pp. 169–178

Identifying Ancient Coins
Deposited with Modern Ships' Ballast:
A Problem for Distribution Studies?

Ryan H. Wilkinson*

As a clear but scattered body of scholarly literature has shown, some ancient artifacts found in coastal locations reached their findspots not during antiquity but through modern transport and dumping of solid shipping ballast. Ballast promotes a floating ship's stability by balancing the vessel and by reducing excess freeboard, lowering the vessel's center of gravity. Because cargo ships in particular lighten significantly after the unloading of cargoes, such vessels generally require additional ballast when they leave a port light or without new cargo. Contemporary ships are able to fill their ballast tanks with seawater, but the crews of early modern vessels (and indeed many into the twentieth century) relied on solid ballast. Although saleable solid cargo with some value was a preferable stabilizer, sailors often simply shoveled aboard gravel, rock, or sand from nearby shorelines. Upon reaching a destination where new weighty cargo was available, crews would shovel the ballast back out, dumping it either into the water or onto shorelines, often very far from the vessel's previous port of call. Such movement and dumping of ballast sometimes involved the inadvertent transport and redeposition of ancient artifacts mixed in with the ballast material; for example, scholars have identified ballast transport as the probable explanation for a number of European artifacts found on American coasts (see, e.g., Jones 1976; for an overview of this phenomenon from an archaeological perspective, see Burström 2017).

As this phenomenon has some potential to distort our perception of an artifact type's geographic range, it should be of interest to any scholar who works

* Ambrose University (Ryan.Wilkinson@ambrose.edu).

on the distribution patterns of small artifacts—and is thus of clear relevance for numismatists. Yet outside a limited body of specialist literature, ballast transport does not seem prominent or well known among scholars of Classical antiquity. In his recent survey of ballast archaeology, Burström observed that "ballast has never made it onto most archaeologists' radar … Ballast has long seemed to be of little or no archaeological interest" (Burström 2017, 101–102). To support Burström's point anecdotally, I might add that although coin distribution is important for my own research, I first learned about ballast transport not from scholarly reading but in a conversation with a non-academic family member (to which I will return below).

Moreover, where archaeologists *have* discussed ballast transport, the focus typically has remained on describing this interesting phenomenon rather than on unpacking its implications for archaeological analysis of find distributions—with a few notable exceptions. The first exception involves the distribution and identification of prehistoric lithic tools (examples in Burström 2017, 27–42). The second involves modern trans-Atlantic movement of artifacts; recognizing the results of ballast transport is important for quashing pseudo-historical claims about early Atlantic crossings by Romans or other pre-modern seafarers (Jones 1976, 45; Burström 2017, 27–32). Back in Europe, the distribution of stone cobbles and construction material drawn from ballast during antiquity or the medieval period has received scholarly attention (Buckland and Sadler 1990); for example, a single cobblestone probably deposited on an Irish shore during the Middle Ages has been the subject of a short study connecting pre-modern ballast transport to pilgrimage and communication (Mohr 2001). Those exceptions aside, however, we have not adequately grappled with the possible implications of ballast transport for European or Mediterranean archaeology, and therefore for numismatics as well. This short article offers some first steps toward such an engagement. I discuss the extent to which ballast transport might be a problem for distribution studies in Europe and the Mediterranean, and then provide some initial methodological recommendations for scholars concerned that a stray coin could have traveled in ballast. Finally, this article reports the discovery of a previously unpublished Roman bronze coin undoubtedly transported to its findspot in exactly that manner.

The small extant literature reporting Greek or Roman coins transported in ballast disproportionately covers finds made in either Scandinavia or North America (see Burström 2017, 29–30). Yet ballast-laden ships navigated not only across the North Sea, Baltic, and Atlantic, but also to every shore around Europe and the Mediterranean. During such modern voyages, ships leaving Mediterranean ports not only took away ballast but also deposited it on other Mediterranean or European shores (and ships embarking on trans-Atlantic voyages often first stopped at multiple Mediterranean or European ports en route). There is therefore a very real chance that some unknown number of stray coins found along coasts in or near the former Roman Empire were deposited as part of modern ballast. We must consider whether the scope of this phenomenon warrants concern—and whether there are any constructive analytical responses to this reality.

The amount of ballast material transported over the centuries has been enormous. The practice has a very long history, with both material and textual evidence indicating solid ballast transport during antiquity (Buckland and Sadler 1990, 115–118; Taylor 1998; Bernard 2014). But the explosive growth of shipping in the modern period has moved far more ballast along the world's shores. As Burström notes, "while it is not possible to come up with a precise figure for the total amount of ballast, it would seem that in the Age of Sail from the sixteenth to the early twentieth centuries there were several million tonnes of it" (Burström 2017, 7). Just as ceramic deposits created Rome's *Monte Testaccio*, ballast dumping has been extensive enough in some locations to create new landforms, such as a "Ballast Island" in the harbor of Seattle or a similar island in the Ångermanälven River in Sweden (Willis 1943, 24; Historical Marker Database; Burström 2017, 77–84). Ironically, both the removal *and* dumping of ballast in early modern Dublin severely exacerbated the shallowness of that city's harbor by building up mass and causing erosion and sedimentation. A 1707 petition complained that "the Port and Channel in the Harbour of Dublin are almost destroyed and choaked up by the irregular taking in and throwing out of Ballast, it being the constant practice of all Masters who come into the Port to take up their Ballast at the sides of the Banks of the Channel, and there upon the Tides roll in great quantities of loose Sand into the Channel, insomuch that Clontarf Pool and Salmon Pool have lost, within a few years, about Two Foot of their former depth of water" (Flood 1975, 149). The relatively early date of these harbor problems should remind us that even coins found under centuries of sediment could have been transported in early modern ballast. As these examples show, ballast transport was no minor practice, but could reshape the geography of important harbors and waterways. Globally, the amount of moved earth that may contain small artifacts (and in some cases clearly did) is very large.

Yet ballast-transported coins are unlikely to pose much of an analytical problem in regions with good datasets, where a given coin type's presence may be attested in multiple locations. The issue becomes more troubling when we turn to scattered or single finds (particularly those not found during controlled excavations) that present anomalous outliers to a coin type's usual distribution pattern. Such outliers can be important for debates about ancient and medieval communication.

Recent studies of Byzantine coinage found in Britain provide a good case in point. Thanks in part to information yielded by the Portable Antiquities Scheme (not to mention other archaeological and textual evidence), we have more and more reason to accept many of these coins as genuine signs of early medieval travel that resulted in primary coin loss, rather than secondary loss during modern times. Older, more skeptical views, according to which few Byzantine coins in Britain were primary losses, now have less support (see important discussions and arguments for this shift in Moorhead 2009, Morrisson 2014, and Morrisson 2017). Although some studies are synthetic and address many coins, the positive reappraisal of such finds has also found expression in the analysis of stray coins, so that, for example, an early Byzantine half-*follis* discovered at Birdoswald as a surface find, rather than in excavation, "appears to be the most northerly example of an ancient loss of an early Byzantine coin" (McIntosh 2014, 368). To be clear, I am not challenging such conclusions (I am quite sympathetic to this line of interpretation); the growing vision of more robust connections with the early medieval north is strongly supported by multiple lines of evidence and by a geographic distribution that does not appear random (Morrisson 2014). Nor do such arguments require a cavalier embrace of all available coins; Moorhead and Morrisson's articles judiciously reject some finds as probable modern losses.

That said, this conversation might benefit from a broader view of the conditions in which modern, secondary deposition could occur. Acknowledging that some secondary loss remained an issue, Moorhead (2009, 263) concedes that multiple "Roman provincial, Roman and Byzantine coins have been shown in the past to have been imported into Britain in recent times by tourists, collectors or even soldiers returning from service abroad." But in light of earlier comments, we certainly should add ballast transport to the list of likely secondary loss mechanisms. At least in coastal and riverine areas, one presumes, ballast dumping was more frequent and consistent than losses by recent tourists wandering about with eastern souvenirs! Therefore, in order to deal more effectively with coastal or riverine stray coins that pose notable outliers to type distributions, it would help numismatists to develop good tests for the likelihood of ballast transport of coins. There may be efficient ways, even from the comfort of the research library, to identify the coins *most* likely to have traveled in modern ballast. Although a full methodology lies well beyond the scope of this short article, I suggest some initial tactics that might help us move forward.

First, we are fortunate to possess a proxy indicator for ballast transport in scholarship from a different field. I refer to the presence of invasive species carried to new ecosystems in ballast; in addition to small artifacts, ballast also brought seeds, whole plants, insects, etc. This phenomenon is extensively discussed in the scientific literature (Lindroth 1957; Ouren 1978; Brawley et al 2009; Bain and Prévost 2010). It has direct application to archaeology, as known ballast deposits can be sourced by identifying the origin of invasive species living around the same ballast (Burström 2017, 85–94, discussing Lindroth 1957). In such cases, researchers may know they are dealing with secondary deposition in ballast, but do not know initially where it came from. This is the opposite situation faced by numismatists placing a stray find on a coin type distribution map; the mint is probably known, along with the typical zone of circulation of coins from that mint, but what is not known is whether specific stray coins traveled in ballast at all. Here, local shipping records might be helpfully indicative, but what if they are unreliable, or unavailable?

I am not aware of any previous scholar suggesting that in such cases we might simply reverse this technique—namely, by using the existence of known invasive species to assess the likelihood that ships sailing from a specific point of origin dumped ballast near a given findspot. Plants or insects native to the region around a mint, or within a coin type's historical circulation area, that are documented near a stray coin's findspot should offer clear warning that ballast transport is a compelling explanation for the coin's presence. It is probably no coincidence that some regions with relatively significant literature on ballast archaeology (e.g., the Canadian Maritimes, Scandinavia) also receive robust attention in the literature on invasive species. Scholars pursuing this approach should take note, however, to distinguish between species probably carried in solid ballast versus very small waterborne species transported in modern water-ballast tanks over the past century, as the latter provides a most unlikely mechanism for artifact transport (there is a substantial literature on invasive species in modern water-ballast tanks: see e.g., Dumont 2006; Briski, Wiley, and Bailey 2012). The earliest date when biologists documented an invasive species' presence is thus important. In some cases, scientific colleagues have already led the way in investigating ballast activities that could have led to coin deposition. Lindroth (1957, 143–211) offers a pioneering and still exemplary combination of biological and historical data for sourcing ballast contents, including detailed study of ballast sources in England; another excellent example is Ouren (1978) on invasive plants in Norway, with a sophisticated and detailed historical discussion of ballast dumping in that country's waters and shores.

In addition to use of invasive species data, we can also draw on better-recognized characteristics of ballast dumping sites. As has already been noted in extant literature (albeit, again, literature in biological sciences), dumped modern ballast sometimes concentrated near shipyards, since ships needed to be emptied of heavy ballast prior to dry-docking for repairs (Ouren 1978, 127). Ballast can be found well beyond the shoreline itself—in both directions; ballast was sometimes carried inland, for example, to private gardens, and modern municipalities often required that ballast be deposited above the maximum high-water line (excessive dumping into water would eventually turn deep water into shallows, or even trap sediment and form bars and islands). Yet sailors often avoided extra work by dumping ballast in the water, either during the final approach to port or even within a harbor itself, against regulations (Emery et al 1968, 1226–1227; Ouren 1978). There is thus no fixed distance from the waterline where we should expect to find ballast coins—and we should keep in mind that coastline changes, (particularly those involving ballast dumping and sedimentation) could lead to an artifact dumped into water centuries ago later being discovered "on land."

In many cases there will be no smoking gun, and uncertainty must continue. Nonetheless, where single coin finds and distribution outliers coincide with invasive species from known minting regions, and especially where evidence for shipyards, dumping or at least extensive modern shipping is available, numismatists and archaeologists have good reason to treat coins without stratigraphic context with even more caution than usual. Where the factors associated with ballast dumping are few or unattested, on the other hand, numismatists and archaeologists have further reason to allow for a primary loss during antiquity. At any rate, numismatists and archaeologists should continue to record ballast-transported coins as they are discovered, so that the scope of this phenomenon relative to other depositional mechanisms can become more apparent.

In that spirit, this is an appropriate context to report the discovery, many decades ago, of a previously unpublished Roman coin undoubtedly transported in ballast. One day during the 1930s, a group of boys stood skipping rocks along the shore of Puget Sound in Seattle (Washington State). Stooping to pick up his next skipping-stone, one of the boys found an ideal choice, a stone round and flat—though coated in mud. Using his thumb and forefinger, the boy scraped off the mud. To his surprise, he realized that he held not a stone but a bronze Roman coin (Fig. 1). That boy was my wife's grandfather, the late Norman Smith, Sr.

Figure 1. Sestertius of Antoninus Pius found at Puget Sound, Seattle.

Smith presented the coin to me as a gift in 2007 (at that date he was a resident of Albion, Nebraska), and it remains in my possession.[1] The coin is a *sestertius* of Antoninus Pius, struck at Rome between ca. 145 and 161 CE. Although the coin is light, probably on account of the heavy wear, the lack of a radiate crown on the portrait precludes identification as a *dupondius*.[2] It is described as follows:

Obverse: ANTONINVS AVG PIVS [P P TR P COS IIII]; laureate head of Antoninus Pius to right.[3]

Reverse: [FELICITAS AVG], S C; Felicitas standing left, holding capricorn and long winged caduceus.

Diameter: 31 mm.

Weight: 19 g.

Reference: RIC III, no. 770.

It was the conversation in which I received this coin that first made me aware of the ballast transport phenomenon. Smith was something of an amateur historian, and was aware both of the history of ballast dumping in Seattle's harbor and of such activity's probable responsibility for transport of this "Puget Sound *sestertius*." As noted above, Seattle's nineteenth-century harbor contained a land-mass named Ballast Island, created by massive ballast dumping in the port. For some time, Ballast Island housed a community of Native American Duwamish tribe-members, until they were eventually further displaced by the expanding

---

1. To avoid a potential conflict of interest, I wish to state clearly that I own the coin in question. The coin is very badly worn and is not for sale; I have no financial interest in reporting this find. I received the coin in person from its finder, who narrated the circumstances of the discovery to me at the time of the gift. Unfortunately, the finder is now deceased, and I am not aware of any further documentation of this find.

2. I am grateful to Carmen Arnold-Biucchi of Harvard University for initial assistance in identifying this coin a number of years ago.

3. Although not easily photographed, the emperor's name is discernible when held in the light.

city. Today, a worn bronze landmark plaque near Alaskan Way South and South Washington Street commemorates the role of marine ballast in shaping Seattle's geography and history, and notes that "in this area, once part of the bay, vessels from ports all over the world dumped their ballast. Untold thousands of tons were unloaded into the water by ships' crews… . The island…was covered in the 1890s by construction of Railroad Avenue (now called Alaskan Way)." (The historical marker was a private gift of the "Yukon Club and Propeller Club;" for discussion and photograph of the marker, see Historical Marker Database (2016). Ballast Island is also discussed in a recollection of a nineteenth-century visit to Seattle: Willis 1943, 24).

It is worth noting, finally, that Lindroth's groundbreaking study of ballast and invasive species in North America mentions limited invasions of European beetles probably carried by ballast to the Pacific Northwest, specifically including Puget Sound (1957, 171–172). As the "Puget Sound *sestertius*" reminds us, coins shipped in ballast may appear in very surprising places, and in company with surprising fellow travelers. This article has aimed to highlight the importance of this under-discussed phenomenon, and to offer some steps toward a constructive methodological response.

REFERENCES

Bain, Allison, and Prévost, Marie-Annick. 2010. "Environmental Archaeology and Landscape Transformation at the Seventeenth-Century Ferryland Site, Newfoundland." *Historical Archaeology* 44.3: 21–35.

Bernard, Seth G. 2014. "Ballast, Mining, and Stone Cargoes in the 'Lex portorii Asiae.'" Zeitschrift für Papyrologie und Epigraphik 191: 182–184.

Brawley, Susan H., James A. Coyer, April M. H. Blakeslee, Galice Hoarau, Ladd E. Johnson, James E. Byers, Wytze T. Stam, Jeanine L. Olsen, and Robert T. Paine. 2009. "Historical Invasions of the Intertidal Zone of Atlantic North America Associated with Distinctive Patterns of Trade and Emigration." Proceedings of the National Academy of Sciences of the United States of America 106.20 (May): 8239–8244.

Briski, Elizabeta, Chris J. Wiley, and Sarah A. Bailey. 2012. "Role of Domestic Shipping in the Introduction or Secondary Spread of Nonindigenous Species: Biological Invasions within the Laurentian Great Lakes." Journal of Applied Ecology 49.5: 1124–1130.

Buckland, P. C. and Jon Sadler. 1990. "Ballast and Building Stone: A Discussion." In Stone Quarrying and Building in England, AD 43–1525, edited by David Parsons, 114–125. Phillimore: Chichester.

Burström, Mats. 2017. *Ballast: Laden with History*. Lund, Sweden: Nordic Academic Press.

Dumont, Serge. 2006. "A New Invasive Species in the North-East of France, *Hemimysis anomala* G. O. Sars, 1907 (Mysidacea)." *Crustaceana* 79.10: 1269–1274.

Emery, K. O., C. A. Kaye, D. H. Loring, and D. J. G. Nota. 1968. "European Cretaceous Flints on the Coast of North America." *Science*, New Series, 160.3833: 1225–1228.

Flood, Donal T. 1975. "The Birth of the Bull Island." *Dublin Historical Record* 28.4: 142–153.

Historical Marker Database. 2016. "Ballast Island: Historical Point of Interest." Submitted 2011, last revised 2016. https://www.hmdb.org/marker.asp?marker=48122.

Jones, William M. 1976. "The Source of Ballast at a Florida Site." *Historical Archaeology* 10: 42–45.

Lindroth, Carl Hildebrand. 1957. *The Faunal Connections between Europe and North America*. New York: Wiley.

Mohr, Paul. 2001. "A Medieval Neapolitan Pilgrimage to Skellig Michael?" *Irish Journal of Earth Sciences* 19: 1–4.

Moorhead, Sam. 2009. "Early Byzantine Copper Coins Found in Britain: A Review in Light of New Finds Recorded with the Portable Antiquities Scheme." In *Ancient History, Numismatics and Epigraphy in the Mediterranean World. Studies in Memory of Clemens E. Bosch and Sabahat Atlan and in Honor of Nezahat Baydur*, edited by Oğuz Tekin, 263–274. Istanbul: Ege Yayınları.

Morrisson, Cécile. 2014. "Byzantine Coins in Early Medieval Britain: A Byzantinist's Assessment." In *Early Medieval Monetary History. Studies in Honour of Mark Blackburn*, edited by Rory Naismith, Martin Allen, and Elina Screen, 207–242. Farnham: Ashgate.

Morrisson, Cécile. 2017. "*Anglo-Byzantina*: monnaies et sceaux outre-Manche (IXe–XIIIe siècle)." In *Οὗ δῶρόν εἰμι τὰς γραφὰς βλέπων νόει. Mélanges Jean-Claude Cheynet* (Travaux et Mémoires 21/1), edited by Béatrice Caseau, Vivien Prigent and Alessio Sopracasa, 471–486. Paris: Association des amis du Centre d'histoire et civilisation de Byzance.

McIntosh, Frances. 2014. "Byzantine Coins from Birdoswald." *The Numismatic Chronicle* 174: 367–369.

Ouren, Tore. 1978. "The Impact of Shipping on the Invasion of Alien Plants to Norway." *GeoJournal* 2.2: 123–132.

RIC III = Mattingly, Harold and Edward A. Sydenham. 1930. *Roman Imperial Coinage, vol. 3, Antoninus Pius to Commodus*. London: Spink & Son.

Taylor, John. 1998. "Late Iron-Age Ballast Quarries at Hengistbury Head, Dorset." *Oxford Journal of Archaeology* 17.1: 113–119.

Willis, Park Weed. 1943. "A Journey to Seattle, 1883." *The Pacific Northwest Quarterly* 34.1: 19–25.

AJN Second Series 32 (2020) pp. 179–218

Emesan Tetradrachms of Caracalla:
An Investigation of their Symbols

Jack Nurpetlian*

The article presents a die study of tetradrachms minted in Emesa during the reign of Caracalla. The primary goal of the study was to understand the meaning of the various field marks on the reverse. Although no solid conclusion could be drawn due to the incomplete nature of the data set, some informative statistics and observations were made that allow for a better understanding of certain characteristics of the coinage and the structure of the mint.

Sometimes we don't even realize what we really care about, because we get so distracted by the symbols.

-Tom Wolfe

The following study was primarily undertaken to explore the significance of the various symbols found on the reverse of tetradrachms minted in Emesa under Caracalla (Fig. 1, below). To this end, a die study was conducted with the expectation that the die links may reveal a coherent pattern, such as a discernible spatial or chronological structure. The results attained were in fact more complicated than anticipated, although it must be emphasized that the sample available for the study, while considerable, is certainly not complete and therefore any results presented here are provisional.[1]

*American University of Beirut (jn21@aub.edu.lb).

1. This study supersedes a smaller die study conducted on 86 Emesan tetradrachms of Caracalla for a PhD thesis (J. Nurpetlian, *Coinage in Roman Syria: the Orontes Valley, 64 BC–AD 253* (London: Royal Numismatic Society), forthcoming.

Figure 1. Emesan AR tetradrachm of Caracalla with bare shoulder. 13.99 g.
CNG Triton V, 1766.

Figure 2. Emesan AR tetradrachm of Julia Domna.
Auktionshaus H. D. Rauch GmbH 99, 181.

The attribution of this series to Emesa is based on the bust of a radiate deity placed between the legs of the eagle on the reverse and the prominence given to Julia Domna (Fig. 2).[2] In total, images of 308 tetradrachms were compiled, 289 of which were utilized for the study, with 14 poorly preserved or photographed, and 5 identified as forgeries (see catalogue below).[3] The sample includes specimens depicting both the busts of Caracalla (226) and Julia Domna (82),[4] as multiple die links indicate that both types were struck concurrently and in the same location.[5] The study does not include tetradrachms of Macrinus and Diadumenian.[6]

2. A. R. Bellinger, *The Syrian Tetradrachms of Caracalla and Macrinus* (New York: American Numismatic Society, 1940), 64. The same deity is also found on bronzes of this city from the reigns of Antoninus Pius, Elagabalus and Uranius Antoninus. Julia Domna is said to be the daughter of the high priest in Emesa (F. Millar, *The Roman Near East: 31 BC–AD 337* [Harvard: Harvard University Press, 1993], 119). However, to date, archaeological or historical evidence for the attribution of these tetradrachms to Emesa is lacking.

3. Data was compiled up to September of 2018. Many specimens were obtained from Michel Prieur's database along with their metrological data; the provenance of some specimens was not listed.

4. Prieur 949–960.

5. Coins with an obverse of Caracalla but struck with a reverse of Julia Domna, and vice versa, have been classified under the person depicted on the obverse; this has not corrupted the statistics since all the coins are treated as a single issue.

6. Prieur 961–968. Since these issues are known in greater numbers and have mostly the same symbols as those of Caracalla, their study in the future may add to any information

The statistical results of the die study are as follows:[7]

n = 289 = the total number of coins in the sample.

d_o = 51 = the number of obverse dies identified in the sample.

d_r = 166 = the number of reverse dies identified in the sample.

D_o = (nd_o) / $(n - d_o)$ = 61.92= the estimated total number of obverse dies produced.

D_r = (nd_r) / $(n - d_r)$ = 390.03 = the estimated total number of reverse dies produced.

d_o / D_o = 82.36% and d_r / D_r = 42.56% provides the coverage of the dies in the sample.[8]

n / d_o = 5.66 and n / d_r = 1.74 are index numbers measuring the average number of coins per die.

D_r / D_o = 6.29 = the ratio of reverse dies to obverse dies.

Altogether eight (possibly nine) groups were identified based on the presence, or absence, of letters and symbols on the reverses as follows: O, H, A, crescent, two pellets, Λ,[9] Γ, and no symbol.[10] The existence of a Δ group remains

provided here; for preliminary results related to them see Nurpetlian, *Coinage in Roman Syria.*

7. Following Esty's method (W. W. Esty, "The geometric model for estimating the number of dies," in *Quantifying Monetary Supplies in Graeco-Roman Times*, ed. F. de Callataÿ [Bari: Edipuglia, 2011], 1–16). See also W. W. Esty, "Estimation of the size of a coinage: a survey and comparison of methods," *NC* 146 (1986), 185–215; W. W. Esty, "How to estimate the original number of dies and the coverage of a sample," *NC* 166 (2006), 359–364.

8. It is apparent that a good portion of the obverse dies have been identified and almost half of the reverses, which implies that observations derived from this study are reasonably reliable, although future specimens may add, or alter, certain results altogether.

9. The Λ may simply be an A missing the horizontal bar, as proposed by M. Prieur and K. Prieur (*The Syro-Phoenician Tetradrachms and their Fractions*. [London/Lancaster, Penn.: Classical Numismatic Group, 2000], 117), but in the present study it is classified as a separate group, since specimens with lambda have been observed for Macrinus also (Caracalla: 2 dies from 3 specimens; Macrinus: 4 dies from 6 specimens, see Nurpetlian, *Coinage in Roman Syria.*

10. Caracalla: O, H, A, crescent, two pellets, Λ, no symbol; Julia Domna: O, H, A, Λ, Γ. The coins with no symbol should not be considered as specimens on which the symbol was forgotten by the engraver, since nine different dies have been identified for this group.

uncertain.[11] The number of dies identified for each group is given in Table 1 in descending order:

Table 1. Symbols on Emesan tetradrachms of Caracalla and Julia Domna

Group	Caracalla	Julia Domna	Total
O	28	18	46
H	28	9	37
A	29	6	35
Crescent	29	4	33
None	9	-	9
Two pellets	2	-	2
Λ	2	-	2
Γ	-	1	1
Uncertain	1	-	1
Total	128	38	166

A secondary investigation was undertaken to see if the various depictions of Caracalla's bust (bare, partially draped, and fully draped; Figs. 1, 3, and 4, respectively)[12] had an intentional significance.[13] Preliminary results indicate that there was no specific preference for the choice of different depictions of the bust,[14] as was the case in Damascus[15] and Tyre[16] for this emperor. The same irrelevance was also observed for the varying position of the symbols placed on the reverse.[17] On one die (O3) Caracalla's bust is supported by an eagle with

11. The letter Δ (see coin no. 221 for Julia Domna and a coin of Caracalla, no. 2, struck from the same reverse die) may simply be an A with a low horizontal bar, considering that this coin has an obverse die link with coins of the A group. The letter Δ is also known for a tetradrachm of Macrinus (CNG EA 225, lot 288) which also has a link with his A group (Nurpetlian, *Coinage in Roman Syria*). Accordingly, further specimens are needed to classify it as a separate group with confidence.

12. Prieur 951–952, 954, 956–959, Prieur 955, 960, and Prieur –, respectively. The latter is known from a single specimen, coin no. 210 (Naville 19, lot 299) in the present catalogue.

13. The emperor is invariably depicted laureate. A radiate portrait is yet unknown for Emesa, unlike at other mints.

14. As an example, dies O9 (partially draped bust) and O12 (bare bust) share a reverse die (R27).

15. J. Nurpetlian, "Damascene tetradrachms of Caracalla," *AJN* 26 (2014), 189–190.

16. J. Nurpetlian, "Tyrian tetradrachms of Caracalla: a quantitative analysis," *Berytus Archaeological Studies* (forthcoming).

17. In front of or behind the eagle's head; behind deity's head; bottom right field; or within legend.

Figure 3. Emesan AR tetradrachm of Caracalla with partially draped bust. 12.67 g.
Tom Cederlind 160, 142.

Figure 4. Emesan AR tetradrachm of Caracalla with fully draped bust. 12.26 g.
Naville 19, 299.

Figure 5. Emesan AR tetradrachm of Caracalla with bust supported by eagle. 13.05 g.
Vcoins Den of Antiquities.

open wings (Fig. 5).[18] Such extraordinary depictions have been referred to as
"introductory" or "inaugural" issues,[19] but based on the position of this die in
the die chain (see Chart 1, fold-out between pp. 186 and 187) this hypothesis
can be neither confirmed nor rejected in the case of Emesa; although it has been
argued in a die study of the Damascene issues that such a depiction of the emperor's bust was unlikely to be the first in the die sequence.[20]

From the number of dies identified, which, in general, should be an indication of the quantities produced in the past, the issues with no symbol, O, H, A,
and crescent seem to have had the largest production, with the remaining issues

18. Prieur 953.
19. P. M. Gilmore, "Syrian officinae under Caracalla and Macrinus," *NCirc* 87.6 (1979), 287;
Prieur, *Syro-Phoenician Tetradrachms*, xxv.
20. J. Nurpetlian, "Damascene tetradrachms," 189.

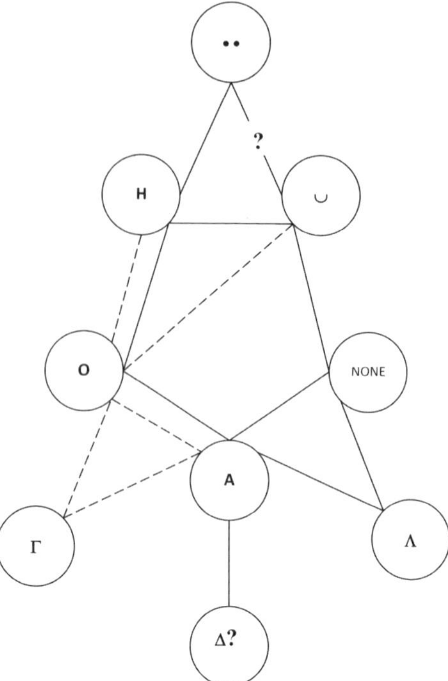

Figure 6. Links between symbols
(solid lines for Caracalla and dashed lines for Julia Domna).

represented by small numbers.[21] In fact, the former group consisting of "primary" symbols seems to have been the core of production, whereas the latter group, involving two pellets, Λ, or Γ, seem to have been "secondary" in nature,[22] as may be discerned from the symbol-link diagram (Fig. 6).[23]

SOME OBSERVATIONS

The average weight of 233 specimens was calculated to be 12.97 g and the average size 25.75 mm (53 specimens).[24] The majority of coins are struck with an upright axis of 12 h, and to a lesser extent 6 h, with 1 h, 5 h, 7 h, 10 h and 11 h also noted.

21. The quantity of coins surviving to date, or at least those compiled for the study, more or less correlate with the quantity of dies identified for each group.

22. Prieur (*Syro-Phoenician Tetradrachms*, 124), in addition to remarking that the issues with two pellets and Γ are small, also noted that they are stylistically distinct and therefore considered them separate from the "main workshops" (see below). Prieur assimilated Λ with A.

23. For the sake of clarity, the diagram was drawn in such a way to avoid lines crossing over one another.

24. The weight ranges from 10 to 16 g and the size from 23 to 29 mm.

Figure 7. Emesan AR tetradrachm of Caracalla with Julia Domna reverse.
Roma Numismatics 7, 896.

Figure 8. Emesan tetradrachm of Julia Domna with Caracalla reverse.
Numismatic Fine Arts 14, 481.

Figure 9. Emesan AR tetradrachm of Caracalla with uncertain reverse inscription.
Roma Numismatics 4, 601.

Figure 10. Emesan AR tetradrachm of Caracalla with ΥΠΑΤΟΣ Π Π legend. 13.44 g.
BnF, CdB 1906.

Figure 11. Emesan AR tetradrachm of Caracalla with "double crescent." 15.02 g.
Yale 1938.6000.1012.

Figure 12. Emesan AR tetradrachm of Caracalla with facing radiate deity. 11.69 g.
BM G.2334.

Figure 13. Tyrian AR tetradrachm of Caracalla with affinities to Emesa. 9.60 g.
Yale 1938.6000.293

Eighteen coins of Caracalla were struck from nine reverse dies intended for
Julia Domna, as attested by the inscription ΔHMAPX EΞ OYCIAC (Fig. 7, above),
whereas six specimens (from four dies) of the Empress had on the reverse the
emperor's title ΔHMAPX EΞ YΠATOC TO Δ (Fig. 8, above), a good indication that
both series were concurrent and that dies were freely shared.

Some minor spelling errors for Caracalla's legends were noticed as follows:
ΔHMAPX EΞ YΠ[A]TOC TO Δ and ΔHMAPX EX YΠATOC T[O] Δ. Five specimens
of the reverse die R3 also have an uncertain relief inscription in the exergue of
the reverse (Fig. 9, above). It may be the remains of the legend [ΔHMAPX E]Ξ [Y]
ΠA[TOC] T Δ possibly resulting from recutting of the die.

A single specimen with the bust of Caracalla (symbol H, coin no. 108) has the
reverse inscription YΠATOC Π Π (Fig. 10, above). It is doubtful that the engraver

deliberately gave the title ΠΑΤΗΡ ΠΑΤΡΙΔΟC to the Emperor; it is more likely that the coin is a mule struck in the reign of Macrinus using a reverse of his and an obverse of his predecessor.[25] A similar case, again from a single specimen, is also known from Tyre (a possible association with this mint is discussed below).[26] Thus, technically, these specimens should be considered to be issues under Macrinus and not Caracalla.

In addition to the main group featuring two pellets as a symbol, on two dies (R25 and R79) a pellet is present along with A and O. It remains uncertain if the addition of this pellet was deliberate or accidental. The same observation is also true for the H group, which includes one die (R10') with two letters H.[27] On one specimen of Julia Domna with a reverse of Caracalla (R29', coin no. 257) the letter O is clearly recut over an A (or Λ).

The tips of the crescent symbol are regularly engraved pointing upward, right or left. Based on the limited die links available no specific pattern was found in their orientation or position in the field, however, an interlocked double-crescent symbol is known from a single die (R107, 5 specimens, Fig. 11), but it may be an upward crescent engraved over a downward crescent (an orientation not known for the series). If this is the case, then this die would imply that the orientation of the crescent was indeed important and therefore corrected.[28]

The radiate deity between the legs of the eagle invariably faces left, but on a single specimen (coin no. 212, British Museum G.2334) the bust is depicted facing (Fig. 12).[29] Both Bellinger and Prieur noted that the style is somewhat different and considered it as an exceptional case.[30]

A noteworthy observation was made during a die study of the tetradrachms of Caracalla minted at Tyre,[31] which depict a murex shell between the legs of the eagle.[32] One specimen (Fig. 13) depicts the emperor's portrait in a style un-

25. This hypothesis can be confirmed upon finding a die pairing between this reverse and an obverse of Macrinus. Worth noting is a specimen struck with the obverse of Macrinus and a reverse of Caracalla (legend ending in TOC TO Δ with crescent symbol, Forum Ancient Coins lot 9032); Nurpetlian, *Coinage in Roman Syria.*

26. Prieur 1552.

27. The "double H" coin is not classified as a separate group, since it is linked with coins with a single H. Note: multiple modern counterfeits of the coin in question are known.

28. Physical inspection of one of these coins may help settle this matter.

29. There does not seem to be a symbol on the reverse, but difficult to confirm due to the poor state of preservation.

30. Bellinger, *Syrian Tetradrachms,* 64; Prieur, *Syro-Phoenician Tetradrachms,* 124.

31. Nurpetlian, "Tyrian tetradrachms."

32. Bellinger *Syrian Tetradrachms,* 86–87; Prieur, *Syro-Phoenician Tetradrachms,* 170–171.

like all other obverses of that city (85 obverse dies identified from 194 coins).[33] Remarkably, the portrait resembles those found on issues of Emesa, while the obverse legend and titulature follow the model of Emesan rather than Tyrian issues.[34] Also notable is the difference in the arrangement of the wreath leaves on the specimen in question. Thus, it may be the case that an obverse die from Emesa migrated to Tyre, or an engraver from Emesa travelled there, or a Tyrian die engraver simply copied from an Emesan coin.[35] Of course, these assumptions of die or engraver sharing can be verified if a die link is established between the two cities, but none was found between this coin and any of the 38 dies (82%) identified for Caracalla in this die study. To the best of the author's knowledge no evidence for shared dies between the mints of Caracalla's tetradrachms has yet been published, although die sharing is known for his bronzes in Asia Minor.[36] However, certain stylistic similarities between tetradrachms from different mints are known, in addition to uncanonical style of dies from the same mint, which reminds us of Butcher's statement that "mints which produced tetradrachms bearing symbols specific to their own cities could have issued coins for other cities which bore symbols specific to those cities."[37] To explore this phenomenon further, an attempt was made to find similarities in style between the Emesan tetradrachms of Caracalla and his bronze coins attributed to that mint, but no solid connection was observed.[38] It is noteworthy that the bronze issues of Emesa, some of which bear dates, do not have field marks,[39] with the exception of those of Antonius Pius, which have the letters A, B, Γ, Δ, E, Ϛ and Z, which seem to be of an alphanumeric nature and not symbolic. Thus, one wonders if the silver and bronze coins of Emesa were produced entirely separately, keeping in mind that the attribution of the tetradrachms remains unconfirmed in the first place.

---

33. The reverse is for Caracalla's third consulship, hence cut under Septimius Severus.

34. Tyre: AYT KAI ANTWNINOC CE; Emesa: AVT K MA ANTΩNEINOC CEB (with slight variants known); the Tyrian specimen in question: AVT K MA ANTΩNEINOC CEB (note the form of omega as well).

35. One wonders if it is also sheer coincidence that to date muled specimens pairing dies of Macrinus and Caracalla are known only from Emesa and Tyre.

36. As an example see K. Kraft, *Das System der kaiserzeitlichen Münzprägung in Kleinasien* (Berlin: Mann, 1972), no. 195.

37. *CRS* 112.

38. Prieur (*Syro-Phoenician Tetradrachms*, 173) had also attempted to do this for the Cypriot mint but without any tangible success. He noted a stylistic similarity between Emesan bronzes of Caracalla and some tetradrachms of Rhesaena, and therefore contemplated whether they should be attributed to Emesa (Prieur, *Syro-Phoenician Tetradrachms*, 104).

39. Some issues under Elagabalus have the letter E (Nurpetlian, *Coinage in Roman Syria*).

An interesting observation made as a result of the present contribution is the reliability of the statistical results derived from die studies in accordance to the quantities studied. The current pool of 289 specimens with the smaller previous study of only 86 specimens is compared in Table 2.

Table 2. Comparison of die statistics between sample groups

n	d_o	d_r	D_o	D_r	d_o/D_o	d_r/D_r	n/d_o	n/d_r	D_r/D_o
86	37	70	64.94	376.25	56.97%	18.60%	2.32	1.23	5.79
289	51	166	61.92	390.03	82.36%	42.56%	5.66	1.74	6.29

The estimated number of original dies, and hence their ratio, is nearly identical, whereas the coverage of the dies changes considerably, and accordingly their index numbers (n/d), rendering the results more reliable.[40] Hence, obviously, the larger the pool the better the results of a die study and a good indication that the results derived from the formula used here to calculate the original number of dies produced in the past is quite consistent.

Table 3 compares the volume of production for the mints of Damascus, Emesa, and Tyre, the three tetradrachm mints for which statistical data is currently available.

Table 3. Comparison of production volume at Damascus, Emesa, and Tyre

	Damascus	Emesa	Tyre
n	91	289	194
D_o	20.90	61.92	151.28
D_r	323.05	390.03	707.12
n/d_o	5.35	5.66	2.28
n/d_r	1.28	1.74	1.27
D_r/D_o	15.45	6.29	4.67

Although Table 3 does provide general patterns in the production of dies and mint output, it would be premature to draw conclusions from the three mints alone. The volume of production, when based on the estimated number of obverse dies originally produced,[41] provides a view of the output "ranking" of each

40. A minimum index number of 2 is required for statistics to be of value (W. W. Esty, "The theory of linkage," *NC* 150 [1990], 217–221). Note that in the second study this was better achieved for the reverse (1.23 vs. 1.74, or 18% vs. 42%).

41. Scholars generally prefer the number of obverse dies for the estimation of output, but various elements such as the ratio D_r/D_o, n/d_o and n/d_r should be taken into consideration. In this study the obverse is preferred since the index number n/d_o is well above 2, in particular for Emesa and Damascus, and therefore more reliable than the index n/d_r.

mint, with Tyre, a prominent mint in the region, leading the group, followed by Emesa. Further studies can provide a better view for the output of silver by mints in the Roman East during the reign of Caracalla.[42] An anomaly in the above table is the high ratio of D_r/D_o at Damascus; future studies are needed to show if this is repeated elsewhere or a one-off case.

THE SYMBOLS

With regards to the meaning of the symbols on Emesan tetradrachms of Caracalla[43] Bellinger identified them as officina marks, but found them to be surprisingly "numerous."[44] Gilmore proposed that the Greek letters (A, H, O, etc.) were initials of the responsible strikers and the (non-alphabetic) symbols (crescent, two pellets, etc.) batch marks for their subordinates.[45] This proposition does not take into account the Greek letters Λ and Γ (and possibly Δ) and the fact that the crescent symbol seems not to be a "subordinate" based on the considerable number of dies identified. Prieur also considered them to be *officinae*, hence his systematic classification as "Officina A," "Officina H," etc.,[46] but later contemplated whether they might represent the "signatures" of elite families or magistrates.[47]

Although it was hoped that the current die study would resolve the above hypotheses, the overall die chart (Chart 1) does not provide a discernible pattern for the linkages between the various symbols. Separate die charts of individual symbol groups are provided as Figures 14–21. The preliminary results indicate that the symbols are linked in a rather haphazard way (see Fig. 6, above), or at least they remain incomprehensible, since not all the dies have yet been accounted for. The symbols are not sequential chronologically, but the numerous links imply that the coinage was struck in the same location. A similar die study of 73 Emesan bronze coins of Antoninus Pius with the letter-numerals A, B, Γ,

---

42. A die study of tetradrachms of Caracalla from the mint of Ptolemaïs (151 specimens) is currently in process by the present author.

43. These field marks are exceptional for they include both letters and symbols (hence the generic reference to them in this article as "symbols"), unlike other Syrian series, in which letters/numbers exclusively replaced the earlier use of pellets by the reign of Domitian in Syria (K. Butcher, "Numerical letters on Syrian coins: officina or sequence marks?" *RBN* 158 (2012), 124).

44. *Syrian Tetradrachms,* 64.

45. Gilmore, "Syrian officinae," 287.

46. Prieur, *Syro-Phoenician Tetradrachms,* 115–124.

47. Keeping in mind that the field marks include non-alphabetic symbols as well (personal communication before his untimely death).

Δ, E, Ϛ and Z on the reverse, which would naturally seem to be of a sequential nature, has also shown that the dies are non-sequential but spatially connected.[48]

Symbols on Roman provincial bronzes have baffled scholars for centuries. It is needless to present a review of all that has been said on the matter here. The reader is referred to the recent work by Kevin Butcher[49] which presents a historical survey, starting in the sixteenth century, with an analysis of various proposals to better understand these markings.[50] It is sufficient to summarize his findings that there is no specific pattern and a simple chronological sequence did not provide an answer to the question, unless random overlaps and erratic gaps are allowed for. The evidence of die deterioration has also demonstrated that the numbers are not necessarily sequential.[51] Also, the letter-numerals do not conform to regnal years or a lunar calendar, nor do they necessarily indicate officina marks, as some are too numerous.[52] They obviously cannot be numbers relating to individual dies, and if they were strictly meant to represent batches of metal, the same erratic results listed above also apply. To add to the confusion, preliminary die studies conducted by Butcher have frequently shown that the field marks are not connected in any discernible pattern, as in the case of the above-mentioned Emesan bronze coins of Antonius Pius. However, despite the anomalies listed above, McAlee finds it plausible that these letters, symbols, and pellets could represent individual workstations without necessarily implying that they were physically separate departments and concludes that "the numeral-letters on the *aes* coins represent different *officinae* of the mint, just as they do on the provincial tetradrachms and on the Roman coins struck at Antioch."[53]

It may simply be the case that this confusion is due to the question being approached in the wrong way when trying to understand field marks through die charts. Consequently, the results would be misleading since the connections

48. Nurpetlian, *Coinage in Roman Syria.*

49. Butcher, "Numerical letters," 123–144. Information in what follows is from this source. See also *CRS* for general observations, in particular, pp. 94–95 and 236–237.

50. For other (non-provincial) Roman coinages with field marks, see R. Witschonke, "The Use of Die Marks on Roman Republican Coinage," *RBN* 158 (2012), 65–86, and B. Woytek, "System and product in Roman mints from the Late Republic to the High Principate: some current problems," *RBN* 158 (2012), 85–122.

51. Following R. McAlee, *The Coins of Roman Antioch* [Lancaster, Penn.: Classical Numismatic Group, 2007], 9), who has also demonstrated that other die deteriorations do demonstrate a sequential order, further adding to the confusion.

52. For example under Trajan at Antioch where 18 numerical letters have been identified (including the "no numeral letter" group) (*CRS* 357).

53. McAlee, *Coins*, 10. He adds that for certain cases the unusually high numbers observed, such as under Trajan as mentioned above, are due to increased output in certain periods.

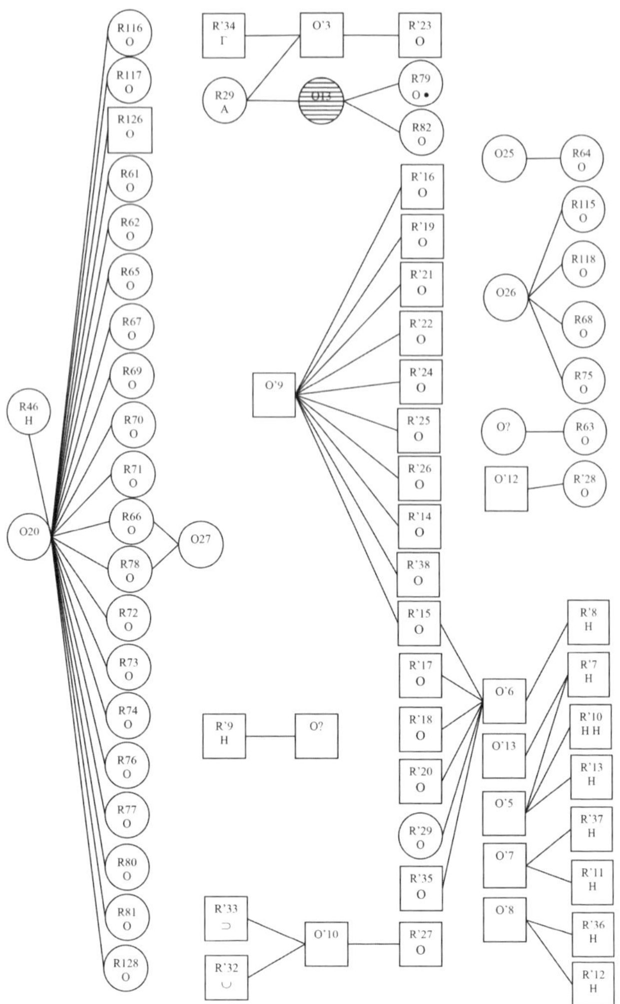

Figure 14. Die links for O tetradrachms of Emesa.

observed could be the result of the so-called "obverse die box" hypothesis,[54] in which obverse dies were freely shared in the mint regardless of the individual marks on the reverses, even if they did indicate separate workstations.[55] In fact,

54. Esty, "The theory of linkage"; G. F. Carter and R. S. Nord, "Calculation of the average die lifetimes and the number of anvils for coinage in antiquity," *AJN* 3–4 (1992), 147–164.

55. McAlee, *Coins,* 10; Woytek, "System and product," 114–115. Consideration should also be made of (obverse) dies lying dormant for a duration of time and later being reactivated for whatever reason (for such an example see K. J. J. Elks, "Coins of Caracalla with altered dies." *NC* 13 [1973], 222–223).

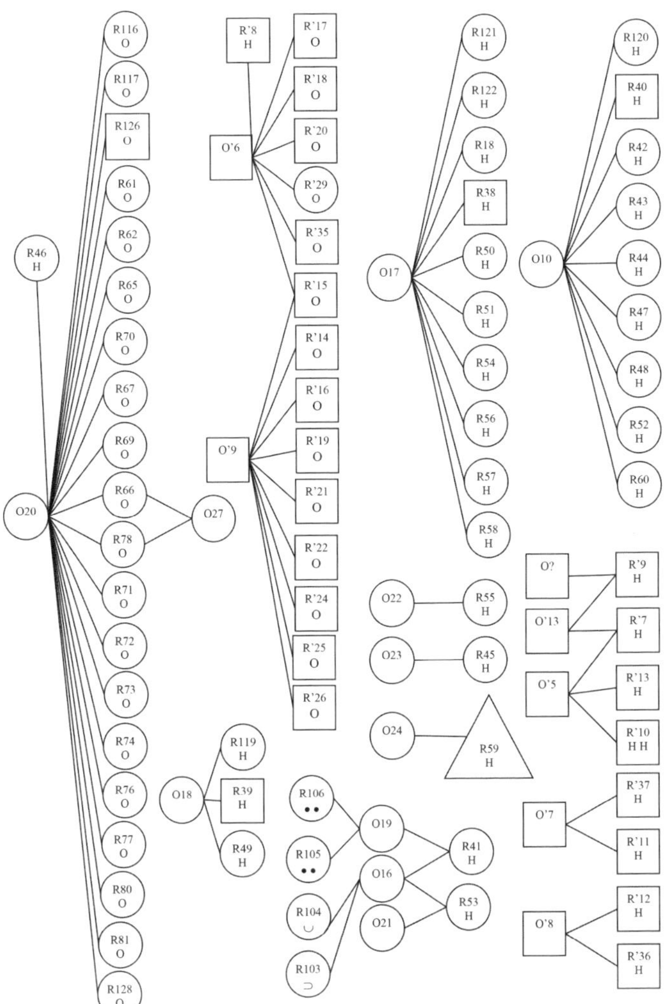

Figure 15. Die links for H tetradrachms of Emesa.

a strong indication of such free use of the obverses at Emesa is evidenced by the frequent use of Caracalla obverses with reverses of Julia Domna and vice versa.[56] Butcher had observed in his preliminary die study of coins of Beroea and Antioch that "if officinae operated using a common pool of dies we might have expected more random links,"[57] but at least in the case of Emesa this has been demonstrated and it is very reasonable to expect more random links between the

56. Also the reverse of Macrinus (ΥΠΑΤΟϹ Π Π, letter H) used with an obverse of Caracalla.
57. Butcher, "Numerical letters," 130.

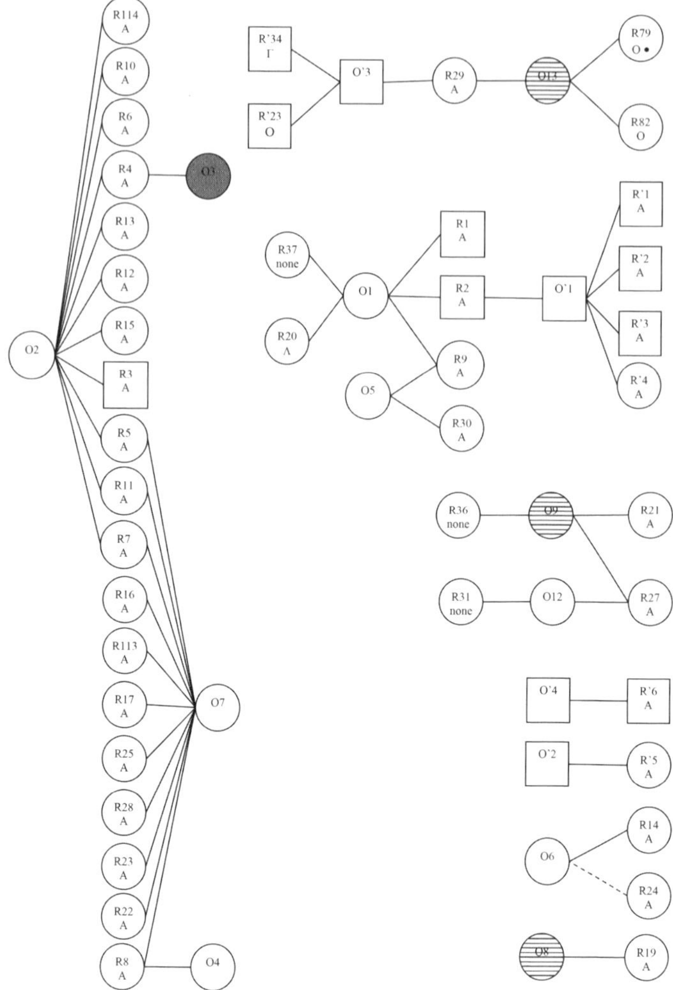

Figure 16. Die links for A tetradrachms of Emesa.

various groups as further specimens emerge in the future, keeping in mind that less than half (42%) of the reverse dies have yet been accounted for. Additionally, a die study of Emesan tetradrachms of Macrinus and Diadumenian could potentially find further links between symbols not established here.

The silver issues of Emesa can in fact be compared to another issue of tetradrachms from the immediate region, albeit from a different time period. Simon Glenn has recently concluded a die study of the Damascene tetradrachms of Alexander the Great, with the primary goal of investigating the meaning of

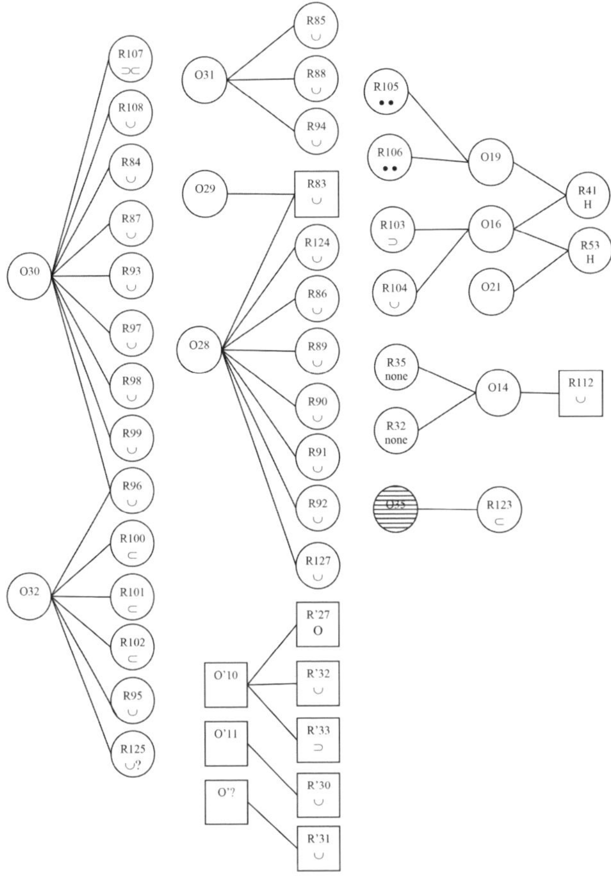

Figure 17. Die links for crescent tetradrachms of Emesa.

the pellets (ranging from one to six) on their reverses.[58] It was naturally anticipated that those with one pellet were used before those with two, two before three, etc., but this did not turn out to be the case. The die links discovered were highly "entangled" leading the author to conclude that there was "no clear pattern of usage among different reverse symbols, which seem to have been used interchangeably with multiple obverse dies."[59] Glenn considered that perhaps the six groups were markings meant to be used after the minting process, whereby

58. S. Glenn, "Exploring localities: a die study of Alexanders from Damascus," in *Alexander the Great. A Linked Open World*, ed. S. Glenn, F. Duyrat and A. Meadows (Ausonius: Bordeaux, 2018), 91–126.

59. Glenn, "Exploring localities," 100.

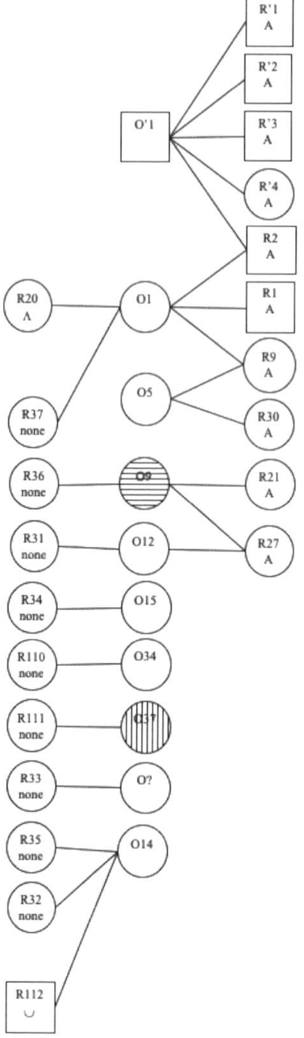

Figure 18. Die links for tetradrachms of Emesa with no symbols.

the processed coins would be tallied for accounting purposes, for example to adjust the overall weight and inspect the batches of raw material distributed to the workstations.[60] Yet another die study of the same Alexandrine tetradrachms

60. For similar proposals see Witschonke ("Use of Die Marks," 80–81, for the Roman Republican period) discussing "secret marks" for recording bags of produced coins in a ledger for purposes of tracing (post-production) any unscrupulous activity in the mint, and also

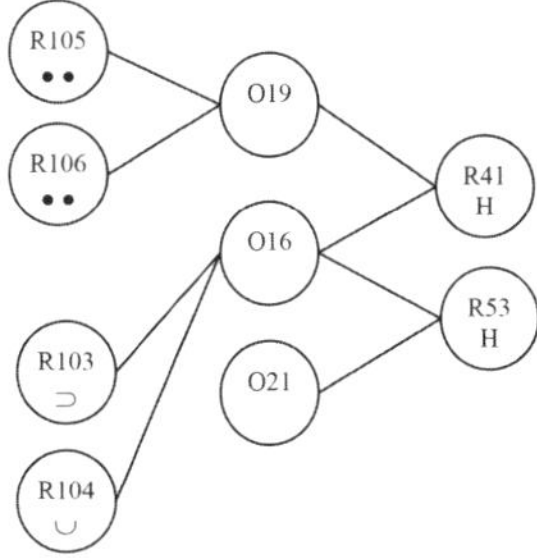

Figure 19. Die links for double-pellet tetradrachms of Emesa.

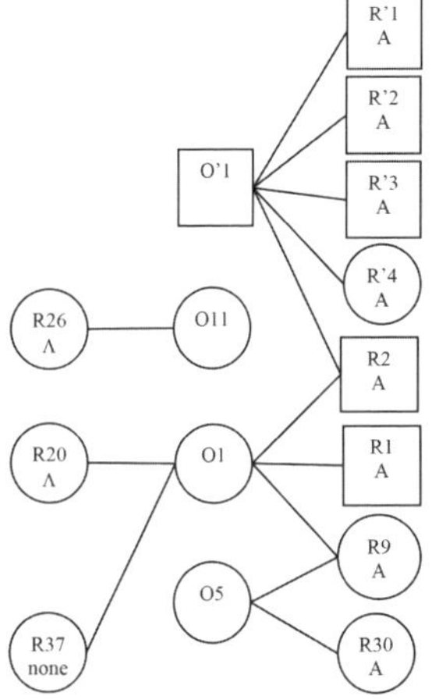

Figure 20. Die links for Λ tetradrachms of Emesa.

has again found a tight interlinking of obverse dies and consequently reached the conclusion that the pellets signify a post-production internal accounting process, since no chronological sequence was observed between the six groups, with the exception of the very first issues.[61]

Currently, there seems to be two generally accepted interpretations for these field marks: the first favors the *officina* hypothesis, as this has been attested for certain coinages, and the second favors the idea that field marks represent batches of metal and accordingly function as an internal accounting system. To the

B. Woytek, "Metal and system in Roman imperial mints. Flan production, quality control and the internal organisation of minting establishments during the Principate," in *Debasement: Manipulation of Coin Standards in Pre-modern Monetary Systems*, ed. K. Butcher (Oxford: Oxbow, 2020), 4, for the early Roman Imperial period).

61. L. W. H. Taylor, "The Damaskos Mint of Alexander the Great," *AJN* 29 (2017), 47–99.

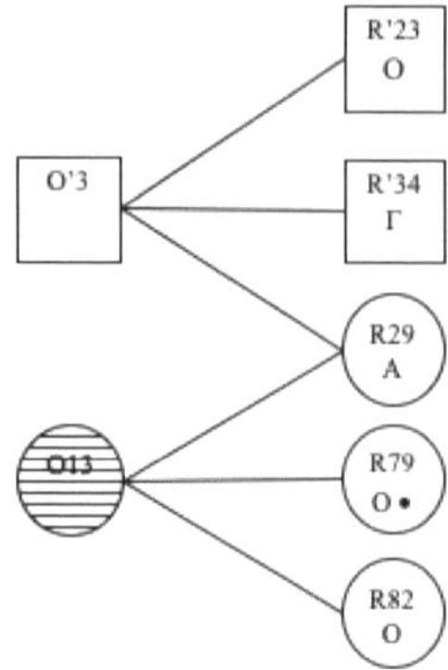

Figure 21. Die links for Γ tetradrachms of Emesa.

latter it should be added that the batches of metal were likely to be in the form of ready-made flans sent to the mint. Tons of metal would have been needed to maintain the output of an average mint and it is not illogical to think that several suppliers would have been needed to provide the large quantities of flans.[62] It is known that in the Roman period flans were outsourced to private contractors (*conductores*) as it was a highly laborious task.[63] The lack of understanding and confusion discussed above may be due to the assumption that these flans were obtained from a single supplier in a chronologically sequential manner (batch A, followed by batch B, then Γ, etc.; or one pellet followed by two pellets, then three, etc.), but it would be more logical to think that the flans were simultaneously, or sporadically, sent from numerous sources throughout the production process and therefore at any given time several batches may have been in concurrent use.[64] This explanation can accommodate the observation made by McAlee of certain die deteriorations being of a non-sequential nature and can even explain the lack of chronological connection between coins having one to six pellets with the exception of the first series, noted by Taylor. The mint may have started the production process with flans initially provided by a single source, but these were supplemented by other suppliers, leading to the inevitable entanglement

62. "The bottleneck that constrained a daily coinage production rate was the manufacture of blanks [which] took longer than the seconds taken to complete a coin strike" (Taylor, "Damaskos Mint," 94 n. 20).

63. Woytek, "Metal and system," using a Trajanic inscription for the mint of Rome. See also A. Burnett, "The Invisibility of Roman Imperial Mints," in *I luoghi della moneta. Le sedi delle zecche dall'antichità all'età moderna. Atti del convegno internazionale 22–23 ottobre 1999 Milano*, ed. R. La Guardia (Milan: Commune di Milano, 2001), 42.

64. "A single issue may exhibit flans produced by more than one method" (*CRS*, 127) when discussing the physical characteristics of coinages in Roman Syria.

of the die links soon after. Thus, if indeed several sources were needed for the acquisition of ready-made blanks, then this would explain why some symbols are represented by a large output and others small (cottage industries?). As for the coins without any symbol, this group may either represent flans produced at the mint itself and/or scrap bullion brought in by individuals for conversion into coins[65] or the recycling of unacceptable coins,[66] such as error strikes.[67]

Conversely, it may be proposed that these field marks represent both workstations and batches of metal. Based on the evidence that in certain cases flan production was farmed out to contractors, one wonders if the actual minting of coins was also farmed out to several contractors, such as workmasters[68] who would delegate the production process in exchange for a commission. Accordingly, each workmaster would be in charge of hiring and presiding over a team of workers operating an anvil,[69] while overseeing that a steady supply of ready-

65. The idea of a "free coinage" in the Roman period remains contested, but is well known from later periods. See B. Woytek, "Exactions and the Monetary Economy of the Late Roman Republic. A Numismatic Perspective," in *Les confiscations, le pouvoir et Rome de la fin de la République à la mort de Néron*, ed. C. Chillet, M.-C. Ferriès and Y. Rivière (Bordeaux: Ausonius, 2016) 183–197. Interesting to note is that the number of identified dies for the group with no symbol at Emesa falls more or less between the groups having a "large" and "small" output.

66. Similar to replacement notes in modern times, which are marked by a symbol, such as a star, instead of the usual alphabetic letters (Bureau of Engraving and Printing, U.S. Department of the Treasury, https://www.moneyfactory.gov/resources/serialnumbers.html)

67. It is reasonable that mints would have employed officials in charge of quality control (see Woytek, "Metal and system"). For "rejected" coins, see Burnett, "Invisibility," 43. Although a considerable number of dies with no symbol have been identified at Emesa and considering that several thousand coins could be struck from a single die, the number of "rejected/recycled" coins would seem to be quite high; however, the ratio of these dies (9) to the overall number of dies identified (166) is approximately 5%, which is not an unreasonable number. As an example of the relatively good production quality of tetradrachms of Caracalla, from a survey of some 3,000 specimens available online, only one brockage coin was found, a ratio of 0.0003%.

68. Similar to the setup in the House of Fabergé which farmed out the production of jewelry as demand increased (U. Tillander-Godenhielm, *Fabergé ja hänen suomalaiset mestarinsa* (Fabergé and his Finnish Workmasters) [Helsinki: Tammi, 2008]).

69. A single workmaster may have employed numerous anvils (as hinted by die links within some of the symbol groups, such as the A group at Emesa, Chart 1, foldout) explaining why some symbols have a high output and others low. It may also be the case that some workmasters may have combined their efforts by merging (similar to McAlee's proposal of *officinae* merging in Antioch: "(BΔ) would represent the merger of the second (B) and fourth (Δ) *officinae*" (McAlee, *Coins*, 10), or one team may have entirely absorbed another, thus explaining why some field marks appear rarely (due to a short run?) or why one symbol may be engraved over another (O recut over A or Λ mentioned above).

made flans, whether outsourced or prepared in house, was in stock.[70] Each workmaster may have also employed a die cutter dedicated (exclusively?) to the relevant team.[71] Thus, each team would have been a self-sufficient unit (not necessarily physically separate from the others) employing a specific control mark for accounting and accountability reasons. The only duty the workmaster would not oversee would be the retention of the dies, which was probably the responsibility of an overseeing official of the mint (moneyers appointed by the central authorities?[72]), whereby the dies would be collected and stored in a safe 'box' at the end of the working day only to be redistributed (randomly in the case of the obverses) the following day;[73] this would explain the presence of the numerous symbols at Emesa, but which all fall under the authority of the main symbol of the mint: the radiate bust.

Yet another equally important question is why this system of marking was not utilized universally, keeping in mind that not all mints employed letters and symbols on their coinages, particularly the numerous mints producing tetradrachms under Caracalla of which the present study is part of.[74] The answer to this question is not known, but perhaps it may be because when the tallying of the struck coins was conducted immediately upon production and in the same location, such traceable marks were not needed,[75] but if done elsewhere and/

70. Noting observations of differences in manufacturing techniques of flans of the same issue.

71. Which can explain why stylistic differences have been observed among dies of the same issue. In fact, Prieur had attempted to study the obverse and reverse styles of the engravers of these Emesan tetradrachms to identify any correlation between them and the individual symbols and managed to make the tentative observation that the 'regular' die-engravers (permanently employed professionals?) were working for the symbols with a large output and the 'irregular' engravers (less qualified freelancers?) for the groups with a small output (personal communication). Interesting to note is a similar observation by McAlee for Antiochene bronze issues under Antoninus Pius where certain issues having numeral letters which appear rarely were noted to be "irregular" in appearance (McAlee, *Coins*, 10).

72. Keeping in mind that 28 mints (based on Bellinger's classification) commence minting under Caracalla, an indication of a centralized initiative (Bellinger, *Syrian Tetradrachms*, 1940, 6; Prieur, *Syro-Phoenician Tetradrachms*, xxv). For the existence of a "technical head" of the mint in Rome and his deputy, see R. A. G. Carson, "System and Product in the Roman Mint," in *Essays in Roman Coinage Presented to Harold Mattingly*, ed. R. A. G. Carson and C. H. V. Sutherland (Oxford: Oxford University Press, 1956), 233–234.

73. The reverse dies may have been marked for allocation to the relevant teams, but the die study indicates that the obverses were freely shared.

74. To provide another example of a similar case, marked and unmarked Roman Republican coins are known to have been produced concurrently (see *RRC*).

75. As an example, Tyre produced tetradrachms under Caracalla with an estimated 707 reverse dies, a number nearly twice that of Emesa, and yet no field marks were utilized.

or later, then these markings would be necessary to retrospectively identify the source.[76]

To sum up, when contextualizing Emesan silver and bronze issues with other similar examples from the region, the result presented here fits in with the general trend observed for the other coinages with symbols/letters/pellets: the lack of any consistent pattern, despite approaching the issue from various angles. This may be because where there is evidence for the free sharing of (obverse) dies, the die study itself is rendered obsolete and the cause of all the distractions. To date there is still no universal explanation for the need or the function of the various field marks on certain coinages despite a considerable amount of research that has been done.[77] However, there is no reason why these symbols should have had a universally adopted function at mints, for they may have signified *officinae*, batches of metal, control marks, an internal accounting system or, perhaps, a combination of all of the above.

CATALOGUE

Caracalla

A

1.	O1	R1*	-	10.78 g	12 h	PC	A behind eagle's head
2.	O1	R2*	-	14.96 g	12 h	PC	A or possibly Δ behind deity.
3.	O1	R9	-	14.94 g	12 h	PC	
4.	O2	R10	-	12.08 g	1 h	market	
5.	O2	R11	-	12.42 g	1 h	van Hoof	
6.	O2	R11	28 mm	11.9 g	-	eBay 391546632382	
7.	O2	R114	-	-	-	Roma 9, 300	
8.	O2	R12	-	-	-	Hirsch 173, 1022	
9.	O2	R13	-	15.24 g	-	Berk 88, 671	
10.	O2	R15	-	12.46 g	-	eBay 2197877391	

76. One should not entirely rule out the possibility that workshops may have been located in various places (with dies being distributed and collected on a daily basis), knowing that this would require added security measures to prevent any unofficial production of coins. For the relative 'uncomplicated' nature of setting up a mint, without necessarily having a dedicated building, see Burnett 2001, 45–46.

77. "There is always the possibility that their meaning will forever evade us" (Butcher, "Numerical letters," 131).

11.	O2	R15	-	-	-	Vosper e-shop 2005	
12.	O2	R3*	25	13.47 g	12 h	Bellinger pl XIV, 6	Uncertain inscription below eagle. Recut die?
13.	O2	R3*		13.49 g	12 h	PC	Uncertain inscription below eagle. Recut die?
14.	O2	R3*	26	12.97 g	12 h	CNG 352, 353	Uncertain inscription below eagle. Recut die?
15.	O2	R3*	-	-	-	G&M 191, 1851	Uncertain inscription below eagle. Recut die?
16.	O2	R3*	-	-	-	Roma 4, 601	Uncertain inscription below eagle. Recut die?
17.	O2	R4	-	13.24 g	-	eBay 150225509981	
18.	O2	R4	-	-	-	Teutoburger Münzauktion Volker Wolframm, 13/09/1999, 298	
19.	O2	R4	-	12.91 g	12 h	CNG 231, 447	
20.	O2	R4	-	13.73 g	-	G&M 191, 1853	
21.	O2	R4	-	-	-	Auktionshaus H. D. Rauch GmbH 91, 522	
22.	O2	R4	-	-	-	Emporium Hamburg 501, 173	
23.	O2	R5	26 mm	-	-	Bellinger pl XIV, 5	
24.	O2	R5	-	14.44 g	1 h	CNG 194, 160	
25.	O2	R6	-	14.1 g	1 h	BnF, HSY 19563	
26.	O2	R7	-	15.4 g	7 h	BnF (Fonds général)	
27.	O2	R7	-	13.6 g	-	PC	
28.	O2	R7	-	-	-	G&M 142, 3462	

No.	Obv.	Rev.		Weight	Axis	Source	Note
29.	O3	R4	-	12.24 g	12 h	PC	Bust supported by eagle
30.	O3	R4	-	13.05 g	12 h	Vcoins Den of Antiquities	Bust supported by eagle
31.	O3	R4	-	-	-	Hirsch 164, 641	Bust supported by eagle
32.	O4	R8	27.5	13.16 g	7 h	Boston 1998.525	
33.	O5	R30	-	13.26 g	12 h	PC	A behind eagle's head
34.	O5	R9	-	11.91 g	-	Rauch 35, 5616	
35.	O6	R14	-	12.34 g	1 h	Market	
36.	O6?	R24	-	-	-	Market	
37.	O7	?	-	-	-	Market	
38.	O7	R11	-	-	-	?	
39.	O7	R113	-	-	-	London Ancient Coins ltd 45, 152	
40.	O7	R16	-	12.23 g	-	CNG 45, 997	
41.	O7	R17	-	13.95 g	12 h	CNG Triton XII, 1282	
42.	O7	R22	-	-	-	Kunst und Münzen Lugano Liste 74, 153	
43.	O7	R22	-	12.33 g	1 h	van Hoof	
44.	O7	R22	-	-	-	Kunst und Münzen Fixed Price List 63, 235	
45.	O7	R22	-	13.00 g	-	Ponterio CICF 97, 1494	
46.	O7	R23	-	12.96 g	12 h	PC	
47.	O7	R23	-	13.49 g	12 h	Market	
48.	O7	R28	-	14.36 g	12 h	CNG MBS 85, 643	A behind eagle's head
49.	O7	R5	-	12.99 g	-	Pegasi 24, 320	
50.	O7	R5	-	12.97 g	12 h	DNW Ancient Coins, 05 10 2009, 5717	
51.	O7	R7	-	13.17 g	6 h	Sokolov I, 62	

52.	O7	R8	-	12.74 g	12 h	Numismatic Fine Arts Mail Bid Sale, 10/1990, 2146	
53.	O7	R8	-	-	-	CNG 218, 540	
54.	O7	R8	24 mm	12.65 g	1 h	CNG 378, 362	
55.	O7	R25	-	12.81 g	1 h	Market	Pellet behind eagle's head
56.	O8	R19	-	12.13 g	12 h	PC	Partially draped bust. Forgery?
57.	O8	R19	25 mm	11.71 g	1 h	Oxford, Amedioz	Partially draped bust
58.	O9	R21	-	12.54 g	6 h	PC	Partially draped bust
59.	O9	R27	-	14.58 g	-	PC	Partially draped bust
60.	O12	R27	-	11.59 g	7 h	BM 1853,1006.10	A behind eagle's head
61.	O13	R29	-	12.33 g	12 h	Numismatic Fine Arts Mail Bid Sale, 10/1988, 947	A behind eagle's head. Partially draped bust
62.	?	R19	-	7.09 g	6 h	PC	Low weight, forgery?

Λ

63.	O1	R20	-	13.25 g	12 h	Market	
64.	O1	R20	-	-	-	ACR Auctions 24, 830	
65.	O11	R26	-	11.65 g	1 h		Unusual reverse style

Η

66.	O10	R120	25 mm	13.29	12	CNG 353, 322
67.	O10	R40*	-	13.8	-	eBay 260068851552
68.	O10	R42	26.4 mm	11.73	12	*SNG Righetti* 2080
69.	O10	R43	-	13.51	12	Market
70.	O10	R44	-	12.45	12	van Hoof

71.	O10	R44	-	11.72 g	-	CNG MBS 49, 1103
72.	O10	R44	-	13.83 g	-	CNG Triton XII, 1280
73.	O10	R44	-	-	-	Roma Numismatics Limited 7, 895
74.	O10	R47	25.5 mm	12.83 g	12 h	Berlin, 11628
75.	O10	R48	-	12.91 g	12 h	market
76.	O10	R52	-	12.34 g	12 h	CNG 205, 310
77.	O10	R60	-	-	-	?
78.	O16	R41	-	13.21 g	11 h	CNG Triton XII, 1284
79.	O16	R53	25 mm	13.69 g	12 h	CNG 356, 349
80.	O17	R121	-	-	-	Dr. Busso Peus Nachfolger 409, 784
81.	O17	R122	-	-	-	G&M 200, 2261
82.	O17	R18	-	12.50 g	-	market
83.	O17	R38*	-	14.41 g	12 h	PC
84.	O17	R38*	-	-	-	Spijkerman pl I, 6
85.	O17	R38*	-	14.06 g	12 h	Vcoins auctions 2009, 223, 69
86.	O17	R50	-	15.13 g	-	Auctiones 29, 812
87.	O17	R51	-	13.10 g	-	Vcoins Pars 2007
88.	O17	R51	-	14.07 g	6 h	Numismatic Fine Arts 9/91993, 501
89.	O17	R51	-	13.10 g	6 h	CNG Triton XI, 511
90.	O17	R54	-	13.66 g	-	Vcoins Zurquieh 07 2010
91.	O17	R56	-	13.73 g	12 h	eBay 8330164760
92.	O17	R56	-	14.46 g	12 h	CNG Triton XII, 1284
93.	O17	R56	-	-	-	eBay 3900881370
94.	O17	R57	-	-	-	eBay 160062055119
95.	O17	R58	-	13.04 g	12 h	market
96.	O18	R119	24 mm	12.14 g	1 h	CNG 348, 554
97.	O18	R39*	-	14.11 g	12 h	Market
98.	O18	R49	-	12.49 g	-	Berk FPL 2005

99.	O19	R41	-	14.76 g	6 h	PC	
100.	O19	R41	-	13.64 g	-	CNG 60, 1366	
101.	O20	R46	-	14.55 g	12 h	CNG 38, 64285	
102.	O20	R46	-	13.95 g	1 h	Berk 59, 518	
103.	O20	R46	-	13.11 g	-	G&M 251, 4715	
104.	O21	R53	-	13.66 g	12 h	CNG 231, 447	
105.	O22	R55	-	14.17 g	12 h	*SNG Righetti* 2081	
106.	O23	R45	-	13.2 g	12 h	Market	
107.	O23	R45	-	13.14 g	12 h	CNG 238, 272	
108.	O24	R59	-	13.44 g	12 h	BnF, CdB 1906	Macrinus reverse (ΥΠΑΤΟC Π Π)
109.	?	R46	-	-	-	Doura Hoard 10, 21	

Crescent

110.	O14	R112*	-	-	-	Roma 7, 896	Crescent in legend
111.	O16	R103	25.5 mm	10.97 g	12	Yale 1938.6000.1013	Crescent left
112.	O16	R104	-	10.78 g	12	CNG 232, 142	Crescent up, behind eagle's head
113.	O28	R124	-	-	-	Teutoburger Munzauktion GmbH 90, 2124	Crescent up
114.	O28	R83*	-	12.59 g	6	PC	Crescent up
115.	O28	R86	-	15.93 g	5	Monnaies et Médailles 461, 64	Crescent up
116.	O28	R89	-	13.39 g	12	PC	Crescent up
117.	O28	R90	-	-	-	Market	Crescent up
118.	O28	R91	-	13.36 g	-	CNG 94, 118	Crescent up
119.	O28	R92	-	14.21 g	12	SNG UK VI, 1771 (Fitzwilliam)	Crescent up
120.	O28	R127	23 mm	13.91 g	12	CNG 418, 406	Crescent up
121.	O29	R83*	25.5 mm	11.59 g	12	Oxford, Amedioz	Crescent up
122.	O29	R83*	-	13.62 g	12	PC	Crescent up

123.	O30	R107	25 mm	15.02 g	12	Yale 1938.6000.1012	Double crescent
124.	O30	R107	-	10.00 g	12	PC	Double crescent
125.	O30	R107	-	-	12	Berk 59, 668	Double crescent
126.	O30	R107	-	13.14 g	12	Giessener Münzhandlung 46, 393	Double crescent
127.	O30	R107	-	12.58 g	12	CNG 45, 998	Double crescent
128.	O30	R108	-	12.37 g	12	Market	Blundered reverse legend or overstrike
129.	O30	R84	-	13.32 g	1	BnF, HSY 19565	Crescent up
130.	O30	R84	-	12.15 g	12	Numismatic Fine Arts 33, 568	Crescent up
131.	O30	R84	-	14.48 g	12	eBay 2224806700	Crescent up
132.	O30	R84	-	13.67 g	-	MM RFA 7, 328	Crescent up
133.	O30	R84	-	13.62 g	12	CNG Triton XII, 1284	Crescent up
134.	O30	R87	25 mm	13.45 g	6	Oxford, Bodleian	Crescent up
135.	O30	R93	25.5 mm	11.24 g	12	Yale 1938.6000.1011	Crescent up
136.	O30	R96	-	-	-	Bland p. 17, no. 29	Crescent up, behind eagle's head
137.	O30	R97	-	13.75 g	6	PC	Crescent up, behind eagle's head
138.	O30	R98	-	13.50 g	1	Müller Solingen 67, 113	Crescent up, behind eagle's head
139.	O30	R99	-	13.48 g	12	G&M 191, 1852	Crescent up, behind eagle's head
140.	O31	R85	-	-	-	Monnaies et Médailles 537, 173	Crescent up
141.	O31	R88	-	15.10 g	-	Peus 315, 426	Crescent up

142.	O31	R88	29.5 mm	11.48 g	12	Oxford, Walker	Crescent up
143.	O31	R94	-	13.72 g	1 h	CNG 210, 129	Crescent up
144.	O32	R100	-	13.72 g	1 h	Sternberg 1976, 601	Crescent right
145.	O32	R101	-	14.91 g	1 h	PC	Crescent right; blundered reverse legend
146.	O32	R102	-	11.48 g	1 h	BnF, HSY 19562	Crescent right
147.	O32	R102	-	12.84 g	-	Market?	Crescent right
148.	O32	R95	-	13.57 g	1 h	BnF, HSY 19561	Crescent up
149.	O32	R95	25 mm	13.37 g	6 h	Yale 2005.6.54	Crescent up
150.	O32	R96	-	12.71 g	1 h	Rauch 48, 766	Crescent up
151.	O32?	R95	-	-	-	PC	Crescent up
152.	O32	R125	26 mm	14.74 g	1 h	CNG 368, 272	Crescent up?
153.	O35	R123	24 mm	10.48 g	6 h	CNG 356, 350	Crescent right; partially draped bust

O

154.	O13	R82	-	11.90 g	11	PC	Partially draped bust; large O behind eagle's head
155.	O13	R79	-	11.93 g	-	Vcoins Zurquieh, 07 2010	Partially draped bust; pellet behind eagle's head
156.	O13	R79	-	12.67 g	-	Tom Cederlind 160, 142	Partially draped bust; pellet behind eagle's head
157.	O20	R116	25 mm	14.14 g	12	CNG 377, 247	

158.	O20	R117	-	-	-	Roma 13, 273
159.	O20	R126*	-	12.58 g	7 h	PC
160.	O20	R61	25.5 mm	10.78 g	6 h	Yale 1938.6000.1024
161.	O20	R62	-	11.69 g	12 h	BM G.2333
162.	O20	R62	-	13.01 g	6 h	PC
163.	O20	R62	-	12.73 g	1 h	?
164.	O20	R62	-	13.45 g	12 h	eBay 8340980596
165.	O20	R65	-	13.09 g	-	PC
166.	O20	R65	-	-	-	Royal Numismatics 1, 359
167.	O20	R66	-	13.83 g	12 h	PC
168	O20	R66	25.9 mm	14.85 g	12 h	Forum Ancient Coins 10736
169.	O20	R67	-	12.49 g	-	market
170.	O20	R69	-	13.58 g	12 h	Kunker 97, 1629
171.	O20	R69	-	-	-	Berk 60, 393
172.	O20	R69	-	-	-	Auktionshaus H. D. Rauch GmbH 101, 1429
173.	O20	R69	-	-	-	Fritz Rudolf Kunker GmbH 97, 1629
174.	O20	R69	-	13.21 g	12 h	Berk 1997, 281
175.	O20	R70	-	-	-	Empire FPL 39, 109
176.	O20	R70	-	-	-	London Ancient Coins 10, 96
177.	O20	R71	-	-	-	Berk 84, 804
178.	O20	R72	-	14.90 g	-	eBay 3923677926
179.	O20	R73	-	11.48 g	-	Vcoins Lodge 2004
180.	O20	R74	-	13.46 g	6 h	Market
181.	O20	R76	-	13.54 g	12 h	CNG 240, 332
182.	O20	R77	-	13.11 g	12 h	CNG 240, 333
183.	O20	R78	-	-	-	Naville 18, 279
184.	O20	R80	-	11.74 g	6 h	BnF, HSY 19564
185.	O20	R128	26 mm	12.38 g	-	Solidus Numismatik 32, 146

No.	Obv.	Rev.				Source	Notes
186.	O20	R81	-	12.86	6 h	PC	Blundered reverse legend
187.	O20	?	-	-	-	Hirsch 168, 709	
188.	O25	R64	26 mm	12.4 g	6 h	*SNG Glasgow* 3163	
189.	O26	R115	26 mm	11.71 g	11 h	CNG 268, 245	
190.	O26	R118	25 mm	10.74 g	-	eBay 371737778416	
191.	O26	R68	-	11.24 g	-	Market	
192.	O26	R75	-	13.34 g	-	Vcoins Den of Antiquity 2008	
193.	O27	R66	23 mm	13.74 g	12 h	CNG 354, 378	
194.	O27	R78	-	13.99 g	-	CNG Triton V, 1766	
195.	?	R63	24.5 mm	12.45 g	12 h	Oxford, Bodleian	

Two Pellets

No.	Obv.	Rev.				Source	Notes
196.	O19	R105	-	14.02 g	12 h	van Hoof	Blundered reverse legend
197.	O19	R105	-	13.54 g	-	Market	Blundered reverse legend
198.	O19	R105	-	12.88 g	12 h	Market?	Blundered reverse legend
199.	O19	R106	-	-	-	PC	
200.	O19?	R105	-	13.75 g	12 h	BnF, HSY 19566	Blundered reverse legend

No Letter or Symbol

No.	Obv.	Rev.				Source	Notes
201.	O1	R37	-	12.31 g	6 h	PC	
202.	O9	R36	-	13.78 g	7 h	Numismatica Ars Classica B, 25/02/1992, 2032	Partially draped bust
203.	O12	R31	-	13.36 g	1 h	PC	
204.	O12	R31	-	-	-	Hirsch 170, 1337	
205.	O14	R32	-	12.67 g	-	Grun 19/05/1992, 181	

No.	Obv.	Rev.	Diam.	Weight	Axis	Reference	Notes
206.	O14	R35	-	13.01 g	12 h	Pegasi-	Double struck reverse
207.	O15	R34	-	9.44 g	12 h	CNG 67, 1143	Low weight and fineness?
208.	O34	R110	-	-	-	Rauch 17, 177	
209.	O34	R110	27 mm	10.94 g	-	eBay 371713714872	
210.	O37	R111	25 mm	12.26 g	-	Naville 19, 299	Fully draped bust
211.	?	R33	-	-	-	eBay 1352396575	
212.	O33	R109	-	11.69 g	12 h	BM G.2334	Deity facing
213.	O36	?	24.5 mm	10.84 g	12 h	Forum Ancient Coins 32990	Contemporary forgery?
214.	O38	?	27.4 mm	11.31 g	1 h	Netherlands 7724	Double struck reverse

Julia Domna

A

No.	Obv.	Rev.	Diam.	Weight	Axis	Reference	Notes
215.	O'1	R'1	-	13.22 g	12 h	BnF, HSY 19567	
216.	O'1	R'1	-	13.13 g	12 h	CNG 137, 111	
217.	O'1	R'2	-	11.66 g	12 h	Leu 42, 360	
218.	O'1	R'2	27 mm	12.36 g	11 h	Vcoins Athena AF450	
219.	O'1	R'3	-	14.34 g	-	G&M 191, 1850	
220.	O'1	R'4*	-	11.93 g	1 h	CNG 79, 650	
221.	O'1	R2	-	15.36 g	6 h	CNG 45, 994	Also struck with Caracalla obverse.
222.	O'2	R'5*	-	12.93 g	12 h	Numismatic Fine Arts 14, 481	A behind eagle's head
223.	O'2	R'5*	-	12.02 g	-	CNG 45, 993	A behind eagle's head

224.	O'3	R'29*	-	-	-	Bland, pl 4, 52	Also struck with Caracalla obverse; A behind eagle's head
225.	O'4	R'6	-	14.04 g	12 h	PC	A to right of wing

H

226.	O'5	R'7	-	13.24 g	10 h	BnF, HSY 19568	
227.	O'5	R'10	-	13.37 g	12 h	PC	HH; forgeries known
228.	O'5	R'13	-	11.85 g	11 h	PC	H in bottom right field
229.	O'6	R'8	-	-	-	Monnaies et Médailles 279, 45	
230.	O'6	R'8	-	-	-	Berk 59, 516	
231.	O'7	R'11	-	-	-	Doura Excavations pl VI, 207	H behind eagle's head
232.	O'7	R'11	-	-	-	market	H behind eagle's head
233.	O'7	R'11	-	-	-	Monnaies et Médailles 212, 51	H behind eagle's head
234.	O'7	R'37	25 mm	12.27 g	12 h	CNG 356, 349	H in bottom right field
235.	O'8	R'12	-	13.26 g	6 h	Market	H in bottom right field
236.	O'8	R'12	-	12.02 g	5 h	Monnaies et Médailles 461, 63	H in bottom right field
237.	O'8	R'12	-	12.65 g	6 h	BnF, Chandon de Briailles 1907	H in bottom right field
238.	O'8	R'12	-	12.76 g	-	CNG 45, 995	H in bottom right field
239.	O'8	R'12	-	-	-	H. D. Rauch 99, 181	H in bottom right field
240.	O'8	R'36	25 mm	12.51 g	6 h	CNG 331, 194	
241.	O'13	R'7	24 mm	12.22 g	12 h	CNG 354, 377	
242.	O'13	R'9	25.5 mm	11.67 g	12 h	Berlin, Imhoof Blumer 1900	

Crescent

243.	O'10	R'32	-	10.10 g	-	Kunker 94, 1990	Crescent up
244.	O'10	R'33	-	14.57 g	12 h	PC	Crescent left
245.	O'11	R'30	-	12.09 g	12 h	Monnaies et Médailles 492, 35	Crescent up
246.	?	R'31	-	14.67 g	6 h	Market	Crescent up

O

247.	O'3	R'23	-	11.44 g	11 h	Bellinger pl XIV, 3	O behind eagle's head
248.	O'3	R'23	-	13.66 g	12 h	CNG 81, 816	O behind eagle's head
249.	O'6	R'15	-	11.20 g	11 h	Revue numismatique 1906, pl VI, 7	
250.	O'6	R'15	25 mm	12.57 g	12 h	CNG 378, 361	
251.	O'6	R'15	-	-	-	Numismatica Ars Classica 84, 1950	
252.	O'6	R'17	-	13.21 g	11 h	Münz Zentrum 53, 1968	
253.	O'6	R'17	-	11.27 g	12 h	Market	
254.	O'6	R'17	-	11.98 g	11 h	CNG 60, 1367	
255.	O'6	R'18	-	13.46 g	12 h	PC	
256.	O'6	R'20	-	12.62 g	-	CNG 51, 989	
257.	O'6	R'29*	-	14.56 g	11 h	eBay 130098909182	O cut over A or Λ
258.	O'6	R'35	26 mm	13.97 g	6 h	CNG 91, 632	
259.	O'6	R'35	27 mm	13.36 g	11 h	CNG 99, 477	
260.	O'6	R'35	27 mm	11.74 g	11 h	Roma Numismatics Ltd E-Sale 42, 415	
261.	O'6	R'15	26.5 mm	13.26 g	-	Naville 36, 694	
262.	O'9	R'14	-	-	-	Cahn 71, 1046	
263.	O'9	R'14	27 mm	13.56 g	11 h	SNG Righetti 2078	
264.	O'9	R'14	-	12.27 g	11 h	CNG 82, 861	
265.	O'9	R'14	26	13.17 g	11 h	CNG 339, 262	
266.	O'9	R'15	-	12.61 g	11 h	Market	
267.	O'9	R'15	-	12.81 g	-	Auctiones 17, 381	

268	O'9	R'15	-	-	-	?	
269.	O'9	R'16	-	-	-	PC	
270.	O'9	R'19	-	14.62 g	12 h	PC	
271.	O'9	R'21	-	12.00 g	-	Lanz 92, 803	
272.	O'9	R'22	-	13.77 g	11 h	CNG 210, 128	
273.	O'9	R'24	-	11.84 g	-	Monnaies et Médailles 411, 195	O behind eagle's head
274.	O'9	R'24	-	13.44 g	12 h	PC	O behind eagle's head
275.	O'9	R'24	-	11.63 g	-	CNG 60, 1368	O behind eagle's head
276.	O'9	R'24	-	-	-	Spink 6026, 182	O behind eagle's head
277.	O'9	R'25	-	12.30 g	5 h	CNG 216, 362	O behind eagle's head
278.	O'9	R'26	-	14.31 g	11 h	BM 1853,1006.1	O in bottom right field
279.	O'9	R'26	-	10.28 g	-	eBay 3912238335	O in bottom right field
280.	O'9	R'24	27.5 mm	11.84 g	11 h	Berlin, 11779	O behind eagle's head
281.	O'9	R'38	27 mm	13.39 g	6 h	Berlin, Loebbecke 1906	
282.	O'9	R'14	26 mm	12.23 g	11 h	Roma Numismatics Ltd E-Sale 43, 406	
283.	O'10	R'27	-	-	-	Bland, pl 4, 51	O in bottom right field
284.	O'10	?	-	14.83 g	-	Hirsch 1979, 792	
285.	O'12	R'28*	-	14.82 g	10 h	Market	

Γ

286.	O'3	R'34	-	13.11 g	5 h	PC	Γ behind deity
287.	O'3	R'34	29 mm	14.80 g	6 h	Boston 1971.391	Γ behind deity
288.	O'3	R'34	-	13.70 g	6 h	?	Γ behind deity
289.	O'3	R'34	27 mm	15.98 g	12 h	Berlin, Loebbecke 1906	Γ behind deity

SPECIMENS NOT INCLUDED DUE TO POOR CONDITION

Caracalla

A

290.	O?	R?	-	-	-	Market
291.	O?	R?	-	-	-	Market
292.	O?	R?	-	-	-	Spijkerman, pl I, 7
293.	O?	R?	-	-	-	Bland pl 3, 28

No Letter or Symbol

| 294. | O? | R? | - | 13.50 g | - | Rauch 35, 5617 |
| 295. | O? | R? | - | 12.78 g | - | eBay 3945711088 |

H

| 296. | O? | R? | - | - | - | Spijkerman, pl I, 6 |
| 297. | O? | R? | - | - | - | ? |

O

| 298. | O? | R? | - | - | - | Hirsch 109, 1244 |
| 299. | O? | R? | - | 13.01 g | 6 | Hirsch 174, 1478? |

Crescent

| 300. | O? | R? | - | - | - | Market |
| 301. | O? | R? | - | - | - | Market |

Julia Domna

Γ?

| 302. | O? | R? | - | 11.62 g | 11 h |

H

| 303. | O? | R? | - | 12.65 g | 12 h |

FORGERIES

Julia Domna

H

304.	O'5	R'10	-	14.21	12 h	Market	HH
305.	O'5	R'10	-	-	-	Market	HH
306.	O'5	R'10	-	10.25 g	11 h	Classical Numismatic Review, Vol. XXIV	HH
307.	O'5	R'10	-	11.00 g	12 h	Forum Ancient Coins	HH
308.	O'5	R'10	-	-	-	Dr. Busso Peus Nachfolger 409, 785	HH

ACKNOWLEDGMENTS

My gratitude to Michel Prieur, Robert Bracey, Kevin Butcher, Frédérique Duyrat, Simon Glenn and the anonymous reviewer for their comments; of course, any oversight remains mine.

BIBLIOGRAPHY

Bellinger, A. R. *The Syrian tetradrachms of Caracalla and Macrinus*. New York: American Numismatic Society, 1940.

Burnett, A. 2001. "The Invisibility of Roman Imperial Mints." In *I luoghi della moneta. Le sedi delle zecche dall'antichità all'età moderna. Atti del convegno internazionale 22–23 ottobre 1999 Milano*, edited by R. La Guardia, 41–48. Milan: Commune di Milano.

Butcher, K. E. T. "Numerical letters on Syrian coins: officina or sequence marks?" *Revue belge de numismatique et de sigillographie* 158 (2012): 123–144.

Carson, R. A. G. "System and Product in the Roman Mint." In *Essays in Roman Coinage Presented to Harold Mattingly*, edited by R. A. G. Carson and C. H. V. Sutherland, 227–239. Oxford: Oxford University Press, 1956.

Carter, G. F., and R. S. Nord. "Calculation of the average die lifetimes and the number of anvils for coinage in antiquity." *American Journal of Numismatics* 3.4 (1992): 147–164.

CRS = Butcher, K. E. T. *Coinage in Roman Syria: Northern Syria, 64 BC–AD 253*. London: Royal Numismatic Society, 2004.

Elks, K. J. J. "Coins of Caracalla with altered dies." *Numismatic Chronicle* 13 (1973): 222–223.

Esty, W. W. "Estimation of the size of a coinage: a survey and comparison of methods." *Numismatic Chronicle* 146 (1986): 185–215.

————. "The theory of linkage." *Numismatic Chronicle* 150 (1990): 205–221.

————. "How to estimate the original number of dies and the coverage of a sample." *Numismatic Chronicle* 166 (2006): 359–364.

————. "The geometric model for estimating the number of dies." In *Quantifying Monetary Supplies in Graeco-Roman Times*, edited by F. de Callataÿ, 1–16. Pragmateiai 19. Bari: Edipuglia, 2011.

Gilmore, P. M. 1979. "Syrian officinae under Caracalla and Macrinus." *Numismatic Circular* 87.6 (1979): 286–289.

Glenn, S. "Exploring localities: a die study of Alexanders from Damascus." In *Alexander the Great. A Linked Open World*, edited by S. Glenn, F. Duyrat, and A. Meadows, 91–126. Scripta Antiqua 116. Ausonius: Bordeaux, 2018.

Kraft, K. *Das System der kaiserzeitlichen Münzprägung in Kleinasien*. Berlin: Mann, 1972.

Prieur, M., and K. Prieur. *The Syro-Phoenician Tetradrachms and their Fractions*. London/Lancaster, Penn.: Classical Numismatic Group, 2000.

Millar, F. *The Roman Near East: 31 BC–AD 337*. Harvard: Harvard University Press, 1993.

McAlee, R. *The Coins of Roman Antioch*. Lancaster, Penn.: Classical Numismatic Group, 2007.

Nurpetlian, J. "Damascene tetradrachms of Caracalla." *American Journal of Numismatics* 26 (2014): 187–198.

————. *Coinage in Roman Syria: The Orontes Valley, 64 BC–AD 253*. Royal Numismatic Society Special Publication. London: Royal Numismatic Society, forthcoming.

————. "Tyrian tetradrachms of Caracalla: a quantitative analysis." *Berytus Archaeological Studies* (forthcoming).

RRC = Crawford, M. H. *Roman Republican Coinage*. Cambridge: Cambridge University Press, 1974.

Taylor, L. W. H. "The Damaskos Mint of Alexander the Great." *American Journal of Numismatics* 29 (2017): 47–99.

Tillander-Godenhielm, U. *Fabergé ja hänen suomalaiset mestarinsa* (Fabergé and his Finnish Workmasters). Helsinki: Tammi, 2008.

Witschonke, R. "The Use of Die Marks on Roman Republican Coinage." *Revue belge de numismatique et de sigillographie* 158 (2012): 65–86.

Woytek, B. "System and product in Roman mints from the Late Republic to the High Principate: some current problems." *Revue Belge de Numismatique et de Sigillographie* 158 (2012): 85–122.

————. "Exactions and the Monetary Economy of the Late Roman Republic. A Numismatic Perspective." In *Les confiscations, le pouvoir et Rome de la fin de la République à la mort de Néron*, edited by C. Chillet, M.-C. Ferriès and Y. Rivière, 183–197. Scripta antiqua 92. Bordeaux: Ausonius, 2016.

————. "Metal and system in Roman imperial mints. Flan production, quality control and the internal organisation of minting establishments during the Principate." In *Debasement: Manipulation of coin standards in pre-modern monetary systems*, edited by K. Butcher. Oxford: Oxbow, forthcoming.

AJN Second Series 32 (2020) pp. 219–272
© 2020 The American Numismatic Society

Kraft in the 21st Century:
A New Listing of Shared Dies
in the Roman Provincial Coinage

George Watson*

This paper gathers together the evidence for the sharing of obverse dies in the Roman provincial coinage. It builds upon the material collected by Konrad Kraft in his 1972 book *Das System der kaiserzeitlichen Münzprägung in Kleinasien*, firstly by offering a number of corrections to Kraft's listing, and secondly by collecting together the numerous instances of die-sharing that have been published since Kraft's book. The paper is accompanied by a website that maps the known instances of die-sharing and will be continually updated as new shared dies are discovered.

It is now nearly 50 years since Konrad Kraft revolutionized the study of the Roman provincial coinage with his book *Das System der kaiserzeitlichen Münzprägung in Kleinasien*.[1] His idea that the cities of Asia Minor were supplied with dies, and probably also coins, by travelling workshops of die engravers necessitated radical revisions to how the provincial coinage was conceived. The vast array of seemingly autonomous mints needed to be replaced by a far more streamlined and centralized system, in which words such as "networks" and "supply areas" took precedence over "cities" and "mints." His principle evidence for this was the fact that a large number of obverse dies were shared between two or more cities. While this phenomenon had long been noted—Friedrich Imhoof-Blumer was the first to publish a shared die in the provincial coinage, in 1883—Kraft vastly

---

*Goethe-Universität Frankfurt am Main (Watson@em.uni-frankfurt.de).

1. K. Kraft, *Das System der kaiserzeitlichen Münzprägung in Kleinasien. Materialien und Entwürfe* (Berlin: Gebr. Mann, 1972).

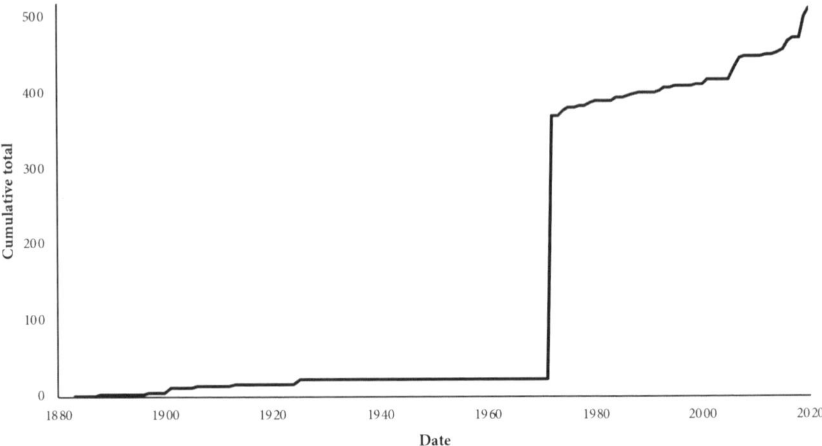

Figure 1. Number of known shared dies in the Roman provincial coinage

increased the number of known die-sharings, from 27 to 373, and also put forward the most developed model yet to explain these occurrences.

However, despite almost universal agreement about the revolutionary nature of Kraft's findings, his model for the system of production has been far from universally accepted. Straight away, in the reviews of Kraft's book, two scholars preferred alternative explanations, one positing a centralized mint, another the loaning of dies directly between cities.[2] Even Ann Johnston, who worked most closely with Kraft's ideas, came to suggest an alternative model, part centralized mint, part itinerant engravers.[3] Other, more recent work, has gone in different directions, but with no clear consensus yet formed.[4] At least some of these varying opinions have been driven by increasing work on die-sharing outside of Asia Minor.[5] Despite the fact that these diverse regions show differing scales of die-

2. W. Kellner, "Konrad Kraft. *Das System der kaiserzeitlichen Münzprägung in Kleinasien.* Review," *SM* 23 (1973), 2930; M. Price, "*Das System der kaiserzeitlichen Münzprägung in Kleinasien. Materialien und Entwürfe* by Konrad Kraft," *CW* 67.5 (1974), 311.

3. A. Johnston, "Aphrodisias Reconsidered," *NC* 155 (1995), 57. For a discussion of the evolution of Johnston's thought, see G. Watson, "Die-sharing and the 'Pseudo-Autonomous' Coinages," *NC* 177 (2017), 201–211.

4. E.g., M. Spoerri Butcher, "L'organisation de la production monétaire au sein de la province d'Asie à l'époque de Gordien III (238–244)," *SNR* 85 (2006), 97–132; G. Watson, *Connections, communities and coinage. The system of coin production in southern Asia Minor, AD 218–276* (New York: American Numismatic Society, 2019).

5. E.g., K. Butcher, "The Colonial Coinage of Antioch-on-the-Orontes c. AD 218–53," *NC* 148 (1988), 70–72; H.-D. Schultz, "Die-sharing in Thrakien," Annotazioni Numismatiche 36 (1999), 829–833; C. Flament, "Die et engraver-sharing dans le Péloponnèse entre le règne d'Hadrien et celui de Septime Sévère," *BCH* 131.1 (2007), 559–614; D. Calomino, "The coin-

sharing and varying degrees of evidence for workshops of engravers, almost all studies take Kraft's book as their starting point.

Amid these discussions of the technicalities of the system of production, the number of known shared dies has continued to grow, both within and outside Asia Minor (Fig. 1).[6] Since 1972, over 130 new shared dies have been published, and the total, correct at press time, now stands at 513. Many of these have been noted in collection catalogues, or are mentioned in passing, without being the subject of a specialist publication, and the references are therefore quite scattered. Moreover, a number of dies published by Kraft have been subject to correction: perhaps further cities have been shown to use the same die, or the die link that Kraft observed has been shown to be the result of tooling of the reverse.

A proper assessment of the system of production of the provincial coinage needs to take all of these newly published shared dies into account, as well as all of the relevant corrigenda. It is no longer valid to discuss die-sharing only on the basis of the links observed by Kraft.[7] To this end, this article collates all new instances of die-sharing that were not published by Kraft, as well as all the corrigenda to Kraft's listing that have appeared in the intervening time. This includes material from outside of Asia Minor, which Kraft deliberately excluded from his study.[8] It may well be the case that these instances of die-sharing arose from a different production system as in Asia Minor, but to exclude them on those grounds would be putting the cart before the horse. Indeed, recent work has tended to stress the possibility of numerous different systems operating within Asia Minor itself.[9] This article therefore offers an overview of a unified evidential phenomenon—shared obverse dies in the Roman provincial coinage—as the basis for a discussion of the reasons for this phenomenon, reasons which may well turn out to be diverse and disassociated.

age of Dionysopolis and the system of coin production in Moesia Inferior at the end of the Severan Age," in *Ex nummis lux: Studies in Ancient Numismatics in honour of Dimitar Draganov,* ed. D. Boteva (Sofia: Bobokov Bros. Foundation, 2017), 261–271; U. Peter and L. Grozdanova, "Philippopolis and Pautalia: A parallel analysis of the coinages," in *Thrace—local coinage and regional identity: Numismatic research in the digital age* (forthcoming).

6. Figure 1 counts only dies that are currently accepted to have been used by more than one city; it does not show instances where a die was once thought to have been shared, but the sharing was later disproved. Similarly, it simply counts shared dies, and does not show when new cities were added for dies that were already known to have been shared.

7. As does, e.g., S. Karwiese, *Die Münzprägung von Ephesos. Band 5. Corpus und Aufbau der römerzeitlichen Stadtprägung. 2. Statistiken, Metrologie und Kommentare* (Vienna: Holzhausen Druck GmbH, 2016), 338–339.

8. That he was aware of instances outside of Asia Minor is shown by the brief discussion at Kraft, *System,* 101–102.

9. Watson, "Die-sharing and the 'Pseudo-Autonomous' Coinages," 207–209.

No mention is made here of the stylistic similarities between obverse dies used at different cities. Since Kraft bound die-sharing to these stylistic similarities in his engraver workshop explanation, the two have tended to be discussed together, but recent research has suggested that this connection may not always be valid.[10] This issue, which gets to the heart of the production process, deserves further investigation. It is hoped that providing an up-to-date listing of the objective side of this equation, namely shared dies, the connection with the more subjective matter of stylistic similarities may be more easily explored.

While addressing questions about the system of production will no doubt be the primary use of this listing of shared dies, it is by no means the only possible use. Whatever model for the production of coinage that one subscribes to, shared dies are representative of some form of inter-*polis* interaction. It should be of interest to anyone investigating the history of individual cities of the eastern Roman provinces, with whom that city shared coins. The fact that, for example, the city of Sibidunda in Phrygia only ever shared dies with Colbasa in Pisidia, and vice versa, is indicative of the regional interactions of those cities, regardless of whether the die-sharing resulted from a shared mint, itinerant engravers, or the loaning of dies. While space does not permit me to explore such questions here, the potential of this material is vast, and this article offers a preliminary step towards its exploitation.

Some general comments may be made on the overall chronological and geographical patterns of die-sharing (Table 1).[11] The earliest known shared die in the provincial coinage dates to the reign of Trajan, though very few are known before the Antonine period.[12] Although the greatest number of shared dies come from the Severan period (*RPC* V and VI), this may simply reflect the longer chronological span of these volumes. Dividing the absolute figures by the number of years covered by each volume shows a high point of die-sharing in the mid-third century for *RPC* VII, VIII and IX, before a decline under Valerian and

10. Watson, *Connections.*

11. Note that the numbers in the columns of Table 1 do not necessarily add up to the total figure given in the last row, since dies were often shared between regions.

12. Shared dies are known in Greek coinages of the pre-Roman period, most notably in Campania in the fifth and fourth centuries BC, on which see N. K. Rutter, *Campanian Coinages: 475–380 B.C.* (Edinburgh: Edinburgh University Press, 1979), 102. On die-sharing in the Hellenistic world, see O. Mørkholm, "The «Behaviour» of Dies in the Hellenistic Period," in *Actes du 9ème Congrès International de Numismatique, Berne, September 1979*, vol. 1, ed. T. Hackens (Louvain-la-Neuve: International Association of Professional Numismatics, 1982), 209–214. There are far fewer occurrences than in the provincial coinage and such that there are should be considered the result of different production systems; for further discussion see Watson, *Connections*, 11 n. 86.

Table 1. Number of shared dies by region and *RPC* volume

Region	*RPC* Volume								TOTAL
	III (98–138)	IV (138–192)	V (193–218)	VI (218–238)	VII (238–244)	VIII (244–249)	IX (249–254)	X (253–276)	
Argolis			1						1
Megaris			1						1
Achaea			1						1
Arcadia			2						2
Laconia			1						1
Messenia			1						1
Macedonia				1					1
Dacia						1			1
Moesia Superior						1			1
Thrace		1	2	3	3				9
Pontus			2						2
Paphlagonia			1	1	3	1	2		8
Bithynia			4	7	8	1	2		22
Mysia		8	8	6	9	3	3		37
Troas	1	5	4	3					13
Aeolis		4	8	10	14	8	3	5	50
Lesbos		4	3	4					11

Table 1 (continued). Number of shared dies by region and *RPC* volume

Region	*RPC* Volume								
	III (98–138)	IV (138–192)	V (193–218)	VI (218–238)	VII (238–244)	VIII (244–249)	IX (249–254)	X (253–276)	TOTAL
Ionia	1	4	27	26	33	20	10	25	143
Caria		4	12	3	8	4	4	5	40
Lydia		18	65	33	14	20	8	14	171
Phrygia		2	30	12	8	13	2	6	73
Lycia					9				9
Pamphylia				13	3	5	3	8	32
Pisidia			5	12	5	4	3	3	32
Lycaonia					2			1	3
Cilicia			1	14	6	6	15	6	48
Commagene				4		2			6
Syria				6			1		7
Judaea		1	3						4
TOTAL	2	33	133	110	89	54	40	57	513

Gallienus (*RPC* X).[13] The general chronological development therefore follows that of the coinage as a whole.[14] Geographically, the largest number of shared dies come from western Asia Minor, in particular the regions of Ionia and Lydia.

Another aim of this article is to offer a standardized form for referencing shared dies. Kraft's book is notoriously difficult to cite, and scholars tend to refer to it in a variety of ways, sometimes citing a page number, sometimes a plate number, and sometimes the numbers that Kraft assigned to individual die-sharings. The aim must be to have a unique number for each shared die, so that the instance of die-sharing can be referred to independent of particular examples. Kraft himself, in fact, began on this path by using a numbering system that, although spread throughout the book, ran continuously from one to 373.[15] These numbers are retained in this publication for all shared dies published by Kraft. Shared dies not included in Kraft's listing are given a number here that continues his numbering system, beginning from 374. Any shared die can thus be referred to by a unique number, which might be given the label "Kraft number." For example, "Kraft no. 205" refers to the die of Septimius Severus shared between Acrasus and Pergamum and published by Kraft; "Kraft no. 74" refers to the die of Gordian III published by Kraft as shared between Magnesia and Metropolis, but shown here to have also been used by Ephesus; and "Kraft no. 472" refers to the die of Tranquillina shared by Amastris and Tium and noted here for the first time. In the future, this form of referencing can be used to refer to any shared die, as well as to make further amendments, and new shared dies can be given numbers according to the same scheme.

This article is accompanied by a website that visualizes the currently known die-sharings cartographically: https://doi.org/10.26608/AJN.31.Watson. The numbering system of the website matches that of this article, and the website will be continually updated as new die-sharings are published.[16] The website offers three basic levels of functionality:

1. Clicking on "Maps & Tools" in the top right, followed by "Layers & Legend" brings up a list of layers, which are ordered by *RPC* volume. This allows a rough chronological overview that also encompasses "pseudo-autonomous" coins. Layers can be toggled on and off using the tick box next to the name.

---

13. The high figures for *RPC* VII are no doubt partly due to the fact that *RPC* VII-1 was published as a die study.

14. A. Johnston, "Greek Imperial Statistics: A Commentary," *RN* 26 (1984), 242.

15. Kraft's book in fact included a number of die-sharings that were illustrated on the plates but were not given a running number; these are assigned a number in the addenda section.

16. The author would be glad to hear of any amendments or additions for the website.

2. Clicking on a line between two cities brings up a pop-up window that lists all shared dies that follow this path, sorted according to *RPC*-layer. Clicking on the number brings up more information about the die, in a format similar to that used in this article.

3. Clicking on a city brings up a pop-up window that lists all shared dies used by that city. The dies are listed twice, once under "*RPC* … Links" and once under "*RPC* … Cities." Clicking on numbers under the "Links" layer brings up the same information as when one clicks initially on a link. Clicking on a number under the "Cities" layer brings up more information about that city, as well as examples of coins that show the use of that particular die at that particular city. Where possible, both examples published in print and images available online have been listed.[17]

Unfortunately the search function at the top of the map does not work with ancient city names.

CORRIGENDA

The corrigenda offered here concern only the cities that used particular shared dies, principally in two forms: new cities that have been added to an already published sharing, and the removal of one or more cities from a sharing, usually because the example on which a link was based has been shown to be tooled. New reverse types or magistrates names associated with a particular shared obverse die are not included here.

Number:	71
Obverse Type:	Gordian III
Published Link:	Ephesus–Metropolis–Samos
Actual Link:	Ephesus–Metropolis–Samos–Colophon
Additional Bibliography:	*RPC* VII-1.348

The *RPC* project has brought to light a specimen of Colophon struck from this die, a link that was unknown to Kraft.

---

17. Note that when both a printed example and an online example are given, they are not necessarily references to the same coin.

Number: 74

Obverse Type: Gordian III

Published Link: Magnesia ad Maeandrum–Metropolis

Actual Link: Magnesia ad Maeandrum–Metropolis–Ephesus

Additional Bibliography: *RPC* VII-1.417

Kraft was apparently unaware of coins of Ephesus struck from this die.

Number: 76

Obverse Type: Gordian III

Published Link: Ephesus–Magnesia ad Maeandrum–Nysa

Actual Link: Ephesus–Magnesia ad Maeandrum–Nysa–Antioch ad Maeandrum

Additional Bibliography: *RPC Consolidated Supplement,* 2015, S3-VII.1-604A

The use of this die at Antioch ad Maeandrum was not noted by Kraft or *RPC* VII-1, but two specimens were recorded in the third *RPC* supplement.

Number: 129

Obverse Type: Elagabalus

Published Link: Hypaepa–Sardis

Actual Link: Hypaepa–Sardis

Additional Bibliography: A. Johnston, "New problems for old: Konrad Kraft on die-sharing in Asia Minor," *NC* 14 (1974), 207

In this instance a correction of a correction is offered. In her review of Kraft's book for the *Numismatic Chronicle*, Ann Johnston wrote "there are occasional inaccuracies: pl. 30, 12 [the illustrations of this link] "Hypaepa" and "Sardis" are actually both Hypaepa as the magistrate's name indicates."[18] It is unclear what Johnston is referring to here, since there is no magistrate's name on the specimen Kraft lists for Sardis. The legend on this specimen is very hard to read, but every indication suggests that it is a *homonoia* coin of Sardis and Hypaepa, and probably struck in Sardis.[19] All subsequent publications have followed this inter-

18. Johnston, "New problems," 207. The same author excludes this link from her later listing the coinage of Sardis: A. Johnston, "Die-sharing in Asia Minor: the view from Sardis." *INJ* 6–7 (1982–1983), 75.

19. Kraft cites another specimen (*BMC* 159) at Sardis from the same obverse die. If this die identity is correct, the matter is settled since this second specimen is not a *homonoia* coin. However both coins are badly worn, and I am not certain that they were struck from the same obverse die.

pretation, and the link therefore should be allowed to stand.[20] The only correction to Kraft's listing should be to replace ΑΤΤΑΛΟΥ in the reverse legend of the Hypaepa coin with ΔΙΟΝΥCΙΟΥ.[21]

Number:	145
Obverse Type:	Philip I
Published Link:	Blaundus–Laodicea–Saitta–Sardis–Tripolis–Carallia
Actual Link:	Blaundus–Laodicea–Saitta–Sardis–Tripolis
Additional Bibliography:	K. Butcher, "Die-sharing in Asia Minor: A Phantom Link," *SM* 219 (2005), 67–68.

Kevin Butcher has demonstrated that the only known specimen from this die at Carallia (*BMC* 7) is in fact a tooled coin of Laodicea.[22] Carallia never shared dies with cities outside of its neighboring region.[23]

Number:	166
Obverse Type:	Severus Alexander
Published Link:	Acrasus–Attalea
Actual Link:	Adramytteum-Attalea
Additional Bibliography:	–

Kraft erroneously lists Acrasus as the mint of *SNG von Aulock* 1060, both in the text and in the catalogue. The coin and its legend are, however, clear, and the correct mint is Adramytteum.

---

20. E.g., P. Franke and M. Nollé, *Die Homonoia-Münzen Kleinasiens und der thrakischen Randgebiete. I. Katalog* (Saarbrücken: Saarbrücker Druckerei und Verlag, 1997), no. 1863 a different specimen from the same dies, listed (erroneously) under Caracalla and (correctly) under Sardis; S. Altınoluk, *Hypaipa. A Lydian City During the Roman Imperial Period* (Istanbul: Ege Yayinlari, 2013), who does not list the coin that Johnston would see as a coin of Hypaepa in his corpus of coins of that city; the coin is also listed under Sardis in the preliminary online database for *RPC* VI.

21. Altınoluk, *Hypaipa*, no. 138A; note, however, that the three specimens that Altınoluk lists for this type are all casts of the same coin.

22. Butcher, "Die-sharing."

23. Watson, *Connections.*

Number: 176

Obverse Type: Severus Alexander

Published Link: Abydus–Eresus

Actual Link: Abydus–Eresus–Methymna–Sestus

Additional Bibliography: D. Calomino, "From Thrace to Lesbos. Coinage and cities across the Hellespont in the 3rd century AD," in *Studies in ancient coinage in honour of Andrew Burnett*, ed. R. Bland and D. Calomino (London: Spink, 2015), link C

Kraft published this die link as between two cities. Dario Calomino has recently shown that a further two cities also used this die.[24] The link thus stretches not just from mainland Asia Minor to the island of Lesbos, but also to the northern shore of the Hellespont.

Number: 190

Obverse Type: Trebonianus Gallus

Published Link: Colossae–Peltae

Actual Link: Colossae–Peltae–Eumenea

Additional Bibliography: *RPC* IX.805

The *RPC* project has brought to light a specimen of Eumenea struck from this die, a link that was unknown to Kraft.

Number: 281

Obverse Type: Commodus

Published Link: Elaea–Pergamum

Actual Link: None

Additional Bibliography: *RPC* IV temp. no. 220

The coin of Elaea on which Kraft based this link (*SNG von Aulock* 7688) is in fact a coin of Pergamum, and this obverse die is thus only used at Pergamum.

Number: 296

Obverse Type: Commodus

Published Link: Euippe–Ephesus

Actual Link: None

Additional Bibliography: –

24. Calomino, "From Thrace to Lesbos," 208–209.

This die link had been published prior to Kraft by J. G. Milne, who had one specimen from each city in his own collection.[25] Milne noted that not only were the obverses struck from the same die, but the reverses were also very similar, apparently differing only with respect to some letters of the legend. He suggested that this was an example of the re-cutting of dies in antiquity, with a pair of dies loaned from Ephesus to Euippe and the reverse being altered so that the ethnic was appropriate for the new city.

Milne's Ephesus specimen, now in Oxford, remains the only known example for that side of the die-sharing.[26] I believe, however, that it is in fact a tooled coin of Euippe. First of all there is the remarkable similarity of the Tyche figure with Milne's Euippe coin. Milne was surely right that these coins were originally struck from the same die—a fact on which Kraft passes no remark—but the tooling appears to have been to the "Ephesus" specimen, and not to the die, as Milne thought. On the "Ephesus" coin the reverse legend is rendered Є=ΦЄ=C=IΩN by all modern catalogues.[27] The final *iota*, however, is not really visible, and the letter between Apollo's head and lyre appears more like a lunate *epsilon* than a lunate *sigma*. The ending -ЄΩN is suitable for Euippe's ethnic, but not for that of Ephesus. Moreover, the reverse type itself is also not suitable for Ephesus. Apollo appears very infrequently on the Ephesian coinage, and when he does he is normally accompanied by Artemis; this coin is the only example of *Apollo Citharoedus*, Apollo the lyre-player.[28] Milne's "Ephesus" coin should therefore be regarded as a modern invention, and there is currently no evidence for the use of this die anywhere but Euippe.

> **Number:** 306
>
> **Obverse Type:** Antoninus Pius
>
> **Published Link:** Pergamum–Hadriani ad Olympum
>
> **Actual Link:** Pergamum–Stratonicea Hadrianopolis
>
> **Additional Bibliography:** –

Coins of Pergamum struck from this die are unproblematic and evidenced through numerous examples. There are two known specimens struck from the same obverse die but naming another city on the reverse, both currently in Par-

25. J. G. Milne, "Two Notes on Greek Dies," *NC* 2 (1922), 45.

26. S. Karwiese, *Die Münzprägung von Ephesos. Band 5. Katalog und Aufbau der römerzeitlichen Stadtprägung mit allen erfassbaren Stempelnachweisen.* (Vienna: Holzhausen Druck GmbH, 2012), 88; *RPC* IV temp. no. 2247.

27. Milne, "Two Notes," 45; *Ephesos. Band 5.1. Katalog,* 88; *RPC* IV temp. no. 2247.

28. Karwiese, *Ephesos. Band 5.2. Statistiken,* 276–277.

is.[29] Although both coins have different reverse types, the reverse legend ЄΠΙ ϹΤΡΑ ΔΙΟΔ ΦΙΛΟΞ ΤΟΥ Κ Γ ΙΟΥ ΑΔΡΙΑΝΟΠ, clearly legible on P 1175, seems to be the same on the other, more difficult to read specimen. On the basis of the abbreviated ethnic at the end of the legend, these coins have traditionally been assigned to Hadrianopolis in Phrygia. They are found in the trays of that city in the Paris collection, and have been published under such an attribution by Babelon, Head, von Fritze, Münsterberg and *RPC* online.[30] Kraft, modifying an older reading given by Pellerin and Mionnet, read the final word of the reverse legend as ΑΔΡΙΑΝΩΝ and thus attributed the coins to Hadriani ad Olympum in Mysia.[31] For him, the sharing of the obverse die with Pergamum was conclusive: "*Die Stempelkoppelung mit Pergamon beseitigt jeden Zweifel.*"

The problem, as Kraft saw it, was the long distance between Pergamum and Hadrianopolis in Phrygia, nearly 400 km as the crow flies. While he himself had shown that long distance links were much more common than previously thought, such distances at such an early stage in the development of die-sharing seem scarcely credible.[32] The problem with his solution is that his reading of the reverse legend is very unlikely, and the reading ΑΔΡΙΑΝΟΠ is almost certain. Moreover, Hadriani ad Olympum is still nearly 180 km distant from Pergamum.

There is, however, another city named Hadrianopolis that lay closer to Pergamum, and to which these coins would be better attributed. The city of Stratonicea ad Caicum in Lydia was given the name of Hadrianopolis by Hadrian on his journey through Asia Minor in 123, and was thereafter known as Stratonicea-Hadrianopolis. It appears that this city has not come into consideration as the mint of the two Hadrianopolis coins under discussion because of the fact that the city usually used the double name on its coinage.[33] However, some of the earliest coins of the city with its new name omit any

---

29. P 1175 and 1177.

30. Inv. Wadd. 6060; *BMC Phrygia*, lxiv; H. von Fritze, *Die antiken Münzen Mysiens. I. Abteilung Adramytion–Kisthene.* (Berlin: Georg Reimer, 1913), 180; R. Münsterberg, *Die Beamtennamen auf den griechischen Münzen* (Vienna: Österreichische Numismatische Gesellschaft, 1911–1914), 164.

31. Kraft, *System*, 192; J. Pellerin, *Mélange de diverses médailles Tome II. Médailles impériales grecques qui manquent dans Vaillant avec des observations sur celles qu'il a publiées* (Paris: H. L. Guerin & L. F. Delatour, 1765), 73; T. E. Mionnet, *Description de médailles antiques, grecques et romaines* (Paris: Testu, 1806–1837), 428–429.

32. A 400 km-sharing would represent the second longest known distance between two cities involved in sharing dies; only Amastris and Neocaesarea (Kraft no. 315) are separated by a greater distance. The average distance between cities that shared dies in the Antonine period was only 65 km.

33. E.g., *RPC* VII-1.183–188A.

reference to Stratonicea, and use only Hadrianopolis.[34] These include some coins naming the magistrate Candidus as *strategos* for the second time, which are likely to be the most recent coins before the reign of Antoninus Pius.

Stratonicea-Hadrianopolis certainly seems a more likely candidate for the issuer of these coins than either Hadrianopolis in Phrygia or Hadriani ad Olympum. Firstly, it was situated just 55 km distant from Pergamum, a much more plausible distance across which the die might be shared. Secondly, the naming of a *strategos* in the reverse legend fits much better at Stratonicea-Hadrianopolis, where it was common practice, whereas at both Hadrianopolis in Phrygia and Hadriani ad Olympum it was more usual to name an *archon*.[35] Finally, despite the difficulties arising from heavy abbreviation, it is also possible that the two names that appear in the reverse legend can be connected to known families in Stratonicea-Hadrianopolis. The magistrate Diod. Philox. may have belonged to the same family as Philoxenos Artemona, known from coins of Elagabalus, while his father, named only as K. G. Iou., could be related to the Kl. Kandidos Ioulianos known as the instigator of the city's coinage under Hadrian.[36]

> **Number:** 309
> **Obverse Type:** Synkletos
> **Published Link:** Mostene–Synnada
> **Actual Link:** None
> **Additional Bibliography:** *RPC* IV temp. no. 2225

The coin of Mostene on which Kraft based this link is in fact a tooled coin of Synnada, therefore this die was only used at Synnada and not elsewhere.

34. E.g., *RPC* III.1779, 1782, 1785, 1788. In some instances (*RPC* III.1781–83) it is not clear whether the abbreviation CT(P) refers to Stratonicea or *strategos* (the office of the named magistrate), but there are enough unambiguous instances to make the point.

35. On the tendency of cities to name just one office on their coins, see P. Weiss, "The cities and their money," in *Coinage and Identity in the Roman Provinces*, ed. C. Howgego, V. Heuchert and A. Burnett (Oxford: Oxford University Press, 2005), 63.

36. On C. Candidus Ioulianus see L. Robert and J. Robert, *Le Carie. Histoire et Géographie historique avec le recueil des inscriptions antiques* (Paris: Adrian Maisonneuve, 1954), 80–84; L. Robert, *Hellenica XI–XII. Recueil d'épigraphie de numismatique et d'antiquités grecques* (Paris: Adrian Maisonneuve, 1960), 59–60 and *RPC* III, p. 215; for Philoxenos Artemona see Münsterberg, *Beamtennamen*, 150.

> **Number:** 312
> **Obverse Type:** Caracalla
> **Published Link:** Gangra–Germanicopolis
> **Actual Link:** None
> **Additional Bibliography:** –

Kraft believed that Gangra was a city in its own right in the vicinity of Germanicopolis.[37] The two are, however, different names for the same city, which returned to its pre-Roman name of Gangra during the early third century AD.[38]

> **Number:** 342
> **Obverse Type:** Severus Alexander
> **Published Link:** Baris–Seleucia Sidera
> **Actual Link:** Baris–Seleucia Sidera–Conana–Prostanna
> **Additional Bibliography:** H. von Aulock, *Münzen und Städte Pisidiens, Teil 2.* Istanbuler Mitteilungen Beiheft 22 (Tübingen: Ernst Wasmuth, 1979), 19 no. 5c

In producing the corpora of a number of smaller Pisidian cities, Hans von Aulock noted that this die was used by two more cities than were recorded by Kraft.[39]

> **Number:** 350
> **Obverse Type:** Philip II
> **Published Link:** Laranda–Perge
> **Actual Link:** None
> **Additional Bibliography:** G. Watson, "Die-sharing in Asia Minor: another phantom link." *SM* 264, 100–102.

It has been shown that the only known specimen of Laranda from this die is in fact a tooled coin of Perge.[40]

---

37. Kraft, *System*, 71.

38. L. Bricault, and F. Delrieux, *Gangra-Germanicopolis de Paphlagonie "Foyer des dieux," Étude de numismatique et d'histoire* (Bordeaux: Ausonius Éditions, 2014), 9–11.

39. Aulock, *Münzen und Städte Pisidiens, Teil 2*, 19.

40. Watson, "Die-sharing in Asia Minor."

Number: 366

Obverse Type: Serapis

Published Link: Aphrodisias–Themisonium

Actual Link: Aphrodisias–Themisonium–Bargasa

Additional Bibliography: D. J. MacDonald, *The Coinage of Aphrodisias* (London: Royal Numismatic Society, 1992), O175; Johnston, "Aphrodisias," 52

That a third city used this die was noted by Johnston in her review of David MacDonald's corpus of the coinage of Aphrodisias.[41] She dated coins from this die to the reign of Septimius Severus, ca. 201–209.[42]

Number: 373

Obverse Type: Elagabalus

Published Link: Hierapolis–Iuliopolis

Actual Link: None

Additional Bibliography: D. H. French, *Roman roads and milestones of Asia Minor. Fasc. 1: The Pilgrim's Road = Haci Yolu* (Oxford: B.A.R., 1981), 44–45; A. Johnston, "Hierapolis Revisited," *NC* 144 (1984), 66

Kraft himself expressed doubt about this die-sharing, and in particular the one example known to him from Iuliopolis.[43] He noted that this was the only coin on which Iuliopolis was named as *neokoros*, and the similarity of the reverse design with coins of Hierapolis suggested the possibility that the reverse legend of a coin of Hierapolis had been tooled to read ΙΟΥΛΙΟΠΟΛΕΙΤΩΝ. He suggested that the matter would only be concluded by the discovery of further examples. In the intervening time, no further evidence of a *neokoria* for Iuliopolis has been discovered,[44] nor do we have any new specimens of that city from this die.[45] The coin in question is generally regarded as tooled, and thus this die-sharing should be removed from the record.[46]

Two shared dies that have been published since Kraft also need to be removed from the record:

41. Johnston, "Aphrodisias," 52.

42. Johnston, "Aphrodisias," 94.

43. Kraft, *System*, 89, 213. Kraft cites the Iuliopolis coin as Abbott 1120, which should in fact be a reference to the catalogue of the sale of the Mabbott collection by Hans M. F. Schulman Gallery in New York on 6–11 June 1969. The lot number is correct.

44. B. Burrell, *Neokoroi. Greek Cities and Roman Emperors* (Leiden: Brill, 2004), 12.

45. According to the initial material for *RPC* VI made available online.

46. E.g. French, *Roman roads*, 44–45; Johnston, "Hierapolis," 66.

Number: –

Obverse Type: Commodus

Published Link: Aphrodisias–Ceretapa

Actual Link: None

Additional Bibliography: MacDonald, *The Coinage of Aphrodisias*, O132;
Johnston, "Aphrodisias," 46–47

The use of this obverse die at Ceretapa is well recorded.[47] MacDonald postulated that *homonoia* coins between Aphrodisias and Ceretapa struck from the same die, currently known only from one poorly preserved specimen, were issued by Aphrodisias, on the basis that Aphrodite, the goddess representing Aphrodisias, appears on the left-hand side.[48] Johnston pointed out, however, that the issuing city did not always place its own divinity in the place of honor on the left-hand side, and that the style of the coin is much better suited to Ceretapa than Aphrodisias.[49] The *homonoia* coins are thus better assigned to Ceretapa, and no die link exists with Aphrodisias.

Number: –

Obverse Type: Severus Alexander

Published Link: Baris–Seleucia Sidera

Actual Link: None

Additional Bibliography: Aulock, *Münzen und Städte Pisidiens, Teil 2*,
19 no. 5b

This shared die was noted by von Aulock, presumably on the basis of his plates.[50] However, there seems to have been some confusion with his illustrations, and the only specimen that he gives from this die at Seleucia Sidera (*vA Pis* 2.1935) is incorrectly illustrated. The original publication of this coin (*SNG von Aulock* 5230) shows that it was struck from a different obverse die. The initial material for *RPC* VI made available online does not show any instance of the use of this Baris obverse at Seleucia Sidera.

---

47. H. von Aulock, *Münzen und Städte Phrygiens, Teil 1* (Tübingen: Ernst Wasmuth, 1980), nos. 492–493.

48. MacDonald, *The Coinage of Aphrodisias*, 5 and 88, noting his own reservations.

49. Johnston, "Aphrodisias," 46–47. Cf. M. K. Nollé and J. Nollé, "Vom feinen Spiel städtischer Diplomatie zu Zeremoniell und Sinn kaiserzeitlicher Homonoia-Feste," *ZPE* 102 (1994), 241–261, for further instances of the issuing city ceding the position of honor on the left-hand side.

50. Aulock, *Münzen und Städte Pisidiens, Teil 2*, 19.

ADDENDA

This list of addenda contains, without distinction, three types of material:
(a) shared dies from Asia Minor published since 1972; (b) shared dies from outside Asia Minor; (c) a small number of shared dies published here for the first
time. In these latter instances references to example specimens has been given
where possible.

The listing is subdivided by *RPC* volume. This is not to say that these shared
dies are necessarily noted by *RPC*—indeed, only two of the relevant volumes
have yet appeared in print—but this division serves rather to offer a rough chronology that also encompasses "pseudo-autonomous" coins.

Bibliography is given here only where the shared die is specifically mentioned.
The reference is, where possible, to an identifying number for the die.[51] Example
specimens can normally be found under these bibliographical references, as well
as on the website that accompanies this article.

RPC IV

Number:	374
Obverse Type:	Marcus Aurelius (Caesar)
Link:	Ephesus–Magnesia ad Maeandrum
Bibliography:	S. Schultz, *Die Münzprägung von Magnesia am Mäander in der römischen Kaiserzeit* (Berlin: Akademie Verlag, 1975), 16 n. 5

Number:	375
Obverse Type:	Faustina II
Link:	Hadrianopolis–Plotinopolis
Bibliography:	H.-D. Schultz, "Die-sharing," 830

Number:	376
Obverse Type:	Commodus
Link:	Gaza–Raphia
Bibliography:	Y. Farhi, "Die-sharing and Other Numismatic Connections in Southern Roman Palestine (Second–Third Centuries CE)." *INR* 10 (2015), 143 no. 6

---

51. The dies in *RPC* VII-1 are numbered for each individual city, meaning that dies used
by more than one city can have more than one number. The reference given is therefore accompanied by a page number, and always points to the first time that the die is mentioned.

Number: 377

Obverse Type: Synkletos

Link: Aphrodisias–Trapezopolis

Bibliography: MacDonald, *The Coinage of Aphrodisias*, O183; Johnston, "Aphrodisias," 52

Notes: Coins struck from this die are dated to the period after 175 by Johnston, "Aphrodisias," 90.

RPC V

Number: 378

Obverse Type: Septimius Severus

Link: Psophis–Thelpusa

Bibliography: Flament, "Die et engraver-sharing," 560

Number: 379

Obverse Type: Septimius Severus

Link: Cleonae–Pellene

Bibliography: Flament, "Die et engraver-sharing," 561

Number: 380

Obverse Type: Septimius Severus

Link: Asine–Pagae

Bibliography: Flament, "Die et engraver-sharing," 561

Number: 381

Obverse Type: Septimius Severus

Link: Anchialus–Marcianopolis

Bibliography: M. Simon, "Stempelkoppelungen aus der Zeit des Septimius Severus für Markianopolis in Moesia Inferior und Anchialos in Thrakien," *Erfurter Münzblätter* 20/21 (2015), 168

Number: 382
Obverse Type: Septimius Severus
Link: Comama–Neocaesarea
Bibliography: Z. Çizmeli, *Le monnayage de Néocésarée et du koinon du Pont* (Milan: Ennerre, 2006), 138

Number: 383
Obverse Type: Septimius Severus
Link: Aphrodisias–Themisonium
Bibliography: MacDonald, *The Coinage of Aphrodisias,* O154

Number: 384
Obverse Type: Septimius Severus
Link: Attalea–Saitta–Thyatira
Bibliography: M. Amandry, "Quelques témoinages numismatiques de cités de la province d'Asie après l'élevation de Caracalla à l'Augustat et de Geta au Césarat en 198." *BSFN* 72.5 (2017), 140.

Number: 385
Obverse Type: Septimius Severus
Link: Gaza–Raphia
Bibliography: Y. Farhi, "Die-Sharing between Gaza and Raphia in the Early Severan Period (Preliminary Report)," *INJ* 16 (2008), 167 no. 1

Number: 386
Obverse Type: Septimius Severus
Link: Gaza–Raphia
Bibliography: Farhi, "Die-Sharing," 168 no. 2

Number: 387
Obverse Type: Septimius Severus, Caracalla & Geta
Link: Dionysopolis–Sebaste
Bibliography: Amandry, "Un coin de Septime Sévère," 138

Number: 388

Obverse Type: Julia Domna

Link: Colbasa–Sibidunda

Bibliography: D. Calomino, *Roma e le Province Orientali. La Collezione Storica di monete "greche imperiali" del Medagliere del Museo Nazionale Romano* (Rome, forthcoming), nos. 513 and 532

Notes: Example specimens:
Colbasa: *vA Col* 9–13
Sibidunda: *vA Pis* 1.1363–71

Number: 389

Obverse Type: Caracalla

Link: Bizye–Perinthus

Bibliography: A. Johnston, "The Denominational Systems of the Greek Imperials of Bizye in Thrace," *NC* 143 (1983), 234

Number: 390

Obverse Type: Caracalla

Link: Ephesus–Magnesia ad Maeandrum

Bibliography: Schultz, *Magnesia,* 16 n. 4

Notes: Since Schultz lists numerous shared dies in the same footnote (many of which were already listed by Kraft), I give here example specimens:
Ephesus: *SNG Cop Ionia* 424
Magnesia: *SNG Cop Ionia* 875
(= Schultz, *Magnesia,* no. 206)

Number: 391

Obverse Type: Caracalla

Link: Ephesus–Magnesia ad Maeandrum

Bibliography: Schultz, *Magnesia,* 16 n. 4

Notes: Since Schultz lists numerous shared dies in the same footnote (many of which were already listed by Kraft), I give here example specimens:
Ephesus: *SNG von Aulock* 1899
Magnesia: Schultz, *Magnesia,* no. 197

Number:	392
Obverse Type:	Caracalla
Link:	Colbasa–Sibidunda
Bibliography:	A. Johnston, "The Intermittent Imperials: the Coinages of Lycia, Lycaonia, and Pisidia." *NC* 140 (1980), 206

Number:	393
Obverse Type:	Caracalla
Link:	Gaza–Raphia
Bibliography:	Farhi, "Die-Sharing between Gaza and Raphia," 169 no. 4

Number:	394
Obverse Type:	Geta
Link:	Gythium–Thelpusa
Bibliography:	Flament, "Die et engraver-sharing," 561

Number:	395
Obverse Type:	Boule
Link:	Aphrodisias–Attuda–Bargasa–Trapezopolis
Bibliography:	MacDonald, *The Coinage of Aphrodisias*, O168; Johnston, "Aphrodisias," 52
Notes:	Coins struck from this die are dated to the period 201–209 by Johnston, "Aphrodisias," 93.

RPC VI

Number:	396
Obverse Type:	Elagabalus
Link:	Hierapolis–Sardis
Bibliography:	Johnston, "Hierapolis," 67

Number:	397
Obverse Type:	Elagabalus
Link:	Hierapolis–Sardis
Bibliography:	Johnston, "Hierapolis," 69

Number:	398
Obverse Type:	Elagabalus
Link:	Carallia–Colybrassus
Bibliography:	*SNG Levante* 327; Watson, *Connections*, E020

Number:	399
Obverse Type:	Elagabalus
Link:	Antioch ad Orontem–Samosata–Seleucia Pieria–Zeugma
Bibliography:	Butcher, "Colonial Coinage," 70
Notes:	Butcher notes that these four cities "consistently share dies" under Elagabalus, but cites specimens only for the one die used by all four. Some other dies shared between these four cities are listed below, where specific instances have been identified. There are almost certainly more.

Number:	400
Obverse Type:	Elagabalus
Link:	Antioch ad Orontem–Samosata
Bibliography:	R. McAlee, *The Coins of Roman Antioch.* (Lancaster, PA: Classical Numismatic Group, 2007), 290

Number:	401
Obverse Type:	Elagabalus
Link:	Antioch ad Orontem–Seleucia Pieria
Bibliography:	Kraft, *System*, pl. 117 no. 13
Notes:	Kraft discussed this die-sharing, and illustrated examples of both cities, but did not assign it a number since it involved cities outside of Asia Minor.

Number:	402
Obverse Type:	Elagabalus
Link:	Antioch ad Orontem–Zeugma
Bibliography:	K. Butcher, *Coinage in Roman Syria. Northern Syria, 64 BC–AD 253* (London: Royal Numismatic Society, 2004), pl. 15 no. 481b

Number: 403
Obverse Type: Elagabalus
Link: Antioch ad Orontem–Zeugma
Bibliography: McAlee, *The Coins of Roman Antioch*, 290

Number: 404
Obverse Type: Julia Maesa
Link: Dionysopolis–Laodicea ad Lycum
Bibliography: H. von Aulock, *Münzen und Städte Phrygiens, Teil 2*, 63

Number: 405
Obverse Type: Julia Maesa
Link: Aspendus–Sillyum
Bibliography: Watson, *Connections*, E004

Number: 406
Obverse Type: Julia Paula
Link: Etenna–Side
Bibliography: Aulock, *Münzen und Städte Pisidiens, Teil 2*, 19 no. 3; Watson, *Connections*, E028

Number: 407
Obverse Type: Julia Paula
Link: Etenna–Side
Bibliography: Watson, *Connections*, E030

Number: 408
Obverse Type: Julia Soaemias
Link: Aspendus–Sillyum
Bibliography: Watson, *Connections*, E016

Number: 409
Obverse Type: Julia Soaemias
Link: Etenna–Side
Bibliography: Aulock, *Münzen und Städte Pisidiens, Teil 2*, 19 no. 4; Watson, *Connections*, E027

Number: 410

Obverse Type: Severus Alexander (as Caesar)

Link: Hierapolis–Sardis

Bibliography: Johnston, "Hierapolis," 72

Number: 411

Obverse Type: Severus Alexander

Link: Pella–Thessalonica

Bibliography: D. Calomino, "Bilingual coins of Severus Alexander in the Eastern provinces," *AJN* 26 (2014), 207–208

Notes: Coins of Thessalonica from this die have an obverse legend in Latin and a reverse legend in Greek, suggesting that the obverse die was erroneously deployed for this mint.[52]

Number: 412

Obverse Type: Severus Alexander

Link: Dionysopolis–Marcianopolis

Bibliography: Calomino, "The coinage of Dionysopolis," 264

Number: 413

Obverse Type: Severus Alexander

Link: Abydus–Cyzicus

Bibliography: Calomino, "From Thrace to Lesbos," 208 link B

Number: 414

Obverse Type: Severus Alexander

Link: Abydus–Methymna

Bibliography: Calomino, "From Thrace to Lesbos," 208 link A

52. A similar instance has been observed in the Peloponnese, where an obverse die with Septimius Severus's name and titles in Latin was coupled with a Greek language reverse for the city of Argos. C. Flament and P. Marchetti, *Le monnayage Argien d'époque Romaine (d'Hadrien à Gallien)* (Athènes: École française d'Athènes, 2011), 41, suggest that the obverse was originally intended for the coinage of Corinth, but the use of the die for Corinth has not yet been observed.

Number: 415

Obverse Type: Severus Alexander

Link: Methymna–Sestus

Bibliography: Calomino, "From Thrace to Lesbos," 209 link D

Number: 416

Obverse Type: Severus Alexander

Link: Cyme–Erythrae–Magnesia ad Sipylum–Phocaea

Bibliography: Kraft, *System*, pl. 3 no. 17

Notes: Although Kraft illustrated this shared die with specimens from all of the above cities, he did not assign it a number.

Number: 417

Obverse Type: Severus Alexander

Link: Germe–Hadrianeia

Bibliography: Shared die unpublished[53]

Notes: Example specimens:
Germe: K. Ehling, *Die Münzprägung der mysischen Stadt Germe in der römischen Kaiserzeit.* (Bonn: Dr. Rudolf Habelt, 2001), no. 93 (V4)
Hadrianeia: Fritze, *Die antiken Münzen Mysiens. I*, no. 476

Number: 418

Obverse Type: Severus Alexander

Link: Hadrianopolis–Peltae

Bibliography: Shared die unpublished

Notes: Example specimens:
Hadrianopolis: *SNG Leypold* 1710
Peltae: *BMC* 8

Number: 419

Obverse Type: Severus Alexander

Link: Aspendus–Sillyum

Bibliography: Watson, *Connections*, A021

---

53. I am grateful to Dario Calomino for bringing this and the following die-sharing to my attention.

Number: 420

Obverse Type: Severus Alexander

Link: Side–Syedra

Bibliography: *SNG Levante* 417; Watson, *Connections*, A103

Number: 421

Obverse Type: Severus Alexander

Link: Baris–Seleucia Sidera

Bibliography: Aulock, *Münzen und Städte Pisidiens, Teil 2,* 19, no. 5a

Number: 422

Obverse Type: Severus Alexander

Link: Etenna–Syedra

Bibliography: Watson, *Connections*, A057

Number: 423

Obverse Type: Severus Alexander

Link: Antioch ad Orontem–Seleucia Pieria

Bibliography: McAlee, *The Coins of Roman Antioch*, 305

Number: 424

Obverse Type: Julia Mamaea

Link: Pogla–Verbe

Bibliography: Aulock, *Münzen und Städte Pisidiens, Teil 2,* 19 no. 6b

Number: 425

Obverse Type: Julia Mamaea

Link: Carallia–Colybrassus

Bibliography: Watson, *Connections*, A033

Notes: The only known specimen from Colybrassus (Gorny & Mosch 196 [Mar 2011] 2237) has an obverse legend reading IOVΛIAN MA-MAIAN, whereas specimens from Carallia read IOVΛIAN MAMЄAN. All other details of the die are, however, identical, and traces of an epsilon underneath the IA of the Gorny & Mosch specimen suggest that this Colybrassus coin has been tooled.[54]

54. See Watson, *Connections*.

Number: 426
Obverse Type: Orbiana
Link: Etenna–Side
Bibliography: Aulock, *Münzen und Städte Pisidiens, Teil 2*, 19 no. 7; Watson, *Connections*, A069

Number: 427
Obverse Type: Maximinus
Link: Aspendus–Selge
Bibliography: Watson, *Connections*, M011

Number: 428
Obverse Type: Maximinus
Link: Ariassus–Magydus
Bibliography: Watson, *Connections*, M002

Number: 429
Obverse Type: Maximinus
Link: Carallia–Colybrassus
Bibliography: Watson, *Connections*, M018

Number: 430
Obverse Type: Maximinus
Link: Coracesium–Syedra
Bibliography: Watson, *Connections*, M031

Number: 431
Obverse Type: Maximinus
Link: Laerte–Syedra
Bibliography: Watson, *Connections*, M045

Number: 432
Obverse Type: Maximus
Link: Aspendus–Side
Bibliography: Watson, *Connections*, M006

Number:	433
Obverse Type:	Maximus
Link:	Perge–Sillyum
Bibliography:	Watson, "Die-sharing in Asia Minor," 101 no. 1; Watson, *Connections*, M063

Number:	434
Obverse Type:	Maximus
Link:	Perge–Sillyum
Bibliography:	Watson, "Die-sharing in Asia Minor," 101 no. 2; Watson, *Connections*, M069

Number:	435
Obverse Type:	Maximus
Link:	Carallia–Colybrassus
Bibliography:	Watson, *Connections*, M016

Number:	436
Obverse Type:	Maximus
Link:	Carallia–Colybrassus
Bibliography:	Watson, *Connections*, M020

Number:	437
Obverse Type:	Maximus
Link:	Coracesium–Laerte–Syedra
Bibliography:	*SNG Levante Suppl.* 66, 68, 71; Watson, *Connections*, M033

Number:	438
Obverse Type:	Maximus
Link:	Laerte–Syedra
Bibliography:	Watson, *Connections*, M044

Number:	439
Obverse Type:	Maximus
Link:	Laerte–Syedra
Bibliography:	*SNG PfPs* 6.874-6; Watson, *Connections*, M046

RPC VII

Number: 440
Obverse Type: Gordian III
Link: Marcianopolis–Odessus–Tomis
Bibliography: A. von Sallet, *Königliche Museen zu Berlin. Beschreibung der antiken Münzen, Erster Band* (Berlin, 1888), 195; D. Calomino, "Die-sharing in Moesia Inferior under Gordian III," *NC* 173 (2013), G1

Number: 441
Obverse Type: Gordian III
Link: Marcianopolis–Tomis
Bibliography: Calomino, "Die-sharing," G2a

Number: 442
Obverse Type: Gordian III
Link: Germe–Hadrianea
Bibliography: *RPC* VII-1, p. 121, AV1

Number: 443
Obverse Type: Gordian III
Link: Germe–Hadrianea
Bibliography: *RPC* VII-1, p. 121, AV2

Number: 444
Obverse Type: Gordian III
Link: Germe–Hadrianea–Miletopolis
Bibliography: *RPC* VII-1, p. 121, AV4

Number: 445
Obverse Type: Gordian III
Link: Cyme–Phocaea
Bibliography: *RPC* VII-1, p. 171, AV3
Notes: This link was in fact noted by Kraft and illustrated at Plate 4, 30a-b, but he did not include it in his numbering.

Number: 446
Obverse Type: Gordian III
Link: Cyme–Smyrna
Bibliography: *RPC* VII-1, p. 171, AV 2

Number: 447
Obverse Type: Gordian III
Link: Elaea–Pergamum
Bibliography: *RPC* VII-1, p. 128, AV 3

Number: 448
Obverse Type: Gordian III
Link: Elaea–Pergamum
Bibliography: *RPC* VII-1, p. 128, AV 4

Number: 449
Obverse Type: Gordian III
Link: Colophon–Metropolis
Bibliography: *RPC* VII-1, p. , 190, AV 27

Number: 450
Obverse Type: Gordian III
Link: Ephesus–Magnesia ad Maeandrum
Bibliography: *RPC* VII-1, p. 195, AV 15

Number: 451
Obverse Type: Gordian III
Link: Ephesus–Metropolis
Bibliography: *RPC* VII-1, p. 195, AV 14

Number: 452
Obverse Type: Gordian III
Link: Ephesus–Metropolis
Bibliography: *RPC* VII-1, p. 195, AV 34

Number: 453
Obverse Type: Gordian III
Link: Smyrna–Temnus
Bibliography: *RPC* VII-1, p. 179, AV 8

Number: 454
Obverse Type: Gordian III
Link: Smyrna–Temnus
Bibliography: *RPC* VII-1, 179, AV9

Number: 455
Obverse Type: Gordian III
Link: Accilaeum–Tiberiopolis
Bibliography: *RPC* VII-1, p. 163, AV2

Number: 456
Obverse Type: Gordian III
Link: Bruzus–Lysias
Bibliography: *RPC* VII-1, p. 262, AV5

Number: 457
Obverse Type: Gordian III
Link: Midaeum–Nacolea
Bibliography: *RPC* VII-1, p. 274, AV1

Number: 458
Obverse Type: Gordian III
Link: Acalissus–Corydalla
Bibliography: H. von Aulock, *Die Münzprägung des Gordian III und der Tranquillina in Lykien* (Tübingen: Ernst Wasmuth, 1974), 30 no. 2

Number: 459
Obverse Type: Gordian III
Link: Aperlae–Cyaneae
Bibliography: Aulock, *Lykien,* 30 no. 5

Number: 460
Obverse Type: Gordian III
Link: Corydalla–Rhodiapolis
Bibliography: Aulock, *Lykien,* 30 no. 6

Number: 461

Obverse Type: Gordian III

Link: Corydalla–Rhodiapolis

Bibliography: Aulock, *Lykien,* 30 no. 7

Number: 462

Obverse Type: Gordian III

Link: Olympus–Trebenna

Bibliography: Aulock, *Lykien,* 30 no. 8

Number: 463

Obverse Type: Gordian III

Link: Olympus–Trebenna

Bibliography: Aulock, *Lykien,* 30 no. 9

Number: 464

Obverse Type: Gordian III

Link: Antioch ad Pisidiam–Iconium

Bibliography: H. von Aulock, *Münzen und Städte Lykaoniens* (Tübingen: Ernst Wasmuth, 1976), 23 no. 2

Number: 465

Obverse Type: Gordian III

Link: Carallia–Colybrassus

Bibliography: *SNG Paris* 2.549 and 579; Watson, *Connections,* G020

Number: 466

Obverse Type: Gordian III

Link: Carallia–Colybrassus

Bibliography: *SNG PfPs* 6.696 and 760; Watson, *Connections,* G021

Number: 467

Obverse Type: Gordian III

Link: Carallia–Colybrassus

Bibliography: *SNG PfPs* 6.693–695 and 759; Watson, *Connections,* G022

Number:	468
Obverse Type:	Gordian III
Link:	Casae–Etenna–Lyrbe
Bibliography:	*SNG Paris* 2.513–514 and 528; Watson, *Connections*, G025

Number:	469
Obverse Type:	Gordian III
Link:	Casae–Lyrbe–Side
Bibliography:	Watson, *Connections*, G028

Number:	470
Obverse Type:	Gordian III
Link:	Laerte–Syedra
Bibliography:	*SNG PfPs* 6.877 and 1222; Watson, *Connections*, G046

Number:	471
Obverse Type:	Gordian III and Serapis
Link:	Dionysopolis–Marcianopolis
Bibliography:	U. Peter, "Religious-cultural identity in Thrace and Moesia Inferior," in *Coinage and Identity in the Roman Provinces*, ed. C. Howgeo, V. Heuchert and A. Burnett (Oxford: Oxford University Press, 2005), 112

Number:	472
Obverse Type:	Tranquillina
Link:	Amastris–Tium
Bibliography:	Shared die unpublished
Notes:	Example specimens: Amastris: *SNG Paris* 7.151 Tium: *SNG von Aulock* 1021

Number:	473
Obverse Type:	Tranquillina
Link:	Etenna–Side
Bibliography:	Watson, *Connections*, G041

Number: 474

Obverse Type: Tranquillina

Link: Etenna–Side

Bibliography: Watson, *Connections*, G043

RPC VIII

Number: 475

Obverse Type: Philip I

Link: Panemoteichus–Perge

Bibliography: Watson, "Die-sharing in Asia Minor," 101 no. 3; Watson, *Connections*, P051

Number: 476

Obverse Type: Philip I

Link: Carallia–Colybrassus

Bibliography: Ziegler 1988, nos. 46 & 66–67; Watson, *Connections*, P014

Number: 477

Obverse Type: Philip I

Link: Carallia–Casae–Colybrassus–Side

Bibliography: Watson, *Connections*, P020

Notes: Watson, *Connections*, P020 is only listed for Casae and Side, but is in fact the same die as Watson, *Connections*, P022 (Colybrassus), and is also attested at Carallia (e.g., Pecunem 6 [Aug. 2013], 284).

Number: 478

Obverse Type: Philip I

Link: Samosata–Zeugma

Bibliography: *BMC Syria*, p. 129; Butcher, "Colonial Coinage," 70 n. 24

Notes: In *BMC* the emperor portrayed on this die is incorrectly identified as Philip II.

Number: 479
Obverse Type: Otacilia Severa
Link: Carallia–Casae
Bibliography: Watson, *Connections*, P014

Number: 480
Obverse Type: Otacilia Severa
Link: Laerte–Syedra
Bibliography: Watson, *Connections*, P042

Number: 481
Obverse Type: Philip II, Caesar
Link: Etenna–Side
Bibliography: Watson, *Connections*, P033

Number: 482
Obverse Type: Philip II, Caesar
Link: Etenna–Side
Bibliography: Watson, *Connections*, P036

Number: 483
Obverse Type: Philip II, Caesar
Link: Prostanna–Sagalassus
Bibliography: Aulock, *Münzen und Städte Pisidiens, Teil 2*, 19 no. 8

Number: 484
Obverse Type: Philip II
Link: Viminacium–*provincia Dacia*
Bibliography: A. Cavagna, *Provincia Dacia. I Conî* (Milan: Società numismatica italiana, 2012), 128 D/51
Notes: Some scholars argue that the mint for the *provincia Dacia* series was located at Viminacium.[55] This does not, however, negate the fact that this obverse die was used for two different series.

55. E.g., F. Martin, *Kolonialprägungen aus Moesia Superior und Dacia* (Budapest/Bonn: Akadémiai Kiadó/Dr. Rudolf Habel, 1992), 10.

Number:	485
Obverse Type:	Philip II
Link:	Samosata–Zeugma
Bibliography:	McAlee, *The Coins of Roman Antioch*, 327

RPC IX

Number:	486
Obverse Type:	Trajan Decius
Link:	Carallia–Colybrassus
Bibliography:	*RPC* IX, 37, no. 29; Watson, *Connections*, D016

Number:	487
Obverse Type:	Trajan Decius
Link:	Carallia–Colybrassus
Bibliography:	*SNG PfPs* 6.764; *RPC* IX, 37, no. 30; Watson, *Connections*, D017

Number:	488
Obverse Type:	Trajan Decius
Link:	Casae–Etenna
Bibliography:	*RPC* IX, 37, no. 25; Watson, *Connections*, D018

Number:	489
Obverse Type:	Herennia Etruscilla
Link:	Casae–Etenna–Lyrbe
Bibliography:	*RPC* IX, 37, no. 26; Watson, *Connections*, D019

Number:	490
Obverse Type:	Herennia Etruscilla
Link:	Laerte–Syedra
Bibliography:	*SNG Paris* 2.601 & 656; *RPC* IX, 37, no. 34; Watson, *Connections*, D043

Number:	491
Obverse Type:	Herennius Etruscus, Caesar
Link:	Laerte–Syedra
Bibliography:	*SNG PfPs* 6.878; *RPC* IX, 37, no. 35; Watson, *Connections*, D044

Number:	492
Obverse Type:	Herennius Etruscus, Caesar
Link:	Lyrbe–Side
Bibliography:	*SNG Levante* 285; *RPC* IX, 37, no. 27; Watson, *Connections,* D048
Number:	493
Obverse Type:	Herennius Etruscus
Link:	Apollonieron–Philadelphia
Bibliography:	*RPC* IX, 37, no. 21
Number:	494
Obverse Type:	Trebonianus Gallus
Link:	Aspendus–Pogla
Bibliography:	*RPC* IX, 37, no. 24; Watson, *Connections,* T004
Number:	495
Obverse Type:	Trebonianus Gallus
Link:	Carallia–Colybrassus
Bibliography:	*RPC* IX, 37, no. 31; Watson, *Connections,* T017
Number:	496
Obverse Type:	Trebonianus Gallus
Link:	Carallia–Colybrassus
Bibliography:	*SNG PfPs* 6.767–70; *RPC* IX, 37, no. 32; Watson, *Connections,* T018
Number:	497
Obverse Type:	Trebonianus Gallus
Link:	Laerte–Syedra
Bibliography:	*RPC* IX, 37, no. 36; Watson, *Connections,* T034
Number:	498
Obverse Type:	Trebonianus Gallus
Link:	Pompeiopolis–Tarsus
Bibliography:	R. Ziegler, *Münzen Kilikiens aus kleineren deutschen Sammlungen* (Munich: C. H. Beck, 1988,) no. 596; *RPC* IX, 37, no. 37

Number: 499
Obverse Type: Trebonianus Gallus
Link: Antioch ad Orontem–Laodicea ad Mare
Bibliography: *RPC* IX, 37, no. 39

Number: 500
Obverse Type: Volusian
Link: Aboutueichus–Tium
Bibliography: *RPC* IX, 36 no. 2

Number: 501
Obverse Type: Volusian
Link: Carallia–Colybrassus
Bibliography: *RPC* IX, 37, no. 33; Watson, *Connections*, T020

Number: 502
Obverse Type: Volusian
Link: Laerte–Syedra
Bibliography: Watson, *Connections*, T035

Number: 503
Obverse Type: Volusian
Link: Lyrbe–Side
Bibliography: *RPC* IX, 37, no. 28; Watson, *Connections*, T037

Number: 504
Obverse Type: Volusian
Link: Pompeiopolis–Tarsus
Bibliography: *RPC* IX, 37, no. 38

RPC X

Number: 505
Obverse Type: Valerian
Link: Isinda–Side
Bibliography: Watson, *Connections*, V051

Number: 506
Obverse Type: Valerian
Link: Colybrassus–Coracesium
Bibliography: *SNG Levante* 344 & 401–3; Watson, *Connections*, V031

Number: 507
Obverse Type: Valerian
Link: Laerte-Syedra
Bibliography: Watson, *Connections*, V059

Number: 508
Obverse Type: Gallienus
Link: Apollonia Salbace-Tabae
Bibliography: A. Johnston, *Greek Imperial Denominations ca. 200–275: a study of the Roman provincial bronze coinages of Asia Minor* (London: Royal Numismatic Society, 2007), 45
Notes: This is the 35+mm denomination with radiate portrait. The other shared die between these two cities referred to by Johnston, *Greek Imperial Denominations*, 45 is Kraft no. 193.

Number: 509
Obverse Type: Gallienus
Link: Aspendus–Lyrbe–Side
Bibliography: Johnston, *Greek Imperial Denominations*, V68 and V72; Watson, *Connections*, V013

Number: 510
Obverse Type: Gallienus
Link: Antioch ad Pisidiam–Iconium
Bibliography: Shared die unpublished
Notes: Example specimens:
               Antioch: Paris 229 (= A. Krzyżanowska, *Monnaies coloniales d'Antioche de Pisidie*. [Warsaw: Editions scientifiques de Pologne, 1970], pl. L, Table 35, obv. I)
               Iconium: Aulock, *Lykaonien*, nos. 405–473

Number:	511
Obverse Type:	Gallienus
Link:	Carallia–Coracesium–Syedra
Bibliography:	*SNG Paris* 2.584; Johnston, *Greek Imperial Denominations,* V10–V12; Watson, *Connections,* V025

Number:	512
Obverse Type:	Salonina
Link:	Perge–Sillyum
Bibliography:	Watson, "Die-sharing in Asia Minor," 101 no. 5; Watson, *Connections,* S038

Number:	513
Obverse Type:	Saloninus
Link:	Ephesus–Metropolis
Bibliography:	Shared die possibly unpublished
Notes:	Example specimens: Ephesus: *SNG Lewis* 4458 Metropolis: *SNG Munich* 700 This is possibly the shared die mentioned by R. Münsterberg, "Über die Namen der römischen Kaiser auf den griechischen Münzen," *NZ* 58 (1925), 39, but he does not illustrate the coins he references, nor are they illustrated in the catalogues he cites.

Number:	514
Obverse Type:	Saloninus
Link:	Attuda–Tripolis
Bibliography:	*SNG Tübingen* 3369 and 3886; W. Metcalf, "The coinage of Temenothyrae under Valerian and Gallienus," in *Rome et les provinces: Monnayage et histoire mélanges offerts à Michel Amandry,* ed. L. Bricault, A. Burnett, V. Drost and A. Suspène (Pessac: Ausonius Éditions, 2017), 367
Notes:	This is possibly the shared die mentioned by Münsterberg, "Über die Namen," 39, but he does not illustrate the coins he references, nor are they illustrated in the catalogues he cites.

A number of shared dies came to my attention after this article was accepted for publication, and their numbering therefore sits out of sequence:[56]

Number:	515
Obverse Type:	Plautilla
Link:	Acrasus–Thyatira
Bibliography:	Shared die unpublished
Notes:	Example specimens: Acrasus: CNG EA 240 (Sep. 2010), 298 Thyatira: G. Hirsch 346 (Feb. 2019), 2744
Number:	516
Obverse Type:	Philip I
Link:	Ephesus–Metropolis
Bibliography:	Shared die unpublished
Notes:	Example specimens: Ephesus: *Ephesos. Band 5.1. Katalog*, no. 942 Metropolis: M&M GmbH 15 (Oct. 2004), 645
Number:	517
Obverse Type:	Philip I
Link:	Phocaea–Thyatira
Bibliography:	Shared die unpublished
Notes:	Example specimens: Phocaea: *BMC* 160 Thyatira: V GR 33452
Number:	518
Obverse Type:	Philip I
Link:	Aspendus–Syedra
Bibliography:	Shared die unpublished
Notes:	Example specimens: Aspendus: VAuctions 273 (Nov. 2011) 282 Syedra: *SNG PfPs* 6.1223 (= Watson, *Connections*, P123)

---

56. They are, however, included in the statistics at the start of this paper, and in the indices.

Number:	519
Obverse Type:	Philip I
Link:	Carallia–Colybrassus
Bibliography:	Shared die unpublished
Notes:	Example specimens:

Example specimens:
Carallia: *SNG Paris* 2.583 (= Watson, *Connections,* P015)
Colybrassus: Naumann 63 (Mar. 2018) 233

I have also been made aware of a number of shared dies amongst cities of Arabia and the Syrian Decapolis during the reign of Elagabalus.[57] The cities involved are Adraa, Canatha, Charachmoba, Dium, Philadelphia, and Rabbathmoba. Unfortunately, work on these die-sharings was not far enough progressed at the time of going to press for them to be included in the catalogue. They will be added to the website, with numbering continuing the scheme employed here, as soon as they are fully published.

INDICES

Two indices are included here, one for cities and one for obverse types. In both indices, entries refer to the number of the die, and not to a page number. The dies indexed include both the material published by Kraft, and the dies listed here; numbers 1 through 373 are to be found in Kraft's book, numbers from 374 upwards are listed here. Dies that have been amended or corrected in the corrigenda section above are marked with an asterisk; shared dies that have been shown to be false are enclosed in square brackets.

The index of obverse types is subdivided by *RPC* volume to aid chronological distinction, and "pseudo-autonomous" types are listed for each *RPC* volume. On occasions it is possible to determine, usually through the occurrence of magistrates' names, that a particular obverse die without imperial portrait was used during the reign of more than one emperor, and should thus appear in more than one *RPC* volume. These dies appear under both relevant *RPC* volumes in this index.

---

57. Dario Calomino pers. comm.

Index of Cities

Index of Cities

BIBLIOGRAPHY

Altınoluk, Sencan. *Hypaipa. A Lydian City During the Roman Imperial Period.* Istanbul: Ege Yayinlari, 2013.

Amandry, Michel. "Quelques témoinages numismatiques de cités de la province d'Asie après l'élevation de Caracalla à l'Augustat et de Geta au Césarat en 198." *Bulletin de la Société Française de Numismatique* 72.5 (2017): 137–143.

Amandry, Michel, and Andrew Burnett. *Roman Provincial Coinage. Vol. III: Nerva, Trajan and Hadrian (AD 96–138).* With the assistance of J. Mairat, W. E. Metcalf, L. Bricault and M. Blet-Lemarquand. 2 vols. London: British Museum Press; Bibliothèque Nationale de France, 2015.

Aulock, Hans von. *Die Münzprägung des Gordian III und der Tranquillina in Lykien.* Istanbuler Mitteilungen Beiheft. Tübingen: Ernst Wasmuth, 1974.

—————. *Münzen und Städte Lykaoniens.* Istanbuler Mitteilungen Beiheft 16. Tübingen: Ernst Wasmuth, 1976.

—————. *Münzen und Städte Pisidiens, Teil 2.* Istanbuler Mitteilungen Beiheft 22. Tübingen: Ernst Wasmuth, 1979.

—————. *Münzen und Städte Phrygiens. Teil 1.* Istanbuler Mitteilungen Beiheft 25. Tübingen: Ernst Wasmuth, 1980.

—————. *Münzen und Städte Phrygiens, Teil 2.* Istanbuler Mitteilungen Beiheft 27. Tübingen: Ernst Wasmuth, 1987.

Bricault, Laurent and Fabrice Delrieux. *Gangra-Germanicopolis de Paphlagonie "Foyer des dieux".* Étude de numismatique et d'*histoire.* Numismatica Anatolica 6. Bordeaux: Ausonius Éditions, 2014.

Burrell, Barbara. *Neokoroi. Greek Cities and Roman Emperors.* Cincinnati Classical Studies 9. Leiden: Brill, 2004.

Butcher, Kevin. "The colonial coinage of Antioch-on-the-Orontes c. AD 218–53." *Numismatic Chronicle* 148 (1988): 63–75.

—————. *Coinage in Roman Syria. Northern Syria, 64 BC–AD 253.* Royal Numismatic Society Special Publications 34. London: Royal Numismatic Society, 2004.

—————. "Die-sharing in Asia Minor: A Phantom Link." *Schweizer Münzblatter* 219: 67–68.

Calomino, Dario. 2013. "Die-sharing in Moesia Inferior under Gordian III." *Numismatic Chronicle* 173 (2005): 105–126.

—————. "Bilingual coins of Severus Alexander in the Eastern provinces." *American Journal of Numismatics* 26 (2014): 199–222.

—————. "From Thrace to Lesbos. Coinage and cities across the Hellespont in the

3rd century AD." In *Studies in ancient coinage in honour of Andrew Burnett*, edited by Roger Bland and Dario Calomino, 207–220. London: Spink, 2015.

———. "The coinage of Dionysopolis and the system of coin production in Moesia Inferior at the end of the Severan Age." In *Ex nummis lux: Studies in Ancient Numismatics in honour of Dimitar Draganov*, edited by Dilyana Boteva, 261–71. Sofia: Bobokov Bros. Foundation, 2017.

———. Forthcoming. *Roma e le Province Orientali. La Collezione Storica di monete "greche imperiali" del Medagliere del Museo Nazionale Romano*. Rome.

Cavagna, Alessandro. *Provincia Dacia. I Conî*. Collana di numismatica e scienze affini 7. Milano: Società numismatica italiana, 2012.

Çizmeli, Zeynep. *Le monnayage de Néocésarée et du koinon du Pont*. Glaux. Collana di Studi e Ricerche di Numismatica 17. Milan: Ennerre, 2006.

Ehling, Kay. *Die Münzprägung der mysischen Stadt Germe in der römischen Kaiserzeit*. Asia Minor Studien 42. Bonn: Dr. Rudolf Habelt, 2001.

Farhi, Yoav. 2008. "Die-Sharing between Gaza and Raphia in the Early Severan Period (Preliminary Report)." *Israel Numismatic Journal* 16 (2008): 166–177.

———. "Die-sharing and Other Numismatic Connections in Southern Roman Palestine (Second–Third Centuries CE)." *Israel Numismatic Research* 10 (2015): 137–154.

Flament, Christophe. 2007. "Die et engraver-sharing dans le Péloponnèse entre le règne d'Hadrien et celui de Septime Sévère." *Bulletin de Correspondance Hellénique* 131.1: 559–614.

Flament, Christophe and Patrick Marchetti. *Le monnayage argien d'époque romaine (d'Hadrien à Gallien)*. Études péloponnésiennes 14. Athènes: École française d'Athènes, 2011.

Franke, Peter R. and Magret K. Nollé. *Die Homonoia-Münzen Kleinasiens und der thrakischen Randgebiete. I. Katalog*. Saarbrücker Studien zur Archäologie und alten Geschichte 10. Saarbrücken: Saarbrücker Druckerei und Verlag, 1997.

French, David H. *Roman roads and milestones of Asia Minor. Fasc. 1: The Pilgrim's Road = Haci Yolu*. BAR International Series 105. Oxford: B.A.R., 1981

Fritze, Hans von. *Die antiken Münzen Mysiens. I. Abteilung Adramytion–Kisthene*. Berlin: Georg Reimer, 1913.

Hostein, Antony and Jerome Mairat. *Roman Provincial Coinage. Vol. IX: From Trajan Decius to Uranius Antoninus*. London: British Museum Press, 2016.

Johnston, Ann. "New problems for old: Konrad Kraft on die-sharing in Asia Minor." *Numismatic Chronicle* 14 (1974): 203–207.

———. "The Intermittent Imperials: the Coinages of Lycia, Lycaonia, and Pisidia." *Numismatic Chronicle* 140 (1980): 205–211.

———. "Die-sharing in Asia Minor: the view from Sardis." *Israel Numismatic Journal* 6–7 (1982–1983): 59–78.

———. "The Denominational Systems of the Greek Imperials of Bizye in Thrace." *Numismatic Chronicle* 143 (1983): 231–239.

———. 1984a. "Greek Imperial Statistics: A Commentary." *Revue Numismatique* 26 (1984): 240–257.

———. "Hierapolis Revisited." *Numismatic Chronicle* 144 (1984): 52–80.

———. "Aphrodisias Reconsidered." *Numismatic Chronicle* 155 (1995): 43–100.

———. *Greek Imperial Denominations ca. 200–275: A study of the Roman provincial bronze coinages of Asia Minor.* Royal Numismatic Society Special Publications No. 43. London: Royal Numismatic Society, 2007.

Karwiese, Stefan. *Die Münzprägung von Ephesos. Band 5. Katalog und Aufbau der römerzeitlichen Stadtprägung mit allen erfassbaren Stempelnachweisen.* Veröffentlichungen des Instituts für Numismatik 14. Vienna: Holzhausen Druck GmbH, 2012.

———. *Die Münzprägung von Ephesos. Band 5. Corpus und Aufbau der römerzeitlichen Stadtprägung. 2. Statistiken, Metrologie und Kommentare.* Veröffentlichungen des Instituts für Numismatik 18. Vienna: Holzhausen Druck GmbH, 2016.

Kellner, Wendelin. "Konrad Kraft. *Das System der kaiserzeitlichen Münzprägung in Kleinasien.* Review." *Sweizer Münzblatter* 23 (1973): 29–31.

Kraft, Konrad. *Das System der kaiserzeitlichen Münzprägung in Kleinasien. Materialien und Entwürfe.* Berlin: Gebr. Mann, 1972.

Krzyżanowska, Aleksandra. *Monnaies coloniales d'Antioche de Pisidie.* Travaux du Centre d'archéologie méditerranéenne de l'Académie polonaise des sciences 7. Warsaw: Editions scientifiques de Pologne, 1970.

MacDonald, David J. *The Coinage of Aphrodisias.* Royal Numismatic Society Special Publications 23. London: Royal Numismatic Society, 1992.

Martin, Ferenc. *Kolonialprägungen aus Moesia Superior und Dacia.* Budapest/Bonn: Akadémiai Kiadó/Dr. Rudolf Habel, 1992.

McAlee, Richard. *The Coins of Roman Antioch.* Lancaster, PA: Classical Numismatic Group, 2007.

Metcalf, William "The coinage of Temenothyrae under Valerian and Gallienus." In *Rome et les provinces: Monnayage et histoire mélanges offerts à Michel Amandry,* edited by Laurent Bricault, Andrew Burnett, Vincent Drost, and Arnaud Suspène, 367–376. Numismatica Anatolica 7. Pessac: Ausonius Éditions, 2017.

Milne, Joseph G. "Two Notes on Greek Dies." *Numismatic Chronicle* 2 (1922): 43–48.

Mionnet, Theodore E. *Description de médailles antiques, grecques et romaines.* 15 vols. Paris: Testu, 1806–1837.

Mørkholm, Otto. "The «Behaviour» of Dies in the Hellenistic Period." In *Actes du 9ème Congrès International de Numismatique, Berne, September 1979*, edited by Tony Hackens. 2 vols, 209–214. Louvain-la-Neuve: International Association of Professional Numismatics, 1982.

Münsterberg, Rudolf. "Die Beamtennamen auf den griechischen Münzen." *Numismatische Zeitschrift* (1911): 69; (1912): 1–111; (1914): 1–98

———. 1925. "Über die Namen der römischen Kaiser auf den griechischen Münzen." *Numismatische Zeitschrift* 58 (1925): 37–48.

Nollé, Magret K. and Johannes Nollé. "Vom feinen Spiel städischer Diplomatie zu Zeremoniell und Sinn kaiserzeitlicher Homonoia-Feste." *Zeitschrift für Papyrologie und Epigraphik* 102 (1994): 241–261.

Pellerin, Joseph. *Mélange de diverses médailles Tome II. Médailles impériales grecques qui manquent dans Vaillant avec des observations sur celles qu'il a publiées.* Paris: H. L. Guerin & L.F. Delatour, 1765.

Peter, Ulrike. "Religious-cultural identity in Thrace and Moesia Inferior." In *Coinage and Identity in the Roman Provinces*, edited by Christopher Howgeo, Volker Heuchert, and Andrew Burnett, 107–114. Oxford: Oxford University Press, 2005.

Peter, Ulrike and Lily Grozdanova. "Philippopolis and Pautalia: A parallel analysis of the coinages." In *Thrace—local coinage and regional identity: Numismatic research in the digital age*. Forthcoming.

Price, Martin J. "Das System der kaiserzeitlichen Münzprägung in Kleinasien. Materialien und Entwürfe by Konrad Kraft." *Classical World* 67.5 (1974): 310–311.

Robert, Louis. *Hellenica XI–XII. Recueil d'épigraphie de numismatique et d'antiquités grecques.* Paris: Adrian Maisonneuve, 1964.

Robert, Louis and Jeanne Robert. *Le Carie. Histoire et Géographie historique avec le recueil des inscriptions antiques.* Paris: Adrian Maisonneuve, 1954.

Rutter, N. K. *Campanian Coinages: 475–380 B.C.* Edinburgh: Edinburgh University Press, 1979.

Sallet, Alfred von. *Königliche Museen zu Berlin. Beschreibung der antiken Münzen. Erster Band.* Berlin, 1888.

Schultz, Hans-Dietrich. "Die-sharing in Thrakien." *Annotazioni Numismatiche* 36 (1999): 829–33.

Schultz, Sabine. *Die Münzprägung von Magnesia am Mäander in der römischen Kaiserzeit.* Berlin: Akademie Verlag, 1975.

Simon, Matthias. "Stempelkoppelungen aus der Zeit des Septimius Severus für Markianopolis in Moesia Inferior und Anchialos in Thrakien." *Erfurter Münzblätter* 20/21 (2015): 167–173.

Spoerri Butcher, Marguerite. *Roman Provincial Coinage. Vol. VII: De Gordien Ier à Gordien III, 1: Province d' Asie.* London and Paris: British Museum Press and Bibliothèque nationale de Paris, 2006.

———. "L'organisation de la production monétaire au sein de la province d'Asie à l'époque de Gordien III (238–244)." *Schweizer Numismatischer Rundschau* 85 (2006): 97–132.

Watson, George. "Die-sharing in Asia Minor: another phantom link." *Schweizer Münzblätter* 264 (2016): 100–102.

———. "Die-sharing and the 'Pseudo-Autonomous' Coinages." *Numismatic Chronicle* 177 (2017): 201–211.

———. *Connections, communities and coinage. The system of coin production in southern Asia Minor, AD 218–276.* Numismatic Studies 39. New York: American Numismatic Society, 2019.

Weiss, Peter. "The cities and their money." In *Coinage and Identity in the Roman Provinces,* edited by Christopher J. Howgego, Volker Heuchert, and Andrew Burnett, 57–68. Oxford: Oxford University Press, 2005.

Ziegler, Ruprecht. *Münzen Kilikiens aus kleineren deutschen Sammlungen.* Vestigia, Beiträge zur alten Geschichte 42. Munich: C. H. Beck, 1988.

AJN Second Series 32 (2020) pp. 273–312
© 2020 The American Numismatic Society

Re-reading the So-called "*Asina* Tokens": Religious Diversity in Late Antiquity

PLATES 23–24   CRISTIAN MONDELLO*

This contribution reassesses the late Roman "*Asina* tokens", whose current scholarly interpretation has been strongly influenced by Andreas Alföldi's thesis, which argued that these artefacts were tools of anti-Christian "pagan" propaganda. This paper provides an updated catalogue of the material as well as a typological, morphological and iconographic analysis of these *tesserae*. This approach clarifies various questions concerning the imagery, production, and role of the tokens while also providing valuable insight into the religious evolution of late Roman society by emphasizing the complex relationship between "pagans" and Christians.

This paper focuses on the so-called "*Asina* tokens", a well-known but still mysterious group of Roman tokens (*tesserae*), generally dated to the end of the fourth or the beginning of the fifth century AD. They are named for the characteristic type of a donkey suckling a foal depicted on some of the reverses, which is sometimes accompanied by the legend *Asina*.

Although these *tesserae* attracted scholarly attention as early as the eighteenth century, no consensus has been reached so far in regard to their authority, chronology or purpose. Moreover, since they have not been treated since the work of A. Alföldi in 1951,[1] these specimens have not been discussed in the context

---

* University of Warwick (Cristian.Mondello@warwick.ac.uk).

1. See A. Alföldi, "Asina. Eine dritte Gruppe heidnischer Neujahrsmünzen im spätantiken Rom" *SNbl* 2.7 (1951), 57–66; A. Alföldi, "Asina II. Weitere heidnische Neujahrsmünzen aus dem spätantiken Rom," *SNbl* 2.8 (1951), 92–96.

of current debates on the contorniates, which are objects most comparable with the *Asina* tokens.

It is therefore necessary to revise and update our understanding of this series in light of the knowledge acquired so far on these pieces as well as the problems they still pose.

1. THE *ASINA* ISSUE:
CLASSIFICATION AND A *STATUS QUAESTIONIS*

The so-called "*Asina* tokens" are a group of ten bronze specimens, all struck and of small size. Indeed, their diameters vary between 11 and 20 mm, while their weight ranges from 1.15 to 3.05 g.

Most of these specimens have unfortunately been lost. Four held in the Cabinet des Médailles (BnF) until the 1950s as well as one kept at the National Museum of Denmark are currently missing;[2] one piece is known only through an eighteenth-century drawing. This leaves only four specimens currently available for study. Among them, this paper includes a new piece (no. 8, Pl. 24,7), which was published by J. P. C. Kent in his study on the fifth-century bronze coinage of Honorius, but which has not been discussed in the context of the other *Asina* tokens.[3]

1.a CATALOGUE

1. AE, 20 mm, 3.05 g (Paris: Cabinet des Médailles, now lost). (Pl. 23, 1)

Obv.: ALEXSΔ–DRI, bust of Alexander the Great left, wearing a lion skin, its paws knotted on his chest.

Rev.: D N IHV XPS DEI FILI–VS, donkey standing right suckling a foal, with a scorpion above.

This specimen was once part of Marcantonio Sabatini's collection and it was described and reproduced in 1719 by Bernard de Montfaucon, who received an "*estampe*" of it from Italy.[4] This piece was later purchased together with a large number of other antique medals by Abbé le Blond, who brought it to France.

---

2. As Dr. Dominique Hollard (BnF) kindly informed me (13/01/2018), four of the six *Asina* tokens kept at the Cabinet des Médailles do not appear amongst the *tesserae* of the late Roman Empire, and therefore they are probably lost. Also the token kept at the National Museum of Denmark (no. 10, Pl. 24, 9) has not been currently located, as kindly communicated by Dr. Helle Horsnaes (13/09/2018).

3. J. P. C. Kent, "The fifth century bronze coinage of Honorius in Italy and Gaul." *RIN* 90 (1988), pl. I, no. 14.

4. B. de Montfaucon, *L'antiquité expliquée et représentée en figures. Tome second* (Paris: Deleaune et al., 1719), 372–373, pl. 168.

According to J. De Witte, the piece was identified with a similar specimen once kept at the Cabinet des Médailles,[5] whose mold was later sent by E. Babelon to F. Lenzi along with that of other *Asina* specimens.[6] The piece has been lost at least since the date of the article of Alföldi.[7]

The legend ALEXSΔ–DRI (= *Alexa-[n]dri*) shows errors as well as a mixture of Latin and Greek letters, while on the reverse the abbreviation IHV (= *Jesu*), instead of IHS (= *Jesus*), does not agree with the name XPS (= *Christus*), in the nominative case.

2. AE, 16 mm, 3.19 g (Paris: Cabinet des Médailles) (Pl. 23, 2).

Obv.: ALEXA–ND [...], bust of Alexander the Great right, wearing a lion skin.
Rev.: Donkey standing right suckling a foal, with a scorpion above.

The specimen was published in 1747–1749 by F. Vettori together with pieces labelled here as nos. 3 (Pl. 23, 3) and 5 (Pl. 23, 5).[8] They existed as part of the collection of the Roman antiquarian Francisco Palatio and, after his death, came into Baldini's collection.[9] This piece, as well as the others two mentioned, were later held in the Cabinet des Médailles.[10]

The specimen is worn while the legend probably read ALEXAND[RI] in the genitive case, as in the case of pieces nos. 1 (Pl. 23, 1) and 4 (Pl. 23, 4).

3. AE, 16 mm, 2.80 g (Paris: Cabinet des Médailles) (Pl. 23, 3).

Obv.: ALEX–XANDR, bust of Alexander the Great right, wearing a lion skin.
Rev.: Hercules standing left holding a club in his right hand and extending his left hand to Minerva, who stands on the right, holding a spear in her left hand, with a shield at her feet.

5. J. De Witte, in C. Cavedoni, "Médailles du temps d'Honorius portant des signes chrétiens mêlés à des types païens," *RN* (1857), 309–310, n. 2.

6. For the photo of the molds see F. Lenzi, "Di alcune medaglie religiose del IV secolo," *Bilychnis* 2 (1913), 113–131.

7. Alföldi, "Asina II," 92.

8. See F. Vettori, *Epistola ad virum cl. P.M. Paciaudi de Musei Victorii emblematae et de non-nullis numismatibus Alexandri Severi secondi curis explanatis* (Romae, 1747); F. Vettori, *De vetustate et forma monogrammatis SS. Nominis Jesu* (Romae, 1747), 60–64; F. Vettori, *Dissertatio apologetica de quibusdam Alexandri Severi numismatibus* (Romae: Zempel).

9. See Alföldi, "Asina," 61, no. 4 (pl. nos. 3 and 3a).

10. For piece no. 2, see inventory no. 17375.

A photo of this piece, kept at the Cabinet des Médailles,[11] was published by Alföldi.[12] The name of Alexander in the obverse legend is expressed with a double X.

4. AE, 12 mm, 1.80 g (Paris: Cabinet des Médailles, now lost) (Pl. 23, 4).

Obv.: ALEXS–ANDRI, bust of Alexander the Great right, wearing a lion's skin over head, its paws knotted on his chest.
Rev.: Erotic scene showing an ithyphallic man standing left, who touches the back of a woman right, leaning against a vase, with her head turned back towards the man.

This specimen, held in the Cabinet des Médailles and described by H. Cohen,[13] is now lost. A photo of the piece was published by Alföldi, who was still able to examine it.[14]

The obverse legend bearing the name of Alexander is characterized by the form XS, which is also attested in piece no. 1 (Pl. 23, 1).

5. AE, 11 mm, 1.15 g (Paris: Cabinet des Médailles, now lost) (Pl. 23, 5).

Obv.: D N V [...], laureate, draped, cuirassed bust of a Roman emperor.
Rev.: Donkey standing right suckling a foal, with a scorpion above.

Once in the collection of Francisco Palatio and then in that of Baldini, this specimen was later acquired by the Cabinet des Médailles but is currently lost. It was photographed by Alföldi.[15] Its poor condition does not allow identification of the legend and portrait of the Roman Emperor on the obverse.[16] The following hypotheses have been proposed for the worn obverse legend: IOVIS FILIVS according to F. Vettori;[17] D N V[ALENTINIANVS] according to P. M. Paciaudi (with reference to Valentinian I) and A. Alföldi (with reference to Valentinian III)[18]—however, previously Alföldi supported Vettori's reading of IOVIS FILIVS;[19] D N

---

11. Inventory no. 17377.

12. See Alföldi, "Asina II," 93, no. 9 (pl. no. 5).

13. H. Cohen, *Description historique des monnaies frappées sous l'Empire romain communément appelées médailles imperials* (Paris: Rollin and Feuardent, 1892), VIII, 322, no. 402.

14. See Alföldi, "Asina II," 94, no. 10 (pl. no. 6).

15. See Alföldi, "Asina II," 92, no. 6 (pl. no. 4).

16. Vettori, *Dissertatio,* 5, reported that the letters on the right of the imperial bust on the obverse were corroded and also partly erased: *etsi literae admodum detritae sint.*

17. Ibid.

18. P. M. Paciaudi, *Osservazioni sopra alcune singolari e strane medaglie* (Napoli: Novello de Bonis Stampatore Arcivescovile, 1748), 42; Alföldi, "Asina II," 92.

19. Alföldi, "Asina," 62.

HONORIVS P F AVG, according to C. Cavedoni and F. Lenzi (by analogy with specimen no. 7, Pl. 23, 6).[20]

6. AE, no weight or diameter recorded (Paris: Cabinet des Médailles, now lost). According to the description made by H. Cohen:[21]

Obv.: D N VA [...] S (?) P F AVG, draped and diademed bust of a Roman emperor (Valentinian II or III?), right.
Rev.: Donkey standing right suckling a foal, with a scorpion above. This piece is missing the legend D N IHV XPS DEI FILI–VS, or the legend was erased.

Only the description made by H. Cohen is available, who did not publish a drawing of the piece. Cohen reports the piece was kept at the Cabinet des Médailles, and the reverse type was the same as the one depicted on piece no. 1 (Pl. 23, 1). Furio Lenzi, who received the molds of the *Asina* tokens held in Paris that were sent by E. Babelon, asserted this specimen was already missing in his day.[22]

7. AE, no weight or diameter recorded (Collection of G. Tanini, now lost) (Pl. 23, 6).

Obv.: D N HONORI–VS P F AVG, pearl-diademed, draped, and cuirassed bust of Honorius, right.
Rev.: ASINA, donkey standing right suckling a foal.

The specimen existed as part of Girolamo Tanini's collection, and is known only through the description and the drawing he published in his *Supplementum* to Banduri's volume.[23] Lenzi reports that this piece was not available in the Cabinet des Médailles.

The piece is currently untraceable. Tanini explicitly mentions the absence of letters in the exergue.[24]

8. AE, 15 mm, 1.25 g (London: British Museum) (Pl. 24, 7).

Obv.: D N HONORI–VS P F AVG, pearl-diademed, draped, and cuirassed bust of Honorius, right.
Rev.: ASINA, donkey standing right suckling a foal.

---

20. Cavedoni, "Médailles," 311; Lenzi, "Di alcune medaglie," 113–114.
21. Cohen, *Description*, VIII, 322, no. 404.
22. Lenzi, "Di alcune medaglie," 114, no. 7.
23. G. Tanini, *Numismatum Imperatorum Romanorum a Trajano Decio ad Constantinum Draconem ab Anselmo Bandurio editorum Supplementum* (Romae: A. Fulgonium, 1791), 352, pl. VIII.
24. Ibid., 352: *absque litteris in exergo*.

This piece is kept at the British Museum,[25] and it came through Spink and Son. It is pierced at 12 o'clock on the reverse to display the donkey side.

Although similar to the piece described by Tanini (no. 7, Pl. 23, 6), this specimen is differentiated from it by the presence of a hole. Moreover, the obverse legend is irregular compared to the more circular arrangement of the legend on piece owned by Tanini, judging from the drawing of his designer.

It is not possible to say if the British Museum token corresponds to the piece described by Alföldi who asked R. A. G. Carson in vain to locate it.[26] In fact, Alföldi did not remember which "big national coin cabinet" kept the specimen in question, and claimed to have lost a rubbing made of it as early as 1947.

9. AE, 14 mm, 2.04 g (London: British Museum) (Pl. 24, 8).

Obv.: PROVI–DENTIA R M, female bust with a crown ending in a crescent shape (Isis?) right, R M below the bust.

Rev.: ROMA, donkey standing right suckling a foal, with a scorpion above. The legend ROMA is placed in the exergue.

This specimen, held in the British Museum,[27] was found by R. A. G. Carson after Alföldi's request (see above). The piece was once part of the collection of the Roman antiquarian Francesco Martinetti.[28] It was pierced at 11 o'clock on the obverse in order to display the side bearing the female bust. The legend in the exergue appears decentralized, and it is flanked by the hole subsequently made on the left side. According to Alföldi, the female bust, which has none of Providentia's typical attributes, should be interpreted as Isis because of her crown, which ends in a crescent shape.

10. AE, 14–15 mm (Copenhagen: National Museum of Denmark, now lost) (Pl. 24, 9).

Obv.: MAXI–MIANI, diademed and draped bust of Maximian (AD 286–305), seen from behind.

Rev: Centaur fighting a hero (Hercules?) holding a stone in his attacking left hand.

---

25. Inventory no. 1922,0317.164.b

26. See Alföldi, "Asina," 59, no. 1.

27. Inventory no. 1940,0401.57.

28. See Collection Martinetti and Nervegna, *Médailles grecques et romaines. Aes grave*, 18 Novembre 1907 et les jours suivants (Paris 1907), lot 2100; Cf. also A. Hess, Römische Münzen, Sammlungen F. A. Walters und P. H. Webb, Montag, den 9. Mai 1932 und folgende Tage, lot 2768.

The specimen, published by Alföldi, was connected with the *Asina* tokens because of what he saw as stylistic and epigraphic parallels with piece no. 1 (Pl. 23, 1).[29] Alföldi argued that this *tessera* is "a positive indication that the emperors of the Tetrarchy were represented on the obverse of our group of coins." He cited as further evidence piece no. 5 (Pl. 23, 5), which he suggested bore the legend IOVIS FILIVS as an allusion to Diocletian as the "Son of Jupiter."[30] However, this specimen has no connection with the donkey image and, as will be explained below, it probably does not belong to the *Asina* series.

1.b Date and Proposed Purposes

Of great rarity, these *tesserae* are connected by two recurring depictions: the portrait of Alexander the Great is represented in the same style, and is accompanied by a legend bearing an abbreviated name, not without some errors; and the type of the donkey suckling a foal on some reverses. The portrait of Maximian Herculius depicted on the obverse of another *tessera*, according to Alföldi, carries stylistic parallels to the representation of Alexander.

Although at times labelled "*Asina* coins" in modern scholarship,[31] these coin-like objects can indubitably be considered tokens or *tesserae*, given the absence of any mintmark as well as the absence of a portrait of the Roman Emperor on some obverses. This is also suggested by the type of the she-donkey and her foal, unusually accompanied by a Christian legend on one or perhaps two specimens, which could not be adopted on official coins having legal validity and economic value.

The *Asina* tokens have been predominantly assigned to the reign of Honorius (AD 395–423), although it is not clear when the minting period began or ended.[32] Moreover, the legend D N VA[...] S (?) P F AVG accompanying the portrait of a Roman emperor (Valentinian I, II, or III?) on a lost specimen (no. 6)[33] could suggest a longer period of production. Nonetheless, Lenzi dated the *Asina* tokens

---

29. See Alföldi, "Asina," 62, no. 7 (pl. nos. 8 and 8a).

30. Ibid., 62.

31. See S. Mazzarino, "Contorniati," in *EAA* (Roma: Istituto dell'Enciclopedia Italiana, 1959), 784–791 ("coins particularly similar to the contorniates"); P. F. Mittag, "Alföldi and the contorniates," in *Andreas Alföldi in the Twenty-First Century*, ed. J. H. Richardson and F. Santangelo (Stuttgart: F. Steiner Verlag, 2015), 264, 266.

32. Before the piece bearing the portrait of Honorius on the obverse was published by Tanini, the *Asina* tokens were assigned to the reign of Severus Alexander by Vettori, *De vetustate*, 60, or the reign of Julian the Apostate by Paciaudi, *Osservazioni*, 56. E. Babelon, *Traité des Monnaies Grecques et Romains. Première Partie: Théorie et Doctrine* (Paris: E. Leroux, 1901), 684, dated these pieces more generally to the end of the fourth century AD.

33. The same legend is probably also on piece no. 5 (Pl. 23, 5).

to the period from 393 (that is, the year the title *Augustus* was given to Honorius) to 423. He argued that the die cutters copied coins of earlier emperors to make issues bearing their portraits under Honorius.

Alföldi proposed a date after AD 410 on the basis of the R M mint mark, which is attested on one previously unknown specimen (no. 9, Pl. 24, 8), and which occurs on bronze coinage from Honorius onwards.[34] The Hungarian scholar thought that the *Asina* tokens were struck during the last years of the reign of Honorius and even under Valentinian III. In his second article on the *Asina* tokens, he suggested that the lost piece no. 5 (Pl. 23, 5) carried the worn legend D N V[ALENTINIANVS]—as in the case of the specimen described by Cohen (no. 6)—and would have imitated, according to him, the bronze coins of Valentinian III.

Production must have been at Rome, as suggested by the letters R M on the obverse as well as the *Roma* legend on the reverse of piece no. 9 (Pl. 24, 8). This is also suggested—as will be explained below—by the close resemblance between some of the images on the *Asina* tokens and the motifs depicted on contorniates, whose place of production was in all likelihood *mainly* Rome. However, their contexts of discovery remain unknown, since the *Asina* tokens existed as part of museum and private collections from at least the eighteenth century. Any find spots thus are lost to history.

Multiple ideas have been proposed as to the purpose of the *Asina* tokens, mainly based on their imagery. Given the combination of "pagan" iconography (e.g., Alexander the Great, Hercules and Minerva, a centaur fighting a hero) and Christian features (i.e., the Christian legend accompanying the donkey image), some scholars have interpreted these *tesserae* as talismans or amulets, connected to magical practices and superstition. In support of this, a passage of John Chrysostom is frequently cited, who, in a homily to the Christian community of Antioch, condemns those who "tie bronze coins of Alexander the Macedonian around their head and feet."[35] We do not know if the coins mentioned by Chrysostom really were coins with the type of the Macedonian king.[36]

34. Alföldi, "Asina," 61 and 63.

35. John. Chrys. *ad illum. catech.* 2, 5 (*PG*, 49, 240). On late antique amulets and the prescriptions against them by Christian authors (with particular attention to John Chrysostom and Augustine), see J. E. Sanzo, "Magic and Communal Boundaries. The Problems with Amulets in Chrysostom, *Adv. Iud.* 8, and Augustine, *In Io. tra. 7.*" *Hen* 39 (2017), 227–246; J. E. Sanzo, "Imagining Illegitimate Ritual in Early Christian Literature," in *Guide to the Study of Ancient Magic*, ed. D. Frankfurter (Leiden: Brill, forthcoming).

36. On the function of the *Asina* tokens, Paciaudi (*Osservazioni*, 52 ff.) considered these tesserae as amulets used by Gnostics—the donkey would have represented one of those "intelligences" to which the Gnostics attributed the reign over earthly things ("Chi avrebbe mai

Conversely, G. Tanini claimed that these *tesserae* were struck as "satirical medals" by pagans to mock the intolerant Christian Emperor Honorius, with the she-donkey alluding to the charge of onolatry (the worship of a god with a donkey's head) levelled against early Christians.[37] This hypothesis was later supported by Alföldi, who interpreted the *Asina* tokens as anti-Christian artefacts, adding them to his collection of late antique pagan propaganda material, which also included the so-called *Vota Publica* coins and the contorniates. The *Vota Publica* coins (also labelled "Festival of Isis coinage") were issued in bronze and brass from the Tetrarchy to at least the reign of Valentinian II. They bear depictions of Roman Emperors and Egyptian deities, and were likely also tokens. The legend VOTA PVBLICA appears on almost all the reverses and is repeated even on some of the obverses.[38] As is well known, the bronze medallions named "contorniates" from their hammered edges were produced from the mid-fourth to the late-fifth century AD, showing a great variety of depictions with a high proportion of subjects related to the games and the circus.[39] According to Alföldi, the "pronounced anti-Christian nature" of the *Asina* tokens was indicated by the image of the donkey suckling a foal—he saw this as an indirect allusion to Jesus, defined as "*Son* of God" by the legend—as well as by the veiled image of Isis as *Providentia*.[40] Indeed, the type of Isis-Providentia led to the suggestion that

immaginato che sotto la figura di un Asino si dovesse intendere espressa una di quelle Motrici Intelligenze […] cui gli Gnostici attribuivano il governo delle cose sublunari?"), while Cavedoni ("Medailles," 314) thought they were employed as "pierres astrifères" and created by "certain evil Christians or the Gnostics or Basilidians [...] to circulate among the people their false and detestable doctrines." Cohen (*Description*, 322–323) classified these pieces as "tessères mystiques," while Lenzi ("Di alcune medaglie," 127 ff.) considered them as propaganda medals produced by a Gnostic sect influenced by dualism, astrology and Mithraism—the donkey would be an eternal health and good symbol since, in his opinion, it would be associated with wine, the sacred drink in Mithraic and Gnostic rituals.

37. See Tanini (*Numismatum*, 352), who stated the image of the donkey suckling a foal could be an allegorical representation of Galla Placidia and Honorius, since Galla, as a true ruler, urged Honorius to exile the Gentiles from the Empire (*CTh* 20, 10). However, this interpretation does not take into account the fact that the donkey type on the reverse is connected not only to Honorius, but also to other subjects (Alexander the Great, Valentinian, *Providentia*), obverse representations which were not all known by Tanini. About the calumny of onolatry against Jews and Christians, we are informed by various ancient authors: Jos. *Ap.* 2, 7; Tac. *Hist.* 5, 4; Min. Fel. *Oct.* 9, 3; Tert. *Nat.* 1, 11–14; Tert. *Apol.* 16. On this point, see, e.g., H. Leclercq, "Âne," in *DACL* (Paris: Letouzey et Ané, 1924), I.2, cols. 2041–2068; Vischer 1951.

38. See Alföldi, *Festival of Isis*.

39. See A. Alföldi and E. Alföldi, *Die Kontorniat-Medaillons. Teil 1: Katalog.* (Berlin: De Gruyter, 1976); A. Alföldi and E. Alföldi, *Die Kontorniat-Medaillons. Teil 2: Text* (Berlin/New York: De Gruyter, 1990).

40. Alföldi, "Asina," 65.

the *Asina* tokens were a secret continuation of the *Vota Publica* coins,[41] which stopped after the battle of Frigidus, because "the pagan party was annihilated in Rome in 394, and [...] the public mint could not have stood at its disposal after this date."[42] Alföldi therefore concluded that the *Asina* tokens should be regarded as 'documents for the existence of a crypto-pagan movement' during the age of Honorius and Valentinian III.[43]

However, specialists have recently strongly criticized Alföldi's interpretation of the *Vota Publica* coins and contorniates as instruments of senatorial propaganda against the Christian Empire.[44] Moreover, a partial revision of the *Vota Publica* coins and a remarkable review of the classification and chronology of the contorniates was recently made by current scholarship.[45]

In view of this, it is necessary to revise the interpretation of the *Asina* tokens, in order to have a better understanding of their iconography, chronology and function, and to identify the arenas in which these objects were distributed.

2. ICONOGRAPHY

The imagery depicted on the *Asina* tokens can be organized thematically into several subgroups. Two main iconographic themes, connecting the objects together, have already been outlined above.

Two other subgroups are connected to these: the imperial portraits, and a "varia"-group including images (e.g., *Providentia*, Hercules and Minerva, a centaur fighting a hero, a *symplegma* or erotic scene) which are represented on both the obverses and reverses of the pieces.

2.a Alexander the Great

The portrait of Alexander the Great as Heracles wearing a lion skin right (or left in one case), is depicted on the obverses of four specimens, and is combined with the donkey suckling a foal (nos. 1–2, Pl. 23, 1–2), Hercules and Minerva (no. 3, Pl. 23, 3) and an erotic scene (no. 4, Pl. 23, 4) on the reverses.

Scholars have repeatedly emphasized the extraordinary appreciation of Alexander and his myth found in Rome in late antiquity. Images of Alexander were

41. Ibid., 63.

42. Alföldi, *Festival of Isis,* 25.

43. See Alföldi, "Asina II," 94, who added: "Man vergesse es nicht, dass für den Fall der Entdeckung der Urheber und Verfertiger dieser Spottmünzen diese der schrecklichste Tod erwartete."

44. See Mittag, "Alföldi," 265–267.

45. For the *Vota Publica* coins of the age of Constantine see Ramskold 2016. For the contorniates see P. F. Mittag, *Alte Köpfe in neuen Händen: Urheber und Funktion der Kontorniaten* (Bonn: Habelt, 1999).

regarded as luck-bringing objects,[46] and his legend was at the heart of a flourishing literature in Latin in the fourth and fifth centuries.[47] There were even efforts to Christianize the figure of Alexander (*Commonitorium Palladii; Collatio Alexandri et Dindimi*), and he was considered as a sort of prophet inspired by Brahman philosophy.[48]

Given the popularity of Alexander, it is not surprising that his iconography was selected for use on contorniates. Alföldi had already highlighted some of the parallels between the *Asina* tokens and the contorniates. However, the number and type of contorniates that have come to light since Alföldi's study may make it possible to further clarify the relations between these two groups of materials.[49]

On contorniates the bust of Alexander occurs on the obverses of 264 specimens (238 struck and 26 cast),[50] which were classified by Alföldi into 22 groups. Two types of Alexander portrait appear: the portrait of Alexander wearing a lion skin (Alexander, I–XIII in Alföldi's catalogue); and the Hellenistic type of Alexander as *basileus*, mostly wearing a diadem (Alexander, XIV–XXII).

On the *Asina* tokens, the portrait of Alexander the Great as Heracles is more or less similar to the first type attested on contorniates, although the quality is much lower. Moreover, according to Alföldi, the head on piece no. 1 (Pl. 23, 1) shows the pearled diadem (“Perlendiadem”) typical of late Roman emperors,[51] representing the traditional iconography of Alexander according to late antique fashion.[52] It is tempting to see a *comparandum* to the *Asina* tokens in the fre-

---

46. SHA *Trig. tyr.* 14, 3–6.

47. See L. Cracco Ruggini, “Sulla cristianizzazione della cultura pagana. Il mito greco e latino di Alessandro dall'età antonina al Medioevo,” *Athenaeum* 43 (1965), 3–60.

48. Ibid., 21 ff. For the “Christian” Alexander see also Simon 1941; G. Cary, “Alexander the Great in Medieval Theology,” *JWI* 7 (1954), 98–114; F. Pfister, *Alexander des Grosse in der Offenbarungen der Griechen, Juden, Mohammedaner und Christen* (Berlin: Akad.-Verl., 1956), 41ff.

49. Indeed, the *magnus opus* on the contorniates, in two volumes, had not been released in its entirety by Alföldi and his wife when he conducted his study of the *Asina* tokens: see Alföldi and Alföldi, *Die Kontorniat-Medaillons 1*; Alföldi and Alföldi, *Die Kontorniat-Medaillons 2*.

50. The full-length type of Alexander is also represented on the reverse of contorniates, but this is not taken into consideration here: see Alföldi and Alföldi, *Die Kontorniat-Medaillons 1*, 18–19, Taf. 22, 7–12; 23, 1–2.

51. So Alföldi, “Asina II,” 92.

52. Although this lost piece is mainly known through an eighteenth-century drawing, the depiction of the diadem is visible also in the photograph of the mold of the *Asina* specimen owned by Lenzi: see Lenzi, “Di alcune medaglie,” pl. 1. Depictions of historical subjects and writers according to the fourth century fashion and style also occurs on contorniates, as for instance in the case of the portrait of Homer: see C. Mondello, “Nuove osservazioni sui contorniati: la serie dei *Literaten-Büsten*,” in *XV International Numismatic Congress Taormina 2015 Proceedings*, ed. M. Caccamo Caltabiano et al. (Roma/Messina: Arbor Sapientiae, 2017), II, 772–776.

quently cited contorniate specimen carrying the bust of Alexander the Great on the obverse and an incised Chi Rho with a tiny circle in the middle, surrounded in turn by a circle, on the reverse.[53] But this Christian monogram is almost certainly a countermark made at a later time with a burin (or another professional instrument), after having erased and smoothed the original design on the reverse of the specimen. Indeed, according to Alföldi's catalogue, this specimen belongs to the XI group of Alexander the Great (no. 40), whose reverse was occupied by a racing scene in the Circus Maximus.[54]

As mentioned above, the *Asina* tokens with the portrait of Alexander unusually show his abbreviated name (i.e., "Alexander" instead of "Alexander the Great/the Macedonian"), which is expressed in the genitive case and carries errors (or uncommon *lectiones* of the name) and even a mixture of Greek and Latin letters. On contorniates, the Greek and Latin legends accompanying the type of Alexander also show his short name although this is usually expressed in the nominative case,[55] or the name is extended by the epithets *Magnus* ("the Great"),[56] *Macedo* ("the Macedonian"),[57] or *Magnus Macedon*/Μέγας Μακεδών ("the Great Macedonian").[58]

Interestingly, the same typology of variants or errors attested on the *Asina* tokens is also found on contorniates. The combination of X and S used in the legends of pieces nos. 1 and 4 (*Alexs–andri*) is also documented in the twelfth and thirteenth groups (Alexander, XII–XIII) of the contorniates with the type of Alexander (*Alexs–ander*).[59] The variant marked by a double X (*Alex–xandri*) on piece no. 3 is also attested in the seventh and eighth groups (Alexander, VII–VIII) of the contorniates with the type of Alexander (*Alexxan–der Mag*).[60] Moreover, the delta in place of the Latin letter A on specimen no. 1 (ALEXSΔ–DRI) evokes the Greek legends referring to Alexander on the contorniates,[61] and it suggests a Greek linguistic influence. On the cast contorniates, there are even

53. Alföldi and Alföldi, *Die Kontorniat-Medaillons 1*, 13, Taf. 15, 9.

54. See C. Mondello, "Using and Reusing Tokens: Some remarks about Christian graffiti on contorniates," in *Tokens: Culture, Connections, Communities*, ed. C. Rowan, A. Crisà and M. Gkikaki. (London: Royal Numismatic Society, 2019), 150.

55. Alföldi and Alföldi, *Die Kontorniat-Medaillons 1*, 8–13 (Alexander, IX–XIII).

56. Ibid., 5–7 (Alexander, VII–VIII).

57. Ibid., 167–168 (I, Alexander, B).

58. Ibid., 1–5 (Alexander, I–V); 17–18 (Alexander, XXI–XXII); 167 (I, Alexander, A).

59. Ibid., Taf. 15, 10; 15, 11.

60. Ibid., Taf. 5, 9–12; 6, 1–12; 7, 1–12; 8, 1–7. Even the legend ALLEXXANDER MAG is attested on one of these specimens: see ibid., Taf. 211, 3.

61. Ibid., 3 (Alexander, IIa = ΑΛΕΞΑΝΔΡΟC–ΜΕΓΑC ΜΑΚΕΔѠΝ), Taf. 3, 12; ibid., 17 (Alexander, XXI = ΑΛΕΞΑΝΔΕΡ ΜΕ–ΓΑC ΜΑΚΕΔΩΝ), Taf. 21, 3.

other variants or errors in rendering the extended name of Alexander, such as
ALEXANDER MAGNVS MHCEDON and ALIXAND–ER MACEDO (*sic!*).[62]

Several depictions of Alexander showing the bust of the Macedonian king
(according to various typologies) as well as images connected with his legend
occur on official issues that were produced, over the second and third centuries, in the eastern part of the Roman Empire.[63] But this evidence does not have
parallels with the types and legends attested on the *Asina* tokens. Furthermore,
Alexander's image does not appear on coins issued in Rome and the Latin West
in the imperial and late antique periods. In terms of iconographic, epigraphic
and stylistic similarities, the contorniate medallions bearing the portrait of Alexander the Great constitute the *comparanda* closest to the *Asina* tokens.

In light of this, the contorniates may have been the archetype used by the
die cutters of the *Asina* tokens. However, the iconography and legends on these
tesserae are not exact reproductions, but reworked, low quality versions of the

62. Ibid., 167 (I, Alexander, A), Taf. 16, 1; 16, 2.6; 16, 3–9; 167–168 (I, Alexander, B), Taf.
16, 10–13.

63. See, e.g., the issues of Nikaia in Bithynia (ca. AD 181–184) combining the portraits of
M. Aurelius (?) and Commodus on the obverse and the head or naked figure of Alexander
on the reverse: Schreiber 1903, 186–187; K. Dahmen, *The Legend of Alexander the Great on
Greek and Roman Coins* (London/New York: Routledge, 2007), 126–127. A later issue showing
Alexander's head on the reverse (as documented by a single coin) was struck again by Nikaia
under Severus Alexander (AD 222–235): see Dahmen, *Legend*, 127. On the image of Alexander as Heracles represented on coins of Apollonia Mordiaion in Pisidia (ca. AD 198–209) see
Rebuffat 1986, 65–71. Alexander's images appear especially on the provincial coinage of Makedonia, which was produced from Elagabalus (AD 218–222) onwards until Philip the Arab
(AD 244–249) in connection with a festival and games (some of which were called *Alexandreia*) in honor of Alexander the Great that were centred on the provincial administrative
capital of Beroia: see H. Gaebler, Die antiken Münzen Nord-Griechenlands. *Die antiken Münzen von Makedonia und Paionia* III, Part 1 (Berlin: Georg Reimer, 1906), 15, 19–24; Dahmen, *Legend*, 136–141. For Alexander's images on coins and medallions, in addition to Dahmen, *Legend*, see L. Müller, *Numismatique d'Alexandre le Grand* (Copenhagen: B. Luno, 1855);
A. B. Marsden, "Some sing of Alexander and some of Hercules: artistic echoes of Hercules and
Alexander the Great on coins and medallions, A.D. 260–269," in *Pagans and Christians: from
antiquity to the Middle Ages. Papers in honour of Martin Henig, presented on the occasion of his
65th birthday*, ed. L. Gilmour (Oxford: Archaeopress, 2007); K. Dahmen, "Alexander in gold
and silver: reassessing third century AD medallions from Aboukir and Tarsos," *AJN* 20 (2008),
493–546; K. Liampi, "Νομίσματα και οικονομία του κράτους του Μεγάλου Αλεξάνδρου,"
in *Μέγας Αλέξανδρος: αναδιφώντας όψεις του περίοπτου: κύκλος σεμιναρίων Μάρτιος–
Απρίλιος 2008* (Peiraias: Idryma Aikaterinis Laskaridi, 2011); P. Moreno, "Immagini di Alessandro Magno: monete e storia," in *Serta antiqua et mediaevalia. 14: Il significato delle immagini:
numismatica, arte, filologia, storia. Atti del secondo incontro internazionale di studio del Lexicon
Iconographicum Numismaticae (Genova, 10–12 novembre 2005)*, ed. R. Pera (Roma: G. Bretschneider, 2012).

contorniate designs. Moreover, they also have new and original features (for example, the use of the genitive case rather than the nominative one in legends, or the pearl diadem attribute).

2.b Donkey suckling a foal (the *Asina* type) and scorpion

The image of the donkey suckling a foal (the *Asina* type), shown on the reverse of seven specimens, is accompanied by the legend *Dominus noster Jesus Christus Dei filius* ("Our Lord Jesus Christ Son of God") (nos. 1 and 6), or by the legends *Asina* (nos. 7 and 8) and *Roma* (no. 9); it also appears without a legend (nos. 2 and 5).

The mysterious *Asina* type, mostly depicted with a scorpion above, was seen by Tanini and Alföldi as an allusion to Jesus as a donkey-headed god, suggesting an alleged anti-Christian use of these artefacts at least during the reign of Honorius. However, this theory is highly speculative: there is no evidence to support the connection of these tokens with onolatry (or ass-worship) attributed by Tacitus and other writers to the Jews and Christians. Some considerations seem to oppose this theory. Indeed, the charge levelled at Christians was that they worshipped just a donkey's head or a donkey-headed god, while the *Asina* type consists of two donkeys, a mother and her young. The legend *Asina* (that is, "she-donkey") stresses the female gender of one of the two beasts, who is depicted in her role as a mother: this does not fit into any ancient tradition of the charge of onolatry ascribed to Judaism and Christianity. Finally, the donkey image on the reverses is connected not only to the portrait of Honorius, but also to obverses showing Alexander the Great, Valentinian and Providentia. Therefore, the image does not refer only to Honorius, and probably has a serious meaning, since it is quite different from the satirical anti-Christian depictions attested in antique material culture.[64]

In the ancient world, the donkey was frequently regarded as a sacred animal and a mount of gods (e.g., Seth, Dionysus, Vesta, Priapus).[65] However, no sig-

---

64. See, for instance, the so-called "Alexamenos graffito" found near the Palatine Hill in Rome: Vischer 1951, 29–30; J. G. Cook, "Envisioning crucifixion: light from several inscriptions and the Palatine graffito," *NT* 50.3 (2008), 262–285; O. L. Yarbrough, "The shadow of an ass: on reading the Alexamenos graffito," in *Text, image, and Christian in the Graeco-Roman world: a Festschrift in honor of David Lee Balch*, ed. A. C. Niang and C. Osiek (Allisan Park, Penn.: Pickwick Publications, 2012), 239–254. Other artefacts perhaps reflecting the charge of onolatry against Christians are discussed by Leclercq, "Âne," cols. 2041–2047.

65. On this point see W. Deonna, "LAVS ASINI. L'âne, le serpent, l'eau et l'immortalité (1e partie)" *RBPH* 34.1 (1956), 5–46; W. Deonna, "LAVS ASINI. L'âne, le serpent, l'eau et l'immortalité (2ᵉ partie)," *RBPH* 34.2 (1956), 337–364; P. Mitchell, *The Donkey in Human History: An Archaeological Perspective* (Oxford: Oxford University Press, 2018).

nificant parallel with the *Asina* type could be found by examining the material of the pagan Graeco-Roman world, where the donkey is predominantly male and is never represented with offspring.

But the image of a she-donkey with her young is documented in early Christian art, appearing in depictions of Jesus's triumphal entry into Jerusalem. From the fourth century, this Gospel episode is represented on sarcophagi with the "continuous frieze" of the Constantinian age, and it is modelled on the imperial *adventus* (the arrival of the emperor) with the intention of contrasting the figure of Christ the King (*Christus rex*) with the Roman Emperor in a chariot. Although denoted by numerous variations, this scene commonly shows Jesus wearing a tunic or a *pallium*, surrounded by the apostles and an acclaiming crowd, riding in from the left on a donkey, or sometimes a donkey accompanied by a young colt.

These two variations representing this episode derive from the fact that written sources also differed in their accounts. Indeed, Matthew, alluding to Zechariah's prophecy, mentions a donkey (ὄνος) and a young colt (πῶλος) as the two beasts alternately mounted by Jesus during his entry into Jerusalem,[66] unlike Mark, Luke and John who refer only to a donkey (πῶλος/ὀνάριον).[67] This scene occurs on at least 21 known sarcophagi, all dated between the first and last quarter of the fourth century.[68] Of these, the donkey and her colt as a mount of Jesus appear on eight sarcophagi,[69] while the donkey alone is depicted on six.[70] Two of the remaining seven sarcophagi fragments carrying this scene could also show the donkey and her young, according to Wilpert's hypothesis.[71] This dem-

---

66. See Zc 9, 9; Mt 21, 1–11.

67. See Mk 11, 1–10; Lk 19, 29–40; Jn 12, 12–15.

68. See Wilpert 1929–1936; F. Deichmann, *Repertorium der christlich-antiken Sarkophage, Rom und Ostia* (Wiesbaden: P. von Zabern, 1967), 1967; D. Goffredo, "Ingresso di Gesù a Gerusalemme," in *Temi di iconografia paleocristiana*, ed. F. Bisconti (Città del Vaticano: Pontificio Istituto di Archeologia Cristiana, 2000), 218, 200–201.

69. G. Wilpert, *I sarcofagi cristiani antichi*, vol I (Roma: Tipografia Poliglotta Vaticana, 1929–1936), I, Taf. 151, 1 (= Deichmann, *Repertorium*, no. 28, Taf. 9); I, Taf. 157, 1 (= Deichmann, *Repertorium*, no. 41, Taf. 13); II, 311, (fig. 195); II, Taf. 212, 2 (= Deichmann, *Repertorium*, no. 772, Taf. 122); II, Taf. 215, 7 (= Deichmann, *Repertorium*, no. 14, Taf. 5); II, Taf. 235, 5 (= Deichmann, *Repertorium*, no. 841, Taf. 136); II, Taf. 235, 7 (= Deichmann, *Repertorium*, no. 21, Taf. 7). In addition to these is a sarcophagus kept at the Metropolitan Museum of Art (MET) (Accession number: 1991.366) (https://www.metmuseum.org/toah/works-of-art/1991.366/).

70. Wilpert, *I sarcofagi*, I, Taf. 13 (= Deichmann, *Repertorium*, no. 680, Taf. 104 and 105); I, Taf. 92, 2 (= Deichmann, *Repertorium*, Taf. 43); I, Taf. 141, 4; II, Taf. 135, 6 (= Deichmann, *Repertorium*, no. 63, Taf. 20); II, Taf. 135, 6 (= Deichmann, *Repertorium*, no. 63, Taf. 20); II, Taf. 218, 2 (= Deichmann, *Repertorium*, no. 40, Taf. 13); Deichmann, *Repertorium*, no. 26, Taf. 8.

71. For these fragments see Wilpert, *I sarcofagi,* I, Taf. 151, 2; II, Taf. 225, 1 (= Deichmann, *Repertorium*, no. 479, Taf. 76); II, Taf. 225, 3 (= Deichmann, *Repertorium*, no. 692, Taf. 110);

onstrates that Matthew's version mentioning the two beasts was used on early Christian sarcophagi, attesting the use and spread of this Christian image from the period preceding the minting of the *Asina* tokens.[72]

In light of this, it seems probable that the donkey and her young on the *Asina* tokens should be interpreted as the mount of the Messiah, as mentioned by the Old Testament and Matthew and attested in the early Christian art at least from the beginning of the fourth century.[73] The Christian legend, *Dominus noster Jesus Christus Dei filius*, accompanying the *Asina* type on two specimens, seems to confirm this identification. The figure of Jesus, who does not appear on these *tesserae*, would therefore be evoked by the legend, whose purpose was probably to qualify the subject represented on the reverse.[74]

It is not easy to explain the scorpion above the donkey. The depiction of this animal on the *Asina* tokens has been considered by some scholars as an astrological symbol, and this theory has arisen out of the idea that these artefacts had an alleged amuletic function.[75] The so-called "Gnostic" gems and intaglios

II, Taf. 230, 5; II, Taf. 235, 2 (= Deichmann, *Repertorium*, no. 506); II, Taf. 235, 4; III, Taf. 291, 4 (= Deichmann, *Repertorium*, no, 38, Taf. 12).

72. Paintings showing the triumphal entry into Jerusalem do not appear before the first half of the fifth century AD, and the first example is attested on a fresco of the hypogeum at Santa Maria in Stelle near Verona depicting only one donkey as a mount of Jesus: see J. M. C. Toynbee, "The early-Christian paintings at Santa Maria in Stelle near Verona," in *Kyriakon: Festschrift Johannes Quasten* II (Münster: Verlag Aschendorff, 1970), 648–653. On the depictions of Christ's entry into Jerusalem in late antiquity and the Middle Ages, see also G. Schiller, *Iconography of Christian Art. The Passion of Jesus Christ* (London: Lund Humphries/New York Graphic Society, 1972), II, 18–23. Moreover, the importance of the episode of the entry into Jerusalem is also attested by the nun Egeria (also called Aetheria), who reports that it was celebrated liturgically with great processions on Palm Sunday in Jerusalem by the fourth century: *Peregr. Eg.* 30–31.

73. This interpretation of the donkey image on the *Asina* tokens was already contemplated but not demonstrated by F. Lenormant, *La monnaie dans l'Antiquité* (Paris: A. Lévy, 1878), I, 43, and Babelon, *Traité*, 684.

74. It is noteworthy that the image of Jesus is never represented on official coins in the fourth and fifth centuries AD. Rather, he is generally evoked by the cross, the *Chi-Rho* and other monograms, which are depicted on the helmet of the Emperor Constantine I as well as the soldiers' labarum. There is a full Christianization of the imperial attributes (e.g., *globus cruciger, manus Dei*, etc.) only from Theodosius I onwards: see K. A. Jacob, *Coins and Christianity* (London: Seaby, 1985), 37–47.

75. So Cavedoni, "Medailles," 312; G. B. De Rossi, "Le medaglie di devozione dei primi sei o sette secoli della chiesa." *Bullettino di Archeologia Cristiana* 7.4 (1869), 61. See also, Mazzarino ("Contorniati,"790), with reference to the *Chronography* of 354. According to Lenzi ("Di alcune medaglie,"130), the scorpion was depicted on the *Asina* tokens as a harmful animal and evil symbol, as opposed to the donkey, which was a good symbol. *Contra* Deonna ("LAVS ASINI 2," 357), who supposed that the scorpion occurs not as an astrological sign,

often depict a scorpion alone or combined with astrological symbols and Egyptian deities[76]—for instance, the gems in yellow jasper were said to protect from the sting of this animal. In two cases the scorpion, alone or as an attribute of Harpocrates, is accompanied by Jewish theonyms (names of god), perhaps as an expression of syncretism and magical influences.[77] Similarly, several late antique amulets written in Greek, consisting of *voces mysticae* and the word "scorpion" or a drawing of a scorpion, contain adjurations against the sting of the scorpion.[78] In addition to these, a group of amulets invoke the names Hôr Hôr Phôr Phôr (probably a reference to the Egyptian god Horus), the Jewish theonyms Iaô Sabaôth Adônai, and a more opaque name Salamantarchi in various configurations along with a first-person formula binding the "Artemisian scorpion" ("I bind you, Artemisian scorpion") and a date.[79] Although the precise association of the scorpion with Artemis is not clear, these amulets invoke a more positive power attributed to scorpions to protect houses against other animals, including poisonous ones.[80] One cannot exclude that the image of the

but because of its "nature phallique" like the donkey. On coins the scorpion appears as a zodiac sign on bronze issues of Antiochus IV Epiphanes (e.g., *RPC* I, 3854) or it is paired with Jupiter in a *quadriga* on the *denarii* of M. Aemilius Scaurus and P. Plautius Hypsaeus (58 BC) (e.g., Crawford 422/1a–b); it is even combined with the bust of Mars on drachmas of Alexandria during the reign of Antoninus Pius (e.g., Dattari 2972). On Hadrian's *denarii*, the scorpion is represented as an attribute of Africa reclining left (*RIC* II, 299). On imperial lead tokens the scorpion is paired with the retrograde legend ASC (Rostovtzeff 3081).

76. Alone: See A. Mastrocinque, "Le gemme gnostiche," in *Sylloge Gemmarum Gnosticarum*, ed. Mastrocinque (Roma: Istituto Poligrafico e Zecca dello Stato, 2003), I, 62; A. Mastrocinque, *Les intailles magiques du Départment des monnaies, médailles et antiques* (Paris: Bibliothèque Nationale de France, 2014), nos. 571–576. With astrological symbols and deities: Mastrocinque, *Les intailles magiques*, 32, no. 49; 52, no. 119; 68–69, nos. 158–162.

77. See *SGG*, I, 385, no. 353: Ιάω (Iaô) Cαβ–αω (= Cαβαωθ/Sabaoth); Mastrocinque, *Les intailles magiques*, 28, no. 33: Ιάω Μιχαὴλ᾿ Αδωναῖ Αβρασαξ (Iaô Michaêl Adônaï Abraxas). In a Christian context, the scorpion is a symbol of heresy at least from the *Scorpiace* of Tertullian, which was perhaps written in AD 203–204 against the Gnostic heretics whose activity is compared to a fatal scorpion bite, murdering the faithful: see, for instance, L. Leclercq, s.v. "Scorpion," in *DACL* XV.2 (Paris: Letouzey et Ané, 1953), cols. 1022–1026; L. Charbonneau-Lassay, *Il Bestiario di Cristo. La misteriosa emblematica di Gesù Cristo.* II (Roma: Arkeios, 1995), 585–587.

78. See T. de Bruyn, *Making Amulets Christian. Artefacts, Scribes, and Contexts* (Oxford: Oxford University Press, 2017), 90–98.

79. *P. Oxy.* VII, 1060; *P. Oxy.* VIII, 1152; *P. Oxy.* XVI, 2061–2063. For the meaning of "Jewish" elements in Christian magic in late antiquity, see R. Boustan and J. E. Sanzo, "Christian Magicians, Jewish Magical Idioms, and the Shared Magical Culture of Late Antiquity," *HThR* 110.2 (2017), 217–240.

80. For a discussion on the scorpion motif in late antique Egypt, see M. Todd, "The Scorpion in Graeco-Roman Egypt," *JEA* 25 (1939), 55–61.

scorpion on the *Asina* tokens was depicted because of the protective and magical function attributed to this animal, as attested in certain Christian contexts.

The combination of the donkey suckling a foal and the scorpion is a unique type, not attested elsewhere in iconographic[81] and literary sources. This may suggest that the meaning of this image, connected with Christian doctrines by virtue of the meaning of the donkey, was known not by a large audience, but by relatively small groups.

2.c Imperial portraits

The imperial portraits of Honorius (nos. 7–8, Pl. 23, 6–7) and a Valentinian emperor (no. 5, Pl. 23, 5; no. 6) are depicted on the obverses of four pieces, which are combined with reverses showing the *Asina* type.

The bust of Honorius on these *tesserae* has stylistic parallels with the obverses of the *Urbs Roma Felix* issue,[82] which was struck almost entirely at Rome in the names of Honorius, Arcadius and Theodosius II during the period 404–408,[83] with a hypothetical revival after Attalus.[84]

According to the internal structure of the *Urbs Roma Felix* issue, there are four main variants: a) head of Roma facing front and b) head of Roma facing right. On the obverses, the imperial bust appears in pearl- and rosette-diadem (variant a and b1), but also with a pearl-diadem only (variant b2 and b3). On *Asina* tokens nos. 7 (according to Tanini's drawing) and 8, the portrait of Honorius appears with the rosette variant while the legend is divided –VS. It might

---

81. The image of the donkey suckling a foal could evoke or have been inspired by the type of the she-wolf suckling the twins which, as is well known, was extremely widespread on Roman coins from the Republic onwards. However, depictions of animals suckling offspring or depicted alongside their young occur on Greek coins, e.g., the mare and her foal on drachmas of Larissa (BCD Thessaly II, 297 var.) and the cow suckling her calf on issues of Illyria from the third century BC (*HGC* 3, 33). Roman coins also show the sow suckling her piglets on Roman asses of Antoninus Pius (*RIC* III, 733) and even a deer suckling the infant Telephus, son of Hercules, on a *tetrassarion* of Heracleopolis during the reign of Geta (Roma Numismatics, Auction XVI, 26 September 2018, lot 485).

82. So Alföldi, "Asina," 59. According to Kent ("Fifth century bronze," 284, n. 6), the type of Honorius on the *Asina* tokens would belong instead to the *Gloria Romanorum* issue, released before 423.

83. A single known specimen in the name of Honorius (obverse legend divided R–I, mint mark SMAQ) shows that there was a small issue of the type struck in Aquileia. See *RIC* X, 130–131.

84. See Kent , "Fifth century bronze," 282–284; *RIC* X, 130–131, 140–141. See also P. Grierson and M. Mays (eds.), *Catalogue of late Roman coins in the Dumbarton Oaks Collection and in the Whittemore Collection. From Arcadius and Honorius to the Accession of Anastasius* (Washington, D.C.: Dumbarton Oaks Research Library and Collection, 1992), 207–209.

then copy variant a (–IVS legend on the obverse) or variant b1 (the –IVS division is prevalent but also the legend divided –VS is found), in which the imperial diadem is formed of pearls or rosettes. However, the style of specimen no. 8—the only one preserved—appears much more crude, as in the variants b2 and b3 with pearl-diadem only, while its diameter of 15 mm is similar to that of variant a.

It is noteworthy that three more tokens bear obverse types that, according to Kent, are similar to variant a of the *Urbs Roma Felix* issue.[85] A specimen published by Alföldi after his article on the *Asina* tokens carries the pearl-diademed bust of Arcadius with legend divided –IVS on the obverse, while on the reverse is the image a man in incuse, standing bent over left, maybe holding an open book in his hands; in front of him is a low bookcase; the letter (or number) E is engraved in right field.[86] The other two *tesserae* with the busts of Honorius and Arcadius with legend divided –IVS could be connected to variant a.[87] The obverse legend of one of these two pieces even reads HONVR–IVS (*sic!*), but this has not yet been noted on a coin.[88] Moreover, the reverses of these two *tesserae*, showing a bearded man in long tunic (XIII in exergue) and a quadruped (XIIII in exergue) both between two palm trees in incuse, suggest that they belong to the same series.[89] The copying of coin types showing Roman Emperors is a phenomenon also attested on a number of contorniates, whose images often reproduce or imitate the portraits depicted on coins of the earlier emperors as well as those reigning beginning with Theodosius the Great.[90] The pearl-diademed, cuirassed, and draped bust of Honorius appears on three contorniate groups. The first two (Honorius, I–II) carry the short legend HONORIO–AVGVSTO, while the traditional imperial titulature (D N HONORI–VS P F AVG) attested on official coins is reproduced on the third group (Honorius, III).[91]

85. See Kent, "Fifth century bronze," 282, n. 1, who considered these specimens as talismans.

86. A. Alföldi, "Heiden und Christen am Spieltisch." *JbAC* 18 (1975), 20–21, no. 2, Taf. 7.12 and 14. Another similar piece was in Henry Platt Hall's collection: see Glendining 16 (21 November 1950), lot 2190.

87. Ibid., 21, no. 2, Taf. 7.13 and 15 (with the bust of Honorius); Kent, "Fifth century bronze," 293, pl. 1, no. 6 (with the bust of Arcadius).

88. So *RIC* X, 131.

89. The problem of the production and interpretation of these specimens will not be discussed in the present paper, since it constitutes the topic of another study by the author that is currently in progress.

90. On this point, see E. Alföldi-Rosenbaum, "Imperial portraits on the contorniates," in *Roman Portraits. Artistic and Literary. Acts of the Third International Conference on the Roman Portraits held in Prague and in the Bechyně Castle from 25 to 29 September 1989*, ed. J. Bouzek and I. Ondřejová (Mainz: P. Von Zabern, 1997), 83–87.

91. See Alföldi and Alföldi, *Die Kontorniat-Medaillons 1*, 149–150.

It follows that the portrait of Honorius on the *Urbs Roma Felix* series, specifically its variant a and b1, may have been the model used for the production of the *Asina* tokens as well as contorniates and other *tesserae* at the beginning of the fifth century. This, as will be explained below, provides a useful framework for determining a relative chronology.

As mentioned above, the poor condition of the two pieces, now lost, that bear a legend related to one of the Valentinian emperors (nos. 5 and 6) does not allow a precise identification. There has been much speculation as to what the worn legend on specimen no. 5 is: *Iovis filius*, an allusion to Diocletian as "Son of Jupiter," or the imperial titulature of Valentinian I or Valentinian III. On contorniates, the only emperor of the Valentinian dynasty to be depicted is Valentinian III, whose type is attested by eight dies (Valentinianus III, groups I–VIII). The consistent occurrence of the type of Valentinian III on contorniates as well as the stylistic parallels of the *Asina* tokens with the late bronze coinage of Honorius could suggest that the *Asina* tokens continued to be struck even under Valentinian III. However, the pieces are too worn to be discussed extensively.[92]

Finally, another *tessera* showing the bust of Maximian Herculius (AD 286–305) on the obverse could be ascribed to the *Asina* issue (Pl. 24, 9). According to Alföldi, the style and iconography of this type belong to the late fourth century; in addition, the obverse legend *Maxi–miani*, the shortened name of the emperor in the genitive case, would appear to be connected to the obverse legend on the *Asina* specimens with the type of Alexander. According to the Hungarian scholar, it should be assumed that even the emperors of the Tetrarchy were represented on this issue.[93]

However, given the absence of any connection with the *Asina* type, one may wonder if the stylistic similarities between this *tessera* and the Alexander type on the *Asina* tokens can be considered sufficient proof to ascribe this specimen to the *Asina* issue. Indeed, there are other kinds of token and medallion issues

92. More evidence is needed in order to identify these imperial busts as those of Valentinian III. In fact, even the portraits of Valentinian I and Valentinian II also occur on late antique tokens, such as the *Vota Publica* coins: see A. Alföldi, *A Festival of Isis in Rome under the Christian Emperors of the fourth century* (Budapest: Dissertationes Pannonicae, 1937), 69–71. In addition, even a coin converted into a token, kept at the British Museum (inventory no. 1936.12.12.2), shows the pearl-diademed bust of the emperor Valentinian II with the legend D N VALENTINIA–NVS IVN P F AVG on the obverse, while on the reverse is the number VIIII incised.

93. See Alföldi, "Asina," 62, who thought the legend "*Iovis filius*" on the worn piece no. 5 (Pl. 23, 5) would be a clue of it. Curiously, the Hungarian scholar has not discussed the piece with the portrait of Maximinian Herculius in his following article on the *Asina* tokens, where he changed his mind and proposed to read the legend D N VA [...] on piece no. 5: see Alföldi, "Asina II," 92.

showing the portrait of Maximian Herculius,[94] and this could also be the case here—the specimen does not need to be connected to a broader series. In light of this, the connection of this *tessera* with the *Asina* issue is to be considered doubtful, and further evidence is needed to determine its attribution.

2.d The "varia" group

The two reverse types of Hercules and Minerva and an erotic scene are combined with the obverse type of Alexander the Great (nos. 3–4, Pl. 23, 3–4). In addition to these, the image of a centaur fighting a hero is associated with the obverse type of Maximian Herculius (no. 10, Pl. 24, 9): although it is unlikely that this specimen belongs to the *Asina* series—as explained above—the question remains open and therefore it seems necessary to discuss also this reverse type.

These depictions were considered by Alföldi to be imitating some of the images sporadically depicted on contorniates.[95] However, the types on the *Asina* issue differ from the contorniates in terms of iconography, style and quality. For instance, on the contorniate dies showing Hercules and Minerva,[96] the centaur fighting Hercules or a hero,[97] the position of the two figures is generally inverted compared to that on tokens, and the contorniates are of undeniably higher quality (Figs. 1–2, below).[98]

The depiction of the *symplegma* (i.e., an erotic scene of a heterosexual couple) on piece no. 4 has no precedent in the *spintriae*. It represents an ithyphallic man standing left, who touches the back of a woman leaning against a vase right, and turned towards the man. This motif should not simply be considered "erotic," since it could allude to one of the *symplegmata* connected to classical myth. Indeed, subjects taken from Graeco-Roman myth are depicted on some

94. For instance, the portrait of Maximian Herculius with the legend D N MAXIMIANO FELICISSIMO SEN AVG appears on issues of the *Vota Publica* coins carrying the imperial busts: see Alföldi, *Festival of Isis*, 937, 59, no. 3, pl. 1.2. W. Froehner ("Variétés Numismatiques." In *Annuaire de la Societé française de Numismatique* XIV (1890), 237–239), described a bronze medal bearing the bust of Maximian with the legend IMP C MAXIMIANVS P F AVG on the obverse, and a number of animals fighting the evil eye ("le mauvais oeil") on the reverse.

95. Alföldi, "Asina," 62; Alföldi, "Asina II," 93.

96. Alföldi and Alföldi, *Die Kontorniat-Medaillons 1*, Taf. 23, 4–6; 193, 6; 119, 8–12; Alföldi and Alföldi, *Die Kontorniat-Medaillons 2*, 123.

97. Hercules: See Alföldi and Alföldi, *Die Kontorniat-Medaillons 1*, Taf. 19, 3; 5, 8; 23, 9–11; 52, 1–3; Alföldi and Alföldi, *Die Kontorniat-Medaillons 2*, 142–143; Taf. 215, 9. Hero: See Alföldi and Alföldi, *Die Kontorniat-Medaillons 1*, Taf. 5, 6–7; 114, 1–4; 144, 10–12; Alföldi and Alföldi, *Die Kontorniat-Medaillons 2*, 142.

98. However, the type of Hercules-Minerva on the *Asina* token appears more similar to the design of Neptune-Minerva on a silver medallion of Hadrian: see Numismatica Ars Classica 18 (29 March 2000), lot 519.

Figure 1. Bronze contorniate with Hercules and Minerva on the reverse.
CNG 50 (23 June 1999), lot 360.

Figure 2. Bronze contorniate with a hero fighting a centaur on the reverse.
Numismatica Ars Classica 100 (29 May 2017), lot 726.

late antique "mythological" cameos, whose production is likely part of the circulation of luxury objects among the aristocratic elite. One of the three cameos reused in the so-called "Cross of Desiderius" shows the love struggle between Hercules, naked and bearded, and a woman largely naked and stripped of her *leonte* (perhaps Omphale); the scene on this gem, dated to the fourth century AD, is depicted according to the erotic Hellenistic tradition of *symplegmata*, which shows satyrs assaulting nymphs or maenads.[99] Although it does not represent a love "struggle" but an apparently consensual erotic scene, the image on the *Asina* token could refer to a subject drawn from classical mythology, rather than representing a purely erotic theme. Given the position of the two figures, this reverse type might evoke a fresco from Pompeii (AD 50–79), which carries the image of a satyr embracing a maenad from behind, who clings to a plant branch.[100]

99. See M. Cadario, M. "Cammei «mitologici» e «di Stato» nella Tarda Antichità. Tre esempi dalla «Croce di Desiderio» a Brescia," *ACME* 56.3 (2003), 65–96.

100. This fresco is held in the Gabinetto Segreto at the Museo Archeologico Nazionale di Napoli (MANN), inventory no. 27693.

However, the image depicted on the token differs from the mentioned fresco because of some details (e.g., the vase in place of the plant branch, the man is ithyphallic unlike the satyr), and therefore the identification of the two figures remains uncertain.[101]

A final obverse shows the type of Isis-Providentia, combined with the *Asina* type (no. 9, Pl. 24, 8). As Alföldi has rightly emphasized, this female bust, accompanied by the *Provi–dentia* legend (with the letters R M below), has none of Providence's attributes. As is well known, the common iconography of Providentia on coins and reliefs consists of a full female figure, standing or sitting left, with or without diadem, holding a scepter in her left hand and a cornucopiae, globe or baton in her right.[102]

However, if the bust on the *Asina* token should instead be interpreted as Isis, there is no need to conclude that the iconography of the Egyptian goddess was disguised as Providentia as a part of a secret continuation of the *Vota Publica* coins after 394.[103] This speculative interpretation was proposed by Alföldi only to support his interpretation of the so-called "anonymous series" of the *Vota Publica* coins, which show busts of Isis and Serapis on the obverse instead of imperial busts: Alföldi thought these were issued as *covert* propaganda and stopped after the defeat of the "pagan party" in Rome.

The female bust on the *Asina* token does not necessarily have to represent Providentia. Indeed, many Roman coins use the image of Providentia in combination with other figures (e.g., the Roman Emperor, Quies-Tranquillitas),[104] or the *Providentia* legend accompanies other imagery. For instance, legends including *Providentia* accompany the image of an altar (PROVID SC) on the *asses* of Vespasian,[105] as well as the figures of Nerva togate and Trajan in military dress (TR P COS III P P PROVID) on the *aurei* and *denarii* of Trajan, eulogizing the emperors for their foresight (Fig. 3, below).[106] The *Providentia Augusti* ("Providence of Augustus") legend also appears on two issues of Commodus, regarded as referring to the African fleet employed by the emperor for the transport of grain from Africa: they show on the reverse a galley with rowers (PROVID AVG P M TR P XI IMP VIII COS V P P S C) and the figures of Hercules and Africa, the

---

101. According to Alföldi, "Asina II," 94, this *symplegma* type occurs on a clay model from Sirmium in Pannonia (second century AD). Lenzi, "Di alcune medaglie," 131, interpreted the erotic scene as an allegory of the abuse of wine, which was also symbolized by the donkey.

102. See Polito 1994; *LIMC*, VII, 2, 432–433.

103. See Alföldi, "Asina," 61 and 63.

104. See Polito 1994, 564, nos. 10–11.

105. *RIC* II, Vespasian 313.

106. *RIC* II, Trajan 28.

Figure 3. Silver *denarius* of Trajan with reverse referring to *providentia*.
ANS 1948.19.1135.

Figure 4. Silver *denarius* of Marcus Aurelius with reverse referring to *providentia*.
Classical Numismatic Group 64 (24 September 2003), lot 1119.

Figure 5. Silver *denarius* of Septimius Severus with reverse referring to *providentia*.
Numismatica Ars Classica 45 (2 April 2008), lot 144.

latter with an elephant scalp on her head and carrying a *sistrum* in her left hand
(PROVIDENTIAE AVG S C) (Fig. 4).[107]

Significantly, on Septimius Severus and Caracalla's *denarii*, all of which perhaps belong to the year AD 207, a reverse type showing the winged head of
Medusa facing (or the variant Medusa-upon-Aegis) is accompanied by the legend *Providentia* (Fig. 5).[108] This non-specific reverse type, combined with the
legend *Providentia*, was considered, by virtue of its connection with the myth
of Minerva, as a reference to the foresight of the two *Augusti*, probably in their
preparation to invade Britain in 208. Medusa was sacred to Minerva, the goddess
of prudence/providence, and her imagery was beloved by the emperors, many of
whom adopted it by adorning their cuirass breastplates with the Medusa head.[109]

The legend *Providentia* on the *Asina* token may have served not to identify
the female bust, but to associate the Greek concept of *pronoia* with the image
depicted on the obverse of the piece. The legend could thus proclaim "foresight",

107. *RIC* III, Commodus 158; 486a and d; 487a and b;Classical Numismatic Group, 24
September 2003, Mail Bid Sale 64, lot 1119.

108. See, for instance, *RIC* IV, part I, 164 (= Numismatica Ars Classica, Auction 39, 16 May
2007, Lot 137); *RIC* IV, part I, 285 (= Numismatica Ars Classica, Auction 45, 2 April 2008,
Lot 144); *RIC* IV, part I, 286 (= Numismatica Ars Classica, Auction 25, 25 June 2003, Lot 57).

109. See S. W. Stevenson, *A Dictionary of Roman Coins* (London: Seaby, 1889), 660.

while the bust of another figure—perhaps Isis—is shown, like the other Graeco-Roman gods and heroes depicted on the remaining pieces.[110] The reception of Graeco-Roman concepts in Christian contexts is also documented on coins, even after the so-called "Constantinian turn." Indeed, ancient symbols of Rome's eternity and personifications (Victoria, Concordia, Roma) continue to appear on issues of Christian Emperors in the fourth and fifth centuries, especially the more sober types regarded as compatible with the Christian faith.[111]

3. CHRONOLOGY

On the chronology of these tokens, at least two points deserve consideration, based on the evidence considered so far.

Firstly, the close resemblance between the portraits of Honorius on the *Asina* tokens and the imperial busts on the *Urbs Roma Felix* series give a *terminus post quem* for these *tesserae* of AD 404. The period 404–408 as the proposed date for the *Urbs Roma Felix* issue, previously ascribed to the years 394–395 by Laffranchi,[112] was recently confirmed by the discovery of a specimen showing the obverse type of the only known bronze emission of Priscus Attalus and the *Urbs Roma Felix* b2 reverse.[113] This makes it sufficiently sure that the *Asina* tokens were struck at least after the start date of the *Urbs Roma Felix* issue, rejecting any previous effort to date them to the end of the fourth century. Moreover, as stated above, it is significant that at least three other *tesserae*, belonging perhaps to this period, bear types and legends that are similar to the obverses of the *Urbs Roma Felix* series. By virtue of the evidence considered, it is likely that the bronze coinage of Honorius was used from AD 404 as an archetype for the production of *tesserae* and coin-like objects.

110. A quite similar female bust is depicted on a bronze token held in the BnF (Inv. no. 17374), which shows a draped, veiled bust of Dysis ("Sunset") left, conveniently identified by the legend ΔVСIС, with a crescent-crown and a torch; on the other side is a radiate bust of Sol or a Roman emperor right, accompanied by the legend ANATOΛI.

111. See Jacob, *Coins*, 44. The concept of *providentia*, associated with the emperor or Caesars by the legend, appears on the reverse of *nummi* issued by the Constantinian dynasty, which bear the type of a camp gate with open doorway, two turrets and star above: e.g., see Roma Numismatics, E-Sale 47 (28 June 2018), lot 827.

112. L. Laffranchi, "Ripostiglio a Porta Collina (Roma)," *RIN* 32 (1919), 42–47; *RIC* IX, 113–114, 134, 135 nos. 67 a–f, 136 nos. 68 a–f; V. Picozzi, "«Urbs Roma Felix». Un problema di cronologia," *RIN* 69 (1967), 63–92.

113. See S. Bruni, "An AE3 of Priscus Attalus: new light on dating the Urbs Roma Felix series," in *XV International Numismatic Congress Taormina 2015 Proceedings*, ed. M. Caccamo Caltabiano et al. (Roma/Messina: Arbor Sapientiae, 2017), II, 700–703.

The comparison with contorniates carrying the type of Alexander the Great does not provide any useful element for determining the relative chronology of the *Asina* tokens, although Alföldi dated the first issue of contorniates before AD 395. Indeed, according to the most appropriate classification of the contorniate production proposed by Mittag, the so-called "regular" contorniates (i.e., the category of contorniates in which the type of Alexander appears), may have been struck until 423.[114] One can only say that, in addition to the *Urbs Roma Felix* series, the contorniate "regular" series, still produced around the first quarter of the fifth century (AD 355/60–395/423), as well as the "imperial" series, issued from Theodosius I (AD 379–472), could have inspired the imagery chosen for the *Asina* tokens.

Secondly, the two letters R M on piece no. 8 were associated by Alföldi with the mintmark R M which, in his opinion, was attested on bronze coinage from AD 410. However, the VICTOR–IA AVGG issue, which first utilized on bronze the letters R M as a mintmark, has been dated by Kent more precisely to late in the reign of Honorius ("Third Period"), although "the exact date of VICTORIA AVGG between 421 and 423 remains uncertain and it may have continued for some time."[115] A high chronology of the *Asina* tokens, perhaps struck even after 425, could be suggested also by the possible representation of Valentinian III on two specimens, but the identification of the subject is far from certain.

One may wonder if the letters R M can be considered as a "Signatur" of the mint of Rome, as Alföldi believed. This is not a mintmark, since these two letters are depicted not on the reverse (as typical for mintmarks on coins from this period), but below the female bust on the obverse. Furthermore, it is not clear why the *Roma* legend is repeated in the exergue on the reverse as well. More probable is that these two legends were a general reference to the city of Rome.[116] According to Kent, specimen no. 8 and the other three *tesserae* with the busts of Honorius and Arcadius, which he considered "talismans," were struck with the same obverse dies used for the *Urbs Roma Felix* and *Gloria Romanorum* issues.[117] However, no die links have been found to date, and these *tesserae* may have imitated or copied the images on official coins—as is frequently the case on contorniates—without having necessarily been struck in the official mint. It

---

114. See Mittag, *Alte Köpfe*, 180.

115. Kent, "Fifth century bronze," 287–288. See also *RIC* X, 136–137.

116. For example, other bronze *tesserae*, perhaps produced in the early imperial period, bear the legend ROMA accompanying the helmeted bust of the goddess Roma: see *Collection Martinetti and Nervegna. Médailles grecques et romaines. Aes grave*, 18 Novembre 1907 et les jours suivants (Paris 1907), lots 3073–3074.

117. See Kent, "Fifth century bronze," 282, 284; see also *RIC* X, 131.

is highly probable that the production of the *Asina* tokens took place in Rome, given their similarities with the contorniates and the official coins of Honorius, as well as the legends referring to Rome.

The precise production location of these *tesserae* poses the same problems as the place of contorniate production. Both are not official products, and the *Asina* tokens and contorniates share features that make it problematic to determine the context of production (inferior quality, incongruous obverse-reverse combinations, errors in titular legends). For contorniates the problem is unsolved and continues to attract scholarly attention. Indeed, it is a matter for debate whether or not the contorniates were produced by the official mint of Rome. While the tendency in earlier literature was to consider the contorniates as produced in the Roman mint,[118] the consensus today follows Mittag's model of private production of "regular" contorniates, ascribed to an unofficial mint because of their inconsistencies. Mittag also proposed that the "regular" series was sponsored privately because of the presence of certain themes and personalities that could have offended the Church (e.g. Nero, Caligula, pagan gods). Moreover, the series of "regular" contorniates has to be distinguished from the "imperial" series and the *Reparatio Muneris* series, which were both produced by the official mint of Rome.[119] However there has been no lack of criticism of this model,[120] and it is not possible at the moment to solve this controversial issue.[121]

118. See Alföldi and Alföldi, *Die Kontorniat-Medaillons 2*, passim.

119. See Mittag, *Alte Köpfe*, 213–214.

120. See A. Holden, "The Abduction of the Sabine Women in Context: The Iconography on Late Antique Contorniate Medallions," *AJA* 112 (2008), 112: "there is […] no evidence that such mints existed in Rome at this time."

121. In fact, if the hypothesis of contorniates as pieces produced by the State within the official mint of Rome were accepted, the recurrent inconsistencies on the contorniates and their rather low quality would remain unexplained. Otherwise, the hypothesis that contorniates were medallions produced by the mint of Rome at the request of private citizens (so e.g., Alföldi and Alföldi, *Die Kontorniat-Medaillons 2*, passim, with reference to the senatorial aristocracy of Rome) closely correlates to the controversial problem of "free coinage", that is the possibility for private citizens to produce coinage themselves through the use of the official mint. For the imperial period, this possibility is rejected by a passage of the jurist Paul, who states that only striking with the *forma publica* marks the transformation of a piece of metal into a Roman coin: *Dig.* 18, 1, 1, pr. (Paul 33 *ad Ed.*) (but might the mint use official dies on behalf of a citizen?). For Republican Rome, see the considerations of B. E. Woytek, "Exactions and the Monetary Economy of the Late Roman Republic. A Numismatic Perspective," in *Les confiscations, le pouvoir et Rome, de la fin de la République à la mort de Néron*, ed. C. Chillet, M.-C. Ferriès and Y. Rivière (Bordeaux: Ausonius, 2016), 188 ff. (Cicero, *Letters to Atticus* 8.7.3. is a key passage cited here). One may wonder if the "rule" described by Paul about the creation of currency as a prerogative of the State should also be applied to the production of pseudo-*monetae* and tokens or, on the contrary, the official mint could be used by private

As with the contorniates, the *Asina* tokens show subjects related, *inter alios*, to Greek and Roman myth as well as the unusual *Asina* type. The choice of the depictions represented on this extremely limited issue, given its historical-political and religious context, seem to suggest private interests and sponsorship. It remains difficult to say whether the production of these *tesserae* took place within the official mint or private workshops, which could have used as models some of the motifs depicted on the official coinage of Honorius as well as the contorniates.[122] This issue can be resolved only through further archaeological and archival finds or, alternatively, the discovery of die links between the *Asina* tokens and the official coins produced by the mint of Rome.

4. AUTHORITY AND FUNCTION: A POSSIBLE SCENARIO

Although it is not possible to determine whether the *Asina* tokens were made by the Roman mint or private workshops, it is difficult to believe they were artefacts produced on behalf of the State, by virtue of their combination of pagan and Christian imagery. It is known that the imperial legislation of Theodosius I and his sons forbade many of the public and private practices of Graeco-Roman cults, which were formerly part of civic life in Mediterranean communities. Also, decrees against "heretical" Christian doctrines which were put on a par with magic were issued by Arcadius (against Eunomians in 398)[123]—and Theodosius II (against Nestorians in 435).[124]

Considering the evidence, two possible interpretations of these tokens could be suggested.

1) These *tesserae* were amulets or talismans, as claimed by Kent and other scholars. However, this hypothesis does not explain the absolute absence of the *Asina* type amongst the imagery of intaglios and magical gems in the imperial period. Furthermore, only the two *Asina* tokens kept at the British Museum have holes, at least by judging from the drawings of the other (non British Museum) pieces, as well as the photos published by Alföldi. In fact, holes and eyelets were generally made on coins and coin-like objects in the Roman period in order to hang the pieces on the neck by a *funiculum* ("cord"), converting them into jewels or amulets. The absence of these interventions on the

citizens in order to produce coin-like objects. The problem of "free coinage" must therefore be considered, especially if the hypothesis of the contorniates as "private" medallions produced by the Roman mint is taken into consideration.

122. Moreover, the wide range of diameters and weight of the *Asina* specimens might suggest that not all pieces were produced in the same context.

123. *CTh* 16, 5, 34, 1.

124. *CTh* 16, 5, 66.

other *Asina* tokens could therefore exclude a possible amuletic or talismanic function for these objects.

2) The choice of imagery and the relatively small number of known specimens suggest the recipients of these tokens may have been private individuals, perhaps non-"orthodox" Christian groups influenced by Hellenism, who used these objects within their own community, perhaps for a ritual purpose or even just to express their religious identity and foster group cohesion.

The latter assumption would fit well with the arrangement of the motifs on these *tesserae* as well as the possible Christian meaning of the *Asina* type, as suggested above. In fact, the she-donkey and foal motif does not constitute one of the symbolic images of Christianity: it alludes to the mount of Jesus mentioned in the Gospel episode of the triumphal entry into Jerusalem and therefore it presupposes an in-depth knowledge of Christian culture, which seems difficult to ascribe to groups supporting Hellenistic and Roman religion. Moreover, the donkey and her colt as a mount of Jesus attracted attention by the biblical exegetes who, at least from Justin Martyr, interpreted the she-donkey mother as the Synagogue of the Jews and her young colt as the pagan people, subject to the yoke of Christ and converted to true faith.[125] However, it is not possible to say if the meaning of this image on tokens reflects the interpretation suggested by Christian exegetes.

The prominence of Alexander's images on the *Asina* tokens should be considered in relation to the appreciation and spread of the legend of the Macedonian king. From the third century AD onwards the figure of Alexander was enriched by the fantastic and colorful stories assembled in Pseudo-Callisthenes's *Alexander Romance*, stories that were later transferred to the medieval Christian and Arab world. For instance, the episode of Alexander's ascension into heaven, transmitted by a single branch of Pseudo-Callisthenes's textual tradition (that is, variant L of the *recensio* β), had a wide popularity throughout the Middle Ages, with numerous depictions in sculpture, miniatures, tapestry, and sumptuary arts.[126] Interpreted as a soteriological allegory of the soul or as an *exemplum superbiae* (the *hybris* of the classical tradition),[127] the iconography of

125. Just. *Tryph.* 53, 1. On this point, see M. P. Ciccarese (ed.), *Animali simbolici. Alle origini del bestiario cristiano* I (Bologna: Edizioni Dehoniane, 2002), 155–176. Moreover, the interpretation of the donkey as a symbol of pagans by the Christian exegesis also applies to other Biblical passages mentioning this animal, which is explained as an allegory of the pagan people become a mount of Jesus: see, for example, Or. *hom.*15, 3; Ambr. *Abr.* 1, 8, 71.

126. See C. Settis Frugoni, "Historia Alexandri elevati per griphos ad aerem. Origine, iconografia e fortuna di un tema," *BIStIAM* 80–82 (1973), 1–360; C. Settis Frugoni, *La Fortuna di Alessandro Magno dall'antichità al Medioevo* (Florence: La Nuova Italia, 1978).

127. Allegory of the soul: Schmidt 1995, 65–69. *Exemplum superbiae*: A. Di Vita and C. Alfano, *Alessandro Magno. Storia e Mito* (Milano: Leonardo Arte, 1995), 320.

Alexander seated on a chariot (*ingenium*) driven by two griffins in order to view the heavens was reproduced, at least from the ninth century, on a number of sculptural works that decorated Romanesque churches in Latin Europe and the Byzantine East, as well as on some mosaic pavements in Apulia's ecclesiastical buildings. Alexander's images depicted on the *Asina* tokens probably constitute one of the first attempts to Christianize the figure of the Macedonian king in the Latin West—this process is attested for the Greek East by John Chrysostom, who reports that images of Alexander on coins were used by some Christian groups in Antioch. This occurred in parallel with the literary tendencies of the imperial period, which focused on the history and myth of the Macedonian king.

From the analysis of the legends, at least another point is striking. The title D(*ominus*) N(*oster*) ("Our Lord") on the obverse legends is used for both the Roman emperor and Jesus. The sacred value of this title is documented for both individuals. The D(*ominus*) N(*oster*) title appears as a part of the imperial titulature on Latin inscriptions from Commodus onwards, while it is attested on coins only after Diocletian's currency reform in AD 294.[128] The Latin word *dominus* and its Greek counterpart *kyrios* referring to Jesus as an attribute of sovereignty—often as opposed to the Roman Emperors worshipped as *kyrioi*—occurs in the New Testament and in much of late antique Christian literature.[129] On the *Asina* tokens, Jesus is also styled *Dei filius* ("Son of God"), a perspective that conformed to the official position of the Church and the Empire after the Council of Nicaea (AD 325), but this was not recognized by all Christian groups.[130] It is not easy to

128. The title *D N* in the imperial titulature is generally regarded as an unofficial title (so L. Berlinger, *Beiträge zur inofiziellen Titulatur der römischen Kaiser,* PhD Diss. [Breslau, 1935], or as "a polite form of speech, implying the superiority of the person so addressed": see *RIC* X, 50. See also A. Chastagnol, "Le formulaire de l'épigraphie latine officielle dans l'antiquité tardive." In La terza età dell'epigrafia, ed. A. Donati (Faenza: Fratelli Lega 1986), 81–82; G. Migliorati, "Lo sviluppo delle titolature imperiali," in *Iscrizioni per la ricostruzione storica dell'impero romano da Marco Aurelio a Commodo,* ed. G. Migliorati (Milan: EDUCatt, 2011), 69–75. Forms of the imperial cult and the reverence paid to imperial images continued to survive even in the fourth and fifth centuries even among the Christians themselves, arousing the debate of the Christian authors: see *RIC* X, 42–44; M. Kahlos, "The Emperor's New Images. How to Honour the Emperor in the Christian Roman Empire?" in *Emperors and the Divine: Rome and its Influence,* ed. M. Kahlos (Helsinki: Helsinki Collegium for Advanced Studies, 2016), 119–138.

129. See, e.g., J. A. Fitzmeyer, "Kyrios," in *Dizionario Esegetico del Nuovo Testamento,* ed. H. Balz and G. Schneider (Brescia: Paoline, 1995), I, cols. 129–138.

130. For instance, Jerome attacked Arius for having considered Christ as a mere creature unlike those who, although non-Christian, would have recognized Jesus as a Son of God: *Nautae atque vectores vere Dei filium confitentur, et Arrius in ecclesia praedicat creaturam* (Hier. *in Mt.* 2). According to Cracco Ruggini, "Sulla cristianizzazione," 16, n. 28, the expression *filius dei* is specifically Christian, since it occurs only rarely among the "pagan" authors, who generally used the noun *deus* in the plural: Cic. *Lael.* 70 (*deorum* [...] *filii*); Festus, *FHG,* 94–95 (*deorum filius*).

establish whether this combination implies the intention of those responsible for these tokens to place the imperial and Christian cults on the same footing. The attribution of the title D(*ominus*) N(*oster*) to both Jesus and the Roman Emperor could even be accidental, due to the fact that the engravers of the *Asina tesserae* reproduced the imperial types of the official coins and their titulature.

The image of the donkey and her young, surmounted by a scorpion, remains a unique symbol, perhaps to be attributed to one of the numerous Gnostic groups.[131] In my opinion, the consideration of J. Eckhel is still valid, who considered the image of *Asina* as a secret symbol adopted by Christians like the *ichthys* symbol, "signifying something understood by themselves though hidden from us."[132] In fact, the use of tokens bearing images and legends that were chosen as a symbol of identity and membership by religious groups and communities is also attested in the earlier imperial period. For instance, the so-called banqueting *tesserae* from Palmyra, produced almost exclusively in clay between the first and third century AD, were adopted as entrance tickets to religious banquets or in distributions following certain sacrifices. They reflect the ways in which people and groups sharing the same religious beliefs acted and interacted on the occasion of religious events (such as ritual dining) and how the functioning of religious and social life of communities in the Roman world was based also on the employment of objects such as *tesserae* and coin-like objects.[133]

The use of the *Asina* tokens could therefore be a continuation of the role played by *tesserae* in religious and cultic contexts during the earlier imperial period. Through their legends and imagery, these objects probably reflected messages and ideas which were known by their recipients, fostering a sense of community and contributing to the formation and expression of one of the many Christian identities in late antiquity.[134]

131. Indeed, there are examples of Christian Gnostic groups, whose worship incorporated elements of pagan myth and sexual rituals, which recall the imagery of the *Asina* tokens. For instance, Epiphanius of Salamis provides a description of the Borborites, a Christian Gnostic sect, whose cosmology included the archon Sabaoth, corresponding to the God of the Jews. He was represented by some Borborites in the form of an ass or a pig: Epiph. *Pan.* 26, 10, 6. According to Epiphanius, the Borborites also adopted elements of sexual sacramentalism and components of pagan myth borrowed from Aphrodite: Epiph. *Pan.* 26, 2, 2; 26, 5, 2; 26, 11, 9.

132. J. Eckhel, *Doctrina numorum veterum* (Vindobonae: sumptibus Frederici Volke, 1798), VIII, 174: *Ergo et asinae lactantis typo aliquid poterant significare notum sibi, nobis ignotum.*

133. See, e.g., C. Dunant, "Nouvelles tessères de Palmyre," *Syria* 36 (1959), 102–110; R. Mesnil du Buisson, *Les tessères et le monnaies de Palmyre* (Paris: E. de Boccard, 1962); R. Raja "Staging «private» religion in Roman «public» Palmyra. The role of the religious dining tickets (banqueting tesserae)," in *Public and Private in Ancient Mediterranean Law and Religion*, ed. C. Ando and J. Rüpke (Berlin/Munich/Boston: De Gruyter, 2015), 165–186.

134. The use of art as sectarian self-assertion by different and competing communities of

CONCLUSIONS

While Alföldi considered the *Asina* tokens as anti-Christian tools like the *Vota Publica* coins and the contorniates, it seems more likely that these *tesserae* were used by some non-"orthodox" Christian groups to express their religious identity and shape their social memory within their community. Although doubts remain on the production context (official mint or private workshops?), further archaeological and archival finds could help to reconstruct the original arrangement of the iconography as well as the exact chronology of these specimens, to be ascribed after AD 404, probably to the last period of the reign of Honorius.

This case study reveals that pagan and Christian imagery existed side by side even at the beginning of the fifth century AD, despite the literary sources often indicating a marked border between Graeco-Roman and Christian culture. Recent studies on pagan-Christian relationships, with reference to Rome and the provinces of the empire, show how a syncretistic process between Christianity and Hellenism took place in late antiquity, often leading to an adaptation and absorption of pagan symbols by Christians.[135] Also the evidence of tokens aligns with other testimonies documented in late antique material culture, by attesting that both pagan and Christian beliefs coexisted with each other even after the so-called "Constantinian turn," in a relationship that did not mutually exclude one from the other.

Roman Christians is attested at least from the third century at Rome: see J. Elsner, "Inventing Christian Rome: the role of early Christian art," in *Rome the Cosmopolis*, ed. C. Edwards and G. Woolf (Cambridge: Cambridge University Press, 2003), 73–75.

135. L. Lavan and M. Mulryan (eds.), *The Archaeology of Late Antique 'Paganism'* (Leiden/ Boston: Brill, 2011); M. R. Salzman, M. Sághy and R. Lizzi Testa (eds.). *Pagans and Christians in Late Antique Rome. Conflict, Competition, and Coexistence in the Fourth Century* (Cambridge: Cambridge University Press, 2016).

ACKNOWLEDGMENTS

This research was funded by the British Academy's Visiting Fellowships Programme under the UK Government's Rutherford Fund. I wish to thank Prof. Clare Rowan for having patiently overseen my research at the University of Warwick (UK) and having offered irreplaceable suggestions for its improvement through her competence on tokens. I also owe her a debt of gratitude for generously correcting my English. I also thank Dr. Richard Abdy for kindly supplying me the inventory numbers as well as the metrological data of the two specimens kept at the British Museum. Finally, special thanks to Prof. Suzanne Frey-Kupper, Prof. Bernhard E. Woytek and Dr. Joseph E. Sanzo for the stimulating discussions as well as for giving me precious suggestions and references. All errors in this paper remain mine.

Publication-permissions are acknowledged to: the British Museum; Bibliothèque nationale de France (BnF); the National Museum of Denmark (I have in vain tried to establish with Dr Helle Horsnaes the ownership of the photo of piece no. 9); Schweizer Münzblätter/Gazette Numismatique Suisse (GNS); Classical Numismatic Group, Inc. (www.cngcoins.com); Numismatica Ars Classica NAC AG (www.arsclassicacoins.com/); CoinArchives (www.coinarchives.com); OCRE (http://numismatics.org/ocre/).

PLATES

Plate 23

1. 20 mm. Alföldi , "Asina." Illustrated at 2:1.
2. 15 mm. Alföldi, "Asina." Illustrated at 2:1.
3. 15 mm. Alföldi, "Asina II." Illustrated at 2:1.
4. 12 mm. Alföldi, "Asina II." Illustrated at 2:1.
5. 11 mm. Alföldi, "Asina II." Illustrated at 2:1.
6. No diameter (approximately 15 mm). Tanini, *Numismatum.* Illustrated at 2:1.

Plate 24

7. 15 mm. British Museum. Illustrated at 2:1.
8. 15 mm. British Museum. Illustrated at 2:1.
9. 15 mm. Alföldi, "Asina." Illustrated at 2:1.

ABBREVIATIONS

FHG = Müller, C. *Fragmenta Historicum Graecorum. Collegit, disposuit, notis et prolegomenis illustravit, indicibus instruxit,* 5 vols. Parisiis: Editore Ambrosio Firmin Didot, 1841–1870.

LIMC = *Lexicon Iconographicum Mythologiae Classicae,* VII, 1–2. Zürich/München: Artemis and Winkler, 1994.

RIC II = Mattingly, H., and E. A. Sydenham. *The Roman Imperial Coinage.* II. *Vespasian to Hadrian.* London: Spink, 1926.

RIC III = Mattingly, H., and E. A. Sydenham. *The Roman Imperial Coinage.* III. *Antoninus Pius to Commodus.* London: Spink, 1930.

RIC IV, part I = Mattingly, H., and E. A. Sydenham. *The Roman Imperial Coinage.* IV, part I. *Pertinax to Geta.* London: Spink, 1936.

RIC IX = Pearce, J. W. E. *The Roman Imperial Coinage.* IX. *Valentinian I—Theodosius I,* London: Spink, 1951.

RIC X = Kent, J. P. C. *The Roman Imperial Coinage.* X. *The Divided Empire and the Fall of the Western Parts. AD 395–491.* London: Spink, 1994.

RPC I = Burnett, A., M. Amandry and P. P. Ripollès. *Roman Provincial Coinage.* I. *From the death of Caesar to the death of Vitellius (44 BC–AD 69),* Paris: Bibliothèque Nationale de France, 1998.

SGG = Mastrocinque, A. *Sylloge Gemmarum Gnosticarum* I. Roma: Istituto Poligrafico e Zecca dello Stato, 2003.

BIBLIOGRAPHY

Alföldi, A. *A Festival of Isis in Rome under the Christian Emperors of the fourth century.* Budapest: Dissertationes Pannonicae, 1937.

————. "Asina. Eine dritte Gruppe heidnischer Neujahrsmünzen im spätantiken Rom." *SNbl* 2.7 (1951): 57–66.

————. "Asina II. Weitere heidnische Neujahrsmünzen aus dem spätantiken Rom." *SNbl* 2.8 (1951): 92–96.

————. "Heiden und Christen am Spieltisch." *Jahrbuch für Antike und Christentum* 18 (1975): 19–21.

Alföldi-Rosenbaum, E. "Imperial portraits on the contorniates." In *Roman Portraits. Artistic and Literary. Acts of the Third International Conference on the Roman Portraits held in Prague and in the Bechyně Castle from 25 to 29 September 1989,* edited by J. Bouzek and I Ondřejová, 83–87. Mainz: P. Von Zabern, 1997.

Alföldi, A., and E. Alföldi. *Die Kontorniat-Medaillons. Teil 1: Katalog.* Berlin: De Gruyter, 1976.

————. *Die Kontorniat-Medaillons. Teil 2: Text*. Berlin/New York: De Gruyter, 1990.

Babelon, E. *Traité des Monnaies Grecques et Romains. Première Partie: Théorie et Doctrine*. Paris: E. Leroux, 1901.

Berlinger, L. *Beiträgezur inofiziellen Titulatur der römischen Kaiser*. PhD Diss., Breslau, 1935.

Boustan, R., and J. E. Sanzo. "Christian Magicians, Jewish Magical Idioms, and the Shared Magical Culture of Late Antiquity." *Harvard Theological Review* 110.2 (2017): 217–240.

Bruni, S. "An AE3 of Priscus Attalus: new light on dating the *Urbs Roma Felix* series." In *XV International Numismatic Congress Taormina 2015 Proceedings*, edited by M. Caccamo Caltabiano et al., II, 700–703. Roma/Messina: Arbor Sapientiae, 2017.

Bruyn, T. de *Making Amulets Christian. Artefacts, Scribes, and Contexts*. Oxford: Oxford University Press, 2017.

Cadario, M. "Cammei «mitologici» e «di Stato» nella Tarda Antichità. Tre esempi dalla «Croce di Desiderio» a Brescia." *ACME* 56.3 (2003): 65–96.

Cary, G. "Alexander the Great in Medieval Theology." *Journal of the Warburg and Courtauld Institutes* 7 (1954): 98–114.

Cavedoni, C. "Médailles du temps d'Honorius portant des signes chrétiens mêlés à des types païens." *Revue Numismatique* (1857): 309–310.

Charbonneau-Lassay, L. *Il Bestiario di Cristo. La misteriosa emblematica di Gesù Cristo*. II. Roma: Arkeios, 1995.

Chastagnol, A. "Le formulaire de l'épigraphie latine officielle dans l'antiquité tardive." In *La terza età dell'epigrafia*, edited by A. Donati, 11–64. Faenza: Fratelli Lega, 1986.

Ciccarese, M. P. (ed.). *Animali simbolici. Alle origini del bestiario cristiano* I. Bologna: Edizioni Dehoniane, 2002.

Cohen, H. *Description historique des monnaies frappées sous l'Empire romain communément appelées médailles imperials*. VIII. Paris: Rollin and Feuardent, 1892.

Cook, J. G. "Envisioning crucifixion: light from several inscriptions and the Palatine graffito." *Novum Testamentum* 50.3 (2008): 262–285.

Cracco Ruggini, L. "Sulla cristianizzazione della cultura pagana. Il mito greco e latino di Alessandro dall'età antonina al Medioevo." *Athenaeum* 43 (1965): 3–60.

Dahmen, K. *The Legend of Alexander the Great on Greek and Roman Coins*. London/New York: Routledge, 2007.

————. "Alexander in gold and silver: reassessing third century AD medallions from Aboukir and Tarsos." *American Journal of Numismatics* 20 (2008): 493–546.

De Rossi, G. B. "Le medaglie di devozione dei primi sei o sette secoli della chiesa." *Bullettino di Archeologia Cristiana* 7.4 (1869): 49–63.

Deichmann, F. *Repertorium der christlich-antiken Sarkophage, Rom und Ostia.* Wiesbaden: P. von Zabern, 1967.

Deonna, W. "LAVS ASINI. L'âne, le serpent, l'eau et l'immortalité (1e partie)." *Revue Belge de Philologie et d'Histoire* 34.1 (1956): 5–46.

————. "LAVS ASINI. L'âne, le serpent, l'eau et l'immortalité (2e partie)." *Revue Belge de Philologie et d'Histoire* 34.2 (1956): 337–364.

Di Vita, A., and C. Alfano. *Alessandro Magno. Storia e Mito.* Milano: Leonardo Arte, 1995.

Dunant, C. "Nouvelles tessères de Palmyre." *Syria* 36 (1959): 102–110.

Eckhel, J. *Doctrina numorum veterum.* VIII. Vindobonae: sumptibus Frederici Volke, 1798.

Elsner, J. "Inventing Christian Rome: the role of early Christian art." In *Rome the Cosmopolis*, edited by C. Edwards and G. Woolf, 71–99. Cambridge: Cambridge University Press, 2003.

Froehner, W. "Variétés Numismatiques." In *Annuaire de la Societé française de Numismatique* XIV (1890): 231–240.

Fitzmeyer, J. A. "Kyrios." In *Dizionario Esegetico del Nuovo Testamento*, edited by H. Balz and G. Schneider, I, cols. 129–138. Brescia: Paoline, 1995.

Gaebler, H. *Die antiken Münzen Nord-Griechenlands. Die antiken Münzen von Makedonia und Paionia* III. Part 1. Berlin: Georg Reimer, 1906.

Goffredo, D. "Ingresso di Gesù a Gerusalemme." In *Temi di iconografia paleocristiana*, edited by F. Bisconti, 200–201. Città del Vaticano: Pontificio Istituto di Archeologia Cristiana, 2000.

Grierson, P., Mays, M. (eds.) *Catalogue of late Roman coins in the Dumbarton Oaks Collection and in the Whittemore Collection. From Arcadius and Honorius to the Accession of Anastasius.* Washington, D.C.: Dumbarton Oaks Research Library and Collection, 1992.

Holden, A. "The Abduction of the Sabine Women in Context: The Iconography on Late Antique Contorniate Medallions." *American Journal of Archaeology* 112 (2008): 121–142.

Jacob, K. A. *Coins and Christianity.* London: Seaby, 1985.

Kahlos, M. "The Emperor's New Images. How to Honour the Emperor in the Christian Roman Empire?" In *Emperors and the Divine: Rome and its Influence*, edited by M. Kahlos, 119–138. Helsinki: Helsinki Collegium for Advanced Studies, 2016.

Kent, J. P. C. "The fifth century bronze coinage of Honorius in Italy and Gaul." *Rivista Italiana di Numismatica e Scienze Affini* 90 (1998): 281–94.

Laffranchi, L. 1919. "Ripostiglio a Porta Collina (Roma)." *Rivista Italiana di Numismatica e Scienze Affini* 32 (1919): 42–47.

Lavan, L., Mulryan, M. (eds.). *The Archaeology of Late Antique 'Paganism.'* Leiden/Boston: Brill, 2011.

Leclercq, H. "Âne." In *Dictionnaire d'Archéologie Chrétienne et de Liturgie*, edited by F. Cabrol and H. Leclercq, I.2, cols. 2041–2068. Paris: Letouzey et Ané, 1924.

———. "Scorpion." In *Dictionnaire d'Archéologie Chrétienne et de Liturgie*, edited by F. Cabrol and H. Leclercq, XV.2, cols. 1022–1026. Paris: Letouzey et Ané, 1953.

Lenormant, F. *La monnaie dans l'Antiquité*. Paris: A. Lévy, 1878.

Lenzi, F. "Di alcune medaglie religiose del IV secolo." *Bilychnis* 2 (1913): 113–131.

Liampi, K. "Νομίσματα και οικονομία του κράτους του Μεγάλου Αλεξάνδρου." In *Μέγας Αλέξανδρος: αναδιφώντας όψεις του περίοπτου: κύκλος σεμιναρίων Μάρτιος–Απρίλιος* 2008. Peiraias: Idryma Aikaterinis Laskaridi, 2011.

Magioncalda, A. *Lo sviluppo della titolatura imperiale da Augusto a Giustiniano attraverso le testimonianze epigrafiche*. Torino: Giappichelli, 1991.

Marsden, A. B. "Some sing of Alexander and some of Hercules: artistic echoes of Hercules and Alexander the Great on coins and medallions, A.D. 260–269." In *Pagans and Christians: from antiquity to the Middle Ages. Papers in honour of Martin Henig, presented on the occasion of his 65th* birthday, edited by L. Gilmour. Oxford: Archaeopress.

Mastrocinque, A. "Le gemme gnostiche." In *Sylloge Gemmarum Gnosticarum* I, edited by A. Mastrocinque, 49–112. Roma: Istituto Poligrafico e Zecca dello Stato, 2003.

———. *Les intailles magiques du Départment des monnaies, médailles et antiques*. Paris: Bibliothèque Nationale de France, 2014.

Mazzarino, S. "Contorniati." In *Enciclopedia dell'Arte Antica*, 784–791. Roma: Istituto dell'Enciclopedia Italiana, 1959.

Mesnil du Buisson, R. *Les tessères et le monnaies de Palmyre*. Paris: E. de Boccard, 1962.

Migliorati, G. "Lo sviluppo delle titolature imperiali." In *Iscrizioni per la ricostruzione storica dell'impero romano da Marco Aurelio a Commodo*, edited by G. Migliorati, 69–75. Milano: EDUCatt, 2011.

Mitchell, P. *The Donkey in Human History: An Archaeological Perspective*. Oxford: Oxford University Press, 2018.

Mittag, P. F. *Alte Köpfe in neuen Händen: Urheber und Funktion der Kontorniaten*. Bonn: Habelt, 1999.

———. "Alföldi and the contorniates." In *Andreas Alföldi in the Twenty-First Century*, edited by J. H. Richardson and F. Santangelo, 259–268. Stuttgart: F. Steiner Verlag, 2015.

Mondello, C. "Nuove osservazioni sui contorniati: la serie dei *Literaten-Büsten*." In *XV International Numismatic Congress Taormina 2015 Proceedings*. Vol. II, edited by M. Caccamo Caltabiano et al., 772–776. Roma/Messina: Arbor Sapientiae, 2017.

———. "Using and Reusing Tokens: Some remarks about Christian graffiti on contorniates." In *Tokens: Culture, Connections, Communities*, edited by C. Rowan, A. Crisà and M. Gkikaki, 145–161. Royal Numismatic Society Special Publication 57. London: Royal Numismatic Society, 2019.

Montfaucon, B. de. *L'antiquité expliquée et représentée en figures. Tome second.* Paris: Deleaune et al., 1719

Moreno, P. "Immagini di Alessandro Magno: monete e storia." In *Serta antiqua et mediaevalia. 14: Il significato delle immagini: numismatica, arte, filologia, storia. Atti del secondo incontro internazionale di studio del Lexicon Iconographicum Numismaticae (Genova, 10–12 novembre 2005)*, edited by R. Pera, 153–170. Roma: G. Bretschneider, 2012.

Müller, L. *Numismatique d'Alexandre le Grand*. Copenhagen: B. Luno, 1855.

Paciaudi, P. M. *Osservazioni sopra alcune singolari e strane medaglie*. Napoli: Novello de Bonis Stampatore Arcivescovile, 1748.

Pfister, F. *Alexander des Grosse in der Offenbarungen der Griechen, Juden, Mohammedaner und Christen*. Berlin: Akademie Verlag, 1956.

Picozzi, V. "«Urbs Roma Felix». Un problema di cronologia." *Rivista italiana di numismatica e scienze affini* 69 (1967): 63–92.

Polito, E. "*Providentia*." In *Lexicon Iconographicum Mythologiae Classicae*, VII, 1, 562–567. Zürich-München: Artemis and Winkler, 1994.

Raja, R. "Staging «private» religion in Roman «public» Palmyra. The role of the religious dining tickets (banqueting tesserae)." In *Public and Private in Ancient Mediterranean Law and Religion*, edited by C. Ando and J. Rüpke, 165–186. Berlin/Munich/Boston: De Gruyter, 2015.

Ramskold, L. 2016. "A die link study of Constantine's pagan Festival of Isis tokens and affiliated coin-like "fractions": chronology and relation to major imperial events." *Jahrbuch für Numismatik und Geldgeschichte* 66: 157–239.

Rebuffat, F. "Alexandre le Grande et Apollonia de Pisidie." *Revue Numismatique* 28 (1986): 65–71.

Salzman, M. R., M. Sághy and R. Lizzi Testa (eds.). *Pagans and Christians in Late*

Antique Rome. Conflict, Competition, and Coexistence in the Fourth Century. Cambridge: Cambridge University Press, 2016.

Sanzo, J. E. "Magic and Communal Boundaries. The Problems with Amulets in Chrysostom, *Adv. Iud.* 8, and Augustine, *In Io. tra. 7.*" *Henoch* 39 (2017): 227–246.

Sanzo, J. E. "Imagining Illegitimate Ritual in Early Christian Literature." In *Guide to the Study of Ancient Magic*, edited by D. Frankfurter. Leiden: Brill, forthcoming.

Schiller, G. *Iconography of Christian Art.* II. *The Passion of Jesus Christ.* London: Lund Humphries/New York Graphic Society, 1972.

Schmidt, V. M. *A Legend and Its Image: The Aerial Flight of Alexander the Great in Medieval Art.* Groningen: E. Forsten, 1995.

Schreiber, T. *Studien über das Bildnis Alexanders des Grossen.* Abhandlungen der philologisch-historischen Klasse der Königlich-Sächsischen Gesellschaft der Wissenschaften 21. Leipzig: Teubner, 1903.

Settis Frugoni, C. "*Historia Alexandri elevati per griphos ad aerem.* Origine, iconografia e fortuna di un tema." *Istituto Storico Italiano per il Medio Evo* 80–82 (1973): 1–360.

———. *La Fortuna di Alessandro Magno dall'antichità al Medioevo.* Florence: La Nuova Italia, 1978.

Simon, M. "Alexandre le Grand, juif et chrétien." *Revue d'histoire et de philosophie religieuses* 21 (1941): 177–191.

Stevenson, S. W. *A Dictionary of Roman Coins.* London: Seaby, 1889.

Tanini, G. *Numismatum Imperatorum Romanorum a Trajano Decio ad Constantinum Draconem ab Anselmo Bandurio editorum Supplementum.* Romae: A. Fulgonium, 1791.

Todd, M. "The Scorpion in Graeco-Roman Egypt." *Journal of Egyptian Archaeology* 25 (1939): 55–61.

Toynbee, J. M. C. "The early-Christian paintings at Santa Maria in Stelle near Verona." In *Kyriakon: Festschrift Johannes Quasten* II, 648–653. Münster: Verlag Aschendorff, 1970.

Vettori, F. *Epistola ad virum cl. P.M. Paciaudi de Musei Victorii emblematae et de nonnullis numismatibus Alexandri Severi secondi curis explanatis.* Romae, 1747.

———. *De vetustate et forma monogrammatis SS. Nominis Jesu.* Romae, 1747.

———. *Dissertatio apologetica de quibusdam Alexandri Severi numismatibus,* Romae: Zempel, 1749.

Vischer, L. "Le pretendu «culte de l'âne» dans l'Église primitive." *Revue de l'histoire des religions* 139.1 (1951): 14–35.

Wilpert, G. *I sarcofagi cristiani antichi.* 3 vols. Roma: Tipografia Poliglotta Vaticana, 1929–1936.

Woytek, B. E. "Exactions and the Monetary Economy of the Late Roman Republic. A Numismatic Perspective." In *Les confiscations, le pouvoir et Rome, de la fin de la République à la mort de Néron*, edited by C. Chillet, M.-C. Ferriès and Y. Rivière, 183–197. Bordeaux: Ausonius, 2016.

Yarbrough, O. L. "The shadow of an ass: on reading the Alexamenos graffito." In *Text, image, and Christian in the Graeco-Roman world: a Festschrift in honor of David Lee Balch*, edited by A. C. Niang and C. Osiek, 239–254. Allisan Park, PA: Pickwick Publications, 2012.

AJN Second Series 32 (2020) pp. 313–337

Coin Molds and a Decentralized Monetary Policy in Tetrarchic Egypt

Irene Soto Marín[*]

The manufacture of non-official coinages in the Roman Empire is a recognized phenomenon. The scale to which clay coin molds are found in fourth-century Egypt, however, is unparalleled, and the location of their findspots near military camps already inspired important scholarship by Alessandra Gara in 1978. This article provides an updated overview of the topic and utilizes recent papyrological and numismatic research to corroborate Gara's hypothesis, namely, that cast coinages were a quasi-official response to the low output of small denominations coins by the Alexandrian mint, signaling the practice of a decentralized monetary policy in Egypt.

INTRODUCTION

In 1948 and 1950, a Franco-Swiss mission directed by Jacques Schwartz excavated the site of Dionysias, modern Qasr Qarun, in the Fayyum Oasis in Egypt.[1] The site contained a fort, unearthed in 1950 (but published only in 1969), that received scholarly attention, since it was mentioned in the *Notitia Dignitatum* as housing the *ala V Praelectorum* around 400 CE.[2] However, equally important for the understanding of the organization of the army and of the monetary economy

*Kelsey Museum of Archaeology and Department of Classical Studies, University of Michigan (irenesm@umich.edu).

1. J. Schwartz and H. Wild, F*ouilles franco-suisses, Rapport I: Qasr-Qarun/Dionysias.* (Paris: Institut Français d'Archéologie Orientale, 1950); J. Schwartz, "La monnaie d'Alexandrie et la réforme de Dioclétien," *SMbl* 13–14 (1963–1964), 98–102.

2. P. Davoli, "The Archaeology of the Fayum," in *The Oxford Handbook of Roman Egypt*, ed. C. Riggs (Oxford: Oxford University Press, 2012), 158.

of Roman Egypt, was a building located close to the fortifications. It contained a rudimentary oven, two channels where soot and ashes where disposed of, and 15,000 coin molds dating to the Tetrarchic and Constantinian period.[3]

Alessandra Gara, an ancient historian at the University of Pavia with a focus on ancient economic history, quickly recognized the economic importance of the presence of these coin molds and published the seminal article "Matrici di fusione e falsificazione monetaria nell'Egitto del IV secolo" in 1978. Gara possessed a rare ability to utilize papyrological and numismatic evidence, and with a sophisticated theoretical analysis, placed it within a wider historical framework. Before her untimely death in 1993, she published monographs and articles dealing with papyri and coinage, as well as a more synthetic piece on the monetary economy of Roman Egypt, published in 1988.[4]

In her 1978 article, Gara contextualized the evidence for wide production of cast coins in Dionysias within the larger setting of the Roman Empire, pointing out that the manufacture of non-official coins was a phenomenon well-known in France and Britain, and therefore she situated Egypt's production of these cast coinages within the greater monetary history of Europe and the Mediterranean.[5] The piece also provided a lengthy discussion of the legal status of these coins, a point to which I will return later in this paper. Based mostly on the coin molds themselves and laws preserved in the *Codex Theodosianus*, Gara was able to challenge the notion that this represented an illegal production of coinage, a claim which continues to be put forward regarding the production of coins outside official state mints,[6] and offered a more nuanced view of cast or molded coins:

> Il problema di fondo sta, infatti, nel significato da attribuire a questa moneta fusa, se sia cioè opera di falsari…o se non si tratti, invece, di una moneta autonoma di emissione non statale, a circolazione locale, comunque tollerata in aree marginali e in periodi storicamente caratterizzati da riv-

3. A. Gara, "Matrici di fusione e falsificazione monetaria nell'Egitto del iv secolo," *NAC* 7 (1978), 234.

4. Besides the article under discussion, her first major monograph *Prosdiagraphomena e circolazione monetaria* published in 1976 became a classic according to R. S. Bagnall ("Alessandra Gara," *BASP* 30 [1983], 79–80).

5. Gara, "Matrici," 232.

6. B. Lichocka ("Les moules égyptiens à monnaies tardives du British Museum," in *Archaeological Research in Roman Egypt. The Proceedings of the Seventeenth Classical Research 2008 Colloquium of the Department of Greek and Roman Antiquities, British Museum, held on 1–4 December, 1993*, ed. D. M. Bailey [Ann Arbor: Journal of Roman Archaeology, 1996], 206) asserts that these cast coins were most likely tolerated given the need for currency by Egypt's population, but the author continues to treat them as illegal productions of coinage.

olgimenti economici e sociali, o da incertezze nella gestione del potere politico.[7]

Gara set the production of cast coinage in Dionysias within the complex political and economic context of late third- and early fourth-century Egypt, and more recent scholarship on coin molds and the hoard evidence from this period has necessitated an even more nuanced view of the role of these "imitation" coinages.[8] Key papyrological texts and an ongoing and more comprehensive hoard analysis of the bronze coinage corroborates Gara's hypothesis that these coins were not only tolerated, but served as a necessity for the highly monetized society of Egypt during the fourth century.

In this article, I will deploy archaeological, numismatic, textual, and papyrological evidence in an attempt to connect the large quantities of fourth-century CE coin molds found in Egypt with the apparent contemporary shortage of the official bronze coins in circulation during this period. I will discuss the information the molded coins can yield regarding the role of the mint of Alexandria, precisely at a moment when Egypt's currency system was, for the first time in over 600 years, the same as in the rest of the Mediterranean. The sets of data are large and complicated and deserve further treatment, but their mere existence demands attention. The questions these coin molds, coin hoards, and single finds raise cannot be solved or answered in one article, especially because much of the evidence is so far unpublished. I hope, however, that by contextualizing and inserting these objects into a broader economic historical frame, we may begin to achieve a more nuanced view of minting and the role of the state in the early fourth-century economy and lay the groundwork for more detailed future investigation. As I will discuss, the widely tolerated practice of producing these cast coinages also raises questions about the application of Roman law in the provinces. Furthermore, the preliminary results of analyzing coin hoards and molds from Egypt suggest ancient roots for a trend that is common in the *longue durée* of later economic history, namely the limited supply of small denomination currency. [9]

7. Gara, "Matrici," 232.

8. See F. Barakat, "Gussmunzen im romischen Agypten." In *L'exception égyptienne? Production et échanges monétaires en Egypte hellénistique et romaine, Actes du colloque d'Alexandrie, 13–15 avril 2002*, ed. F. Duyrat and O. Picard (Paris: Institut Français d'Archéologie Orientale, 2005), 213–233; Lichocka, "Bilan des découvertes," for more information on the actual manufacture of the cast coinage.

9. The so-called imitation coinages and their production are not an unknown phenomenon in economic history. T. J. Sargent and F. Velde (*The Big Problem of Small Change* [Princeton: Princeton University Press, 2002]) have introduced a model showing the recurrent scarcity

HISTORICAL BACKGROUND

Ptolemy I, son of Lagos, officially introduced Greek coinage into Egypt soon after he took power there following Alexander's death in 323 BCE.[10] In 306 BCE a fiscal crisis was precipitated by the Ptolemaic defeat at the battle of Salamis, and the ongoing war against the Antigonids forced Ptolemy I to seek extra revenues for state expenses. Ptolemy decided to recoin his tetradrachms, moving from the Attic silver standard of 17.2 grams to a lower silver standard of 15.7 grams, and all non-Ptolemaic coinage was banned from use within the Ptolemaic kingdom. Throughout the Hellenistic and Roman periods, Egypt remained a separate currency zone. Recent studies on the economic transition between Hellenistic and Roman Egypt, following Octavian's conquest in 30 BCE, have concluded that there is no evidence of an attempt at that time to integrate the province monetarily with the rest of the empire, as was done with the province of Asia. As Blouin and Burnett have concluded:

> The one time of potential real co-ordination across the whole empire was the reign of Nero, when substantial changes took place in Rome, Crete, Syria, Cappadocia and Egypt, all intended to recover silver for the Roman government. But it was (remarkably) the only moment of such coordination, the only occasion in the first or early second centuries that any monetary reform was attempted empire-wide."[11]

Blouin's and Burnett's analysis of the coinage transition between Hellenistic and Roman Egypt seems to be in line with much of the picture recently drawn by Andrew Monson regarding the domains of administration, land management

and depreciation of small change in medieval and early modern Europe, mainly stemming from the expensive pressure on the state to provide a constant stream of coinage. In summary, the minting of small currency was not profitable to the state, but its shortages were harmful to the state because they hurt trade and caused further inflation and depreciation. The authors used case studies mainly from medieval Florence and Venice and sixteenth-century France and were able to isolate and distinguish various monetary "symptoms": Free minting, bullion famine, ghost monies, and units of accounts (along with attempts by the state to fix prices). A full comparison to fourth-century Egypt would necessitate a lengthy exposition, which is outside the scope of this article. Nonetheless, the similarity in small-change problems identified by the authors is undeniable and demonstrates the relevance of Late Antique Egyptian political economy to later stages of economic history.

10. C. C. Lorber, "The Coinage of the Ptolemies," in *The Oxford Handbook of Greek and Roman Coinage*, ed. W. E. Metcalf (Oxford: Oxford University Press), 212.

11. K. Blouin and A. Burnett, "From kings to emperors: The development and integration of the Egyptian monetary system into the Roman Empire," in *L'argent est roi: L'économie monétaire en Égypte des Perses aux débuts de l'Islam, Orléans, du 29 au 31 octobre 2015*, ed. T. Faucher (Paris: Institut Français d'Archéologie Orientale, 2020), 284.

and tenure, taxation, and the agricultural economy, where the Roman conquest seems to have not have been as disruptive for the economic systems of Egypt as had sometimes been thought.[12]

Accordingly, throughout the Roman period, until the reforms of Diocletian at the end of the third century CE, the currency of Egypt retained the Ptolemaic system of denominations and dating.[13] Coins continued to be made of billon and bronze and minted only in Alexandria, which was the only official mint of the province throughout the Hellenistic and Roman periods. For over six centuries, entering Egyptian territory had necessitated currency exchange at its borders in order to have currency usable locally for the purchase of goods. This barrier allowed very close control of the metal supply and the minting schedule, as well as the extraction of coinage within the province. Yet this system also separated Egypt from the rest of the Roman Empire and gave it an isolated economic status relative to the rest of the provinces, a characteristic perhaps acceptable or even desired during the early empire, but one that was strongly at odds with Diocletian's political ideal of a well-integrated empire. Furthermore, during periods of rebellion, usurpers were known to mint their own coins, and thus after the revolt of L. Domitius Domitianus in 297/298 CE, Diocletian could have seen the retention of Egypt's separate currency system as an invitation for further political unrest.

To restore and stabilize the empire, Diocletian had to maintain his expanded administrative apparatus and his presumably larger army; and this required him to streamline tax collection and enhance revenues throughout the Roman Empire.[14] Thus, Diocletian instituted empire-wide economic reforms in 296 CE, one of which introduced a new set of coinages. In the wake of this, he abolished Egypt's isolated monetary zone in 297/8 after the revolt of Domitianus had

---

12. A. Monson, *From the Ptolemies to the Romans. Political and Economic Change in Egypt* (Cambridge: Cambridge University Press, 2012), 214.

13. A. Geissen, "The Coinage of Roman Egypt," in *The Oxford Handbook of Greek and Roman Coinage*, ed. W. E. Metcalf (Oxford: Oxford University Press, 2012), 566.

14. E. Luttwak (*The Grand Strategy of the Roman Empire* [Baltimore: Johns Hopkins University Press, 1967], 177) and A. H. M. Jones (*The Later Roman Empire, 284–602: A Social, Economic, and Administrative Survey* [Baltimore: Johns Hopkins University Press, 1964], 17) both argue for an increase in the number of legions, but the size of the legions was reduced; therefore the actual number of soldiers enlisted did not increase as much as one would have initially supposed looking at the increase in legions and units. More recently, P. Heather (*The Fall of the Roman Empire: A New History of Rome and the Barbarians* [Oxford: Oxford University Press, 2005]) has argued for an increase of size of the army by at least 33%.

been put down.[15] The immediate effects of this reform on the Alexandrian mint and the Egyptian economy are unclear. On the one hand, the large quantities of fourth century CE bronze coins present in the archaeological record throughout Egypt (in single finds and in hoards) would seem to point both to a large production of bronze coinage within the territory and to the utilization of coins imported from mints abroad. However, the archaeological record also provides thousands of coin molds, which have been interpreted, as we have seen, as representing an illegal production of bronze coins, and which circulated alongside Alexandrian coins and those minted elsewhere in the empire.[16] This paradox needs close examination.

BRONZE COINAGE

After the reform of 297/8 CE in Egypt, the two most common coins were a billon *nummus* of 10 g and a smaller 3 g piece of bronze. The precise chronology and composition of this coinage is problematic, since it appears that both reform coinage and the older pre-reform Alexandrian coinage circulated together in the beginning. By 301 the official monetary system in use in Egypt included the *aureus* (*solidus*), *argenteus*, *nummus* of billon, a radiate *aes*, and a laureate *aes*; the latter two were eventually dropped.[17] The billon *nummus* weighing ca. 10 g contained around 4% silver and on the basis of the prices in the Edict of Maximum Prices issued by Diocletian in 301, would have been overvalued by 70%.[18] The *nummus* underwent a progressive debasement starting in 308 CE, going from a piece with 4% silver content to one with 1.4% by 341.[19] The continuous debasement of the *nummus* could represent the struggle of the state mints to supply enough small-value currency to meet the needs of the highly monetized

15. Although the coinage reform took place in earlier years (294–295 CE) in other provinces of the empire. Schwartz ("La monnaie d'Alexandrie") initially argued that the reform took place in August 296 CE in Alexandria, based on his analysis of the coinage issued by the usurper L. Domitius Domitianus. D. J. Thomas ("The Date of the Revolt of L. Domitius Domitianus," *ZPE* 22 [1977], 253–279) convincingly argued for a later date of the revolt, in 297/8, based on papyri, ostraca, and literary evidence; the latter date is now widely accepted.

16. B. Lichocka, "Bilan des découvertes monétaires dans les fouilles polonaises d'Alexandrie," in *L'exception égyptienne? Production et échanges monétaires en Egypte hellénistique et romaine, Actes du colloque d'Alexandrie, 13-15 avril 2002*, ed. F. Duyrat and O. Picard (Paris: Institut Français d'Archéologie Orientale, 2005), 309–311.

17. Gara, "Matrici," 248.

18. R. S. Bagnall and G. Bransbourg, "The Constantian Monetary Revolution," ISAW Papers 14 (2019), http://dlib.nyu.edu/awdl/isaw/isaw-papers/14/#works-cited.

19. R. S. Bagnall, *Currency and Inflation in Fourth Century Egypt* (Atlanta: American Society of Papyrologists, 1985), 31, 37. See table 1 in this article for a chronology of the weight and silver content of the *nummus* throughout the fourth century.

empire, and thus to produce more coins, it lowered the official required quantity of the precious metal. The effect that the debasement actually had on the volume of output of both the Alexandrian mint and other mints of the empire remains to be explored. The archaeological record does not seem to reflect a higher quantity of coins in circulation, however, and preliminary analysis of hoards and single finds in Egypt shows, as we shall see, that evidence of official billon and bronze coinage minted between 298–330 is scarce. *Solidi* and *argentei* are also non-existent in the archaeological record before 337 CE, and Alexandria did not habitually mint gold coins.[20]

While the discussion of the role of high-value precious metal currency is outside of the scope of this article, it is worth mentioning the archaeological absence of coined silver and gold during this period in Egypt, because it corresponds to the papyrological evidence that shows the state's extraction of precious metal bullion through compulsory sales, a kind of "hidden tax", which will be discussed further on in this paper.

From the fourth century, the billon and bronze pieces are indeed by far the most common coin types found in Egypt, but the chronological distribution of the coins tends to skew sharply towards the latter half of the century. The database I have compiled of fourth-century bronze coinage includes more than 27,500 coins from published hoards and single finds documented in Egypt up to the year 2000, when Hans-Christoph Noeske published his catalogue of fourth- and fifth-century coinage in Egypt and Syria.[21] The analysis of these hoards is still ongoing, but some preliminary patterns are worth mentioning in order to aid in our discussion of the role of coin molds. First, of the 27,500 coins accounted for in the publication record, only 499 are precisely dated to the period

---

20. The Alexandrian mint produced few *aurei* and *solidi* during the Roman period, and only to mark the occasion of the visit of the emperor to the province of Egypt. Small issues of gold coins were minted for Vespasian, Septimius Severus, Maximian, Diocletian, Licinius, Justin II, and Heraclius. See *RIC* VII, Alexandria.

21. H.-C. Noeske, *Münzfunde aus Aegypten. Prolegomenza zu einer Geschichte des spaetroemischen Münzumlaufs in Aegypten und Syrien/1, die Münzfunde des aegyptischen Pilgerzentrums Abu Mina und die Vergleichsfunde aus den Dioecesen Aegyptus und Oriens vom 4.–8. Jh. n. Chr.* (Berlin: Gebr. Mann Verlag, 2000). This database was utilized for this author's dissertation, finished in 2018. In September 2020 a project led by the author at the University of Basel concluded, in which further results from H.-C. Noeske, *Münzfunde aus Ägypten* II, *Die griechisch-römischen Münzfunde aus dem Fayum* (Mainz: P. von Zabern, 2006) as well as O. Picard, et al. *Les monnaies des fouilles du Centre d'études alexandrines: Les monnayages de bronze à Alexandrie de la conquête d'Alexandre à l'Egypte moderne* (Paris: Centre d'études alexandrines, 2012), and other unpublished material were included. The overall results, however, do not change the analysis offered in this article.

between 297/8 and 330. Of these 499, only 24 are stated to be legible enough to be traced to a mint, as represented in Table 1.

Table 1. Coins with identifiable mint attributions

Mint	Number of coins
Alexandria	6
Antiochia	3
Heraclea	3
Roma	3
Ticinium	3
Thessalonica	2
Siscia	2
Treveri	2

Since 24 coins are a minute fraction of the whole, I will refrain from analyzing the mints of these coins as evidence for any circulation patterns in the early fourth century. What is clear at first glance, however, is that there is a low quantity of bronze coinage attributable to this period. It is less clear why this should be so. Numerous factors could have contributed to this apparent scarcity. Coins minted in these decades could have been melted and the metal reused (perhaps on the occasion of a recall of coinage) or simply not hoarded to the same extent as issues of later periods. However, the presence of the large quantity of coin molds paired with the comparatively low ratio of early fourth-century coins to coins dating to the later half of the fourth century, seems to point at a shortage of officially struck small change during the first decades after the reform. This observed pattern is nothing necessarily new and in fact it is not even unique to Egypt. Shortage of coinage during the Tetrarchy has been noted in the rest of the Roman Empire,[22] and in fact a recent monetary analysis of this period actually proposes an explanation to this phenomenon.

A major monetary change happening during the reign of Constantius II, specifically between 351 and 353 has been pinpointed recently by Bagnall and Bransbourg. Bagnall shows a price discontinuity in Egypt between prices before

---

22. I thank the anonymous reviewer for this observation. See J. Chameroy et al. "L'officine De Faux-Monnayeurs De La Coulonche (Orne): Nummi Coulés De La Tétrarchie En Occident." *NC* 174 (2014), 153–191; R. Gaspar, "Counterfeiting Roman Coins in the Roman Empire I–III A.D. Study on the Roman provinces of Dacia and Pannonia." *Journal of Ancient History and Archaeology* 2.4 (2015), 31–74.

351 and those after 353, and Bransbourg identifies a hoard discontinuity around 348–354:[23]

> Then comes evidence of a rare demonetization, as *C. Th.* IX, 23, 1 (354) implies that a range of coins is by then forbidden and that everyone knows about it—the *maiorina*, the *centenionales communes*, and *ceteras vetitas*. Since the actual demonetization must have preceded such an edict, we have a clear chronological compatibility between the 351–353 price increase, the replacement of the AE2/AE3 348–352 *fel. temp. reparatio* series by the new Falling Horseman AE3,[24] and the implication in 354 that some coinage demonetization had taken place not long ago."[25]

This monetary change is evident in the quantity of hoards deposited after the 350s, compared with the first half of the fourth century, and is also evident in the absence of any *solidi* dating before the 340s found either in hoards or as single finds. Therefore, when questions of integration during the fourth century arise, particularly when analyzing data from hoards, it is imperative to recognize that much of the coinage in circulation prior to Constantius was of lower quality and may have subsequently been recalled. Since a large quantity of the dataset I have presented (73%) stems from hoards, they naturally will tend to show the same coin series, and given the hoard discontinuity presented by Bransbourg, this skews drastically the quantification of the coins to the latter half of the fourth century. Therefore, the absence of early Tetrarchic coinage in the archaeological record does not mean necessarily that they were simply not in circulation at all. The exact output may indeed have been lower, but Bagnall and Bransbourg have shown that the situation may have been more nuanced.

Accordingly, the database documents 20,000 coins which can be dated to the latter half of the fourth century, i.e., after the reform of Constantius II, most of

---

23. Bagnall and Bransbourg, "The Constantian Monetary Revolution," 27.

24. See ibid., cf. 23: "The dating of the demonetization remains uncertain: the 354 edict implies a prior date, although nothing would have prevented such a measure from being implemented at different moments throughout the empire. A step by step scenario starting in 349 in Constantinople and Antioch, in late 350 or early 351 in the Balkans, reaching Italy after September 352 and Gaul in late 353 as Constantius II reunified the empire, is offered in Kent 1957, 81—although such an early date for Egypt does not fit with the papyrological evidence, which places the price jump after early 351. Broadly speaking, J. P. Callu ("The Distribution and the Role of the Bronze Coinage from A.D. 348 to 392," in *Imperial Revenue, Expenditure, and Monetary Policy in the Fourth Century A.D.; the Fifth Oxford Symposium on Coinage and Monetary History*, ed. C. E. King [Oxford: BAR Publishing, 1980], 227–228) dates the introduction of the new AE3 between 352 and the spring of 354."

25. Bagnall and Bransbourg, "The Constantian Monetary Revolution," 32.

which can be dated and traced to a mint. For now, it is sufficient to repeat the remarkable facts that of the 27,500 coins that have been recorded so far from the fourth century, only 499 come from the first third of the fourth century, and of those only 24 may be securely traced to a mint. This caesura between 298 and 330 is not only evident in hoards, where their absence might be attributed to a lower rate of hoarding; it is also found in the seriation of single coin finds from specific sites, such as Hawara, Abu Mena, Kellia, and Pelusium, which also present coins from before 297/8 and after 330, but not a single one dating to the aforementioned 35-year period.[26] It is therefore difficult to attribute the scarcity of coins from this period to patterns in hoarding or other causes. The remainder of the 27,500 bronze coins from the fourth century, about 7,000 in number, have been categorized in their respective publications or by Noeske as illegible, and thus may not be specifically dated to a period within the fourth century.

In Michael Ford's 2000 compilation of fourth- and fifth-century CE coin hoards from Egypt, the author continually references the original editors' and authors' remarks on the poor quality and illegibility of numerous coins within these hoards.[27] The illegibility is often dismissed as a product of the decay or extensive circulation of the coin, which may well be the case in many instances, as all bronze coinage, struck or mold-made, is susceptible to wear and corrosion. Molded or cast coins tend to have a smaller diameter, and the contour of the imagery is blurrier in later periods of the fourth century.[28] To the numismatist, however, this difference in diameter is not always diagnostic of manufacturing technique, since struck coins can be blurry as well, depending on the level of preservation of the coin and how long it was in circulation before being deposited. Thus little attention has been paid in the past to the measurements of individual coins when analyzing a hoard, nor to other physical traits, such as finesse, that may be indicative of the manufacturing technique of each coin. Much analysis thus needs to be done again on these bronze hoards. Given the quantity of coin molds found dating to the first half of the fourth century CE, however, one wonders where are these thousands of coinages produced from the clay molds? Perhaps they cannot be easily differentiated from struck coins at all.

Correlating coin molds to coins is not a straightforward endeavor; sets of evidence need to be reconciled. Metallurgical analyses on various types of bronze coins could perhaps offer further insight as to which coins were struck

---

26. This hoard analysis is still ongoing and thus unpublished, but the raw data may be found compiled in Noeske, *Münzfunde*, 15–207, 222–234, 235–242, 291–343.

27. M. Ford, "The Coin Hoards of Late Roman/Early Byzantine Egypt from the Reform of Diocletianus to the Reform of Anastasius, AD 294–491," *NC* 160 (2004), 335–367.

28. Lichocka, "Les moules," 197.

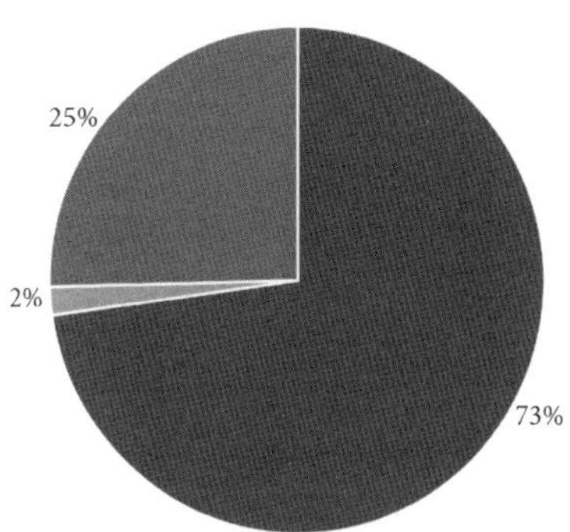

Figure 1. Number of coins.

and which were cast, if one accepts the assumption that the silver content in cast coins would be more irregular than in officially struck coins, or even non-existent. How much care was devoted to the composition of the molten metal poured into molds remains unknowable, but a metallurgical analysis of silver content in bronze coins from this period would offer substantial insight into the manufacturing process of non-official coinage and should be done to advance our understanding of the production of these coins. It would be beneficial to present an overview of the periods of the coin molds in order to place them more precisely in chronological periods within the fourth century. In fact, the exact chronology and typology of the clay coin molds in Dionysias has only been superficially studied and a future project has been announced in 2019 by the IFAO, which will quantify and study the chronology and series of the coin molds from Dionysias in depth.[29]

To summarize the argument up to this point: the archeological record provides remarkably small numbers of officially struck bronze *nummi* securely dated to the first third of the fourth century, whereas *nummi* minted between 340–408 CE are found by the tens of thousands. (Fig. 1) A large percentage of the bronze *nummi*, namely the 7000, are of such a poor quality as to be illegible and undatable at first instance but perhaps a focus on their physical character-istics, such as their diameter, will be able to place them more precisely during

29. J. P. Ghihard, *Contrefaire la monnaie dans la Vallée du Nil au début du Ive siècle. Un nouvel examen des moules en terre cuite de Dionysias (Qasr-Qārūn, Égypte) dans le cadre d'une mission scientifique Attribuée par L'IFAO (Institut français d'archéologie orientale, Le Caire)* (blog) (March 22, 2019), https://craham.hypotheses.org/2038?fbclid=IwAR2cSH1BzmNxAV ohtMUmzZXF39l9Cwn-jgZ5WcuwEetOto3u6OV6P8AQxYo.

the fourth century. A closer study and quantification of the illegible coinages will ensure the likeability of this, and perhaps it would solidify this hypothesis. What remains clear is that in Egypt a deficiency of small denomination coinage struck at the official mint at Alexandria during the early fourth century may be identified, based on the skimpy archaeological record of bronze coins and on the presence of tens of thousands of coin molds from the same period.

COIN MOLDS

Official coins from the mint of Alexandria during the Graeco-Roman period were usually struck. A fresh flan would be placed over a die, which contained the obverse negative of a coin, and then it was struck with a mallet, which contained the negative impression of the reverse type. Due to the malleability of the metal in the flan, the crisp definition of the obverse and reverse impressions in the die, and the force used to strike the flan, officially struck coins are easily recognizable if they have not been subject to extensive wear and use. If they have been in lengthy circulation, however, and subject to constant handling and weathering, the quality of the impression may decline until it becomes hard to tell if the coin has been officially struck or made from the mold of another coin. Therefore, the identification of a cast versus a struck coin depends substantially on the state of preservation of the object, which is an uncontrolled variable.

By contrast, coin molds are unmistakable. There are two main types of coin molds. One of them consists of a cylinder formed from various clay disks impressed with the obverse and reverse of a coin. Once the cylinder contains about 10 molds, a triangular incision is made along its length, into which the metal is poured. Once used, the clay molds were discarded. It is in these depositional contexts that thousands of used molds are found in Dionysias (Fig. 2). The second type consists of a clay disk into which a coin has been impressed multiple times; a channel is incised connecting each impression left by the coin and then molten metal is poured into the mold. Once the metal has hardened, the mold is broken, and the coins are separated and polished.[30]

The existence of coin molds in Egypt can be traced to the very beginning of the presence of coinage. In 2009, for example, excavations at the Karnak temple complex uncovered ceramic coin molds from the Ptolemaic period.[31] The practice was in continuous use, and one can find examples from various periods in

---

30. For a full description on the manufacturing process and useful illustrations, see Barakat, "Gussmunzen."

31. T Faucher, "Des monnaies grecques en Thébaïde : trouvailles monétaires dans Karnak ptolémaïque," in *La présence grecque dans la vallée de Thèbes*, ed. G. Gorre and A. Marangou (Rennes: Presses universitaires de Rennes, 2015), 141–146.

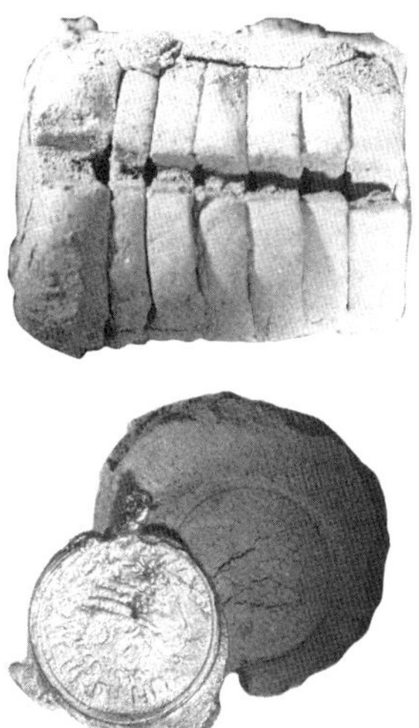

Figure 2. Coin mold from Dionysias.

Graeco-Roman Egypt up until the seventh century CE.[32] Even so, the scale on which they are found following Diocletian's reform is unparalleled. Just in the published material, we have nearly 2,888 molds found at Hermopolis Magna[33] and 15,000 at Dionysias; in a later campaign another 2,768 were excavated.[34] Excavations in a sector of Alexandria in 1880 uncovered 356 molds, and J. G. Milne published 153 molds from the 1903–1905 excavations at Oxyrhynchos.[35] There are 1,054 unpublished pieces (dating to 295–317 CE) present in the Cabinet des Médailles in Paris. There is also a small group of 14 molds dating to the Tetrarchic period in the Australian Center for Ancient Numismatics[36] and 6 molds

32. H.-C. Noeske, "Finds of Coins and Related Objects from the Monastery of Apa Shenute at Suhag," in P. Grossman, et al. "Second Report on the Excavation in the Monastery of Apa Shenute (Dayr Anba Shinuda) at Suhag," *Dumbarton Oaks Papers* 63 (2009), 210. Excavations at the White Monastery unearthed a clay mold for casting *dodecanummi* in the name of the emperor Phocas.

33. Schwartz and Wild, F*ouilles*, 39–48; M. Jungfleisch and J. Schwartz, *Les moules de monnaie imperials romaines* (Paris: Institut Français d'Archéologie Orientale, 1952), 250; Schwartz, "La monnaie d'Alexandrie," 99–105; Noeske, *Münzfunde*, 408.

34. Lichocka, "Les moules," cf. no. 2; Schwartz and Wild, *Fouilles*, 99–105; J. Schwartz, "La circulation monétaire dans l'Egypte du IVe siècle," *SMbl* 9 (1959), 11–17; J. Schwartz, "Sur quelques trésors du 4e siècle," *SMbl* 24 (1974), 45–48.

35. J. G. Milne, "The Coins from Oxyrhynchus," *JEA* 8.3–4 (1922), 158–163.

36. C. E. V. Nixon "Late Roman coin moulds in the Collection of the Australian Centre for Ancient Numismatic Studies (ACANS), Macquarie University, NSW," *JNAA* 24 (2013), 23–38.

in the University of Winnipeg collection.[37] Furthermore, Thomas Faucher has remarked (personal communication) that there are thousands of fourth century coin molds in storage in the Egyptian Museum in Cairo and about 16,000 uncatalogued molds at the Institut Français d'Archéologie Orientale in Cairo.[38] The British Museum contains a small collection of about 20 molds dated to 337–395 CE, very similar in size and clay composition to the ones found in Kom el-Dikka in Alexandria.[39] I have noted in the text above the instances when we know the date of these coin molds from their publication, however a further analysis and chronological seriation of the coin series represented in them is necessary.

The blurriness and poor quality of the ceramic molds often makes them illegible and thus hard to date, but it is not always impossible to do so. Chameroy compiled and dated the available coin molds, and by analyzing the differently combined impressions of the reverses of coins he identified two main production phases: 312–313 and 316–317 CE.[40] To put this in a wider chronological context, according to C. E. King there were nine recognized periods of coin-copying between the first century BCE and the fifth century CE. Of these nine, four occur during the fourth century in a nearly consecutive manner, between 310 and 360 (specifically in 310–318, 318–325, 330–348, and 348–360).[41] These periods, unsurprisingly, are also periods of strong debasement.

Debasement and coin mold production may not be directly related, however I believe that the occurrence of the two at a period in which we also have papyrological evidence for compulsory extraction of silver and gold bullion in kind from wealthy landowners may hint at the lack or at the very least at an extra need for precious metal by the state. To illustrate this point, I reproduce the following table from Bagnall, *Currency*, cataloguing the periods of debasement and the size of the largest *nummus* piece in each (Table 2).

The first period of debasement begins around 308, and this is also precisely the time to which the earliest and most numerous *nummi* coin molds are dated. Moreover, it has already been established by Bagnall, among other scholars, that

---

37. Lichocka, "Les moules."

38. Faucher, personal communication.

39. Lichocka, "Les moules."

40. J. Chameroy, "Münzgussformen des 3. Jahrhunderts in den Sammlungen des Römisch-Germanischen Zentralmuseums Mainz," *Jahrbuch des Römisch-Germanischen Zentralmuseums* 54 (2007 [2010]), 533–572.

41. C. E. King, "Roman Copies," in *Coin Finds and Coin Use in the Roman World—the 13th Oxford Symposium on Coinage and Monetary History 25–27 March 1993*, ed. C. E. King and D. G. Wigg (Berlin: G. Mann, 1996), 237–263.

these periods of debasement match periods of inflation identified on the basis of prices in the papyrological record.[42]

Table 2. Weight and Silver Content of *Nummus* by Period

Period	Weight of largest *Nummus*	Percentage of Silver
296–307	10 g	4% or 400 mg
308–312	7.75 g	3.8% or 295 mg
312–318	5.25 g	3.8% or 200 mg
318–324	3.4 g	3.3% or 112 mg
324–325	3 g	0.12% or 3.6 mg
325–330	3.05 g	2.1% or 63 mg
330–335	2.48 g	1.1% or 27 mg
336–337	1.61 g	1.5 % or 24 mg
337–341	1.64 g	1.4% or 23 mg
352–357	2.5 g	1.2% or 30 mg
357–358	< 2.5g	?
359–362	< 2g	?
363–364	2.9 g	?
364–375	2.3–2.4 g	0.2% or 4.7 mg

PRECIOUS METAL SUPPLY: COEMPTIONES, AND PAYMENTS TO THE ARMY

Bronze, gold, and silver coinages had different roles in ancient economic practice. The purchasing power of a bronze coin was far less than that of a silver or gold issue. Bronze facilitated the ease of exchange for quotidian transactions, while silver and gold were used for larger transactions, including purposes that were more central to the state, such as paying soldiers' salaries. If silver and gold were not available for these larger transactions, then large quantities of small-value bronze currency would have been needed to make larger payments.

There is in fact papyrological evidence from Egypt that clearly points to a shortage of silver and gold bullion for state needs during the first quarter of the fourth century. *P. Columbia* VII 138, 139, and 140, dated to 307/8 CE, are receipts for gold and silver bullion from Karanis, which form part of the archive of Aurelius Isidoros. Bagnall edited and analyzed these texts and concluded that these exactions did not represent an imposition on landowners, who were required to provide gold and silver bullion for purchase by the government at a

42. Bagnall, *Currency*, 31, 37.

determined price. The quantity of bullion was calculated based on the amount of taxes paid in wheat by the landowners, quantified in artabas, and it was then purchased by the state, with the amounts of gold and silver apparently equal in value. Because the state treated the relative value of the two metals as being at a ratio of 12:1, they required twelve times the quantity of silver as of gold. [43]

The requisitions present in these papyri do not exist in a vacuum and have actually been assessed by Jean-Michel Carrié in 1994, and widely accepted, as part of Diocletian's newly implemented fiscal and coinage reforms. In light of other literary evidence, Carrié proposed that these Tetrarchic requisitions, the *coemptiones* of precious metal in Egypt, are not particular to this province but part of exactions occurring throughout the empire, which later would be turned into a regular tax by Constantine.[44] The question of whether or not these requisitions were paid in kind or cash remains open, however, an unknown which has been delineated by Bransbourg most recently.[45]

While this requisitions of precious metal by the state may not be directly linked to the production of coinage, it is hard to imagine that during this period the representatives of the Roman state in Egypt (and the mint in Alexandria by extension) had access to large quantities of silver bullion. Furthermore, the need for this bullion is justified by papyrological evidence from the period detailing the payment of soldiers, a point that Jean-Michel Carrié initially suggested over four decades ago, and which he has recently reiterated in light of new evidence, and which Bransbourg has expanded upon with a monetary analysis.[46]

Using the Panopolis papyri, Carrié first suggested that the 2,500 *denarii donativum* mentioned in the texts likely implied a "625-denarii gratification for simple soldiers in 300 CE," a figure that Bransbourg has stated "works very well as a multiple of a coin worth 12.5 *denarii*—50 coins—rather than in *argentei*—12.5 coins…" As Bransbourg points out further in his analysis, this does not mean that silver coins were not incorporated into the pay, but it proves the need for a

---

43. See R. S. Bagnall, "Bullion Purchases and Landholding in the Fourth Century," *Chronique d'Égypte* 52 (1977), 322–336.

44. J.-M. Carrié, "Dioclétien et la fiscalité," *Antiquité Tardive* 2 (1994), 50, 56. See also Bransboug 2010.

45. G. Bransbourg, *Politique fiscale et enjeux de pouvoir dans le monde romain*. PhD diss. (Paris: École des Hautes Études en Sciences Sociales, 2010), 14–30.

46. J.-M. Carrié, "Finances militaires et fait monétaire dans l'Empire romain tardif," in *Les "dévaluations" à Rome. Époque républicaine et impériale. (Rome, 13–15 novembre 1975)*, ed. C. E. King (Rome: École française de Rome, 1978); J.-M. Carrié, "Aspects concrets de la vie monétaire en province." *RN* 159 (2003), 175–203; G. Bransbourg, "Inflation and monetary reforms in the fourth century: Diocletian's twin edicts of AD 301," in *Debasement. Manipulation of Coin Standards in Pre-Modern Monetary Systems*, ed. K. Butcher (London: Routledge, forthcoming).

base coinage to complete these payments.[47] Furthermore, the use of the terms "βαλλαντιον and αττικη represents a reasonable proof that billon and silver coins were both used to settle the monetary components of military pay."[48] Whether a *stipendium* (salary), *donativa* (gratifications) or *alimenta* (supplies), it is clear that base coinage was used to some extent to settle the payments during this period.

The state's limited access to supplies of precious metal and a strong need for base coinage could partially explain the need for alternative minting in the province. At present there are no metallurgical analyses of the silver content of cast coins, nor a clear identification of these in hoards or in the archaeological record, in order to provide comparative data for the officially minted series. Gara concluded that an uncontrolled quantity or complete absence of silver in the bronze currency in circulation would be particularly problematic for the minting authorities, who controlled the amount of precious metal in each official coin.[49] The fact that a large quantity of coin molds are dated to the same period, in which there is both a scarcity of officially minted coins, evidence for forced requisitions of precious metal, and evidence for the payment of soldiers using base coinage, clearly demonstrates that these phenomena are related. The mint at Alexandria could have been closed for a period of time due to this lack of silver bullion, or the *officinae* were reduced, creating an immense need for small-value currency.[50] The contemporaneous lack of high denomination currency could have fostered the use of small change for large monetary transactions, such as payments of the troops, which would mean that, given the difference in value, more and more billon or bronze coinage was needed for purchases, putting stress on a mint whose political situation had been tenuous for the preceding decades.[51]

47. Bransbourg, "Inflation." Bransbourg goes on to explain as a detailed analysis using the hypothesis proposed by Carrié, "Finances militaires," 235–238.

48. Bransbourg, "Inflation."

49. Gara, "Matrici," 248.

50. Ibid., 238.

51. W. E. Metcalf, "Aurelian's reform at Alexandria," in *Studies in Greek Numismatics in Memory of Martin Jessop Price*, ed. R. Ashton and S. Hurter (London: Spink, 1998), 269–276.

THE LEGALITY OF CAST COINAGE

Gara already offered a lengthy discussion of the legality of the coinage in her article, which allows me to summarize her conclusions:

- they can be distinguished from struck ones;
- they were not necessarily made using coins that were in circulation at the time;
- they were accepted without any evident resistance by their intended users;
- they tended to imitate the weight of the *nummus* (but without silver); thus they must represent the lowest (or one of the lowest) denominations in circulation;
- they are clearly, in the case of Dionysias, tied to and dependent on the military.[52]

Aspects of the numismatic evidence published since, and which I have discussed, however, seems to challenge or at least problematize part of Gara's conclusions. The first and foremost issue is that the Tetrarchic coin molds from Dionysias are considered in tandem with other forms of imitation coinages. Through the work of various scholars published in the last 40 years, which I have cited throughout this article, it is evident that this issue is not as straightforward. From the beginning of the fourth century and up until the time of Constantine the monetary situation in Egypt was undergoing continuous change, corroborated by papyrological evidence for prices.[53] Therefore, the cast coinages made during the Tetrarchic period may correspond to different realities than those manufactured in the latter fourth century.

Given the challenge of identifying cast coins within hoards, I believe they cannot be so easily differentiated from struck *nummi* of the time, particularly if the latter have been in circulation for a while before deposition. Therefore a many of Gara's assumptions and conclusions were made without there having been proper identification of these cast Tetrarchic *nummi*, let alone proper metallurgical analysis that would confirm the metal composition and weight.

We can assume they were accepted given their wide manufacture, but since evidence for actual use in a transaction remains obscure, we therefore have little clue as to how easily they were accepted, or if their users would be able to differentiate them from struck *nummi* (or if they even cared to differentiate). This

---

52. Gara, "Matrici," 245.

53. Bagnall, *Currency*. It was also treated more recently in Bagnall and Bransbourg, "The Constantian Monetary Revolution," 2–13.

kind of evidence, to my present knowledge, seems to have escaped even the papyrological evidence.

The large-scale presence of coin molds challenges the allegedly illegal status of imitation coinage in the empire, and points to a monetary system that relied on non-state coinage production for part of its needs. The clearly widespread use of these coin molds indicates that the practice of manufacturing cast coins could not have been a concealed practice in Egypt, a point that has been made ever since Schwartz initially published this discovery. Schwartz and Wild concluded that neither the nature of the work nor the resultant smoke emissions from the building in Dionysias manufacturing the coins could have possibly been concealed.[54]

Although the findspot for the molds at Dionysias was located about 100 meters from the local military camp,[55] the connection to the army is not lost. Another large workshop of imitative cast *nummi* has been discovered at the site of Bibe near Epernay, in Gallia Belgica. The fact that the two largest workshops producing imitative *nummi* have been found near military camps further asserts the view that these coinages were meant to serve the army stationed in these sites.[56] The army was the biggest consumer of local goods and was in constant need of coinage to maintain troops and pay soldiers' salaries. Furthermore, the army involvement in cast production could essentially legitimize the industry, a point which J.P. Callu has also reiterated.[57]

Gara concluded that given the papyrological evidence from the archive of Abinnaeus, prefect of the *ala V Praelectorum* and commander of the fort in Dionysias, the cast coinage was an autonomous local response on the part of agents of the state to the needs of the local villages, to make it possible to conduct monetary exchanges. The archive dates between 342 and 351 CE and elucidates the role the army played within the rural population in Egypt; they offered protection and provision of justice to the local villages in the Fayyum. Therefore, the cast coin could be seen as an official response to the large local need for currency.[58]

<hr>

54. Ibid., 234; Schwartz and Wild, *Fouilles*.

55. Gara, "Matrici"; Callu, "Distribution," 102.

56. Carrié, "Aspects," 195; J.-M. Carrié, "Ressources métalliques, politiques monétaires, production et circulation des espèces dans l'Empire romain tardif," in *Produktion und Recyceln von Münzen in der Spätantike / Produire et recycler la monnaie au Bas-Empire*, ed. J. Chameroy and P.-M. Guihard (Mainz: Römisch-Germanischen Zentralmuseums, 2016), 3–27.

57. J.-P. Callu, *La politique monétaire des empereurs romains de 238 à 311* (Paris: Écoles Françaises d'Athènes et de Rome, 1969).

58. Gara, "Matrici," 247.

As mentioned in the introduction, the question of the role of these cast coins in light of the legal texts has also been analyzed by Gara and thus I will not go into extensive detail of them in this article and will rather offer some brief thoughts on the matter. The laws preserved in the late antique codices of Roman law repeatedly condemn the practice of fusing coined metal. However, Gara has theorized that the army could be seen acting as a local minting authority in a time when the mint at Alexandria, for one reason or another, was not able to provide the needed supply of small-value currency. Therefore, as the producers of the coins were acting in an official role legitimized by the army, the laws forbidding the fabrication of cast coins could not be applied in this scenario; at any rate, the authority most likely to enforce the laws was the one implicated in their apparent violation.

Furthermore, the laws in the Theodosian code forbidding the illegal manufacture of coinage seem to evolve over time slightly, and specify a special concern and focus on the precious metal that was melted down from older coins in order to manufacture more.[59] The Constantinian law from 326 CE severely punishes the manufacture of illegal coinage, (*si quis nummum falsa fusion formaverit…*)[60] but years later, in 349, *Codex Theodosianus* IX.21.6 explicitly mentions *quam crebre separato argento ab aere purgare*, perhaps implying that it was the act of extracting the silver from official coinage that concerned the state the most.[61] Even if the official status of these coins was that they were illegal, it does not necessarily mean that the local authorities in Egypt frowned upon their use. Perhaps a more important question that remains unanswered is the value that these coins held in the market. Even if they were modeled after the *nummus*, were they accepted at the same nominal value?[62] Were they then a response to price inflation or a product of the state's lack of access to bullion? As I have shown, any single explanation for the existence of coin molds and their coins and their relationship to the precious metal supply would no doubt be an oversimplification of the multifaceted currency system and the complex market price relationships between metals.[63]

---

59. From Lichocka, "Les moules": *C. Th.* IX. 21.1,3,6,9,10; 23.1, *C. Just.* XI.11.2

60. *C. Th.* IX.21.3

61. For a more thorough discussion and primary sources on the legality of cast coins see Gara, "Matrici," 240–250. The author points to the complicated nomenclature for the different sets of coinages in circulation during this period as indicative of the complex numismatic reality.

62. Gara, "Matrici," 252.

63. See conclusions in Gara, "Matrici" and Bagnall, *Currency,* for more on the currency and inflation during the fourth century CE.

CONCLUSIONS

Identification and metallurgical analyses of the cast coinages are necessary in order to understand fully the role that they played in the monetary economy. The fact that cast-coin production was a widespread phenomenon in Egypt shows that at least for the first third of the fourth century the currency system was not being fully maintained by the Alexandrian mint alone, or even with imports from other imperial mints.

If there was a decentralized and autonomous mint at Dionysias, as with other centers where these coinages were produced, then the tolerated imitative coinage of low intrinsic value brings us into a functioning monetary economy made possible, in part, by freely minted coinage. This directly implies the practice, even if not theory, of a decentralized monetary policy in Egypt. The coin molds are a sign that the provision of coinage by the Alexandrian mint, and other mints outside of Egypt for that matter, must have not sufficed to maintain the highly monetized economy. Rathbone's 1991 analysis of the Heroninos archive from the third century CE concluded that Egyptian society was wealthy and highly monetized during this period. I am assuming, based on the evidence presented in this article, that the heavy dependency on a large quantity of coinage must have continued well into the fourth century.

Though the historical question of the legitimacy of coin molds has been debated in the past, numismatic analysis and papyrological evidence have corroborated Gara's hypothesis that these coins were quasi-official and functioned in response to a low output of small denominations by the Alexandrian mint. This case study of integrating analyses of coin molds, hoards, and papyri offers not only a preliminary understanding of the monetary situation in Egypt during a difficult period for historians to unravel but also reinforces the need for the utilization of multiple sets of data for historical analyses.

ACKNOWLEDGMENTS

This paper is a direct result of the research conducted at the American Numismatic Society's Eric P. Newman summer seminar in 2013. I would like to express my profound gratitude to Roger Bagnall and Gilles Bransbourg for their continuous guidance and editorial input throughout this process. The anonymous reviewer of this paper also made invaluable comments, which undoubtedly improved and focused my ideas. For that I am thankful.

BIBLIOGRAPHY

Bagnall, R. S. "Bullion Purchases and Landholding in the Fourth Century," *Chronique d'Égypte* 52 (1977): 322–336.

————.*Currency and Inflation in Fourth Century Egypt.* BASP Supplement 5. Atlanta: American Society of Papyrologists, 1985.

————. "Alessandra Gara," *Bulletin of the American Society of Papyrologists* 30 (1993), 79–80.

Bagnall, R. S., and G. Bransbourg. "The Constantian Monetary Revolution." ISAW Papers 14. http://dlib.nyu.edu/awdl/isaw/isaw-papers/14/#works-cited

Barakat, F. 2005. "Gussmunzen im romischen Agypten." In *L'exception égyptienne? Production et échanges monétaires en Egypte hellénistique et romaine, Actes du colloque d'Alexandrie, 13-15 avril 2002,* edited by F. Duyrat and O. Picard, 213–233. Paris: Institut Français d'Archéologie Orientale, 2019.

Blouin, K., and A. Burnett, "From kings to emperors: The development and integration of the Egyptian monetary system into the Roman Empire." In *L'argent est roi: L'économie monétaire en Égypte des Perses aux débuts de l'Islam, Orléans, du 29 au 31 octobre 2015,* edited by T. Faucher, 231–285. Paris: Institut Français d'Archéologie Orientale, 2020.

Bransbourg, G. *Politique fiscale et enjeux de pouvoir dans le monde romain.* PhD diss. Paris: École des Hautes Études en Sciences Sociales, 2010.

————. "Rome and the Economic Integration of Empire." *ISAW Papers* 3 (2012).

————. "Inflation and monetary reforms in the fourth century: Diocletian's twin edicts of AD 301." In *Debasement. Manipulation of Coin Standards in Pre-Modern Monetary Systems,* edited by K. Butcher. London: Routledge, forthcoming.

Bruun, P. M. *Roman Imperial Coinage* VII, *Constantine and Licinius A.D. 313–337.* London: Spink and Son, 1966.

Callu, J. P. *La politique monétaire des empereurs romains de 238 à 311.* Bibliothèque des Écoles Françaises d'Athènes et de Rome 214. Paris: Écoles Françaises d'Athènes et de Rome, 1969.

————. "The Distribution and the Role of the Bronze Coinage from A.D. 348 to 392."In *Imperial Revenue, Expenditure, and Monetary Policy in the Fourth Century A.D.; the Fifth Oxford Symposium on Coinage and Monetary History,* edited by C. E. King, 95–124. BAR International Series 76. Oxford: BAR Publishing, 1980.

Carrié, J.-M. "Finances militaires et fait monétaire dans l'Empire romain tardif." In *Les "dévaluations" à Rome. Époque républicaine et impériale. (Rome, 13–15 novembre 1975)*, edited by C. E. King, 227–248. CÉFR 6. Rome: École française de Rome, 1978.

———. "Dioclétien et la fiscalité." *Antiquité Tardive* 2 (1994): 33–64.

———. "Aspects concrets de la vie monétaire en province." *Revue Numismatique* 159 (2003): 175–203.

———. "Ressources métalliques, politiques monétaires, production et circulation des espèces dans l'Empire romain tardif," in *Produktion und Recyceln von Münzen in der Spätantike/Produire et recycler la monnaie au Bas-Empire*, edited by J. Chameroy and P.-M. Guihard, 3–27. Tagungen des Römisch-Germanischen Zentralmuseums 29. Mainz: Römisch-Germanischen Zentralmuseums, 2016.

Chameroy, J. "Münzgussformen des 3. Jahrhunderts in den Sammlungen des Römisch-Germanischen Zentralmuseums Mainz." *Jahrbuch des Römisch-Germanischen Zentralmuseums* 54 (2007 [2010]): 533–572.

Chameroy, J., et al. "L' officine De Faux-Monnayeurs De La Coulonche (Orne): Nummi Coulés De La Tétrarchie En Occident." *Numismatic Chronicle* 174 (2014): 153–191.

Davoli, P. "The Archaeology of the Fayum." In *The Oxford Handbook of Roman Egypt*, edited by Christina Riggs, 152–170. Oxford: Oxford University Press, 2012.

Heather, P. *The Fall of the Roman Empire: A New History of Rome and the Barbarians*. Oxford: Oxford University Press, 2005.

Ford, M. "The Coin Hoards of Late Roman/Early Byzantine Egypt from the Reform of Diocletianus to the Reform of Anastasius, AD 294–491." *Numismatic Chronicle* 160 (2004): 335–367.

Faucher, T. "Des monnaies grecques en Thébaïde : trouvailles monétaires dans Karnak ptolémaïque." In *La présence grecque dans la vallée de Thèbes*, edited by G. Gorre and A. Marangou, 141–146. Rennes: Presses universitaires de Rennes, 2015.

Gara, A. "Matrici di fusione e falsificazione monetaria nell'Egitto del iv secolo." *Numismatica e Antichità Classiche* 7 (1978): 229–252.

Gaspar, R. "Counterfeiting Roman Coins in the Roman Empire I–III A.D. Study on the Roman provinces of Dacia and Pannonia." *Journal of Ancient History and Archaeology* 2.4 (2015): 31–74.

Geissen, A. "The Coinage of Roman Egypt" in *The Oxford Handbook of Greek and Roman Coinage*, edited by W. E. Metcalf, 561–582. Oxford: Oxford University Press, 2012.

Ghihard, P. M. *Contrefaire La monnaie dans la Vallée du Nil au début du Ive siècle. Un nouvel examen des moules en terre cuite de Dionysias (Qasr-Qārūn, Égypte) dans le cadre d'une mission scientifique Attribuée par L'IFAO (Institut français d'archéologie orientale, Le Caire)* (blog). March 22, 2019. https://cra-ham.hypotheses.org/2038?fbclid=IwAR2cSH1BzmNxAVohtMUmzZXF39l9 Cwn-jgZ5WcuwEetOto3u6OV6P8AQxYo

Jones, A. H. M. *The Later Roman Empire, 284–602: A Social, Economic, and Administrative Survey.* Baltimore: Johns Hopkins University Press, 1964.

Jungfleisch, M., and J. Schwarz. *Les moules de monnaie imperials romaines.* Suppl. ASAE, Cahier 19. Paris: Institut Français d'Archéologie Orientale, 1952.

King, C. E. "Roman Copies." In *Coin Finds and Coin Use in the Roman World— the 13th Oxford Symposium on Coinage and Monetary History 25–27 March 1993,* edited by C. E. King and D. G. Wigg, 237–263. Berlin: G. Mann, 1996.

Lichocka, B. "Les moules égyptiens à monnaies tardives du British Museum." In *Archaeological Research in Roman Egypt. The Proceedings of the Seventeenth Classical Research 2008 Colloquium of the Department of Greek and Roman Antiquities, British Museum, held on 1–4 December, 1993,* edited by D. M. Bailey, 197–206. JRA Suppl. 19. Ann Arbor: Journal of Roman Archaeology, 1996.

———. "Bilan des découvertes monétaires dans les fouilles polonaises d'Alexandrie." In *L'exception égyptienne? Production et échanges monétaires en Egypte hellénistique et romaine, Actes du colloque d'Alexandrie, 13-15 avril 2002,* edited by F. Duyrat and O. Picard, 309–311. Paris: Institut Français d'Archéologie Orientale, 2005.

———. "Late Roman coin-finds from Kom el-Dikka in Alexandria." In *XIII Congreso internacional de numismática. Actas—Proceedings—Actes* I, edited by C. Alfaro, C. Marcos and P. Otero, 763–769. Madrid: Ministerio de cultura, Subdirección general de museos estatales, 2005.

Lorber, C. C. "The Coinage of the Ptolemies." In *The Oxford Handbook of Greek and Roman Coinage,* edited by W. E. Metcalf, 211–234. Oxford: Oxford University Press, 2012.

Luttwak, E. *The Grand Strategy of the Roman Empire.* Baltimore: Johns Hopkins University Press, 1976.

Metcalf, W. E. "Aurelian's reform at Alexandria." In *Studies in Greek Numismatics in Memory of Martin Jessop Price,* edited by R. Ashton and S. Hurter, 269–276. London: Spink, 1998.

Milne, J. G. "The Coins from Oxyrhynchus." *Journal of Egyptian Archaeology* 8.3–4 (1922): 158–163.

Monson, A. *From the Ptolemies to the Romans. Political and Economic Change in Egypt.* Cambridge: Cambridge University Press, 2012.

Nixon C. E. V. "Late Roman coin moulds in the Collection of the Australian Centre for Ancient Numismatic Studies (ACANS), Macquarie University, NSW." *Journal of the Numismatic Association of Australia* 24 (2013): 23–38.

Noeske, H.-C. *Münzfunde aus Aegypten. Prolegomenza zu einer Geschichte des spaetroemischen Münzumlaufs in Aegypten und Syrien/1, die Münzfunde des aegyptischen Pilgerzentrums Abu Mina und die Vergleichsfunde aus den Dioecesen Aegyptus und Oriens vom 4.–8. Jh. n. Chr.* Berlin: Gebr. Mann Verlag, 2000.

———. *Münzfunde aus Ägypten II, Die griechisch-römischen Münzfunde aus dem Fayum.* Mainz: P. von Zabern, 2006.

———. "Finds of Coins and Related Objects from the Monastery of Apa Shenute at Suhag." In P. Grossman, et al. "Second Report on the Excavation in the Monastery of Apa Shenute (Dayr Anba Shinuda) at Suhag." *Dumbarton Oaks Papers* 63 (2009): 167–219.

O. Picard, et al. *Les monnaies des fouilles du Centre d'études alexandrines: Les monnayages de bronze à Alexandrie de la conquête d'Alexandre à l'Egypte moderne.* Paris: Centre d'études alexandrines, 2012.

Rathbone, D. *Economic Rationalism and Rural Society in Third-Century A.D. Egypt: The Heroninos Archive and the Appianus Estate.* Cambridge: Cambridge University Press, 1991.

Sargent, T. J., and F. Velde. *The Big Problem of Small Change.* Princeton: Princeton University Press, 2002.

Schwartz, J. "La circulation monétaire dans l'Egypte du IVe siècle." *Schweizer Münzblätter* 9 (1959): 11–17.

———. "La monnaie d'Alexandrie et la réforme de Dioclétien." *Schweizer Münzblätter* 13–17 (1963–1967): 98–102.

———. "Sur quelques trésors du 4e siècle." *Schweizer Münzblätter* 24 (1974): 45–48.

Schwartz, J., and H. Wild. *Fouilles franco-suisses, Rapport I: Qasr-Qarun/Dionysias.* Paris: Institut Français d'Archéologie Orientale, 1950.

Thomas, D. J. "The Date of the Revolt of L. Domitius Domitianus." *Zeitschrift fur Papyrologie und Epigraphik* 22 (1977): 253–279.

AJN Second Series 32 (2020) pp. 339–388

Construction Sites, State Collections, Sixteenth-Century Spanish and Maltese Coins: The Via Maqueda Hoard in Context (Palermo, 1872)

PLATES 25–37   ANTONINO CRISÀ*

This article presents an account of the so-called Via Maqueda Hoard and offers, for the first time, documentary evidence and numismatic data traced at the Archaeological Museum "A. Salinas" and the Palermo City Council Archive. The hoard, found in Palermo's downtown area in 1872 within an urban construction site, was originally buried in the late sixteenth century. It contained 89 silver coins issued in Sicily, Spain, and Malta, which potentially reflected the island's contemporary coin circulation. This discovery generated a sensation in Palermo involving the city council authorities— Giovanni Fraccia, director of the National Museum, and Antonino Salinas, well-known numismatist and professor at the local university. The hoard was finally acquired by the museum, where it is still preserved.

INTRODUCTION

The history of archaeology and museum collections in Sicily during the post-Unification period (1861–1918) has recently raised interest among scholars due to fresh investigations in Italian archives and significant exhibitions held at local museums, such as the one dedicated to Antonino Salinas[1] and the National Mu-

*Marie Skłodowska-Curie Research Fellow, Department of Archaeology, Ghent University, Sint-Pietersnieuwstraat 35, B-9000 Ghent, Belgium (Antonino.Crisa@ugent.be).

1. Antonino Salinas (1841–1914) was mainly an archaeologist and numismatist. After having been a soldier of Giuseppe Garibaldi, he trained in Germany and then became one the first Italian professors of archaeology in Palermo, and was museum director for almost forty years (1873–1914). He was interested in ancient, medieval, and modern history; archaeology; and the numismatics of Sicily, with a strong regional perspective. Among his most remarkable works we

seum in Palermo (2014). This has consequently encouraged publications focusing on the impact of archaeology on local communities, the role of national and regional authorities dealing with casual discoveries, the evolution of archaeological methods and the formation of new state museum collections (Moscati and Di Stefano 2006, 14–21; Spatafora and Gandolfo 2014; Crisà 2018).

When the Kingdom of the Two Sicilies collapsed and Sicily became a region of the new Italian nation in 1861, the museum of the University of Palermo was rearranged in the former Oratory of the Fathers of Saint Philip Neri at Piazza Olivella, which was confiscated from the Church in 1866. Its first directors were Giovanni D'Ondes Reggio (1863–1870),[2] Giovanni Fraccia (1870–1873),[3] and especially Antonino Salinas (1874–1914), who shaped the museum as a regional representation of Sicilian history. The Commission of Antiquities and Fine Arts, a prestigious body created by the Bourbon government in 1827 to grant excavation and export licenses and offer advice on the safeguarding of antiquities, was operational until 1875, when it was superseded by the Ministry of Public Education in Rome (Pelagatti 2001; Crisà 2018, 34–36).

After the Unification period, urban development bloomed in Sicily, especially in major centers like Catania, Messina, and Palermo. New roads and railways were built starting in the mid-1860s, resulting in fresh numismatic discoveries, such as occurred in Cerda (Palermo, 1869), when a coin hoard was found along the new track construction (Crisà 2014a). Although poverty, lack of education, epidemics, and criminal associations caused some social tensions, the state capital of Sicily markedly developed and many construction sites opened in the downtown area between the late 1860s and 1870s. These comprised the erection or renovation of buildings and the creation or reconstruction of urban roads. Of course, construction involved digging activities in vast urban areas, generating archaeological discoveries, which often have been neglected by scholars.

---

can list *Le monete delle antiche città di Sicilia* (1867), *Del Museo Nazionale di Palermo e del suo avvenire* (1874) and *Breve guida del Museo Nazionale di Palermo* (1901) (La Corte Cailler 1907; Cagiati 1914; Pace 1926; Spatafora and Gandolfo 2014; Crisà 2018, 31–37).

2. Giovanni D'Ondes Reggio was interested in arts and archaeology. He was also a well-known novelist. Among his works we mention: *Roberto ossia il barone siciliano* (1838), *Giovanni Barresio signore di Militello* (1847) and *Sopra tre anelli antichi Greco-siculi* (1892).

3. Giovanni Fraccia (1824–1892) was a numismatist and archaeologist. After having directed the Palermo Museum, he became Director of the Cagliari Museum in Sardinia. He published some works on Sicilian archaeology and numismatics, like *Egesta e i suoi monumenti* (1859), *Antiche monete siciliane pubblicate pel primo dal Cav. Giovanni Fraccia* (1889–1890) and *Su due contromarche di monete romane* (1889).

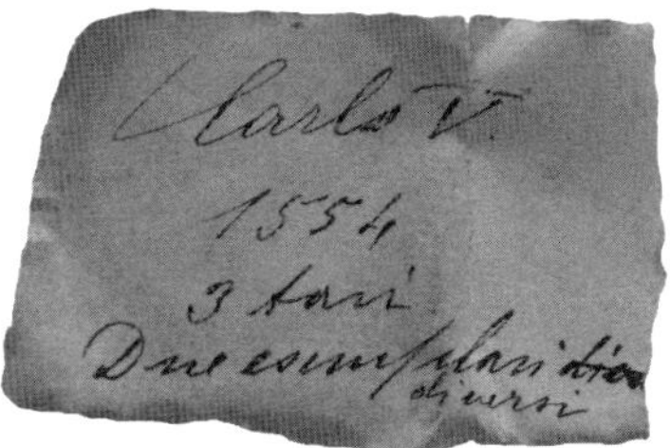

Figure 1. One of the cataloguing tags written by Salinas, still kept at the Palermo Museum (photograph by the author, by permission of the Archaeological Museum of Palermo).

Thanks to recent research carried out at the Palermo Museum (Museo Archeologico "A. Salinas") and the City Council Archive (Archivio Comunale di Palermo) in 2016–2017, we know that a hoard of silver coins issued in Sicily, Spain, and Malta during the sixteenth century was found in Via Maqueda in Palermo in 1872. This paper aims to offer a detailed account of this remarkable discovery and assess all documentary, archaeological, and numismatic data regarding the coin hoard. Such information is worth analyzing and is presented for two reasons: first, the discovery represents a significant case study in the history of Sicilian archaeology in the post-Unification period, shedding new light on state and regional authorities dealing with casual discoveries and all the bureaucratic procedures associated with antiquities protection and find acquisition by museum institutions. Second, the hoard, which has never before been studied, offers new data on hoarding trends and coin circulation in sixteenth-century Spanish Sicily, which was dynamic and also embraced Maltese coins.

First, the essay offers a historical reconstruction of the archaeological discovery by assessing all archival records. Second, it sheds new light on the hoard, giving a detailed analysis of its composition and outlining the historical background of sixteenth-century Sicily. Lastly, we provide final remarks on the Via Maqueda Hoard, placing it in a wider historical context and providing some hypotheses on its concealment. Records have been faithfully copied and chronologically arranged (Appendix A), as have the coins, which are properly catalogued and organized by kings and authorities (Appendix B), with reporting on the tags written by Salinas (Fig. 1).

VIA MAQUEDA: CONSTRUCTION SITES
AND CONTRACTORS IN PALERMO

Via Maqueda can be considered one of Palermo's main arterial roads, connecting Via Oreto (S–E) to Via Ruggiero Settimo (N–W) and crossing Via Vittorio Emanuele at "Quattro Canti" (Piazza Vigliena). In the early 1870s, the city council funded an extensive reconstruction of the road, sidewalks, and lighting, including replacement of old sewers and the laying of "Billiemi stone" paving slabs, extracted from local quarries outside Palermo. Since building operations would have been unmanageable, the city council made several public announcements (*avvisi per appalti*) to subdivide and subcontract the massive construction in preset sections.

One such subcontract was published on 30 August 1871, for bids on construction of the 500-meter section between Via dei Calderai and Porta di Vicari (Piazza Giulio Cesare, central railway station) junctions (Fig. 2). Local contractor Francesco D. Crisa obtained the tender, which was worth 492,475.31 *lire*. Construction began by late 1871 and ended on 26 April 1873, when an inspection by the city council established that the whole endeavor was properly realized, including the "Billiemi stone" slab installation (Fig. 3); a short section was open to the public as early as October 1872 (Appendix A, nos. 1, 6–7, 10–12, 26–27).

Records shed new light on contracting in late nineteenth-century Palermo, showing how any potential accident, fraud, or inaccurate execution might cause delays and damage. For instance, on 24 May 1872, contractor Crisa wrote to the Technical and Public Works Office of the Palermo City Council, complaining that gas pipelines had been previously installed at 0.5 meters depth (instead of 1.0 meter). This caused substantial delays and unforeseen costs to excavate, remove, and reinstall the pipelines. It is evident that the previous contracting company, called Faeres, operated dishonestly (Appendix A, nos. 7, 10–12).

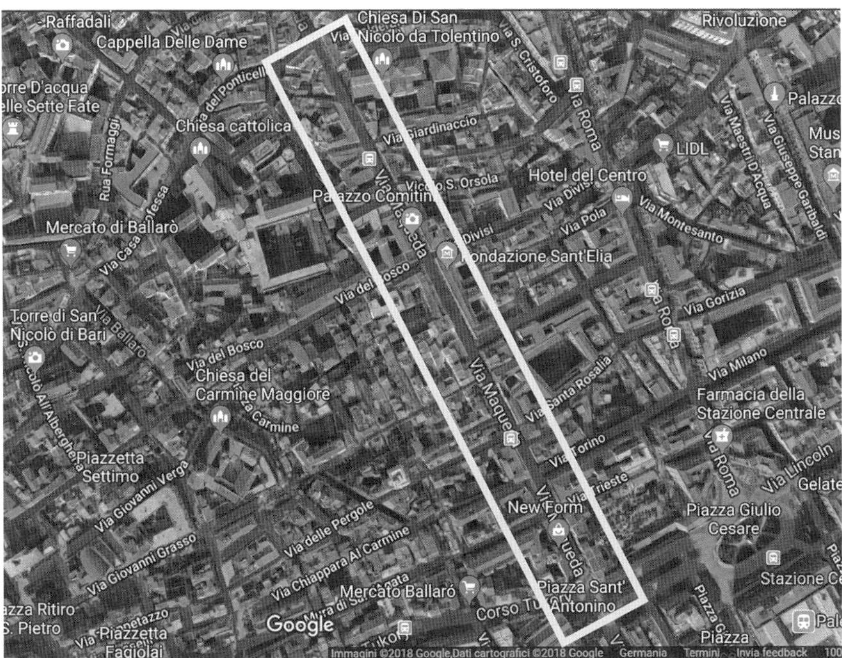

Figure 2. Map showing road section of Via Maqueda between Via Calderai and Porta di Vicari (map data © Google, from Google Maps).

Figure 3. View of Via Maqueda at Via Calderai-Ponticello crossroad and the Billiemi stone sidewalk in Palermo's downtown, in the area where the hoard was presumably discovered (photograph by the author).

DISCOVERY OF THE HOARD, ANTONINO SALINAS,
AND THE PALERMO MUSEUM

Construction and reconstruction activities involved excavation and substantial soil removal. Of course, this happened in Via Maqueda, where workers dug trenches between 0.5 and 1.0 meter in depth. Archaeological discoveries could occur within these operations. In the early post-Unification period, Sicily benefited from a well-established system of antiquities protection, derived from Bourbon legislation. The system was somewhat efficient, thanks to the activity of the Commission of Antiquities and Fine Arts, still active until 1875. If discoveries were not properly documented, finds might be lost, scattered, or sold on the antiquities market (Di Stefano 1956, 362–367; Giuffrida 1984; Crisà 2018, 120–122).

Luckily, the Via Maqueda Hoard was properly preserved in 1872, although our documentation lacks specific data regarding the exact place and date of the discovery. As records traced at the Archivio Comunale di Palermo clearly prove, the only main construction site in Via Maqueda was located between the Via dei Calderai and Porta di Vicari junctions. In this section of the road, workers found the hoard. Unfortunately, we do not know in front of which urban block or house the treasure was discovered. The exact date of discovery is also unknown; from the records, it can only be argued that the hoard was unearthed between January and the end of April 1872.

We know that D. Peranni, the mayor of Palermo, wrote to Salinas and the Commission of Antiquities and Fine Arts on 16 May, saying that a treasure of Spanish silver coins had been casually found in a pot (evidently made of ceramic). Authorities were able to seize only 76 coins. It is evident that many coins were scattered, and the hoard actually might have been much more substantial. Peranni sent those "surviving" coins to Salinas, asking for a detailed numismatic analysis and evaluation. Including 13 additional coins, recovered on 23 May, Salinas received 89 specimens (Appendix A, nos. 3–4, 8).

The most significant record is certainly Salinas's numismatic report on the Via Maqueda Hoard (Appendix A, no. 9). It is a nine-page, undated document, probably written in May 1872, that offers essential data on the hoard's composition and its acquisition by the Museum; it also provides a detailed list of coins. At the time, Salinas had been a professor of archaeology at the University of Palermo since 1867, and he was already a well-known numismatist, having published *Le monete delle antiche città di Sicilia* (1867). He was often appointed to evaluate coins to be acquired by the Palermo Museum. For instance, he had studied two

Greek coins of Queen Philistis in 1868 and had analyzed an eighteenth-century coin hoard, found in the Palermo-Cerda railway construction site in 1869 (Crisà 2014a; Crisà 2014b, 280–281).

A detailed analysis of the hoard is provided in the following section. At this point, it is crucial to explain how Salinas assessed the hoard and why he recommended its acquisition to the Palermo Museum. First, he declared that the silver coins were extremely common in the current antiquities market in Sicily and did not have any value. In fact, Salinas had a deep knowledge of the market, considering his thick network of contacts in Palermo, the main Sicilian center for the antiquarian trade. On the other hand, Salinas, confirming that the coins were not valuable, cleverly encouraged Palermo's city mayor to get rid of them through an official donation to the Museum.

Second, Salinas asserted that no one (neither private collectors nor public institutions) had been interested in collecting and keeping modern Sicilian coins in the past. This explained why they did not have any value on the market in the 1870s. Salinas had declared the same when assessing the eighteenth-century Cerda Hoard. Above all, the majority of public numismatic collections in Bourbon Sicily were essentially formed of Greek and Roman coins (Appendix A, no. 9: "…nel commercio degli oggetti antichi non si dà ad essere valore alcuno, perché privati e musei pubblici non pensarono sia oggi a formare raccolte di monete siciliane recenti") (Crisà 2012, 53–54; Crisà 2014a, 347–348).

Salinas stated that he was promoting a remarkable numismatic collection at the Palermo Museum—atypical for contemporary collecting trends—featuring coins of all Sicilian kings from the Normans to the Bourbons. Thus, the donation of the Via Maqueda Hoard would have been much welcomed for historical and numismatic studies, as well as for the wider public in Palermo. We know Salinas had similarly justified acquisition of the Cerda Hoard in 1869, even though he had opted to acquire only a selection of well-preserved eighteenth-century Sicilian coins lacking from the museum collection (Appendix A, no. 9: "Ho sempre promesso nel nostro Museo la formazione di una serie non interrotta di monete siciliane dai tempi Normanni"; "opera di grande utilità agli studj storici e numismatici") (Crisà 2014a, doc. no. 3, 351–52).

Salinas was successful. The Municipal Council of Palermo approved the donation of the Via Maqueda Hoard to the Royal Museum on 25 May 1872; the coins were offered through a permanent "safekeeping" gift. Peranni wrote to both Salinas and the Museum director on 28 May, reporting the donation (Appendix A, nos. 13, 15–17).

Once the coins were donated, on 4 June Peranni contacted the editorial staff of the *Giornale di Sicilia*, one of the main Sicilian newspapers based in Palermo. Thereafter, an unknown journalist wrote a brief article in the night edition of the newspaper (issue no. 127), announcing the donation of the hoard (Appendix A, no. 21). Meanwhile, G. Fraccia wrote a new numismatic report on the coin hoard, which is not dissimilar to Salinas's evaluation. The hoard was finally registered in the museum's *Giornale d'Entrata* as object no. 107 (including 89 coins) on 5 June. Two days later, Fraccia wrote to Giovanni Daita, head of the Commission of Antiquities and Fine Arts, announcing the acquisition. Lastly, Giuseppe Misasi and Carmelo Mustaca, two Calabrian workers who had discovered the hoard while working in Via Maqueda, obtained deserved awards (15 and 5 *lire*, respectively) offered by the Palermo City Council (Appendix A, nos. 22–25).

COMPOSITION AND BURIAL OF THE VIA MAQUEDA HOARD

Before analyzing the composition of the hoard, it is important to provide some historical insight into sixteenth-century Sicily, when the treasure was formed and finally buried. Sicily was ruled by the Spanish. Ferdinand II the Catholic (1479–1516), one of the most powerful kings in Europe, promoted a significant alliance between the Church, Venice, Spain, the Holy Roman Empire, and England (1511). Sicily played a leading role in Europe for its commercial routes and busy ports. Subsequently, Charles V of the House of Habsburg (1516–1556), ruler of the Holy Roman Empire and the Spanish Empire, offered Malta to the Knights of Saint John, since they had just lost Rhodes to the Ottomans. The knights of the Order, led by Grand Master Philippe de Villiers de l'Isle-Adam (1464–1534), officially took possession of the island in 1530. Malta, controlled by the Spanish, was a pivotal point of strength for maritime commerce and economy in the Mediterranean, like Sicily, whose coasts and ports were sacked by Barbarossa Hayreddin Pasha (1478–1546). Once the king defeated the fearsome pirate in 1535, Sicilians greeted Charles as a savior. Philip II (1554–1598) established a vital monetary reform, introducing new silver issues: the *scudo* (or 10-*tarì*), *mezzo scudo* (or 5-*tarì*), 3-*tarì*, 1-*tarì*, and *mezzo tarì* (Mack Smith 1968, 171–180; Trasselli 1969, 28–30; Trasselli 1970, 208–209; Battlori 1977; Trasselli 1982a, 48–53; Trasselli 1982b; Sant 1983, 233–234; Pannuti and Riccio 1984, 90–91, 106–107; Giuffrida 2006, 11–12; Travaini 2013, 36–38; Locatelli 2017, 1138).

As far as we know from archival records, the Via Maqueda Hoard contained at least 89 silver coins. This is the quantity of coins finally donated to the Palermo Museum; it can be argued that the original hoard, found in a pot, contained more specimens, which were partially scattered. At present, we have traced and fully catalogued 76 coins at the museum (Appendix B, nos. 1–76), which have not undergone conservation. However, their preservation is fairly good; it seems that some specimens did not circulate extensively, like the 11 *scudi* of Philip II (Appendix B, nos. 54–64).

The Via Maqueda Hoard contains silver coins issued between 1516 and 1581, under five Spanish and Maltese rulers. The oldest coins were issued by Charles V (Charles I of Spain and Charles II of Sicily, 1516–1556), while the most recent were released by Jean l'Evesque de la Cassière (1572–1581) in Malta. The hoard mostly includes coins of Philip II (47, 61.8%) and Charles V (13, 17.1%) and Maltese issuers (12, 15.8%) (Table 1).

Table 1. Issuers represented in the Via Maqueda Hoard

Issuer	Number of Coins	%	Appendix B (Catalogue)
Charles I (1516–1556) or Philip II (1556–1598) with the names of Ferdinand II and Isabella I	4	5.26	1–4
Charles V (1516–1556)	13	17.10	5–17
Philip II (1556–1598)	47	61.84	18–64
Jean Parisot de Valette (1557–1568)	10	13.15	65–74
Pietro del Monte (1568–1572)	1	1.31	75
Jean l'Evesque de la Cassière (1572–1581)	1	1.31	76

The hoard shows coins with a wide range of face values, which possibly reflects contemporary coin circulation in Sicily. On the whole, it is possible to identify 51 Sicilian (67.1%) and 25 "foreign" issues (32.9%). The most frequently attested coins are the Sicilian 4-*tarì* (15, 19.7%), 3-*tarì* (14, 18.4%), *scudo* (or 10-*tarì*) (11, 14.5%) and 5-*tarì* (or ½-*scudo*) (7, 9.2%), chiefly used for transactions of medium value. The 2-*tarì* is less attested (4, 5.3%). Among the "foreign" currency, Spanish 4-*reales* (10, 13.2%) and Maltese 4-*tarì* (8, 10.5%) are the most common (Fig. 4, below).

Coin provenance is varied, showing a prevalence of Sicilian issues and also some foreign ones from the Mediterranean area (Fig. 6, below). The hoard contains 51 coins struck by the mint of Messina (67.1%), which was the main coin supplier in sixteenth-century Sicily, followed by Malta (12, 15.8%), the Spanish mints of Seville (8, 10.5%), Valladolid (2, 2.6%), and Barcelona, Cuenca, and Toledo (1 specimen for each mint, 1.3%) (Fig. 5, below).

In his numismatic report, Salinas provided us with a basic interpretation of the hoard's date. Considering the condition of the most recent coins, which

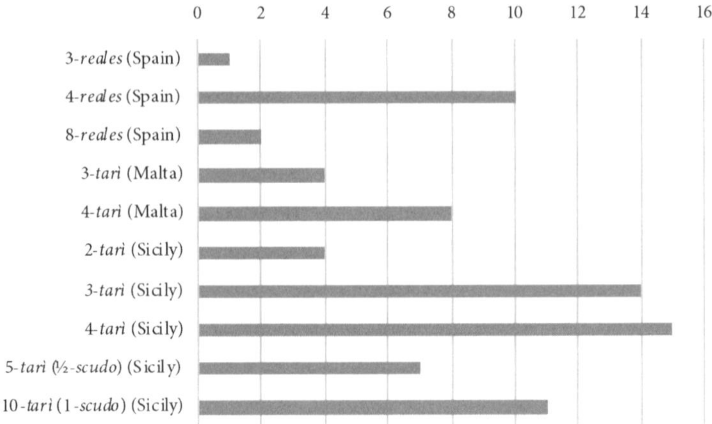

Figure 4. Graph showing the number of coins of each denomination represented in the Via Maqueda Hoard.

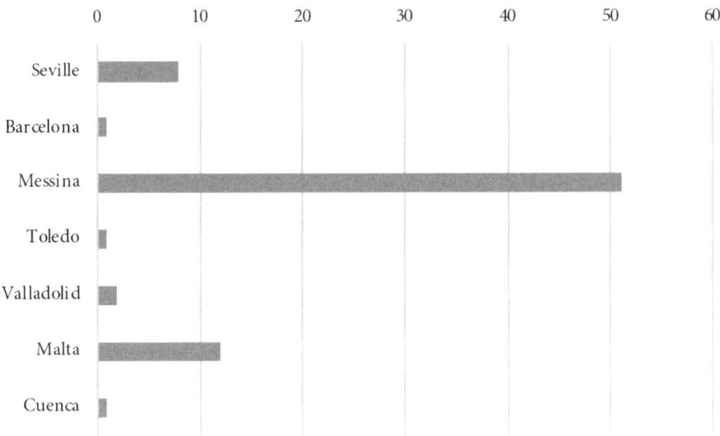

Figure 5. Graph displaying the number of coins of each mint represented in the Via Maqueda Hoard.

probably did not extensively circulate, the hoard was buried between 1581 (Salinas erroneously reported 1582), the last year that Jean l'Evesque de la Cassière served as Grand Master of the Order of Malta, and 24 July 1600, when the Spanish government began to build up Via Maqueda (Appendix A, no. 9: "La freschezza di conservazione delle ultime monete che ho citato provano che quel tesoretto dovette essere sepolto negli ultimi decenni del sec. XVI"). Lasting for

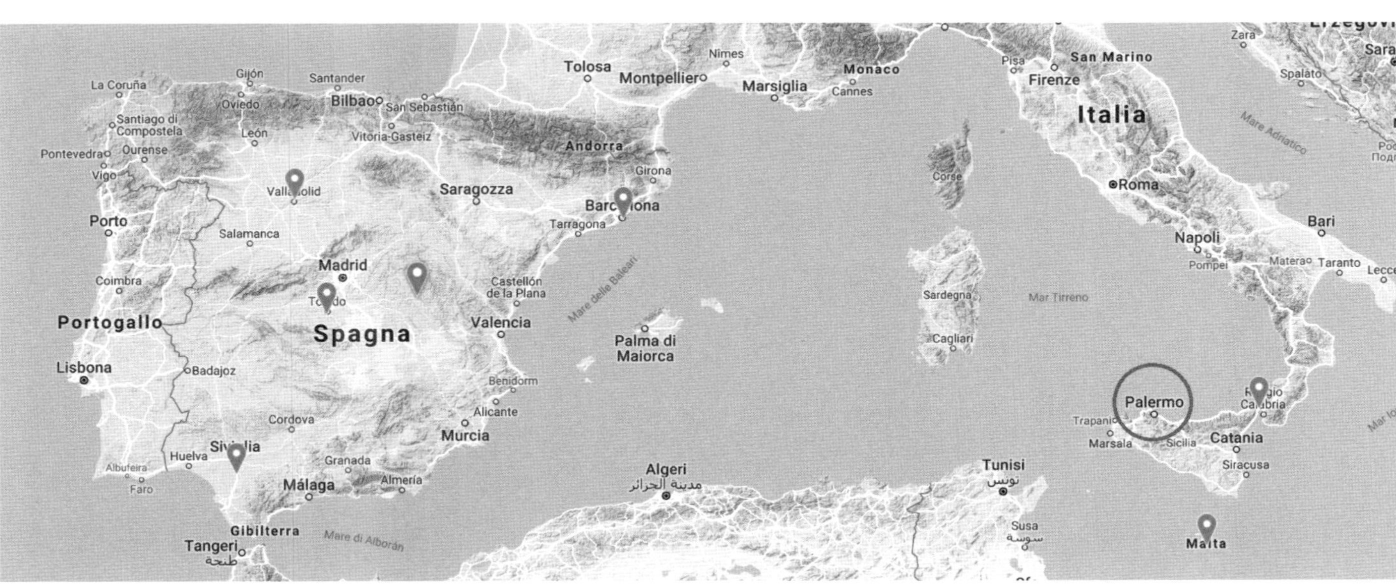

Figure 6. Map showing the Sicilian and foreign mints represented in the Via Maqueda Hoard (map data © Google, via Click2Map.com).

many years due to various delays and lack of funding, the initial construction in Via Maqueda, which was extensive and very costly, attracted investors and markedly transformed Palermo's downtown plan (Trasselli 1970, 202–203; Di Fede 1995, 111; De Seta and Di Mauro 2002, 76–77, 84; La Lumia 2004, 30–31; Vesco 2015).

The nineteen-year span proposed by Salinas for the hoard's concealment is certainly plausible, even though we can argue that the hoard was potentially buried in the 1580s, since we do not have any coins issued following this period.

FINAL REMARKS

Benefiting from archival, archaeological, and historical data, our assessment of the Via Maqueda Hoard has revealed significant insights into post-Unification Palermo, showing how a casual discovery could generate a sensation, involving entrepreneurs, workers, safeguarding authorities, a city mayor (Peranni), a famous numismatist (Salinas), and a museum curator (Fraccia). These characters were part of a network—such as those identified in the Palermo and Messina provinces (Crisà 2018, 124–125)—which provides us much information on how they acted and collaborated with each other. Furthermore, the hoard analysis improves our knowledge on hoarding trends and coin circulation in sixteenth-century Sicily. The scope of this section is to provide some final remarks and considerations on these aspects.

The Via Maqueda Hoard has to be contextualized in its contemporary Sicilian historical context, in order to better understand its role in the island's economy. When the hoard was buried (presumably in the 1580s), Sicily played a leading role in the economy of the Mediterranean basin, as a central pole or merging point for commercial routes between the Iberian Peninsula, northwestern Italy, northern Africa, and Malta, despite the harmful incursions of pirates. Sicily was also a primary exporter of grain, fish, pottery, silk, and sugar, generating an impressive movement of goods, transactions, and shipping in its flourishing ports, especially in Messina, Palermo, and Trapani. Even the slave trade prospered. As said, coin circulation was dynamic, including foreign currencies (such as Maltese), which were accepted in transactions and could obviate the problem of substantial forgeries of silver coins. Genoese bankers and merchants operated successfully, as well as foreign investors (Mack Smith 1968, 172–173; Trasselli 1970, 225, 230–232; Trasselli 1977; Sant 1983, 234–235; Giuffrida 2006, 60–61; 76, 96, 114; Locatelli 2017, 1140).

In such a context, as Trasselli has clearly proved in assessing vital records, Gentile, a powerful Genoese banker based in Palermo in the 1570s, managed the funding and saving of the Maltese *Ricevitoria*, directed by Friar Onofrio Acciaiuoli. The Order of Malta, which mobilized substantial current assets in Sicily, therefore had a local revenue office branch in Palermo for this purpose. Once they moved to Malta in 1530, thanks to Charles V, the Knights enjoyed many privileges in Sicily as well (Mifsud 1918, 207–208; Trasselli 1970, 203–204; Giuffrida 2006, 11–12, 16, 22–23, 41–42).

Maltese coins (15.7%) play a significant role in the Via Maqueda Hoard. They had been accumulated and finally buried together with various Spanish and Sicilian coins, which were certainly circulating much more in late sixteenth-century Sicily. It is evident that Maltese coins were fully accepted in Sicily for important reasons. First, L. Travaini argued that those coins circulated substantially in Sicily due to a "local silver famine" on the island and in southern Italy (Travaini 2013, 39; Locatelli 2017, 1140).

Second, both Sicily and Malta were on the same commercial routes and in the orbit of the powerful Spanish dominions; this also had an impact on Mediterranean economics. Therefore, Maltese currency was welcomed in daily-life transactions in Sicily. Third, Maltese and Sicilian silver *tarì* could be easily exchanged and used in transactions on both islands due to their similar weight and intrinsic value (e.g., average weights: Maltese 4-*tarì*, 11.31 g; Sicilian 4-*tarì*, 11.53 g).[4]

The hoard composition certainly reflects that of one of the other contemporary hoards discovered in Sicily. The so-called Lipari 2 Hoard, found in the *Castello* of Lipari (Messina) in 1958, contained 296 silver coins, mostly minted in Messina (80%) by Ferdinand II of Aragon, Charles V, and Philip II. In addition to those coins, Locatelli identified Iberian issues (mints of Burgos, Granada, La Coruña, Segovia, Seville, and Toledo) as well as Maltese issues of Juan de Homedes (1536–1553), and even Jean de Valette (1557–1568), whose coins are also attested in the Via Maqueda Hoard. Both hoards can be considered in line with contemporary coin circulation, containing mostly Sicilian coins associated with foreign currency from Malta (Locatelli 2017, 1139–1140). Maltese silver coins have been also documented in other sixteenth-century coin hoards discovered in Sicily (e.g., Girgenti-Agrigento 1905: 4-*tarì* of Jean Parisot de Valette) (Cassarino Tranchina 1995, 212 n. 9).

Records from the archives in Palermo's Museum and city council have provided us essential data on the discovery of the hoard, even if some aspects are still unknown. For instance, we do not know where exactly the hoard was found.

---

4. Averages have been calculated on the following specimens: Maltese 4-*tarì*, issued by Jean Parisot de Valette, Pietro del Monte and Jean l'Evesque de la Cassière (Appendix B, nos. 69–76); Sicilian 4-*tarì* issued by Philip II (Appendix B, nos. 38–46).

Was it buried in former private or public land on Via Maqueda? A quick hint to a land parcel or building lot would have been very useful in tracing the original findspot of our hoard, by affording the ability to view a relevant map in the local archives (e.g., the real estate registry office). At present, our records do not show these data, but future investigations and discoveries in the archives might clarify this aspect.

What was the final destiny of missing and scattered coins? As said, we do not know the exact number of coins found in the pot in Via Maqueda, although records show two Calabrian workers were rewarded by the city council for having honestly ceded the coins. However, it can be inferred that some coins were stolen by dishonest workers and maybe illegally sold to local silversmiths, who were very keen on purchasing and melting down ancient and modern coins. This often occurred in nineteenth-century Sicily, of course including Palermo (Lagumina 1895, 360; Crisà 2012, 52–53; Crisà 2018, 111).

In terms of museum studies, the acquisition of the Via Maqueda Hoard by the Palermo Museum is remarkable. Undoubtedly it confirms how acquiring finds could be very successful for museum authorities at that time. Donations by the Palermo City Council (or other institutions) and private donors were always advantageous, since the museum could acquire finds at no cost.

The role of Salinas appears essential in this process. As a coin expert, he evaluated the coin hoard professionally. Clearly, Salinas's policy of promoting donations to increase ancient and modern collections became known before he was appointed as a museum director. His action clearly shows his thick network of contacts in Palermo on a civic, curatorial, and institutional scale. Furthermore, the Via Maqueda Hoard event holds a strong political aspect. Salinas, Peranni, and Fraccia represent a network themselves, interacting with each other and personally operating to obtain prestige on local, regional, and national scales. The first aspired to increase his reputation as a numismatist and potential curator; the second, as a city mayor, could demonstrate his effective interest in promoting local cultural heritage and the study of Sicilian history among his citizens (and voters, of course); the third demonstrated a willingness to promote and increase the museum collections (although Salinas had evaluated them).

Records from the Palermo Museum offer some essential information on the role of the press (e.g., the regionally widespread *Giornale di Sicilia*) in nineteenth-century Sicily. As has previously emerged (Crisà 2018, 114–115), it is evident how local curators, museum directors, and safeguarding authorities contacted and used the press to disseminate casual discoveries and find acquisitions by public institutions. This process contributed not only to thanking those authorities who were personally involved, but also boosted their political prestige and reputation among the wider public.

Studying and assessing a coin hoard always implies speculation on the reasons why a hoard has been concealed. Regarding the treasure found in Via Maqueda, we can opt for two hypotheses. First, it is possible that it represented a provisional store of coins, temporarily collected by a local businessman who may have been involved in shipping and naval commerce (e.g., grain, silk, or sugar). As a temporary deposit, coins were probably ready to be invested in buying merchandise or building and construction activities in late sixteenth-century Palermo (Trasselli 1970, 202). Second, it is possible that the hoard was concealed by a foreign merchant who came to Palermo to invest his small wad of coins. Of course, we will never know why the owner did not recover his hoard.

Lastly, our investigation of the Via Maqueda Hoard has shed new light on an essential case study about hoarding trends in sixteenth-century Sicily, and also on the role of Salinas and local authorities dealing with casual discoveries in Palermo. Such information represents a remarkable tessera to reconstruct the history of archaeology and museum collections in post-Unification Sicily, a subject which constantly needs to be supported by fresh archival and historical research.

APPENDIX A: ARCHIVAL RECORDS

1. ACP, busta 886, headed paper, 1 side

S.P.Q.P.

AVVISO PER APPALTO

Dovendosi dare in appalto la ricostruzione della via Macqueda dai Calderaj a Porta di Vicari e delle strade che come necessarj raccordi ne dipendono, la cui spesa è stata estimata per L. 492475,31 s'invitano tutti coloro che volessero concorrere a detto appalto a presentare le loro offerte al Sindaco; perché potesse indi mettersi all'asta pubblica, ne' modi di legge, quella che a giudizio della Giunta Municipale presenterà le maggiori convenienze.

Si previene all'uopo, che il progetto de' lavori, la relazione della spesa, ed il Capitolato dell'appalto sono depositati presso l'ufficio de' Lavori Pubblici, dove chiunque potrà prenderne conoscenza—E che nell'offerta dovranno particolarmente specificarsi le condizioni seguenti cioè: tempo da impiegare ne' lavori, modo di pagamento degli stessi, avuto riguardo alle condizioni finanziare del Comune, cauzione per garenzia de' lavori medesimi.

Palermo 30 agosto 1871.

Il Sindaco – D. PERANNI

Off. tip. diretto da B. Lima.

2. AMARAS, U.A. 420, headed paper, 1 side

Categoria 7

Cassetta 1

Fasc. 76

DIREZIONE DEL MUSEO NAZIONALE DI PALERMO E DEGLI SCAVI

1872

OGGETTO: Deposito (in entrata) Monete d'oro[5] rinvenute nella via Maqueda.

3. AMARAS, U.A. 420, headed paper, 1 side

MUSEO [NAZIONA]LE DI PALERMO | 26 APR. 73 | N. 3
CITTÀ DI PALERMO
UFFICIO CENTRALE

---

5. This is a mistake, because the hoard contains only silver coins.

N.º 2406.
Oggetto: Per illustrazione di monete

Palermo 16 Maggio 1872.

Egregio Prof. Antonio Salinas

Occasionalmente alla ricostruzione della via Macqueda si rinvenne una pentola
con una quantità di monete di argento dell'epoca spagnuola, delle quali il Municipio ne ha finora ricuperato N. 76 pezzi.
Però volendo conoscere il valore e la importanza storica per le ulteriori determinazioni che converrà prendere io non saprei meglio dirigermi che alla S.V.
Illma, la quale essendo maestra in questo genere di studi, potrebbe agevolmente favorirmi dei suoi lumi sul riguardo.
Mi permetto quindi farle tenere le succennate monete nel numero sopra indi-
cato, e fiducioso che avrà la bontà di accogliere la mia preghiera, standomi in
attenzione de' suo' favori colgo intanto l'occasione per segnarmi co' sensi della
più alta considerazione.

Il Sindaco
D. Peranni

4. AMARAS, U.A. 420, headed paper, 1 side
Palermo 16 Maggio 1872.
CITTÀ DI PALERMO
UFFICIO CENTRALE
N.º 2406.
Oggetto: Per illustrazione di monete.

Al Sig. Presidente della Commissione di Antichità e Belle Arti

Le monete rinvenutesi occasionalmente alla ricostruzione della via Macqueda
sono state da me trasmesse al Prof. Salinas, con preghiera di esaminarne il
valore e l'importanza storica per le ulteriori determinazioni che converrà prendere.
Mi riserbo quindi riscontrare la sua pregiata lettera d'oggi stesso col N. 319, che
tratta di dette monete appena avrò il bene di essere favorito dal prelodato Prof.
Salinas.

Il Sindaco
D. Peranni

5. AMARAS, U.A. 420, unstamped paper, 1 side

Palermo 16. Mag 72

Al Signore Sindaco della Comune di Palermo

Palermo
N. 319.
Circa li monete rinvenute nella via Macqueda.

Come reca nota a questo Comune, che la S.V. fece ultimate le procedure in cor-
so avrebbe regalato a questo museo un esemplare per uno della diversa specie
tanto per grandezza quanto per anno di coniazione, delle monete rinvenutesi
nella via Macqueda, occasionalmente ai lavori di risistemazione del suolo, che
[…] concedendolo, […] mi permetto […] volere fin da ore secondar questa
Commissione, […] il nostro Museo con tal dono.[6]
Sicuro di presentare riguardo porgo anticipatamente ossequi.

Il Presidente.

6. ACP, busta 1108, headed paper, 1 side
− 3 − 3 −
N. 76

Addì, 21 Maggio 1872.

CITTÀ DI PALERMO
UFFICIO TECNICO E DEI LAVORI PUBBLICI
N.° 919.
Oggetto: Tubolature di Gas nella via Macqueda.

Sig.ᵣ Assessore dell'Ufficio di Pubblica Illuminazione
Pria che si perdano le tracce è interessante di far controllare opportunamente la
profondità dei tubi del gas tanto nella via Macqueda che nella strada Calderai
ambo in ricostruzione.
E a risparmio di tempo e di scrittura ulteriori è pur conveniente di far controllare la profondità dei tubi stessi in tutte le altre strade che si hanno a ricostruire
dipendentemente dalla via Macqueda, delle quali per l'oggetto di ambedue il
notamento.

L'Assessore
Granelligola

6. The handwriting is unclear and not fully understandable.

7. ACP, busta 1108, unstamped paper, 3 sides

{1}   22 Maggio 1872

3 – 3 –
N. 114
Sig.ʳ Mascuzza
Ingegnere Comunale
L'Assessore dei lavori pubblici mi ha fatto tenere l'annessa nota accompagnata
con lettera così composita:
/ si trascriva /
E comecché una tale verifica debbesi eseguire, come pel passato, dagli Ingeg-
neri comunali; Io mi rivolgo a lei perché, mano mano che le vie in detta nota
descritte si vanno ricostruendo, faccia constatare la profondità dei tubi da gasi,
diffidando in pari tempo l'impresa Faeres, se non si trovino alla dovuta profondità, ed informando del ri-{2}sultato di siffatta verifica l'Ufficio scrivente per le
ulteriori pratiche a fare.

L'Ingegnere
[signed]

8. AMARAS, U.A. 420, headed paper, 1 side

MUSEO [NAZIO]NALE DI PALERMO | 26 APR. 73 | N. 4

CITTÀ DI PALERMO
UFFICIO CENTRALE
N.° 2554.
Oggetto: Per altre 13 monete rinvenute nella via Macqueda.

23 maggio 1872.

Al Signor Professore Antonino Salinas
Avendo ricuperato altre 13 monete di quelle che si rinvennero nella via
Macqueda, mi affretto a farle tenere alla S.V. per comprenderle nel lavoro, di
cui la pregai colla precedente lettera del dì 16 del corrente mese di N. 2406.
E stommi in attenzione de' suoi favori –

Il Sindaco
D. Peranni

9. AMARAS, U.A. 420, unstamped paper, 9 sides

{1} Ad eseguire l'incarico dalla S.V. commessomi intorno alle monete rinvenute nella via Maqueda mi pregio restituirle gli originali disposti in piccoli involti secondo il notamento qui racchiuso. Di quelle monete tutte di argento, e appartengono 64 alla Sicilia, alla Spagna 13, e all'Isola di Malta 12. Le più antiche fra tutte sono spagnuole di Ferdinando II il Cattolico e Elisabetta, la quale potrebbe essere della fine del sec. XV; tutte le altre sono del XVI. e vanno sino al gran Maestro di Malta Giovanni {2} l'Eveque de la Classierè,[7] il quale governò dal 1572 al 1582. L'ultima moneta con data è siciliana, di Filippo III con l'anno 1573.

La freschezza di conservazione delle ultime monete che ho citato provano che quel tesoretto dovette essere sepolto negli ultimi decenni del sec. XVI, cioè poco prima che si desse mano alla costruzione la via Maqueda, il che accadde a' 24 di luglio 1600.

In ordine al pregio di queste monete devo dichiarare che nel commercio degli oggetti antichi non si dà ad essere valore alcuno, perché privati e musei {3} pubblici non pensarono sia oggi a formare raccolte di monete siciliane recenti. Da questa trascuranza la S.V. comprenderà agevolmente quanto di questa mancanza debba soffrire lo studio la storia nostra economica, non che quello delle nostre arti; e da parte mia ho sempre promesso nel nostro Museo la formazione di una serie non interrotta di monete siciliane dai tempi Normanni. Le monete ora rinvenute, per lo più parte di ottima conservazione hanno il pregio di rappresentare {4} quasi per intero la storia monetaria dei regni di Carlo V e di Filippo II (I di Sic.); per la qual cosa ove il Municipio palermitano volesse destinare a questo museo i 49 esemplari di conio diverso ora rinvenuti farebbe, a parer mio, opera di grande utilità agli studj storici e numismatici e porgerebbe testimonianza del suo amore pe' pubblici stabilimenti scientifici – {5}

Scelti.
Sicilia.   N.

Carlo V. imp.

1551.	2 *tarì*	1.
1554.	4. 3. 2. *tarì*	4.
1555	4. 3. 2. *tarì*	3
1556	4 *tarì*	1.
———		——
	9	

7. Jean de la Cassière (1502–1581).

Filippo II (I di Sic.)

1556	4.3. *tarì* 4.
57.	4. 3. *tarì* 3.
58.	3. 2. 2.
59.	3. 1.
156..	4. 1.
61	3. 1.
65	12. 6. 3. 3.
66.	12. 1
67	4 1

————

17 {6}

70	4 1.
71	12. 6. 3. 3
72.	12 1
73	6. 1

————

6

17

————

Filippo

23

9

————

32 Sic.

Fil. II.

1559	4 *tarì* 1
1566.	12 t. 1.
1567.	12 t. 1

————

35 {7}

Sic.	Spagna	Malta	
35	7	5	64
15	4	7	13
6	2	————	12
————	————	12	————
56.	13.		89
8			

————

64. {8}

Spagna
Filippo II   5 es.
Ferd. II e Elisabetta   1
Carlo V.   1
————
7

Malta
G. De la Vallette 1558–1572   1
G. l'Evêque de la Cassierè 1572–1582   1
————
5 {9}

Duplicati –
Carlo V.   6.
Filippo II.   15.
Spagna (Ferd. II e Fil. II.) 4.
Malta (G. de la Vallette)   7
————
32 –
Spagna Filippo II.   1
Sic. Carlo V.   1
Filippo II   7.

23
9
32

32
Sicilia   32
Spagna   7
Malta   5
44
————
76

[Antonino Salinas][8]

8. This record was written by A. Salinas, as can be inferred from his handwriting. Unfortunately, the report is not dated. However, it can be argued that the document was produced between 16 and 25 May 1872.

10. ACP, busta 886, headed paper, 1 side

3–3–10 del 1872

Addì 23 Maggio 1872.

Città di Palermo
UFFICIO TECNICO e dei Lavori Pubblici
Oggetto:

23–5–72
Dare prima rapporto.

Al Signore
Signor Ingegnere Capo
Recatomi oggi stesso a verificare la profondità della tubolatura del gas nella via
Calderai e nella via Macqueda a contare dal quadrivio della sud.ᵃ via Calderai,
trovai che la profondità media del detto condotto è di centimetri cinquanta in
media, a contare dalla superficie dell'antico lastricato.
Dovrebbe inoltre scriversi con urgenza all'ufficio della P. Am.ᵉ per la rimozione
dei detti tubi, stanteché non si può dar principio alla collocazione del lastricato
di quel tratto di strada, e non si sistemi la canalizzazione del gas.

L'Ingegnere Capo
T. Tamburello

11. ACP, busta 886, unstamped paper, 1 side

{1}   Palermo li 24 Maggio 1872.
515 3–8–10 del 1872
N.2

25 Mag.º 1872
Intendenti

Per sistemare il gas della via Macqueda in costruzione.

All'Ill.º Signore
Sig.ʳᵉ Assessore dei Lavori Pubblici in Palermo

Illmo Signore
Onde gli appaltatori sottoscritti pella ricostruzione della Via Macqueda proce-
dere ai lavori di espletamento del primo tratto di detta via, hanno per diverse
volte invitato il Sig. Ingegnere Direttore di detti lavori acciò scrivere al Sig.ʳ
Favier appaltatore del Gas di questa, per sistemare i tubi col nuovo livello, e

sino a questo punto non hanno veduto nessun lavorante di modoché i sottoscritti si vedono costretti a sospendere i lavori per detto 1.° tratto, ed è perciò
che gli stessi si fanno un dovere darne avviso alla S.V. Ill.ᵃ per prenderne nota e
risolvere su tale assunto.

Lo appaltatore
Domenico Cordaro

12. ACP, busta 1108, headed paper, 1 side

– 3 – 3 –
N. 85

24 Maggio 1872.

CITTÀ DI PALERMO
UFFICIO TECNICO E DEI LAVORI PUBBLICI
N.° 943.
Oggetto: Via Macqueda

Al Signore
Assessore della Illuminazione
Non si può dare principio alla costruzione del lastricato nel primo tratto della
via Macqueda e via Calderai, se non si rimuove e sistema la canalizzazione del
gas.
I tubi furono trovati dall'ingegnere ad un'altezza media di centimetri cinquanta
a contare dalla superficie dello antico lastricato –
Prego pertanto la S.V. a voler dare con urgenza gli opportuni provvedimenti.

L'Assessore
Granello […]

13. ACP, Deliberazioni Giunta Municipale, 03/02/1872–19/08/1874, unstamped
paper, 1 side

Seduta del 25 Maggio 1872.

Monete antiche
Per la relazione del Prof. Anton.° Salinas sulle monete rinvenute nella via
Macqueda, e per di lui proposta, delibera che dette monete si mandino al R.
Museo che a titolo di deposito potrà conservarle ed esporle allo studio.

14. ACP, busta 1108, unstamped paper, 2 sides

{1}   26 Maggio 1872

3–3
N. 120

Non possono continuarsi i lavori stradali nelle vie Macqueda e Calderaj se non
si sistema la tubolatura del gas. Ella quindi si metterà di accordo coll'Ingegnere
direttore dei lavori e col macchinista Municipale e sotto la di costoro sorvegli-
anza eseguirà la sistemazione in parola.
La prevengo che per questo fatto il Municipio non pagherà alcuna spesa poiché
{2} i detti tubi furono trovati a 50 centimetri di profondità dell'antico suolo,
mentre se fossero stati posati all'epoca dell'impianto alla profondità di un metro
voluta dal contratto, non sarebbe nato il disagio di remuoverli.

L'Ing.
[signed]

15. AMARAS, U.A. 420, headed paper, 1 side

MUSEO [NAZIO]NALE DI PALERMO | 26 APR. 73 | N. 5
CITTÀ DI PALERMO
UFFICIO CENTRALE
N.° 2643.
Oggetto: Monete rinvenute nella via Macqueda.

28 maggio 1872.

Al Signore Prof. A. Salinas
Nella tornata del 25 corr. la Giunta municipale ha preso la infrascritta deliberazione:
"La Giunta. Scritta la relazione del Sig. Salinas sulle monete rinvenute nella
via Macqueda. Mentre fa un voto di ringraziamento al sullodato Professore,
l'egregio lavoro da lui fatto, secondando le di lui proposte.
Delibera che le monete di cui si tratta si mandino al R. Museo, che a titolo di
deposito potrà ivi conservarle ed esporle allo studio, di cui è cenno in detta
relazione.
Tale deliberazione ho il piacere di comunicare alla S.V. aggiungendo a quelli
espressi dalla Giunta i miei particolari ringraziamenti per la sua detta relazione.

Il Sindaco
D. Peranni

16. AMARAS, U.A. 420, headed paper, 1 side

A 28. maggio 1872.

CITTÀ DI PALERMO
UFFICIO CENTRALE
N.º 2643.
Oggetto: Monete antiche rinvenute nella via Macqueda.

Illmo Signore
Presidente del R. Museo di Palermo
Nella tornata del 25 corr. la Giunta municipale ha preso la infrascritta delibera-
zione:
"La Giunta letta la relazione del Prof. Salinas sulle monete rinvenute nella via
Macqueda.
Mentre fa un voto di ringraziamento al sullodato Professore per l'egregio lavoro
da lui fatto, secondando le di lui proposte.
"Delibera che le monete di cui si tratta, si mandino al R. Museo, che a titolo
di deposito potrà ivi conservarle ed esporle allo studio, di cui è cenno in detta
relazione".
Tale deliberazione ho il piacere di comunicare alla S.V., trasmettendo le
monete, di cui è parola.

Il Sindaco
D. Peranni

Per di 28
Si consideri eseguiti.
Si consegnino al Direttore Museo
[…] al prof Salinas

Il Sig. Salinas […] le monete direttamente al Sindaco, il Sig. Patricolo […]
quindi che fare col Direttore.
29 Mag 72.

17. ACP, Deliberazioni Giunta Municipale, 03/02/1872–19/08/1874, unstamped
paper, 1 side

Seduta del 29 Maggio 1872.

Acquisto di 13 monete antiche
Autorizza sulle impreedute generali l'esito di £ 92 per l'acquisto già fatto di N.º
13 delle monete rinvenute sotto la strada Macqueda, che fan parte di quelle che

si mandarono in deposito al R. Museo colla illustrazione che ne fece il Prof. Salinas.

18. AMARAS, U.A. 420, unstamped paper, 1 side

Palermo 4 Giugno 72
Al S.E. Illma
Il Sig. Direttore del Giornale di Sicilia
Palermo
N. 365.

La Giunta Communale di questa città ricevendo nella tornata del 25. Maggio ultimo la perizia del Prof. Antonino Salinas deliberava dover darsi al Museo Palermitano in titolo di deposito e per seguirci allo studio del pubblico le monete di cui seguito ricuperateci da quel Municipio tra quelle rinvenute nella via Macqueda.
Quelle monete già trovavansi in questa Commune, si concessero al convenuto Museo.
Facci altro modo deliberato alla di Lei cortesia ove volesse rendere ciò di esecuzione pubblica perché il pubblico convenne la decisione delle Giunta Communale Palermitana.

Il Presidente

19. AMARAS, U.A. 420, unstamped paper, 1 side

Palermo 4 Giugno 72
Al Sindaco di Palermo
N. 362

Riguardo a nota 18 Mag. 72. N. 2643

Mi acquisisco la sua nota pervenutami da V.S. col pregevole foglio a manco ricordato e da non ultimi la deliberazione pervenutaci sull'avvenuta seduta della Giunta, secondo la quale, la prego, di farmi interprete di ringraziamenti di questa Comune, e vicini.
Con questa occasione la rendo nota, da uno facendomi al parere espressato dalla Giunta precedentemente ricordata, ho disposto, che si espongano quelle monete alla osservazione richiestaci, considerando vantaggiosamente ciò di pubblica cognizione secondo [...] del Giuramento della Provincia.

Il Presidente

20. AMARAS, U.A. 420, unstamped paper, 2 sides

{1} Palermo 4 Giugno 72
Al Direttore del Real Museo
Palermo
N. 363.

Invio di monete

Il Prof. Salinas Antonino incaricato dal Sig. Sindaco di questa Città, apprestava il suo parere sulle monete rinvenutesi non è guari nella via Macqueda, e proponeva a quel funzionario di donare al Museo Palermitano le monete ivi rinvenute.
Convenevole della nostra Città tale prosecuzione deliberai che nella tornata del 25 Maggio ultimo inviando le monete anzidette al Museo di Palermo in titolo di deposito per rimanerci in quel luogo ed esservi nelle esecuzioni de' studiosi. Accettando questa Comune tale deposito incaricavami di {2} dare alla S.V. quella sua nota e […] in Maggio, non pure di volermene restituire uno munito di sua firma.

Il Presidente.[9]

21. AMARAS, U.A. 420, newspaper, 1 side

Palermo 1872

Martedì 4 Giugno

Numero 127

GIORNALE DI SICILIA
OFFICIALE
Edizione della sera

La Giunta Comunale di questa città secondando nella tornata del 25 maggio ultimo, la proposta del prof. Antonino Salinas, deliberava mandarsi al Museo palermitano a titolo di deposito, e per esporsi allo studio del pubblico, le monete di argento ricuperatesi da questo municipio, tra quelle rinvenutesi in via Macqueda.
Quelle monete si conservano ora nel ricordato R. Museo.

---

9. The handwriting is not clear.

22. AMARAS, U.A. 420, unstamped paper, 3 sides[10]

{1} Notamento di monete di argento di Sicilia, Spagna, e Malta dalla fine del secolo XV. alla fine del secolo XVI. trasmesso dalla Commessione di Antichità e Belle Arti, e firmato dal Direttore del Museo, giusta quanto era oggetto della nota di Essa Commessione del 4. Giugno 1872 N.° 363.

Scelte

Spagna
Filippo II   N.° 2.
"   1566.   N. 12.   N.° 1.
"   1567.   "   N.° 1.
Duplicati
Sicilia
Filippo II.   1559.   N. 4.   N.° 1.
"   N. 7.   N.° 7.
Carlo V   N. 3.   N.° 1.
                             ————
                             N.° 13.   N.° 13.

Sicilia
Filippo II
"   156.   N. 4.   N.° 1.
"   1566.   N. 3.   N.° 3.
"   "   N. 3.   N.° 1.
"   1557.   N. 3.   N.° 2.
"   "   N. 4.   N.° 1.
"   1558.   N. 2.   N.° 1.
"   "   N. 3.   N.° 1.
"   1559.   N. 3.   N.° 1.
"   1561.   N. 3.   N.° 1.
"   1565.   N. 6.   N.° 1.
                             ————
                             N.° 13.

{2}
Riporto N.° 13.   N.° 13.
Filippo II.   1565.   N. 3.   N.° 1.

10. AMARAS also keeps a handwritten copy of this record.

"	"	N. 12.	N.° 1.
"	1566.	N. 12.	N.° 1.
"	1567.	N. 4.	N.° 1.
"	1570.	N. 4.	N.° 1.
"	1571.	N. 3.	N.° 3.
"	"	N. 12.	N.° 1.
"	"	N. 6.	N.° 1.
"	1572.	N. 12.	N.° 1.
"	1573.	N. 6.	N.° 1.

————

	N.° 23	N.° 23.

Sicilia

Carlo V.	1551.	N. 2.	N.° 1.
"	1554.	N. 4.	N.° 1.
"	"	N. 2.	N.° 1.
"	"	N. 3.	N.° 2.
"	1555.	N. 3.	N.° 1.
"	"	N. 4.	N.° 1.
"	"	N. 2.	N.° 1.
"	1556.	N. 4.	N.° 1.

————

	N.° 9.	N.° 9.

Malta

Giov. de la Vallette Gran Maestro

1557.1568.	N. 3.	N.° 3.

Pietro del Monte Gran Maestro

1568.1572.		N.° 1.

Giov. l'Evesque de la Cassiere Gran Maestro

	N.° 1.

————

	N.° 5.	N.° 5.

————

	N.° 50.

{3}

Riporto N.° 50.

Spagna

Filippo II. esemplari	N.° 5.	
Carlo V.	N.° 1.	
Ferdinando II ed Elisabetta	N.° 1.	
	——————	
	N.° 7	N.° 7

Spagna Duplicati

Ferdinando II. e Filippo II	N.° 4.	
Malta		
Giov. de la Vallette G.M.		
N.° 7 esemplari	N.° 7.	
Carlo V esemplari	N.° 6.	
Filippo II. esemplari	N.° 15.	
	——————	
	N.° 32.	N.° 32.
	——————	

Totale   N.° 89.

Dico Numero Ottantanove

Il Direttore
G.i Fraccia

23. AMARAS, *Giornale d'Entrata*, 1869–1883, unstamped paper, 1 side

107 | 5. Giugno 1872 | Ottantanove monete di argento rinvenute nella via
Macqueda depositate per deliberazione della Giunta Comunale di Palermo |
Da uno scavo in via Macqueda | Nota 4. Giugno 72 N.° 363 e 174 Prot:°. | 89 |
Segretario della Commne | Alla Direzione.

24. AMARAS, U.A. 420, headed paper, 1 side

Palermo li 7. Giugno 1872.

DIREZIONE DEL REAL MUSEO DI PALERMO
N. 199.
Oggetto: Dono di monete rinvenute nella via Macqueda

All'Illmo Signore
Sig.[r] Presidente della Commessione di Antichità e Belle Arti
Palermo

Ricevutesi in questa Direzione le Numero Ottantanove monete di argento rive-
nutesi nella via Maqueda, e che dalla Giunta Comunale di questa Città manda-
va in questo Museo per conservarvisi a titolo di deposito, mi pregio annetterle
uno dei due consimili notamenti di esse monete dalla Sig.a Vra trasmessomi
con la pregiata lettera del 4. stante N.° 363; in piè del quale ho apposta la mia
firma, giusta il volere della Sig.a Vra nella precalendata lettera espresso.

Il Direttore
Giovanni Fraccia

25. ACP, Deliberazioni Giunta Municipale, 03/02/1872–19/08/1874, unstamped
     paper, 1 side

Seduta del 12 Giugno 1872.

Monete antiche
Delibera accordarsi sulle impre.[e] gen.[i] una regalia di £ 15 al calabrese Gi-
useppe Misasi, ed altra di £ 5 al calabrese Carmelo Mustaca, lavoranti nella via
Macqueda, per aver trovate le monete antiche, dal Municipio ora raccolte.

26. ACP, busta 886, headed paper, 1 side

774.
3-3-10 del 1871

Addì 2 Ottobre 1872.

5-1-1
CITTÀ DI PALERMO
UFFICIO TECNICO E DEI LAVORI PUBBLICI
N.° 1864
Oggetto: Apertura al transito di un tratto della via Macqueda.

All'Illmo Sig.[r] Sindaco
Se a giudizio dell'ufficio tecnico lo […] si può aprire senza correggere l'opera a
cui inizia.
Si è compiuto il 1.° tratto della via Macqueda dai Calderai alla via del Bosco;
e siccome per contratto, l'Amme comunale può dividere in due parti uno dei
tratti della via Macqueda così la S.V. Illma è chiamata a decidere se intenda far

aprire al pubblico transito l'intero primo tratto di già compiuto, ovvero dividere questo in due ed ordinare la sola apertura dalla via Calderai a quella del Giardinaccio.

L'Assessore
[signed]

27. ACP, busta 888, headed paper, 2 sides

{1} CITTÀ DI PALERMO
UFFICIO TECNICO E DEI LAVORI PUBBLICI
Oggetto: Consegnazione diffinitiva della via Macqueda tra Calderai e Palazzo Comitini
Raccordi
Via Ponticello
Via Viola
Via SS. 40 Martiri
Vicolo S. Orsola

L'anno 1800settantatrè il giorno 26 del mese di Aprile in Palermo.
Io qui sottoscritto Tommaso Tamburello ing.^re assistente presso l'Ufficio Tecnico Com.^le per disposizione del Sig.^r Assessore dei LL.PP. con foglio del 25 del sud.^o Aprile, mi son recato nel sud.^o giorno alle ore 9. a.m. nella via Macqueda dietro invito fatto ai Sigg.^i Domenico Cordaro e Vincenzo Schimicci App.^ri per la recostruzione della via Macqueda tra la via Calderai e la Porta di Vicari e suoi raccordi ed al Sig.^r Francesco D Crisa App.^re per la manutenzione del Mandamento Palazzo Reale riguardante le strade interne. I suddetti sono intervenuti per la consegna che dovrà farsi dai detti Sigg.^i Cordaro e Schimicci all'App.^re D. Crisa Francesco del tratto della via Macqueda compresa tra la via Calderai e la entrata del Palazzo Comitini, essendo scorso il termine di fida per la costruzione non ché dei raccordi della stessa che sono: Via Ponticello, della via Macqueda alla 2^a cantonata della via Amadei—Vicolo Viola, dalla via Macqueda alla piazzetta del Ponticello—Via S.S. Martiri, dalla via Macqueda allo sbocco della Piazza dell'istesso nome—Vicolo S. Orsola, dalla via Macqueda, alla gradinata in fondo.
Il sud.^o Appaltatore D. Crisa dopo aver {2} percorso la della via Macqueda e raccordi della stessa accertarle in perfetto stato di manutenzione assieme alle opere d'arte sotto stradali così come trovansi specificate nella misura finale all'uopo redatta.

La Via Macqueda trovasi lastricata a botte con basole di calcare compatto lavorate a scalpello per m. 0,08 nelle giunture, e con marciapiede con mattoni quadrati Billiemi e bordatura con fronte a gola pure di calcare compatto di Billiemi martellinati di fino.

Le altre strade sudette formanti raccordi della stessa sono lastricate a botte con basole di massa lavorate a scalpello per m 0,05 nelle giunture.

Quindi ho chiuso il presente verbale il giorno e mese come sopra da me firmato e dagli Appaltatori.

Tommaso Tamburello
Vincenzo Schimicci
Francesco D. Crisa
Domenico Cordaro

Abbreviations Used in the Archival Documents

{X}	progressive page number
£, L.	Italian lira
2ª	seconda
ACP	Archivio Comunale di Palermo
Am.ᵉ, Amme	Amministrazione
AMARAS	Archivio del Museo Archeologico Regionale "Antonino Salinas" (Palermo)
Anton.º	Antonino
App.ʳᵉ	Appaltatore
App.ʳⁱ	Appaltatori
APR.	Aprile
Com.ˡᵉ	Comunale
Commne	Commissione
corr.	corrente
esempl.	esemplari
fasc.	fascicolo
Ferd.	Ferdinando
Fil.	Filippo
G., G.i, Giov.	Giovanni
G.M.	Gran Maestro
gen.ⁱ	generali
Ill.º, Illmo	Illustrissimo
imp.	imperatore
impre.ᵉ	impreviste

Ing., ing.^{re}	ingegnere
LL.PP.	Lavori Pubblici
m	metri
Mag, Mag.^o	Maggio
N., N.^o	numero
Off.	Officina
P.	Pubblica
Prof.	Professore
Prot.^o Prot:^o	Protocollo
R.	Real
S.	Sant'
S.P.Q.P	Senatus Populusque Panormitanus
S.S., SS.	Santissimi
S.V.	Signoria Vostra
Sic.	Sicilia
Sig., Sig.^r, Sig.^{re}	Signor
Sig.^a	Signoria
Sigg.ⁱ	Signori
sud.^a	suddetta
sud.^o	suddetto
t.	*tarì*
Tip.	Tipografica
U.A.	unità archivistica
Vra	Vostra

APPENDIX B: COIN CATALOGUE[11]

Charles I of Spain (1516–1556) or Philip II of Spain (1556–1598) with the names of Ferdinand II the Catholic and Isabella

AR, 4-reales

1. Inv. no. 68336 | Ø 30.4 mm | th.: 2.3 mm | 11.95 g | Seville | 1516–1566

Obv.: FERN[ANDVS·ET·ELIS]ABET; crowned coat of arms of Spain; S in the left field; *Rev.:* REX·ET·REGINA·CAS[...]; bundle of six arrows. | References: Calicó et al. 1998, 47 no. 169.

2. Inv. no. 68315 | Ø 32.5 mm | th.: 2.4 mm | 13.65 g | Seville | 1516–1566

Obv.: FERNANDVS·ET·ELISAB; crowned coat of arms of Spain; S–O/IIII; *Rev.:* REX·ET·REGINA·CASTELE; bundle of six arrows; P in the right field. | References: Calicó et al. 1998, 47 no. 170.

3. Inv. no. 68339 | Ø 33.3 mm | th.: 2.1 mm | 13.93 g | Seville | 1516–1566

Obv.: FERNANDV[S·ET]·ELISAB; crowned coat of arms of Spain; S–O/IIII; *Rev.:* REX·ET·REGINA·CASTELE·L; bundle of six arrows; P in the right field. | References: Calicó et al. 1998, 47 no. 170.

4. Inv. no. 68354 | Ø 32.9 mm | th.: 2.0 mm | 13.76 g | Seville | 1516–1566

Obv.: [FE]RNANDVS·ET·ELISABE; crowned coat of arms of Spain; S–O/IIII; *Rev.:* [R]EX·ET·REGINA·CASTELE·LEGIO; bundle of six arrows; P as a square in the right field. | Tag: "Ferdinando II ed Elisabetta". | References: Calicó et al. 1998, 47 no. 179.

Charles V (1516–1556)

AR, 3-reales

5. Inv. no. 68362 | Ø 28.9 mm | th.: 1.7 mm | 8.52 g | Barcelona | 1521–1556

Obv.: CAROLVS·[QVINTVS]·IMPERATO[R]; crowned coat of arms of Spain and eagle displaying wings; *Rev.:* [HIS]PANIARVM[·ET·VTR]IVSQ3·SIC[...]; ornate cross, showing crown flanked by flames at each end. | References: Calicó et al. 1998, 127 no. 26/77.

---

11. The catalogue is arranged by coin issuers and value, following a chronological order. Spanish coins always precede Sicilian ones. We also report original tags, written by Antonino Salinas in 1872, once the hoard was acquired by the Palermo Museum.

AR, 2-tarì

6. Inv. no. 68310 | Ø 24.6 mm | th.: 1.6 mm | 5.57 g | Messina | 1551

Obv.: CAR[O]LVS·[IM]PERATOR; crowned and cuirassed bust left; *Rev.:* REX·SICILIE·1551; crowned eagle facing, head right, displaying wings; below M-A. | Tag: "Carlo V. 1551 2 *tarì*". | References: Spahr 1959, 141 no. 233; Varesi 2001, 71 no. 292/12.

7. Inv. no. 68363 | Ø 27.5 mm | th.: 1.4 mm | 5.83 g | Messina | 1554

Obv.: CAROLVS·IMPERATOR; crowned and cuirassed bust right; *Rev.:* REX·SICILIAE·1554; crowned eagle facing, head right, displaying wings. | Tag: "Carlo V. 1554 2 *tarì*". | References: Spahr 1959 141 no. 233; Varesi 2001, 71 no. 293/3.

AR, 3-tarì

8. Inv. no. 68361 | Ø 28.8 mm | th.: 1.5 mm | 7.41 g | Messina | 1552

Obv.: CARO[LVS]·V·[IMP]ERATOR·; crowned and cuirassed bust right; below 3 dots; *Rev.:* ET·D·G·REX·SI[CI]LIAE·1552; ornate cross, showing crown flanked by flames at each end; M−A. | Tag: "Carlo V. 1554. 3 *tarì*. Due esemplari diversi".[12] | References: Spahr 1959, 136 no. 180 (similar); Varesi 2001, 70 no. 289.

9. Inv. no. 68305 | Ø 29.1 mm | th.: 1.6 mm | 8.78 g | Messina | 1555

Obv.: CAROLVS·V·IM[P]ERATO·; crowned and cuirassed bust right; below 3; *Rev.:* D·G·REX·SICILI[AE]·1555; ornate cross, showing crown flanked by flames at each end; G−M. | References: Spahr 1959, 137 no. 181; Varesi 2001, 70 no. 290/1.

10. Inv. no. 68309 | Ø 27.0 mm | th.: 1.8 mm | 7.19 g | Messina | 1555

Obv.: [CAROLVS]·V·[IMPERATOR]; crowned and cuirassed bust right; [below 3]; *Rev.:* [D·G·REX·SIC]ILIAE·1555; ornate cross, showing crown flanked by flames at each end; T−P. | Tag: "Carlo V. 6 esemplari".[13] | References: Spahr 1959, 136 no. 180; Varesi 2001, 70 no. 290/1 (similar).

11. Inv. no. 68308 | Ø 30.5 mm | th.: 2.0 mm | 8.79 g | Messina | 1556

Obv.: CAROLVS·V·IMPERATO·; crowned and cuirassed bust right; below 3; *Rev.:* D·G·REX·[S]ICILI·1556; ornate cross, showing crown flanked by flames at each end; G−M. | References: Spahr 1959, 137 no. 185; Varesi 2001, 70 no. 290/2.

---

12. "Due esemplari diversi": inv. nos. 68361–68362.
13. "6 esemplari": inv. nos. 68304–68309.

12. Inv. no. 68303 | Ø 28.7 mm | th.: 1.8 mm | 8.76 g | Messina | 1556

Obv.: CAROLVS·V·IMPERATO·; crowned and cuirassed bust right; below 3; *Rev.:* D·G·R[E]X·SICILI[AE]·[155]6; ornate cross, showing crown flanked by flames at each end; G–M. | Tag: "Carlo V (Sicilia) N. 1." | References: Spahr 1959, 137 no. 185; Varesi 2001, 70 no. 290/2.

AR, 4-tarì

13. Inv. no. 68307 | Ø 30.4 mm | th.: 1.6 mm | 9.70 g | Messina | 1552

Obv.: [CA]ROLVS·V·IMPERATOR; crowned and cuirassed bust right; below 4 dots; *Rev.:* ET·D[·G]·REX·SICILIAE·1552; crowned eagle standing and displaying her wings; M–A and 4 dots. | References: Spahr 1959, 134 no. 159; Varesi 2001, 69 no. 286.

14. Inv. no. 68311 | Ø 33.2 mm | th.: 1.7 mm | 10.50 g | Messina | 1552

Obv.: CA[R]OLVS·[V]·IMPERATOR; crowned and cuirassed bust right; below 4 dots; *Rev.:* ET·D[·G]·REX·[SI]CILI[AE]·1552; crowned eagle standing and displaying her wings; M–A. | References: Spahr 1959, 134 no. 159; Varesi 2001, 69 no. 286.

15. Inv. no. 68360 | Ø 34.5 mm | th.: 1.9 mm | 11.62 g | Messina | 1552

Obv.: CA[R]OL[V]S·IMPERATOR; crowned and cuirassed bust right; below 4 dots; *Rev.:* ET·D·G·REX·SIC[I]LIAE·1552; crowned eagle standing and displaying her wings; M–A. | Tag: "Carlo V. 1554 4 *tarì* – Municipio".[14] | References: Spahr 1959, 134 no. 159; Varesi 2001, 69 no. 286.

16. Inv. no. 68304 | Ø 31.2 mm | th.: 2.0 mm | 11.69 g | Messina | 1555

Obv.: C[A]ROLVS·V·I[MPER]AT[O]R; crowned and cuirassed bust right; below 4; *Rev.:* [ET]·D·G·[RE]X·SICILIA[E]·1555; crowned eagle standing and displaying her wings; G–M. | Tag: "Carlo V. 6 esemplari".[15] | References: Spahr 1959, 135 no. 164; Varesi 2001, 69 no. 287/1.

17. Inv. no. 68306 | Ø 32.2 mm | th.: 2.1 mm | 11.64 g | Messina | 1556

Obv.: [CA]ROLVS·V·[IMPERA]TOR; crowned and cuirassed bust right; below 4; *Rev.:* ET·D·G·R[E]X·SICI[LIAE]·1556; crowned eagle standing and displaying her wings; G–M. | References: Spahr 1959, 135 no. 164; Varesi 2001, 69 no. 287/2.

---

14. "1554" is wrong.

15. "6 esemplari": inv. nos. 68304–68309.

Philip II (1556–1598)

AR, 4-reales

18. Inv. no. 68313 | Ø 31.5 mm | th.: 2.6 mm | 13.69 g | Seville | 1556–1598

Obv.: PH[ILIPPV]S·II·[D]EI·GRATIA; crowned coat of arms of Spain; S–O/IIII; *Rev.:* [HISP]A[NIA]RVM·RE[X]; coat of arms within a tressure; P in the field. | References: Calicó et al. 1998, 169 no. 311.

19. Inv. no. 68314 | Ø 32.4 mm | th.: 2.3 mm | 13.86 g | Seville | 1556–1568

Obv.: PHIL[IPPV]S·[II·D]EI·GRATIA; crowned coat of arms of Spain; S–O/IIII; *Rev.:* [HISP]ANIARVM REX; coat of arms within a tressure; P in the field. | References: Calicó et al. 1998, 169 no. 311.

20. Inv. no. 68357 | Ø 30.7 mm | th.: 2.3 mm | 13.77 g | Seville | 1556–1568

Obv.: PHILI[...]A; crowned coat of arms of Spain; S–O/IIII; *Rev.:* [HIS]PANIA[RVM REX]; coat of arms within a tressure; F in the field. | References: Calicó et al. 1998, 169 no. 313.

21. Inv. no. 68355 | Ø 33.5 mm | th.: 2.3 mm | 13.71 g | Toledo | 1556–1598

Obv.: PHI[LIP]PVS·II·DEI·GRATIA·; crowned coat of arms of Spain; M/T; *Rev.:* HISPANIA[R]VM REX·; coat of arms within a tressure. | Tag: "Filippo II. 5 esemplari"[16] | References: Calicó et al. 1998, 170 no. 330.

22. Inv. no. 68356 | Ø 31.5 mm | th.: 2.3 mm | 13.78 g | Valladolid | 1556–1598

Obv.: [PHILIPPV]S·II·DEI·GRA[TI]A; crowned coat of arms of Spain; small flag on the left and A/O/IIII on the right; *Rev.:* [HISP]ANIARVM R[EX]; coat of arms within a tressure. | References: Calicó et al. 1998, 171 no. 363.

23. Inv. no. 68358 | Ø 32.2 mm | th.: 2.2 mm | 13.76 g | Cuenca | 1556–1568

Obv.: PH[I]LIPPVS·II·DEI·GRATI[A]; crowned coat of arms of Spain; C/I–O/IIII; *Rev.:* H[I]SPANIA[RV]M·R[EX]·; coat of arms within a tressure. | References: Calicó et al. 1998, 165 no. 266.

AR, 8-reales

24. Inv. no. 68312 | Ø 37.8 mm | th.: 3.1 mm | 27.41 g | Seville | 1556–1598

Obv.: PHI[LI]PPVS·[II]·DEI·GR[A]TIA; crowned coat of arms of Spain; S-; *Rev.:* [HIS]

---

16. "5 esemplari": inv. nos. 68355–68359.

PANIA[R]VM [RE]X·; coat of arms within a tressure; P in the right field. | Tag: "<u>Spagna</u> (Ferdinando II. e Filippo II) 4 esempl."[17] | References: Calicó et al. 1998, 156 no. 182.

25. Inv. no. 68359 | Ø 39.0 mm | th.: 3.0 mm | 27.35 g | Valladolid | 1556–1598

Obv.: PHILIPPVS·II·DEI·GRA[TIA]; crowned coat of arms of Spain; small flag on the left and A/O/IIII on the right; *Rev.:* HI[SP]ANIAR[V]M REX·; coat of arms within a tressure. | References: Calicó et al. 1998, 160 no. 215.

AR, 2 tarì

26. Inv. no. 68333 | Ø 24.4 mm | th.: 1.6 mm | 5.82 g | Messina | 1556

Obv.: [PHILI]PPVS·D·G[RATIA]; armored bust right; *Rev.:* [RE]X·[S]ICILIAE·1556; crowned eagle facing, head right, displaying wings. | References: Spahr 1959, 167 no. 75; Varesi 2001, 79 no. 325.

27. Inv. no. 68316 | Ø 26.0 mm | th.: 1.6 mm | 5.81 g | Messina | 1558

Obv.: PHILIPPVS·D·G; armored bust right; *Rev.:* REX·SICILI[AE]·1558; crowned eagle facing, head right, displaying wings; T–P. | Tag: "Filippo II. 1558. 2 *tarì*". | References: Spahr 1959, 167 no. 76; Varesi 2001, 79 no. 324/3.

AR, 3-tarì

28. Inv. no. 68365 | Ø 26.8 mm | th.: 1.8 mm | 7.26 g | Messina | 1556

Obv.: [PH]ILIPPVS·D·GRATIA; armored bust right; T; *Rev.:* [R]EX·SICI[LIAE]·1556; ornate cross, showing crown flanked by flames at each end; [Y]–A. | Tag: "Filippo II. 1556. 3 *tarì*". | References: Spahr 1959, 164 no. 44; Varesi 2001, 78 no. 319 (generic).

29. Inv. no. 68318 | Ø 29.5 mm | th.: 2.0 mm | 8.69 g | Messina | 1557

Obv.: PHILIPPVS·D·G; armored bust left; *Rev.:* REX·SICILI[A]E·1557; ornate cross, showing crown flanked by flames at each end; T–P. | Tag: "Sicilia Filippo II. N. 7".[18] | References: Spahr 1959, 164 no. 49; Varesi 2001, 78 no. 319/2.

30. Inv. no. 68335 | Ø 30.8 mm | th.: 1.8 mm | 8.71 g | Messina | 1557

Obv.: PHILIPPVS·D·; armored bust left; *Rev.:* REX·SICI[L]IAE·1557; ornate cross, showing crown flanked by flames at each end; T–P. | References: Spahr 1959, 164 no. 49; Varesi 2001, 78 no. 319/2.

---

17. "4 esempl.": inv. nos. 68312–68315.
18. "N. 7": this reference is potentially wrong.

31. Inv. no. 68353 | Ø 27.3 mm | th.: 2.0 mm | 8.78 g | Messina | 1558

Obv.: PHILIPPVS·D·G; armored bust left; *Rev.:* REX·SICIL[IAE]·1558; ornate cross, showing crown flanked by flames at each end; T–P. | References: Spahr 1959, 164 no. 49; Varesi 2001, 78 no. 319/3.

32. Inv. no. 68366 | Ø 28.8 mm | th.: 1.8 mm | 8.20 g | Messina | 1558

Obv.: PHILIPPV[S]·D·[G]; armored bust left; *Rev.:* REX·SICILIAE·1558; ornate cross, showing crown flanked by flames at each end; T–P. | Tag: "Filippo II. 1558 3 *tarì*". | References: Spahr 1959, 164 no. 49; Varesi 2001, 78 no. 319/3.

33. Inv. no. 68320 | Ø 29.2 mm | th.: 1.7 mm | 8.70 g | Messina | 1560

Obv.: [P]HILIPPVS·[D]·G; armored bust left; *Rev.:* REX·S[I]CILIA[E]·1560; ornate cross, showing crown flanked by flames at each end; T–P. | References: Spahr 1959, 164 no. 49; Varesi 2001, 78 no. 319/5.

34. Inv. no. 68368 | Ø 29.2 mm | th.: 1.8 mm | 8.76 g | Messina | 1556

Obv.: PHILIP[P]V[S]·D·G; armored bust left; *Rev.:* REX·SICILIA[E]·1561; ornate cross, showing crown flanked by flames at each end; T–P. | Tag: "Filippo II. 1561 3 *tarì* –". | References: Spahr 1959, 166 no. 67; Varesi 2001, 78 no. 319/6.

35. Inv. no. 68330 | Ø 25.1 mm | th.: 2.0 mm | 7.92 g | Messina | 1565

Obv.: PHILI[PPVS]·D·G·[R·SI]·[1]565; armored bust right; *Rev.:* Crowned coat of arms of Spain; [C]–G. | Tag: "TAV. 53 ARM. 6" (by unknown author). | References: Spahr 1959, 179 no. 216; Varesi 2001, 78 no. 320/5.

36. Inv. no. 68325 | Ø 25.7 mm | th.: 2.1 mm | 7.87 g | Messina | 1571

Obv.: PHILIP[P]VS·D·[G·R·SI]·1571; armored bust right; *Rev.:* Crowned coat of arms of Spain; P–P. | References: Spahr 1959, 180 no. 236; Varesi 2001, 78 no. 320/11.

AR, 4-tarì

37. Inv. no. 68327 | Ø 32.2 mm | th.: 1.8 mm | 11.02 g | Messina | 1556

Obv.: PHILIPPVS·D·G; armored bust right; *Rev.:* REX·SIC[I]L[I]AE·1556; crowned eagle facing, head left, displaying wings; T–P. | Tag: "Filippo II 1556 4 *tarì* Municipio". | References: Spahr 1959, 161 no. 13; Varesi 2001, 77 no. 317/1.

38. Inv. no. 68337 | Ø 33.0 mm | th.: 1.8 mm | 11.68 g | Messina | 1556

Obv.: [PH]ILIPPVS·D·GRATIA; armored bust right; *Rev.:* REX·SICILIAE·15[5]6; crowned eagle facing, head left, displaying wings; T–P. | References: Spahr 1959, 161 no. 13; Varesi 2001, 77 no. 316/2.

39. Inv. no. 68338 | Ø 32.6 mm | th.: 1.9 mm | 11.70 g | Messina | 1556

Obv.: PHI[LI]PPVS·D·G; armored bust right; *Rev.:* REX·SICILIAE·1[5]56; crowned eagle facing, head left, displaying wings; T–P. | References: Spahr 1959, 161 no. 13; Varesi 2001, 77 no. 317/1.

40. Inv. no. 68364 | Ø 32.6 mm | th.: 2.0 mm | 11.73 g | Messina | 1556

Obv.: PHILIPPVS·D·GRATIA; armored bust right; *Rev.:* REX·SICILIAE·[15]56; crowned eagle facing, head left, displaying wings; Y–M. | Tag: "Filippo II. 1556 4 *tarì*. 3 esemplari diversi".[19] | References: Spahr 1959, 160 no. 2; Varesi 2001, 77 no. 316/1.

41. Inv. no. 68372 | Ø 32.7 mm | th.: 2.0 mm | 11.67 g | Messina | 1556

Obv.: PHILIPPVS·D·GRATIA; armored bust right; *Rev.:* R[EX]·SICILIAE·1556; crowned eagle facing, head right, displaying wings; Y–M. | Tag: "Filippo II 1567 4 *tarì*". | References: Spahr 1959, 160 no. 2; Varesi 2001, 77 no. 316/1.

42. Inv. no. 68317 | Ø 33.3 mm | th.: 1.9 mm | 11.70 g | Messina | 1557

Obv.: PHILIPPVS·D·G; armored bust right; *Rev.:* REX·SICI[L]IAE·1557; crowned eagle facing, head left, displaying wings; T–P. | Tag: "Filippo II. 1557 4 *tarì*". | References: Spahr 1959, 161 no. 13; Varesi 2001, 77 no. 317/2.

43. Inv. no. 68374 | Ø 31.0 mm | th.: 2.1 mm | 10.94 g | Messina | 1557

Obv.: PHILIP[PV]S·D·G; armored bust right; *Rev.:* [RE]X·SIC[I]LIA[E]·1[5]57; crowned eagle facing, head left, displaying wings; [T]–P. | Tag: "Filippo II. 1570 4 *tarì*". | References: Spahr 1959, 161 no. 12; Varesi 2001, 77 no. 317/2.

44. Inv. no. 68319 | Ø 30.4 mm | th.: 2.0 mm | 11.67 g | Messina | 1559

Obv.: PHILIP[PV]S[·D·G]; armored bust right; *Rev.:* REX·SI[C]ILIAE·1559; crowned eagle facing, head left, displaying wings; T–P. | Tag: "Filippo II. 1559. 4 *tarì*". | References: Spahr 1959, 161 no. 13; Varesi 2001, 77 no. 317/4.

---

19. "3 esemplari diversi": inv. nos. 68364–68366.

45. Inv. no. 68373 | Ø 32.5 mm | th.: 1.8 mm | 11.66 g | Messina | 1561

Obv.: [PH]ILIPPVS·D·G; armored bust right; *Rev.:* [R]EX·SICIL[IAE]·1561; crowned eagle facing, head left, displaying wings; T–P. | Tag: "Filippo II. 156. 4 *tarì*". | References: Spahr 1959, 161 no. 12; Varesi 2001, 77 no. 317/6.

46. Inv. no. 68367 | Ø 30.9 mm | th.: 1.8 mm | 10.57 g | Messina | 1562

Obv.: [PHILI]PPVS·D·G; armored bust right; *Rev.:* [REX·S]ICILIAE·[15]62; crowned eagle facing, head left, displaying wings; T–P. | Tag: "Filippo II. 1559 3 *tarì* –". | References: Spahr 1959, 163 no. 39; Varesi 2001, 77 no. 317/7.

AR, mezzo scudo (or 5-tarì)

47. Inv. no. 68326 | Ø 28.9 mm | th.: 2.2 mm | 12.93 g | Messina | 1563–1567?

Obv.: PHILIP[P]VS·D·G·REX·SI·15[...]; armored bust left; *Rev.:* Crowned royal coat of arms within grain ear wreath; C–G. | References: Spahr 1959, 177 (generic); Varesi 2001, 76 no. 313 (generic; variant with SI legend).

48. Inv. no. 68340 | Ø 29.6 mm | th.: 2.4 mm | 13.24 g | Messina | 1564

Obv.: PHILIPPVS·D·G·REX·1564; armored bust left; *Rev.:* Crowned royal coat of arms within grain ear wreath; C–G. | References: Spahr 1959, 177 no. 181; Varesi 2001, 76 no. 313/6.

49. Inv. no. 68301 | Ø 29.2 mm | th.: 2.7 mm | 13.12 g | Messina | 1565

Obv.: PHILIP[PVS]·D·G·REX·1565; armored bust left; *Rev.:* Crowned royal coat of arms within grain ear wreath; C–G. | Tag: "Spagna Filippo II n. 2".[20] | References: Spahr 1959, 177 no. 181; Varesi 2001, 76 no. 313/7.

50. Inv. no. 68369 | Ø 30.6 mm | th.: 2.4 mm | 13.21 g | Messina | 1565

Obv.: PHILIPPVS·[D·G]·REX·1565; armored bust left; *Rev.:* Crowned royal coat of arms within grain ear wreath; C–G. | Tag: "Filippo 2° 1565 6 *tarì*". | References: Spahr 1959, 177 no. 181; Varesi 2001, 76 no. 313/7.

51. Inv. no. 68334 | Ø 30.8 mm | th.: 2.4 mm | 13.25 g | Messina | 1568

Obv.: PHI[L]IPPVS·D·G·[R]EX·1568; armored bust left; *Rev.:* Crowned royal coat of arms within grain ear wreath; P–P. | References: Spahr 1959, 178 no. 204; Varesi 2001, 76 no. 313/11.

---

20. "N. 2": inv. nos. 68301–68302.

52. Inv. no. 68302 | Ø 30.1 mm | th.: 2.4 mm | 12.97 g | Messina | 1572

Obv.: [PHI]LIPP[VS·D·G]·REX·SI·1572; armored bust left; *Rev.:* Crowned royal coat of arms within grain ear wreath; P–P. | References: Spahr 1959, 179 no. 208; Varesi 2001, 77 no. 314/3.

53. Inv. no. 68321 | Ø 28.9 mm | th.: 2.2 mm | 12.86 g | Messina | 1572

Obv.: [PH]ILIPPVS·D·G·REX·[S]I·1572; armored bust left; *Rev.:* Crowned royal coat of arms within grain ear wreath; P–P. | References: Spahr 1959, 178 no. 204; Varesi 2001, 77 no. 314/3.

AR, scudo (or 10-tarì)

54. Inv. no. 68322 | Ø 36.0 mm | th.: 3.0 mm | 26.37 g | Messina | 1565

Obv.: [P]HILIPPVS·D·G·REX·1565; armored bust left; below C–G; *Rev.:* PVBLI/CAE·COM/MODIT/ATI within grain ear wreath. | References: Spahr 1959, 174 no. 146; Varesi 2001, 75 no. 311/4.

55. Inv. no. 68329 | Ø 35.7 mm | th.: 3.2 mm | 26.47 g | Messina | 1565

Obv.: PHI[L]IPPVS·D·G·REX·1[5]65; armored bust left; C·G; *Rev.:* PVBLI/CÆ·COM/MODITA/TI within grain ear wreath. | References: Spahr 1959, 174 no. 146; Varesi 2001, 75 no. 311/4.

56. Inv. no. 68323 | Ø 35.7 mm | th.: 3.2 mm | 26.25 g | Messina | 1566

Obv.: [P]HILIPPVS·D·G·[REX·]SI[·15]66; armored bust left; below C–G; *Rev.:* PVBLI/CÆ·COM/MODIT/ATI within grain ear wreath. | References: Spahr 1959, 174 no. 149; Varesi 2001, 75 no. 311/6.

57. Inv. no. 68324 | Ø 35.5 mm | th.: 3.3 mm | 26.36 g | Messina | 1566

Obv.: PH[I]LIPPVS·D·G·REX·[SI·]1566; armored bust left; below C–G; *Rev.:* PVBLIC/AE·COM/MODITA/TI within grain ear wreath. | References: Spahr 1959, 174 no. 150; Varesi 2001, 75 no. 311/6.

58. Inv. no. 68328 | Ø 37.0 mm | th.: 3.3 mm | 26.45 g | Messina | 1566

Obv.: PHILIPPVS·D·G·REX·SIC·1566; armored bust left; below C·G; *Rev.:* PVBLI/CÆ·COM/MODIT/ATI within grain ear wreath. | Tag: "Filippo II. N. 15".[21] | References: Spahr 1959, 174 no. 149; Varesi 2001, 75 no. 311/6.

59. Inv. no. 68370 | Ø 35.9 mm | th.: 3.0 mm | 26.40 g | Messina | 1566

---

21. "N. 15": this reference is not clear.

Obv.: PHILIPPV[S·D]·G·REX·SI·1566; armored bust left; below CG; *Rev.:* PVBLICÆ/ COMMOD/ITATI within grain ear wreath. | Tag: "Filippo II 1566 12 *tarì*". | References: Spahr 1959, 175 no. 153 (reported as PVBLICA) (new specimen); Varesi 2001, 75 no. 311/6.

60. Inv. no. 68371 | Ø 36.4 mm | th.: 3.1 mm | 25.55 g | Messina | 1567

Obv.: P[HI]LIPP[V]S·D·G·REX·S·1567 [7 on 6 overdate]; armored bust left; below C·G; *Rev.:* PVBLIC/Æ·COMM/ODITA/TI within grain ear wreath. | Tag: "Filippo II. 1567 12 *tarì*". | References: Spahr 1959, 175 no. 154 (variant); Varesi 2001, 75 no. 311/7.

61. Inv. no. 68331 | Ø 36.9 mm | th.: 2.8 mm | 26.29 g | Messina | 1571

Obv.: PHILIPP[V]S·D·G·REX·SI·1571; armored bust right; P·P; *Rev.:* PVBLI/ CAE:COM/MODITA/TI; within grain ear wreath. | References: Spahr 1959, 175 no. 160; Varesi 2001, 76 no. 312/2.

62. Inv. no. 68332 | Ø 33.0 mm | th.: 2.9 mm | 21.35 g | Messina | 1571

Obv.: PHILIPPVS·D·G·[REX·SI]·[15]71; armored bust right; P·P; *Rev.:* PVBLI/ CAE·COM/MODITA/[TI]; within grain ear wreath. | References: Spahr 1959, 175 no. 160; Varesi 2001, 76 no. 312/2.

63. Inv. no. 68375 | Ø 37.2 mm | th.: 3.0 mm | 26.28 g | Messina | 1571

Obv.: [PH]ILIP[PVS]·[D]·G·REX·S[I]·1571; armored bust right; below P·[P]; *Rev.:* PVBLI/CAE·COM/MODITA/TI within grain ear wreath. | Tag: "Filippo II. 1571 12 *tarì*". | References: Spahr 1959, 175 no. 160; Varesi 2001, 76 no. 312/2.

64. Inv. no. 68376 | Ø 37.7 mm | th.: 3.0 mm | 26.43 g | Messina | 1572

Obv.: PHILI[P]PVS·D·G·REX·[S·]1572; armored bust right; below P·P; *Rev.:* PVBLI/ CAE:COM/MODITA/TI within grain ear wreath. | Tag: "Filippo II. 1572 12 *tarì*". | References: Spahr 1959, 176 no. 165 (reported without P·P; new specimen); Varesi 2001, 76 no. 312/3.

Jean Parisot de Valette (1557–1568)

AR, 3-tarì

65. Inv. no. 68344 | Ø 30.5 mm | th.: 1.8 mm | 8.71 g | Malta | 1557–1568

Obv.: F·IOANNES·DE·VALLET[E]·M·HO·[H]; arms of the Grand Master of Malta; *Rev.:* [S]VB·HOC·SIGNO·MILIT[A]MVS; cross of the Order. | References: Restelli and Sammut 1977, 1:48 no. 62.

66. Inv. no. 68345 | Ø 31.4 mm | th.: 1.5 mm | 8.76 g | Malta | 1557–1568

Obv.: [F·IO]ANN[ES]·DE·[V]ALLETE·[M·H]O·H; arms of the Grand Master of Malta; *Rev.:* SV[B]·HOC·SIGNO·MILITAMVS; cross of the Order. | References: Restelli and Sammut 1977, 1:48 no. 62.

67. Inv. no. 68346 | Ø 28.3 mm | th.: 1.5 mm | 7.45 g | Malta | 1557–1568

Obv.: F·IOANNES·DE·VALL[ET]E·M·HO·H; arms of the Grand Master of Malta; *Rev.:* S[V]B·HOC·SIGNO·MILITAMVS; cross of the Order. | References: Restelli and Sammut 1977, 1:48 no. 62.

68. Inv. no. 68350 | Ø 31.3 mm | th.: 1.71 mm | 8.74 g | Malta | 1557–1568

Obv.: F·IOANNES·[D]E·VALLETE·M·HO·H; arms of the Grand Master of Malta; *Rev.:* SV[B]·HOC·SIGNO·MIL[IT]AMVS; cross of the Order. | References: Restelli and Sammut 1977, 1:48 no. 62.

AR, 4-tarì

69. Inv. no. 68341 | Ø 33.9 mm | th.: 1.7 mm | 11.76 g | Malta | 1557–1568

Obv.: F·IOANNES·[DE]·VALL[ETE]·[M·HOSP]·HIER; coat of arms of the Grand Master of Malta; *Rev.:* PROPTER·VERITATEM·ET·IVSTICIAM; head of John the Baptist. | Tag: "Malta (Giov. de la Valette) G. M. 7 esemplari".[22] | References: Restelli and Sammut 1977, 1:46 no. 44.

70. Inv. no. 68342 | Ø 30.9 mm | th.: 2.0 mm | 10.42 g | Malta | 1557–1568

Obv.: F·IOANNES·[DE·]VAL[LETE·]M·HOSP·HIE; coat of arms of the Grand Master of Malta; *Rev.:* [PR]OPTER·VERITATEM·ET·IVS[TICIA]M; head of John the Baptist. | References: Restelli and Sammut 1977, 1:45 no. 37.

71. Inv. no. 68343 | Ø 34.1 mm | th.: 1.9 mm | 11.80 g | Malta | 1557–1568

Obv.: F·IOANNES·DE·VALLETE·M·HOS[P·HIE]; coat of arms of the Grand Master of Malta; *Rev.:* PROPTER·VERITATEM·ET IVSTI[C]IAM; head of John the Baptist. | References: Restelli and Sammut 1977, 1:45 no. 37.

72. Inv. no. 68347 | Ø 34.1 mm | th.: 1.9 mm | 11.61 g | Malta | 1557–1568

Obv.: F·IOANNES·DE·VALLETE·M[·H]OSP·HI[E]; coat of arms of the Grand Master of Malta; *Rev.:* P[R]OPTER·V[E]RITATEM·ET·IVSTICIAM; head of John the Baptist. | References: Restelli and Sammut 1977, 1:45 no. 37.

22. "7 esemplari": inv. nos. 68341–68347.

73. Inv. no. 68349 | Ø 36.2 mm | th.: 1.7 mm | 11.56 g | Malta | 1557–1568

Obv.: F·IOANNES·D[E]·VALLETE·M·HOSP·HIER; coat of arms of the Grand Master of Malta; *Rev.:* PROPTER·VERITATEM·ET·IVSTICIAM; head of John the Baptist. | Tag: "Malta Giov. de la Vallette Gran Maestro (1557–1568) 3 esemplari diversi".[23] | References: Restelli and Sammut 1977, 1:46 no. 44.

74. Inv. no. 68351 | Ø 30.3 mm | th.: 1.8 mm | 10.23 g | Malta | 1557–1568

Obv.: F·[IOAN]NES·DE·VALLETE·M·[HOSP·]HIER; coat of arms of the Grand Master of Malta; *Rev.:* PROPTER·VERITATEM·E[T·IVSTICIA]M; head of John the Baptist. | References: Restelli and Sammut 1977, 1:46 no. 44.

Pietro del Monte (1568–1572)

AR, 4-tarì

75. Inv. no. 68352 | Ø 35.0 mm | th.: 1.9 mm | 11.55 g | Malta | 1568–1572

Obv.: F·PETRVS·DE·MONTE·M·HOSP·HIER; coat of arms of the Grand Master of Malta; *Rev.:* PROPTER·V[E]RITATEM·ET·IVSTICIAM; head of John the Baptist. | Tag: "Malta Pietro Del Monte Gran Maestro (1568–1572)". | References: Restelli and Sammut 1977, 1:57 no. 2.

Jean l'Evesque de la Cassière (1572–1581)

AR, 4-tarì

76. Inv. no. 68348 | Ø 35.1 mm | th.: 1.8 mm | 11.60 g | Malta | 1572–1581

Obv.: IO·LEVESQVE·DE·LA·CASSIERE·M·HOSP·H; coat of arms of the Grand Master of Malta; *Rev.:* PROPTER·[VE]RITATEM·ET·IVSTICIAM; head of John the Baptist. | Tag: "Malta Giov. l'Evesque de la Cassìere Gran Maestro (1572–1582)"; "TAV. 54 ARM. 6" (by unknown author). | References: Restelli and Sammut 1977, 1:63 no. 8.

---

23. "3 esemplari diversi" = inv. nos. 68349–68351.

ACKNOWLEDGMENTS

I am very grateful to the Royal Numismatic Society, which funded my research trips in Palermo between 2016 and 2017. I am also thankful not only to Caterina Greco and Francesca Spatafora, current and former directors of the Archaeological Museum of Palermo, who authorized me to study the Via Maqueda Hoard (prot. no. 436 of 29 August 2016 and no. 4867 of 10 November 2020), but also to Lucina Gandolfo and Costanza Polizzi (especially for her kind support and assistance during my stay at the Salinas Museum). All personnel at the Archivio Comunale di Palermo also were very helpful in tracing archival records on construction sites in Via Maqueda. Finally, special thanks go to Alberto Corrado (University of Oxford) and Carlo Lualdi (University of Warwick), who helped me to trace essential bibliographical material.

REFERENCES

Battlori, M. 1977. "Ferdinando il Cattolico e il Reame di Napoli." In *Atti del Congresso internazionale di studi sull'età del Viceregno*, edited by F. M. De Robertis and M. Spagnoletti, 29–33. Bari: Grafica Bigiemme.

Cagiati, M. 1914. "Antonino Salinas." *Rivista Italiana di Numismatica* 27: 125–131.

Calicò, F., F. X. Calicò, and J. Trigo. 1998. Las monedas españolas desde Fernando e Isabel a Juan Carlos I: Años 1474 a 1998. Barcelona: X. C. Estivil.

Cassarino Tranchina, P. 1995. "Soprintendenza ai Beni Culturali ed Ambientali di Siracusa. Siracusa. Gabinetto Numismatico. Ripostigli di età medievale e moderna." *Annali dell'Istituto Italiano di Numismatica* 42: 209–225.

Crisà, A. 2012. *Numismatic and Archaeological Collecting in Northern Sicily during the First Half of the Nineteenth Century*. British Archaeological Reports International Series 2411. Oxford: BAR Publishing.

———. 2014a. "An Eighteenth-Century Sicilian Coin Hoard from the Termini-Cerda Railway Construction Site (Palermo, 1869)." *American Journal of Numismatics* 26: 339–362.

———. 2014b. "Coin Collectors and Museum Donors: Contextualizing Delfino Trucchi and Antonino Salinas in Early Post-Unification Sicily (1868–73)." *Journal of the History of Collections* 26, no. 2: 277–286.

———. 2018. *When Archaeology Meets Communities: Impacting Interactions in Northern Sicily Over Two Eras (Messina, 1861–1918)*. Oxford: Archaeopress.

De Seta, C. and Di Mauro, L. 2002. *Palermo. Le città nella storia d'Italia*. Rome–Bari: Laterza.

Di Fede, M. S. 1995. "Architettura e trasformazioni urbane a Palermo nel Cinquecento: La committenza viceregia." *Espacio, Tiempo y Forma* 8: 103–118.

Di Stefano, G. 1956. "Momenti e aspetti della tutela monumentale in Sicilia". *Archivio Storico Siciliano* 8: 343–369.

Giuffrida, R. 1984. "L'amministrazione per la tutela dei Beni culturali della Sicilia in epoca borbonica (1778–1860)." *Beni Culturali e Ambientali Sicilia* 5, nos. 3–4: 127–153.

———. 2006. *La Sicilia e l'Ordine di Malta (1529–1550). La centralità della periferia mediterranea*. Palermo: Mediterranea.

La Corte Cailler, G. 1907. "Onoranze al Prof. Antonino Salinas." *Archivio Storico Messinese* 8: 148–149.

La Lumia, I. 2004. *Palermo e il suo passato, i suoi monumenti*. Palermo: Antares Editrice.

Lagumina, B. 1895. "Di un pregevole ripostiglio di monete arabe trovato a Palermo." *Archivio Storico Siciliano* 20: 360–374.

Locatelli, S. 2017. "Aspects of the Monetary Circulation of the Kingdoms of Naples and Sicily in the Sixteenth Century. Two Unpublished Coin Hoards from the Island of Lipari." In *Proceedings of the XV International Numismatic Congress, Taormina 21–25 September 2015*, edited by M. Caccamo Caltabiano, vol. 2, 1138–1142. Rome: Arbor Sapientiae.

Mack Smith, D. 1968. *A History of Sicily, Vol. 2: Medieval Sicily, 800–1713*. London: Chatto & Windus.

Mifsud, A. 1918. "L'approvigionamento e l'Università di Malta nelle passate dominazioni." *Archivium Melitense* 3, no. 5: 163–212.

Moscati, S. and Di Stefano, C. A. 2006. *Palermo. Museo Archeologico*. Palermo: Novecento.

Pace, B. 1926. "Antonino Salinas e il Museo di Palermo." *Emporium* 63: 152–162.

Pannuti, M. and Riccio, V. 1984. *Le monete di Napoli: dalla caduta dell'Impero Romano alla chiusura della zecca*. Lugano: Nummorum Auctiones.

Pelagatti, P. 2001. "Dalla Commissione Antichità e Belle Arti di Sicilia (CABAS) alla Amministrazione delle Belle Arti nella Sicilia post-unitaria. Rottura e continuità amministrativa." *Mélanges de l'École Française de Rome, Italie et Méditerranée* 113.2: 599–621.

Restelli, F. and Sammut, F. 1977. *The Coinage of the Knights in Malta (1530–1798)*. Malta: E. Said Publishers.

Salinas, A. 1867. *Le monete delle antiche città di Sicilia*. Palermo: Francesco Lao.

Sant, M. A. 1983. "Gold and Silver Coinage in Malta, 1530–1798: The Order's Stand against Falsification of Money." *Hyphen* 3, no. 6: 233–244.

Spahr, R. 1959. *Le monete siciliane dagli Aragonesi ai Borboni (1282–1836)*. Palermo: Banco di Sicilia.

Spatafora, F. and Gandolfo, L., eds. 2014. *Il Salinas ricorda Salinas, 1914–2014. "Del Real Museo di Palermo e del suo avvenire", Museo Archeologico Regionale "Antonino Salinas", Palermo 8 luglio–4 novembre 2014*. Palermo: Regione Siciliana, Assessorato dei Beni Culturali e dell'Identità Siciliana, Dipartimento dei Beni Culturali e dell'Identità Siciliana.

Trasselli, C. 1969. *Appunti di metrologia e numismatica siciliana per la Scuola di Paleografia dell'Archivio di Stato di Palermo. Lezioni tenute negli anni 1968 e 1969*. Palermo: Archivio dello Stato.

———. 1970. "Un banco genovese a Palermo nel 1570." *Revue internationale d'historie de la banque* 3: 177–236.

———. 1977. "Problemi monetari siciliani nei secoli XVI–XVII." In *Atti del Congresso internazionale di studi sull'età del Viceregno*, edited by F. M. De Robertis and M. Spagnoletti, 283–296. Bari: Grafica Bigiemme.

———. 1982a. *Da Ferdinando il Cattolico a Carlo V: l'esperienza siciliana*. Soveria Mannelli: Rubbettino.

———. 1982b. "Sull'economia siciliana del Quattrocento." *Archivio Storico Messinese* 33: 5–29.

Travaini, L. 2013. *Le collezioni della Fondazione Banco di Sicilia. Le monete: le monete siciliane dal Vespro al 1836*. Cinisello Balsamo: Silvana Editore.

Varesi, A. 2001. *Monete italiane regionali: Sicilia*. Pavia: Numismatica Varesi.

Vesco, M. 2015. "Dal rettifilo alla croce: L'apertura di strada Maqueda a Palermo." *Archistor* 2, no. 4: 4–25.

AJN Second Series 32 (2020) pp. 389–414

François Declos, Barber?
A Reconsideration of the F D Countermarks from Trinidad

Guy Chamberland[*]

By the middle of the nineteenth century, Port of Spain, Trinidad, seems to have been reasonably well supplied with a vast array of copper and bronze coin, from the British halfpenny to the Venezuelan *centavo*, American large cent, and a wide range of Canadian, European, and South-Asian penny- and halfpenny-sized coins. None of this small change, however, fit well into the "street economy" which was based on the stampee (2½ cents or 1¼ pence) and half-stampee (1¼ cents), for example in the sale and purchase of one's daily loaf of bread. To remediate this situation, some shop owners undertook an extensive operation of countermarking coins, roughly halfpenny-sized, to raise them to the value of a half-stampee. Deeply incused F D marks became synonymous with this scheme. Until now, however, the identity of "F D" and the purpose of his countermarks have been largely misunderstood. This paper aims at rectifying this situation by introducing primary evidence unknown to Chalmers and the other numismatists who have researched the F D countermarks in the past 125 years.

The small Caribbean islands offer a rich numismatic history, mostly because Spanish-American and other "dollars" were officially cut and counterstamped in the eighteenth and nineteenth centuries to provide for local currencies.[1] Some

---

* Thorneloe University at Laurentian University (gchamberland@laurentian.ca).

1. I accept here the terminological convention that a counterstamp is official in character while a countermark is private. For a summary of different views, see Baker (2006, vi–vii). See also Krause (2015, 11; or the introduction of any recent Krause world coin catalogue).

more alterations were made privately by merchants and traders so that official currencies were at times supplemented with what amounted to private token coinages. The aim of this paper is to contribute to our knowledge of one such private alteration, the large and deeply incused F D countermarks attributed to Port of Spain resident François "Declos" and his imitators.[2]

1. WHAT WE THINK WE KNOW

One of the few things we think we know about "Declos," besides his counter-marking of hundreds, if not thousands, of coins and tokens from the 1850s to the 1870s, is that he was a barber. Since the late nineteenth century the verdict of numismatists, to all intents and purposes, has been unanimous on this. The earliest reference is a footnote in Robert Chalmers's *History of Currency in the British Colonies* (Chalmers 1893, 123):

> It is worthy of note that in the middle of the century a local barber, François Declos, stamped his initials on all pence and half-pence (valued at 2 cents and 1 cent) which came into his hands, and issued the stamped coins for 2½ and 1¼ cents respectively. These "Stampees" were freely received at the barber's valuation.

Chalmers, most unfortunately, did not cite his source. All later numismatic publications which claim that F D stands for a barber named "François Declos" go back to Chalmers in some way or other. Especially worthy of note are Howland Wood (1914, 110), Fred Pridmore (1961, 168–169; 1965, 221–222), Robert Lyall (1989, 167), and Greg Brunk (1989, 58; 2003, 332). Ray Byrne (1971, 114, quoted below, Appendix 2) and Warren Baker (2006, 107) accepted Chalmers's account, but more hesitantly. Frank Duffield, in his pioneering work on counter-marks, likewise reported that the F D countermark is "*said to be* for Francois Declos, a barber, for local use" (1919–21, 93; italics mine).

This is not to say that there has not been any progress in our understanding of the F D countermarks since Chalmers. Much credit goes to Fred Pridmore, who was the most able to review Chalmers's account on the basis of the primary evidence, i.e., the coins themselves. Although Pridmore's views will need to be revised extensively, it is worth quoting him at some length, not least because his catalogue is now out of print and rather difficult to obtain:

---

2. I use quotation marks around "Declos" and "Duclos" until the name issue is addressed further on in the paper. When quoting, too, I spell the first name exactly as in the source, i.e., Francois or (correctly) François.

Figure 1. British halfpenny, bronze, 1864, with F D countermark deeply incused. This seems to be the best attested set of letter punches and may well be Declos/Duclos's original. 25.7 mm, 5.28 g.

Figure 2. US large cent, copper, 1844, with F D countermark from the same punches as in Fig. 1 (the differences in the F are attributable to how it shifted when punched on the 1864 halfpenny). 27.5 mm, 10.09 g.

Figure 3. British halfpenny, copper, 1831–1837, with F D countermark deeply incused. 27.9 mm, 7.65 g.

> Coins stamped with the F D initials occur with varying styles which show that more than one set of punches were used. The actual coins themselves include English copper and bronze halfpence; 18th and 19th century English and Colonial tokens; coins of Austria, Denmark, France, Russia, Spain and the United States of America, in fact a whole miscellany. But of all the specimens traced, including a local collection of 30 pieces, not ONE piece corresponds in size to the English copper penny. Every coin, whether struck in copper or bronze, corresponds approximately in size to either the English copper or bronze halfpenny (Pridmore 1965, 222).

While this was a perceptive analysis of the evidence, the conclusions that immediately followed were not all sound:

Figure 4. Unidentified coin or token, copper or bronze, with F D countermark deeply incused. 28.4 mm, 7.36 g.

Figure 5. Province of Nova Scotia halfpenny, copper, 1832, with F D countermark deeply incused. The punch letters are inferior in workmanship. 28.1 mm, 7.48 g. On the possible Canadian origin of this F D punch, see note 21.

Figure 6. British halfpenny, bronze, 1872, with F D countermark not as deeply incused as in Figs. 1–5. The punch letters are inferior in workmanship. 25.6 mm, 5.45 g.

> The impression gained from this study of the available material is that only ONE VALUE was intended by the barber, and that the counter-marked coins, irrespective of their origin or denomination, simply passed as a "stampee" (= 2 Cents or Penny). They are catalogued accordingly until further proof is forthcoming (Pridmore 1965, 222).

It was certainly reasonable to formulate the hypothesis that only one value was intended, but the assumption that the value of the countermarked coins was thereby doubled to a stampee worth a penny or two cents was unjustified.[3] New

3. This remains the accepted view (Lyall 1989, 167–168; Brunk 2003, 332). Brunk, however, also accepts Chalmers's values, which cannot be reconciled with Pridmore's. An *AJN* referee points out to me that the Jamaican William Smith penny token countermarked F D and sold on May 2, 2014, at the Raymond Brandon auction (Brandon 2014, lot 923 with plate) was, at

documentary evidence now shows that Chalmers was right with regard to the value of the F D countermarked coins and tokens.

The current wisdom can be summarized thus (adding some well-known details not introduced above):

1. Coins and tokens were countermarked from the 1850s to the 1870s with large and incused F D letters by a Port of Spain barber, François Declos, and his imitators.
2. Their value was thereby augmented, perhaps doubled.
3. Given that we know of at least eighteen different sets of punches,[4] it is probable that many residents started to punch F D initials in imitation of Declos in order to get a share in the profit-making scheme.
4. This activity ceased with the adoption, in 1874, of the Trinidad Coin Ordinance, section 9 of which made coin defacement a misdemeanor.

Most of these points can and will be challenged in some way or other in the next sections. Yet, before moving on, a further, enigmatic piece of evidence should be introduced. In two of his books Brunk (1989, 58; 2003, 332) cites a personal note he received from Pridmore in 1976 (my filling out of abbreviations is within square brackets; everything else is exactly as transcribed by Brunk):[5]

> Most FD c[ounter]m[arked] pieces are contemp[orary] forgeries. It seems the major part of the population got in the project and seem to have so stamped FD on every copper or bronze piece that reached the island. So when the local authorities requested F[rançois] D[eclos] to redeem his pieces, he paid out … (many) more than he had coined.

about 29 mm in diameter, certainly too small to pass for a penny in Trinidad. I should add that at 9.61 g, it is slightly lighter than the American large cent, a common host for the F D countermark (Pridmore 1965, 110). On the "stampee," which originally was a French colonial coin called "stampé" (i.e., "marked"), see Dyroff (1987) and Pridmore (1965, 222, also 215–216 about the Tobago stampee). On the Trinidadian monetary system see Appendix 1.

4. Compare Figs. 1–6. Pridmore knew of fourteen sets (1965, 222), but Lyall claimed that there were at least eighteen (1989, 168). He informed me via email on Feb. 19, 2019, that he did not have the evidence any longer but assured me that he "would have checked each punch." Brunk also gave the number of eighteen (1989, 58), again without evidence, but he may have taken the figure from Lyall whose book he cites elsewhere on the same page. It is also possible that he got an updated figure from Pridmore. On Brunk's correspondence with Pridmore, see next note.

5. I got in touch with Professor Brunk via his editor, Rich Hartzog, until the latter's untimely death at the age of 70 in November 2017. Since Brunk has almost entirely lost his sight, Hartzog read him my letter over the phone. One of my questions was whether the full version of Pridmore's letter added anything to the excerpt quoted by Brunk in his books. The answer is presented below, section 4.

This is not supported with any reference to sources and cannot be traced back to Pridmore's writings on Trinidad (1961; 1965, 219–226, 333–338), but a 1948 booklet relates much the same story:[6]

> There being at one time an insufficiency of change, pieces were stamped out of the dollars and circulated, at the value of 10¢ each, under the name of "escalin clou." Even these were not sufficient, however, so shopkeepers began to issue their own tokens, called "marks" locally, of very small value. When these private tokens along with other confusing coinage were later replaced by sterling at the instance of Sir Ralph Woodford, some traders whose total value of outstanding tokens were swollen by counterfeits were reduced to near bankruptcy. One such merchant, a M. Francois Declos, whose tokens were stamped "F.D.," was called upon to cash an amount estimated as high as 500 per cent over that which he had issued (Pitts 1948, 13).

Harold Pitts, who wrote these lines, did not cite any sources to support them. As a matter of fact, he did not cite sources anywhere in his book, nor did he provide any bibliographical references. One cannot even determine whether he used any official documents. An estimate of "as high as 500 per cent" would not go back to an official order of recall—if any ever existed—but to a later account. Perhaps two or more sources were used, including possibly some official document. Still, there are obvious historical problems in the passage quoted which are compounded by the very lack of references. The spelling "Declos," which is almost certainly wrong, would suggest that Pitts used Chalmers or Wood, but neither says anything of the alleged recall, nor do they use the term "marks" for or instead of "half-stampees." What is more, no source other than Pitts seems to record "mark" as a colloquial term for a currency unit in Trinidad, which suggests that it was *his* translation of the term "stampee."[7] The mention of Sir Ralph Woodford inspires even less confidence, since he was governor of the island from 1813 to 1828, as Pitts knew well (1948, 21–25), a quarter of a century before "Declos" even began to stamp his initials on coins. The whole passage,

---

6. In light of his book, Harold Pitts was no historian, but he was not foreign to research since he had co-written a book on the calypso in 1944.

7. Cf. Winer (2009, s.v. "mark"). As for "escalin clou," while I have not been able to find this expression in any nineteenth-century document, Borde reports that in his days the term "escalin" (on its own) was still used in the island to mean a coin worth approximately "12 sous" (Borde 1882, 99), which actually corresponds to Pitts's "10¢." The term "clou" ("nail" in French) was used for cut coins (cf. Winer 2009, s.v. "escalin clou"). Zay (1892, 361) records it for French Cochinchina, where it was the triangular eighth of a cut Mexican dollar, but I have not been able to find any Caribbean example.

oddly, was inserted among a series of facts about Trinidad at the time of the British conquest in 1797.

To rescue the excerpt in any way, and perhaps Pridmore's letter to Brunk, it is necessary to examine documents that have been neglected or ignored so far, as well as several pieces of legislation which were issued in the middle decades of the nineteenth century until the 1870s, when the erratic currency situation was finally addressed.

2. OLD TEXTS, NEW EVIDENCE

None of the writers presented so far seems to have been aware of three non-numismatic sources (two by the same author) that contradict the current wisdom in significant ways: two of them use the name "Duclos" and one, in addition, makes it clear that he was *not* a barber. The three also contribute significantly to our understanding of the economic incentive for "Duclos" and his imitators to countermark coins—so much so that most of what we thought we knew will have to be discarded.

It will be easier to start with the two later sources, which are reminiscences by Lewis O. Inniss (1848–1940), first published in 1910 as a book chapter and expanded into a small book in 1932. The author recalled, among many other things, the chaotic state of the currency in his youth (see Appendix 1). In his earlier publication, Inniss had this to say about small change:

> The half-bit or five cent piece was the most popular coin, and the half of that was called a stampee. As there was no coin to represent this, it was made up of a penny and a farthing and when for some reason farthings became scarce the shopkeepers simplified matters by cutting the half-bit into two pieces, and the mutilated coin passed current in all the shops as a stampee. Some went further and cut the 'bits' into four triangles, to make stampees, and these were also cheerfully accepted over the counters. A half-stampee was also a recognized value, but as no coin could be found to represent it (1¼ cents) the ingenious shopkeepers again came to the rescue, for they stamped their initials upon a one-cent piece and then both gave and accepted it in change for a half-stampee or one and a quarter cents (Inniss 1910, 92–93; also quoted in Elliott 1914, 31)!

In the 1932 version, Inniss was more specific about the countermarked coins. It is worth quoting him at some length, even though there is some overlap with the passage just given:

> The copper coinage was mostly British pennies and half-pennies. [...] As
> time went on and the money market got tighter, the necessity for a half-
> stampe was felt and this need was got over by shopkeepers stamping their
> initials on the half-penny and giving and receiving it over the counter as a
> half-stampe... One Francois Duclos started the custom with F.D. stamped
> on a half-penny piece and lots of others imitating him. Quite a Patriar-
> chal way of adapting the currency to the needs of the population. After a
> while the Government woke up to the necessity of putting its monetary
> house in order and straightened out the Currency chaos. An Ordinance
> was passed calling in all foreign coins and making British the only legal
> tender thenceforward (Inniss 1932, 18–19; quoted in Brown 1989, 17–18;
> Brown 1990, 35–36).

This Port of Spain resident remembered F D as being François Duclos. He could
be remembering incorrectly, but in light of the sharpness of his remarks about
the currency situation and the fact that he was a resident of Port of Spain, his
account should be taken as a serious challenger to Chalmers's.

The two sets of reminiscences support Pridmore in some but not all aspects
of his analysis. First, in terms of what coins were countermarked, Inniss recalled
only halfpennies though he was aware that pennies were also circulating at that
time. Admittedly, he is somewhat inaccurate since a wide variety of coins and
tokens were actually countermarked, but his account suggests that halfpenny-
sized pieces were by far the most commonly (if not the only) countermarked
coins. Second, the variety of marks (which, interestingly, he remembered better
than the variety of host coins) was to be explained by Duclos's imitators, which
was the view taken by Pridmore. If others imitated Duclos by stamping their *own*
initials, as Inniss relates, the fact that only one such mark can be documented so
far[8] indicates that they were not successful and abandoned the practice quickly,
or else they swallowed their pride and went with the F D mark that everybody
trusted.

With regard to the currency of such tokens, however, Inniss's account vindi-
cates Chalmers' since he claims the countermarked halfpennies were circulating

---

8. Late in 2016 an 1858 Venezuelan *centavo* was auctioned on eBay with an F D stamped over
an R G countermark. R G might have been a Venezuelan, but it seems just as likely that he was
a pioneer or early imitator of the practice so successfully taken over by "Duclos." Names that
immediately come to mind are those of Robert Guppy, father (quoted below as a member of the
1886 Taxes and Trade Commission) and son (see Guppy 1882), but neither was a trader, merchant, or shopkeeper. A doubtful A D countermark is discussed in Appendix 2.

as half-stampees, or 1¼ cents coins.[9] It is significant that for Inniss, the countermarking was a "way of adapting the currency to the needs of the population." The incentive given by most numismatists since Pridmore, that of a quick profit (Pridmore 1965, 222; Byrne 1971, 114; Lyall 1989, 167–168; Brunk 1989, 58; Brunk 2003, 332), apparently did not cross his mind. If Inniss is right, the countermarks did not increase significantly (let alone double) the value of the pieces.

From a historian's perspective, the next document, which includes a brief but most significant mention of the F D tokens, is invaluable. Not only is it earlier than Chalmers by seven years, it also originated in Trinidad. What is more, the context is an official enquiry into the trade and taxes situation in the island, for which Governor William Robinson struck a Commission in August 1886. The Chairman, Sir John Gorrie, was a British judge with much experience in the colonies. He had been appointed Chief Justice of Trinidad in 1885 and landed on the shores of the colony early in the following year.[10] Most of the other thirteen members were Port of Spain residents, such as Henry J. Clark, Government Printer, and Louis A. A. de Verteuil, Member of the Legislative Council, former Mayor of Port of Spain, and a prominent personality in many other respects; he had, four years earlier, published the second edition of his important study of the geography, natural resources, and administration of Trinidad (de Verteuil 1884). The Government Printing Office published each day of the evidence-gathering as individual pamphlets; this was done so quickly that the commissioners and witnesses sometimes made reference to earlier pamphlets. The entire proceedings were published soon after the Commission completed its deliberations. These facts are important since they contribute to the reliability of the evidence about to be presented.

On the eighth and ninth days of its deliberations, the Commission invited several witnesses who were flour traders or bakers. The following exchange took place on the ninth day, September 23, the witness being Mr. A. Mendez, a "provision dealer" who dealt in flour:

> Mr. Mendez: Our coin is now shillings and pence, of course; but we always sell by the old five cents—what we call a half-a-bitt; and before it used to be a stampee, and then a half stampee would be a cent and a quarter, and there was no coin for the half stampee, which used to be a cent stamped with the name of some responsible shopkeeper in town with the

9. The value of the stampee is reported in several other sources, for example de Verteuil (1884, 217) and Commission (1886, 22, 31; quoted below).

10. See Brereton (1997, 226–258) on Gorrie's first Trinidad appointment in 1886–1889; the Commission is discussed on pages 241–242.

permission of the Government, and he used to give it out and the people would give it in exchange, but it would be returned to buy with in the place where it was issued; but if he was a wealthy man people would have no objection to take that stampee. I remember the time when all the half stampees were stamped "F. D."

Mr. Hoffmann: It was stopped long ago.

Mr. Clark: "F. D.", François Duclos, was a baker, and it was done in order to get a coin to represent the half stampee loaf. It was not done with any sanction from Government.

Mr. Mendez: We had in English coin the five stampees (12½ cents). That was in English money.

The Chairman: But where you have a mass of poor population in a town of this kind, why should not there be the farthing? For example, you would give these two little loaves[11] for a cent, but why should not a little child be able to get one of those loaves for a farthing. You say there are farthings?

Mr. Mendez: I suppose there are some, but I have never seen them lately. I believe that is a great want of exchange for the poorer class. There is no small coin.

Mr. Hoffmann: Many of the merchants import their own coins here, because the Colonial Bank does not keep a sufficient stock (Commission 1886, Ninth Day, 31–32).

This exchange leaves no doubt that F D was François Duclos, not "Declos." In addition, he was not a barber but a baker. Mendez and Clark agree (with no-one present objecting) that the countermarks were meant to set the value of foreign coppers at a half-stampee, the price of a small loaf of bread. The point, therefore, was to facilitate trade, not to make a quick profit out of the manipulation of the currency, as Pridmore's hypothesis would have it.

Barber tokens were sometimes issued in the nineteenth and early twentieth century, for example in Britain and the United States, but bread tokens were much more common. While barbers provide a number of services at a variety of prices,[12] bread comes in standard sizes. In many countries or regions, bakers

---

11. The Chairman had at his disposal a number of loaves of different sizes and kinds.

12. In the United States (and presumably elsewhere), besides shaves and haircuts, barbers sometimes provided services such as drinks (in dry jurisdictions) and slot machines (Akin et al. 2016, 102; bakery tokens are briefly discussed on 101). Both referees for this article pointed

issued tokens GOOD FOR 1 LOAF, which were often complemented with GOOD
FOR ½ LOAF tokens. In Trinidad, now that we have established that Duclos's
pieces were bread tokens,[13] it might be useful to look at another local issue: the
Rapsey half-stampee tokens.

3. FLOUR, BAKERS, LOAVES

Horatio Edwin Rapsey was a baker and grocer at 9, Frederick Street, Port of
Spain. He had his own half-stampees minted in the 1860s.[14] The obverse reads
HALF / STAMPEE / REDEEMABLE AT / H.E. RAPSEYS and the reverse, BAKERY &
GROCERY / 9 FREDERICK ST PORTOFSPAIN. Whether Duclos or Rapsey initiated
the local practice of issuing tokens is not clear. What Mr. Mendez says in the passage quoted above indicates that a large number of coppers had been stamped
with the initials F D. This may suggest that Duclos and his imitators initiated
the practice and upheld it for many years, probably until 1874 as we will see.
Pridmore estimated that the countermarking took place over two decades and,
therefore, suggested 1854 as an approximate starting date (1965, 222). At any
rate, Rapsey seems to have been unsuccessful in issuing his half-stampees since
they are now very scarce. Interestingly, some are attested with the F D countermark (e.g., Brunk 2003, 332 = Krause 2015, no. Tn1.2).

Rapsey is known to numismatists for his tokens, but not for his testimony
before the 1886 Commission. On the eighth day of inquiry, beside pointing out
that he had been "a baker for thirty years standing" (Commission 1886, Eighth
Day, 4),[15] he says something of the kind of baker he is:

> Vast quantities of bread in this country are made into cent loaves, and
> three loaves are sold for a penny. We don't do anything in that trade. We
> leave that, of course, to the other bakers. We don't go anything beyond the
> penny loaf. Others give three for a penny. That is good for the labouring
> classes (Commission 1886, Eighth Day, 11).

out that it would have been easy for Chalmers to misread "barber" where his correspondent
wrote "baker." Since it seems unlikely that "k" could be misread "rb," even in the clumsiest of
handwriting, my own hypothesis is that the correspondent overstretched his "a" to make it
look like "ar"; it would then be easy to read "b" instead of "k."

13. They obviously gained much wider acceptance; see next section.

14. Pridmore 1965 no. 5 = Lyall 1989 no. 508 = Krause 2015 no. Tn3. It was presented at
the February 20, 1868, session of the Numismatic Society of London (*Numismatic Chronicle*,
8, 1868, "Proceedings of the Numismatic Society. Session 1867–1868," 6); this is the earliest
known print reference to this piece.

15. He had, however, retired four or five years earlier (Commission 1886, Eighth Day, 7), and
turned the business over to his son (cf. Commission, Eighth Day, 5), by which he means John
Alfred Rapsey (Bissessarsingh 2012).

This indicates that Rapsey's tokens, valued at a half-stampee, were not intended primarily to purchase bread. Admittedly, much time had passed between the 1860s, when he issued his tokens, and 1886, but in light of his testimony, there is no reason to think that Rapsey's trade had ever been in buying other than the best flour to bake the best bread. He was not alone in this since another baker, Charles Haynes (Commission 1886, Ninth Day, 13–25), stressed that he did the same, and that "it is not ignorant people but the better class that buy the bread" (Commission 1886, Ninth Day, 15). Both agreed, therefore, that beside those Rapsey called "gentlemen bakers" (Commission 1886, Eighth Day, 5–6), there were, as Haynes put it, "cheap bakers that make cheap bread with an inferior class of flour" (Commission 1886, Ninth Day, 17). Given the success of his half-stampees, it is very likely that Duclos belonged to the latter category—which the Chairman more respectfully called "ordinary bakers" (Commission 1886, Ninth Day, 17).

Rapsey's testimony is useful in other ways as well. He insists that a cancellation of tariffs on flour would have no impact on the price of individual loaves; ordinary folks, therefore, would not benefit from any such measure. The reduction of the duty on flour, he added, "would amount to one farthing on the penny loaf, and there is no coin in the country to represent it. It does not amount to a farthing" (Commission 1886, Eighth Day, 5).[16] Further on, he is particularly honest:

> When the duty on flour was lowered from 5 s[hillings = $1.20] down to 80 cents, it was not possible that any baker or any retailer in a shop could make any difference to the consumer. When the Government took off that 40 cents, they put 40 cents a barrel into my pocket, for all the years that I carried on the business under the reduced tariff of 80 cents a barrel (Commission 1886, Eighth Day, 5).

Later on Chairman Gorrie pointed out that the cancellation of tariffs could save a penny on a dozen of loaves but Rapsey insisted here (Commission 1886, Eighth Day, 14) and at several other points that the people of Trinidad buy only small quantities of bread at any time.

Of relevance to the shortage of small change is the issue of the legislation regarding the sale of bread. This was raised many times (e.g., Commission 1886, Eighth Day, 5–6), but several questions remained unanswered by Rapsey (who obviously was not a lawyer) or the commissioners. Fortunately Mr. Clark there-

---

16. Mr. William Kell, a businessman but not a baker, said basically the same thing (Commission 1886, Seventh Day, 23).

after investigated the issue further and presented his research on the ninth day (Commission 1886, Ninth Day, 22–24). Ordinance 3 of 1835, he reported, regulated the price and weight of the stampee, half-bit, bit, and two-bit loaves. It also required bakers "to keep 'a Beam and Scales with proper Weights,' and to weigh when required, any Bread sold by them, in the presence of the purchaser." A table prescribed the weight of each category of bread according to the average price of a barrel of flour, between $7 and $10 (Commission 1886, Ninth Day, 22). The stampee loaf, for example, was to weigh 7 oz 10 dwts when flour was at $7/barrel and 5 oz 15 dwts when it was at $10/barrel. The 1835 Ordinance was repealed by Ordinance 12 of 1846 which, Clark pointed out, was still in force (Commission 1886, Ninth Day, 23). While the weight of the loaves was mentioned, there was no accompanying table, so that bakers were pretty much free to sell any size of bread:

> The Chairman: I see section 3 is that they should sell by weight, but section 14 allowed them to fix the loaf at any size or weight.

> Mr. Clark: Exactly so. It has been suggested to me that the want of copper coins may have been the reason why a new assize was not introduced; that it would have been necessary to regulate it according to the coins used in the Colony, and that it was intended to bring in such an assize later on (Commission 1886, Ninth Day, 24).

Just a few minutes earlier, Clark had reported that in 1846 Governor Harris had "stated that the objection to the existing Ordinance (3 of 1835) was that the poor man who purchased a stampee loaf was obliged to take his change in an article he did not want, from the want of a smaller coin than the stampee" (Commission 1886, Ninth Day, 23). This is all very useful to understand the consequences of the shortage of small change, even though it is inaccurate with regard to the legislation, for another commissioner, Mr. Robert Guppy, Mayor of San Fernando, commented:

> I remember that Ordinance very clearly. [… A]t the time [...] the laws with regard to assize in England had been abolished, and it was the intention that it should be the same here. It was not by a side-wind that the assize of bread was done away with; it was intended that the trade in bread should be free, but only that for the protection of the purchaser it might be insisted upon that the bread should be weighed in order that he should know the weight of the bread that he purchased for his money (Commission 1886, Ninth Day, 24).

It seems likely, therefore, that the Ordinance brought about an unintended consequence since bakers were now better able to adjust the size of their loaves to match the available currency. If so, this was far from satisfactory given that Duclos's token scheme would be so successful a decade or so later.

It may be useful at this point to introduce two interesting observations gathered from Clark's notes. First, the 1835 Ordinance did not mention the half-stampee loaf (Commission 1886, Ninth Day, 22). The stampee loaf, it should be noted, probably would have been paid for in silver most of the time, i.e., with one half of a cut 5¢.[17] Second, copper coins came into more general circulation in the later 1830s (Commission 1886, Ninth Day, 24). By about 1850 the colony may have been supplied reasonably well with copper and bronze coin since Ordinance 15 of that year intended to limit legal tender to four pence.[18] The evidence presented so far suggests that few of the copper and bronze coins were of penny or farthing size and that most, therefore, must have been halfpennies or foreign coins roughly the size of the halfpenny. The hosts of the F D countermarks, if they are representative in any way of the copper and bronze in circulation towards the middle of the nineteenth century, confirm this hypothesis (Brunk 2003, 332; see also Lyall 1989, 168–169).[19] Besides the single lightweight penny token already mentioned,[20] and no farthing, there are several dozen halfpennies and halfpenny-size pieces which have been reported. They include, among others, British halfpennies from George III to Victoria (at least 10, including 7 from 1861–1872); early nineteenth-century British halfpenny tokens (7); halfpennies, cents, and other coins of similar size from the British possessions of Ireland, Gibraltar, and India (3); mid-nineteenth-century halfpenny tokens and large cents from Canada, Nova Scotia, Prince Edward Island, and Newfoundland (16);[21] also, American coins and tokens, 1837–1853 (10, including 3 large

17. I.e., half of a half-bit. Most of the half-bit pieces were French silver 25-*centimes* (Chalmers 1893, 121). Inniss claimed that the bit was sometimes cut in four (1932, 18–19 quoted above).

18. This, however, was disallowed by the Queen on advice of the Treasury (Parliamentary Papers 1852–53 no. 268, 14–16). In light of this documentation, Pridmore was probably wrong to believe that copper coins were uncommon before about 1850 (1961, 168).

19. Pridmore (1965, 222) quotes the 1862 "Blue Book" where it is stated that "[c]opper coins of all descriptions pass current owing to the scarcity of British copper money."

20. It is possible that the idea of a large *copper* stampee was not well received by the population.

21. There are so many of these that it seems possible that another F D was doing business and countermarking coins in one of the British North American colonies (Baker 2006, 33–34, 107). I have myself acquired a Nova Scotia 1832 halfpenny with deeply incused F D letters (Fig. 5); it may be significant that the seller was based in Canada.

cents); French and French colonial coins, 1767–1855 (10); Venezuela *centavo* pieces, 1852–1862 (5); and coins from Austria, Denmark, Portugal, Spain, Italy, Sardinia, and Russia, 1771–1859 (8). Most of these pieces were "upgraded" from a halfpenny or a cent to 1¼ cents, i.e., a half-stampee. All were turned into half-stampees, whatever their intrinsic value (but see note 21).

François Duclos's scheme was very successful, with others imitating him and stamping *his* initials on halfpenny-size coins. He may just have been the first to try to rectify the uneasy relationship between the local customs and the copper coins actually circulating. Based on the evidence presented so far, his half-stampees were widely accepted beyond their original purpose as bread tokens. This is summarized very well in the testimony of Mr. Mendez already quoted. For values smaller than the half-bit, people on the street usually did business in stampees and half-stampees, denominations which were going back to the *stampé* or *estampé* of the largely French and Créole population in Spanish colonial times.[22] Duclos and his imitators understood the importance of local customs and the need for a standardized copper and bronze coinage for small transactions. In economic terms, it could be said that they created conditions to increase the velocity of money. They were successful, the people went along, and as Mr. Mendez remarked, "if he [who stamped his initials] was a wealthy man people would have no objection to take that stampee." What Inniss remembered of the cutting of silver coins into halves and quarters is significant in this context since these cut pieces, too, were private alterations.[23] Merchants, traders, and their patrons, therefore, took the street economy into their own hands in the absence of a coherent policy on the part of the colonial government. Chalmers, writing about the Trinidad of his own days, remarked:

> As no ordinance has ever been passed in this island prescribing sterling denominations of account, (i) private persons continue to reckon exclusively by dollars and cents, whilst (ii) in the Government offices accounts are kept both in £. s. d. and in $ currency (Chalmers 1893, 123).

It should be noted, however, that a piece of legislation then only two decades old was of great consequence for the circulation of small change. It was left unmentioned by Chalmers and later writers, including Pridmore,[24] until Lyall noticed it. Ordinance no. 1 of 1874, section 9, making coin defacement a criminal of-

---

22. See above, note 3, and Frey (1916, 228, s.v. "Stampee", 236 s.v. "Tampé"). Great Britain seized Trinidad from Spain in 1797. This was formally recognized in the Treaty of Amiens, 1802.

23. Bits and half-bits had been officially cut for the last time in 1804 (Pridmore 1965, 220, 223).

24. He discusses only the version relevant to Barbados (Pridmore 1965, 78).

fence, must have put an end to the F D countermarking; this is supported by the fact that the latest coins attested with the F D initials are 1872 halfpennies (Lyall 1989, 168) (Fig. 6). From a socio-historical perspective, however, much more can be said.

4. STAMPEES, ORDINANCES, PENNIES

It will be well to start with the British version of the text, i.e., section 16 of the Coinage Offences Act (24 & 25 Victoria [= 1860–1862] cap. 99), which was used in the writing of the subsequent colonial versions:

> Whosoever shall deface any of the Queen's current gold, silver, or copper coin,[25] by stamping thereon any names or words, whether such coin shall or shall not be thereby diminished or lightened, shall, in England and Ireland, be guilty of a misdemeanour, and in Scotland of a crime and offence, and being convicted thereof shall be liable, at the discretion of the court, to be imprisoned for any term not exceeding one year, with or without hard labour.

Except for the underlined parts which were removed, and for minor punctuation variants, the text was identical for the following colonies: Hong Kong (Law 10 of 1865, section 16), New Zealand (31 Victoria [= 1867/68] Law 2, section 16), Barbados (Law 4 of 1868, section 16), and Jamaica (Law 21 of 1872, section 18).[26] For some other colonies and dominions (such as Canada) the content was in essence the same, but the text was rearranged. In Trinidad, however, while the British formulation was adopted, there were some substantial insertions (underlined) and a minor deletion (crossed out):

> Whosoever shall deface any of the Queen's current gold, silver, or copper coin, or the gold, silver, or copper coin of any foreign state, prince, or country, whether ordered or permitted to be current in this Colony or not, by stamping or otherwise putting thereon any names, or words, or letters, or by cutting any marks on the same, or by perforating the same, whether such coin shall or shall not be thereby diminished or lightened, shall be guilty of a misdemeanour, and being convicted thereof shall be liable, at the discretion of the court, to be imprisoned for any term not exceeding one year with or without hard labour.

---

25. Section 1: "the expression 'the Queen's copper coin' shall include any copper coin and any coin of bronze or mixed metal […]."

26. This is not meant to be a comprehensive list. I am just reporting examples I was able to find in electronic repositories such as the Internet Archive and Google Books.

It seems most likely that the legislators, in drafting section 9 of the Coin Ordinance, had the F D countermarks in mind. The wording of section 16 in the British act was too narrow since it did not consider individual letters (including of course initials) as a possible form of defacement.[27] Just as significant is the fact that the legislation applied not only to legal tender, but to any coin, while the British legislation did not prevent anyone from stamping foreign coins with names or words.

The immediately following article (10) must have been a major concern to Duclos and the others who had invested the most energy in the countermarking scheme:

> No tender of payment in money made in any gold, silver, or copper coin so defaced as in the last preceding section mentioned shall be allowed to be a legal tender, and whosoever shall knowingly and wilfully tender, utter, or put off, any coin so defaced shall on conviction thereof before any stipendiary justice of the peace be liable to forfeit and pay any sum not exceeding five pounds, or at the discretion of the said justice to be imprisoned, with hard labour, for any term not exceeding three months.

Why were the legislators so hard on the half-stampee, the coin of the lower classes? Probably because this denomination, unlike the bit and half-bit, was at odds with the sterling legal tender. While rates such as 1 penny = 2 cents, or a half-bit = 5 cents = 2½ pence, were easy to calculate and widely accepted, the F D half-stampee was a 1¼-cents coin which could not be converted into sterling. What is more, British halfpennies imported into the island were being defaced and converted into this local, unofficial currency. And what if you tendered two identical halfpennies, only one countermarked? It is probably at this time, therefore, that the half-stampee was in all but name demonetized—or rather criminalized—and disappeared as a currency unit. What Rapsey called the "cent loaf" as he was standing before the 1886 Commission (Eighth Day, 11), a thing he would not bake, was probably the successor of the half-stampee loaf on the stalls of the "cheap" or "regular" Trinidadian bakers.

According to Pitts and Pridmore, as we saw, the authorities requested Duclos to redeem his tokens, but I have not been able to find any piece of legislation to confirm this. Perhaps common people did not need any legislation; once

---

27. An interesting case occurred in the early 1900s, when the Dunlop Tire Co. stamped their trademark of two hands on Canadian coins. This became a concern for the government of the Dominion, but the Ministry of Finance decided that no legal case could be brought against Dunlop since the criminal code provided only for defacement caused by stamping names or words (Brunk 1998, 193).

words about the Ordinance got around, possibly hundreds rushed to the baker with their half-stampees and asked for sterling in return. A folktale may well have grown up about it, and Inniss may provide some further hints of what happened. In the later version of his reminiscences, in the excerpt already quoted, he claimed that an ordinance was passed which both called in all foreign coins and made British sterling the only legal tender. There is no piece of legislation that fits this description exactly. The closest match is an ordinance which demonetized Spanish and Spanish-American silver "dollars" and granted one month to holders of such coins to take them to the Colonial Treasury to exchange them. This was Ordinance 7 of 1876, passed only two years after the Coin Ordinance. If a folktale started to grow around the Duclos mishap, one would expect other coin-related stories to contribute in its embellishment. This is all very speculative, but overall one can certainly put more trust in Inniss's version of what happened than in Pitts's. In August 2017, I got in touch with the world authority on merchant countermarks, Gregory Brunk, via Rich Hartzog, his editor at the Exonumia Press (see n. 5). Hartzog reported that Pridmore had written Brunk several times, relating the information contained in the letter quoted in his two books, but "Brunk, and most likely Pridmore, had no referential basis for it. Brunk says it was probably a story handed down, a 'good story' that was probably true, but Brunk has no evidence, and he thinks Fred [Pridmore] did not either" (R. Hartzog, email communication, August 24, 2017).

Before concluding this paper, two more numismatic items should be taken into consideration. First, a coin described as a "Halfpenny, countermarked I STAMPEE" was listed in the Caldecott 1912 auction catalogue (lot 439). It was then mentioned by Wood (1914, 110), Frey (1916, s.v. "Stampee"), and Pridmore (1961, 168), but none of them was able to trace its wanderings after 1912. Assuming for a moment that the attribution to Trinidad is right, the denomination of 1 stampee would have more than doubled the value of this halfpenny. It is probable, therefore, that the piece should not be attributed to Trinidad and that it actually is a forgery. As a matter of fact, the sale contained a number of items which we now know to be forgeries, such as a Spanish-American dollar countermarked G R 5 ORD (Caldecott 1912, lot 388, cf. 389).

The other piece is a farthing token issued by J. G. D'Ade & Co., Port of Spain (Pridmore 1965 no. 6 = Lyall 1989 no. 498 = Krause 2015 Tn3). Without providing evidence Pridmore (1965, 224) dated it to about 1874. Lowsley seems to have been unaware of its existence when he was "stationed in Trinidad from 1867–1869, and again a year or two later" (Lowsley 1895, 214), so Pridmore may well be right, though a slightly later date should not be ruled out. John D'Ade himself informed Lowsley in a letter dated March 1, 1889, that he had 10,000 struck but had not seen any in circulation for many years (Lowsley 1895, 214). That would confirm the exchange between Gorrie and Mendez already quoted about the lack of farthings. By the mid 1880s, therefore, neither D'Ade's nor British farthings were seen in circulation. But what about the mid-1870s? It would be interesting to know whether D'Ade issued his farthings in response to the 1874 Ordinance. Since he was a dry goods merchant, he may well have been selling a broad range of items for a stampee; issuing a farthing (or half-cent) would have provided some badly needed small change after the stampee was killed by the legislation.

5. FRANÇOIS DUCLOS, BAKER

A reader who has reached this far is likely to see François Duclos as a rather elusive character. His name indicates that he was of French descent, but he never speaks for himself. We do not know when and where he was born, whether he married and had children, or when he died. He seems to have done very well as a baker for the lower classes, at least for a time. So he may have had much in common with Mr. Les Chaloupés, a baker who was a witness before the 1886 Commission (Ninth Day, 25–29). During his testimony (translated from French) Les Chaloupés said that he was buying his flour in the local market, not abroad, and that he was generally making second-quality bread: "I make two different qualities of bread; one cheaper for the poorer people. […] I make very little of the first quality, I work for the people" (Commission 1886, Ninth Day, 25–26). He must have been doing quite well since he then pointed out that he had "three different bakeries in the town" (Commission 1886, Ninth Day, 26). Interestingly, he disagreed with the "gentlemen bakers" about the proposition of taking off the duty on flour:

> I am of opinion that if you take off the duty from flour I will be able to give the poor people more bread for the price and give them a better quality; because there are certain marks of flour which I cannot buy at present because the cost is too high. When flour goes down these brands will be available for me to use, either separately or mixed, and therefore the poor people will get bread not only of better quality, but more bread.

Les Chaloupés' testimony reveals a wider gap between the lower and upper economic classes than Rapsey was willing to admit. In this context, if Duclos—however wealthy he came to be—was perceived as a baker for the poorer classes, this may explain in part why we know so little about him. Someday, perhaps, a local historian will take up the challenge and search the Port of Spain archives for him. Yet, the basic facts are now clear enough from a numismatic point of view.

APPENDIX 1: THE CURRENCY SYSTEM

The currency system used on the Port of Spain street and described by Chalmers, Pitts, Inniss, Borde, and Mendez is rather complex. The following table will, hopefully, clarify things for the reader:

Table 1. Trinidad currency system: lower denominations, mid-nineteenth century

Sterling	farthing	halfpenny		penny	1¼ pence	2½ pence	5 pence
Decimal	half-cent	cent	1¼ cents	2 cents	2½ cents	5 cents	10 cents
Colloquial			half-stampee		stampee	half bit	bit, *escalin, escalin clou*

Only the lower denominations are included. These rates are somewhat at odds with those of the higher denominations circulating on the island. Borde, a Trinidadian, pointed out that in his day the term *escalin* was still used to mean the Spanish *real sencillo*, i.e., "plain real" (Borde 1882, 99) which in theory was an eighth of a Spanish dollar. The 1866 "Blue Book" gives the value of the Spanish, Mexican, or Colombian silver dollar at 4s. 6d. sterling or exactly $1.00 Trinidad currency (Hart 1866, 188). By 1881, however, the Trinidad dollar currency was worth 4s. 2d., so that 1d. equalled 2¢ (Guppy 1882, 87).

The main difficulty seems to be in the values to attribute to the more colloquial terms "bit" and "*escalin.*" Like the *escalin*, the bit should be the Spanish or Spanish American real, i.e., an eighth of a dollar. The table, nevertheless, presents no internal contradiction and is faithful to all the authors quoted in this paper for the evidence they provide about the use of small change in the Port of Spain street economy.

APPENDIX 2: "ANTOINE DECLOS"

Ray Byrne described the F D tokens thus:

> Copper Stampees (usually ½d size coppers bearing deeply incused letters "F D" (presumably the initials of a local barber, Francois Declos) were circulated and accepted to pass at 2 cents (tokens) for convenience only. Further and later examples marked with letters "A D" (brother Antoine Declos??) also circulated here (Byrne 1971, 114 [punctuation mine]).

The author mentioned, without reference to his source, a possible brother to François, Antoine, who was not known to Chalmers, Wood, or even to Pridmore just six years earlier.[28] Interestingly, a specimen of the A D countermark was listed in 1968 at the van Loan Gaines auction in the care of Hans M. F. Schulman of New York. This was Lot 1122, described thus (van Loan Gaines 1968, 110):

> 1122 Worn copper ¼ anna Bengal. Ctspd large "AD" for Antoine Declos, brother of Francoise, to pass for 1½ cents. H. Wood #86. Ex-Guttag Coll.

Although it is blurry, the picture makes it clear that this lot was not a coin from the Bengal Presidency, but an 1835 East India Company quarter-anna (Krause 446.2). There is another mistake, in François's first name, which makes it easy to trace the information back to a catalogue of the same auctioneer, only two years earlier, for one of the several Howard D. Gibbs auctions. Lots 1940 and 1941 were described thus (Gibbs 1966: 127):

> 1940 Worn ½ Penny George III, also ½ Penny (Victoria) counterstamped F(RANÇOISE) D(ECLOS) for value of 1½ cents. H. W. 86. Ex Guttag coll. 2 pcs. Stamps - Fine.
>
> 1941 Worn ¼ Anna of Bengal, counterstamped A(NTOINE) D(ECLOS) for 1½ Cents. Stamp - Fine.

The coin had previously been auctioned in New York, August 1941, as part of Lot 2269 at a Kosoff and Schulman auction of the Guttag collection (Guttag 1941, 80, without photo):[29]

---

28. Byrne's view was unchanged four years later when he sold his collection (Byrne 1975, 114).

29. Here, unlike in the previous quotation, the reference to Wood is rightly applied to the F D tokens; Wood did not discuss any A D countermark.

> 2269 4676. Two copper pennies counterstamped with the initials of bar-
> ber F. Declos. Wood 86. Added copper coin counterstamped A.D.
> Very good. (3 pcs.)

It is to be noted that there is no attempt to identify the author of the A D countermark, but it is important to point out as well that the coin was *added* to a lot of
two F D coins that had previously been listed as no. 4676 (hence that reference)
in the 1929 publication of the Julius Guttag collection of Latin American coins
(Guttag 1929, 498):

> 4676 "F D" initials of Francois Declos. Wood, Fig. 86, Page 109.

Between 1929 and 1941, therefore, Guttag added not just the A D coin but a
second F D coin as well. Since pennies were unknown to Pridmore, it seems
very likely that neither of the F D coins was a penny as described in the 1941
auction, which is actually confirmed by the correction made 25 years later. Nevertheless, the fact remains that in 1966 Gibbs and Schulman made two lots, one
for the two F D coins and the other for the A D coin, and two years later van
Loan Gaines and Schulman made a single lot of, most certainly, the same three
coins. The front cover of the 1966 auction booklet points out that the collection
was "as catalogued by Howard D. Gibbs." Was it he who first filled in the name
A(ntoine) D(eclos)? If not, one can certainly narrow the search down to between
the years 1941, when the Kosoff and Schulman—i.e., the same Hans M. F. Schulman—auction took place, and 1966. If, as seems likely, Gibbs himself obtained
the three coins at the 1941 auction, he was *the first collector to acquire them in a
single lot*, as is clear from the lot description. Later, although he split them into
two lots, he listed them side by side, as they certainly were all those years in his
collection. All these circumstances make it very likely that Gibbs himself was
the originator of the hypothesis that the initials A D stood for Antoine Declos,
brother of François.

That Gibbs was wrong in his description of Lot 1941 is certain beyond the
shadow of a doubt for the simple reason that the name "Declos," as we saw, is
wrong. In looking for François's siblings, one would need first to discover what
the real name is in order for the inquiry to get anywhere. It is, therefore, most
probable that Gibbs *assumed* that the F D and A D coins were connected, and
that he did so solely on the basis of shared attributes, i.e., the large size and thick-
ness of the letters, the fact that they were incused, the final initial D, and the fact
that the hosts are copper coins of comparable size. At some point, Gibbs looked
at this assemblage and, in all likelihood, gathered that A D was perhaps François's
brother, suggesting the name "Antoine" for a reason that would obviously not

make its way into an auction catalogue. As time passed numismatists have either reported this hypothesis, as Byrne did with a double question mark, or ignored or overlooked it, as did Brunk. It needs to be stressed that the grouping of the F D and A D countermarks on the basis of their perceived similarities is unwarranted. It can even be challenged since the A D punch looks like the work of a skilled blacksmith when compared to the more amateurish F D punches. What is more, until evidence is presented to prove otherwise, there is no reason to even assume that the A D countermark originated in Trinidad. There are actually good reasons to reject that assumption:

1. The strongest argument in support, that François and Antoine were brothers, is unfounded.
2. The 1941 Guttag auction catalogue, where (to my knowledge) it first gets recorded, does not say anything of its provenience.
3. The host is an 1835 East India Company quarter-anna which, indeed, could have found its way to Trinidad but is far from being well attested there, as the list of known hosts for the F D countermarks suggests.
4. The A D coin discussed so far is one of only two that I am aware of. All references but one are to *this* coin and all photographs are of *this* coin. The other coin is an undated Danish India *kas* (or cash) of Frederick IV (1699–1730) (Stack's 1991, Lot 713, where the identification with Antoine Declos is suggested). Since (1) "A D" are common initials, (2) the two coins are separated by a century, and (3) a *kas* is too small (about 9.5 mm diam.) for the "A D" initials found on the quarter-anna (26.2 mm diam.), it is almost certain that they are the initials of two distinct individuals. What is more, arguing that they are of the same individual would make it likely that "A D" was active in colonial India, not Trinidad.

After the 1968 van Loan Gaines auction, the quarter-anna can be spotted in the collections of Alcedo Almanzar (1968?–1977) and Edward Roehrs (1977–2010); the current owner is unknown to me. The photo in the van Loan Gaines catalogue leaves no doubt that it is the same coin that was later sold at the Roehrs auction (Roehrs 2010, lot 320 with photo). Who "A D" was and where he came from will have to remain a mystery.

ACKNOWLEDGMENTS

I would like to thank Mark Beadle, Rich Hartzog†, Lise Winer, and Pierre-Jean Darres for their help. Much gratitude goes as well to Patricia Bissessar and the members of the Facebook group "Angelo Bissessarsingh's Virtual Museum of Trinidad and Tobago," especially Roger Edghill and Sean Ng Wai. Lastly, I would like to thank two anonymous *AJN* referees for their judicious comments. All remaining mistakes are mine.

The six coins illustrated in this article are from my personal collection and were photographed by me.

REFERENCES

Akin, M. H., J. C. Bard, and K. Akin. 2016. *Numismatic Archaeology of North America: A Field Guide*. New York and London: Routledge.

Baker, W. 2006. *Marked Impressions. A Catalogue of the Joseph Foster Collection of 19th Century Canadian Countermarked Coins*. Montréal: Warren Baker.

Bissessarsingh, A. 2012. "John Rapsey—Creator of Hops Bread and Biscuit Cake." *Trinidad and Tobago Sunday Guardian*. 18 November: A25.

Borde, P.-G.-L. 1882. *Histoire de l'île de La Trinidad sous le gouvernement espagnol*, Vol. 2. Paris: Maisonneuve.

Brandon, R. 2014. "Coins, Tokens and Medals of the Caribbean from the Late Raymond Brandon Collection." In *An Auction of Ancient, British and World Coins, Tokens, Jetons, Medals and Books*. London: Dix Noonan Webb, 2–3 April 2014. Last accessed online July 2018.

Brereton, B. M. 1997. *Law, Justice and Empire. The Colonial Career of John Gorrie, 1829–1892*. Kingston, Jamaica: University of the West Indies Press.

Brown, D. 1989. *History of Money and Banking in Trinidad and Tobago from 1789 to 1989*. T. W. Farrell & P. Forde eds. Port of Spain: Central Bank of Trinidad and Tobago.

————. 1990. "The Response of the Banking Sector to the General Crisis: Trinidad, 1836–56." *Journal of Caribbean History* 24: 28–64.

Brunk, G., ed. 1976. *World Countermarks on Medieval and Modern Coins*. Lawrence, MA: Quarterman.

Brunk, G. 1989. *Merchant Countermarks on World Coins*. Rockford, IL: World Exonumia Press.

————. 1998. "Purposive Canadian Countermarked Coins and What Is Known about Their Issuers, Part I." *Canadian Numismatic Journal* 43: 190–196.

————. 2003. *Merchant and Privately Countermarked Coins*. Rockford, IL: World Exonumia Press.

Byrne, R. 1971. "The British West Indies. Cut, Holed and Counterstamped Coins." In Remick *et al.* 1971: 96–115.

———. 1975. *Coins and Tokens of the Caribbees.* Public Auction, Jess Peters, Inc., Sale No. 78.

Caldecott, J. B. 1912. *Catalogue of the Collection of Coins and Tokens of the British Possessions and Colonies Formed by J.B. Caldecott, Esq.* London: Sotheby, Wilkinson & Hodge.

Chalmers, R. 1893. *A History of Currency in the British Colonies.* London: Eyre and Spottiswoode.

Commission. 1886. *Trade and Taxes Commission, Trinidad, 1886.* Port-of-Spain: The Government Printing Office.

Duffield, F. G. 1919–1921. "A Trial List of the Countermarked Modern Coins of the World." *The Numismatist* 32–34. Reprinted in Brunk 1976: 27–110, with Duffield's three supplementary lists, 110–120, and Brunk's supplement and corrections, 121–136.

Dyroff, J. M. 1987. "The Quaint and Curious Stampee." *The Numismatist* 100: 756–760.

Elliott, L. E. 1914. "The History of Trinidad." *Pan-American Magazine* 18 (October): 23–31.

Frey, A. R. 1916. *A Dictionary of Numismatic Names, Their Official and Popular Designations. American Journal of Numismatics* 50: v–x, 1–311.

Gibbs, H. D. 1966. *Coin Auction: The Howard D. Gibbs Collection of Counterstamped, Necessity and Siege Coins of the Americas as Catalogued by Howard D. Gibbs, March 18, 19, 1966.* New York: Hans M. F. Schulman.

Guppy, R. J. L. 1882. *The Trinidad Official and Commercial Register and Almanack for the Year of Our Lord 1882.* London: Trübner & Co.

Guttag, J. 1929. *Catalogue of the Collection of Julius Guttag, New York, N.Y., U.S.A., Comprising the Coinage of Mexico, Central America, South America and the West Indies.* Arranged by Edgar H. Adams. New York: Julius Guttag.

———. 1941. "The Guttag Latin American Collection. Part V — West Indies." In *Auction Sale: Rare Coins, Decorations, Patterns, Books, and Paper Money to Be Held at the Numismatic Gallery.* New York: A. Kosoff and Hans M. F. Schulman: 62–81.

Hart, D. 1866. *Trinidad and the Other West India Islands and Colonies,* 2nd ed. Trinidad: The "Chronicle" Publishing Office.

Inniss, L. O. 1910. *Trinidad and Trinidadians: A Collection of Papers, Historical, Social, and Descriptive, about Trinidad and Its Peoples.* Port-of-Spain: Mirror Printing Works.

————. 1932. *Reminiscences of Old Trinidad from 78 Years Ago*. Port of Spain: Clifford Sealy.

Krause. 2015. *Standard Catalogue of World Coins 1801–1900*, edited by G. S. Cuhaj, 8th ed. Iola, WI: Krause Publications.

Lowsley, B. 1895. "Coins and Tokens of Ceylon." *Numismatic Chronicle* 15: 211–268.

Lyall, R. 1989. *The Tokens, Checks, Metallic Tickets, Passes, and Tallies of the British Caribbean and Bermuda*. Lake Mary, FL: Token and Medal Society.

Pitts, H. C. 1948. *100 Years Together. A Brief History of Trinidad from 1797 to 1897*. Port of Spain: Trinidad Publishing.

Pridmore, F. 1961. "Notes on Colonial Coins—Trinidad." *Numismatic Circular* 69: 141–142, 168–169.

————. 1965. *The Coins of the British Commonwealth of Nations to the End of the Reign of George VI, 1952, Part III: Bermuda, British Guiana, British Honduras, and the British West Indies*. London: Spink and Son.

Remick, J., S. James, A. Dowle, and P. Finn. *A Guidebook and Catalogue of British Commonwealth Coins, 1649–1971*. Winnipeg: Regency Coin and Stamp Co.

Roehrs, E. 2010. *The Roehrs Collection of West Indies Cut and Countermarked Coins (Part I) (28 September 2010)*. London: Dix Noonan Webb. Last accessed online July 2018.

Stack's. 1991. *Ancient and Modern Coins of the World and the United States. Mail Bid Sale. Closing Date Wednesday, April 10, 1991*. New York: Coin Galleries, Stack's.

van Loan Gaines, A. 1968. *A Selection from the Collection of Alvin van Loan Gaines and Other Consignments. Public Auction Sale, May 24 and 25, 1968*. New York: Hans M. F. Schulman.

de Verteuil, L. A. A. 1884. *Trinidad: Its Geography, Natural Resources, Administration, Present Condition, and Prospects*, 2nd ed. London: Cassell & Company.

Winer, L., ed. 2009. *Dictionary of the English/Creole of Trinidad and Tobago*. Montreal/Kingston: McGill/Queen's University Press.

Wood, H. 1914. "The Coinage of the West Indies with Especial Reference to the Cut and Countermarked Pieces". *American Journal of Numismatics* 48: 89–128. Reprinted in Brunk 1976: 211–250.

Zay, E. 1892. *Histoire monétaire des colonies françaises*. Paris: Montorier.

AJN Second Series 32 (2020) pp. 415–450

When the Magic Has Gone:
Coin Collecting and the Senses

Heinz Tschachler[*]

Encapsulating coins has become standard practice with collectors. While it is evident to everyone that to preserve and protect one's coin collection makes sense, collectors nevertheless are denied a fuller sensory perception of their precious coins, which are so perfectly suited to their purpose that it seems natural, almost instinctive, to hold them directly. But "slabbing," as encapsulation is commonly called, not only disallows touch and sensory cognition beyond sight but also guards against what is natural, bodily, raw, or unclean. On the deepest level, slabbing provides a defense against the transitory and precarious nature of our existence, thus against death. Slabbing is not, however, natural, as sensory perceptions are shaped and determined by historical, social, and cultural factors. They have meanings, and they articulate the values and norms of distinctive groups of people. Ultimately, therefore, sonically sealed plastic holders are neither a sufficient nor a necessary condition for collecting coins but are, simply, contingent.

This article seeks to engage with the paradox that emerges from the practice of encapsulating coins. Encapsulated coins are no longer "history we hold in our hands," to paraphrase numismatist James Earl Jones;[1] instead, they are more like history in a holder in our hands. On the other hand, it is evident to everyone that to preserve and protect one's coin collection makes sense. Collectors thus are

*Alpen-Adria University, Klagenfurt, Austria (Heinz.Tschachler@aau.at).

1. "Money: History in Your Hands," narrated by James Earl Jones, Colorado Springs: American Numismatic Association, 1995, DVD.

faced with an uncomfortable choice: either to experience to the full the sensory qualities of coins, and accept that this will gradually destroy them, or to preserve them from any interaction beyond the visual but thereby limit that experience. In the remaining space I will try to deconstruct this paradox.

"Slabbing," as encapsulation is commonly called, is done not only for the sake of protecting and preserving one's precious coins. Encapsulated coins come with condition grading, which means that the company providing the service encloses a label certifying that this particular coin grades to the stated condition (e.g., Mint State 61). By attaching grade descriptors of this kind, a coin is classified. Classification is a practice that originated with Carolus Linnaeus. Beginning in the 1730s, this Swedish botanist and physician organized natural phenomena into groups according to their physical characteristics, that is, according to "natural" differences between "species." For Linnaeus, species were immutable prototypes, perfectly designed for their role in a divinely created chain of beings. "There are as many species as there are forms produced in the beginning by the Infinite Being," Linnaeus wrote in 1735, "no new species are produced."[2] The father of modern taxonomy, as Linnaeus is known, considered his work done once he had classified an organism, assigned it a fixed place and attached a label to it. Henceforth the organism could be identified until all eternity. From its origin, however, taxonomy has been an eminently visual practice, a fact that, as we will see presently, is not without importance for coin collecting. Taxonomy of course is at work in museums of natural history with their collections of butterflies and other insects, but it is equally common in various coin collections, not least in Vienna's famous Münzkabinett (Fig. 1).[3]

Collections of this kind bear testimony to a preset uniformity in which the full sensory qualities of coins are of little or no account.[4] This is also true for the practice of encapsulation, which not only disallows touch and sensory cognition beyond sight but, as I will try to demonstrate, also guards against what is natural, bodily, raw, or unclean. On the deepest level, encapsulation provides a defense against the transitory and precarious nature of our existence, thus against death. Alternatively, we may insist on the sensate qualities of coins and currency, quali-

---

2. C. Linnaeus, "Systema Naturae," in *Readings in Early Anthropology*, ed. J. S. Slotkin (Abingdon and New York: Routledge, 2011), 180.

3. For a virtual tour of the Vienna Münzkabinett, go to https://www.khm.at/besuchen/sammlungen/muenzkabinett/, accessed June 6, 2018.

4. Cf. S. M. Pearce, *Museums, Objects, and Collections: A Cultural Study* (Washington, DC: Smithsonian Institution, 1993); Pearce, *On Collecting: An Investigation into Collecting in the European Tradition* (London: Routledge, 1995).

Figure 1. Hall 1, Münzkabinett, Kunsthistorisches Museum Wien
(image courtesy of the KHM-Museumsverband).

ties that pertain, respectively, to their symbolism, their design, and, importantly, their material qualities—the rustling of crisp new bills, their smell, the clanging of coins, or the feel of them in our hands. Many colloquialisms attached to money likewise refer to a sensory experience, especially to nourishment—such as "bread" or "beans" (on the analogy of it being a staple of life). In literature and the arts, too, coins have been treated as pleasure-giving objects, though in most instances writers and artists only draw out the degeneracy resulting from the fetishization and idolization of precious coins.

All this is to say that coin collecting articulates norms and creates meanings. Sensory perceptions are shaped and determined by historical, social, and cultural factors. Already the young Marx wrote: "The forming of the five senses is a labour of the entire history of the world down to the present."[5] There exist, then, collective models of perception or sensory models that attempt to order and understand the senses. If we accept that the sensorium is an ever-shifting social and historical construct, sensory perceptions are not just the product of a human consciousness working in a vacuum, as phenomenologists after Merleau-

5. K. Marx, "Private Property and Communism," *Economic and Philosophic Manuscripts of 1844*, §4, Marx Engels Archive, accessed May 7, 2018, https://www.marxists.org/archive/marx/works/1844/manuscripts/comm.htm.

Figure 2. United States gold 1 dollar, 1849, encapsulated.

Ponty have assumed.[6] Phrased differently, sensory perceptions are constructivist, are means and ways of giving meaning to and interpreting the world, and they are acquired and internalized through socialization. They do not happen directly but are mediated through social codes. They have meanings, and they articulate the values and norms of distinctive groups of people. Collecting is not therefore merely an act of consumption, but also one of production: "Collectors," Russell Belk wrote,

> create, combine, classify, and curate the objects they acquire in such a way that a new product, the collection, emerges. In the process they also produce meanings…they participate in the process of socially reconstructing shared meanings for the objects they collect.[7]

My interest in the norms and meanings produced by and articulated in the act of collecting originated with some business about rare coins, one fictional, the

6. On the sensorial turn in the humanities and social sciences, see D. Howes, "Charting the Sensorial Revolution," *The Senses and Society* 1.1 (2006), 113–28. For a critique of phenomenology's assumption that one's subjective model of perception is universally valid, see D. Howes, *Sensual Relations: Engaging the Senses in Culture and Social Theory* (Ann Arbor: University of Michigan Press, 2003), 236 n4.

7. R. W. Belk, *Collecting in a Consumer Society* (London: Routledge, 1995), 55.

Figure 3. Gold Brasher doubloon, 1787. ANS 1969.62.1.

other real. First, the fictional one. Raymond Chandler in one of his crime novels has his hero, private detective Philip Marlowe, receive a cheap little 2½-inch box. When he opens it, Marlowe finds himself "looking at a gold coin about the size of a half dollar, bright and shining as if it had just come from the mint." Marlowe doesn't just look at the coin, which turns out to be a Brasher doubloon from 1787, but takes it in his hand: "I turned the coin over on my palm. It was heavy and cold and my palm felt moist under it."[8] Marlowe is a lucky fellow, unlike this author. At work on a book about the monetary imagination of Edgar Allan Poe, a scornful screed Poe launched in the Southern Literary Messenger of June 1849 on the occasion of the debut of the gold dollar coin prompted me to place an order for one such coin.[9] When it finally arrived, I noticed that it was encased in a solid plastic slab (Fig. 2).

There was some consolation in the fact that the $1 gold dollar was considerably less expensive than a Brasher doubloon (Fig. 3), which is a true rarity. In 2005 one specimen was sold at auction for $2.5 million; in 2011 a New York-based investment company bought another one for $7.4 million. The tiny gold coin that Poe chose to deride is no doubt of considerable numismatic interest, too. Poe is largely remembered for his writings about ravens and tell-tale hearts, but he also cast a critical eye on America's coinage. He never tired of bemoaning the absence of a stable federal paper currency and often pointed to the disastrous consequences of private currencies on banking, the economy at large, politics, and the country's collective psyche. He was also aware of the fact that from the beginning United States coinage had been overvalued and therefore was rarely

8. R. Chandler, *The High Window* (New York: Knopf, 1945), 89.

9. "The Romans worshipped the standards; and the Roman standard happened to be an eagle. Our standard is only one tenth of an Eagle—a Dollar—but we make all even by adoring it with tenfold devotion." E. A. Poe, "Marginalia," in *Essays and Reviews*, ed. G. R. Thompson (New York: Library of America, 1984), 1455; H. Tschachler, "'Adoring with Tenfold Devotion': Edgar Allan Poe, America's Money and the 1849 Gold Dollar," *The Numismatist* 126.10 (October 2013), 32–39.

Figure 4. United States gold 1-dollar, 1849. ANS 2010.37.1.

seen in circulation. For the most part, gold and, to a lesser extent, silver coins were either hoarded or were exported and melted at their destination, which in most cases was London. To make matters worse, until the discovery of gold in California, lack of precious metal led to the widespread use of foreign coins, which came mostly from Spanish mints in Latin America (significantly known in English as "dollars" since the 1500s).

The discovery of gold in California in 1848 had profound effects on America's money. Within two years, the face value of the nation's coinage rose from $4 million to $31 million, climbing to more than $62 million the following year. In Spring 1854, a mint was opened in San Francisco. By that time, the Liberty Head Gold Dollar, designed by James Barton Longacre, had been in circulation for five years (Fig. 4). (Shown here is the original "open wreath type.")

The legislation set the weight of the gold dollar at 25.8 grains (about 1.2 grams) and its fineness at .900. The tiny dollar was instantly popular as a substitute for the significantly larger silver dollar, which was still produced in small quantities, but rarely seen in commercial channels. The gold coin, in contrast, was produced in considerable quantities and became widely used. Today it has the distinction of being the smallest ever United States issue; at a minuscule 13 mm it is smaller than the dime, which is 17.9 mm in diameter, and smaller also than the 1 euro cent coin at 16.25 mm. After being hoarded for its bullion value in 1861, the gold dollar never returned to general circulation, though it remained the darling of collectors and jewelry manufacturers. Although production was discontinued in 1889, the coin continued in circulation in the West until 1917, when World War I led to a lapse in the gold standard. Westerners then learned to use paper money, and after that time the gold dollar was no longer seen in daily commerce. It became a "lame duck," like all United States gold coins, given as gifts and eventually stashed away in jars and drawers.[10]

For me, the question was what to do with my encapsulated coin. Pretend that it's a telephone and hold it to my ear, saying "hello"? When I tried to open the coin's protective case, I found that this was utterly impossible. (I have since learned that I should have tapped a mallet along the edge until the sonic weld is loosened to open the plastic holder.) My initial disappointment led to anger

---

10. D. W. Lange, "Lame Ducks," *The Numismatist* 128.12 (December 2015), 17–18.

and frustration. I felt deprived, but of what exactly? I had expected to be able to touch the coin, hold it in my hand, smell it, perhaps even take it into my mouth, and surely listen to "that clinking clanking sound…that makes the world go 'round," as Liza Minelli famously sang. I could look at my little coin, but that was as far as it would go. In fact, what I was holding in my hand rather resembled a dead insect behind glass. When I thought about this some more it dawned on me that I felt deprived of a fuller sensory perception of my precious little coin which, like all coins, is so perfectly suited to its purpose that it seemed natural, almost instinctive, to hold it directly. Yet encapsulated as it was in solid plastic, the magic, in the words of Joe Cocker, had gone.

Encapsulating coins has become a standard practice among collectors and dealers. State-of-the-art plastic holders, we are told, offer "a solid defense" (Fig. 5, below). The question is, defense against what? This is what the advertisers promise:

1) Defense against potentially irreversible problems, such as corrosion or unsightly residues;
2) defense against mechanical damage and tampering; all this in the interest of
3) protecting one's legacy and its value. After all, one's coins are more than a collection. They are treasured heirlooms that will be passed down for generations and thus are also in need of certification and, even, of being submitted to registries offered by major coin grading companies.

These are good, rational arguments. It must be evident to everyone that to preserve, protect, certify and, if necessary, have registered one's coin collection makes sense, in particular when we talk about rare, well-preserved, and expensive specimens that are to be taken care of for their next owner. While such coins may well be considered untouchable, criticism need not and should not accept the face value of what is being said. What I propose, borrowing words of the dramatist Georg Buechner, is to follow the slogans through to the point where they turn into flesh and blood.[11] Or, using a more contemporary conceit, to set my article up as a kind of decompiler—in goes the rhetoric, the actual words and phrases, out come the cultural codes and ideological drives that power the apparatus. In doing so, we shall see that encapsulation also offers

4) defense against touch and sensory cognition beyond sight. Those "lower" senses—touch, smell, hearing, and taste—have been under suspicion since classical antiquity; in a more general sense, therefore, slabbing also provides

11. G. Buechner, "Danton's Death" (1835), in *Complete Plays, Lenz and Other Writings*, ed. and trans. John Reddick (Harmondsworth: Penguin, 1993), 3:3, 49.

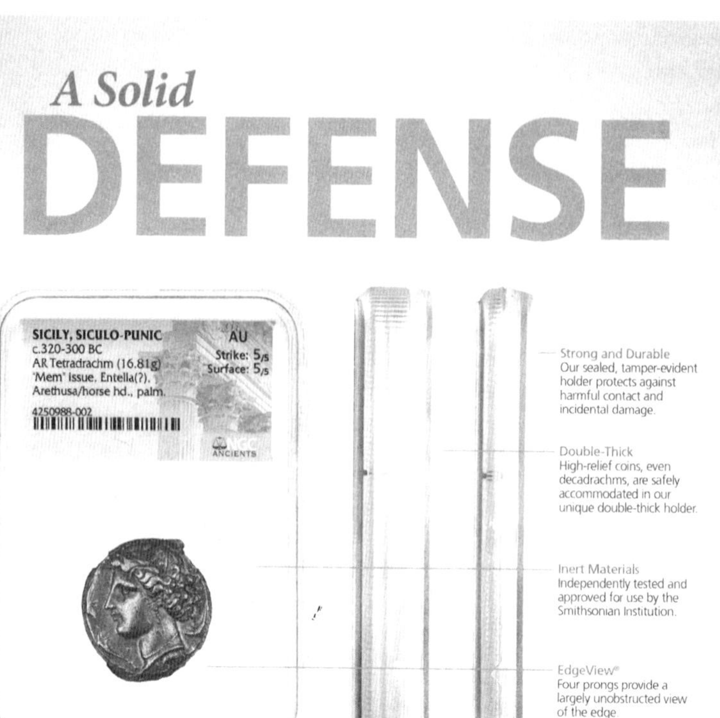

Figure 5. "A Solid Defense." Advertisement for Numismatic Guaranty Corporation
(NGC), *The Numismatist* 131.2 (February 2018), 26
(image courtesy of Numismatic Guaranty Corporation).

5) defense against what is natural, bodily, "raw," unclean, and, from a psychoanalytical perspective, against the identification of coined money, feces, and sexuality. In the last analysis, slabbing provides

6) defense against the transitory and precarious nature of our existence, thus against death.

Let's first consider the rational arguments:

1) Defense against corrosion and surface contaminants such as unsightly residue and encrustations: A common problem are coin holders ("flips") that contain polyvinyl chloride (PVC). PVC makes holders soft and pliable, but the chlorine leaches out of the holder, reacting with a coin's surface and eventually leading to corrosion. Copper and bronze specimens that feature mint luster are also reactive, namely with the sulfur and paper dust found in coin albums. Advanced environmental damage is often caused by water, most frequently found as humidity in the air. It may include staining (oxidation) and, later, corrosion. On silver coins, for instance, staining leaves opaque milky-white areas, whereas corrosion appears black. Copper and nickel specimens, in contrast, turn red, orange, and greenish-blue from corrosion. Corrosion may appear in the form of raised spots, but may also affect the entire surface, creating a rough texture. Coins that are buried in soil commonly develop a thick, opaque, reddish-orange residue. Oily fingerprints or tiny droplets of sweat or saliva are also perilous. Even gold can fall victim to improper storage or environmental damage. While it is rare, it is not impossible that gold coins develop small, reddish surface blemishes ("gold spots"), especially when they contain copper (hence "copper spots"), or else, that they present a dull, salmon-pink hue. And unlike what is often believed, modern coins are afflicted in pretty much the same way that more classic examples are, the only difference being that on the former, the negative visual impact (a light haze or a light toning) often is more apparent.[12]

2) Defense against mechanical damage and tampering: Previous generations used wooden cabinets, preferably of mahogany and fitted with felt or velvet-lined trays, paper envelopes, cardboard pages, or cardboard albums to protect coins. All of these materials set in motion chemical processes that slowly change

---

12. C. Shappell, "Damaging Effects," *The Numismatist* 129.12 (December 2016), 109; Shappell, "Common Misconception," *The Numismatist* 130.12 (December 2017), 103; Shappell, "Looking Ahead," *The Numismatist* 131.2 (February 2018), 91; Shappell, "Nature or Nurture?" *The Numismatist* 131.7 (July 2018), 107; Shappell, "Early Intervention," *The Numismatist* 132. 1 (January 2019), 103. For a different view, see M. S. Shutty, Jr., "Awful Beauty: The Allure of Relic Coins," *The Numismatist* 130.8 (August 2017), 55–57.

a coin's surface. They also offer little protection against mechanical damage (the "wrinkles of history") and tampering. Vinyl coin albums were also used, though they are very destructive and should not be used at all.[13] Holders made of Mylar™ (polyethylene terephthalate film) are better options; ensuring long-term preservation without encasing, Mylar holders enable historians, archaeologists, and other researchers still to handle coins, even with gloves.

While I've been told that for archaeologists in particular, the very idea of encasing is bizarre, for collectors "slabbed" coins (that is, coins encapsulated in inert plastic) have become the norm. They may now even go for the new Multi-Coin Holder—a single slab that can encapsulate two or more coins, promoted as a visually appealing and convenient display option for matched pairs or sets of specimens.[14] There is a further ramification of the phenomenon. Since February 2015, subscribers to the *Sample Slab Update Newsletter* have been offered discussions of "sample and related coin and currency slabs, including news, market information, and research." The newsletter (and the accompanying website) are not even about collecting encapsulated coins for the coins' sake; they are about collecting the plastic capsules themselves.[15]

The technique used in slabbing is called "ultrasonic welding," promoted as a "safe, clean and secure process that helps to protect coins and reveal attempts at tampering."[16] The airtight coin holders offer resistance to environmental factors, slowing down chemical processes, and they protect against mechanical damage and tampering. Thus, they are said to provide collectors and dealers "with unparalleled peace of mind." To make (as in Raymond Chandler's novel) an imitation of a coin by producing, through a method then employed by dental technicians, a model from the original coin, would be impossible.[17] In the end, all these defensive measures serve to

13. P. Grierson, *Numismatics* (Oxford and New York: Oxford University Press, 1975), 182–84. Mahogany was the timber of choice for coin storage and display because of all woods it contains the least amount of coin-damaging oils and resins. H. Spiller, *Keep the Change: A Collector's Tale of Lucky Pennies, Counterfeit C-Notes, and Other Curious Currency* (New York: Princeton Architectural Press, 2015), 14 and, for "wrinkles of history," 25.

14. See "Better Than One: NGC Introduces a Two-Coin Holder," *The Numismatist*, 132.3 (March 2019), 24.

15. See D. Schwager, "Sample Slab Book.com," accessed August 13, 2018, https://sites. google.com/site/sampleslabbook/.

16. Numismatic Conservation Services (NCS), "FAQs," accessed February 27, 2018, https:// www.ngccoin.com/ncs-conservation/.

17. Chandler, *The High Window*, 221–22. For "unparalleled peace of mind," see the NGC advertisement in *The Numismatist* 131.8 (August 2018), 106.

3) protect one's legacy and its value. As one of the slabbing companies trumpets in an advertisement (Fig. 6, below), "It's your legacy. Protect it."

Encapsulating coins debuted in the mid-1980s in response to the ever-growing problem of "coin doctoring." Third-party encapsulation is the business of companies such as NGC (Numismatic Guaranty Corporation) or PCGS (Professional Coin Grading Service). These companies at first marketed their products as protection for numismatic investors who spend substantial sums on rare coins. The encapsulation has two purposes in relation to the grading: to minimize the possibility of any changes in the certified condition of the coin, but just as importantly to ensure that the certification label remains with that specific coin rather than being put with some other, inferior specimen. Moreover, an extra sale value may accrue to a coin that comes with an authentic signature from a great name in numismatics or that is documented or certified (i.e., on the label in the plastic slab) as having been in a famous past collection. And just to be on the safe side, collectors have turned to submitting their collections of slabbed coins to registries offered by major coin-grading companies.

But third-party grading is not perfect, as is evident from the recent rise of "stickering" by the Certified Acceptance Corporation (CAC), which acts as a "fourth party" to assess the third-party determinations. Sometimes the CAC imprimatur means that a stickered specimen is solid, better than average, or even higher than the grade on the holder. (Stickers come in different colors.) This can provide a welcome boost in market value and demand from potential buyers.[18] Third-party grading is nevertheless highly useful, even essential, as a common basis for evaluation.

Evaluation has its price, though. At present, the going rate is 4% of the "fair market value". Nor is collecting coins the exclusive domain of investors. According to a study, nearly 10% of American men report collecting coins, which, like other hobbies, they consider as "a constructive leisure time activity." As a result, coin certification and encapsulation have gone well beyond high-end items. Coins valued at no more than $300 can be certified and placed in sonically sealed holders for $20 under the "Economy" tier. For specimens dated 1955 and later, this fee drops to just $16 per coin, with a value limit of $1000 each. But encapsulation can also suggest a surplus value. Often, low-value pieces are listed on eBay at vastly inflated "Buy It Now" prices. This is good business, in the process of which "raw" coins are being transformed into something more noble.[19]

18. M. Sanders, "Getting Started," *The Numismatist* 131.10 (October 2018), 108; A. Doyle, "Green Beans," *The Numismatist* 132.4 (April 2019), 19.

19. D. W. Lange, "Dollars & Sense," *The Numismatist* 129.11 (November 2016), 95. For collecting as a "constructive leisure time activity," see Belk, *Collecting in a Consumer Society*, 55.

Figure 6. "It's Your Legacy. Protect It." Advertisement for Numismatic Guaranty Corporation (NGC), *The Numismatist* 131.3 (March 2018), 4 (image courtesy of Numismatic Guaranty Corporation).

"Raw" coins are coins not encased in sonically sealed plastic holders.[20] Does the opposite term, "cooked," then apply to encased coins? In a figurative sense it does. The French social anthropologist Claude Lévi-Strauss has used the binary opposition of raw vs. cooked food to mark the difference between non-human and human. The food we consume, Lévi-Strauss argued, establishes an identity between us as human beings (our culture) and our food (nature). Cooking is, then, the universal means by which nature is transformed into culture. Put differently, cooking represents the archetypal transformation of nature into culture. Thus, the process of civilization is one that progresses from "raw" to "cooked." Cooked food is regarded as raw fresh food that has been changed or transformed by cultural means.[21]

Classifying food as raw or cooked is a means by which we make sense of the world and construct meanings. This is true of all classificatory systems or taxonomies, and it extends to the act of collecting coins. It even permeates Raymond Chandler's fictional universe, in which a coin dealer's office contains "wall cases of tarnished coins in tilted slots with yellowed typewritten labels under them" as well as "long-legged tables with glass tops and more coins under the glass tops."[22] Collecting that is done with an eye on taxonomy is based on the premise of a rigid sense of order, an order in which the only sense appealed to is sight. (While this is evident from the collections of the Vienna Münzkabinett or the coin dealer Elisha Morningstar, the same can be said about coin descriptions in numismatic handbooks or auction catalogs.)

Not all information is visual, however, and restricting the sensory perception of coins to sight is no trivial affair. In a famous tract published in 1930, Sigmund Freud ruminated over civilization's discontents. The discontents, Freud found,

20. C. Shappell, "Handle with Care," *The Numismatist* 130.10 (October 2017), 103: "Proper handling of a 'raw' coin (one that is not encased in a slab) involves holding it by its edge with clean hands (or while wearing clean cotton gloves) and steering clear of the surface."

21. C. Lévi-Strauss, *Le cru et le cuit* (Paris: Plon, 1964), trans. *The Raw and the Cooked* (New York: Harper & Row, 1975). There is another transformation, in Lévi-Strauss's triangle, from raw to rotten: rotten food is fresh raw food that has been transformed by natural means. In general terms, cooking is a language in which we "speak" about ourselves and our places in the world. Consider, for instance, the kinds of food we eat on holidays and what constitutes "everyday fare"; or else, the foods we refuse to eat, other people refuse to eat; or the foods we would eat, etc. "What we eat", the cultural studies analyst Kathryn Woodward wrote, "can tell us a lot about who we are and about the culture within which we live. Food is a medium through which people can make statements about themselves. It may also suggest changes over time as well as across cultures. … food is a bearer of symbolic meanings, and can act as a signifier." K. Woodward, *Identity and Difference: Culture, Media, and Identities* (London: Sage, 1997), 31–32.

22. Chandler, *The High Window*, 55.

result from culture's flip side, the restrictions of and limitations to the satisfaction of our drives. This means that the pleasure principle, which makes us strive for an increase of pleasure, must remain unfulfilled and is replaced by the reality principle. Culture, Freud claimed, cannot therefore be separated from the denial of drive satisfaction. "One feels inclined to say," he wrote, "that the intention that man should be 'happy' is not included in the plan of 'Creation.'" Still, Freud considered the pleasure principle as vital and indispensable: "The programme of becoming happy, which the pleasure principle imposes on us, cannot be fulfilled; yet we must not—indeed, we cannot—give up our efforts to bring it nearer to fulfillment by some means or other."[23]

Following Freud, then, the denied access to the object of my desire, the little gold dollar encased in a plastic slab, is the price I have to pay for civilization's progress, the loss of happiness. I nevertheless am confident that I am not suffering from a neurosis (which might be a consequence of the denial of pleasure, Freud would have said). On the contrary, I now know how to crack the coin out of its wretched plastic slab. Nor has my lustful destructiveness been transformed into a sense of guilt (another consequence according to Freud). It is quite possible, however, that my destructiveness lives on in sublimated form, in the deconstructive reading attempted in this article. Following the slogans through to the point where they turn into flesh and blood shows that the much-vaunted "solid defense" also means

4) defense against touch and sensory cognition beyond sight. Numismatists have long employed the idea of a "hierarchy of materials," from gold to silver to copper to aluminum to paper.[24] By slabbing, however, differences in weight and density are made to disappear, the lightness of aluminum as opposed to the heft of a silver coin, for instance. Some Americans may still remember the time when, as a wartime measure introduced in 1943, the penny no longer was copper but zinc-plated steel; in 1944–1946, the pennies were a copper-zinc bronze lacking the tin content of the pre-war bronze; it was only in 1947 that they returned to the original copper-zinc-tin alloy of 1864. By the same token, the "nickel" between 1942 and 1945 no longer contained any nickel, but was an alloy of silver, copper, and manganese. The sense of sound is also irrelevant in the case of slabbed

<hr>

23. S. Freud, "Civilization and Its Discontents," in *The Standard Edition of the Complete Psychological Works of Sigmund Freud*, trans. James A. Strachey, vol. 21 (London: Hogarth Press, 1986), 76, 83.

24. N. Klüßendorf, "Gold—Silber—Kupfer—Aluminium—Papier. Materialhierarchien in der Münz- und Geldgeschichte," *Anzeiger des germanischen Nationalmuseums* 110 (1995), 107–114.

coins. Drop but a coin on a table top and you'll hear different "rings": bronze vs. zinc-plated steel, gold or silver vs. copper-nickel. Coin designs are no more than a few hundredths of an inch deep, yet differences in relief are still visible and perceptible to the touch. A penny from the 1960s, for instance, has a noticeably greater depth than another from the 2000s. A "raw" penny, that is, not a slabbed one. Slabbing also makes it impossible to feel the sharp edges of a new coin, so different from the smoothness of a well-worn coin, whose loss of detail betrays decades of hand-to-hand history.[25]

People generally give very little thought to what happens when they hold a coin in their hands, turning it over, touching it. In fact, what happens is that the coin as it were returns the touch. The scientific term for this phenomenon is "proprioception," that is, the ability to sense stimuli that arise within the body. The sense of proprioception is activated also through the use of a so-called "hand caresser." A "hand caresser" (*Handschmeichler* in German) is really any object that fits snugly in a human palm and that because of its shape and surface structure leads to pleasant sensations when touching it. Examples of "hand caressers" are qigong balls, semiprecious stones (jades or rose quartzes), a horse chestnut—or else, a coin attached to a key ring, usually a gold or silver coin, as subsidiary coins are considered less "caressing."[26]

The popularity of "hand caressers" is no coincidence. The sense of touch is truly essential. Already Aristotle knew that we would not survive without haptic or active touch perception. (He also knew that many organisms have no or only a very limited sense of sight, much as all other senses only serve our wellbeing.) Indeed, we are sensorily equipped for a three-dimensional environment. The sense of touch therefore is the primary sense, which the fetus develops in the seventh or eighth week of pregnancy, prior to all other senses. Moreover, touch is the only sense not associated with a particular organ, thus the closest experience we have of our central nervous system. For babies, too, touch is essential—babies put everything in their mouths. It is also a truism to say that if we stop putting things into our mouths (and, later, into our fingers or hands), our sense of touch will atrophy, and we will be unable to grasp anything, both in a literal and in a figurative sense. "The sense of touch is the sense of the intellect," the French physiologist Philippe Pinel wrote as early as 1800. This pioneering physician deemed touch more reliable than sight in many instances, most notably in certain medical treatments. And modern studies have shown that writing

---

25. M. Sanders, "Hand-to-Hand History," *The Numismatist* 126.10 (2013), 111.

26. R. Sheldon and A. Arens, ""Make it Snuggle in the Palm'. The Commodification of Touch," in *The Book of Touch*, ed. Constance Classen (Oxford: Berg, 2005), 426–428.

something down by hand leads to more and better memorizing than by typing into a computer.[27]

Our sensory equipment responds to weight, surface structure, pressure, color, taste, smell, sound, and noise. In 1658, the Moravian theologian and teacher Johann Amos Comenius depicted the five "external" or bodily senses in a schoolbook, *Orbis sensualium pictus*.[28] Comenius's spectrum of "external" or bodily senses faithfully follows Aristotle.[29] The philosophers among Comenius's contemporaries, however, distrusted the senses. They—most notably Descartes, Hobbes, Spinoza, and Leibniz—put their trust in reason, the intellect. For Descartes in particular, all of the senses, vision included, were fallible. When thinking philosophically, therefore, Descartes rejected the senses: "I shall now close my eyes, I shall stop my ears, I shall call away all my senses."[30] Thinking was, then, Descartes's only way of being certain of his own existence. "*Cogito, ergo sum.*"[31]

About a century after Descartes, the German philosopher Alexander Gottlieb Baumgarten published a passionate plea for "the perfection of sense cognition as such."[32] The proposition is based on a definition of taste, in its wider meaning, as the ability to judge according to the senses, instead of according to the intellect. Such a judgment of taste he saw as based on feelings of pleasure or displeasure. Deducing general rules or principles of artistic or natural beauty from individ-

---

27. M. Grunwald, *Homo hapticus. Warum wir ohne Tastsinn nicht leben können* (Munich: Droemer Knaur, 2017); Aristotle, *De Anima*, in *The Basic Works of Aristotle*, ed. Richard McKeon (New York: Random House, 1941), 413b, 434b. Philippe Pinel, as cited in J. Riskin, *Science in the Age of Sensibility: The Sentimental Empiricists of the French Enlightenment* (Chicago and London: University of Chicago Press, 2002), 65.

28. J. A. Comenius, *Orbis Sensualium Pictus / Die sichtbare Welt* (Nuremberg: M. Endteri, 1658), 86–87, Augustana, Augsburg, accessed March 6, 2018, http://www.hs-augsburg. de/~harsch/Chronologia/Lspost17/Comenius/com_0041.html.

29. Aristotle, *De Anima*, 424b.

30. R. Descartes, "Third Meditation," cited in D. Howes, "Skinscapes: Embodiment, Culture and Environment," in *The Book of Touch*, ed. C. Classen (Oxford: Berg, 2005), 37.

31. R. Descartes, *Principia Philosophiae* (Amsterdam: apud Ludovicum Elzevirium, 1644), part 1, article 7. On the disregard for sensory perception in the early Enlightenment see A. Gottlieb, *The Dream of Enlightenment: The Rise of Modern Philosophy* (New York: Liveright, 2016).

32. "The end of aesthetics is the perfection of sense cognition as such." A. Baumgarten, *Aesthetica* (Frankfurt an der Oder: J. C. Kleyb, 1750–58; reprinted Hildesheim and New York: Georg Olms, 1970), §14: *Aesthetices finis est perfectio cognitionis sensitivae, qua talis*. No English translation exists. For translations of the original Latin into English I have therefore drawn here on Mary Gregor's fine article "Baumgarten's *Aesthetica*," *Review of Metaphysics* 37.2 (December 1983), 357–385.

ual "taste" would, therefore, lead to an independent science of sense cognition (*scientia cognitionis sensitivae*). As a science (really, as a method of discovery), aesthetics would deal with perceptual objects, as distinct from rational objects. The senses, Baumgarten argued, provide materials for the intellect to work with; thus, the perfection of sensory perception was eminently important, much more so than the sensory perception of perfection. Phrased differently, Baumgarten rejected the common reduction of aesthetics to the formal qualities of a work of art, instead drawing attention to the concrete nature of the aesthetic (read, sensory) experience.[33]

Baumgarten's *Aesthetica* draws on the Greek root of the word "aesthetics"— *aisthesis* (Gr. αἴσθησις)—which explicitly refers to the ability to receive stimulation from one or more of the five bodily senses. *Aesthetica* thus is Baumgarten's protest against the devaluation of sense cognition through "arid" intellectual knowledge (*cognitio intellectualis*), derived solely through reason. Reason, he writes, abstracts. While it is "more exact" than the senses, it is "also poorer" because it deals exclusively with "distinct ideas," as opposed to the "confused and indistinct ideas" generated by the senses (*cognitio sensitiva*).[34] Sense perception thus may be of a "lower cognitive power" (in contradistinction to the "higher cognitive power" of reason), yet it binds together ideas below the level of full consciousness, introducing into our present perceptions echoes of what has disappeared from memory. These echoes constitute "the base of the soul," that is, the unconscious, which may be difficult or even impossible to deal with rationally. The perfection of sensory perception, of a "disposition to sense acutely," thus means attending to the nature of sensory experience in itself, rather than trying to rationalize perception.[35]

Baumgarten died in 1762, leaving *Aesthetica* unfinished. Although he had an influence on Kant,[36] he became largely forgotten. Rediscovery began around the middle of the twentieth century, when the American philosopher Su-

33. Baumgarten, *Aesthetica*, §1 (*scientia cognitionis sensitivae*), §3 (*aesthetica...scientiis... bonam materiam parare*), and §17–20. On the distinction, in *Aesthetica*, between "perfection as perceived" and "perfect perception," see Gregor, "Baumgarten's *Aesthetica*," 376–377.

34. Baumgarten, *Aesthetica*, §8, §560, §619; Gregor, "Baumgarten's *Aesthetica*," 364–365.

35. Baumgarten, *Aesthetica*, §38 (*facultates inferiores...facultates cognoscitivae superiores*), §80 (*fundus animae*), §30 (*dispositio...acute sentiendi*); Gregor, "Baumgarten's *Aesthetica*," 367.

36. In his *Critique of Judgment*, Kant conformed to Baumgarten's new usage and employed the word aesthetic to mean the judgment of taste or the estimation of the beautiful. For Kant, an aesthetic judgment is subjective in that it relates to the internal feeling of pleasure or displeasure and not to any qualities in an external object. See H. Caygill, "Aesthetics and Civil Society: Theories of Art and Society, 1640–1790" (PhD thesis, University of Sussex, 1982).

sanne Langer revived Baumgarten's concept of aesthetics as "the education of perception."[37] In Langer's wake, American Studies scholar Jürgen Peper developed a general theory of culture premised on the gradual emancipation of *cognitio sensitiva* from *cognitio intellectiva* (and ultimately from a *cognitio religiosa*). Peper was my teacher at the University of Graz. He now considers my interest in the sensory dimension of coins and currency ("die sensuelle Seite des Geldes") as further proof of his general theory of culture, a perfect example of the "re-aestheticization of everyday life."[38] Credit for rediscovering Baumgarten also goes to the philosopher Gottfried Gabriel. In *Ästhetik und Rhetorik des Geldes*, Gabriel applies Baumgarten's *cognitio sensitiva* to the sensate qualities of coins and currency.[39] These qualities pertain, respectively, to their symbolism, their design, and, importantly, their material qualities—hence Professor Gabriel's privileging

37. S. K. Langer, *Philosophy in a New Key: A Study in the Symbolism of Reason, Rite and Art* (Cambridge, MA: Harvard University Press, 1942), 202–3; Langer, *Feeling and Form: A Theory of Art Developed from Philosophy in a New Key* (New York: Charles Scribner's Sons, 1952), 28. On Langer's indebtedness to Baumgarten, see F. Sparshott, *The Structure of Aesthetics* (Toronto: University of Toronto Press, 1963), 4. In a recent collection of essays on touch in early modern Western culture, Misty Anderson introduces us to the work of the maverick seventeenth-century natural philosopher and dramatist Margaret Cavendish, Duchess of Newcastle. "I believe," Cavendish wrote, "that the Eye, Ear, Nose, Tongue and all the Body, have knowledge as well as the Mind." This is at odds with the then prevailing rationalism of Hobbes and Descartes—who ignored her. Cavendish for her part responded by writing, in 1688, a play titled *The Convent of Pleasure*, in which she invented a "space of freedom," a place where the senses may be delighted rather than denied. Nor did Cavendish shrink from scientific debates. In *Grounds of Natural Philosophy* (1668) or *The Blazing World* (1666) she took on those natural philosophers who imagined "that all mysteries can be comprehended through extending the power of sight." M. Anderson, "Living in a Material World," in *Sensible Flesh: On Touch in Early Modern Culture*, ed. Elizabeth D. Harvey (Philadelphia: University of Pennsylvania Press, 2003), 191–204; and C. Classen, T*he Color of Angels: Cosmology, Gender and the Aesthetic Imagination* (London: Routledge, 1998), 98–106.

38. "(Wieder-)Ästhetisierung des Alltagslebens," letter to this author, February 10, 2016. On Baumgarten's importance for the theory of a "Counter-Enlightenment" ("Gegenaufklärung"), see J. Peper, *Ästhetisierung als zweite Aufklärung. Eine literarästhetisch abgeleitete Kulturtheorie*, 2nd ed. (Bielefeld: Aisthesis Verlag, 2012), esp. 16, 63–64, 334, 378. Other leading works on the aestheticization of everyday life include M. Featherstone, *Consumer Culture and Postmodernism* (London: Sage, 1991); J. M. Malnar and F. Vodvarka, *Sensory Design* (Minneapolis: University of Minnesota Press, 2004); and G. Schulze, *Die Erlebnisgesellschaft: Kultursoziologie der Gegenwart* (Frankfurt am Main and New York: Campus Verlag, 1993), chap. 1.

39. G. Gabriel, *Ästhetik und Rhetorik des Geldes* (Stuttgart and Bad Canstatt: Frommann-Holzboog, 2002). In his more recent *Präzision und Prägnanz: Logische, rhetorische, ästhetische und literarische Erkenntnisformen* (Paderborn: Mentis, 2019), Gabriel goes even further, arguing for a philosophical "complementarism," that is, a plurality of different forms of cognition that, taken together, would lead to a more comprehensive knowledge of the world.

of the rustling of crisp new bills, their smell, the clanging of coins, or the feel of them in our hands. Gabriel is interested in delicate, almost unconscious sensory perceptions, not so much of sight as of smell, taste, sound, and touch.[40] In doing so, he goes beyond Baumgarten, for whom signs must be audible (the clanging or jingling of coins, the rustle of bills), visual (colors, forms, images, and symbols), or tactile (solidity, firmness, smoothness) in order to be picked up. Baumgarten largely ignored smell and taste, as we cannot make our thoughts known to others, or know their thoughts, through odor or flavors. In contrast, Gabriel's aesthetics of money describes and evaluates all sensory manifestations of coins and currency.

As admirable as Gabriel's efforts at adapting Baumgarten's writings to modern needs are, works that explore the material qualities of coins and currency are still rare. An exception is Mark Tomasko, who excitedly writes about the "feel of steel," by which he means "that tactile experience one gets from well-printed bank-note engraving."[41] In my own work with students I have made some surprising discoveries concerning coins and currency as sensate things. "Cold hard cash," for instance, preserves the original meaning of the word "cash" as referring to coins or specie. It also preserves the long-standing contest in the United States between coin and paper currency, a contest that was effectively decided because of the Civil War, whose uncertainties instantly drove gold and silver coins into hiding. Alternative forms of sensory perception of monetary tokens survive in residual or marginal cultures, where people still bite on a coin to see if it is real, or where they say things like "It ain't worth a plug nickel" when referring to counterfeit coins. Other terms preserve echoes of money as substance (which is self-evidently open to sensory perception), in particular names of monetary units such as "shekel", "pound", "mark", or "lira"—all originally terms for units of weight, reminding us that gold and silver (copper, too) once passed by weight. Many colloquialisms attached to money likewise refer to a sensory experience,

40. Gabriel, *Ästhetik und Rhetorik*, 27–38; Gabriel, "Aesthetics and Political Iconography of Money," in *Pictorial Cultures and Political Iconographies: Approaches, Perspectives, Case Studies from Europe and America*, ed. U. J. Hebel and C. Wagner (Berlin and New York: de Gruyter, 2011), 419–428.

41. M. Tomasko, T*he Feel of Steel: The Art and History of Bank-Note Engraving in the United States* (New York: American Numismatic Society, 2012), xiii. For an overview of the current state of research see two articles by Christian Thiel: Thiel, "Der schöne Schein. Banknoten als Untersuchungsgegenstand einer visuellen Soziologie," *Soziale Welt* 64 (2013), 191–216; and Thiel, "Banknoten im Blickpunkt der Wissenschaft: Fragen – Perspektiven – Desiderata," in *Der schöne Schein. Symbolik und Ästhetik von Banknoten*, ed. S. Hartmann and C. Thiel (Regenstauf, Germany: Gietl Verlag, 2016), 45–76.

especially to nourishment: "bread" or "beans" (on the analogy of it being a staple of life); "cheddar" or "chedda" (perhaps from the concept of cheese distributed by the government to welfare recipients); "cabbage" or "lettuce" (for paper money, from its color); "clams" for dollars (perhaps from the onetime use of seashells as currency); "spondulix" for money (possibly from *spondylus*, a Greek word for a shell once used as currency); "dough" (because everyone "kneads" it). Hiphop has likewise valorized money throughout its existence, measuring wealth in terms of "ducats," "cheddar," "cheese" or "c.r.e.a.m." ("Cash Rules Everything Around Me").[42]

To look at and explore monetary tokens as sensory phenomena is potentially iconoclastic. "Looking alone is not enough," Gottfried Gabriel writes, calling to mind that traditionally, sight has been regarded as the noblest of our senses, touch as the lowest. Smell, the olfactory sense, also has had a low prestige. Aristotle considered smell the least advanced of the five senses. The strict hierarchy of the senses, declining from face to feeling, survived from classical antiquity and resurfaced during the Renaissance, together with the symbolism attached to individual senses.[43] Taste became a metaphor for aesthetic discrimination, but was also associated with sexual experience; so was touch, which was also associated with power. Sight, the number one sense, became the twin brother of reason, the rhetorical flagship of the early Enlightenment. Ironically, though, sight is the least reliable of our senses—the entertainment value of optical illusions is legendary. Regardless, professional conservation likewise privileges sight, not feeling or bodily experience. As NCS (Numismatic Conservation Services) proclaim in an advertisement (Fig. 7), "Professional conservation...substantially improves [a coin's] visual appeal."[44]

The meticulous descriptions in guide books or auction catalogs are also proof

42. H. Tschachler, *The Greenback: Paper Money and American Culture* (Jefferson, NC: McFarland, 2010), 26–28; and for a much longer, alphabetized list, H. Spiller, *Keep the Change,* 82–85.

43. Aristotle, *De Anima,* 424b. See also M. M. Smith, *Sensing the Past: Seeing, Hearing, Smelling, Tasting, and Touching in History* (Berkeley and Los Angeles: University of California Press, 2008), 1–18. For "Looking alone is not enough," see Gabriel, *Ästhetik und Rhetorik,* 51: "Mit einem Hin-Sehen im buchstäblichen Sinn, mit einem optischen Blick auf die Objekte, ist es nicht getan" (my translation). Gabriel clearly addresses here the philosophical distinction, established by Bertrand Russell, between "knowledge by description" and "knowledge by acquaintance": B. Russell, "Knowledge by Acquaintance and Knowledge by Description," *Proceedings of the Aristotelian Society* 11 (1910–1911): 108–28.

44. Cf. the publicity on NGC's homepage: "From within a state-of-the-art secure facility, NCS uses a variety of proprietary techniques to remove harmful surface contaminants, stabilize and protect a coin's surfaces, *and improve eye appeal.*" NGC, February 27, 2018, https://www.ngccoin.com/ncs-conservation/, emphasis added.

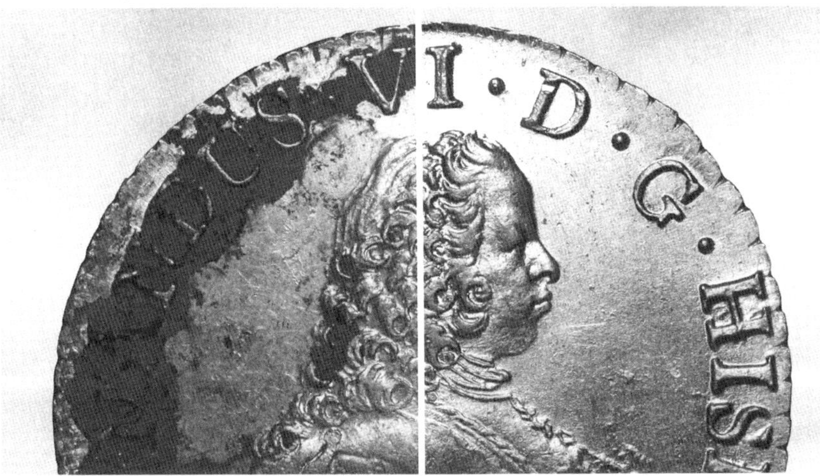

Figure 7. "Reveal Your Coins' True Beauty." Advertisement for Numismatic Conservation Services (NCS), *The Numismatist* 131.1 (January 2018), 33 (image courtesy of Numismatic Conservation Services).

that among numismatists the perceptual experience is fed primarily through the eye—the most despotic of our senses, as the Romantics knew.[45] Ironically, their alternative to the prevailing "oculocentrism" was to extol the "inward eye," insight or intuition.[46] Yet other means to "thwart this tyranny"[47] of the visual exist. Free-thinker and nature enthusiast Henry David Thoreau, for instance, considered sensory phenomena as food and drink for the parched spirit: "A man should feed his senses with the best that the land offers," he wrote in his journal on September 12, 1851.[48] Shortly after the Civil War, Walt Whitman declared in *Song of Myself*, "I am the poet of the Body."[49] On the other side of the Atlantic, Friedrich Nietzsche in *Zarathustra* defined aesthetics as "applied physiology" ("*angewandte Physiologie*"), as absolute bodily immanence, a full sensory experience; elsewhere he wrote about the olfactory sense in terms of a detective sensitivity, a nose that could "smell a lie as a lie."[50]

The lies Nietzsche's nose targeted in the final years of the nineteenth century were those of theologians, German idealist philosophers, and historicists. Today, he might well direct his olfactory sense towards the general suspicion the "lower" senses are put under among numismatists and collectors. What he would smell is that slabbing also offers a solid

45. For William Wordsworth, for instance, sight "is in every stage of life / The most despotic of our senses": *The Prelude; or, Growth of a Poet's Mind* (New York: D. Appleton, 1850), Book 12, 322. For further discussion and analysis, see K. McSweeney, *Language of the Senses: Sensory-Perceptual Dynamics in Wordsworth, Coleridge, Thoreau, Whitman, and Dickinson* (Montreal: McGill-Queen's University Press, 1998), chap. 4, 41–60.

46. On "oculocentrism" as the heritage of the Enlightenment, see D. Kleinberg-Levin, *Modernity and the Hegemony of Vision* (Berkeley, CA: University of California Press, 1993); P. Maltby, *The Visionary Moment: A Postmodern Critique* (Albany: State University of New York Press, 2002), 34–35.

47. Wordsworth continues by saying that he would "Gladly" "endeavour to unfold the means / Which Nature studiously employs to thwart / This tyranny": Wordsworth, *The Prelude*, 322.

48. H. D. Thoreau, *The Writings of Henry D. Thoreau, Journal*, vol. 4, *1851–1852*, ed. Leonard N. Neufeldt and Nancy Craig Simmons (Princeton: Princeton University Press, 1992), 75.

49. W. Whitman, "Song of Myself," §21, in *Leaves of Grass*, ed. Sculley Bradley and Harold W. Blodgett (New York and London: Norton, 1973), 48. For a discussion of Whitman's poetics of the body, which owed a great deal to the practice of preserving and learning from cadavers or body parts during the Civil War era, see L. Tuggle, *The Afterlives of Specimens: Science, Mourning, and Whitman's Civil War* (Iowa City: University of Iowa Press, 2017).

50. "Applied physiology" ("*angewandte Physiologie*"): F. Nietzsche, *Also sprach Zarathustra* (*Thus Spake Zarathustra*), in *Sämtliche Werke. Kritische Studienausgabe in 15 Einzelbänden*, ed. Giorgio Collio (Munich and Berlin: dtv and de Gruyter, 1999), 4:577; "smell a lie as a lie" ("*die Lüge als Lüge riechen*"): Nietzsche, "Nietzsche contra Wagner" (1888), in *Sämtliche Werke*, 6:366.

5) defense against what is natural, bodily, "raw," and unclean, and also, from a psychoanalytical perspective, defense against the identification of coined money, feces, and sexuality. In "The Ontogenesis of the Interest in Money" (1914), Sándor Ferenczi argued that money derives from the infantile impulse to play with feces, sublimated by the impingement, on this play impulse, of a repudiation of feces. Feces, Ferenczi wrote, is "one of the first toys of the child." From this, the child "is to be weaned only through deterrents and threats of punishment." As the "sense of cleanliness" increases, children will devote themselves to "cleaner" toys: sand, putty, rubber, then pebbles, glass beads, marbles, buttons, and finally, "shining pieces of money"—in the form of coins. These are treasured "less for their economic value than for their own sake as pleasure-giving objects," pleasure to *all* the child's senses.[51]

Ferenczi's piece on money followed a 1908 essay by Sigmund Freud titled "Character and Anal Eroticism," in which the master linked coprophilia (the love of filth) to the love of (filthy) lucre, calling it a "specific identification of gold with faeces."[52] Freud himself drew on various visualizations of this identification, such as the *Dukatenscheisser* ("shitter of ducats"), a colloquialism for someone who knows how to create or increase money, or else for a wealthy spendthrift. Freud also knew that the *Dukatenscheisser* is a variant of the *Dukatenesel* (the "gold-ass"), a fairy-tale figure. In the Brothers Grimm's "The Wishing-Table," for instance, a donkey begins to defecate coins (ducats).[53]

In the Christian tradition, excreting coins is the prerogative of the devil. There is no dearth of money devil cartoons showing the devil defecating precious coins, thus articulating the dislike of money in Christendom, not only for its association with avarice, but also for its form, which used to evoke the com-

51. S. Ferenczi, "The Ontogenesis of the Interest in Money [1914]," in *First Contributions to Psychoanalysis,* trans. Ernest Jones (London: Hogarth Press and the Institute of Psycho-Analysis, 1952), 321, 322, 327; cf. M. Kelly, "The Smell of Money: Mary Kelly in Conversation with Emily Apter," in *Imaging Desire* (Cambridge, MA: MIT Press, 1996), 148–149; and N. O. Brown, *Life Against Death: The Psychoanalytical Meaning of History* (Middletown, CT: Wesleyan University Press, 1977), esp. chap. 15 on "Filthy Lucre," 234–304.

52. S. Freud, "Character and Anal Eroticism," in *The Standard Edition of the Complete Psychological Works of Sigmund Freud,* trans. James A. Strachey, vol. 9 (London: Hogarth Press, 1959), 174. On money as fetish and sexual connotations of money, see E. Bornemann, *The Psychoanalysis of Money* (New York: Urizen Books, 1976). For a summary of the "money complex" in psychoanalytical writings, see M. Shell, *Money, Language, and Thought: Literary and Philosophic Economies from the Medieval to the Modern Era* (Baltimore and London: Johns Hopkins University Press, 1993), 196–99.

53. The full title of the tale is "The Wishing-Table, the Gold-Ass, and the Cudgel in the Sack" (original German name "Tischlein deck dich, Goldesel und Knüppel aus dem Sack"). On the *Dukatenscheisser,* see Freud, "Character and Anal Eroticism," 174.

munion wafer. The coin-excreting money devil is conceived of as a figure who has to be eliminated but never is, not even by cleansing the temple with whips and scourges.[54] As for the modern era, Martin Luther especially focused on the fecal filth of the money devil; thus, he too saw the need to cleanse the temple. (The theme of cleansing the temple also made it into Franklin Delano Roosevelt's first inaugural address of 1933, in which the President said that the United States had been shamefully betrayed by the "money changers" but fortunately for America they had now fled "from their high seats in the temple."[55])

Depictions of the money devil are known from the late fourteenth century, usually showing St. John's vision, and with a crowned Antichrist as a sidekick. By the seventeenth century, the coin-covered money devil had become a worn theme, abounding in France, England, Italy, Holland, Russia, and Germany, such as a caricature of the money devil that now is among the holdings of the Germanische Nationalmuseum in Nuremberg (Fig. 8).[56]

Also noteworthy is a mid-nineteenth-century book on Flemish folk life by the Belgian writer Hendrik Conscience that bears the money devil in the title: *De geldduivel* (Eng. trans. *The Demon of Gold*, German trans. *Der Geldteufel*).[57] Yet another instance is a German movie from 1923, which is likewise titled *Der Geldteufel*.[58] Hardly more uplift comes from writers and artists who actually treat coin money as pleasure-giving objects. Two examples from novels, one British, the other American, illustrate the degeneracy resulting from the fetishization and idolization of precious coins.[59]

In George Eliot's *Silas Marner* (first published in 1861) an embittered weaver lives isolated and alone near the rural village of Raveloe. His only comfort are his craft and the gold and silver coins he earns and hoards from his weaving. When

54. M. Shell, *Art and Money* (Chicago and London: University of Chicago Press, 1995), 64.

55. F. D. Roosevelt, "Inaugural Address," March 4, 1933, online by Gerhard Peters and John T. Woolley, *The American Presidency Project*, accessed July 7, 2018, http://www.presidency. ucsb.edu/ws/?pid=14473; reference is to Matt. 21:12 (and see Mark 11:15). Note that in the biblical reference there is greater stress on agency: "Jesus...cast out all them...." Also note that Roosevelt by using Matthew carefully avoids the rhetoric of class and class struggle. Additionally, Roosevelt's choice of words is symptomatic of a discursive practice that construes capitalism as religion.

56. Marc Shell, *Art and Money*, 69, fig. 49, erroneously dates the picture to 1720; the work, a copper engraving by Abraham Aubry, actually dates to ca. 1660.

57. H. Conscience, *The Demon of Gold* (Baltimore and Philadelphia: John Murphy and Lippincott, 1857).

58. The film *Der Geldteufel*, which was directed by Heinz Goldberg and produced by the Berlin-based Wörner-Filmgesellschaft, is listed in the International Movie Database (IMDb), accessed May 16, 2018, https://www.imdb.com/title/tt0482981/?ref_=nv_sr_1.

59. For an exhaustive discussion of artworks, see Shell, *Art and Money*.

Figure 8. "The Money Devil," copper-plate engraving by Abraham Aubry, *ca.* 1660, Germanisches Nationalmuseum, Nuremberg.

his treasure is stolen, he sinks into a deep gloom. At one point, a small girl child finds her way to Silas's house. Silas keeps and raises her and, through her, finds a place in the rural society and a purpose in life. In the end, even Silas's robbed treasure is found, and the money duly returned to him. As Silas finds happiness with his now extended family, the gold no longer serves as the substitute god it was at the beginning, when

> at night came his revelry: at night he closed his shutters, and made fast his doors, and drew forth his gold. Long ago the heap of coins had become too large for the iron pot to hold them, and he had made for them two thick leather bags, which wasted no room in their resting-place, but lent themselves flexibly to every corner. How the guineas shone as they came pouring out of the dark leather mouths! The silver bore no large proportion in amount to the gold, because the long pieces of linen which formed his chief work were always partly paid for in gold, and out of the silver he supplied his own bodily wants, choosing always the shillings and

sixpences to spend in this way. He loved the guineas best, but he would not change the silver – the crowns and half-crowns that were his own earnings, begotten by his labour; he loved them all. He spread them out in heaps and bathed his hands in them; then he counted them and set them up in regular piles, and felt their rounded outline between his thumb and fingers, and thought fondly of the guineas that were only half-earned by the work in his loom, as if they had been unborn children....[60]

McTeague is a novel by Frank Norris, first published in 1899. It tells the story of the dentist McTeague and his wife Trina, their courtship and marriage, and their subsequent descent into poverty, violence, and finally murder as a result of jealousy and greed (*Gier nach Gold*, greed for gold, is the title of the novel's German translation). Trina wins $5,000 from a lottery ticket but is too parsimonious to touch the principal, not even when McTeague loses his dental practice. From her own work, Trina has accumulated a few hundred dollars, penny-pinched savings that she keeps in a locked trunk:

At times, when she knew that McTeague was far from home, she would lock her door, open her trunk, and pile all her little hoard on her table. By now it was four hundred and seven dollars and fifty cents. Trina would play with this money by the hour, piling it, and repiling it, or gathering it all into one heap, and drawing back to the farthest corner of the room to note the effect, her head on one side. She polished the gold pieces with a mixture of soap and ashes until they shone, wiping them carefully on her apron. Or, again, she would draw the heap lovingly toward her and bury her face in it, delighted at the smell of it and the feel of the smooth, cool metal on her cheeks. She even put the smaller gold pieces in her mouth, and jingled them there. She loved her money with an intensity that she could hardly express. She would plunge her small fingers into the pile with little murmurs of affection, her long, narrow eyes half closed and shining, her breath coming in long sighs.[61]

The money, which amounts to roughly $10,000 in today's value, does not bring Trina any happiness. One day, McTeague beats her to death and takes the entire

60. G. Eliot, *Silas Marner, the Weaver of Raveloe* (Oxford and New York: Oxford University Press, 1996), chap. 2, 20–21.

61. F. Norris, *McTeague. A Story of San Francisco*, ed. Donald Pizer (New York: Norton, 1977), chap. 16, 173. On sexual pathology in McTeague see W. B. Michaels, *The Gold Standard and the Logic of Naturalism: American Literature at the Turn of the Century* (Berkeley: University of California Press, 1987), 119–123.

hoard with him, only to end up stranded, alone and helpless, in the arid waste of Death Valley.

Idolization and fetishization of money go back a long way. Around 110 CE, the Roman historian Suetonius portrayed the Roman Emperor Gaius Caligula (37–41 CE) as being seized "with a mania for feeling the touch of money [so that he would] pour out huge piles of gold pieces in some open place, walk over them barefooted, and wallow in them for a long time with his whole body."[62] Both Silas Marner and Trina McTeague can be seen as reincarnations of Caligula in literature. No doubt the best-known reincarnation stems from popular culture, as a cartoon figure by the name of Scrooge McDuck, also known as Uncle Scrooge, or rather, "$crooge," as the "S" is usually realized as a dollar sign. Donald Duck's wealthy uncle came into being in 1947 when comic-book cartoonist Carl Barks (a former story man for Disney cartoons) needed a miserly old relative for a story, "Christmas on Bear Mountain." In this tale, Scrooge serves as a mere story prop, a simple caricature of his namesake from Dickens's *A Christmas Carol*, Ebenezer Scrooge. Barks later claimed that he originally intended to use Scrooge only once, but eventually was able to draw more from him. In an interview, Barks said that he had always looked at the ducks as caricatured human beings. Scrooge McDuck, who is supposed to have made his fortune between 1890 and 1920, in many ways recalls the robber barons and industrialists of that era. Thus, he proudly asserts, "I made it by being tougher than the toughies and smarter than the smarties!" Yet he is also allowed to say of himself, "*And I made it square!*"[63] Scrooge McDuck thus is the noble capitalist of the Cold War era who by luck and by pluck has risen from obscure and humble origins in the Old World. This is not a very original idea. In this regard, the Scrooge stories are very much like the Horatio Alger stories of the late nineteenth century—or like *Acres of Diamond*, the famous inspirational lecture of Russell Cromwell, of the same era. They all suggest that escape from suffering and poverty lies in "the individual plugging away, searching for a break, and walking away a millionaire."[64]

Scrooge is usually depicted not with dollar bills but with gold coins. (He also searched for gold on several occasions throughout his long career.) "Buckaroo,"

62. Suetonius, *De Vita Caesarum: Caius Caligula*, trans. John C. Rolfe (Cambridge, MA: Harvard University Press, 1920), 1:465.

63. Wikipedia, "Scrooge McDuck," modified July 21, 2018, accessed July 26, 2018, https:// en.wikipedia.org/wiki/Scrooge_McDuck.

64. A. Brinkley, *Culture and Politics in the Great Depression* (Waco: Markham Press Fund/ Baylor University Press, 1999), 11. For a reading of Barks's Disney books as anti-modern fables, see T. Andrae, *Carl Barks and the Disney Comic Books: Unmasking the Myth of Modernity* (Jackson: University Press of Mississippi, 2006).

a known alias for Scrooge McDuck, thus is a somewhat unhappy choice of name in that, through its allusion to "buck," it evokes paper money rather than gold. Considering the hero's predilection for gold, the McDuck stories foreground the sensory experience of money, which is so much stronger and more direct with coins. Tellingly, Scrooge's favorite "sport" is diving into his money like a dolphin, burrowing through it like a gopher, and throwing coins in the air to feel them fall upon his skull. In Carl Barks's 1974 painting "The Sport of Tycoons," Scrooge's piles of coins are breaking the 90-foot level, and his money bin is ripe for the ritual bath, Scrooge's sacred act of the rich man.[65]

Scrooge McDuck's miserliness bears a closer look. In "Character and Anal Eroticism" Freud describes the character traits that are typical of anal eroticism in terms of 1) orderliness (bodily cleanliness, conscientiousness in carrying out small duties, trustworthiness), 2) parsimoniousness (stinginess, an exaggerated form of avarice), and 3) obstinacy (defiance, together with rage and revengefulness)—all found in the figure of the miser, including of course Scrooge.[66] Anal eroticism begins with childish anal retention. Once again following Freud, Sándor Ferenczi speaks of childish anal retention in terms of the desire to hoard "dejecta" as so many "savings" for the future. Civilization, we have seen, prohibits the accumulation of excrement itself but it sanctions its sanitized substitutes— sand, putty, rubber, glass beads, and later, money in the form of coins. Ferenczi calls these material samples of odorless and dehydrated filth "copro-symbols." To the extent that money is derived from anal eroticism, it is "nothing other than odorless dehydrated filth that has been made to shine. *Pecunia non olet.*"[67]

There are, then, good reasons for associating Scrooge McDuck with coins rather than with bills. Wallowing in coins increases pleasure, even though the coins are mere "copro-symbols," and, following Freud, the increase in pleasure is only in "moderated and tamed" form and "inhibited in its aim."[68] But it is pre-

65. The painting, measuring 14 × 18 inches, is based on the tale "Only a Poor Old Man"; it was first published in Carl Barks, *The Fine Art of Walt Disney's Donald Duck* (Scottsdale, AZ: Rainbow Publishing, 1981), 215. On November 16, 2011, the painting was sold at Heritage Auctions for $262,900.00. See "Swimming in Money," bleedingcool.com, November 17, 2011, accessed July 26, 2015, http://www.bleedingcool.com/2011/11/17/swimming-in-money-carl-barks-scrooge-mcduck-painting-goes-for-record-262900/?sa=X&ved=0CBUQ9QEwAGoVC hMI4I-1ofL4xgIVg5EsCh2Z3QU9. Disney Enterprises, Inc., after a five-months wait decided that they were unable to grant permission to reproduce the image in the pages of the *AJN*.

66. Freud, "Character and Anal Eroticism," 169.

67. Ferenczi, "The Ontogenesis of the Interest in Money," 321, 327.

68. Ferenczi, "The Ontogenesis of the Interest in Money," 327; S. Freud, "Civilization and Its Discontents," 121: "The instinct of destruction, moderated and tamed, and, as it were, inhibited in its aim, must, when it is directed towards objects, provide the ego with the satisfaction

cisely the symbolic form, together with moderation and inhibition, that makes Scrooge's childish posturing appear tolerable. With regard to the connection between coins and sensoriness, however, everything has not yet been said.

6) The fundamental suspicion against sensory perception inevitably leads, Jürgen Peper argues, towards a culture that has lost the aesthetic without any compensation.[69] Loss of the aesthetic means an absence or denial of sensory experience in an effort to defend against the transitoriness of all things and, in the final analysis, against death. For collectors, the goal is to preserve the beauty and integrity of their coins at all costs. Preservation, needless to say, is a fundamental dogma of museum cultures. "Collect—Preserve—Make Accessible" is the motto that graces the website of the Museum of the State of Carinthia, Austria.[70] A similar note is struck by an article in a numismatic magazine: "...*a coin, medal, token or bank note should look the same when it leaves your collection as it did when it entered your collection.*" From this commandment we are led to the "cardinal rule of numismatics: do not clean any numismatic collectible—ever."[71] The injunction must have escaped Trina McTeague, who "polished the gold pieces with a mixture of soap and ashes until they shone, wiping them carefully on her apron."[72] The job of cleaning coins, we learn from the numismatic article, should be done by professionals, and it should be the preliminary stage to encapsulation, the *conditio sine qua non* for the preservation of beauty and youth. Once a coin has become encased in a solid plastic slab, it will neither change, age, decay, nor die.

Death is, of course, a threatening scenario, and humans will always try to transcend their mortality, by various heroic acts (such as climbing Everest without additional oxygen) or, in a general sense, by symbolic "immortality projects." The term "immortality project" belongs to Ernest Becker, the author of a book titled *The Denial of Death*.[73] The book was originally published in New York. There, as well as in the United States in general, people don't usually die. Sometimes they are killed in mass shootings, and then President Trump sends them

of its vital needs and with control over nature."

69. "[E]ine kompensationslos wegästhetisierte Kultur": Peper, *Ästhetisierung als zweite Aufklärung*, 371.

70. Landesmuseum Kärnten, Rudolfinum, "Sammeln—Bewahren—Erschliessen," accessed May 10, 2018, http://www.landesmuseum.ktn.gv.at/210227_DE%2dLMK%2dMuseen.?aussenstelle=6.

71. M. Sanders, "Preserve & Protect," *The Numismatist* 129.10 (October 2016), 119, emphasis added.

72. F. Norris, *McTeague*, chap. 16, 173.

73. E. Becker, *The Denial of Death* (New York: Free Press, 1973).

"thoughts and prayers," but mostly they pass away. For some, this is not the end, though. Certain people have themselves deep-frozen, in order to be thawed out at a future date. (Do they ever reflect that the world may not even exist anymore then?) I find even more bizarre the efforts of Aubrey de Grey, self-styled medical gerontologist, editor-in-chief of the journal *Rejuvenation Research*, and co-author of *Ending Aging*, whose research is rooted in the belief that defeating aging and death is both feasible and desirable.[74] Cultural practices of this kind may seem ludicrous, but as the bioethicist George J. Annas so aptly put it, America is "a death-denying culture that cannot accept death as anything but defeat." Americans, Annas continues, "prepare for any and every disease and screen for every possible 'risk factor,' but are utterly unable to prepare for death."[75]

If Americans are unable to prepare for their own deaths, how should they be able to prepare for the death of the coins they collect? Coins that come in sonically sealed plastic holders don't die. They are truly odorless and dehydrated, removed from any association with dirt, physicality, or natural processes. Slabbing, done in order to preserve beauty and youth, thus may legitimately be called an "immortality project." Ultimately, however, sonically sealed plastic holders are neither a sufficient nor a necessary condition for collecting coins. These holders are simply contingent. Thus, the universe of plastic slabs is merely one possible construct. While acceptance of that world is not mandatory, as there are all kinds of ways to ensure long-term preservation without encasing, neither is acceptance of a world in which the sensory qualities of coins can experienced to the full. Collectors will always have to face an uncomfortable choice. This may be cold comfort to those readers who perhaps expected a definitive answer to the paradox that emerges in the act of collecting coins. But coming as I do from Austria, I have learned not to make a decision, living with ambivalences instead. As the dramatist Franz Grillparzer wrote during the upheavals that shook mid-nineteenth-century Europe: "This is the curse of Hapsburg's noble house: Halfway to halt, and doubtfully to aim at half a deed, with half considered means."[76]

<hr>

74. A. de Grey, with M. Rae, *Ending Aging: The Rejuvenation Breakthroughs That Could Reverse Human Aging in Our Lifetime* (New York: St. Martin's Press, 2008).

75. G. J. Annas, *Worst Case Bioethics: Death, Disaster, and Public Health* (New York: Oxford University Press, 2010), 12.

76. F. Grillparzer, *Family Strife in Hapsburg*, trans. Arthur Burkhard (Yarmouth Port, MA: Register Press, 1940), 2:2, 53–54. German original (1848), *Ein Bruderzwist in Habsburg*: "Das ist der Fluch von unserm edlen Haus: Auf halben Wegen und zu halber Tat mit halben Mitteln zauderhaft zu streben."

ACKNOWLEDGMENTS

The author wishes to thank David Yoon as well as the two anonymous reviewers for their helpful comments. While their suggestions and critiques no doubt greatly improved this article, the faults it may still have are entirely mine.

BIBLIOGRAPHY

Anderson, Misty. "Living in a Material World." In *Sensible Flesh: On Touch in Early Modern Culture*, edited by Elizabeth D. Harvey, 191–204. Philadelphia: University of Pennsylvania Press, 2003.

Andrae, Thomas. *Carl Barks and the Disney Comic Books: Unmasking the Myth of Modernity*. Jackson: University Press of Mississippi, 2006.

Annas, George J. *Worst Case Bioethics: Death, Disaster, and Public Health*. New York: Oxford University Press, 2010.

Aristotle. "De Anima." In *The Basic Works of Aristotle*, edited by Richard McKeon, 535–606. New York: Random House, 1941.

Barks, Carl. *The Fine Art of Walt Disney's Donald Duck*. Scottsdale, AZ: Rainbow Publishing, 1981.

Baumgarten, Alexander Gottlieb. *Aesthetica*, 2 vols. Frankfurt an der Oder: J. C. Kleyb, reprinted in 1 vol. Hildesheim-New York: Georg Olms, 1970.

Becker, Ernest. *The Denial of Death*. New York: Free Press, 1973.

Belk, Russell W. *Collecting in a Consumer Society*. London: Routledge, 1995; reprinted 2001.

"Better Than One: NGC Introduces a Two-Coin Holder." *The Numismatist* 132.3 (March 2019): 24.

Bornemann, Ernest. *The Psychoanalysis of Money*. New York: Urizen Books, 1976.

Brinkley, Alan. *Culture and Politics in the Great Depression*. Waco: Markham Press Fund/Baylor University Press, 1999.

Brown, Norman O. *Life Against Death: The Psychoanalytical Meaning of History*. Middletown, CT: Wesleyan University Press, 1977.

Buechner, Georg. *Complete Plays, Lenz and Other Writings*, edited and translated by John Reddick. Harmondsworth: Penguin, 1993.

Caygill, Howard. "Aesthetics and Civil Society: Theories of Art and Society, 1640–1790." PhD thesis, University of Sussex, 1982.

Chandler, Raymond. *The High Window*. New York: Knopf, 1945.

Classen, Constance. *The Color of Angels: Cosmology, Gender and the Aesthetic Imagination*. London: Routledge, 1998.

Comenius, Johannes Amos. *Orbis sensualium pictus / Die sichtbare Welt*. Noribergae [Nürnberg]: M. Endteri, 1658. Augustana, Augsburg. http://www.hs-augsburg.de/~harsch/Chronologia/Lspost17/Comenius/com_0041.html. Accessed March 6, 2018.

Conscience, Hendrik. *The Demon of Gold* [orig. *De geldduivel*, 1856]. Baltimore: John Murphy / Philadelphia: Lippincott, 1857.

De Grey, Aubrey, with Michael Rae. *Ending Aging: The Rejuvenation Breakthroughs That Could Reverse Human Aging in Our Lifetime*. New York: St. Martin's Press, 2008.

Descartes, René. *Principia philosophiae*. Amstelodami: apud Ludovicum Elzevirium, 1644.

Doyle, Al. "Green Beans." *The Numismatist* 132.4 (April 2019): 19.

Eliot, George. *Silas Marner, the Weaver of Raveloe*. Edinburgh: William Blackwood and Sons, 1861; reprinted Oxford/New York: Oxford University Press, 1996.

Featherstone, Mike. *Consumer Culture and Postmodernism*. London: Sage, 1991.

Ferenczi, Sándor. "The Ontogenesis of the Interest in Money." In *First Contributions to Psychoanalysis*, translated by Ernest Jones, 319–31. London: Hogarth Press and the Institute of Psycho-Analysis, 1952 (originally published 1914).

Freud, Sigmund. "Character and Anal Eroticism." In *The Standard Edition of the Complete Psychological Works of Sigmund Freud*, translated by James A. Strachey, 9.167–75. London: Hogarth Press, 1959 (originally published 1908).

———. "Civilization and Its Discontents." In *The Standard Edition of the Complete Psychological Works of Sigmund Freud*, translated by James A. Strachey, 21.57–145. London: Hogarth Press, 1986 (originally published 1930).

Gabriel, Gottfried. "Aesthetics and Political Iconography of Money." In *Pictorial Cultures and Political Iconographies: Approaches, Perspectives, Case Studies from Europe and America*, edited by Udo J. Hebel and Christoph Wagner, 419–428. Berlin and New York: de Gruyter, 2011.

———. *Ästhetik und Rhetorik des Geldes*. Stuttgart and Bad Canstatt: Frommann-Holzboog, 2002.

———. *Präzision und Prägnanz. Logische, rhetorische, ästhetische und literarische Erkenntnisformen*. Paderborn: Mentis, 2019.

Der Geldteufel. International Movie Database (IMDb). Accessed May 16, 2018. https://www.imdb.com/title/tt0482981/?ref_=nv_sr_1.

Gottlieb, Anthony. *The Dream of Enlightenment: The Rise of Modern Philosophy*. New York: Liveright, 2016.

Gregor, Mary J. "Baumgarten's Aesthetica." *The Review of Metaphysics* 37.2 (December 1983): 357–385.

Grierson, Philip. *Numismatics*. Oxford and New York: Oxford University Press, 1975.

Grillparzer, Franz. *Family Strife in Hapsburg*, translated by Arthur Burkhard. Yarmouth Port, MA: Register Press, 1940.

Grunwald, Martin. *Homo hapticus. Warum wir ohne Tastsinn nicht leben können*. München: Droemer Knaur, 2017.

Howes, David. "Charting the Sensorial Revolution." *The Senses and Society* 1.1 (2006): 113–28.

———. *Sensual Relations: Engaging the Senses in Culture and Social Theory*. Ann Arbor: University of Michigan Press, 2003.

———. "Skinscapes: Embodiment, Culture and Environment." In *The Book of Touch*, edited by Constance Classen, 27–39. Oxford: Berg, 2005.

Jones, James Earl. *Money: History in Your Hands* [DVD]. Colorado Springs, CO: American Numismatic Association, 1995.

Kelly, Mary. "The Smell of Money: Mary Kelly in Conversation with Emily Apter." In *Imaging Desire*, 142–157. Cambridge, MA: MIT Press, 1996, reprinted 1998.

Kleinberg-Levin, David Michael. *Modernity and the Hegemony of Vision*. Berkeley: University of California Press, 1993.

Klüßendorf, Niklot. "Gold—Silber—Kupfer—Aluminium—Papier. Materialhierarchien in der Münz- und Geldgeschichte." *Anzeiger des germanischen Nationalmuseums* 110 (1995): 107–114.

Landesmuseum Kärnten Rudolfinum. "Sammeln—Bewahren—Erschliessen." http://www.landesmuseum.ktn.gv.at/210227_DE%2dLMK%2dMuseen.?aussenstelle=6. Accessed May 10, 2018.

Lange, David W. "Dollars & Sense." *The Numismatist* 129.11 (November 2016): 95.

———. "Lame Ducks." *The Numismatist* 128.12 (December 2015): 17–18.

Langer, Susanne K. *Feeling and Form: A Theory of Art Developed from Philosophy in a New Key*. New York: Charles Scribner's Sons, 1952.

———. *Philosophy in a New Key: A Study in the Symbolism of Reason, Rite and Art*. Cambridge, MA: Harvard University Press, 1942.

Lévi-Strauss, Claude. *Le cru et le cuit*. Paris: Plon, 1964. Vol. 1 of *Mythologiques*. English trans. *The Raw and the Cooked*. New York: Harper & Row, 1975.

Linnaeus, Carolus. *Systema Naturae*. In *Readings in Early Anthropology*, edited by J. S. Slotkin. Chicago: Aldine, 1965; reprinted Abingdon and New York: Routledge, 2011 (originally published 1735).

Malnar, Joy Monica, and Frank Vodvorka. *Sensory Design*. Minneapolis: University of Minnesota Press, 2004.

Maltby, Paul. *The Visionary Moment: A Postmodern Critique.* Albany: State University of New York Press, 2002.

Marx, Karl. "Private Property and Communism." *Economic and Philosophic Manuscripts of 1844.* Marx Engels Archive. Accessed May 7, 2018. https://www.marxists.org/archive/marx/works/1844/manuscripts/comm.htm.

McSweeney, Kerry. *Language of the Senses: Sensory-Perceptual Dynamics in Wordsworth, Coleridge, Thoreau, Whitman, and Dickinson.* Montreal: McGill-Queen's University Press, 1998.

Michaels, Walter Benn. *The Gold Standard and the Logic of Naturalism: American Literature at the Turn of the Century.* Berkeley: University of California Press, 1987.

Münzkabinett. Kunsthistorisches Museum Wien. Accessed June 6, 2018. https://www.khm.at/besuchen/sammlungen/muenzkabinett/.

Nietzsche, Friedrich. *Sämtliche Werke. Kritische Studienausgabe in 15 Einzelbänden.* Edited by Giorgio Colli and Mazzino Montinari. Munich and Berlin: DTV and de Gruyter, 1999.

Norris, Frank. *McTeague. A Story of San Francisco.* New York: Doubleday & McClure, 1899. Reprinted New York: Norton, 1977.

Numismatic Conservation Services (NCS). "FAQs." 2018. Accessed February 27, 2018. https://www.ngccoin.com/ncs-conservation/.

Pearce, Susan M. *Museums, Objects, and Collections: A Cultural Study.* Washington, DC: Smithsonian Institution, 1993.

———. *On Collecting: An Investigation into Collecting in the European Tradition.* London: Routledge, 1995.

Peper, Jürgen. *Ästhetisierung als Zweite Aufklärung. Eine literarästhetisch abgeleitete Kulturtheorie,* 2nd ed. Bielefeld: Aisthesis Verlag, 2012.

Poe, Edgar Allan. *Essays and Reviews.* Edited by G. R. Thompson. New York: Library of America, 1984.

Riskin, Jessica. *Science in the Age of Sensibility: The Sentimental Empiricists of the French Enlightenment.* Chicago and London: University of Chicago Press, 2002.

Roosevelt, Franklin D. "Inaugural Address," March 4, 1933. Online by Gerhard Peters and John T. Woolley. *The American Presidency Project.* Accessed July 7, 2018. http://www.presidency.ucsb.edu/ws/?pid=14473.

Russell, Bertrand. "Knowledge by Acquaintance and Knowledge by Description." *Proceedings of the Aristotelian Society* 11 (1910–1911): 108–128.

Sanders, Mitch. "Getting Started." *The Numismatist* 131.10 (October 2018): 107–108.

————. "Hand-to-Hand History." *The Numismatist* 126.10 (October 2013): 111.

————. "Preserve & Protect." The Numismatist 129, no. 10 (October 2016): 119.

Schulze, Gerhard. *Die Erlebnisgesellschaft: Kultursoziologie der Gegenwart.* Frankfurt am Main and New York: Campus Verlag, 1993.

Schwager, D. "Sample Slab Book.com." Accessed August 13, 2018, https://sites. google.com/site/sampleslabbook/

Shappell, Chris. "Common Misconception." *The Numismatist* 130, no. 12 (December 2017): 103.

————. "Damaging Effects." *The Numismatist* 129.12 (December 2016): 109.

————. "Early Intervention." *The Numismatist* 132.1 (January 2019): 103.

————. "Handle with Care." *The Numismatist* 130.10 (October 2017): 103.

————. "Looking Ahead." *The Numismatist* 131.2 (February 2018): 91.

————. "Nature or Nurture?" *The Numismatist* 131.7 (July 2018): 107.

Sheldon, Roy, and Egmont Arens. "'Make it Snuggle in the Palm'. The Commodification of Touch." In *The Book of Touch*, edited by Constance Classen, 426–28. Oxford: Berg, 2005.

Shell, Marc. *Art and Money.* Chicago and London: University of Chicago Press, 1995.

————. *Money, Language, and Thought: Literary and Philosophic Economies from the Medieval to the Modern Era.* Berkeley and Los Angeles: University of California Press, 1982. Reprinted Baltimore: Johns Hopkins University Press, 1993.

Shutty, Michael S., Jr. "Awful Beauty: The Allure of Relic Coins." *The Numismatist* 130.8 (August 2017): 55–57.

Smith, Mark M. *Sensing the Past: Seeing, Hearing, Smelling, Tasting, and Touching in History.* Berkeley and Los Angeles: University of California Press, 2008.

Sparshott, Francis. *The Structure of Aesthetics.* Toronto: University of Toronto Press, 1963.

Spiller, Harley J. *Keep the Change: A Collector's Tales of Lucky Pennies, Counterfeit C-Notes, and other Curious Currency.* New York: Princeton Architectural Press, 2015.

Suetonius: C. Suetonius Tranquillus. *De Vita Caesarum: Caius Caligula.* Translated by John C. Rolfe. Cambridge, MA: Harvard University Press, 1920. Internet Ancient History Sourcebook. 1998. Accessed July 7, 2009. http://www. fordham.edu/HALSALL/ANCIENT/suetonius-caligula.html.

"Swimming in Money." Bleedingcool.com. November 17, 2011. Accessed July 26, 2015. http://www.bleedingcool.com/2011/11/17/swimming-in-money-carl-barks-scrooge-mcduck-painting-goes-for-record-262900/?sa=X&ved=0 CBUQ9QEwAG0VChMI4I-1ofL4xgIVg5EsCh2Z3QU9.

Thiel, Christian. "Banknoten im Blickpunkt der Wissenschaft: Fragen—Perspektiven—Desiderata." In *Der schöne Schein. Symbolik und Ästhetik von Banknoten,* edited by Stefan Hartmann and Christian Thiel, 45–76. Regenstauf: Gietl Verlag, 2016.

———. "Der schöne Schein. Banknoten als Untersuchungsgegenstand einer visuellen Soziologie." *Soziale Welt* 64 (2013): 191–216.

Thoreau, Henry David. *The Writings of Henry D. Thoreau. Journal.* Vol. 4: 1851–1852. Edited by Leonard N. Neufeldt and Nancy Craig Simmons. Princeton: Princeton University Press, 1992.

Tomasko, Mark D. *The Feel of Steel: The Art and History of Bank-Note Engraving in the United States.* New York: American Numismatic Society, 2012.

Tschachler, Heinz. "'Adoring with Tenfold Devotion': Edgar Allan Poe, America's Money and the 1849 Gold Dollar." *The Numismatist* 126.10 (October 2013): 32–39.

———. *The Greenback: Paper Money and American Culture.* Jefferson, NC: McFarland, 2010.

Tuggle, Lindsay. *The Afterlives of Specimens: Science, Mourning, and Whitman's Civil War.* Iowa City: University of Iowa Press, 2017.

Whitman, Walt. *Leaves of Grass.* Edited by Sculley Bradley and Harold W. Blodgett. New York and London: Norton, 1973.

Wikipedia. "Scrooge McDuck." Modified July 21, 2018. Accessed July 26, 2018. https://en.wikipedia.org/wiki/Scrooge_McDuck.

Woodward, Kathryn. *Identity and Difference: Culture, Media, and Identities.* London: Sage, 1997.

Wordsworth, William. *The Prelude; or, Growth of a Poet's Mind.* New York: D. Appleton, 1850.

Plates

Arados II	**Other Mints**

1. Av5. Cat. No. 10

Sidon, Year 7. Price 3482

2. Av6. Cat. No. 13

Sidon, Year 13. Price 3500

3. Av11. Cat. No. 22

Miletos. Price 2096

4. Av12. Cat. No. 23

Miletos. Price 2078

Tyre, Year 33. Price 3284

5. Av17. Cat. No. 33

Macedonia. Price 164

On the Reattribution of some Byblos Alexanders to Arados II

Plate 2

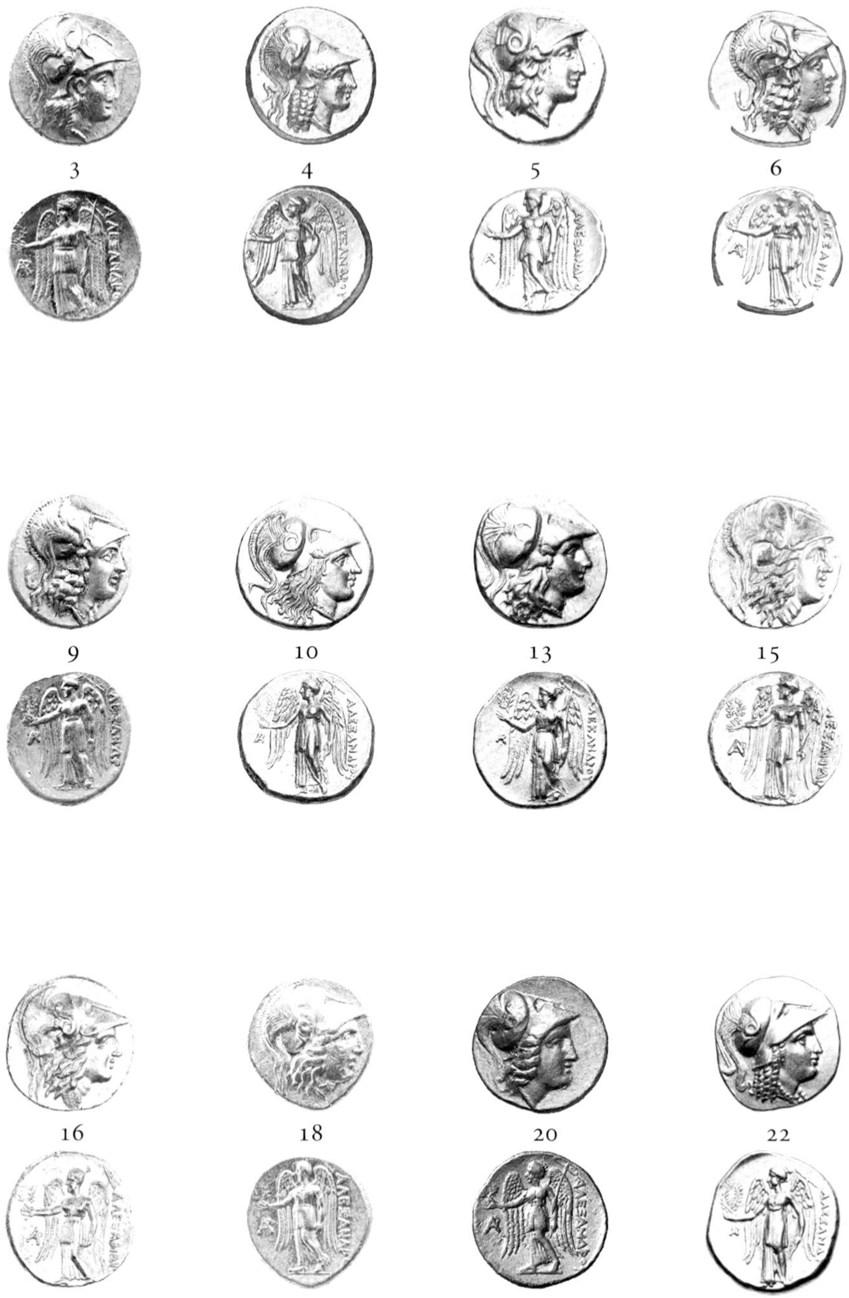

On the Reattribution of some Byblos Alexanders to Arados II

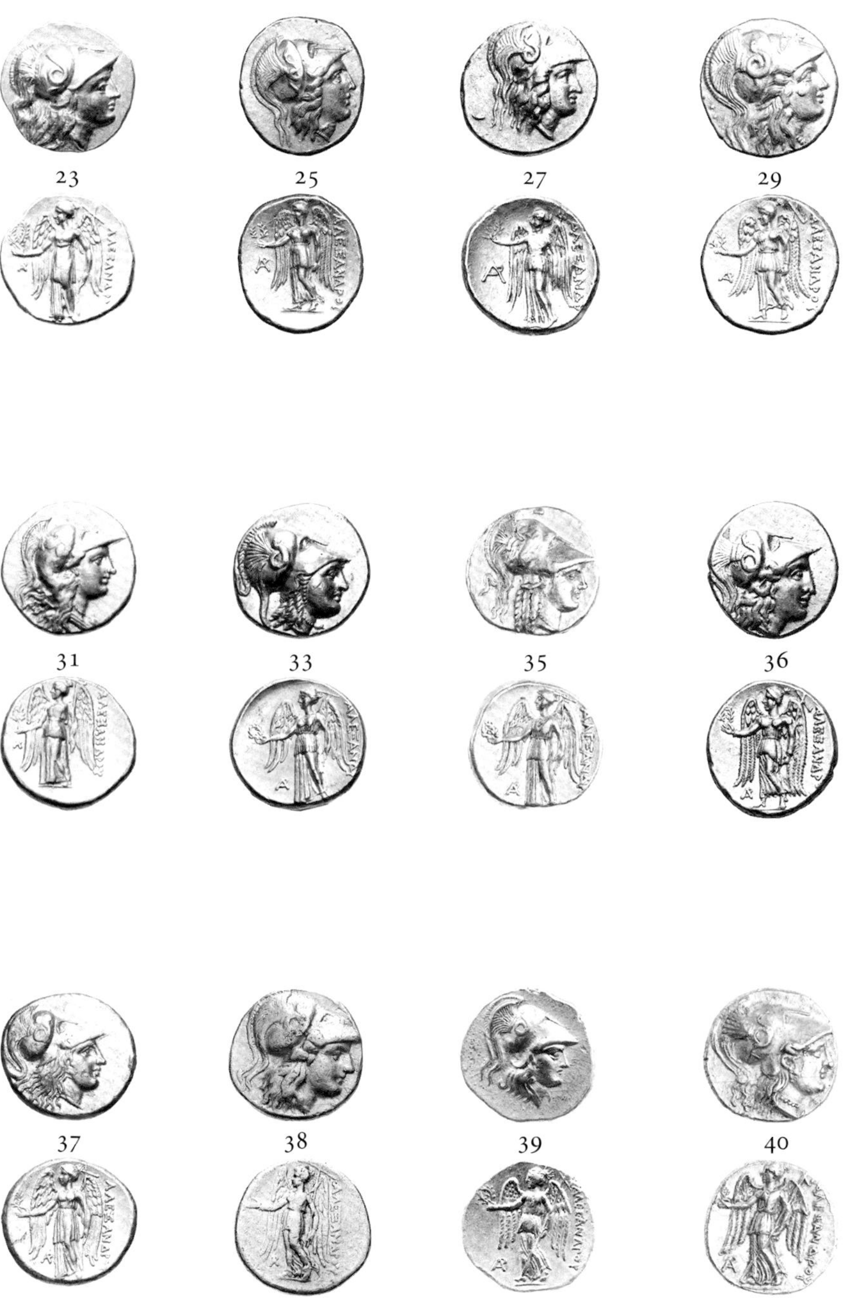

23   25   27   29

31   33   35   36

37   38   39   40

On the Reattribution of some Byblos Alexanders to Arados II

Plate 4

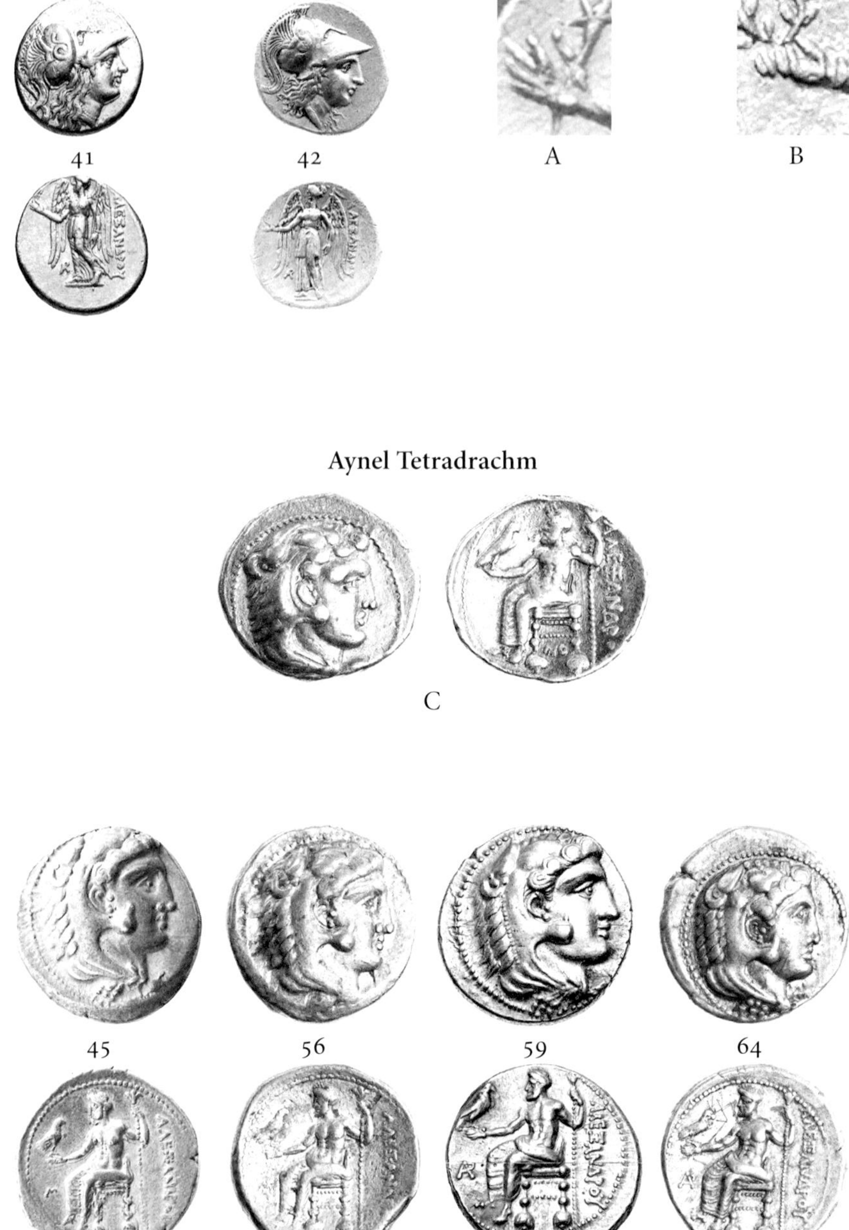

On the Reattribution of some Byblos Alexanders to Arados II

On the Reattribution of some Byblos Alexanders to Arados II

On the Reattribution of some Byblos Alexanders to Arados II

On the Reattribution of some Byblos Alexanders to Arados II

169   171   182   183

184   187   199   203

205

On the Reattribution of some Byblos Alexanders to Arados II

On the Reattribution of some Byblos Alexanders to Arados II

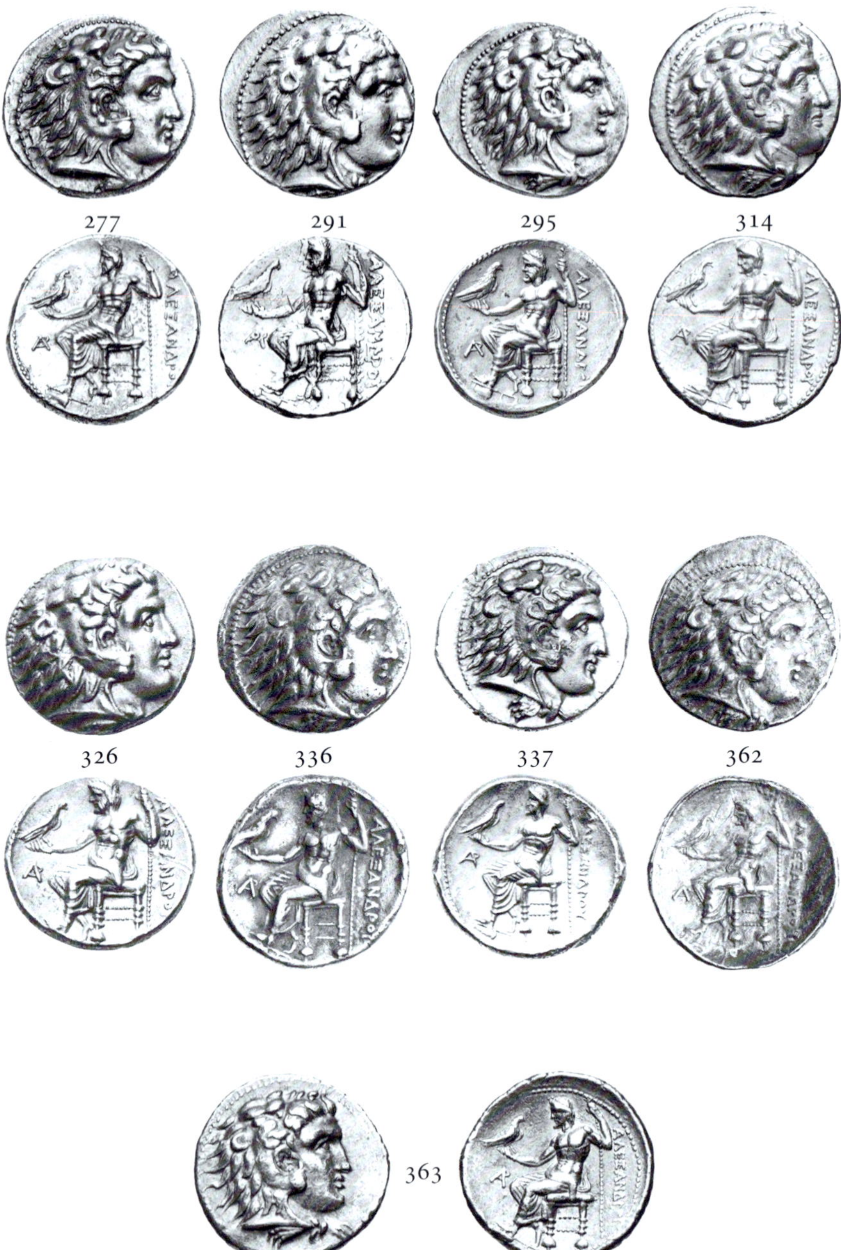

277   291   295   314

326   336   337   362

363

On the Reattribution of some Byblos Alexanders to Arados II

On the Reattribution of some Byblos Alexanders to Arados II

Plate 12

On the Reattribution of some Byblos Alexanders to Arados II

458   459   460   461

465   467   474   475

476

On the Reattribution of some Byblos Alexanders to Arados II

On the Reattribution of some Byblos Alexanders to Arados II

500 502 504

506 507 508

On the Reattribution of some Byblos Alexanders to Arados II

Late Hellenistic Tetradrachms of Parion and Lampsakos

Late Hellenistic Tetradrachms of Parion and Lampsakos

10   11   12

13   14   15

Late Hellenistic Tetradrachms of Parion and Lampsakos

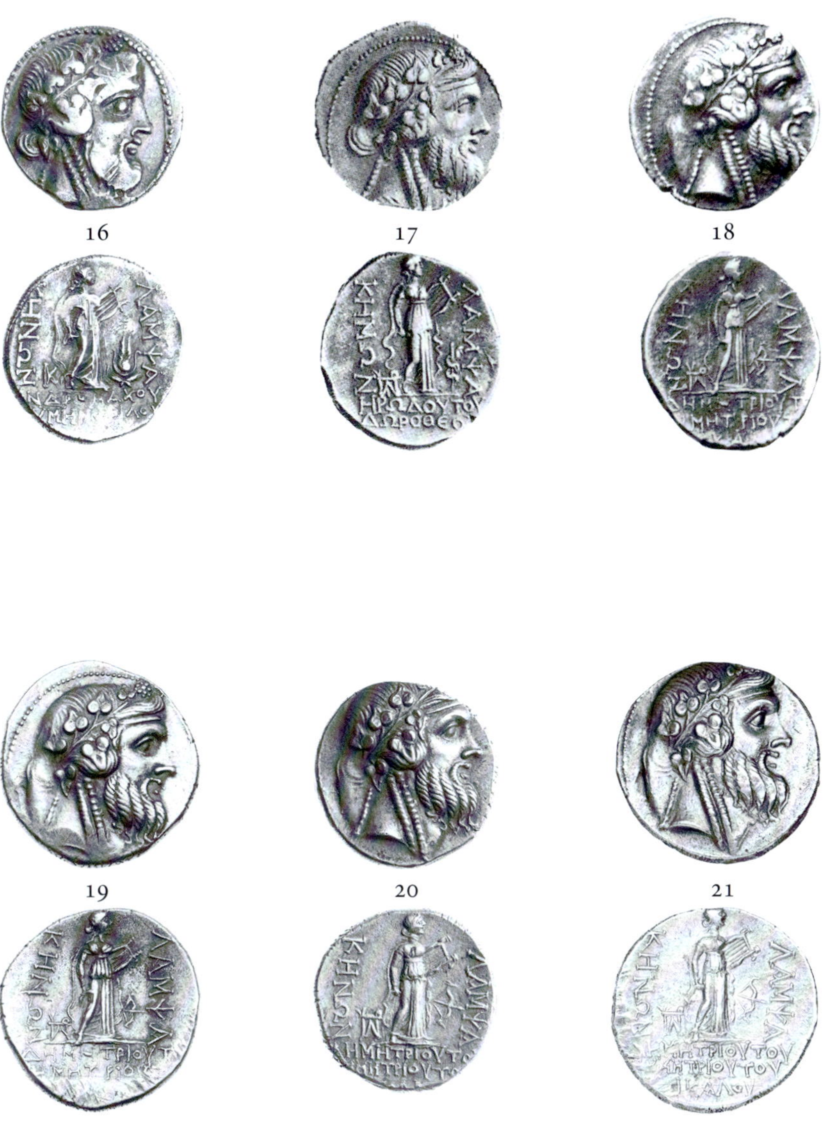

Late Hellenistic Tetradrachms of Parion and Lampsakos

Late Hellenistic Tetradrachms of Parion and Lampsakos

New Evidence for the Introduction of the Roman *Denarius* System

New Evidence for the Introduction of the Roman *Denarius* System

Re-reading the So-called "*Asina* Tokens"

7

8

9

Re-reading the So-called "*Asina* Tokens"

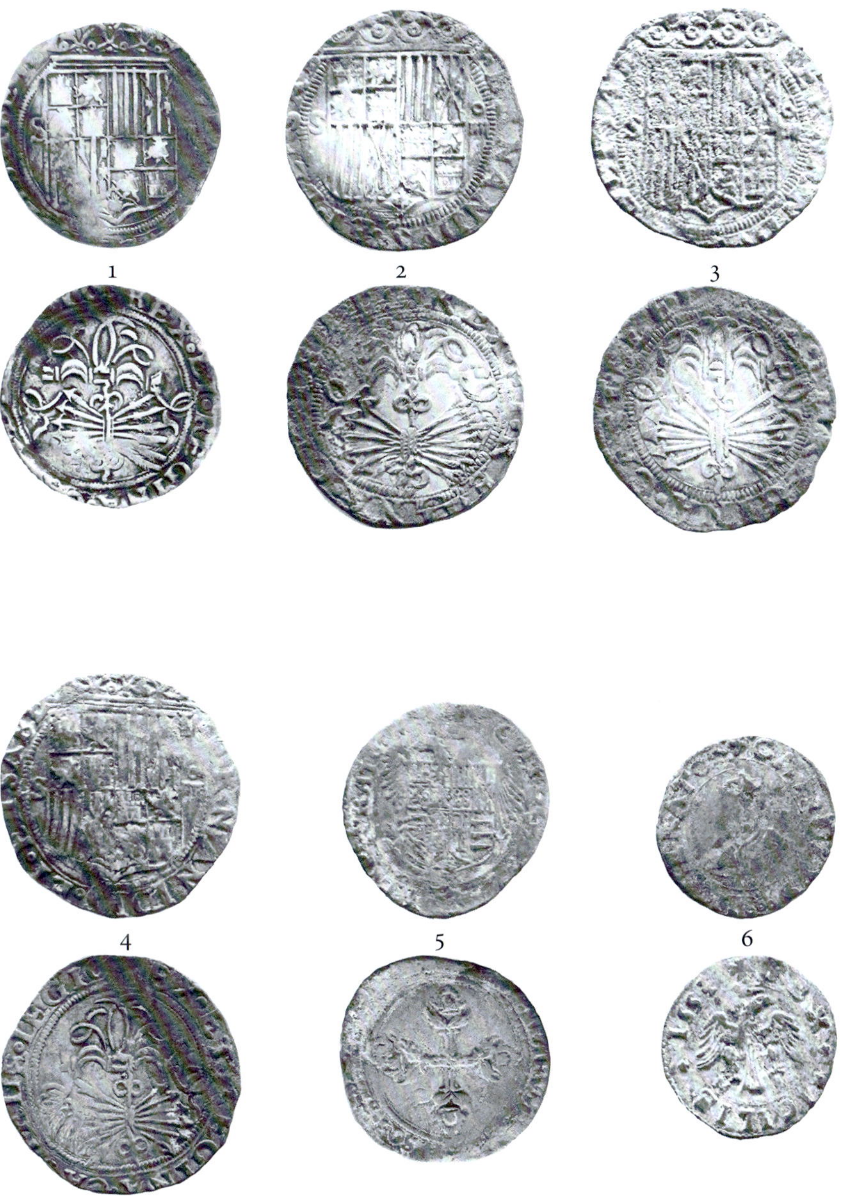

1   2   3

4   5   6

The Via Maqueda Hoard in Context (Palermo, 1872)

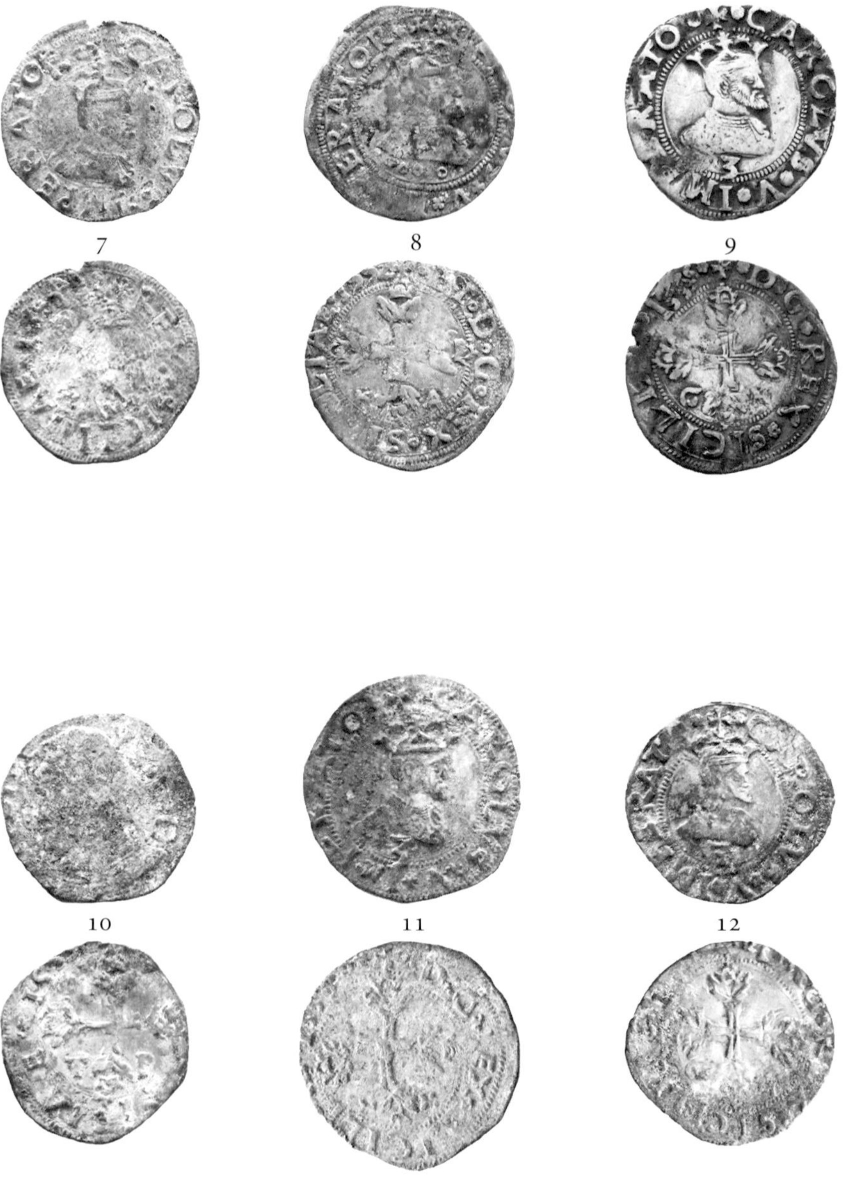

The Via Maqueda Hoard in Context (Palermo, 1872)

The Via Maqueda Hoard in Context (Palermo, 1872)

The Via Maqueda Hoard in Context (Palermo, 1872)

25 26 27

28 29 30

The Via Maqueda Hoard in Context (Palermo, 1872)

The Via Maqueda Hoard in Context (Palermo, 1872)

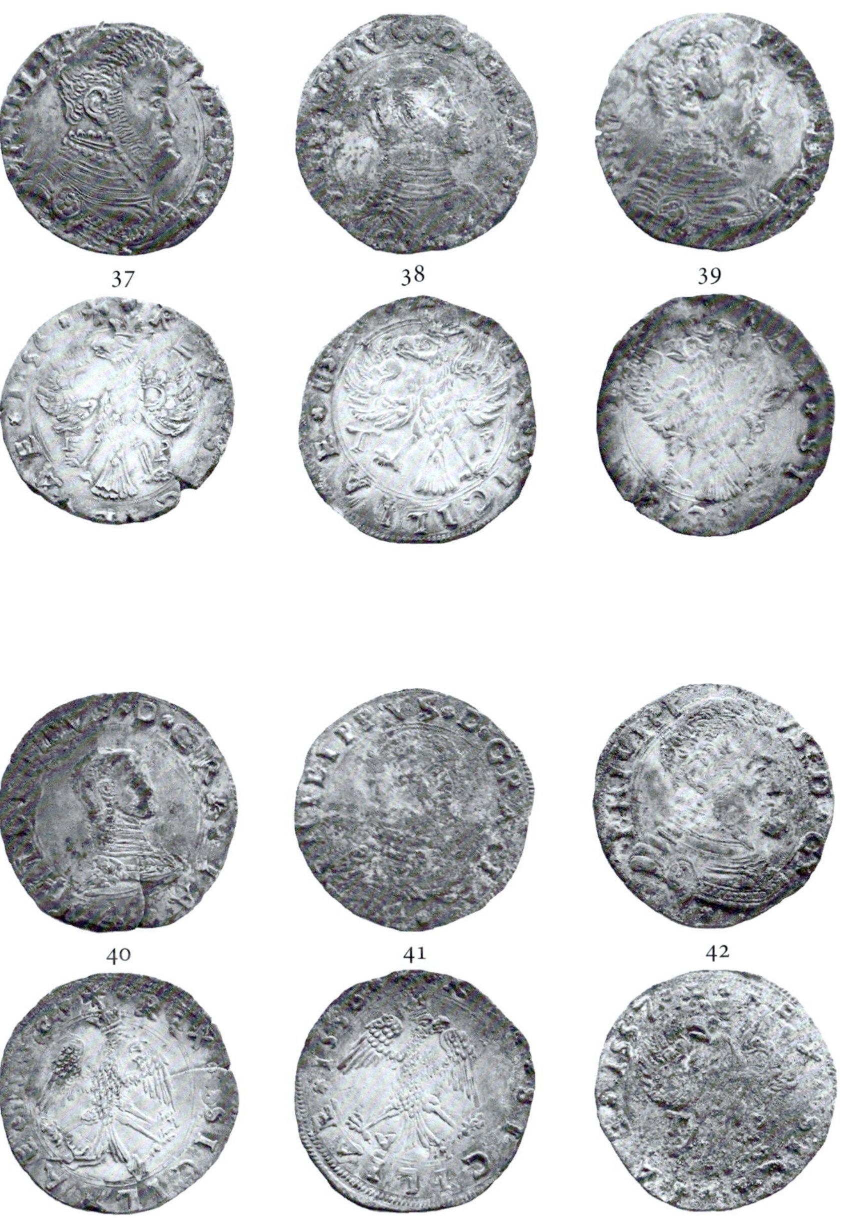

37   38   39

40   41   42

The Via Maqueda Hoard in Context (Palermo, 1872)

43

44

45

46

47

48

The Via Maqueda Hoard in Context (Palermo, 1872)

The Via Maqueda Hoard in Context (Palermo, 1872)

The Via Maqueda Hoard in Context (Palermo, 1872)

61

62

63

64

65

66

The Via Maqueda Hoard in Context (Palermo, 1872)

67 68 69

70 71 72

The Via Maqueda Hoard in Context (Palermo, 1872)

73

74

75

76

The Via Maqueda Hoard in Context (Palermo, 1872)